Family Therapy
in Clinical Practice

"The world of family therapy has long awaited Murray Bowen's book. Heretofore, his writings have appeared in scattered journals and books. Now, for the first time, the developments of Bowen's thinking is collected into one volume.

"As every mental health professional knows, the growth of family theory and therapy over the past several decades has been astonishing. Among the various theories of family system functioning, Bowen's is probably the most influential. So many of his concepts, such as differentiation, triangulation, and fusion, have become part of the language of family therapists and are used so automatically that there is a tendency to forget their origin.

"Clinically, Bowen deals with the fundamental question of how one can deal with his family's craziness without giving the family up. Bowen's quantum leap in the understanding and treatment of intimate relationships goes beyond family boundaries. His theoretical contributions have profound implications for man and society. Most of the papers in this volume have become classics.

"The publication of Murray Bowen's collected papers is an unusual event in the history and evolution of psychiatric thinking. It records the steady, unrelenting dedication of an explorer whose initial curiosity about the schizophrenic riddle led to unexpected ports of call. His journey from regarding schizophrenia as an intrapsychic entity to one rooted in hitherto unrecognized disturbed transactions among family members is well documented.

"The triumphant application of the Bowen Theory is brilliantly presented in *Toward the Differentiation of Self in One's Family of Origin*. This paper represents the natural conceptional trajectory from Socrates, whose injunction 'know thyself' can easily and readily be translated into 'know your family' and how its roots feed into you and your progeny. The focus of attention on the absence of behavioral phenomena strongly supports the view that nothing is objective; one's preconceptions are rooted in personal experiences too numerous to count and categorize, most of which one is incapable of recalling.

"Bowen's papers represent a beacon which has already led to fruitful investigation of both psychological and physical disorders. His rich and fertile thought will inevitably serve as a springboard in the unending search for man's understanding of himself and his behavior. Bowen follows in the footsteps of such heretics as Darwin and Freud."

James L. Framo, Ph.D.

Family Therapy in Clinical Practice

MURRAY BOWEN, M.D.

JASON ARONSON
Northvale, New Jersey
London

THE MASTER WORK SERIES

First softcover edition 1994

Copyright © 1985, 1983, 1978 by Jason Aronson Inc.

ISBN: 1-56821-011-6
Library of Congress Catalog Card Number: 84-45863

Manufactured in the United States of America. Jason Aronson Inc. offers books and cassettes. For information and catalog write to Jason Aronson Inc., 230 Livingston Street, Northvale, New Jersey 07647.

Acknowledgments

Chapter one was presented at the sessions on Current Familial Studies at the Annual Meeting of the American Orthopsychiatric Association, Chicago, March 8, 1957.

Chapter two was presented at the Annual Meeting of the American Orthopsychiatric Association, San Francisco, May 1958. It was first published in the *American Journal of Psychiatry*, vol. 115 (1959), pp. 1017-1020. Copyright © 1959, the American Psychiatric Association. Reprinted by permission.

Chapter three originally appeared in *Schizophrenia—An Integrated Approach*, edited by Alfred Auerback, pp. 147-178, copyright © 1959, Ronald Press. Reprinted by permission of John Wiley & Sons, Inc.

Chapter four, "A Family Concept of Schizophrenia," is reprinted from *The Etiology of Schizophrenia*, edited by Don D. Jackson, pp. 346-370, copyright © 1960 by Basic Books, Inc., Publishers, New York.

Chapter five is reprinted with permission from The *American Journal Of Orthopsychiatry*, volume 31, no. 1, January 1961, pp. 40-60; copyright© by the American Orthopsychiatric Association, Inc. It was presented in 1959 at a workshop, The Family as the Unit of Study and Treatment, Stephen Fleck, M.D., chairman.

Chapter six was a contribution to a panel discussion, The Group Therapeutic Approach in Extramural Settings, and is reprinted from *Proceedings of the 24th Annual Meeting of the Medical Society of Saint Elizabeths Hospital*, published by Saint Elizabeths Hospital, Washington, D.C, 1961.

Chapter seven appeared originally in *Family, Church, and Community*, edited by A. D'Agostino, pp. 81–97, P.J. Kennedy and Sons, New York, 1965. Reprinted by permission. Copyright © 1965, Macmillan Publishing Co., Inc.

Chapter eight appeared originally in *Intensive Psychotherapy*, edited by I. Boszormenyi-Nagy and J. Framo, pp. 213-243, 1965. Reprinted by permission of Harper and Row, Hagerstown, Md.

Chapter nine originally appeared in *Comprehensive Psychiatry* 7:345-374. Reprinted by permission of Grune & Stratton, Inc.

Chapter ten is reprinted from *Comprehensive Group Psychotherapy*, edited by H. Kaplan and B. Sadock, pp. 384-421, Baltimore, Williams and Wilkins, 1971.

Chapter eleven is reprinted from *Systems Therapy*, edited by J. Bradt and C. Moynihan, pp. 388-404, Washington, D.C., 1971.

Chapter twelve is originally appeared in *Annals of the New York Academy of Sciences*, vol. 233 (1974), "The Person with alcoholism," eds. F. Seixas, R. Cadoret, and S. Eggleston, pp. 115-122. Reprinted by permission of the New York Academy of Sciences.

Chapter thirteen was presented at the Nathan W. Ackerman Memorial Conference, Venezuela, February 1974. A condensed version appeared under the same title in *Energy: Today's Choices, Tomorrow's Opportunities*, ed. A. Schmalz, Washington, D.C., World Future Society, 1974.

Chapter fourteen, "Family Therapy after Twenty Years," is reprinted from the *American Handbook of Psychiatry*, Second Edition, edited by Silvano Arieti, Volume 5, edited by Daniel X. Freeman and Jarl E. Dyrud, copyright © 1975 by Basic Books, Inc., Publishers, New York.

Chapter fifteen is reprinted from *Family Therapy*, edited by Philip Guerin, pp. 335-348, New York, Gardner Press, 1976.

Chapter sixteen is reprinted from *Family Therapy*, edited by Philip Guerin, pp. 42-90, New York, Gardner Press, 1976.

Chapter seventeen is reprinted from *The Family*, vol. 3 (1976), pp. 50-62. It is an interview conducted by David Berenson, M.D., at a CFL Workshop on January 24, 1976.

Chapter eighteen is an amplified version of a paper presented at the Georgetown Family Symposium, 1973, and appearing in *Georgetown Family Symposia*, vol. 2 (1973-1974), edited by F. Andres and J. Lorio, Washington, D.C., Department of Psychiatry, Georgetown University Medical Center.

Chapter nineteen originally appeared in the *American Journal of Psychiatry*, vol. 116 (1959), pp. 514-517, copyright © 1959, the American Psychiatric Association. Reprinted by permission.

Chapter twenty is reprinted from *Georgetown Family Symposia*, vol. 1 (1971–1972), edited by F. Andres and J. Lorio, Washington, D.C., Department of Psychiatry, Georgetown University Medical Center, 1974.

Chapter twenty-one was published anonymously in *Family Interaction: A Dialogue Between Family Researchers and Family Therapists*, edited by J. Framo, pp. 111–173, copyright © 1972, Springer Publishing Company, Inc. New York. Used by permission. It was presented at the Family Research Conference, 1967.

Chapter twenty-two is reprinted from *Georgetown Family Symposia* vol. 1 (1971–1972), edited by F. Andres and J. Lorio, Washington, D.C., Department of Psychiatry, Georgetown University Medical Center, 1974.

Contents

Contents

Introduction

This volume is a collection of my most important papers from 1957 to 1977. The papers represent the evolution of Family Systems Theory from the earliest descriptive papers in 1957, to the first orderly presentation of the theory in 1966, to the refinements in therapy and the extensions of theory over the past ten years. The development of this theory has paralleled most evolutionary processes. It began slowly when several key ideas began to coalesce into a different way of understanding the human phenomenon. The ideas quickly led into so many new areas it became a busy balancing act to follow all at the same time; it would have been conceptually inaccurate to try to stay on one without conceptual violence to the whole. The rapid evolution of the theory is largely responsible for the fact I have gone twenty years and have not yet written a book.

Family Systems Theory contains no ideas that have not been a part of human experience through the centuries. The task of the theorist is to find the minimal number of congruent pieces from the total bank of human knowledge that fit together to tell a simple story about the nature of man, or whatever other phenomenon he attempts to describe. The theorist needs a formula or blueprint as a guide in selecting the pieces. Without it he is vulnerable to the use of attractice but discrepant pieces of knowledge that can defeat his long-range goal. In my papers I have described the disciplined effort to select consistent theoretical concepts that might someday conceptualize emotional illness as a product of that part of man he shares with the lower forms of life. After 1957 there was a consistent effort to work toward systems theory and get beyond the conventional concepts I had long held as "truth." I have tried to be scientifically accurate in the use of such terms as *hypothesis, concept,* and *theory.* These terms have come into such misuse that it is common for people to say "I have a theory" when it would be accurate to say "I have an idea" or "a wild guess."

The first important nodal point in the development of the theory was a research study conducted during the years 1954–1959 at the National Institute of Mental Health. In this study entire families lived on the ward with the schizophrenic patients. The baseline for this study had been developed in clinical work with schizophrenia at the Menninger Clinic in the period from 1946 to 1954. The live-in project was the source of a wealth of new facts about schizophrenia. In 1955 it led to the development of a method of family therapy. By 1956 it was leading to new theoretical ideas about schizophrenia. When it had become possible to see the relationship patterns in families with schizophrenia, it was then possible also to see less intense versions of the same patterns in milder forms of emotional illness, as well as in normal people. It was the comparison of the intense patterns in schizophrenia with the less intense patterns in others that eventually became the basis for the theory. By 1956 there were informal outpatient studies of less severe forms of emotional illness. Another parallel project had to do with the use of research knowledge with my own nuclear and extended families. In the 1940s I had tried to understand my own families with conventional psychoanalytic theory. This led to the inevitable emotional impasses and was discontinued until 1955, when new facts emerged from the family research. There was no way for writing to keep pace with the clinical investigation on several fronts. There were informal presentations to small professional groups during 1955 and 1956, but the first formal presentations to national meetings were in the spring of 1957. The papers were simple clinical description based mostly on conventional psychiatric theory. They were never published, because their content was incorporated in subsequent papers. One of these early papers is included in this volume for the sake of history.

The lag between the idea, the clinical application, the writing of a paper, and its publication is illustrated by "A Family Concept of Schizophrenia," which was started in 1957, finished in 1958, and finally published in 1960 as a chapter in *The Etiology of Schizophrenia*. The area of family therapy was being neglected. A companion to the "Family Concept" paper, entitled "Family Psychotherapy," was finally published in January 1961. The original family research had been focused on schizophrenia and there was a commitment to write about it before proceeding to new projects. Therefore the papers published between 1957 and 1961 convey little about the parallel studies I had undertaken. The live-in project was terminated in 1959 and I moved to the Georgetown University Medical Center, where the main focus was on less severe emotional problems. In 1959 I signed a contract for a book about the live-in research. I was at the time deeply involved in theory. When the first draft of the book was finished in 1960, an editor believed I was close enough to a new theory to spend a few more years on that. This fitted with my preoccupation and the book was never written.

The period from 1960 to 1965 was focused on the theory. I gave up the use of clinical description in writing, which is more popular with professional audiences, and shifted toward the use of theoretical concepts. The goal was to gain experience with less severe emotional problems and to refine the family therapy as a method consistent with the theory. The few papers from this period reflect a mixture of detail about schizophrenia and some of the same issues as applied to less severe problems. A noteworthy paper from that period is "Family Psychotherapy with Schizophrenia in the Hospital and Private Practice," written in 1963–64 in response to a request for a book chapter about schizophrenia. It for the most part drew on my earlier experience with schizophrenia. Also, between 1959 and 1962 detailed multigenerational research was carried out with a few families, including one case in considerable detail going back more than 300 years. Such efforts are so time-consuming that one could spend a lifetime with a few families. But by 1960 it was clear that all families were pretty much alike. I decided that my own family would provide as much detail as any and would be more accessible. That was the beginning of the mulitgenerational study of my own family. Until that time I knew no more about my family than most people do of theirs: fair knowledge about grandparents and sparse knowledge about great-grandparents. In six generations one is the product of 64 families of origin. Beyond that, the figure mounts rapidly. In ten generations it is 1024 and in fifteen generations 32,768. Since the early 1960s I have developed reasonable knowledge about 20 of my 64 families of origin for periods that range from 100 to 300 years. During the five years to 1965 the six interlocking concepts of Family Systems Theory were developed in detail. Then came the problem of conceptualizing the concepts as parts of a unified theory and presenting it in writing. This writing was done in 1965–66 and was one of the most difficult, frustrating, and satisfying experiences of my life. The paper was finally finished in August 1966 and published in October of the same year. I saw that as a time, finally, to write a book about both the theory and the family therapy.

Later that same August there occurred an event in my family of origin which evolved into the most important turning point in my entire professional life. It began with a small emotional crisis in the family. I automatically used new knowledge about triangles, developed in writing the theory paper, plus knowledge from the multigenerational family study, in relating to my own family. There was a spectacular result that led to a breakthrough in both theory and clinical practice. In March 1967 at a national family conference, I talked about my own family experience in lieu of presenting a formal didactic paper. This helped focus national attention on the importance of one's own family to therapists. Later that month I began using the new knowledge in teaching young family therapists. Several of them began going home to use detriangling knowledge with their parental families. They would return to the conference with reports of successes and failures. I had for some years encouraged young mental health professionals to work out their own personal problems in family therapy with their spouses, instead of in personal psychotherapy or psychoanalysis, and had accumulated years of experience conducting family therapy with such people. Within a year I discovered that the training conference members, none of whom were in any kind of psychotherapy, and none of whom had more than thirty minutes a month for discussion of their own families in conference, were making as much or more progress in dealing with their spouses and children as were comparable professionals in weekly formal family therapy with their spouses. The following months and years went into a careful check of this chance finding. By 1970 this working with the family of origin, instead of with the nuclear family, was developed into a fairly well defined method. By 1971 it had become one of the most important parts of the postgraudate training programs. No single development in almost twenty-five years in family research and family therapy has changed me and my approach to families as much as that one.

In January 1966 began the development of a special method of multiple family therapy designed to keep the focus on the emotional process within a family and to prevent group process between the families. This was developed into a rather excellent therapeutic method which later ran parallel to the work with families of origin. The biggest development of the past decade began in 1972 with an invitation from the Environmental Protection Agency to do a paper on predictable human response to crisis situations. I had long been interested in the specific ways that emotional process within a family interconnects with emotional process in society. I had planned to talk in general terms about the issues. In the months of research that went into the writing of this paper, I was able to define the process sufficiently well to satisfy my own theoretical curiosity. In 1974 this was added as a new concept to the total theory. The interest in societal issues continues, and sometime in the not too distant future I will write about this in sufficient detail to make it more understandable to others.

I began using the term Family Systems Theory in 1966. As the "systems" concept came into wider use in the late sixties and early seventies, the terms Family Systems Theory and Family Systems Therapy were being used to cover a broad and various spectrum of theoretical and therapeutic approaches. I looked for qualifying terms and adjectives to more specifically define this theory and this method of therapy. Much as I have always disliked the use of proper names in such situations, I in 1974 changed the name of this theory to the Bowen Family Systems Theory, or, more succinctly, the Bowen Theory.

I have attempted here a brief summary of the evolution of this theory and this method of family therapy in the two decades since 1957. I hope it conveys an over-all view of the multiple interconnecting forces that influenced the theory, a view perhaps not readily available from an initial reading of the papers.

Murray Bowen, M.D.

I
Schizophrenia and the Family

Chapter 1

Treatment of Family Groups With a Schizophrenic Member

With the collaboration of Robert H. Dysinger, M.D., Warren M. Brodey, M.D., and Betty Basamania, M.S.W.

A small research project was started two and a half years ago to study the relationship between mothers and schizophrenic patients. Normal family members have lived on the ward with hospitalized schizophrenic patients. Individual psychotherapy was provided for both patients and mothers. After one year, fathers were included in the family groups and a plan was devised to treat the family as a single unit rather than treating individuals in the unit. During the second year, two family groups consisting of father, mother, patient, and normal sibling were admitted.

An important development was the conceptual change from thinking of schizophrenia as a process confined within the patient to thinking of it as the manifestation of an active dynamic process involving the entire family. A corresponding change in treatment was the shift from psychotherapy for the individual to psychotherapy for the family as a unit.

This presentation will be a brief description of the hypothesis on which the original project was based, a description of some of the striking observations and clinical experiences that led to the conceptual change, the experience in adapting the changed hypothesis to treatment, and some of the impressions from 14 months of clinical experience since the change. No attempt is made to go into the various and voluminous data from the project except as it has a relationship to the thesis of this presentation.

The original hypothesis was based on a premise that the basic character problem, on which clinical schizophrenia is later superimposed, is an unresolved symbiotic attachment to the mother. It considered psychological symbiosis to be the same order of phenomenon as biological symbiosis. It considered that the mother physically gives up her child in the birth process but that she is unable to psychologically give up the child. This can result in a state of relative physical maturity along with a state of marked psychological immaturity. According to the thinking, the process is initiated by the emotional immaturity of the mother who uses the child to fulfill her own emotional needs. The mother feels guilty about this use of the child and while she covertly does things to block the child's development, she simultaneously tries to force the child to achievement. The child, once entangled, tries to perpetuate the symbiosis along with the opposite effort to grow up. The father passively permits himself to be excluded from the intense twosome and marries his business or other outside interests. Symbiosis was seen as a developmental arrest which at one time was a normal state in the mother-child relationship.

The hypothesis also considered that there is a wide range of symbiotic attachments from the more intense attachments in which mother and child remain together, to the mildest nonclinical attachments. This would include the large group in which the child disrupts the tie to mother only to duplicate it in marriage or other relationships throughout life. Hill (1955) speaks of symbiotic marriages among the fathers and mothers of schizophrenic patients. This project was designed to deal with a very narrow range of symbiosis.

The project might more properly be called a study of symbiosis as seen in schizophrenia and a specific treatment effort focused on the symbiosis rather than on the schizophrenia. Three chronic schizophrenic young women and their mothers were chosen for the initial study. A goal was to find the most intense possible clinical examples of attachments between schizophrenic patients and their mothers in which the symbiotic process was still active. This was done on the grounds that it would be easier to first observe the characteristics of the symbiotic relationship in the most exaggerated possible form. Intensity of symbiotic attachment was considered more important than the intensity or configuration of schizophrenic symptoms. It was assumed that this degree of symbiosis would imply a maximum degree of personality impairment which in turn would also result in a slower therapeutic response. The mothers were given a choice of participation which ranged from rooming with the patient to living outside the hospital and spending daytime hours with the patient. The most impaired mother chose to room with the patient and the other two chose to live outside. Women patients were chosen because the ward would adapt to all women better than to all men or to mixed groups.

The treatment program was planned from the hypothesis. For instance, the symbiosis was considered to be an arrest in psychological development which had been initiated by a psychological deficit in the mother. The premise was that if this psychological deficit could be dealt with to the extent that it no longer exerted an influence on the patient, then the psychological arrest in the patient could begin to move toward a higher level of maturation on its own motivation. A cornerstone of the treatment program was a supportive therapeutic relationship for the mother. A specific relationship with a social worker was chosen as the one that most nearly fulfilled the hypothesized criteria. A medical psychotherapist was provided for the patient. The basic treatment design evolved from the hypothesis was: (1) move the original symbiotic mother-patient pair into the hospital; (2) introduce a supportive therapeutic relationship for the mother; and (3) influence the natural course of psychological events between mother and patient as little as possible by the ward environment. The ward milieu was planned to furnish maximum neutral emotional support and at the same time to exert minimal influence on the relationship.

Observations and Clinical Experiences

There were a number of striking clinical observations in the first year of study of the three mother-patient family groups.

1. *Symbiotic relationship patterns.* The patterns of relationship were seen more clearly than had been the experience in other clinical settings. It is an opinion that the unstructured ward setting was the most important factor in this. Support from the ward staff also seemed important. The most characteristic relationship pattern has been referred to as the "closeness-distance cycles." When left to their own devices, the mothers and daughters would get overclose, fight, separate, come back together again, and repeat the cycles over and over. There was great variation in the frequency of the cycles. During a very intense period, one family could go through as many as two complete cycles in one day. The time for the average cycle varied between several days and several months. In the closeness phases the mother and patient seemed interested only in each other, and their relationships to outside figures were calm. As the closeness increased, the anxiety would increase to intense incorporation

anxiety. Then they would fight and separate until separation anxiety set up a reunion and a new cycle. In the distance phases each was hostile to the other and each attempted to duplicate the symbiotic relationship with outside figures. These outside relationships were difficult, demanding, and anxious for the outside figures. The mothers and patients never seemed to have the *inner* strength to control the intensity of the cycles. They attempted to get *outside* rules, advice, or structure to control the vigor of the cycles. When staff unwittingly did furnish this outside structure, the clarity of the closeness-distance cycles was less plainly distinguishable.

2. *Transfer of anxiety.* There was a high level of fluidity in the relationship between patient and mother that was not accounted for in the original hypothesis. The hypothesis had considered the symbiosis to be a rather fixed and rigid state with a high degree of personality fusion and of the order of phenomenon described by a patient who once said, "But doctor, you do not understand how it was between my mother and me. The only way that we could be separated was for me to kill her and if she died, I would die too." There were frequent observations consistent with this "fixed fusion" hypothesis such as: when the patient belched while sitting at the dinner table the parent sitting alongside followed with, "Excuse me."

The surprising observation was the marked mobility, fluidity, and pervasiveness of the process. It is an opinion that the difference between hypothesis and observation resulted from the hypothesis having been developed from clinical experience with individuals and the observations came from watching the daily living of the family as a unit. The fluidity was on the order of transfer of anxiety, of weakness, of sickness, or of psychosis from one member to another.

(a) *Description of transfer of anxiety.* The most common example of the transfer of anxiety was from mother to patient. Mother would become anxious and then her thinking would focus on the sickness in the patient. The timing of this seemed related to the mother's own functioning rather than to the reality of the patient's functioning. Mother's verbalization would include repeated emphasis on the patient's sickness. Very soon the mother's anxiety would be less and the patient's psychotic symptoms would be increased. This mechanism was so common that any increase in mother's anxiety would alert the staff for an increase in the patient's psychosis. Just as the emotional calm or tension in an infant can be a most sensitive indicator of the functioning of a mother, so the psychotic patient in daily living contact with mother can be a more sensitive indicator of the functioning of mother than direct observation of mother herself. There was a quality about this that suggested almost a quantitative transfer of anxiety. There were less frequent examples of transfer from patient to mother. A most striking one occurred when a newly admitted patient was making a vigorous effort to move out of a prolonged chronic regression. She made her steps positively and firmly. She showed little concern when her mother said, "You are weak, go slow," or "Remember the last time you tried things too fast, you cracked up." Each time she made a new positive step the mother, within a few hours, would go to bed with a physical illness of several days' duration. She maintained this command of the situation for several months and then relinquished it. This transfer of anxiety pattern is presented as the description of a mechanism observed to occur between the mothers and daughters, in which both play *active* roles.

(b) *Patterns of transfer anxiety.* There were variations in one prominent pattern by which these transfers seemed to take place. These seemed to occur at points along the same scale. At one end of the scale was the mother who seemed to force the anxiety or psychosis onto a resisting, fighting, victimized, reluctant patient. The mother would make frequent comments directly to the patient, aside to others in the patient's presence, or in confidence to others, to say that the patient was sick, stupid, weak, incompetent, inadequate, confused, or schizophrenic. The mother sought medical and other authoritative opinion to support the pronouncement. The term *schizophrenia* was used frequently after it was part of the mother's vocabulary. The patient member would fight back with mechanisms ranging from denial to counterattack—"*You* are the one who is sick"—to psychotic hostility against the accuser. These examples seemed to occur when the patient was integrated enough to fight back. There were few examples of this in these very impaired families. Most of the examples in these families occurred in the middle of the scale. In these, the parent actively forced the pronouncement onto the patient member and the patient member actively reached out to accept it. This implies the concept of activity on the part of both. At the other end of the scale was the patient member who actively sought to be called sick and weak and the parent who was reluctant to go along with it. This occurred rarely, except in one family unit. It occurred often in the family in which mother was really more impaired than the daughter. It occurred in situations when the mother attempted to force the daughter to be more responsible and to give (mothering) to the mother. At this point the daughter would work actively to be more irresponsible and helpless than the mother and to have this confirmed with a label of stupid. This occurred on one occasion with a more adequate mother and daughter when the daughter reached a level of functioning more adequate than mother. The daughter seemed threatened by any further move that might make her responsible for the mother and the mother seemed threatened at permitting herself to depend on the daughter. An important point was the activity that went into the situation to maintain an emotional status quo. Either mother or patient could portray themselves as being victimized by the other when status quo was threatened. Searles in his recent (1956) paper, "The Effort to Drive the Other Person Crazy," has described similar observations from psychotherapy with schizophrenic patients.

(c) *Dynamics of transfer of anxiety.* There has been some tentative initial thinking about the dynamics of this relationship fluidity. All three of the original mothers and the two later mothers are insecure women in whom the use of denial, reaction formation, and projection is pronounced. Their passive wishes (wish to be mothered) are great, but equally great is their inability to accept help. They deny their own wish to be mothered with: "It is weak to want mothering. I am not weak. I am strong. I only want to mother my child." Three mothers had somatic mechanisms by which it was possible to permit themselves to have some attention. The other two were the only ones who were consistently dominating and dogmatic. Under calm conditions, all five mothers seemed to do fairly well with the use of denial and reaction formation. In periods of stress, projection came into use. The projection involved primarily the mother's own feelings of helplessness, weakness, and inadequacy. None of the families had any sense of discrimination between feeling and reality. To them, to feel helpless is to be helpless. A tentative dynamic formulation suggested by observations is that mother projects her own weak self into the child which results in a psychological orientation in which she is completely strong and the child is weak. With her adequate self she mothers her weak self which is perceived to be in the child. An example was the mother who fed her child when she herself felt hunger. The giving is then governed by her own wishes rather than the reality needs of the patient. At times when her own wish for mothering is intense she can force the child to accept her attention whether the child wants it or not. She could quote an authority who advocated unlimited giving to children. At times when her own need to be mothered is not great she can neglect the child beyond any reality needs of the child as a person and then justify herself with another authority who advises parents to be firm with their children. There were repeated observations to indicate the mother's attention was determined from inside herself rather than the reality of the situation.

3. *Relationships of family members to staff.* There was an intense cohesiveness in the closeness phases of the closeness-distance cycles and an

equally intense disruptiveness in the distance phases. There was a quality of magnetic pulling together in the closeness phases and explosive fragmentation in the distance phases. When the central cohesive closeness suddenly fragmented, the symbiotic pairs attempted to form outside relationships which had the same qualities as the central symbiotic relationship. The outside figures included other relatives, staff members, social agencies, or other receptive figures. This process of "combining with" outside figures seemed to take place on an unconscious level in which both the family members and outside figures played active roles. This was the process which constituted the one most difficult operating problem for the staff. The phenomenon was anticipated in the hypothesis and much teaching and discussion was devoted to techniques to help the staff members remain objective and relate to the families without taking sides or becoming incorporated into the family process. The staff had an excellent intellectual understanding of the phenomenon but the process continued on an unconscious level. There were constantly occurring situations when a staff member would become involved and then through a chain of intrastaff relationships involve the entire staff in a state of turmoil. The family would then be more free of anxiety. The staff would lose objectivity and therapeutic effectiveness. The anxiety could also involve the hospital community or even the outside community. The patterns of the closeness-distance cycles disappeared during these periods. The details of staff involvements with the families are not the subject of this paper. It is the aim to say that there was an intense shift of anxiety between the symbiotic pairs and, especially in the separation phases, the anxiety or the sickness or the problem could shift to a variety of receptive figures inside or outside the family.

4. *Relationships to other family members.* Other family members were also intensely vulnerable to involvement in the mother-patient relationship. One mother could separate from the hospitalized daughter and within hours her anxiety would be less and a younger son would have disabling neurotic symptoms. Clinical impressions of the dynamics of this shift are not the subject of this paper.

5. *Other observations.* It was always a new and surprising experience for the staff to see and feel the intensity of a mother's involvements. There has been an intellectual awareness of this for a long time, but each new observation causes a reaction as if the staff member is experiencing this for the first time. It has the quality of an emotional experience that can be tolerated only for brief periods without re-repression.

Summary of Observations

The observations described here were among those which were different from the original hypothesis, and which led to the extension of the hypothesis. The most striking was the fluid, shifting character of the mother-patient attachment. It was more than a state of two people *responding* and *reacting* to each other in a specific way but more a state of two people *living and acting and being for each other*. There was a striking lack of definiteness in the boundary of the problem as well as lack of ego boundaries in the symbiotic pairs. The relationship was more than two people with a problem involving chiefly each other; it appeared to be more a dependent fragment of a larger family group. There was this quality referred to as "transfer anxiety" in which the anxiety or sickness or psychosis could shift from one to the other, or to other family figures or, to a lesser degree, to staff members. The results with psychotherapy also suggested the symbiotic pair to be a weak undifferentiated fragment of a larger group and to lack within itself the strength to differentiate into two autonomous people.

Extension of Hypothesis and Change in Treatment Plan

It was the repeated clinical experiences similar to those described which led to the extension of the hypothesis to consider the schizophrenic symptoms in the patient member to be part of an active dynamic process that involves the entire family. The previous thinking about the symbiosis was not changed except it was now seen as part of a larger, active, shifting unit. It was decided to include fathers in new families to be admitted. The parents were to have lived away from their own immediate families, to have one severely impaired child, and not more than two children. It was suggested that this would be families in which the intense process would be contained within four people without involving inlaws or multiple siblings. The parents were to be as young and healthy as possible with a potential for major changes within themselves for their own gains.

Two complete family units were admitted the second year. The first was admitted fourteen months ago. The father was fifty-one, the mother forty-five, the schizophrenic daughter twenty-three, and the normal daughter fifteen years old. The patient had been constantly in a regressed assaultive panic for four years with no remission from treatment with massive shock and drug therapies. The second family was admitted seven months ago. The parents were in their forties, their catatonic son was twenty, and the normal son was thirteen years old. The patient has become progressively worse during four years of constant treatment. All parents were now required to live on the ward. Normal siblings who have been in school have stayed on the ward over weekends.

After admission of the first complete family, a different treatment approach was tried to see if it would be possible to think of the family as a unit and treat the family as a unit. A weekly meeting, in use for some months, had been fairly successful in dealing with discordant issues between the families and staff. It had not been possible to accomplish this with staff meetings alone. There had been a clinical experience to illustrate this. One of the mothers could speak to a staff person and within minutes relay a distorted version of the staff comment to the daughter who would then act on the distortion. One distortion added to another, involving multiple staff members, could become complicated. A rule was made that only one person, the ward psychiatrist, would speak to either mother or patient about important issues. This structure did not work well either. Then a rule was made that no one would speak to either mother or daughter about these issues until mother, patient, and all staff on duty were in the same room together. This worked satisfactorily.

Most of the emotion between staff and families was focused on ward policy and nursing procedures. Open meetings to include all staff and family members were held to discuss the discordant issues. The project director presided. Both staff and family members were enthusiastic about the meetings. Discussion of reality problems led to discussion of personal problems. Observation of the entire group in a meeting provided the first clear picture of the way intrafamily tensions could be reenacted between staff and family or entirely within the staff group. For the first time the tensions between staff and families were on a workable level.

These were the meetings adapted to the family unit therapy. The meetings were held in the ward lounge for an hour each day. An average of eighteen people, about equally divided between staff and family members attended. This was to be a trial period. The new family was asked to forego individual psychotherapy and to use the meetings to discuss individual problems. The psychiatrists and social worker assumed a therapeutic responsibility to point out and clarify relationship patterns between family members, between families and staff, and between staff members when appropriate. All meetings have been tape recorded. Three additional simultaneous written records include a set of process psychotherapy notes, a process sociogram, and a summary of content. Meetings are unstructured and any member can introduce any subject at any time.

Another change was made for the staff. Routine staff meetings, to discuss family problems, were discontinued. This included staff conferences and ward rounds. The staff was asked to use the large meetings for such communications. Of course it was not possible to discontinue all meetings, but staff was asked to report about these to the group. A rule was adopted, similar to one used by Jones in "The Therapeutic Community," that any communication presented in confidence could be brought up in the group. If one can picture a distraught family, each member with anxiety and angers and secrets about the others, afraid to mention these things to the one involved, seeking a nurse or outside figure with whom to share problems; each staff person wanting to be helpful and wishing to listen and promising to keep confidence; and each staff and family member being the keeper of many secrets—then one can get an idea of the anxieties and tensions that can pervade the group. The family members had little problem in being able to speak in the group, and most important, in front of the other members of their families. The staff was more anxious about speaking in the presence of family members but the initial anxiety about this subsided in a short time.

The meeting plan was designed to encourage family participation in the problems of each other, to discourage practices which had been found to encourage fragmentation of the family, and to encourage free relationships between staff and families. Relationships can become distant and hostile when there are secrets. For the first time the staff had a satisfactory structure to handle the problems encountered with the family members. The staff person could refuse to relate to a family member in reference to a personal subject by saying, "Take it up in the group." When a family member did make a personalized communication, the staff member could report it in the group. The staff could encourage relationship on neutral subjects. Most of the meetings are very active. Family members press for time to be heard, and have competed in bringing up difficult subjects. There is rarely a meeting without vigorous emotion.

This presentation will permit only a brief mention of the therapeutic effort. Family members all have poorly defined ego boundaries, if that be a satisfactory way to conceptualize it. Considerable effort goes into helping the individual define his own "self" and to differentiate self from others. A common observation is a kind of family projection process in which the family weakness is projected to the patient who resists noneffectively and then accepts it. Projection is consistently pointed out in the group. Much time goes to defining intrafamily relationship patterns and especially defining the part played by staff when a staff member provokes a repetition of the family pattern in the staff. There are many ego supportive moves such as support from a family member who gets anxious in his effort to differentiate self from the "family ego mass."

There have been some consistent relationship patterns in both the complete families. The mothers were the active, decision making, dominant family members who assumed roles of strength and adequacy. Both patients were helpless, irresponsible babies. Both fathers were weak, conforming, and devoted in the relationship to the mother. Both normal siblings appeared more mature than their years. The day to day clinical course, especially in the early months, was characterized by much disagreement, high emotion, defensiveness, blaming, and contradiction. Over a period of months there were some patterns. On admission, both mothers devoted themselves to the patients with the same patterns of overprotectiveness, babying, demands, criticism, and fighting as had been observed in the three mother-patient families. The process had the pattern of something the mothers and patients had to continue to exhaustion or disruption. The fathers sat helplessly on the periphery. They did not seem to have an identity of their own but saw the struggle in terms of siding with one or the other. When a father did get into the relationship, he seemed to become mother's agent, using her words, and the patient related to him the same as to mother. The patients' psychoses seemed to be directed specifically at mother, almost point for point, at the old issues between them. When the patients' anxieties would reach a high level, the psychoses seemed to "spray" to everyone except mother, leaving mother free to stay close by. The first members to change in both families were the fathers. They were the first to become interested in their own problems and their part in the family dilemma. They both worked hard at finding their own identities. Their first efforts at having convictions of their own (instead of borrowed convictions) were weak and authoritative in telling others what to do and say and believe. Even this much activity usually brought a period of calm to the family. Through this period, the mothers continued their preoccupation with the patient, denying that they had problems, insisting their lives were devoted to the welfare of the patient, and particularly attacking the father at any show of strength. The second father is still in this stage. The first father gradually reached the point of a "declaration of independence" delivered to the head nurse but which seemed for his own mother. This was five months after admission. For the first time his strength seemed greater than the mother's attack and within ten days she went out alone with him for the first time. Up to this point she insisted tht the psychotic daughter accompany them. They went through two months referred to as "the honeymoon." During this time the daughter's psychosis was like a tremendous temper tantrum designed to win mother back to her. The mother was kind, firm, motherly, and objective and the daughter made some gains. At seven months the younger daughter reverted to a very rebellious infantile demanding state. There was one episode in which she lay with her head on mother's lap threatening to run away and get married. The mother immediately had a relationship with this daughter similar to the one with the psychotic daughter. The daughter's brief intense panic made the family fear she would become psychotic too. The father immediately reverted to the weak, authoritative role. This new cycle went through five months until the father advanced again which was followed by a second change in mother. The striking point is that both of these mothers and patients seemed to be in the same helpless bind as the symbiotic pairs and remained so until the father could firmly establish himself as a person in the family. Only then was it really possible for the mother to understand or accept psychotherapeutic interpretations.

The staff has considered the family unit therapy to have answered a number of problems for the project. There has been a marked decrease in anxiety on the entire project. There were periods during the first year when there were doubts that it would be possible to continue the project. The families are more comfortable and the anxieties are more understood and contained. Research observations are more complete and are considered more accurate. The observations made from watching and hearing a family member in relationship to his family is different than composite observations assembled from other sources. It is suggested that a family member is different when in relationship to family symbiotic attachments than in relationship with other figures. The meetings also provide a clearer picture of staff involvements with the families. The therapists have felt themselves to be in more of an objective relationship to schizophrenia than they had found possible in doing or supervising individual psychotherapy.

The group is difficult to assess as a psychotherapeutic agent. In the beginning the group was regarded as a preliminary therapeutic method which would probably be followed by individual psychotherapy. The staff now feels that the group may answer the family's total treatment program. There are questions about the size of the group and the participation of so many people not trained for psychotherapy. As seen by the staff, some such group is necessary to make the milieu program workable.

In summary, this is a project that is going into its third year with voluminous data on five families. The total number of clinical subjects and families is too small to know how the observations can supply to a wider clinical group. The most that can be said at this point is that these are observations made on five families with chronic psychotic family members, and that the observations were made in terms of the specific theoretical orientation presented in the paper. A striking change in the staff's perception of schizophrenia began to occur when the entire family group was seen together. In terms of therapeutic response, there have been significant changes in the fathers and mothers and the staff. The patients are much quieter and calmer, but they are still regressed and infantile. The change to the treatment of the family as a unit is considered to have advantages worth a more detailed exploration.

Chapter 2

The Role of the Father in
Families With a Schizophrenic Patient

With the collaboration of Robert H. Dysinger, M.D.,
and Betty Basamania, M.S.W.

The father often plays a peripheral part in the intense conflict in a family with a psychotic patient. The intensity of conflict between mother and patient can defocus his importance in the family problem. This paper will focus on the function of the father in ten families currently participating in a clinical research study. Lidz was one of the first to focus specifically on the role of the father in these families (Lidz et al. 1957).

Four families, consisting of father, mother, and severely impaired schizophrenic patients have lived together on a psychiatric ward in a research center and participated in family psychotherapy for periods up to two and a half years. An additional six families with fathers, mothers, and overtly psychotic schizophrenic patients have been treated in out-patient family therapy for periods up to two years. The details of the theoretical and psychotherapeutic orientation have been presented in other papers (Benedek 1949, Bowen 1957a). Theoretically, the psychosis in the patient is regarded as a symptom of a process that involves the entire family. Psychotherapeutically, the family is treated as if it were a single organism. This report contains material from all ten families. Detailed twenty-four hour daily observations have been made on each member of the in-patient families. The study is thus a longitudinal one in which the day to day adjustment of the families has been followed for fairly long periods.

This paper describes the father as he functions in the day to day life of the family. The term "function" is probably more accurate than the term "role" as used in the title of the paper. This viewpoint could be compared to a familiar model like a football team. We could describe a quarterback in terms of his physical and psychological makeup; or we could describe his individual adaptation to the requirements of the quarterback position; or we could describe his function with the team in an entire season of play. The latter would be similar to the viewpoint from which we have tried to observe family members as they function together as a family unit. A football coach knows his players as individuals but, when he watches the team in action, he focuses first on the team as a functioning unit and then on the functioning of individual team members. We believe there are theoretical and therapeutic advantages in viewing the family as a unit and also in following the family as it functions under varying situations over a long period of time. In our experience, each family member functions in a variety of ways, determined quite as much by the reciprocal functioning of other family members as by forces inside himself. For instance, we often hear that "the father is jealous of the mother's attention to the patient." In these ten families, this might be descriptively accurate for a single situation but descriptively misleading if applied to a total father-daughter relationship. To summarize this point, the father is viewed as he functions as part of the family unit over a prolonged period of time.

The primary family threesome is father, mother, and patient. Normal siblings have also participated in the family studies but the intense conflict remains pretty much confined to the father-mother-patient group. The other siblings soon isolate themselves from the "round robin of conflict" between father, mother, and patient. Another clinical point has been most striking. The family members are quite different in their relationships to figures outside the family than they are toward those within the family. A parent might function successfully and efficiently in outside business and social relationships and yet, within the family group, find self paralyzed by indecision, immaturity and inefficiency.

Functionally, there is a marked emotional distance between the parents in all ten families. There is considerable variation in the way the distance is maintained. One set of parents had a positive but very formal and controlled relationship. They had few overt differences. They saw their marriage as ideal. They reported an active and satisfying sexual relationship. They used conventional terms of endearment with each other but wide areas of personal human experience were obliterated from their thinking and discussions. At the other end of the scale, one set of parents could not remain long in physical proximity with each other without arguments, shouting, and disagreement. In social situations they were congenial. In the middle of the scale, eight sets of parents had adjustments with varying combinations of controlled positiveness and overt disagreement. They were aware of differences but they consciously avoided the touchy points. They maintained sufficient impersonal distance to keep disagreements at a minimum. The families with the most open disagreements have done the best in family psychotherapy.

The fathers and mothers appear equally immature. The surface distance controls a deeper interdependence on each other. One denies the immaturity and functions with a facade of overadequacy. The other accentuates the immaturity and functions with a facade of inadequacy. Neither can function in the midground between overadequacy and inadequacy. In their day to day living, the overadequacy of one functions in reciprocal relationship to the inadequacy of the other. In situations requiring team action, one functions as the overadequate one and the other as the inadequate one. Ackerman (1956) and Mittelman (1956) are among those who describe reciprocal functioning in marriages. A clinical manifestation of the problem is the "domination-submission" issue. The overadequate one is seen as "dominating" and the inadequate one as "forced to submit." Both complain of "domination by" and of being "forced to submit to" the other. Both avoid the responsibility of "dominating" and the anxiety of "submission." Another clinical issue involves decision-making. The families are incapable of decisions that are routine for other families. One father stated this clearly when he said, "We cannot decide together on anything. I suggest we go shopping Saturday afternoon. She objects. We argue. Neither will give in to the other. We end up doing nothing." This example is characteristic of other decisions, both minor and major. Important decisions can remain undecided to be resolved by time, by circumstance, or the advice of an expert. Decisions that are "problems to be solved" by other families become "burdens to be endured" by these families. This paralysis of indecision creates the impression of "weak families." The paralysis subsides when one parent "dominates" the family."

In all ten families the parents hold emotionally charged, intense, opposite viewpoints about the proper treatment for the patient. This conflict exists when there are no other conflicts. One father said "The only question on which we never agree is how to raise children and how to raise parakeets. Neither ever changes a stand and neither ever gives in." The mothers most often get their way while the fathers oppose, either actively or passively. After her way has failed, the father institutes his plan while the mother becomes his critic and the predictor of his failure. The cycle repeats over and over.

There is a constant family relationship pattern in all the families. The parents are emotionally separated by the distance barrier. They cannot have a close relationship with each other but either can have a close relationship with the patient, if the other parent permits. The mother is usually close to the patient and the father is excluded, or he permits himself to be excluded, from the intense mother-patient twosome. The term "intense" describes a close ambivalent relationship in which the thoughts of both, either positive or negative, are invested in each other. The pattern is most frequently changed by the mother, who withdraws from conflict with the patient, and leaves the patient with the father. In these situations, the fathers function as substitute mothers. The father may change the pattern with his own activity but he cannot win the patient until he has somehow dealt with the mother's opposition. In these situations, the fathers have become cruel and dominating and the mothers inadequate and whining. The patient's psychosis is an effective mechanism to rearrange family patterns. In our experience, it is easier for the mother to win the patient from the father than for the father to win the patient from the mother.

The fathers and mothers often divide the patient's time just as divorced parents share their children. This has been striking in the five families with schizophrenic sons. The parents had long been concerned about the son's attachments to their mothers. The mothers blamed the attachments on the father's lack of interest in the sons. Both parents agreed that boys needed close relationships with fathers. All five fathers tried hard to get this closeness. One became a boy scout troop leader to encourage closeness with his son. Another father maintained a regular schedule of father-son activities. Another tried "to be pals" with his son, and another tried a continuing "man-to-man" approach. The mothers approved the father-son efforts, but they did not give up their prior intense attachments, and the fathers' efforts all failed. To summarize this point, the parents have an emotional divorce from each other but either parent can have a close relationship with the patient if the other parent permits.

The family configuration emerges clearly in family psychotherapy. All three members attend therapy hours together. The therapeutic effort is to analyze the existing intrafamily relationships. There are periods when one of the threesome is absent from the hours. When all three family members are present, when the therapist does not structure the hour, and when the family follows the plan of working on its own problem in the hour, then the family group cannot avoid running into intense family conflict, and disagreement. This results in high anxiety, action, and progress in therapy. Any two members of the family threesome can successfully avoid anxiety issues and the therapy becomes a more intellectual, more sterile, and less profitable pursuit.

The relative functioning of the father has been revealed clearly in the sharp changes that occur in the course of family therapy. The usual family begins therapy with a compliant, nonparticipating father and a mother locked in emotional turmoil with a hostile infantile patient. The initial hours deal with the conflict between mother and patient. When the father begins to participate, the conflict shifts to the father-mother relationship. As the father begins to assert his strength, the mother becomes more aggressive, more challenging, and then more overtly anxious. Her anxiety and tears can cause him to retreat from his stand. When the father is "no longer soluble in the tears of the mother" and he can maintain himself as head of the family in spite of her anxiety, the mother goes into several days of intense anxiety. One mother who had been aggressive, hostile, and dominating, changed in a few days to a kind, objective, motherly person. She said, "It is so nice to finally have a man for a husband." Another mother said, "I was so happy to see him stand up for himself. I couldn't help fighting him. It was automatic. All the time I was hoping and hoping he would not get concerned about my anxiety and the things I said." Another mother said, "If he can keep on being a man, then I can be a woman." These changes can last until the parents encounter anxiety. Then they revert to their former way of functioning but the changes repeat with greater frequency and less turmoil. The pattern suggests that a fairly normal family is a flexible one in which parents can shift their functioning according to the prevailing reality without threatening either. The first to change in these families has been the parent in the inadequate position, whether it be father or mother.

When the parents change their functioning, the patient becomes more disturbed. The first real change in the patients has taken place when the mothers can maintain a firm stand against the infantile clinging of the patient. During one change in the parents, the staff referred to the parental closeness as "the honeymoom." When the parents can maintain a closeness in which they are more invested in each other than either is invested in the patient, then the patients have made rapid gains. When either parent becomes more invested in the patient than in the other parent, the psychotic process becomes intensified.

There was a change in one family which was different from the above. A son dominated a home with his psychotic demands. His parents, especially the father, was fearful of physical harm if they opposed him. The anxiety reached a peak in which the father took a stand. The patient attacked. The father subdued the son physically. There was immediate peace and quiet in the house. Within a week the patient's psychotic symptoms subsided and he returned to school. The father policed the home for a month. His relationship to the son had changed and the son's relationship to the mother had changed but there had been no change between father and mother. The father said, "I can't take it any more." He gave up his strong stand, the mother resumed her picking on the patient, and the patient resumed his psychotic behavior. The parents had each changed their relationship to the son without a change between themselves.

Summary. A small number of fathers, mothers, and schizophrenic patients have been studied as a group and treated in family psychotherapy for periods up to two and a half years. The view of the family as a single organism provides a broader, more distant perspective than is possible with close up views of individual family members. An effort is made to avoid the use of terms and descriptions that are associated with the more familiar individual perspective.

The father is described as he is seen to function in terms of the broader family perspective. Several prominent patterns have emerged when the family has been viewed from this position. The family members, particularly the father and mother, function in reciprocal relation to each other. They are separated from each other by an emotional barrier which, in some ways, has characteristics of an "emotional divorce." Either father or mother can have a close emotional relationship with the patient when the other parent permits. The patient's function is similar to that of an unsuccessful mediator of the emotional differences between the parents. The most frequent family pattern is an intense twosome between mother and patient which excludes the father and from which he permits himself to be excluded. The family pattern changes under varying individual and family circumstances in the course of daily living.

Chapter 3

Family Relationships
in Schizophrenia

Two hundred years ago, Laurence Sterne (1762), in his novel *The Life and Opinions of Tristram Shandy*, described family relationships in a way that is strikingly appropriate today. Tristram Shandy said, "Though in one sense, our family was certainly a simple machine, as it consisted of a few wheels, yet there was this much to be said for it, that these wheels were set in motion by so many different springs, and acted one upon the other from such a variety of strange principles and impulses—that though it was a simple machine, it had all the honor and advantages of a complex one—and a number of as odd movements within it, as ever were beheld in the inside of a Dutch silkmill."

In this paper some relationship patterns observed in families with a schizophrenic son or daughter are to be described. The families have been part of a clinical research project in which fathers, mothers, schizophrenic patients, and normal siblings have lived together on a psychiatric ward in a research center. Four of these in-residence families have now participated in the research study and in family psychotherapy for periods up to two and a half years. The average length of in-residence participation has been one and a half years. An additional six families consisting of fathers, mothers, and moderately disturbed psychotic patients have been treated in outpatient family psychotherapy for periods up to two years. The study is an intensive longitudinal one which has followed the clinical course of ten family groups for fairly long periods of time. The most important part of the research study has been the four in-residence families. The parents assume the major responsibility for the psychotic family member. The structure permits a parent to work and the normal sibling to attend school, but it requires the family to attend the daily family psychotherapy hours. There are detailed around-the-clock observations on each family member. This longitudinal view of the families, as they live, eat, play, and work together through periods of success, failure, crisis, and physical illness provides our best source of subjective and objective research data.

The theoretical orientation and the psychotherapy approach for this project was developed from experience during the first year of the project. During that year three schizophrenic patients and their mothers lived together on the ward. Each patient and each mother had individual psychotherapy. The details of that part of the study have been reported in other papers (Bowen et al. 1957, Bowen 1957a, 1960). To summarize briefly, there had been increasing experience to suggest that the mother-patient relationship was a dependent fragment of a larger family problem and that the father played an important part in it. The research hypothesis was extended to consider the psychosis in the patient as the symptom manifestation of a problem that involved the entire family. The research plan was changed to permit entire family groups to live on the ward together. The psychotherapy plan was changed to make it more consistent with the research hypothesis. The new plan was one in which family members attended all psychotherapy hours together. We[1] have called this *family psychotherapy*. There are two important concepts in this theoretical orientation. The first is the concept of the family unit. We attempt to think of the family and to relate to the family as though it were a single unit or single organism. The second is the concept of family psychotherapy. We attempt to direct the psychotherapy to the family unit rather than to the individual.

A major problem has been the orientation of ourselves to a family-unit way of thinking. We have all been trained to think of emotional problems in terms of the individual. The entire body of psychoanalytic and psychological theory is oriented to the individual. All our diagnostic and descriptive terms apply to the individual. It has been difficult to change this automatic way of thinking in ourselves. Even after the staff had achieved some success at thinking of the family as a unit, we found that the use of familiar psychiatric terms could result in an immediate associative shift back to "second-nature" individual orientation. To facilitate the shift to family-unit thinking, we have tried to avoid the use of terms associated with the individual and to force ourselves to use simple descriptive words. Another difficulty in the family-unit orientation is an emotional tone. In our daily living experience, we all constantly participate emotionally in the life about us. We identify ourselves with the victim, we applaud the hero, and we hate the villain. A family in daily living contact with a psychotic members has a high level of anxiety and emotion. There are frequent emotional crises that portray one member as victim, another as hero, and another as villain. It is easy for the observer to become so involved in the emotion that he loses objectivity. The emotional situation is further complicated by the efforts of each family member to find a staff ally for his or her emotional point of view. Staff members have tended to detach themselves emotionally to the point that they can work with the families without becoming overinvolved in the vigorous ebb and flow of conflictual emotion.

We believe there are certain distinct advantages to having a family-unit orientation in addition to our more familiar individual orientation. When it is possible to defocus the individual, to find a perspective that permits the entire family into vision at once, and to continue the observations for long periods, it is then possible to get a much clearer view of over-all patterns. We have compared this to changing the lens of a microscope from the oil-immersion to a low-power lens, or to moving from the playing field to the top of the stadium to watch a football game. The view from the top of the stadium makes it possible to see broad patterns of movement and team functioning that are obscured by the close-up view. It is easier to see the team as a unit from this perspective. This in no way detracts from the value of the individual orientation. In fact, the distant view enhances the close-up view. For instance, the high magnification of the oil-immersion lens is far more meaningful after it has been possible to see the larger area through the low-power lens. The broader viewpoint, maintained over long periods of time, helps to put clinical fragments into place. For example, we often hear statements like, "The father was seductive toward the daughter." In our experience with these families, this might be descriptively accurate in describing an occasional or transient phase in their relationship but inaccurate and misleading if applied to their over-all relationship. We agree with those who would like to have a family diagnosis in addition to individual diagnoses. Ackerman (1956) has worked toward defining interlocking pathology in family relationships. Mittelman (1956) has described reciprocal relationships between family members. After working at this problem for over three years, our effort has been going toward some kind of concept that deals with the *function* of one person in relation to another, rather than with the more static situation implied in a diagnostic label. Spiegel (1957) includes the idea of function in his work on role theory, though it is not specifically stressed.

In this paper I wish to focus on the *functioning* of one person in relation to another and on broad *patterns* of behavior that are more easily seen from "the top of the stadium." I shall defocus, as much as possible, the more specific relationship characteristics which have been reported in other papers. In this regard, our observations of specific characteristics have much in common with the work of Lidz et al. (1957; also Lidz 1958), Jackson and Bateson (1956), and Wynne et al. (1958). The main part of this paper will be devoted to the clinical course of a single family. Before considering the single family, however, some of the over-all *patterns* of family *functioning* that appear to us to be most important are here reviewed. These patterns of functioning have been presented in more detail in other papers (Bowen 1960, Bowen et al. 1959), but they are of sufficient importance to the understanding of this presentation to be reviewed here.

There has been a high level of emotional conflict in the research families. For brief periods the conflict may be equally present in several family members. The conflict tends to localize in the family member who is in the weakest and most inadequate position. The localization occurs through a process of reciprocal functioning in which all family members participate. The conflict tends to localize in the schizophrenic member. When the emotional conflict is "fixed" in the weakest member by means of a diagnosis and by the designation of *patient*, the family problem becomes more crystalized in the person of the patient, and anxiety in the family is greatly increased. When the parents and patients are brought together in a living situation in a hospital ward, and the designation *patient* is purposely left ambiguous, the family conflict again becomes more fluid and shifting. Parents begin to develop intense anxiety and conflict. Such a family can accurately be called a *disturbed family*.

Family members, and especially the parents, are quite different in their business and social relationships outside the family from what they are to those within the family. The parents might function adequately and successfully in outside business and social relationships while they are immature, indecisive, and inadequate within the family. The primary family members involved in the family conflict are the father, mother, and the patient. Other family members are involved to a much lesser extent. This was particularly striking in the families in which normal siblings lived in residence as long as one year. There were times when the normal siblings were intensely involved, but they could always separate themselves from the conflict and leave the father, mother, and patient to continue in cyclical conflict. We have referred to the father, mother, and patient as the *interdependent triad*.

There is a striking emotional distance between the parents in all the families. We have called this the *emotional divorce*. As I see it, the situation began early in the marriage with alternating periods of overcloseness and overdistance which then settled down to the more fixed, and less anxious, emotional distance. Some parents maintain the distance with a very formal, positive, and controlled relationship. These marriages have the words and actions to give a superficial appearance of closeness, but feeling and emotion is obliterated from the parental relationships. Other parents have so much emotion and disagreement that they use physical distance to maintain the "divorce." Most parents use combinations of controlled positiveness and physical distance.

The parents in all the families have a constant pattern of functioning in their relationship together. We have called this the *overadequate-inadequate reciprocity*. Both parents are equally immature. In any teamwork activity, the one who makes decisions for the two of them becomes the overadequate one and the other becomes the inadequate or helpless one. Neither is able to find mid-ground functioning between the two extremes. The overadequate one is seen as dominating, authoritative, or stubborn and the inadequate one as helpless, compliant, and forced into submission by the dominant one. Either mother or father can function in either position though they eventually find an equilibrium in which one is overadequate in most areas and the other overadequate in fewer areas. They tend to solve the anxiety of the overadequate-inadequate reciprocity in rather consistent ways. They can reduce the areas of joint activity and increase their individual activities. It is common for fathers to devote themselves almost entirely to business and for mothers to be completely in charge of home and children. When they do encounter a decision in the area of joint activity, they have either to avoid the decision, postpone it, or face the anxiety and conflict when one "takes the bull by the horns" and assumes the overadequate position. An example is a father who has no problem in important decisions at work but who can end up in an emotional, paralyzing deadlock when he and the mother try to decide which movie to see.

All the parents have highly charged opposing viewpoints about how to relate to the psychotic patient. This seems to be their one joint activity about which conflict remains most intense. They do not reveal such conflict about the normal siblings. The parents may not become aware of the disagreement about the patient until psychotherapy is under way. A familiar pattern is one in which the mother had her way while the father retreated and said nothing about his intense opposing viewpoint. The mother may go many years believing the father to be in agreement with her viewpoint and then be completely surprised to hear of his long-term opposition. If the parents disagree openly, they may alternate their plans for the patient, each one "letting the other have his way to prove him wrong."

There are some constant relationship patterns within the interdependent triad. The parents are separated from each other by the emotional divorce. They cannot have a close relationship with each other, but either can have a close relationship with the patient if the other permits. Functionally, this is similar to the way divorced parents share their children. The mother usually has the primary relationship or "custody" of the patient while the father is excluded or permits himself to be excluded from the intense mother-patient relationship. There are repeating situations that follow the same pattern. The mother does things to keep the patient attached to her. Verbally, she blames the father for his lack of interest in the patient. The father has actually been making a long-term effort to win the patient to his side. He sees his poor relationship with the patient as his failure to be a good father. When the mother accuses him of neglecting the patient, he tries to get close to the patient. If the patient shows too much interest in the father, the mother moves to intensify the patient's attachment to her. There are several variations to the pattern. Mothers arrange for fathers and patients to spend regular time together, but they initiate it and the father in such a case functions more like a baby sitter than a father. The psychotic patient can become so hostile and aggressive that the mother rejects the patient or goes away. The father then moves into what would appear to be a close relationship, but, in our experience, the father still functions as a substitute mother and the mother can usually win back the patient, even after long absences. As I currently see it, the father has somehow to deal directly with the mother before he can have a real father relationship to the patient.

Now to a consideration of family psychotherapy and to some of the sharp, clear changes in family functioning that have occurred during the course of family psychotherapy. These changes have been of crucial importance in the research study. The first such change came unexpectedly some six months after the first family was admitted. The father had slowly changed from a passive compliant fellow to a man of more strength and conviction. When he had reached a point of self-assertion that was greater than the mother's aggression and domination, she immediately went through a series of dramatic changes. She had long been the resourceful and overadequate one in the family. Within a few days she became tremulous, tearful, and overtly anxious. She was fearful and felt helpless. The father maintained his stand in spite of her anxiety and within two weeks she had changed to a calm, objective, firm, motherly person. She said, "If he can keep on being a man, then I can be a woman." The emotional divorce was resolved and the father and mother were as devoted to each other as a teen-age couple in love for the first time. They were so much invested in each other that neither was overinvested in the patient. Both were then able, for the first time, to be objective toward the patient. At this point, the schizophrenic daughter began some significant changes toward more adequate functioning. The new functioning level lasted a month and then the family suddenly reverted to the old way of functioning; but thereafter, it was easier for the father to pull up to more adequate functioning and less threatening for the mother to give up the overadequate position. It was this change and similar changes in other families that highlighted facets of the problem not particularly noted before. It was the changes in the families during family psychotherapy that led to the concept of the functioning of one person in relation to another. Before this experience, we had thought in terms of "the father *is* one kind of person, the mother *is* another kind of person, and the patient *becomes* another kind of person." The research operation had first gone toward defining what we believed to be the fixed characteristics of each family member. After we had seen changes in one family member followed by immediate complementing changes in other family members, and after we had seen changes in characteristics formerly considered to be fixed, we began to work toward the concept of the functioning of one person in relation to another.

The techniques of the family psychotherapy were developed from clinical observation in the research study. After a clinical pattern had repeated itself sufficiently to permit an extension in theoretical thinking, the working hypothesis was extended. Then the psychotherapy approach was changed to make it as consistent as possible with the research hypothesis. In this way the theoretical thinking and the psychotherapy complemented each other. We have attempted to differentiate family psychotherapy from individual and from group psychotherapy. Individual psychotherapy focuses on psychological understanding of the individual in terms of concepts developed for the individual. The analysis of the transference relationship between patient and therapist is an important part of the treatment process. One of our goals in family psychotherapy is to leave the already existing intense relationships within the family group and to analyze the relationships *in situ* rather than to permit transfer to the relationship with the therapist. An effort has been made to define and to avoid those things which encourage the individual relationship with the resulting transference to the therapist. We believe it is technically possible for the analyst to remain in a fairly objective relationship to the family organism in this way. Of course, the analyst hopefully remains objective when he is in an individual relationship with a psychotic patient, but the patient has the potential of creating a crisis which can force the analyst into dealing with, rather than analyzing the crisis situation. In family psychotherapy, the parents are present to deal with the upset in the patient and the therapist is free to remain an observer and to analyze the situation in which one side of the family organism acts up against the other side. It should be obvious that the therapist is not permitted to participate in the intense emotional process in the family. Even when the therapist takes sides without expressing it, the other family members can become aware of it and react negatively toward this countertransference participation. When the therapist can avoid individual relationships, there usually develops a dependent relationship with the family unit which is then analyzed.

Family psychotherapy is also clearly differentiated from group psychotherapy. A psychotherapy group is an assembly of people brought together with a therapeutic goal. Group members are comparative strangers in contrast to the intense interdependent relationships between family members. A goal of group therapy is to understand the individual in the context of his relationships in a group of other individuals.

The clinical course of a single family in outpatient psychotherapy with a single therapist will be used to illustrate the changes in family functioning during psychotherapy and to illustrate the principles of family psychotherapy as developed in the research project. A single therapist with a single family is the simplest example of our psychotherapy effort. The impatient families become involved in complex relationships with the staff, other family groups, and with the hospital environment. As a group the outpatient families have progressed more rapidly in family therapy.

The family to be described is one that has progressed most rapidly and that has shown striking changes in relationship functioning. The family history is very similar to that of several families in the study. The parents were in their fifties. The psychotic patient was a daughter in her late twenties who had been overtly psychotic for six years. The father was a quiet, soft-spoken businessman who had devoted most of his energies to business. He often worked nights and weekends. At home he functioned as the provider and the one responsible for repairs and maintenance of the home. All his life he had worried about financial security. The mother was an outgoing, aggressive resourceful woman who managed to keep going even when she did not feel like it. During their thirty years of marriage, the mother had devoted herself to the children and the home while the father had devoted himself to the business. Within the family the mother was the overadequate decision-making one while the father remained on the periphery of the family circle. The daughter had been the helpless inadequate one since her first acute psychotic break while still in college. She was the oldest of two daughters. The other daughter, three years younger, had been relatively uninvolved in the family turmoil. She separated herself from the family after college and has made a good adjustment.

The family was prominent and respected in the small town in which they lived. The father had moved to this town as a single man to establish his business. He met the mother through a business acquaintance when she visited the town. They had a brief courtship. He took a few days from his business for the wedding. The business did well. After a few years they built a new home in one of the better sections of town. This house is still the family home. The family group consisted of father, mother, and the two daughters. The mother wanted children for "my fulfillment as a woman." The father wanted to wait until their financial future was more secure. The mother was overinvested in the child by the time she knew she was pregnant. Her overinvestment was expressed in fears, concerns, and worries that the child would be defective or born dead. Her worries about the child were more intense when she was emotionally detached from the father. The worries decreased when she was closer to the father. She felt a great relief when she first saw the baby and could see for herself that it was alive and well. She was impressed by the "tiny helplessness" of the baby. She felt a surge of maternal instinct to protect and care for the child. The second daughter never occupied this position of importance in the mother's thoughts.

The mother's overinvestment in the first daughter continued over the years. When the second child was born, she was impressed with the reaction of the older child and decided, "she needs me more than the baby." Through the years she worried about the daughter's development, her appearance, her dress, her hair, her complexion, her social life, and many other such items. There was much less concern about the second daughter who, "somehow was able to get along by herself." In childhood the daughter was shy, immature, and compliant. She was bright and she learned quickly but she was very attached to the mother and "she never learned how to relate with other children." The father and mother had become increasingly distant in their relationship. He was completely involved with the business while the mother was devoted to doing a good job with the children. She felt there was no sacrifice too great for the children, especially the older daughter, who seemed to need so much more from the mother. Socially the parents were congenial. Their social relationships were not close but they belonged to social and civic clubs and they were active in their home town. At home they had sharp differences in opinion and frequent arguments, but they avoided touchy points to keep disagreements to a minimum.

There were several changes in the family during a two-year period when the daughter reached adolescence. The daughter was much attached to the mother. She began to act very grown-up and to deny the need for the mother. She had been shy and inhibited in her school relationships. Now she became outgoing, overactive, and pushed in her drive for friends.

The mother was offered a job and she began to work. The father had some business reverses, but he took on additional business responsibility and began to work longer hours. The parents moved to separate bedrooms at home. The family kept up this increased tempo of living for several years. The daughter was vaguely aware of her dependence on the mother, but she looked forward to college and living away from home to bring about an emancipation from the family.

The daughter developed her first acute psychotic break while living away at college. This was the beginning of a six-year period of psychosis and family prostration. The psychotic daughter was hospitalized and for the next several years she was either acutely psychotic and in a hospital or living at home on a borderline adjustment. The mother pulled up to her most overadequate level of functioning. She assumed responsibility for the daughter and made the decisions for hospitalization against the daughter's protests. The father had a series of business reverses and within a year after the psychosis in the daughter, he lost his business. The mother was the decision-making breadwinner for the family. Her thoughts were almost totally invested in the daughter. The father worked at a number of different jobs, but he was at the most ineffective period in his life. He was opposed to the mother's decisions about the daughter but, on the surface, he went along with her. The only one who changed during this period was the younger daughter, who finished college and became a schoolteacher in a distant state.

During hospitalizations the daughter was an overactive assaultive patient who spent much time in packs and restraints. She was treated with intensive individual psychotherapy, electroshock treatment, and tranquilizer drugs. During her periods at home she usually isolated herself or became overactive in responding to delusional thinking. The family home was mortgaged to finance private treatment. Eventually the family finances were completely exhausted and she was transferred to a state institution. The father was able to get another business of his own started about this time. The daughter returned home after about six months in the state hospital. Family life at home was stormy with much family turmoil and psychotic acting-out by the patient.

It was at this point, six years after the onset of the psychosis, that the father, mother, and daughter began family psychotherapy. The mother inquired about individual psychotherapy for the daughter. Family psychotherapy was discussed in the initial interview. She was enthusiastic about the idea of family treatment. She was to discuss the idea with the father and daughter. There was no space for this family in the inpatient study. We agreed to do outpatient family therapy if the family wished to proceed with that plan, or we could refer them elsewhere for individual psychotherapy. Since there was no space on the inpatient ward, it would be necessary for them to again use the state hospital if the daughter required hospitalization. The father was noncommittal. The daughter said she needed freedom, not treatment. There was another family fight. The mother moved away from home saying that she would return only after the father and daughter had made the first appointment for family therapy. About ten days later the fater called and asked for an appointment.

This series of events has been a common pattern with the research families. The parent in the adequate decision-making position is usually the one who asks about treatment. It is common for other family members to oppose either actively or passively. The decision-making parent usually asks the therapist to persuade the opposing members in favor of the psychotherapy effort. The therapists have been complete failures at this, but the adequate parent, the functioning leader of the family, has ways to overcome the resistance. We have made it a basic rule to respect the one in the adequate position as family leader and negotiator. For instance, the therapist may say that he wants one family member to be the spokesman and negotiator for arrangements, like making or changing appointments, but the family may designate another spokesman any time they wish. The families with the most active intrafamily resistance, emotion, and disagreement have done the best in psychotherapy.

Now to a summary of eighty-four hours of family psychotherapy that has now covered a period of fifteen months. The mother decided to begin with two hours a week. Our first basic rule is that the family work on its own problem in the hour while the therapist observes from the sideline and attempts to understand and analyze the emotional process between the family members. The goal is to get the family to work together on the problem. When the family attempts to follow this therapy structure, intense anxiety develops. There are several ways in which the family attempts to avoid the anxiety. The most frequent is for the decision-making family member to engage the therapist in conversation. In addition to avoiding the family problem, it tends to encourage an individual relationship with the therapist, and the decision-making family member thus becomes more dependent on the therapist. Some families have been able to keep this going with the therapists for weeks but when the therapist is able to structure himself out of the "working-together effort" of the family, preferably by analyzing the family effort to avoid the structure, another series of anxiety-avoiding mechanisms is seen. The next most frequent is for the parents to talk to the psychotic one about the psychosis. There is the emotional divorce between the parents. It is extremely difficult for parents to discuss personal problems about themselves, but it is comparatively easy for either parent to talk directly to the patient, and this frequently changes rapidly to criticism of the patient. Other ways the parents avoid anxiety between themselves is by small talk or by silence.

The mother in this family opened the therapy with comments to the daughter about her psychotic behavior. The daughter responded with denial. This soon became a highly emotional denial and contradiction of the mother's statements. The mother said, "It is your unreasonableness and screaming that try my soul." The daughter said, "It is the things you do that make me scream." The mother continued to refer to the daughter as "sick" and to prove her statements with historical material. In response to the word *sick* the daughter's emotion and anxiety would increase. When her anger at the mother would increase to a certain level, she would suddenly shift to paranoid delusions and with greatly increased emotion scream that she would kill the boy friend who had wronged her. This boy friend had sided with the mother in one of the issues between the mother and daughter. The mother would yell, "Shut up, you will disturb other people." The daughter would cry. The mother would cry and say it was hopeless. The father would move to silence the daughter and say to the mother, "Don't cry. It is not so bad." Few things disturb the parents as much as hostile psychotic expressions from the patient. Family members are distressed by tears, especially tears in the overadequate mother.

The intense conflict between mother and daughter continued for about twenty hours at two to three hours a week. There were two consecutive hours that went about as follows: The mother began with a story that conveyed that she had been a good mother but that the daughter had been a terrible and ungrateful daughter. The daughter responded with stories to deny the mother's accusations, more stories to prove that she had been a good daughter, and more stories to prove the mother had been a poor mother. The mother would relate incidents to deny the accusation, more incidents to prove she had been a good mother, and still more incidents to support the thesis that the daughter was selfish and ungrateful. The daughter would then deny the accusation, offer proof that she was a good daughter, and more proof that the mother was a terrible mother. This cycle repeated itself over and over in these hours.

In our experience, a therapist can lose his way if he permits himself to become involved in evaluating the dramatic historical material that comes up in such hours. In these hours the therapist confined himself to pointing out the "proof that I am wonderful—proof that you are terrible" pattern. The vigor of the daughter's stand against the mother seemed a good prognostic sign. The inactivity of the father was most striking during this period. He was more a spectator than participant in the family problem. Both the mother and daughter tried to get him to take sides, but he successfully stayed on the periphery. The therapist then began to focus on the passivity of the father.

Clinical experience with passive fathers had a long background in the family therapy effort. The one most striking pattern in the research families has been that of the aggressive mother and the passive peripheral father. In the first year or so of the project, we described this by saying, "The problem in the family is as much an act of omission by the father as it is an act of commission by the mother." There had been two families with dramatic changes similar to the family reported earlier in this paper. In these families the first to change had been the fathers, and there had been striking changes in the entire family when the fathers became active, assertive participants in the family problem. These changes would usually last for a few weeks and then the family would revert to the former functioning. Two fathers reverted to the inadequate functioning when they developed minor physical illnesses. After the first change had been possible, however, it became increasingly easy for the fathers to pull up to more adequate functioning and less threatening for the mothers to give up the overadequate functioning. From these experiences, we would postulate that a fairly normal family is one in which parents can function in either the strong or the weak position, according to the demands of the situation, without threatening either one.

The project staff had been quite impressed with the changes in the families when passive fathers began to participate in the family problem. We reasoned that if the first change to be expected was activity from the passive father, then the psychotherapy might be facilitated by focusing on the passivity of the father. Eventually this was abandoned. One family in particular helped to point up our therapy problem. The therapist had been making comments about the father's withdrawal and apologies. Gradually the father became more active and assertive if the mother was at home. She, as all the mothers have done, challenged his strength. She asked him where he got his ideas. He said, "The doctor told me I should do it this way." This was one of the incidents which caused the therapists to stick to analyzing what went on in the families instead of trying to influence the families in a particular direction.

This phase of the therapy with this outpatient family occurred at the time that the therapists were focusing on the passivity of fathers. The therapist said to the father, "You never express opinions about family problems. It cannot be that you do not have opinions." The father said softly, "Well, I do think mother picks on her sometimes." The mother responded vigorously, "What was that? What was it you said?" The father said, "Well, I do think you start some of these fights." The mother said, "Name one! Just name one. Come on and get specific. Give me just *one* example." The father turned to the therapist and said, "See, I was squelched." The therapist said, "I just watched you get yourself squelched."

During the next hour the father was in a more inadequate position than he had been before. For the first time there was some mention that the father's new business might fail. During the next hours the daughter became increasingly psychotic, the mother increasingly strong, and the father increasingly peripheral and inadequate. The schizophrenic patients in our families have been like sponges for absorbing family anxiety. This daughter rushed in to bolster the anxious father, except that her help came out in psychotic schemes which she acted out in town. The parents began to hint at hospitalization for the daughter. She opposed them vigorously. This was a crucial period in family therapy. The parents wanted support for their view that the daughter should be hospitalized and the daughter wanted support for her view that she was functioning better all the time. To agree with the parents would be to support the family forces to "fix" the problem in the daughter. To agree with the daughter might delay the parents taking steps to protect the community from the daughter's paranoid annoyance of people in town. The therapist tried to remain neutral. He made statements like the following: "It is the parents' responsibility to determine when you are no longer able to carry on at home. People go to mental hospitals when the family or when society asks for it. Many very upset people continue to live with their families. It is a family decision to determine when the family can no longer remain together at home. Mental hospitals do impose difficult situations for patients but the human organism is capable of growth when it has to adjust to difficult situations." The therapist said they should make their own decision if they did decide to hospitalize the daughter.

The mother made the decision and the arrangements to hospitalize the daughter. This occurred after ten weeks and twenty-six hours of family therapy. There were many telephone calls preceding the hospitalization.

This brings in some of our other basic rules of family therapy. One is the rule about individual communications from family members who attempt to influence the therapist to an individual viewpoint through telephone calls, letters, and messages. The rule is that the therapist will discuss such individual communications at the next meeting of the family group. Frequently a family member will test this rule by communicating personal information by the telephone. Another rule is that family psychotherapy can continue with only two family members present, but, if only one member can attend, the meetings will be discontinued until at least two can again be present. If only one member attended, it would be considered individual therapy. It has been our experience that when father, mother, and patient are present together and the therapist is able to maintain the therapy structure, the family soon encounters conflict and disagreement. This results in high anxiety, action, and progress in therapy. Any two members of the father-mother-patient threesome can successfully avoid anxiety issues and the therapy becomes more intellectual, more sterile, and less profitable. There was a marked calm between the parents the day the daughter was hospitalized. The mother reduced the appointments to once a week. The parents talked about visits to the hospital, the comments of the hospital doctors, and the status of the liquidation of the father's business.

The daughter remained in the hospital for three months. She spent half the time on a disturbed ward where she fought, defied the staff, and spent time in seclusion. She was especially antagonistic to doctors who called her "sick." She was psychotically angry with the mother for "forcing her into the hospital" and "controlling the doctors who kept her there." There were explosive scenes when the mother visited. The mother decided against visits "for the good of the daughter," but she encouraged the father to go regularly. After the acute upset had subsided, the mother visited again. The daughter agreed not to mention the paranoid delusions which upset the mother. She kept the promise but took up another equally sensitive issue which created a scene. She wrote one letter to the therapist in which she wondered how the therapist stood the parents and asking him to help her get out of the hospital. The therapist read the letter at the next hour with the parents saying that since this was family therapy, family matters would be discussed with those able to attend. If they wished, they could convey to the absent family member that he had received her letter and that she was probably more familiar than he with requirements for discharge from the hospital. Her acute upset subsided on tranquilizer drugs.

The daughter asked to return to the therapy hours. The parents arranged a hospital pass for her to attend one family meeting. She returned on the thirty-seventh hour after having missed ten hours. The following week she attended two hours. She was in a state of amazing intellectual insight but emotions were very controlled. Events shifted rapidly in the next two months. She remained home on a trial-visit status; the therapist went on a vacation; the mother went on vacation for three weeks; and she began to work. The absence of the therapist in family cases causes much less of a problem than in individual therapy. There was an anxious period before the mother left. The daughter presented a "I cannot get along without you" picture to the mother. The mother started to cancel a trip planned sometime before. The therapist asked if the mother was treating the daughter as if she really were helpless. The day after the mother left, the daughter found a job as a file clerk. She worked, kept house for the father, and cooked. She was extremely anxious and concerned that she would be fired, but the father's unexcited do-nothing attitude seemed helpful. If the mother had been present she undoubtedly would have been on the telephone to fight the daughter's battles. Therapy hours were calm and uneventful during the absence of the mother. The therapist made comments like, "What will happen if she is fired? Will she collapse or disintegrate, or will she learn from the experience?" The girl lost her job the week the mother returned, but she immediately found another on her own initiative.

The therapy remained uneventful after the mother returned. There had been some changes. The daughter was working but still very anxious. The mother was more detached and less influenced by the daughter's anxiety. Instead of becoming overhelpful and advising, she could now say, "Make up your own mind what you want to do and do it." The daughter complained of lack of motivation. She said, "My spirit, my imagination, my fight is all gone. Unless I can get back my fight, I am sunk. It is the tranquilizers. It is awful not to be anxious in situations in which anyone would be anxious." She begged the doctors to stop the drug. The mother insisted that it be continued. The question of "sick" came up again.

This issue and the use of diagnostic labels is very important in these families. In all ten families there is a pattern in which the patient becomes the scapegoat of the family problem. It is inaccurate to say that the patient is a "victim" in this process. In our experience, the parents and patients all participate in this process by which the family problem locates in the patient. This has been a long-term shifting process in the family.

On the day the shifting process is finally given a diagnostic label and is officially located in the person of the patient, a big change takes place in the family. The shifting process is then more fixed and crystallized in the patient. This was one of the factors that led to our concept of schizophrenia as a process that involves the entire family and especially to our effort to treat the family as a single unit. Generally we have avoided the use of diagnostic labels and have especially avoided agreeing with the family process to fix the problem in the patient. In my opinion, this would be one of the main advantages if we had a family diagnosis instead of individual diagnoses. This issue about "sick" came up again in this family. They asked the therapist for his opinion. He said it made no difference to him what label they used. If they wanted to use the term *schizophrenic* he would insist that the family be called *schizophrenic*. If the parents were called *normal* then he would insist the daughter also be called *normal*. The issue never came up again.

An impasse in therapy continued for about six weeks after the return of the mother. No one agreed or disagreed. Each would wait for the other to begin the hours. No one had a problem. They attempted to engage the therapist in social conversation. The therapist made several unsuccessful attempts to break up the impasse. The daughter was the one who was most alive and the one who introduced more issues into the hours. The therapist wondered if her functioning would improve if he devoted time to her problems. He decided to respond directly to her the next time she spoke directly to him. This was an individual relationship between the therapist and one family member. So, the next time she directed a comment to him, he responded as in individual psychotherapy. The daughter liked it. She came to life. The parents became interested spectators. At one point the mother started to say something. The father said, "Sh-h-h, let's see how he does it." Within the week the daughter telephoned the therapist twice. One message was, "something inside me tells me to resign my office job and get a job as a waitress or dishwasher. Unless I do, I am afraid the 'real me' may get blocked. I know mother is against it. What can I do? Can you help me figure it out?" The therapist abandoned the trial at an individual relationship after one hour.

During the next hour of family therapy he made another effort. He said, "The family acts as if you are waiting on me, or time, or Fate for the answer to your problems. Somewhere I may have led you to believe I knew some answers. Actually, psychiatry has never found an answer to schizophrenia, though the premise of family therapy is that the family can find its own answers if they work on it." He said he was going to fall back and become a nonparticipating, note-taking observer. At the end of the hour the mother said, "Does this mean you will not see us again when you say we have to do it ourselves?" The therapist asked the others for their perception of his comments. The mother was amazed that she was the only one to hear the comments this way. This was the beginning of family discussions at home to find differences in the way each heard such comments.

The reason for the impasse in therapy became clearer. The mother had not resumed her adequate function as family leader since her vacation. The lead position had been dropped and the family sat and looked at the therapist. This helped to clarify our position on another basic rule: this is to support the family member who motivates the situation. When therapists have become critical of the family member who gets things done, they have found themselves with passive, complaining families that wait for the therapists to supply answers. This has been a greater problem with hospitalized families. It is very easy for the staff to become critical of the parents' actions and then for the parents to become inactive. Now, we would say to recognize the effort of the one who motivates the family, even if his actions appear traumatic or "schizophrenogenic." We have seen patients respond favorably to such activity from a parent.

In this family the mother was clearly the adequate one before her vacation. She was still the breadwinner. As soon as the therapist began to recognize her position, she moved immediately into the family lead and, after a two-month impasse, family therapy was under way again. She went into a vigorous attack on the inadequacy of the father. She said with great feeling, "I am tired supporting you. I wonder how I got myself into this position. You remain an unemployed executive while your family starves." This was the first real conflictual emotion between the parents. Previous conflict had involved mother and patient. The father made a plea for his inadequate position. He said, "This is the way you have always been. I am down and I need your help. All I get is your bitter tongue and your lashing out." The mother held her stand. She said, "You ask for my help! I have been supporting you for years. All I have done all my life is support you. Do you want me to support you the rest of our lives?" This phase continued for three weeks. The father made some changes. On a business trip he developed an acute intestinal upset and was hospitalized. An elective operation was advised. He returned home for the operation. He was hospitalized for two weeks and missed three appointments. It is not unusual for a parent in an inadequate position to develop a physical illness when he attempts to pull up to more adequate functioning.

The mother made her greatest progress during the absence of the father. This was nine months and sixty hours after the start of therapy.

She became intensely aware of how much her thoughts were devoted to the daughter. She wondered why this happened. She wondered why she always had the same feelings and emotions as the daughter. She recalled an incident when the daughter, then a child, had injured her head. Instantly, her own head had begun to hurt in the exact spot where the daughter's head was injured. She pondered the *why* of this. She concluded that her own life was connected with the daughter in some very complex way. She decided to "put an invisible wall between us so I can have my life and she can have hers." The daughter confirmed this fusion of feelings. She had never been able to know how she herself felt. She had depended on the mother to tell he how she felt. When she occasionally had some feeling different from what the mother said, she discounted it and felt the way her mother said she felt. She depended on her mother to tell her how she looked, if colors matched, and other such things. Away at school she could have some feelings of her own unless a teacher or some such person suggested she must feel a certain way. When she returned home she would again lose her ability to have her own feelings. The daughter then described her ability to know how her mother felt. The mother arrived at the conclusion that parents should let their children lead their own lives. Although she must have heard this hundreds of times, she reacted as if she had just discovered a fresh new truth for herself.

The mother activated this emotional disengagement from the daughter during the absence of the father. The daughter responded with pleas of helplessness to the mother. The mother said firmly, "It is your life. You decide." In the meanwhile the daughter had been very successful at work. She won the admiration of fellow employees for her ability to get along with a dominating woman boss. She resigned after three months to take a better job in the field of her college training. Her old employer offered to meet the new salary if she would remain. The office gave her a going-away party at which she cried.

The mother relinquished her lead position and there were two weeks of little activity in therapy. Then the daughter picked up the lead and began moving forward. She suddenly became popular socially. Her relationships with men were intense. She began dating several nights a week and staying out very late. She began going to parties in men's apartments. The question of sexuality came up. The mother said she would have to make her own decisions about this. The father was anxious. He objected on the grounds of late hours, the opinions of neighbors, and working with so little sleep. After about six weeks of this, the daughter called the therapist to ask for ten minutes alone with him at the end of the next hour. She said her problem was too personal to discuss with the parents. The therapist refused. He said this was family therapy and he would not change the rule. If she just had to talk personally, she would have to find someone else. The daughter talked about her problem early in the next hour. She said a boy friend was making demands for a sexual relationship. The mother said it was the daughter's own problem to work out. The father was very anxious but he spoke only of propriety. These comments seemed to be directed more for the parents' reactions than for their reality value. During the week, the daughter, without telling the parents, arranged a date to terminate the relationship with the boy friend. She returned home late. The mother went to bed early but the father remained up. This was another striking change in the parents. Before this, it had been the mother who was anxious about the daughter and the father who was calm and objective. Now the father was the one who worried about the daughter. He awakened the mother to tell her that the daughter was still out. She fussed at the father for disturbing her rest. When the daughter and her date returned, the father created a "behind-the-scenes" scene by talking loudly so the daughter and date could hear him. In the following therapy hour the daughter told the father that she was not pleased that he got mad but if he had to get mad, at least he should have been man enough to speak directly to the boy instead of yelling like an angry child.

This series of events brought about a new equilibrium between father and daughter. The next hour, the seventy-seventh in fifty-three weeks, was another neutral hour. The daughter had a new hairdo and was as charming, assured, and self-contained as a young lady could be. The parents beamed with parental pride and satisfaction. The talk of sex and dates had disappeared. The daughter had met her old friends from college days. She had been avoiding them since her first psychotic break. She felt she would never be acceptable to them again. She felt she could not risk the pity they might feel for her. She had met one of the boys, a successful young businessman who asked her to a party with the "old gang." They knew about her long struggle with psychosis but they accepted her as before, without pity or anxiety. She said she had changed her ideas about people's attitudes to former mental patients. She said formerly she had thought they were reacting to her but they were really reacting to their own fears about mental illness. She was meeting new people who asked how she had stayed single so long.

The next five hours the mother shifted from her old adequate position to a weak, complaining, helpless position. Each time one family member makes a significant change, complementing changes in the others follow almost immediately. When the psychotic one improves, it is usually the mother who becomes symptomatic. Before this time the daughter would have become more helpless in response to the mother's symptoms. This time the daughter held the family lead. She said to the mother, "Don't try to dump your troubles on me. I have my own life to bother about." The mother said, "You can just move out on your own." The daughter said, "Sometime I intend to marry and leave but I will go when I choose and not before." The next hour the mother suggested that the daughter go on in individual therapy. She said the daughter was now in a position to be free and on her own. The father and daughter opposed this. The therapist said he thought they had not exhausted the advantages of family therapy and he would not change to individual therapy. In the eighty-fourth hour the daughter was still in the adequate position. The father had been employed for several weeks and he now was moving toward a more adequate position in relation to the mother. This is the present status of a family that continues in family psychotherapy.

Summary. A clinical research project for the study and treatment of schizophrenic patients and their families was organized on a ward in a research center. Fathers, mothers, patients, and normal siblings have lived together on the ward as long as two and one-half years. The theoretical hypothesis regarded the schizophrenic symptoms in the patient as a manifestation of an active process that involved the entire family. A psychotherapeutic approach, consistent with the working hypothesis, was developed. The family members attended all psychotherapy hours together. Four in-residence families and six outpatient families have participated in the research study and have been treated in family psychotherapy.

An attempt has been made to observe and to relate to the family unit rather than to the individual family member. From this viewpoint, certain relationship patterns became clear that had been obscured by the more familiar focus on the individual. Some of the broad patterns of relationship functioning, observed in these ten research families, have been described. There was an emotional distance between the parents which we called the *emotional divorce*. The family conflict seemed to remain pretty much in the father-mother-patient triad and to involve normal siblings less than was anticipated. The parents were separated from each other by the emotional divorce, but either one could have a close relationship with the patient if the other parent permitted it. The most common family configuration was one in which the overadequate mother was attached to the helpless patient and the father remained peripheral to the intense mother-patient twosome.

During the course of family psychotherapy there were some unexpected changes in the family patterns. A change in one family member would be followed by complementing changes in the other two members of the father-mother-patient triad. When the parent in the inadequate or weak position became more assertive and active in the family, the parent in the overadequate or strong position would shift to the inadequate position. This we have called the *overadequate-inadequate reciprocity* between parents. In those families in which parents could resolve the emotional divorce, the psychotic patient began to change toward more mature functioning.

A course of family psychotherapy with an outpatient family was presented. This was a family with some of the most striking changes, though the change between the father and the mother was less marked, and the change between mother and patient was more dramatic than changes in other families. It is our opinion that the theoretical view of the "family as a unit" can provide valuable theoretical additions to our usual individual concepts and that family psychotherapy may open up a whole new range of therapeutic possibilities.

Note

1. "We" refers to the staff of the research project. This includes the author, Robert H. Dysinger, M.D., Warren M. Brodey, M.D., and Betty Basamania, M.S.S. In this paper the words "we" or "our" will be used to refer to ideas generally accepted by the staff and included in the operating policy of the project. "I" and "my" will refer to points in my thinking that are not part of the operating policy of the project.

Chapter 4

A Family Concept
of Schizophrenia

The schizophrenic psychosis of the patient is, in my opinion, a symptom manifestation of an active process that involves the entire family. This orientation has evolved during the three and one-half years of a clinical research project in which schizophrenic patients and their parents have lived together on a psychiatric ward in a research center. The family unit is regarded as a single organism and the patient is seen as that part of the family organism through which the overt symptoms of psychosis are expressed.

This volume is devoted to papers about the etiology of schizophrenia. When schizophrenia is seen as a family problem, it is not a disease in terms of our usual way of thinking about disease, nor does it have an etiology in terms of the way those of us in the medical sciences have been trained to think of etiology. However, a family orientation does permit us to talk in terms of the origin and development of schizophrenia. When the family is viewed as a unit, certain clinical patterns come into focus that are not easily seen from the more familiar individual frame of reference. In this paper, I will describe some of the prominent clinical observations from the family research study and convey some thoughts about the way schizophrenia develops in the family group.

I will present my material in four sections. The first section will deal with some important over-all considerations. The second section will include pertinent background information about the family research study. The third, and most important section, will include clinical material from the research project and theoretical considerations of the family concept. The fourth section will include a summary of the family concept and some thoughts about how this is related to the over-all problem of schizophrenia.

General Considerations About Schizophrenia

As this book demonstrates, the problem of schizophrenia is so basic and pressing that it has been approached from many angles and from the points of view of many different disciplines. Each of these disciplines— whether it be psychology, endocrinology, sociology, genetics, clinical medicine, or any other—has learned to think about data in a certain way and also to ignore data that it feels to be irrelevant to the study at hand. It could hardly do its work otherwise. But since each of these disciplines tends to ignore or minimize data that may be very important to those in another, it is not surprising that the study of schizophrenia sometimes seems to be nearly as confused as the patient, with, it is true, a great profusion of theories stemming from certain evidence but tending to ignore or overlook the evidence procured by other disciplines with a very different theoretical background and direction of thinking.

In this connection, we might do well to recall the

> . . . six men of Indostan
> To learning much inclined,
> Who went to see the Elephant
> (Though all of them were blind),
> That each by observation
> Might satisfy his mind (Saxe 1949).

Was the blind man who perceived the elephant as a wall more accurate than he who felt a tree or he who felt a fan? Perhaps they did not have time to feel the whole elephant, but certainly they would have proceeded more intelligently by pooling their information rather than by quarreling over partial concepts.

In the study of schizophrenia we are handicapped by the same sort of "blindness." What is needed is no less than a unified concept of man, a frame of reference that will enable us to understand the necessary connections between cell and psyche, and perhaps between psyche and the entity we know as soul. We are far from capable of such thinking at this time, but the recognition of the partial "blindness" and the limitations of each discipline should go far to discourage the sort of limited thinking that mistakes the part for the whole.

These initial thoughts are presented for several reasons. One is to reiterate a belief that the understanding of schizophrenia is right in front of our "eyes," that it has been there for a long time, and that more progress can be made in understanding why man thinks as he does about schizophrenia than in understanding why the schizophrenic patient thinks as he does. Another reason is to remind the reader that the family concept presented in this paper is based on psychological thinking. Even though we have made an effort to find a broader viewpoint from which to "see the elephant," we must remember that a psychological orientation has its own conceptual boundaries, and that, in the long run, the family concept is the perception of yet another "blind man."

Background Data About the Family Study

This research study was started in 1954. The initial working hypothesis had been developed several years before during the course of individual clinical work with schizophrenic patients and also with their mothers. The hypothesis considered schizophrenia to be a psychopathological entity in the patient which had been influenced to a principal degree by the mother. It considered that the basic character problem in the patient, on which schizophrenic symptoms are later superimposed, was an unresolved, symbiotic attachment to the mother.[1] The initial focus of the study was on the mother-patient relationship. Three mothers and their schizophrenic daughters lived on the ward and participated together in the milieu treatment program. Each patient and each mother had individual psychotherapy. When mothers and patients were in a living situation together, certain facets of the relationship came into focus that had not been anticipated from work with each individually or from joint interviews with the two together. The details of the mother-patient relationship will be discussed later in the paper. To summarize it briefly, there was increasing evidence that the mother was an intimate part of the patient's problem, that the mother-patient relationship was a dependent fragment of a larger family problem, and that the father played an important part in it.

At the end of one year, the hypothesis was extended to make it more consistent with the clinical observations. The psychosis in the patient was now considered to be a symptom of the total family problem. The research plan was revised to admit new families in which both father and mother could live with the patient on the ward. The psychotherapy plan was revised to make it more consistent with the new working hypothesis. The new psychotherapy plan, which we have called "family psychotherapy," was one in which the family members attended all therapy hours together.[2]

Four families consisting of father, mother, and patient have now lived on the ward and participated in family therapy for periods up to two and one-half years. Normal siblings have lived with two of the families for periods up to one year. The ward living space accommodates three families at a single time. Thus, a total of three mother-patient families and four father-mother-patient families have now participated in the in-patient study. Among these seven families, the maximum period of participation has been three years, the minimum period has been six months, and the average period of participation has been eighteen months. An additional seven families consisting of father, mother, and moderately disturbed psychotic patient, have been treated in out-patient family therapy for periods up to two years. This is a total of fourteen families in the research study. An additional twelve families groups have been seen in detailed preadmission evaluation studies as well. These families were not admitted to the research project, but the evaluation data has supplemented certain areas of data from the fourteen research families.

A major part of the staff effort went into the creation of a ward milieu that would permit the family to remain with the patient in the ward setting. The patients were chronically and severely disturbed. All had been hospitalized, continuously or periodically, for a number of years before admission to the project. The ward administration was adapted, as nearly as possible, to permit the family to function as it would at home. Twenty people have worked full time on the combined clinical and research operation; three psychiatrists and a social worker make up the clinical research team, and twelve nurses and attendants staff the ward in eight hour shifts, seven days a week. The remainder of the staff includes an occupational therapist and various clerical and technical assistants. Consultants and members of other professional disciplines have participated on a part-time basis.

The parents assumed the principal responsibility for the care of the patients, but the medical and nursing staff worked toward making services available at the family's request. The parents were soon asking, and demanding, that the staff "come into the family problem" and solve it for them so that there was never a problem with the staff's "intruding into" or "being excluded from" the family situation. The close "helping" relationship of the staff made it possible for them to know the families better but it created new technical problems for the treatment program.

There have been discussions about how our observations made in the ward setting might differ from those obtained by an observer in the home. This is impossible to answer. An essential element in our observations is equivalent to a psychotherapist's view of the patient in a psychotherapy relationship.

The ward living situation has provided an opportunity for subjective and objective research observations that has not been equaled by any other in our experience. It enables us to see the family as a whole in action as no other method could. To explain briefly, each family member has a perception of the family that is different from the perception of any other family member. Each family member is different in outside relationships from what he is in the presence of other family members. The psychotherapist, who meets with the family group in "talking" hours, has a view of the family different from any possible in any, or in all, individual perceptions of the family. This "family-unit" view of the family, which is crucial to our theoretical orientation, will be discussed later. The ward living situation provides an additional "talking and action" view of the family drama that has not been possible in the more structured family therapy hours. There are views of the family eating, sharing, working, and playing together. There are views of the family relating to other families, to the ward staff, and to the outside environment. There are longitudinal views of the family adjustment to success, failure, crisis, and serious illness.

All of the changes in our working hypothesis and treatment approach have been based on clinical observations from the in-patient families. The nurses on each shift record observations on each individual family member, on the family unit, and on the relation of the family group to the environment. Each family therapy hour is tape-recorded while three additional written records are also made. Written records include a set of process psychotherapy notes, a summary of the verbal content, and a sociogram of the meeting. The daily material is then summarized into weekly and monthly summaries. The data from the out-patient families have been almost entirely supplemental to the more detailed data from the in-patient families.

The concept of the "family unit" or the "family as a single organism" is crucial to our way of thinking about schizophrenia. In addition to the theoretical reasons, which I will present later, there were practical reasons to institute the "family-unit" approach. A family, in constant living contact with a psychotic family member, is in a state of intense conflict and emotional turmoil. Each family member solicits outside support for his particular emotional point of view. It is difficult for therapists and personnel to remain objective even if they are trained in handling countertransference problems. A nonparticipant observer might aspire to scientific objectivity, but, in the emotional tension that surrounds these families, he begins to participate emotionally in the family drama just as surely as he inwardly cheers the hero and hates the villain when he attends the theater. Clinical staff members have been able to gain workable objectivity by detaching themselves emotionally from the family problem. When it was possible to attain a workable level of interested detachment, it was then possible to begin to defocus the individual and to focus on the entire family at once. Even though the family-unit orientation appeared to have a theoretical advantage, it was the presence of the family group on the ward, and the clinical necessity of dealing with the situation, that forced the staff to work toward a family-unit orientation. Once it was possible to focus on the family as a unit, it was like shifting a microscope from the oil immersion to the low power lens, or like moving from the playing field to the top of the stadium to watch a football game. Broad patterns of form and movement that had been obscured in the close-up view became clear. The close-up view could then become more meaningful once the distant view was also possible.

Other factors have made the family-unit orientation difficult. We have all been trained to think of emotional problems as individual ones. The entire body of psychological and psychoanalytic theory was developed from perceiving the family through the eyes of the patient. Diagnostic and descriptive terms apply to the individual. It has been difficult to change this automatic way of thinking in ourselves. To facilitate the shift to family-unit thinking, we have attempted to discard as much of the "second nature" psychiatric terminology as possible and to force ourselves to use simple descriptive words. I do not like the terms "maturity" and "immaturity," as used later in the paper, but I have used them descriptively in an attempt to avoid terms with an association automatically connotative of an individual orientation. The conceptualization of the family has been a problem for others working in the field. We agree with those who would like to a have a family diagnosis in addition to our individual diagnosis. Ackerman (1956) and his group have attempted to define the interlocking of individual defense mechanisms. Mittelman (1956), working with different members of the same family, has described the reciprocal relationships between family members. After wrestling with this problem for over three years, we are working our way toward some kind of system that deals with "function" rather than with the static situation conveyed by a diagnostic label. This functional orientation has been approached by a number of investigators. Spiegel (1957) emphasizes function in his work on role theory. Jackson (1958) suggests a functional system in his stable-satisfactory, unstable-satisfactory, stable-unsatisfactory, unstable-unsatisfactory classification. Regensburg (1954) suggested a functional classification of the marital relationship from her experience in social casework. It is probably part of the change in climate from static to dynamic concepts.

Development of Schizophrenia in a Family: a Theoretical Concept

Since the beginning of our family study, I have come to regard schizophrenia as a process that requires three or more generations to develop.[3] The clinical and research data will be presented in chronological order, beginning with the grandparents and progressing in successive stages to the acute psychotic eruption in the patient. It has been possible to obtain some fairly detailed historical data in line with the three-generation idea, but this area remains as the one where thinking is most speculative and supporting data are weakest.

This brief history from one of the families will be used to illustrate the points that I currently consider to be most important in the three-generation process: The paternal grandparents (first generation) were relatively mature and highly respected members of the farming community in which they lived. Their eight children were also relatively mature except for a son (second generation), who was the father of the patient and who was much less mature than his siblings. As a child he was very dependent on his mother. The other siblings regarded him as mother's favorite, but she either denied this and affirmed that she loved all her children equally, or she implicitly agreed and said that she would have done as much for any of the other children if they had needed as much attention as this son. With the need to begin functioning in the outside world that came with adolescence, he suddenly became distant and aloof from his mother and began to function much more adequately outside the home. He applied himself to school and later to his business. He became more successful in business than his siblings and colleagues, but he was aloof, shy, and uncomfortable in close personal relationships. He never rebelled against his parents, but he maintained a distant, compliant relationship with them.

There was a similar pattern on the mother's side of the family. The maternal grandfather (first generation) was a respected professional man in a small town. It was the oldest daughter (second generation) who became the mother of the patient. She was the one in her sibling group who had the most intense attachment to her mother. At adolescence, she reacted to the parental attachment in a different way from that in which the father reacted in his family. He attained his area of adequacy outside the home, while she gained her area of adequacy in the home. She suddenly changed from a shy, dependent girl who could do nothing without her mother to a socially poised and resourceful young woman who could run the home without help. Here were two people with high levels of immaturity, but both had managed to deny their immaturity and to function adequately in certain areas. Both were lonely people and somewhat aloof in their relationships with others. They met while he was working in the town where she lived. Neither had been serious about marriage before they met. On one level there was a "made only for each other" quality about the relationship, but on the surface they appeared casual or even indifferent to each other. The casual relationship continued for a year. They married suddenly, a few days before the husband was transferred to a job in another state. Their relationship became conflictual as soon as they began to live together.

According to the speculative three-generation idea, these two people will have at least one child with a very high level of immaturity, and this child may develop clinical schizophrenia in an attempt to adapt to the demands of growing up. It is stressed that this is not a specific proposition about the origin of schizophrenia but that such a pattern has been present in several of the families. We have speculated about the implications of this pattern. It suggests that one child in each sibling group acquires a higher level of immaturity than the other siblings, that the immaturity is in the one who had the most intense *early* attachment to the mother, and that the immaturity is roughly equivalent to the combined levels of immaturity in the parents. It is a consistent clinical experience, among those who work with husbands and wives, that people choose spouses who have identical levels of immaturity but who have opposite defense mechanisms. To summarize this three-generation idea, the grandparents were relatively mature but their combined immaturities were acquired by one child who was most attached to the mother. When this child married a spouse with an equal degree of immaturity, and when the same process repeated itself in the third generation, it resulted in one child (the patient) with a high degree of immaturity, while the other siblings are much more mature. We have not worked with families with complicated family histories involving the death of a parent, divorces, remarriages, or multiple neuroses and psychoses in the same sibling group.

There are some characteristics of the early married life of the parents that are important in our theoretical thinking. A constant finding in all eleven father-mother-patient families has been a marked emotional distance between the parents. We have called this the "emotional divorce." There is considerable variation in the ways parents have maintained this distance. At one extreme was a family in which the parents maintained a very formal and controlled relationship. They had few overt differences. They saw their marriage as ideal. They reported an active and satisfying sexual relationship. They used conventional terms of endearment with each other, but it was difficult for them to share personal feelings, thoughts, and experiences. At the other extreme was a family in which the parents could not remain for long in each other's presence without arguments and threats. In social situations they were congenial. They controlled the conflict with physical distance from each other. They referred to their marriage as a terrible twenty-five years. In the middle of the scale were nine families in which the parents maintained the emotional divorce with various combinations of formal control and overt disagreement. They were consciously aware of their differences but they avoided the touchy points to keep arguments at a minimum. They saw their marriages as difficult situations to be endured.

In all the families, the parents have definite patterns of functioning in the emotional-divorce situation. Both parents are equally immature. One denies the immaturity and functions with a facade of overadequacy. The other accentuates the immaturity and functions with a facade of inadequacy. The overadequacy of one functions in reciprocal relationship to the inadequacy of the other. Neither is capable of functioning in the midground between overadequacy and inadequacy. The terms *overadequate* and *inadequate* refer to functioning states and not fixed states. Overadequate refers to a functioning facade of strength that is greater than realistic. Inadequacy refers to a functioning facade of helplessness that is as unrealistic as the facade of strength is unrealistic in the other direction. When the mother functions as the overadequate one, she is dominating and aggressive and the father is helpless and compliant. When the father functions as the overadequate one, he is cruel and authoritarian and the mother is helpless and whining.

There are some constantly recurring situations that accompany the overadequate-inadequate reciprocity. One is the "domination-submission issue." On personal issues, especially decisions that affect both parents, the one who makes the decision becomes the overadequate one and the other becomes the inadequate one. The overadequate one sees self as being forced to take responsibility and the other as a shirker. The inadequate one sees self as being "forced to submit" and the other as "dominating." The "domination-submission" term was introduced by the inadequate one who complains the most. This brings in the problem of "decisions." One of the outstanding clinical characteristics of the families is the inability of the parents to make decisions. They avoid responsibility, and the anxiety of "submission," by avoiding decisions. All levels of decisions are left undecided, to be decided by time, by circumstance, or by advice from experts. Decisions that are routine "problems to be solved" by other families become "burdens to be endured" by these families. The inability to make decisions creates the impression of weak families. One father illustrated the decision problem clearly. He said, "We can never decide together on anything. I suggest we go shopping Saturday afternoon. She objects. We argue. We end up doing nothing." When decision paralysis becomes intense, the mothers more often assume the decision-making function against the passive resistance of the fathers.

There is a fairly constant pattern in the conscious reasons of the parents for having chosen each other as mates. These are the kinds of personal things that are rarely said to each other. This material is usually fragmented and distorted until after they are comfortable in family psychotherapy. The fathers say they admired the mothers' strength, social confidence, and directness. One mother said, "I was so scared in social groups I would start chattering. It just came out. Now, after twenty-five years I hear my husband thought I was a brilliant conversationalist." The mothers say they admired the fathers' kindness, intelligence, and reliability. One father said, "I was too scared to do anything but agree and she thought it was kindness." The qualities they consciously admired in each other were qualities that were prominent in the facades of overadequacy.

In most of the families, the parental conflict began in the first few days or weeks after the marriage. The conflict began over decisions that dealt with routine problems of living together. A striking example of this occurred between an intern and nurse who were secretly married two years before they finished their hospital training. The marital relationship was calm and satisfying until they began to live together. According to our current thinking, the marital partners encountered the anxiety of overadequate-inadequate reciprocal functioning as soon as they were in a teamwork living situation. Parents have described "arguments over nothing" in situations like golf, a game of cards, or a work project for just the two of them. They found ways to avoid this anxiety. The usual mechanism was for each to work independently and to avoid joint activity. The conflict was less when a third or fourth person was present. Several couples spent much time visiting others or entertaining friends in their home. Marriage tensions would be reduced when one went to his or her parents for a visit. One father reviewed the dilemma of this prechildren period quite clearly. He said, "Our life was a cycle of too much closeness, too much distance, and fights. We fought when we got too close. Then we stayed mad and spoke only when necessary. One would start to make up. Then there would be a good period of a few hours or a few days until there would again be a cycle of too much closeness, a fight, and another cycle." When asked what he meant by too much closeness, he said, "When we were close, I would start acting like a little boy and she would make demands like a bossy mother. If I continued to act like a helpless child, she would purr like a kitten. The problem was that I gave up part of me when I was helpless. I had a choice. I could give in to her or balk. If I gave in, she would stay calm. If I balked, she would get nasty, I would get nasty, and we would fight." Of the distance phases, he said, "I did my best work when we were far apart. It was far from ideal. That is when I would get depressed and call myself names but I could somehow work better then." About the closeness phases, he said, "They occurred when either of us started to make up. I would be determined to have nothing to do with her but when she would start to make up, it was like a piece of bait I could not resist. I think it was the longing for closeness in both of us that made us respond so fast."

The decision to have a child was the most difficult of all decisions in these families. This problem began with the earliest thinking about having a baby. A history from a family in which the oldest child became schizophrenic will illustrate some of the crucial issues. The wife had a great desire for children for "my fulfillment as woman." The husband opposed passively with comments about money and the right time. His opposition obscured her fears that she might not be able to have a normal baby. The wife became pregnant at a time when her wish for a baby was great. She immediately was in great conflict about the pregnancy. From the beginning of the pregnancy, her thoughts were almost totally invested in the developing fetus. Her thoughts were expressed as doubts, worries, and concerns about the normality and health of the child. When she was emotionally close to the husband, her thoughts were more invested in him and there was less preoccupation with the child. During periods of greatest distance from the husband, she wished she could abort to relieve the conflict. This mother did not have the same intense conflict during a later pregnancy with a normal child. She had the same kind of fantasies, but they were much less intense. The conflictual state continued until after the mother could see that the child was alive and healthy. The mother said she had not been able to permit herself to realize, until after the child was born, how important this baby was to her. For her, the pregnancy had been a constant frustration between "promise of fulfillment" and a "threat that it could never be true." She worried so much that the baby would be deformed, or born dead, or be abnormal and die later, that she reached a point of saying to herself, "If it is going to be abnormal and die, I would rather abort now" and "I know I can never have a normal baby. I wish I could go on and have a miscarriage."

A significant shift in the husband-wife relationship began when the wife first knew she was pregnant.[4] At this point she became more emotionally invested in the unborn child than in the husband. The conflict of anticipating the baby continued until the baby was born. Another important shift in family relationships began the moment she could see that the baby was alive and well. Her thoughts immediately went toward caring for the baby. When she first saw this child, she thought, "This tiny, tiny, helpless little thing. I am its mother and I am the one who has to *protect it and care for it.*" She described an overwhelming surge of maternal instinct to do things for the baby. The intensity of the maternal instinct was much less with the second child who grew up to be normal. When she first saw the second baby, she thought, "A new baby is so tiny. It is a wonder that such a tiny thing *can grow up and become an adult.*" The first child came closer to completing "fulfillment" of the mother's need for an important other person than any other person in her experience.

As I currently see the mother-child equilibrium, the mother was securely in the overadequate position to another human being, this human belonged to her, and it was realistically helpless. She could now control her own immaturity by caring for the immaturity of another. With her emotional functioning more stabilized in the relationship with the child, the mother became a more stable figure for the father. He could better control his relationship to her when her functioning did not fluctuate so rapidly. He tended to establish a more fixed position of aloof distance from the mother, similar to his relationship with his own mother. This new emotional equilibrium came to be a fixed way of functioning for the father, mother, and child. I have referred to this as the "interdependent triad." The child was the keystone. Through the relationship with the child, the mother was able to stabilize her own anxiety and to function on a less anxious level. With the mother's anxiety more stabilized, the father was able to establish a less anxious relationship with the mother.

Two other mothers described maternal feelings of similar intensity when they first saw the child who later became schizophrenic. The memory of this feeling experience remained with them just as another person remembers the most striking emotional experience in his life. The similar, but less intense, feelings with other babies were not particularly noted at the time. The meaning of the baby to these mothers is reminiscent of a psychotic girl who said many times, "I wish I could have a baby of my own. I do not know how I could ever become pregnant, but if I could ever have a baby of my own, I would never be lonely again." Freud (1914), in writing about the narcissistic mother, said, "In the child to whom they give birth, a part of their own body comes to them as an object other than themselves, upon which they can lavish out of their narcissism, complete object love."

For the purpose of this presentation, the period from the birth of the child to development of the acute psychosis in the patient will be considered as a single stage in the development of schizophrenia in the family. The research data will be summarized in terms of the mother-child relationship, the child-mother relationship, and the relationships of the father.[5] The characteristics of the relationships are most pronounced during periods of stress.

Perhaps it will make the discussion of general characteristics of such relationships clearer if I present a brief chronological history of one of the families for this period. This was a family with a psychotic older daughter and a normal younger daughter. The father and mother continued their emotional divorce in the marriage. To those outside the home, the marriage was considered to be happy. After a difficult few years, the father did well in his own business. The mother devoted herself to the child and to the home. The father put his energy and thoughts into the business. The daughter did well intellectually, but she was extremely shy. Her problem was similar to that described for most of the patients in the research families. The parents said, "She had few close friends. She was more comfortable with adults. She never seemed to know what to do or what to say around other children." After adolescence, she was much more active and outgoing in school. Her psychotic break came the first year she was away from home at college. The father's business failed during the year after the daughter became psychotic. The second daughter, four years younger than the patient, was unusually outgoing and successful with minimal effort.

The mother-child relationship is the most active and intense relationship in the families. The term *intense* describes an ambivalent relationship in which the thoughts of both, whether positive or negative, are largely invested in each other. The mother makes two main demands on the patient. The most forceful is the emotional demand that the patient remain helpless. This is conveyed in subtle forceful ways that are out of conscious awareness. The other is the overt, verbalized, "hammered home" demand that the patient become a gifted and mature person. An example from a hospitalized family will illustrate these separate simultaneous levels of process. A psychotic son was eating a late lunch alone. The mother stopped to help him. She buttered his bread, cut his meat, and poured more milk for him. At the same time she was urging him, on an intellectually mature level, to become more grown up and to learn to do more for himself. It is incidental that the patient stopped eating. If the action story could be separated from the verbal story, there would be two separate themes. The action story would be appropriate between a mother and small child and the verbal one would fit best between a mother and teenage child. Dysinger (1957) made an attempt to isolate the action story in one of the research families. To summarize this point, we think of two levels of process between the mother and the patient. Much of the emotional demand that the patient remain a child is conveyed on an action level and out of conscious awareness of either mother or patient. The verbal level is usually a direct contradiction to the action level.

A prominent feature of every mother-patient relationship is the mother's worries, doubts, and concerns about the patient. This is a continuation of the mother's overinvestment that began before the child was born. In the research families, there are some definite patterns to the worries of the mothers. In general, the worries are focused on the patients' development, growth, behavior, dress, and other such personal items. Each mother has a special grouping of worries that have to do with her own feelings of inadequacy. For instance, one mother was always concerned about disease and the inadequacy of her own internal organs. Her worries focused on her son's bowels, skin, sinuses, and endless other items about impaired organs. The son had multiple physical complaints. Several mothers had feelings of inadequacy in which they doubted their own physical attractiveness. Their worries focused on the patients' teeth, hair, complexion, posture, body build, dress, masculine or feminine characteristics, and other related subjects. These patients tended to be exaggerated examples of what the mothers had "fought against." The mothers doubted their own intellectual capacities. Their worries tended more toward intelligence tests, grades in school, and intellectual functioning. The patients in these two families appeared intellectually dull. To summarize this point, the subjects of the mothers' overconcerns about the patients and the focus of their "picking on the patients" are the same as their own feelings of inadequacy about themselves. This point is so accurate on a clinical level that almost any point in the mothers' list of complaints about the patient can be regarded as an externalization of the mother's own inadequacies. If a therapist or other outside figure suggests this, the mother and even the father and patient will attack or withdraw, or both. However, if either the patient or father confronts the mother with this, there is a significant beneficial emotional reaction.

The degree of negative response in the patients seems directly related to the intensity of the campaigns to *change* the "inadequacies" in the patients. The mothers' efforts to change the patients are timed with anxieties in themselves, and not with the reality situation in the patients.

We have used the term "projection"[6] to refer to the most all pervasive mechanism in the mother-child relationship. It has been used constantly by every mother in every aspect of her relationship with the patient. According to our thinking, the mother can function more adequately by ascribing certain aspects of herself to the child, and the child accepts. This is of crucial importance in the area of the mother's immaturity. The mother denies her own feelings of helplessness and her wish to be babied. She projects the denied feelings to the child. Then she perceives the child to be helpless and to wish to be mothered. The child, and even the entire family, accepts the mother's perception as a reality in the child. The mother then "mothers" the helplessness in the child (her own projected feelings) with her adequate self. Thus, a situation that begins as *a feeling in the mother, becomes a reality in the child.* There have been many examples of this mechanism in the families. One mother fed her child when she herself was hungry. When she was most anxious, she would force attention on the child and justify her actions by quoting an authority who recommended unlimited love for children. When she was not anxious, she would be relatively neglectful of the child and justify herself by quoting an authority who recommended firmness with children. In one sense, by using the child as an extension of herself, the mother was able to take care of her own inadequacies without having to depend on others. An example of another level of "projection" occurred in a mother who unrealistically perceived her daughter to have a voice of operatic quality. The daughter soon realized, from experiences outside the home, that this was not true. At home, she would sing for her mother's friends and act as if the good-voice myth were true. Outside the home, she related herself according to the reality of the situation. She said she continued the unreality at home to make her mother feel better. This daughter had a neurotic problem. In a family with a psychosis, neither daughter nor mother could have recognized the boundary between reality and unreality and both would have acted out the good-voice myth in all their relationships.

The "projection" occurs also on the level of physical illness. This is a mechanism in which the *soma of one person reciprocates with the psyche of another person.* There have been innumerable examples in which an anxiety in one person could become a physical illness in another. Before the ward internist was fully aware of this, there were many situations in which an overtly anxious mother would describe the patient's symptoms to the doctor. The patient would agree with the symptoms. The doctor would make a diagnosis and prescribe medication. Within a few hours, a process could change from anxiety in the mother to pain in the patient that had been diagnosed and was being treated. Pediatricians have told us that this is a troublesome problem in their practice. It is much easier to treat the compliant patient than to attempt to deal with the underlying problem. The somatic reciprocation often includes definite physical pathology. A striking series of such reciprocations occurred in a mother in response to rapid improvement in a regressed patient. Within a few hours after each significant change in the patient, the mother developed a physical illness of several days' duration. The somatic responses included a febrile respiratory infection, laryngitis with severe edema of the vocal cords, gastroenteritis, and severe urticaria. These marked reciprocating mechanisms are most common in, but not limited to, the mother-patient relationship. I believe the mechanism belongs primarily in the functioning reciprocation of extreme unrealistic overadequacy to extreme unrealistic inadequacy.

Another facet of the complex mother-child relationship was described by a mother and daughter who were far along in the process of untangling themselves from each other. The mother began to notice how much time she spent in thinking about the daughter. She had never been consciously aware of this before. She said she had always felt the same feelings and emotions as the daughter. She wondered about her intuitive ability to feel what another felt. She recalled an incident from the daughter's childhood. The child fell and injured her head. The mother's own head began to hurt in the exact spot the daughter's head was injured. She pondered the reason for this. She concluded that her own life was connected with the daughter's in some complex way. She decided to "put an invisible wall between us so I can have my life and she can have hers." The daughter confirmed this fusion of feelings. She had never been able to know how she herself felt. She had depended on the mother to tell her how she felt. When occasionally she had a feeling that was different from what the mother said, she discounted her own feeling and felt the way the mother said she felt. She had depended on the mother for many other things. She never knew how she looked, if clothes were becoming, or if colors matched. She depended on the mother for this. Away at school for long periods, she could begin to have her own feelings. When she returned home she would again lose the ability to know her own feelings. Then the daughter described the same intuitive ability to know how the mother felt.

Now to a consideration of the child's function in the child-mother relationship. An oversimplified description is to say that the mother "projects" her inadequacies to the child and the child automatically "introjects" the mother's inadequacies. In more detail, the child is involved in the same two levels of process as the mother, except that the mother actively initiates her emotional and verbal demands and the child is more involved in responding to the mother's demands than in initiating his own demands. In this sense, the child's life course is one in which he tries the best he can to remain the mother's baby and at the very same time to become a mature adult. I believe this is the same dilemma described in different terms by Bateson et al. (1956) in their concept of the double bind.

In the research families, the response of the patient to the mother's demands varies with the degree of functional helplessness of the patient and the functional strength of the mother. A very helpless and regressed patient will comply immediately to emotional demands and pay little attention to verbal demands. A less regressed patient offers token resistance to emotional demands but disagrees vigorously with verbal demands. It requires a fairly high level of functional strength for the patient to oppose an emotional demand actively with comments like, "I refuse to let you get me upset." In response to such a stand the mother can become overtly anxious or physically ill. The compliance of an inadequate patient to the mother's emotional demand is almost instantaneous. As soon as the overtly anxious mother is in direct contact with the patient, the mother becomes less anxious and the patient more psychotic and regressed. The more adequate mother then babies the less adequate patient. It seems that anxiety in the mother is an automatic signal for the patient "to help the mother" by becoming her baby. The patient participates so actively in this process that I do not see the patient as a "victim" of the situation. In a certain sense, patients philosophically accept this position as a mission for which they were born. Of this, one patient said, "I was born when my mother needed someone. It could have been my brother or my sister if they had been born when I was." The patient lives his life as if the mother would die without his "help" and if the mother died, then he would die too.

The child makes his emotional and verbal demands on the mother by exploiting the helpless, pitiful position. Patients are adept at arousing sympathy and overhelpfulness in others. All the research families have eventually found their homes geared to the demands of the patient. The parents are as helpless in taking a stand against the patient as the patient in taking a stand against parents.

Now to a consideration of the father's relationships in the interdependent triad. His emotional divorce from the mother remains rather constant, but he can have a close relationship to the child any time the mother permits it. The parents follow a pattern very much like divorced parents who share their children. The mother, the overadequate one in relation to the inadequate child, is in charge of the child. The child has no direct voice in choosing between the father or mother, but the child can harass the mother until she goes away and leaves the child with the father. The father is then in the functioning position of a substitute mother. Even though he may function in this position a long time, he still remains a representative of the mother. In our experience it has not been possible for a father to have a primary relationship with the patient until he has first been able to change his own emotional divorce with the mother.

All eleven research families have followed the basic pattern of overadequate mother, helpless patient, and peripherally attached fathers. All the mothers have been concerned about the intensity of the child's attachment to themselves. The mothers see the attachment as due to the fathers' disinterest in the child. The fathers agree with this. This was especially true in the six families with psychotic sons. The parents all worried about implications of homosexuality if the sons remained attached to their mothers. All the parents agreed that sons needed close relationships with their fathers for proper masculine identification. All six fathers tried to be close to their sons. Every effort failed. The most successful was one in which the father and son spent an afternoon a week together for several years. The father was in the position of the mother's hired attendant for the son. One father initiated his own effort to win his son. He became a boy scout troop leader with the secret hope his son would become interested in the boy scouts. The mother did not relinquish any of her attachment to the son, and he never attended a scout meeting.

Our experience with normal siblings has been of great interest. At the beginning of the study, I thought all the siblings were heavily involved in the family problem. With increasing experience, I now lean strongly to the belief that the essential process is confined in the father-mother-patient triad. From the histories, and from superficial observation, there were data to indicate that every family member was somehow involved. A case will illustrate the point. A mother had the usual attachment to the older psychotic daughter. The family story indicated that the father and the younger daughter were as attached as the mother and older daughter, and observations during the first six months tended to confirm this. During the next two years the younger daughter sided with all three members of the basic family triad, but she was never involved to the point that she could not withdraw and leave the family. Over and over, normal siblings and in-laws have become involved for a time in the family conflict but they have always withdrawn so that the basic family triad remains, linked in the triangular interdependency.

Before attempting to follow the family pattern to the point of psychotic disruption, I will return to the beginning of the mother-child relationship and review some of the points that are crucial to the psychosis. According to our present thinking, the child becomes the "important other" to the mother. Through the child, the mother is able to attain a more stable emotional equilibrium than had otherwise been possible for her. The "tiny helplessness" of the infant permits her to function securely in an overadequate position. The emotional stabilization of the mother then enables the father to have a less anxious relationship with the mother. Thus, the functional helplessness of the infant makes it possible for both parents to have a less anxious adjustment. Even though both parents have a conscious wish for the child to grow and develop normally, they both automatically do things to keep the child in the helpless position. I have already described mechanisms by which the mother attempts to keep the child helpless. The father does this too. If the mother's effort to "make the child behave" is not immediately successful, the father will add his weight to her effort. I believe anxiety is the crucial issue. The research families all have a low tolerance for anxiety. They operate on a "peace at any price" principle. They quickly compromise important life principles to relieve anxiety for this moment. Of course, this "peace at any price" policy immediately causes greater anxiety for tomorrow, but they continue the compromising attitudes to relieve the anxiety of the moment.

The mechanisms by which either the mother or child can feel the same as the other, or "be for the other," are difficult to conceptualize. A number of possible explanations have been proposed in the literature. Why does the child enter into this situation in the first place? I believe the child is automatically protecting his own interests by doing the things that will insure a less anxious and more predictable mother. However, once the child enters into this "being (helpless) for the mother" and the mother enters into the opposite "being (strong) for the child," they are both in a functional bind of "being for each other." When the child's self is devoted to "being for the mother," he loses the capacity of "being for himself." I stress the functional *"being* helpless" rather than the fixed *"is* helpless" viewpoint. In other words, I regard schizophrenia as a functional helplessness in contrast to concepts that regard it as a constitutional helplessness. There are valid data on both sides of this issue.[7]

The process in which the child begins to "be for the mother" results in an arrest in his psychological growth. His physical growth remains normal. Each year there is a wider discrepancy between physical growth and psychological growth. The relationship requires that the child devote himself completely to the mother and that the mother devote herself to the child. The symbiotic state is precariously balanced at best. As the years pass and the child is no longer a baby in size, it is even harder to keep the symbiosis in emotional equilibrium. Each is threatened by change in the other. The child is treatened by any sign of aging, sickness, anxiety, weakness, or change in the mother's attitude that might prevent her always being the strong, adequate mother. The mother is threatened by growth, sickness, or any circumstance that might prevent the child being always her baby. However, it is inevitable that they both change and inevitable that the relationship will one day be disrupted. The feelings that each experience in regard to the loss of the other are equated with death.

The mother threatens the child in many ways. Most important is the threat that she might have another baby and desert the child. I believe the mother's selection of a particular child for such an intense relationship is determined by her unconscious functioning in the prevailing reality situation. A good percentage of mothers will retain the initial relationship with the first child. One mother said the oldest was so pitiful when the second was born that the oldest needed her more. Other mothers have successive attachments to each new child and finally retain the youngest as "my baby." Other choose children from the middle of the group. One mother with five children had successive attachments with the first two and retained an attachment to the third, a daughter who looked like the mother. Another mother had normal relationships with her first two children and then an intense attachment to the third, who was born shortly after the death of her own mother. The birth of a physically deformed child might come closer to "fulfillment" of the mother's emotional needs than a normal child.

The main threat to the continuation of the mother-child symbiosis is the growth process in the child. The relationship might remain fairly calm and erupt into separation anxiety symptoms only during periods of rapid growth in the child. The growth can bring out threats, rejections, demands, and retaliation in both. Described as a phenomenon, the symbiosis attempts to make two lives stand still at a particular pleasurable phase in both life cycles. In the beginning, the mother-infant symbiosis is a normal stage in the course of a life from birth to death. When it is perpetuated, it becomes a foreign thing, threatened by the biological progression of the very life process of which it was once a part.

Now to a consideration of events that lead to the acute psychosis. The rapid growth of the child at adolescence interferes with the functioning equilibrium of the interdependent triad. There is an increase in anxiety for all three members. The automatic mechanisms of the mother—and also the father—go toward forcing the child back into a more helpless position, and the automatic mechanisms of the child go toward compliance. The adolescent period is one in which the growth process repeatedly upsets the equilibrium and the emotional process attempts to restore it. The conscious verbal expressions demand that the child be more grown up.

The child's course from adolescence to the acute psychosis is one in which he changes from a helpless child, to a poorly functioning young adult, to a helpless patient. I will focus on the changes in the child without specifically describing the continuing reciprocating mechanisms in the parents. Adolescence activates intense anxiety in the symbiotic relationship. Before adolescence, the mother had remained calm as long as the child was infantile. He had handled his wishes to grow up with fantasies of future greatness. The growth period causes anxiety in the child and anxiety in the mother, until the symbiotic relationship itself becomes a serious threat. When the child is more grown up, the mother infantilizes. When he is childish, she demands that he grow up. After years of functioning as a helpless child, he has little "self" of his own and he is poorly equipped to do anything without the mother. His dilemma is one of finding a course between the opposing forces. The problem is much greater than that of the normal adolescent who can expect help from parents in growing up and who is basically capable of making a start outside the family. The child in this dilemma has to deal first with the mother's effort to hold him back and then with his own urge to return to her, before he can get to the problems of the normal adolescent. Once free of the mother, he faces outside relationships without a self of his own. Of this dilemma a male patient said, "It takes a lot of doing to hold your mother's hand and play baseball at the same time." A young woman patient said the situation was like a "magnetic field" around the mother. When she was too close to the mother, she would suddenly be "pulled into the mother" and lose her own identity; when she was too far away from the mother, she had no "self" at all.

Our patients used denial and isolation, while still living in the home, to escape the mother's "magnetic field." One of our patients collapsed into psychotic helplessness at fifteen years old after failing in his initial efforts to function without his mother. Most of our patients were successful in their first efforts to function without their mothers. This was the case with the daughter described in the brief family history. She became more outgoing and comfortable with those outside the family. The family was sure that adolescence had solved her "adjustment problem." She looked forward to becoming completely free of the family when she went away to college. By increasing the denial and reassuring herself, she made it through one semester of college. Her work became impaired during the first examination period. The psychotic collapse developed over a period of a few days while she was still increasing the denial and redoubting her effort to "do it myself." In terms of our theoretical viewpoint, the psychosis represents an unsuccessful attempt to adapt the severe psychological impairment to the demands of adult functioning. The patient's denial of incapacity and her protestations of strength were now expressed in the distorted verbalization, while her helplessness was acted out by the psychosis.

The psychosis represented a disruption of the symbiotic attachment to the mother and a collapse of the long term interdependent father-mother-patient triad. Anxiety in the family became high. The mother handled her anxiety with an increased facade of strength, especially toward the father and the staff at the mental hospital. She had assumed responsibility for the hospitalization. The daughter was hostile and openly rebellious to the mother for the first time. The mother dealt with the daughter's total rejection by saying, "It is because she is sick," implying that the daughter would not behave this way if she were well. The father, without being aware of it, had automatically slipped back to inadequate functioning in relation to the extremely overadequate mother. His business began to fail. He went into bankruptcy within a year without any awareness that his bankruptcy could have any relation to the functional interdependency of the central family triad.

I believe that unresolved symbiotic attachments to the mother vary from the very mild to the very intense, that the mild ones cause little impairment, and that schizophrenic psychoses develop among those with the most intense unresolved attachments. There are a number of ways in which the individual with an intense attachment may find some solution to his dilemma. Certain individuals are able to replace the original mother with mother substitutes. The functional helplessness may find expression in somatic illness. The person with a character neurosis uses a flight mechanism to deal with the helplessness. The patients in our families attempted to find distant relationships. The psychotic collapse is seen as an effort at resolution that failed.

I have used the terms *emotional demand* and *emotional process* to describe the emotional responsiveness by which one family member responds automatically to the emotional state of another, without either being consciously aware of the process. Perhaps this can be understood as nonverbal communication, but I have chosen to use these terms descriptively. The process is unconscious in the sense that neither person is consciously aware of it, but it is not unconscious in our usual use of the term. This "emotional process" is deep and it seems somehow to be related to the *being* of a person. It runs silently beneath the surface between people who have very close relationships. It operates during periods of conflict and periods of calm harmony. In most of our families there is much conflict and open disagreement and many stories of injustices and misdeeds between family members. It is easy for the observer to become preoccupied with the conflict and turmoil. There are families with schizophrenic family members that have little or no conflict and no history of the factors we ordinarily associate with schizophrenia. I believe this emotional process may be intimately associated with schizophrenia and that the "silent" family may provide more clues to the process.

The question of "rejecting mothers" comes up. We have not had a rejecting mother in our small number of research families. Every mother in our group has been "called rejecting" by the patients. The amount of attention the mothers give the patients depends on their level of anxiety. When mothers are anxious, they are hovering and infantilizing. When mothers are not anxious, they give much less attention. The patients experience this decrease in attention as "rejection." My impression of the real rejecting mother is one whose baby could never be part of her defense system for her own emotional needs, so that she has to desert the baby to find her gratification elsewhere.

Among the families who have done well in family therapy, we have seen changes in the usual, fixed, family patterns. For instance, a change in one member would be followed by changes in the other two. It was observation of the changes that led to the description of the "overadequate-inadequate reciprocal functioning."

There are some other changes from the course of therapy that are of theoretical interest. The following is a brief account of some changes in a father-mother-daughter family. The intense conflict between the mother and psychotic daughter occupied the first several months of family therapy hours. The father remained on the periphery, and in an inadequate position. Gradually the father began to participate in the family problems. The conflict shifted to the mother-father relationship. As the father began to take some stands against the overadequate mother, she became much more anxious, challenging, and aggressive toward him. Eventually he assumed a position as head of the family, in spite of her marked anxiety, tremulousness, and protest. In a few days she rather quickly changed to a kind, motherly, objective person. She said, "It is so nice finally to have a man for a husband. If he can keep on being a man, then I can be a woman." The emotional divorce disappeared, and for two months they were as completely invested in each other as two young lovers. The patient tried to win back her lost symbiotic partner, but the mother remained firm and the patient made some solid progress. Under stress, they each fell back to their former ways of functioning, but thereafter it became easier for the father to move into an adequate position and less threatening for the mother to lose the overadequate position.

The striking observation was that when the parents were emotionally close, more invested in each other than either was in the patient, the patient improved. When either parent became more emotionally invested in the patient than in the other parent, the patient immediately and automatically regressed. When the parents were emotionally close, they could do no wrong in their "management" of the patient. The patient responded well to firmness, permissiveness, punishment, "talking it out," or any other management approach. When the parents were "emotionally divorced," any and all "management approahces" were equally unsuccessful.

Conclusion

The working hypothesis for this research project has been based on the theoretical assumption that the psychosis in the patient is a symptom of a larger family problem. This assumption is in contrast to the usual theoretical position which considers it a disease or pathological phenomenon in the patient. It has not been possible to run the clinical and the research operation in complete harmony with our theoretical position. Our own limitations and the generally accepted view that it is a disease in the individual make it necessary to retain part of the individual orientation. In other words, we may say that we regard psychosis as a family problem, but, in many basic ways, we must relate to it as a disease in the individual. However, our research institution has afforded unusual experimental flexibility, and it has been possible to achieve a reasonable degree of harmony between the hypothesis and the research operation. The more we have been able to see the psychosis as a family phenomenon, the more we have been able to see a different picture of schizophrenia. Thus, the working hypothesis is based on a theoretical assumption. The research operation, based on the hypothesis, has provided observations different from those possible from other theoretical viewpoints. The family concept is a correlation of research obserations with the hypothesis. Our research project has been in operation four years. The hypothesis and operational approach has been modified, to some degree, every year. In this sense, the family concept, as here presented, could be called our current working conceptualization of schizophrenia as a family problem.

At the beginning of the paper I said our theoretical problem with schizophrenia was somewhat analogous to the problem of the blind men and the elephant. The analogy is probably more apt for those who work with the family than for others, but I have been surprised to find that schizophrenia viewed from the family orientation is very different from schizophrenia viewed as an individual problem. The schizophrenia did not change; the only change was in the eyes that saw it. In this sense, the family concept provides another position from which to view one of man's oldest dilemmas.

Notes

1. This type of symbiotic relationship had already been discussed by a number of authors. Benedek (1949) had discussed the theoretical aspects of the mother-child symbiosis. Mahler (1952) had discussed clinical implications in her work with autistic and symbiotic children. Hill (1955), Lidz and Lidz (1952), and Reichard and Tillman (1950) had considered symbiosis as it applies to the adult schizophrenic patient. Our present views about symbiosis have much in common with those of Limentani (1956).

2. Details about these early clinical observations of the families, and the initial efforts at family psychotherapy, have been presented in another paper (1957).

3. The investigation of the three-generation idea began in 1955 with the statement of our consultant, Dr. Lewis Hill, that it requires three generations for schizophrenia to develop. This was an extension of the thinking in his book *Psychotherapeutic Intervention in Schizophrenia* (1955). Dr Hill died in February 1958 while this paper was being written, but I believe the three-generation idea as expressed here is a fairly accurate representation of his thinking.

4. Caplan (1960) points out the shift in parental relationships during a pregnancy. He also suggests that the mother's relationship to the child can be predicted from her fantasies during the pregnanacy.

5. Our clinical findings are in close agreement with that of Lidz et al. (1957). Bateson et al. (1956), Wynne, et al. (1958), and others working with schizophrenic patients and their families. In many cases the main difference is the use of different terms to describe the same phenomenon. For instance, I have used the term *reciprocal functioning*, Wynne uses *pseudomutuality*, and Jackson (1958) uses *complementarity* to describe the same relationship phenomenon.

6. The "projection" from the mother to the patient has been described in the literature. Reichard and Tillman did an excellent description of it in 1950. "Projection" accurately describes a mechanism in the individual, but, in a two-person relationship, it does not describe the reciprocating "introjection" of the other. The combined term "projection-introjection" also does not account for all the essential aspects of this complex mechanism.

7. Bayley, Bell, and Schaefer (n.d.) are among those investigating the early mother-infant relationship. They are searching for clues as to whether the character of the relationship is determined by inherent qualities in the infant to which the mother responds, or whether the character of the relationship is determined by factors in the mother.

Chapter 5

Family Psychotherapy

The family psychotherapy for this research project was developed directly from the theoretical premise "the family as the unit of illness." Some knowledge of the theoretical premise is crucial to a clear understanding of the therapeutic approach. I shall deal first with the theoretical premise "the family as the unit of illness," and then with the psychotherapeutic approach "the family as the unit of treatment."

The development of the theoretical premise, presented in detail in other papers (Bowen 1957a, 1960; Bowen et al. 1957), will be summarized briefly. The first working hypothesis for the project was developed from previous experience in psychoanalytic psychotherapy with schizophrenic patients and with their parents. Improvement had been more consistent in the patients whose parents were also in psychotherapeutic relationships. Schizophrenia was regarded as a psychopathological entity within the person of the patient, which had been influenced to a principal degree by the child's early relationship with the mother. The basic character problem, on which psychotic symptoms were later superimposed, was considered to be an unresolved symbiotic attachment to the mother. The symbiotic attachment was regarded as an arrest in the normal psychological growth process between mother and child, which was initiated by the infant's response to the emotional immaturity of the mother, which neither wanted and against which both had struggled unsuccessfully over the years. This latter point was important. When the hypothesis avoided "blaming" the mothers, new theoretical and clinical flexibilities became possible. I believe "blaming" is inherently present, no matter how much it is toned down or denied, in any theory that views one person as "causal" to the problem in another. The hypothesis further postulated that mother and patient could begin to grow toward differentiation from each other with individual psychotherapy for both.

The research plan in the first year provided for mothers and patients to live together on the ward, for staff persons to interfere as little as possible in the relationship problems between the two, and for each to have psychotherapy. The working hypothesis, formulated from experience with mothers and patients individually, had accurately predicted the way each would relate to the other as individuals. It did not predict, nor even consider, a large area of observations that emerged from the living-together situation. The "emotional oneness" between mother and patient was more intense than expected. The oneness was so close that each could accurately know the other's feelings, thoughts, and dreams. In a sense they could "feel for each other," or even "be for each other." There were definite characteristics to the way the "oneness" related to fathers or other outside figures. This emotional oneness is quite different from the emotional separateness between the mothers and their normal children. There were repeated observations to suggest that the mother-patient oneness extended beyond the mother and patient to involve the father and other family members. The mothers and patients used individual psychotherapy more to restore harmony to the oneness than to differentiate from each other.

With the change to the family-unit hypothesis, the focus was on the "family oneness" rather than on individuals. At that point we could have kept the familiar individual orientation and focused on characteristics of individual relationships, but we had the research facility to make an exploration into the different way of thinking, and there were observations to support the "family-unit" hypothesis as a profitable way to approach the problem. The hypothesis was changed to regard the psychosis as a symptom of an active process that involved the entire family. Just as a generalized physical illness can focus in one organ, so schizophrenia was seen as a generalized family problem which disabled one member of the family organism. The research plan was changed to admit new families in which fathers, mothers, patients, and normal siblings could live together on the ward. The research design was adapted to the family unit instead of the individual. For instance, the ward milieu was adapted for family activity rather than individual activity, and the staff attempted to think in terms of the family unit rather than the individual. The psychotherapy was changed to "the family as the unit of treatment" approach.

The theoretical concept "the family as the unit of illness" is basic to every aspect of the research and clinical operation. It is the theoretical foundation from which family psychotherapy was developed as a logical orderly system. The terms *family as a unit* and *family unit* are used as short forms of "the family as the unit of illness." On one level this concept appears so simple and obvious that it hardly deserves second mention. On another level, the concept is subtle and complex, with far-reaching implications that involve a major shift in the way man thinks about himself and illness, and in the theory and practice of medicine. In an effort to communicate as clearly as possible about the concept, I shall describe some of the experiences of the staff in shifting from the individual to the family-unit orientation.

The staff experienced three main levels of awareness of the family-unit concept. The first was the level of *intellectual awareness*. It was relatively easy to understand the concept intellectually.

The second was the level of *clinical awareness*. It was infinitely more complex to put the concept into clinical operation than to understand it intellectually. First it was necessary to further clarify and define our own thinking. All existing theories, terminology, literature, teaching, the rules of society that deal with sick people, and the rules and principles that deal with the practice of medicine, are based on the familiar individual orientation. It was hard for the staff to give up this "second nature" way of thinking. Then came the problem of operating in a medical center which regarded "the individual as the unit of illness." The individual orientation in medicine is strict. It requires that the individual be called "patient" and that individual pathology be defined with tests and labeled with a "diagnosis." Failure to focus on the individual can be regarded as medical irresponsibility. Our problem was to find a way to operate a "family-unit" project in an institution with an individual orientation. Our research center permitted certain flexibilities not possible in a strict clinical setting. For instance, the center permitted a "For Research Study Only" diagnostic label. In general, the minimal individual requirements of the center were met, but within the research ward the use of *diagnoses* and the term *patient* was avoided. The same problem had come up in our writing. It becomes so complicated to avoid terms such as *patient* and *schizophrenia* that we have temporarily resolved the dilemma by sparing use of familiar terms. In the course of implementing the family-unit concept into the clinical operation, we came to "know" the concept in a way that was quite different from the intellectual awareness.

The third level was that of *emotional awareness*. There was a definite process in changing from emotional identifications with the individual to an emotional awareness of the family unit. The first emotional reaction in a new staff member was usually overidentification with one family member, usually the patient, and anger at the family member most involved with the patient, usually the mother. Family members work constantly to get staff members to support their individual viewpoints. The second emotional reaction was usually that of alternating overinvolvements, first with one, and then with another family member. Gradually, there would come an emotional detachment from the stressful overinvolvements and a beginning capacity to become aware of the over-all family problem.

As I see it, the theoretical focus on the family unit, plus the constant daily contact with the living together situation, set the stage for this automatic detachment from the individual and the growing emotional awareness of the family. The detachment proceeded most rapidly in those who had the best control over countertransference overinvolvement. Some staff members were never free of overinvolvements with one family member and angers at other family members. It is essential that the family psychotherapist relate himself to the family and that he avoid overinvolvement with the individual. There are constant forces within the family and within himself to cause him to revert to the familiar individual orientation. When anxiety is high, the family members exert more pressure for individual relationships. When the therapist is anxious, he is more likely to respond with his second nature individual orientation that "feels right." I found that the use of terms associated with the individual orientation was sufficient stimulus to cause me to revert to individual thinking. I was responsible for the family psychotherapy. In an effort to maintain a family-unit orientation, I avoided the use of many familiar psychiatric terms associated with the individual and forced myself to use simple descriptive terms. Other staff members have been freer to use familiar terms.

Early in the study we used a term which was discarded because it has certain inaccuracies, but it does convey a fairly clear notion of the hypothesized psychological unity in the family. The term *undifferentiated family ego mass* suggests a central family oneness. Some siblings are able to achieve almost complete differentiation from the family while others achieve less. The one who becomes psychotic is an example of one who achieves little differentiation. On one level each family member is an individual, but on a deeper level the central family group is as one. Our study was directed at the "undifferentiated family ego mass" beneath the individuals. In the literature the concept that appears to be closest to our family-unit idea was presented by Richardson in *Patients Have Families* (1948). He did not develop his concept as specifically as we have done, but one section of his book is headed "The Family as the Unit of Illness" and another "The Family as the Unit of Treatment." With the increasing number of family research studies, terms such as *family unit* and *family as a unit* have become commonplace. Most investigators have used theoretical thinking based on individual theory, and *family-unit* terms that refer in a nonspecific way to a group of individual family members. According to our hypothesis this would be a "family group" rather than a "family unit." The term *family psychotherapy* is also used frequently. We have used the term to refer to psychotherapy directed at the hypothesized emotional oneness within the family. According to our hypothesis, a psychotherapy based on individual theory and directed to a group of individuals in the same family would be "family group psychotherapy," which is quite different from the method "family psychotherapy" as presented here.

In an effort to remove the psychotherapy from the status of an empirical trial-and-error method, it was incorporated into the research hypothesis so that the hypothesis determined the course of the psychotherapy and psychotherapy observations could be used to change the hypothesis. There were three main steps in adapting the hypothesis to the clinical operation. Each step had its own unique resistances. The first was to *think* in terms of the family-unit rather than the individual. This step was incorporated into the hypothesis. Resistance to this was within the staff. It was difficult to give up "second nature" individual thinking. The second step was to *relate* to the family unit rather than to individuals. This step was incorporated into the research design. Resistance was both in the staff and in the families. In periods of high anxiety, the tendency to revert to the individual orientation was present both in the families and in the staff. The third step was to *treat* the family psychotherapeutically as a single organism. This step was incorporated into the research as "family psychotherapy." Obviously it was necessary to first *think* of the family as a unit and to be reasonably successful at *relating* to the family unit before it was possible to *treat* the family as a unit.

Now to a consideration of the way the family psychotherapy was integrated into the total research plan. The first step was to state the hypothesis in great detail (see Bowen 1957a, 1960, Bowen et al. 1957). Every possible clinical situation was anticipated, explained according to the hypothesis, and recorded as predictions to be checked against clinical observations. The working hypothesis was thus a theoretical blueprint which postulated the origin, development, and clinical characteristics of the family problem, which served as a basis for knowing the clinical management before a clinical situation arose, and which predicted clinical response in family psychotherapy. This corresponds to the *thinking* step outlined above. The second step was the development of a research design through which the working hypothesis could be put into clinical operation. The ward milieu was changed to fit the hypothesis as nearly as possible. For example, occupational therapy was planned for the family unit instead of the individual. This step corresponded to the *relating* step outlined above. The third step was the development of a psychotherapy consistent with the hypothesis.

Thus the entire operation came under the direction of the working hypothesis. Clinical predictions came to have great use. There were constant checks between predictions and actual observations. There were areas in which the predictions were amazingly accurate, and others with great inconsistency. The areas of inconsistency then became areas for special study. Eventually, when there were sufficient clinical observations to support a change, the working hypothesis was reformulated, the research design and the psychotherapy modified to conform to the reformulated hypothesis, and new predictions made. In this way the psychotherapy was linked point by point with the hypothesis, and observations that recurred consistently in psychotherapy could eventually become the basis of a change in the hypothesis. It was possible at any time to make changes in the psychotherapy but only *after* it was possible to reformulate the hypothesis and to *make the changes on the basis of theory*, rather than make changes in clinical emergencies that were based on "clinical judgment" or "feelings." The working hypothesis, which is also our current theoretical concept of schizophrenia, has been presented in detail in another paper (Bowen 1961a).

There is a wealth of dramatic clinical observations in a project such as this. The main problem is selecting and classifying data. I have focused on broad patterns of behavior rather than detail, and specifically on broad patterns present in all the families. There are a number of these which have been incorporated into the working hypothesis, which then served as the basis for modification of the psychotherapy. These relationship patterns have been described in other papers (Bowen 1959, 1960; Bowen et al. 1959), but they have played such an important part in the development of the psychotherapy that it is necessary to summarize some of them here.

Family members are quite different in their outside business and social relationships than in those within the family. It is striking to see a father who functions successfully and decisively in business but who, in relation to the mother, becomes unsure, compromising and paralyzed by indecision. In all the families there has been emotional distance between the parents which we have called the "emotional divorce." At one extreme were the parents with a calm controlled distance from each other. The parents had few overt disagreements and they saw the marriage as ideal. The marriages had the *form* and *content* of closeness in that they went through the actions of closeness and used terms of endearment associated with closeness, but *emotion* was obliterated. Neither husband nor wife could communicate inner thoughts, fantasies or feelings to each other, although both could communicate thoughts and feelings to others. At the other extreme were parents who fought and argued in their brief periods of closeness and who spent most of their time in a "cold war" distance from each other. Most of the parents maintained the distance with varying combinations of calm control and overt disagreement.

Both parents are equally immature. In outside relationships both could cover up the immaturity with facades of maturity. In their relationship with each other, especially when they attempted to function together as a team, one would immediately become the adequate or overstrong one and the other the inadequate or helpless one. Neither could function in the mid-ground between these two extremes. Either could function in either position, depending on the situation. Overadequate fathers were cruel and authoritative and inadequate mothers were helpless and complaining. Overadequate mothers were dominating and bossy and inadequate fathers were passive and compliant. We have called this the "overadequate-inadequate reciprocity." The one who makes a decision for the two of them immediately becomes the overadequate one who is seen as "dominating" the other, who is "forced into submission." When neither will immediately "give in" they fight and argue. Neither wants the responsibility of "dominating," the anxiety of "submitting," nor the discomfort of fighting. The emotional divorce is a mechanism to make the relationship more comfortable. They keep the distance, avoid teamwork decisions, seek individual activities and share inner thoughts and feelings with relatives, friends, children, or other outside figures. As the years pass, the parents tend to develop fixed patterns in which one is usually overadequate and the other inadequate. The overadequate-inadequate reciprocity and the decision paralysis create a state of extreme *functional helplessness* in the family.

There is an intense interdependence between father, mother, and patient which we have called the "interdependent triad." It is usual for normal siblings to become rather involved in the family problem, but not so deeply that they cannot separate themselves from the triad, leaving the father, mother, and patient interlocked in the family oneness. There are constant patterns of functioning within the triad. Either parent can have a close relationship with the patient, provided the other parent permits it. The parents, separated from each other by the emotional divorce, share the patient much as divorced parents share their children. The most familiar pattern is one in which the mother, in an extreme overadequate position to the helpless patient, has the "custody" of the patient, while the father is distant and passive. There are situations in which the mother-patient relationship is disrupted, following which the father then functions very much as does the mother in the close attachment to the patient.

The parents hold strong opposing viewpoints about many levels of issues in their lives together. The one issue about which there is strongest disagreement is the management of the patient. A father and mother with a high level of overt disagreement said, "We agree on everything but politics. Isn't that strange?" Other parents with a low level of overt disagreement said, "We agree on everything except how to raise children, and how to raise parakeets." It is important for the psychotherapist to know that the parents hold these opposite viewpoints about the patient, even though the opposing viewpoint is not expressed. Opposing viewpoints appear to be related more to opposing the other than to real strength of conviction. There have been exchanges of viewpoints in which each parent comes to argue the viewpoint formerly used by the other. The opposing viewpoints seem to function in the service of maintaining identity. For instance, the ones who "give in" have described a "loss of identity," "loss of part of myself," and "inability to know what I think and believe." "Speaking up" seems to be a way of maintaining identity. The "differences" constitute a pressing daily problem for the parents. To them, the answer lies in reaching an agreement and ". . . that is impossible." Actually, their own effort to talk out the difference results in greater difference! The more clearly one states a viewpoint, the more vigorously the other raises the opposition.

Some definite *principles, rules, and techniques* of family psychotherapy have been developed. The principles are derived directly from the working hypothesis. The rules establish the structure for adapting principles to the psychotherapy operation. The techniques are devices used by the therapist to implement the rules. For instance, one of the principles considers the family as a psychological unit. The rule requires the family to participate as a unit in the family psychotherapy. The techniques are devices used by the therapist to implement the rules. In this paper I shall focus on the more simple structure of a single family in family psychotherapy with one therapist, and avoid the more complex situations with multiple therapists and atypical family groups.

The initial goal is to get the family unit into a continuing relationship with the therapist in which family members attempt to "work together" in the hour to discuss and define their own problems. The therapist works toward a position of unbiased detachment, from which position he is able to analyze intrafamily forces. If we think of the family as a single organism, the situation has certain analogies to the structure of psychoanalysis. The family "working together" is similar to the patient who attempts to free associate. The therapeutic effort is to analyze existing intrafamily relationships *in situ*, rather than to analyze the transference relationship between patient and analyst. When the therapist is successful in relating to the family unit and in avoiding individual relationships, the family unit develops a dependence on the therapist similar to neurotic transference, which is quite unlike the intense primitive attachment of psychotic patient to therapist.

We begin the psychotherapy with a simple explanation of the theoretical premise of the project and of the "working together" structure in the hours. The working together may appear simple on the surface but it is directed at the heart of the problem. The "emotional divorce," the "overadequate-inadequate reciprocity" and the problems of the "interdependent triad" stand in the way. The structure demands that one member function as leader and start the hour. When the family is able to start, deep anxiety is stirred up. There are definite mechanisms (equivalent to resistance in individual psychotherapy) by which the family avoids the anxiety of working together. When anxiety mounts, the family effort can become blocked. As I see it at this point, one of my main functions is that of an "enabler" who helps them get started at working together, who follows along when they can work together, and who helps them start again when there is a block.

A family with a psychotic family member is a functionally helpless organism, without a leader, and with a high level of overt anxiety. It has dealt helplessly and noneffectively with life, it has become dependent on outside experts for advice and guidance, and its most positive decisions are made in the service of relieving anxiety of the moment, no matter how many complications this may cause tomorrow. How does the therapist help this kind of family into a working-together relationship? Some of our most important principles and rules are directed at this area. In broad terms, the goal is to find a leader in the leaderless family, to respect the family leader when there is a functioning leader, and to find ways to avoid individual relationships and the position of omnipotence into which the family attempts to place the therapist. A review of the research families will illustrate some of the problems with family leaders.

In the fifteen families with fathers, there were eight in which the mothers functioned clearly as the overadequate ones in relation to helpless patients and as decision-makers for the family. The fathers were distant, passive, resisting critics of the mothers' activities. Even though the fathers did not express it openly, their thoughts focused on what the mothers were doing wrong and on what the *mothers* should do to correct it, but not on any initiative or action for themselves. These mothers could motivate the family effort, overcome the fathers' and patients' resistance to coming to the hours, and initiate the "working together." These families have done best in family psychotherapy.

There were four families in which the fathers functioned as spokesmen for the mothers, who remained behind the scenes. A parody of this situation might go as follows: The mother tells the father that he has to decide what to do. He says he doesn't know what to do. She tells him he has to decide and then gives him an idea to help him decide. He says he will do it that way. Such a father is as helpless as he was when his own mother told him what to do, what to wear or when to get a haircut. With this family in the unstructured working-together situation, the helplessness of the father is clearly demonstrated. He has to begin the hour. He turns to the mother. In this situation she is silent, although she may lecture him after the hour ends. Then he turns to the therapist, using all his ingenious mechanisms to have the therapist tell him what to do. These families have done poorest in family psychotherapy. One family went over a year before the parents could begin to work together. The fathers are skillfull at reading "instructions" into the therapist's facial expressions or casual remarks.

There were three families in which the fathers appeared to have functioned as the leaders and decision-makers, but they were comparatively weak and more like "acting leaders." The mothers were active with the patients, but in relation to the fathers they were relatively silent. They seemed to be important somewhere behind the scenes. One of these mothers finally explained her version of this. She said, "If I make a direct suggestion, he opposes it. So, I keep working it around and eventually it will come out of him as his idea. The only problem is that he often misses the point and changes it around, and then I have to start all over." These families made slow progress in family psychotherapy.

It was relatively easy for the overadequate decision-making mothers to initiate working together. Two mothers were able to start at the beginning of the first hour. The mother, separated from the father by the emotional divorce, would direct the first comment to the patient. If anxiety was high, she would criticize the patient. If anxiety was low, she might use an understanding approach, such as, "Tell us what you think.

Tell us what you don't like about us." Eventually there would be an angry exchange between mother and patient. The passive father, in silent disagreement with the mother, would remain quiet, expecting the therapist to "put her right." Later he might ask the therapist to express a professional opinion. The request for a professional opinion usually comes when there is a difference of opinion between the parents. The therapist who expresses an opinion not only takes a side, but also misses the "why" of the question. In the disharmony between mother and patient, the father usually identifies with the patient's viewpoint, yet, when the patient asks him for support, he remains passive. If the patient becomes aggressive with the mother, he will respond to the mother's request to make the patient behave. The decision-making mother can become very aggressive and even cruel in her attempts to deal with the family.

In the beginning we tended to point out the mother's aggression, the illogic of her comments, and the father's passivity. This would result in the mother's stopping the aggression and, along with it, giving up the position of family leader. The therapist could then find himself faced with a helpless "what do we do now" family. The passive father would usually respond with a half-hearted attempt to be more active, but with a compliant "the doctor told me to" attitude. Now we avoid comments which might reduce the initiative of the family leader. We make comments designed to "support" the family leader, such as, "You are having a hard time trying to get your family to pull together." These people have lived together for years. They are all perfectly capable of dealing with each other. When the therapist is able to deal with his own concerns, then the family members are more capable of utilizing their own spontaneous resources. Eventually the passive father moves, on his own initiative, to oppose the aggressive mother, and the main conflict shifts from the mother-patient relationship to the mother-father relationship. The father usually retreats when the mother becomes angry, anxious, or tearful but eventually he can maintain a stand that is "no longer soluble in the mother's tears." It is an important milestone when the father can maintain his strong position. The mother will go through a few days of intense anxiety and then settle down to a period of calm, kind, firm objectivity. One such mother said, "I am so pleased with him. If he can keep on being a man, I can be a woman." This new level will continue a few days or a few weeks before they lapse back to the familiar dominant mother-passive father positions, but after the first such shift, it is easier for new shifts to occur.

My opinion about the "dominating" mother has been changed by this experience. As long as she feels the weight of the family problem, she is highly motivated for change. If the therapist can keep her in that position, she can cause the family to change. However, she will relax her effort and turn the problem over to the therapist at the first opportunity. For instance, she will ask the therapist to convince the father to give up his opposition to the family psychotherapy. She is quite capable of dealing with the father but the therapist will fail. If the therapist tries to help her deal with the family, he will suddenly discover that she has changed to a helpless complaining person who waits for him to motivate her helpless family. Some of the most significant family changes have occurred when the mothers have become "fed up" and have exploded in anger. One mother said, "I wish I could get mad more often. Acting mad doesn't work. I have to be really mad." Most of our therapeutic impasses have occurred when we have failed to identify the family leader. The therapist tells the family he expects one member to be the responsible spokesman for the family on arrangements concerning the psychother- apy. The family can change the spokesman as it wishes, as long as the therapist has one person who can speak for the family. The selection of spokesman forces the family to a beginning resolution of the leadership problem. It also creates a workable structure for the therapist.

There are a number of mechanisms to avoid the anxiety of working together. The most prominent is the effort to involve the therapist in individual relationships. This mechanism, and techniques for dealing with it, are discussed throughout the paper. There are frequent joking comments about the working together, such as, "we do that at home. How can that help?" One father who had previously been in individual psychotherapy said, "Doesn't it strike you as crazy for us to come here to say the same things we could say at home?" The therapist responded, "Any crazier than for you to go to a therapist alone and act as though he were your father?" A subtle and difficult mechanism is one by which the parents represent the psychotic one as the therapist's patient and themselves as assistant therapists. The assistants become helpless and the therapist is responsible for three helpless individuals. The parents may urge the patient to talk and thus create a situation in which the patient fills the time with psychotic chatter while the parents attempt to enlist the therapist in interpreting symbolic meaning. Several of the families, from their long experience with psychiatry, had an excellent intellectual graps of psychoanalytic theory. Another mechanism is "chit- chat." Silence can occur in less disturbed familes. When the family is disturbed, the one with the highest anxiety will start chattering. The more functionally helpless the family, the more ingenious the family at invoking these mechanisms. The families with fathers who spoke for the mother were the most skillful in the use of avoidance mechanisms.

The avoidance mechanisms that involve the therapist in the emotional problems of the individual are of more immediate importance to the family psychotherapy than the avoidance mechanisms that are contained within the family unit. The family is not able to work together successfully, nor is the therapist able to see the family unit objectively when he is emotionally involved with a single family member. It probably is not possible for the therapist to relate to the family without occasional involvements with individuals. My efforts have gone toward recognizing individual involvements when they occur, and toward finding more efficient ways to regain and to maintain emotional detachment. An important part of the therapist's overinvolvement comes from his own unconscious functioning. For instance, when I feel myself inwardly cheering the hero, or hating the villain in the family drama, or pulling for the family victim to assert himself, I consider it time for me to work on my own functioning. Some of our most important psychotherapy rules have been made to structure an environment favorable for the therapist. Note-taking has been an efficient device to help me remain detached. The rationale for the detachment and for my use of note-taking to achieve this is explained to the family at the beginning of treatment.

Family members are skillful at making individual communications outside the family psychotherapy hours. They will stop at the end of the hour to tell the therapist something "too unimportant for the family hour." They write personal notes, make telephone calls between hours, or find occasion to tell the therapist "secrets" about other family members that the therapist should know, but that would be "hurtful" if mentioned in the family hour. Not all of these communications are "loaded," but a blanket rule that the therapist will report all outside communications at the next family hour was successful in preventing emotional involvements that resulted from certain of these individual messages.

There are times when, for reality reasons such as illness or business, it is not possible for a family member to attend hours. In the beginning we had a strict rule that a family hour would not be possible unless at least two family members were present. This rule was designed to prevent an individual relationship with a single family member. Recently we have been making one exception to the two-person rule. When the family leader is not motivated to overcome family resistance we see the leader alone, but the orientation remains on the family, the leader is seen as the official representative of the family, and discussion of the leader's personal problems is avoided. For instance, one family leader began the hour by talking about her own fears. The therapist shifted the discussion to the family problem. Personal material will eventually emerge in the family sessions when it is possible to see the emotional reaction of other family members to the personal material. Results from seeing the leader alone have been good. When the other parent is alone, he will represent himself as sick or helpless, or solicit aid in dealing with the leader's injustice. When the patient is seen alone, the parents relax their efforts and leave the problem between patient and therapist.

The therapist remains relatively inactive when the family is able to work together. We have continued as long as twelve consecutive hours with no more comment than a greeting at the beginning of the hour and an announcement that time was up. In one such period, the father asked what the therapist was supposed to do in the hours. The therapist replied, "I create the atmosphere. It is my presence that counts." The father began calling the therapist "Dr. Presence." When the working together goes smoothly, communication barriers begin to decrease. Those in the controlled, inhibited families find it is possible to express thoughts in the family hours that could not be expressed at home. One mother said, "It is a revelation to come here and find out so many things about the others that I never knew before." Those in the fighting, arguing families find they can talk much more calmly than at home. One father said, "We have stopped fighting at home. We agreed to reserve the emotional issues and the fights until we get here. We do not get as mad here and it is harder to get mad and walk out." The period of free communication will stop when the communications again arouse anxiety. Then there is a period of resistance with comments such as, "We are getting nowhere. The family situation is worse than when we started." From experience, we have found that certain "feeling" communications arouse deep anxiety, which can be followed by emotional arguments over trivial points. It can be fairly easy for the family to resume working together if the therapist can relate the "explosion" to the specific feeling communication.

There are inquiries about the kinds of comments and interpretations we make in family psychotherapy. There is infinite material of interest to any psychotherapist. The working together, the family leader structure, and the emotional detachment of the therapist always get immediate attention. Comments about intrafamily avoidance mechanisms are withheld until the therapist can speak without impeding the working together. A comment that causes the family to shift attention from its own problems to the therapist was probably ill-timed. The family member in the most helpless position (usually the patient) tells dramatic stories of trauma, rejection, hardship and injustice. Other family members disagree with the reality of the stories. If the therapist becomes involved in the dramatic stories, he can lose his way in a swamp of conflicting detail. We avoid content interpretations and focus on the process. Detailed content material for the research was obtained in separate information-gathering meetings. Such comments as, "The mother uses one voice in speaking to the patient, and another voice in speaking to the father" and "The father looks at the patient when he speaks to him, but not at the mother when he speaks to her," seem to be helpful at any time. The more therapists have limited their comments, the more active family members become in interpreting for each other. For a time we followed the practice of "summing up" at the end of the hour. Families began to stop five minutes before the end to wait on "the word" from the therapist. When family members were asked to do their own summaries, they were able to do rather well.

One of our most important principles has to do with the therapist's attitude about anxiety. These families have a low tolerance for anxiety. They fear it, withdraw from it, and treat it as an awful thing to be avoided at any cost. They compromise important life principles for "peace at any price." The anxiety inhibits every relationship in the family. The parents are afraid to relate spontaneously with each other lest they do or say something to "hurt" the other. Parents are particularly afraid to relate to the patient. Convinced they did something "wrong" to cause the problem in the patient, they are afraid to touch the patient lest they make the problem worse. In family psychotherapy, the families quickly encounter deep anxiety. It is essential that the therapist have some way to help them with the anxiety. Throughout the entire course of family psychotherapy, the therapist maintains an attitude which conveys, "Anxiety is inevitable if you solve the problem. When anxiety increases, one has to decide whether to give in and retreat or carry on in spite of it. Anxiety does not harm people. It only makes them uncomfortable. It can cause you to shake, or lose sleep, or become confused, or develop physical symptoms, but it will not kill you and it will subside. People can even grow and become more mature by having to face and deal with anxiety situations. Do you have to go on treating each other as fragile people who are about to fall apart?"

In my opinion these families are not *really* helpless. They are functionally helpless. The parents are adequate, resourceful people in their outside relationships. It is in relationship to each other that they become functionally helpless. When the family is able to be a contained unit, and there is a family leader with motivation to define the problem and to back his own convictions in taking appropriate action, the family can change from a directionless, anxiety-ridden, floundering unit, to a more resourceful organism with a probelm to be solved. The parents had all spent years seeking answers outside themselves. They had read extensively, attended lectures, and sought the advice of experts for answers to what they had done "wrong" and what they should do "right." When parents could eventually reach the point of acting on convictions from inside themselves, they might do things that others would consider harmful, but the patient and the rest of the family would respond positively.

In the effort to focus on the family, the parents' emphasis on the "sickness" of the patient was defocused. For example, a son who avoided stepping on cracks in the sidewalk was upset unless the father also avoided the cracks. The father, to avoid hurting the son, went along with his irrational behavior.[1] The father focused on changing the "sickness" in the son. The therapist asked how the father managed to get himself into the position of skipping over cracks. At the beginning of treatment all the parents were solicitous and infantilizing to the sick, incompetent patients. As the parents began to assume leadership responsibility, there would be arguments between the parents about the patient. One parent, basing opinons on "knowing how the patient felt," would say that behavior was caused by "sickness" and advocate understanding, love, and kindness for the patient. The other parent would conclude that it was not all "sickness" and advocate management based on what the patient did, instead of feelings. The arguments seemed to have little to do with the functioning of the patient at the time. In those families in which both parents could eventually tone down the sickness theme and relate to the patient on a reality level, the patients changed. After one family had emerged from their unreality, the patient said, "As long as they called me sick and treated me sick, I somehow had to act sick. When they stopped treating me sick, I had a choice of acting sick or acting well."

Individuals in the family went through a process of "differentiation of self" from other family members. An important part was emotional differentiation. One mother said she was putting an invisible wall between herself and the daughter, "so I can feel what I feel and she can feel what she feels; so I can have my life can she can have hers." It was common for the mother's tears to "hurt" the rest of the family more than the mother. The therapist asked many questions to define the emotional overlap between family members. Another part of the differentiation was the "establishment of identity" which is similar to the discovery of self in individual psychotherapy. An example was a father who said, "If we spent less time working on our son and more time trying to find out what we believe and what we stand for, it would be easier for him to find himself." The family leaders were the first to begin working on differentiation of self. The other parent changed more slowly, usually in relation to the leader parent. When the family leader changed, the new leader was the one who changed next. The patient usually lagged far behind; their changes came after the parents were fairly definite about themselves.

There was one family which illustrates the degree to which parents go along with irrational behavior, the dramatic change when a passive father took a positive stand, and the marked change when the therapist refused to call the patient "sick."

The 17-year-old psychotic son was the only child of parents in their early forties. He dominated the home with his psychosis. A guidance center recommended hospitalization. The parents wanted to keep the son at home. They were referred to our family project for consultation. There was no space on the "in-residence" ward, but we agreed to outpatient family psychotherapy as long as the parents would maintain the son at home.

The son spent much time in his room with the door locked. He insisted that window blinds be closed to prevent attack from enemies outside. He crawled across the floor beneath the windows lest his enemies see through the blinds. He became angry unless his mother sat with feet and hands in a certain position. He would demand special food, throw it in the garbage because the mother did not prepare it right, and demand more.

The first hour the therapist did little more than wonder how the parents came to be privates and the son the general in the family. The father made a weak effort to take a stand. The son twisted the father's arm. A dramatic change came after four months (eight hours) of family psychotherapy. The son had been unusually aggressive and the parents unusually helpless. The father expressed concern that the son might kill him. The therapist suggested hospitalization if this was the case. The father said he would not attend the next hour; he was going on a vacation and would let the mother and patient settle their own differences. Father, mother, and son were together for the next hour, three days later. The family was calm and congenial; there were no psychotic symptoms. After the previous hour the father had announced that he was tired living in a darkened morgue and that he was going to open the blinds to let the sunshine in. The son threatened to kill the father if he touched the blinds. The father opened the blinds. The father and son fought briefly and the father won. The psychotic symptoms disappeared. The father policed the home for a month. The son did well. The father-son relationship had changed and the son-mother relationship had changed, but the father-mother relationship did not change.

After a month the father told the mother he could not take it any longer. He gave up his firm stand, the mother resumed her picking on the son, and the son resumed the psychosis. The family continued for some months with the chronic psychotic adjustment. There was a pattern in which the parents would "gang up" on the son to prove him "sick" and the son would argue vigorously, using paranoid delusions to support his arguments. The parents would then use the delusions as proof of sickness. In an effort to give more status to the son, the therapist referred to the family as a debating society, indicating that debating rules permit the debater to argue illogical points if he wishes. The son kept arguing, but within a week he was choosing to argue reality points to support his viewpoints. After sixteen months (seventy-three family psychotherapy hours) the son said, "For years I have been trying to find what to do about my parents' brainwashing me. Now I know. The trick is to brainwash them before they brainwash me."

The family achieved a good symptomatic result. They reduced appointments to once a month and continued for ninety-four hours over three years. The son made a good social adjustment. He finished high school and went on to college. The mother is employed for the first time in her life.

This was a family with an "acting leader" father. The parents in these families have not achieved as much basic change in the parental relationship as families with more definite family leaders.

Outside the formal research study we have used family psychotherapy in a number of families with character disorders and neurotic problems. The family relationship patterns first observed in the "in-residence" families were also present in all other families. However, there were also striking differences. In families with neurotic problems, the patterns were more flexible and resilient. The separation in the emotional divorce could be as great but it could fluctuate more easily. The "overadequate-inadequate reciprocity" could be as marked but there was not so much anxiety, rigidity, and decision paralysis. In families with severe character disorders, the family relationship patterns appeared to be essentially the same as in families with psychoses. Families with neuroses were much better able to distinguish feeling from fact and to act on the basis of reality. Families with psychotic-level problems were more inclined to evaluate a situation with feelings, to consider the feelings as factual, and to act on the basis of feeling. Families with neurotic problems were more capable of objective consideration of the problem without "acting it out," involving the therapist, and becoming paralyzed by indecision. According to my current thinking, there is nothing in schizophrenia that is not also present in all of us. Schizophrenia is made up of the essence of human experience many times distilled. With our incapacity to look at ourselves, we have much to learn about ourselves from studying the least mature of us.

In considering change in the research families, we have come to think more in terms of change in the parental relationship than of change in psychotic symptoms. The parents can change in relationship to each other. When there is a change in a fixed rigidity of the parental relationship, there follows a change in the patient, irrespective of the immediate level of psychotic symptoms. Psychotic symptoms can change dramatically in relation to one parent. There have been other examples of temporary change similar to the change in the family described above. The most characteristic and definite changes occurred in outpatient families with decision-making mothers. The most dramatic changes occurred when the fathers assumed family leadership against the mothers' protests. This was usually followed by a period of calm resolution of the emotional divorce and objectivity in taking stands against the patients' demands. Then the patients would change. Until observing these shifts, we had considered "dominant mothers" and "passive fathers" as fixed personality characteristics. The fathers would lapse into inactivity, passively permit the mothers to resume the leadership, and a new cycle would begin. These shifts were repeated once or twice a year, with successive shifts becoming calmer and easier.

One family went on to a fairly good resolution of parental relationship problems. The patient achieved a good adjustment. Two other families, still in family psychotherapy, appear to be going in this direction. Two families terminated psychotherapy in helpless disharmony when the family-leader structure was lost. Two families with "acting leader" fathers, including the family described in this paper, achieved gradual symptomatic improvement with minimal change in the parental relationship. The outpatient families did much better in family psychotherapy. This did not appear directly related to the long-term maximum degree of psychosis in most of the in-residence patients. The degree of chronic impairment was almost as great in some of the outpatient families. The seven in-residence father families with hospital staff nearby, were never able to deal with their helplessness. One in-residence family achieved some change between the parents and, with two other families, sufficient decrease in symptoms for the patients to live at home. Four families participated only six months. In two of these there was no change. The patients are in institutions. The other two families are now in outpatient family psychotherapy.

Summary

This paper describes a method of family psychotherapy developed as part of a family research project. The research was based on the theoretical premise "the family as the unit of illness." The psychotherapeutic approach "the family as the unit of treatment" was developed from the theoretical premise and incorporated as an integral part of the research project. The goal of this paper has been to present a broad over-all view of both the theoretical and the clinical aspects of the psychotherapy. To achieve this, the theoretical premise "the family as the unit of illness" has been described in some detail. The description of family psychotherapy has been focused more on broad principles and the rationale for structuring the psychotherapy than on description and clinical details.

Note

1. Lidz and Fleck (1960) have referred to this as the families who provide training in irrationality.

Chapter 6

Out-Patient Family
Psychotherapy

It is difficult to describe a relatively new method of psychotherapy in a brief presentation. In an effort to be as concise and brief as possible, I will focus on the theoretical orientation and on broad clinical principles. The theoretical orientation is based on the concept of an "emotional oneness" that involves certain key figures in the family. Descriptively, the emotional oneness is equivalent to an "intrafamily psyche," or "family self," or to a "family ego." The psychotherapy is directed to the "family ego" rather than to individuals in the family.

How does one conceptualize an intrafamily psyche, or a family ego? In 1956-1957 I used a term which was discarded becasue of certain conceptual inaccuracies, and then revived because of its usefulness in describing the "emotional oneness." It is the term *undifferentiated family ego mass*. According to the theoretical concept, children grow up to achieve varying levels of "differentiation of self" from the undifferentiated family ego mass. Some children achieve almost complete differentiation of self to become autonomous individuals with clear ego identities. This is equivalent to our familiar concept of a "mature person." These people function as contained emotional units. They do not become emotionally enmeshed in new "emotional onenesses" with others. According to the concept, people marry spouses with identical levels of "differentiation of self." When a person with a high level of differentiation of self marries a spouse with equal maturity, they can be emotionally close and each can maintain clear individuality and identity without the "fusion of selfs" that occurs in marriages of less differentiated individuals.

If the degree of differentiation of self is put on a percentile scale, the person who later develops a clinical neurosis will belong somewhere in the middle of the scale. The person who becomes a parents of a schizophrenic offspring has a very low level of differentiation of self and would belong far toward the lower end of the scale. The person who later develops a schizophrenic psychosis has the lowest level of differentiation of self and would belong at the extreme lower end of the scale.

The characteristics of parents of a schizophrenic offspring will help to illustrate the concept. These are people with a very low level of differentiation of self who somehow manage to function fairly well in their life adjustments. As children they do not "grow away" from the family ego mass as do their more differentiated siblings. They remain emotionally attached to their parents. After adolescence, in an effort to function without the parents, they "tear" themselves away" to attain a "pseudo-self" with a "pseudo-separation" from the family ego mass. Some achieve this with denial and an exaggerated facade of independence while still living with the parents. Others achieve this with denial and physical distance. Their adjustment depends on maintaining an emotional distance from people. They can do well in business and academic pursuits as long as they do not become involved in close emotional relationships. In marriage to a spouse with an equally poor differentiation of self, they become deeply involved emotionally. The new spouses "fuse together" into a new undifferentiated family ego mass in which ego boundaries between them are obliterated. The same kind of phenomenon takes place between spouses with higher levels of differentiation of self but the process is not as intense and striking as between spouses with poor differentiation of self.

Children who later become psychotic are examples of those with the lowest level of differentiation of self. The main difference here is that these people do not achieve even a working level of "pseudo-self." They continue to function as dependent appendages of the family ego mass. Some achieve so little differentiation of self that they collapse in psychosis in their first efforts to function independently of the parents. Others achieve brief or tenuous periods of "pseudo-self" but any long-term separation from the parents is maintained only by finding new dependent attachments to other people who will guide and advise them, and from whom they borrow enough self to function. Their adjustment depends on the all-important dependent attachment to others. They can collapse in situations in which the dependent attachments are disrupted or threatened.

There are characteristic dynamics in the new husband-wife undifferentiated family ego mass. Both have intense longings for closeness but when they are close, their individual "selfs" fuse together into an emotional oneness with a "common self." This results in loss of individual identity, emotional turmoil, and conflict. They retreat to sufficient aloofness and distance from each other for each to maintain as much identity and autonomy as possible. This emotional distance, which I have called the *emotional divorce*, helps prevent the loss of identity and conflict that comes with closeness. The greater their emotional dependence on each other, the more intense the turmoil and conflict within the marriage. The intensity of the turmoil can be reduced by maintaining important but distance relationships within their own families or with new friends. Each seems to derive some "self" and support from outside relationships. However, the problem between them is always present. Both experience "loss of self" and each sees the other as "dominating" or taking away his or her "self." In marriages in which both work actively to maintain identity, neither will "give in" to the other and there is constant marital conflict. The conflict is avoided when one will "give in" but this results in an exchange in which the dominant one "gains strength" at the expense of the other who "loses strength." The one who "gives in" often spontaneously describes a "loss of identity," "confusion," and "inability to know who I am and what I stand for," while the other functions with greater confidence and effectiveness. In some marriages, one will volunteer to be the dependent one who automatically "gives in" and the other becomes the dominant one. Such families may find a fairly comfortable equilibrium with each in their respective roles, and without undue incapacity in the submissive or adaptive one. Others do not find an equilibrium so easily. The process in which the dominant one becomes stronger at the expense of the weaker one can continue until the weaker one becomes incapacitated with a physical illness, with an emotional illness, or with impaired social and personal functioning such as drinking, irresponsibility, and work inefficiency. A brief presentation does not permit sufficient clinical examples to illustrate the points, but one family illustrates two facets of the concept. In the first marriage, the wife was the dominant, resourceful one to a husband who became weaker to the point that drinking and irresponsibility prevented him from working. In her second marriage, the wife resolved to avoid the pitfalls of the first marriage, and to "become more dependent and feminine." Three years later, after increasing lack of confidence and "loss of identity," she found herself hospitalized with an acute psychosis.

In some families, the emotional disharmony of the husband-wife oneness is contained pretty much within the "oneness," or within the circle of their outside relationships. For some reason, their children remain relatively uninvolved. In other families, the full weight of the problem is transmitted to one or more children. The parental problem appears to be almost completely "solved" by the children. In an overwhelming percentage of families, there is a combination of parental conflict and problems in the children, but there is this small percentage of families with very great parental conflict and relatively little involvement of the children, and also a small percentage at the other end of the scale in which the parental relationship is calm and harmonious and in which the first manifestation of a family problem is a neurotic or psychotic problem in a child. I believe this small percentage of families is of critical importance as living proof that *parental conflict within itself cannot* cause *a neurosis or psychosis in children* and also that *major emotional problems can develop in families in which there has been no overt parental conflict.* In my clinical experience with 156 families, 49 percent sought help for a problem in one spouse or for a marital problem, and 51 percent sought help for a problem in a child. In many of these one would be hard pressed to decide whether the parental problem or the problem in the child was greatest, but it was striking that the chief complaints, for which they sought help, divided the families into almost equal groups.

This method of psychotherapy is directed to the family ego mass rather than to the individual problems of a group of family members. This approach evolved from a research project for families with one maximally impaired schizophrenic offspring. Both parents, the psychotic offspring, and normal siblings attended all psychotherapy hours together. The "normal" siblings were not strong "selfs" but, in every case, the normal siblings soon found reason to separate themselves from the families, leaving the two parents and the psychotic offspring interlocked in an intense emotional interdependency which I called the *interdependent triad.* This is an emotional oneness that is above and beyond all other emotional ties. The child who becomes psychotic is emotionally "welded" into the ego oneness with the parents where he has long functioned as an "ego nothing" which permitted the parents to be an "ego something," until his growth and the passing years made this into an untenable solution. These three people can be physically separated from each other but it is extremely difficult for any one of them to differentiate a "self" from the other two. After months of psychotherapy, one parents would develop a clearer "self" or "identity," then the other parent would develop more identity and then the patient would "grow up a little" I had hoped this process might continue the cyclical course until all three could differentiate themselves into autonomous individuals. This did not work out. Once they reached a point of decreased symptoms, the motivation for further differentiation would decrease.

Recently I have modified the psychotherapy approach. Now, I work with the triad until each is able to see that each has a part in the family problem. Then I begin seeing the parents together with the explicit goal of helping them to separate themselves from the patient, and helping the patient to separate from them. The patient is seen alone with the explicit goal of helping him develop his own autonomy, and to resist his built-in emotional urge to "save the parents" by surrendering his "self" to them. Better clinical results have come with this approach.

Families with a neurotic or behavior problem in a pre- or postadolescent child will help to illustrate both the theoretical concept and the family psychotherapy. In these families, the basic dynamisms, including the husband-wife "emotional divorce," and the triadic involvement of one child, are exactly the same as in families with a psychotic offspring, except the levels of differentiation of self in the parents is much higher. It is easier for the parents to "get outside the emotion" and see the problem objectively, and the response to therapy is much faster. For about three years I worked with parents and child together in the hours. This psychotherapy followed a definite course. Parents would begin with a working premise that they had done something "wrong" with the child, and that the problem would be solved when they had discovered the "wrong" and corrected it. Parents would work for months at trying to understand and interpret the child's problem and at devising programs to favorably influence the child. Parents avoided problems between themselves. Consistent effort by the therapist might bring the parental problem briefly into focus, but either the parents or the child would quickly shift the focus back to the child. If the parents did not find some old issue for which to criticize the child, then the child would do or say something to anger the parents and draw the focus back to himself. This process could continue for months, or for a year or two, and terminate with decreased symptoms in the child, more activity in passive fathers, and less aggressiveness in anxious mothers, but the basic family dynamisms did not change.

Experience with twenty such families suggested that the parental problem was transmitted to the child through *making a project out of the child*, and that the problem in the child could be created and perpetuated just as surely by a "project" that was psychologically "correct" as by a "project" that was "psychopathological." Two years ago I began a new psychotherapeutic approach designed for *the parents to make a project out of themselves*. Parents were asked if they could accept the working premise that the basic problem was between themselves, and if they could leave the child out of the psychotherapy, and devote their effort to searching out problems between themselves. Some of the best clinical results have come with a group of families in which parents were emotionally capable of focusing on themselves. In three families, I have never seen the symptomatic child for whom the family first sought treatment. In other families the "sick" child has been seen no more than twice. There is often a dramatic decrease in the child's symptoms within a few weeks after the parents have been successful in keeping the focus on themselves. The psychotherapy proceeds in several distinct phases. The first weeks or months the parents discuss their stored up discontents with each other. This is usually accompanied by "hurt" feelings, mild conscious or unconscious retaliation against the other (acted out feelings), and with abrupt decreases and increases in the emotional divorce. Then comes a calmer phase in which each is more capable of dealing with inner emotional problems as they emerge in the other. This phase is one in which inner thoughts, feelings, and fantasies are communicated. I often structure this as "communication of inner self" to the other. This introspective focus of each leads to the emergence of unconscious, infantile, and sexual material, and then to each working out old problems with his or her own parents. Some of the greatest therapeutic benefit comes from analyzing the intense emotional response that each experiences in dealing with deep emotional material from the other. When the process reaches this point, the emotional divorces begins to resolve permanently and the child is free of the emotional process between the parents.

The favorable results with parents who could make a project out of themselves was a turning point in both the theory and practice of family psychotherapy. The problem in the child would almost completely disappear by the time parents were seriously occupied with each other. When parents encountered intense anxiety during therapy, the child's symptoms would recur briefly, but by the time parents were engaged in dealing with their deeper emotional problems, there simply was never a thought or reason to consider individual psychotherapy for the child. Older teenage children who were trying to "tear themselves away from parents" were offered psychotherapy appointments separate from the parents, on the premise that they had more of an individual internalized problem that would not respond to change in the parents. The average teenager did not continue this. In every family in which parents could continue the focus on themselves, the teenage child would give up "tearing himself away," and establish a new emotional closeness with the family, and then proceed to a more orderly "growing up" and "growing away" from the family. There was one 22-year-old "problem child" away at college who had no individual help and only brief vacation contacts with the parents. The response to parental change was almost as dramatic as that of a preadolescent child who lives with the parents.

More experience is needed to know the extent of family change that follows change in the parents.

Now to a brief consideration of the parents who can go through the motions of making a project out of themselves, but who are simply not capable of making it work. Some parents are so emotionally invested in the child and so much of their thoughts, worries, and psychic energies go to the child that it is difficult for them to think or speak about anything else. Efforts to direct thoughts elsewhere can be as strained and artificial as the anxious person who tries to make conversation at a party. In other families, the child functions as an "emotional shunt" between the parents. Deprived of the physical presence of the "shunt," they argue and fight. Such parents are so "hurt" by what the other says and thinks, and "acting out" accusations, and retaliatory "hurting the other" can become so intense, that therapy is disrupted. If emotion does not get too high, they might be able to continue together. If the conflict is disruptive, it is more productive to work with the most motivated parent alone (this point will be discussed later) until the two can work together. The ability of parents to work together on their own problems depends on the basic level of differentiation of self in the parents.

Now, to family psychotherapy with husband-wife families. My approach to this is very much the same as with the parents from families in which the initial problem was primarily in a child. The therapy begins with husband and wife focusing on each other but the therapy can be more difficult than when the initial focus was on a child. Husbands and wives with the primary problem between themselves seem to have more rigid defenses against each other than those who have displaced part of the problem to a child. Problems in a husband-wife family are manifested in one, or a combination of two general areas. One is the area of marital conflict. The other is the area of illness or impaired functioning in one spouse. All levels of problems can be present in a single family, such as a severe impairment in a child, marital conflict of physical violence intensity, and a borderline psychosis in one parent.

"Conflictual spouses" might be able to continue to attend the hours together if the conflict is in a toned-down "armed truce" or "cold war" state, and the "acting out" and retaliation does not become disruptive. When conflict is high, one spouse usually wants the psychotherapy while the other is resistive or even vehemently opposed. Their conscious and unconscious mechanisms are so involved in offensive and defensive maneuvers that neither can focus on self in the presence of the other. In these families I work with one alone until they are able to work productively together. The goal can be stated on several levels. One is to help the motivated one toward a higher level of differentiation of self.

Another is to help the motivated one gain some emotional distance, some understanding of the attack-counterattack mechanisms, some ability to observe the phenomenon without responding emotionally, and some awareness of the part he or she plays in acting out and perpetuating the conflict. The therapist avoides "side-taking," emotional identification with either, participation in accusations against the other, or permitting infantile material to come into focus. Discussion of infantile material comes after the other spouse is present. I do not permit this phase of therapy to become "individual" therapy, nor to be called "individual" therapy. When the motivated one can engage the family problem constructively and gain some confidence and mastery over becoming involved in emotional couter-responses, it is usually not long before the other expresses a positive wish to join the effort. Then the two are in a position to proceed toward a calm, orderly course of family psychotherapy.

When one spouse is "sick" or incapacitated, or has been labeled "patient," it might require months of individual therapy before this can be seen as a family problem. This is usually the product of a long-term situation in which one, with a "need to be strong," has functioned as the dominant one, and the other, with a "need to be dependent," has functioned as the weak one. The motivation is toward alleviation of symptoms rather than toward changing the familiar and comfortable situation behind the symptoms. Both work actively to maintain their familiar dominant and dependent positions. It is difficult for them to work toward resolving the underlying problem until something shifts. When it is the dominant one who seeks help, the weak one is usually in a severe collapse. The dominant one want symptoms removed and often discontinues at this point. It is easier when the weak one seeks help. I usually continue with this one alone, leaving it to the "patient" to decide when, or if the other is to join the therapy. An effort is made to help the "patient" define the part he has played in the family problem. When the "patient" gains some strength and confidence, he often prevails on the other spouse to change the "individual" psychotherapy to family psychotherapy.

In summary, I have presented some over-all characteristics of a method of family psychotherapy which regards the basic problem as a "fusion of egos" or undifferentiated family ego mass, and in which the psychotherapy is directed to the family ego mass, or to those family members most involved in the undifferentiated emotional oneness of the family. An over-all goal of the therapy is to enable involved family members to proceed toward a higher level of differentiation of self or toward ego identity. In certain situations it is most profitable to include all family members in the family psychotherapy hours. In other situations it is more profitable to work with the single family member who is most motivated for change at that time. Experiences with different kinds of clinical problems have been presented in terms of the over-all theoretical premise and broad clinical principles.

II
Family Systems Theory

Chapter 7

Intrafamily Dynamics
in Emotional Illness

During the last ten years there has been a rapidly increasing interest in family treatment of emotional problems. I shall here present the broad outlines of a family theory of emotional illness and a method of family psychotherapy developed from it. To put this theory into a wider perspective I shall review briefly the background of the current interest in "the family."

Theoretical interest in the family goes back to the beginning of psychoanalysis when Freud made his original formulations about the part played by parents in "causing" emotional illness. This was followed by a period of more than fifty years with only minor changes in theory and with treatment focused almost entirely on the "patient." The only exceptions were in child psychiatry and some social casework and counseling efforts. In the early 1950s efforts were begun to involve the family in treatment. There was a sudden increase in family research in order to further understanding of family dynamics. Some of the research resulted in new theories or modifications in existing theory. This was followed by innumerable variations in psychotherapeutic techniques designed to involve multiple family members in the treatment process. In the last six or eight years the number of people working with families has multiplied each year, and terms such as *family psychotherapy* and *family therapy* have come into common usage to refer to a wide variety of methods and techniques.

There is little agreement about what makes up the "family" part of family psychotherapy and even less agreement about what is involved in the "psychotherapy" part of family psychotherapy. I am one of several investigators who support the view that certain key concepts of the theory of the individual simply cannot be adapted to profitable work with families. A number of investigators are working toward new theoretical frames of reference to explain the family phenomenon. Most of the increasing numbers of therapists working with families are using variations in group therapy techniques, with less attention to the theoretical problems. The main point to be conveyed here is that the current interest in the "family" is new, that it has grown vigorously in the few years since it began, that it is currently in an unstructured transitional state of chaos, but that it is a healthy new movement that holds much promise for the future.

The family orientation to be presented here is different from our familiar individual orientation in a number of important ways. It has been difficult for me to communicate this orientation to others. First, it was difficult to get it clear in my own thinking. Then it was even more difficult to present it so it could be heard by others who thought automatically in terms of individual theory. As I have found better ways to conceptualize the thinking, and as more people are able to "hear" the family orientation, communication has become easier. In this presentation I have chosen to review important steps in my thinking as I shifted from an individual to a family orientation, in the hope that this will be an effective way to communicate the family orientation.

My shift from "individual" to "family" began fifteen years ago while doing individual psychotherapy with schizophrenic patients and with various members of their families. In this situation it is impossible to ignore the relationship system between family members. Attention was focused on the cyclical nature of the symbiotic relationship between mother and patient in which they could be so close that they were emotional Siamese twins, or so distant and hostile that they repelled each other. The characteristics of the symbiotic relationship were incorporated into a hypothesis to explain the origin and development of schizophrenia.

The next major step in the shift toward a family orientation came early in a formal research study started in 1954.[1] The hypothesis from the previous work was incorporated into a research plan for mothers to live "in-residence," on the ward with the patients. As the research was supplemented by clinical work with outpatient families, new and unanticipated discoveries could be made. The symbiotic mother-patient relationship was more intense than hypothesized and it was not a circumscribed entity confined to the mother-and-patient relationship. Instead, it was a fragment of a larger family emotional system in which fathers were as intimately involved as the mothers, which was fluid and shifting, and which could extend itself to involve the entire central family unit, and even nonrelatives. Family relationships alternated between overcloseness and overdistance. In the closeness phases, one family member could accurately know the thoughts, feelings, fantasies, and dreams of another family member.

This "fusion of selfs" could involve every area of ego functioning. One ego could function for that of another. One family member could become physically ill in response to emotional stress in another family member. Emotional conflict between two family members could disappear with the simultaneous development of conflict between two other family members. In the distance phases the "emotionally fused" family members would separate and each "refuse" with other family members, with members of the hospital staff, or with other vulnerable nonrelatives. There was a fluid shifting of strengths and weaknesses from one family member to another. It was as if the family were a giant jigsaw puzzle of strength and weakness with each family member holding parts of the same puzzle, and with much trading of pieces.

At the end of one year the notion of a symbiotic "emotional oneness" between mother and patient was extended to that of a "family emotional oneness"; the research plan was changed to permit both parents and normal siblings to live on the ward with the schizophrenic patients; and the psychotherapy was changed to a method in which all family members attended the psychotherapy hours together. This was an effort to bring the important parts of the family jigsaw puzzle into the live-in research study, and to devise a method of psychotherapy directed at the total "puzzle" rather than to parts of it. The formal research study, focused on families with a schizophrenic offspring, was continued for five years. In 1959 the research was moved to a new setting.[2] Since that time the effort has been to extend the theoretical orientation from a "family concept of schizophrenia" to a "family theory of emotional illness" and to adapt the family psychotherapy to the entire range of emotional illness.

The striking observations of the mother-patient relationship first came into view during the early months of the "live-in" research study. Why had these observations not been possible in the previous study? The theoretical hypothesis and the clinical problems were the same as in the earlier study. The living-together closeness could account for the increased intensity in the symbiotic relationships, but the most important factor is one that could be called "observational blindness" in the investigator. Man can fail to see what is in front of his eyes unless it fits into his theoretical frame of reference. Some excellent examples of this followed Darwin's theory of evolution. For centuries man had been stumbling over the bones of prehistoric animals without "seeing" them. Man believed the world had been created as it appeared before his eyes. The bones did not belong to animals living at that time and they were considered to be "artifacts." After Darwin had formulated his theory, it was possible finally to "see" the evidences of man's evolutionary development that had been there all the time.

My original theoretical background was the firm individual orientation of psychoanalysis. It was in the practice of this orientation, individual psychotherapy with different members of the same family, that the first shift toward a family orientation occurred. Attention was focused on the symbiotic relationship between mother and patient. Clinical evidence of the larger family phenomenon was present at that time. Why was the focus on the mother-patient relationship? One can offer support to the thesis that this relationship was so noisy and obvious that it obscured the view of the larger family. I believe attention went to the mother-patient relationship because the larger view was obscured by fixed individual thinking. It was easier to see the symbiotic relationship because it had already been described in the literature as an extension of individual theory. A detailed study of the symbiotic phenomenon became the basis of a hypothesis to explain the total phenomenon of schizophrenia!

The next step toward a family orientation occurred in the creation of the formal live-in research study in 1954. The theoretical thinking and the clinical problems were the same as in the previous study, but the act of creating a living-together situation represented a shift toward the family. The shift, with the intensity of the mother-patient relationship in the living-together situation, finally made it possible to "see" something that had been present all the time. After the phenomenon was clearly seen the first time, it was then possible to see it in its less intense form in families with neurotic problems, and even in "normal" families.

The important turning point between individual and family theory came at the end of the first year of the "live-in" family research. Important issues came into focus which will help to distinguish differences between the two orientations. To this point the research had been focused on the mother-patient relationship. The theoretical thinking had been based on *individual* theory, each mother and each patient had *individual* psychotherapy, and the research had focused on the interlocking of *individual* psychopathology. Theoretical thinking favored a family orientation, but practical issues were strongly in favor of continuing the individual orientation. Family theory was poorly defined and family psychotherapy seemed incomprehensible. The operation involved considerable clinical responsibility, and individual theory and individual psychotherapy were within known acceptable methods of theory and practice. A compromise approach might relieve some of the pressures but any possible compromise was theoretically inconsistent. There had been evidence, which was later confirmed, that intrafamily tensions could be toned down while any involved member of the family unit was in individual psychotherapy, only to recur when treatment ended. The alternative was to treat the family, not the individual, as the patient.

I had the strongest misgivings about the idea of "family psychotherapy." At that time I still believed that the only way to emotional maturity was the careful analysis of the transference relationship between the patient and the therapist. I believe now that family psychotherapy can be more than a preparation for eventual individual psychotherapy for each family member. Individual psychotherapy was thus discontinued in spite of protests and the operation committed to "a good hard try at family psychotherapy before returning to individual." It was the total commitment that opened the doors to exciting new dimensions of clinical observations and psychotherapy previously obscured by individual thinking. Later experience has confirmed the early impression that the "individual-family" issue is an "either-or" proposition. Any compromise in maintaining a strict family orientation is immediately utilized by family dynamics to make it an individual approach, and the unique advantages inherent in family psychotherapy can be lost.

For eight years I have been looking for the best way to conceptualize the idea of a "family emotional oneness." The most useful concept found thus far is conveyed by the term *undifferentiated family ego mass*. There are some inaccuracies in the term but it aptly describes the over-all family dynamics and no other term has been as effective in communicating the idea to those who think in terms of individual theory. I conceive of a fused cluster of egos of individual family members, with a common ego boundary. Some egos are completely fused into the family ego mass and others are less fused. Some egos are intensely involved in the family ego mass during periods of emotional stress and are less involved at other times. During periods of emotional calm the family ego mass may include only a small number of the most involved family members. During periods of stress the fusion may extend itself to include multiple members of the extended family network, and even nonrelatives. Live-in servants can be more emotionally fused into the family emotional system than certain blood relatives. The ego fusion is most intense in the least mature families. In a family with a schiziphrenic family member, the fusion reaches maximum intensity. Theoretically, the fusion is present to some degree in all families except those in which family members have attained complete emotional maturity. Theoretically, a mature person is a contained emotional unit who is able to maintain his ego boundaries under stress without becoming involved in emotional fusions with others.

In family psychotherapy the undifferentiated family ego mass is considered equivalent to a single ego. The family psychotherapy is directed to the family ego mass without specific regard for the individual family members involved in the family ego mass at the time. The family psychotherapist relates himself to the family ego in the same way a psychotherapist relates himself to the individual ego in individual psychotherapy. The family psychotherapist may choose to approach the family ego mass with all the involved members present in the therapy hours, with any combination of family members, or with a single family member present. The specific members whom I include in the psychotherapy hours depend on the dynamics within the family ego mass, the immediate therapeutic goal, and the stage of family psychotherapy.

Family psychotherapy with a single family member is difficult to explain to those with a different theoretical orientation. The family psychotherapist who relates to the family ego mass *through* a single family member employs a psychotherapeutic principle similar to the individual therapist who relates himself to the most intact portion of a person's ego, or to the mature side of the individual ego. The two spouses, or the two parents in families with children, are equally and maximally involved in the family ego mass. The most rapid and productive family psychotherapy occurs when these two most involved family members are able to work as a team in family psychotherapy. Many peripheral issues can be avoided when this is possible. The final stages of successful family psychology invariably includes the two spouses working together on their individual and joint problems.

The Family Theory

According to the family theory, children grow up to achieve varying levels of differentiation of self from the undifferentiated family ego mass. Some achieve almost complete differentiation of self and become clearly defined individuals with well-defined ego boundaries. This is equivalent to our concept of the mature person. These individuals are contained emotional units. Once differentiated from their parental families, they can be emotionally close to members of their own families or to any other person without fusing into new emotional onenesses. People select spouses who have identical basic levels of differentiation of self. When the well-differentiated person marries a spouse with an equally high level of differentiation of self, the spouses are able to maintain clear individuality, and at the same time to have a comfortable, nonthreatening emotional closeness with each other. These spouses do not become involved in the "fusion of selfs" that occurs in marriages of less differentiated spouses. In the use of this terminology I would consider "differentiation of self" to be equivalent to "identity" or "individuality," provided one does not confuse "identity" with the psychoanalytic concept of "identification." "Identity" and "individuality" are equally good terms if one can avoid the notion of individuality as "different from." A person with a high level of "differentiation of self," or "identity," or "individuality," is one who can be emotionally close to others without emotional fusions or loss of self, or loss of identity, because he has attained a higher level of differentiation of self.

In this family theory of emotional illness I have put the entire range of human functioning on a single scale with the highest possible level of differentiation of self (theoretical complete maturity) at the top of the scale and the lowest level of maladaptation and the severest forms of emotional illness at the bottom. According to the theory, the person who has, or who later develops, a neurosis would belong somewhere in the mid-section of the scale. The character disorder type of problems would develop in a person with a lower level of identity and belongs well down in the lower half of the scale. The person who becomes the parent of a schizophrenic offspring belongs far toward the lower end of the scale. The person who develops severe schizophrenia belongs at the extreme lower end of the scale.

People who become the parents of a schizophrenic offspring illustrate an important point in this theory. These are people with very low levels of differentiation of self who manage to function reasonably well in their life adjustments. As children they do not begin the steady process of "growing away" from their parents as do their more differentiated siblings. Instead, they remain emotionally attached to their parents. After adolescence, in an effort to function without their parents, they "tear themselves away" to establish "pseudo-selfs" with a "pseudo-separation" from their parents. This may be achieved by denial while still living at home, or it might be reinforced by physical distance. The young adult who runs away from home never to see his parents again may have more basic attachment to his parents than other siblings who continue to live with their parents.

The Achilles' heel of these people is the close emotional relationship. They may function in business and professional relationships as long as they keep their relationships casual and brief. They are vulnerable to the close emotional relationship. In a marriage to a spouse with equally low differentiation of self, they become deeply involved emotionally. The new spouses "fuse together" in a new family ego mass and the tenuous ego boundaries between them are obliterated. This is a replica of the former emotional fusions with their parents. This same process, on a less intense level, occurs in people with higher levels of differentiation of self. It is most striking, however, in the lower levels of differentiation of self.

The person who later becomes schizophrenic illustrates another important facet of this theory. The main difference here is that these people are never able to "tear themselves away" to achieve a workable level of "pseudo-self." They continue always to function as dependent appendages of the family ego mass. Some achieve so little differentiation of self that they collapse into psychosis during their first efforts to function independently of their parents, even while living at home. Some achieve sufficient pseudo-self to function independently for very brief periods, but any longer term separation from the parental ego mass is possible only when there is another waiting ego mass to which they can attach themselves. Their life adjustment depends on the all-important attachment to another person who will guide and advise them, and from whom they can borrow enough self to function. They might be able to keep these dependent attachments in equilibrium throughout life and continue to function without serious trouble, but they are extremely vulnerable to any threatened or actual loss of the important other, and they can collapse into psychotic nothingness with life events that threaten or disrupt their dependent attachment.

The dynamics within the husband-wife ego mass involve some of the most important concepts in this theory. At the time of the marriage, or at the time they establish a living-together interdependence, the new husband and wife fuse together into a new family ego mass. The lower the level of differentiation of self, the more intense the fusion. Both long for emotional closeness but when they are close, the pseudo-selfs merge into a common self, with obliteration of the tenuous ego boundary between them, and with loss of self to the common self. To avoid the anxiety of fusion, they keep sufficient emotional distance between themselves for each to function with as much pseudo-self as possible. In general, the pattern and the future course of the new family ego mass are determined first by the dynamics between the two spouses, second by the maintenance of relationships to those outside the new family ego mass, and third by the intensity of the ego fusion.

The dynamics between the new husband and wife are determined by the way they fight for, or share, the ego strength available to them. They go into the marriage with equal levels of "self," but they quickly fuse into a common self (perhaps even during the emotional interchanges during courtship) and thereafter one spouse usually functions with more than an equal share of the available ego strength. When both spouses fight for their rights, a conflictive marriage results. The conflict subsides when either "gives in," but the one who "gives in" "loses self" to the other who "gains self."

This "losing" and "gaining" of self are examples of the fluid shifting of strengths and weaknesses that can occur within the family ego mass. There is a large group of marriages in which differences are settled by one spouse who reluctantly "gives in" after a brief period of contesting rights. Thre is another large group in which one spouse actively works to become the dependent one. This spouse volunteers to "give in" and to become a "no-self" to strengthen the self of the other, on whom he is dependent. A spouse who habitually "gives in," either reluctantly or voluntarily, can reach a state of sufficient "no-self" to become incapacitated with (1) a physical illness, (2) an emotional illness, or (3) a social dysfunction such as work inefficiency, drinking, and social irresponsibility. A marriage might become permanently stabilized with one spouse chronically incapacitated with a chronic illness which seems to absorb the ego deficit between them. Such a marraige can remain emotionally harmonious as long as the disabled spouse does not recover from the physical illness.

Relationships to those outside the new family ego mass can influence the intensity of the process between the spouses. For instance, if one or both maintain sufficient emotional attachment back to their parental ego masses, the emotional intensity between them can be toned down. A wife who works might keep the marital relationship relatively stabilized as long as she maintains the emotional attachments at work. Termination of the work relationships, without a satisfactory replacement, can result in marital tension and conflict. The stabilizing outside relationship can also become a source of conflict and disharmony in the marriage. If the stabilizing outside relationship becomes unstabilized, it not only loses its stabilizing value, but it can become a source of added emotional pressure within the marriage.

Some spouses maintain their most important outside relationships to the past generation, their parents or aunts or uncles; others maintain their most important relations within the present generation, their siblings or friends in their own age group; and others to the future generation, their children or students. Most will spread their important relationships to more than one generation. A small group of spouses will keep their emotional problems confined to one small area. Examples of this are those who keep the emotional investment almost exclusively in each other, which results in a conflictive marriage or one with a chronically disabled spouse. There are conflictive marriages in which the conflict is so contained within the marriage that there is little or no emotional involvement of the children. Other examples are the spouses who transmit the entire weight of the parental problem to one or more children, resulting in a marital relationship that is calm and harmonious and a major impairment in the child. The average family maintains relationships in a number of areas, and the family receives support from, or transmits its emotional problems to, a number of areas.

The intensity of the husband-wife ego fusion is one of the important determinants of the pattern of events in the new family ego mass. As a general rule, spouses with lower levels of differentiation of self will have more intense ego fusions and more serious problems to be stabilized than spouses with higher levels of identity. However, the clinical course can depend more on the effectiveness of mechanisms to stabilize the problem than on the intensity of the problem. For example, there are the spouses with very low levels of identity who find fairly effective long-term or permanent stabilizing mechanisms. The parents of a child who later becomes schizophrenic can, by transmitting a major portion of the parental problem to the child, maintain a relatively calm adjustment until the child develops the psychosis and can no longer function. A permanent physical incapacity in one spouse can effectively stabilize a low-identity marriage as long as the incapacitated one lives. Spouses with relatively high levels of identity generally are able to find a wider range of effective stabilizing mechanisms, but when the stabilizing effort fails, these spouses can experience almost as much anxiety and stress as a family with low identity.

Any family is motivated to seek outside help when its own stabilizing mechanisms have failed and family efforts to solve the problem result in "making it worse." Families with the higher levels of identity make the best of psychotherapy prospects. They are much more motivated to keep at the psychotherapy until some kind of permanent resolution is reached. Families with lower levels of identity are seeking for immediate relief and another adaptive mechanism that works a litte better than the last. If they succeed in slight relief, they can be glowing in their praise of the psychotherapy. If they fail, they can accept the inevitable and leave the future course to chance.

Family Psychotherapy

The family psychotherapy was developed as an integral part of the family theory. A few of the principles of the psychotherapy will illustrate the clinical approach to the family ego mass.

Theoretically, a family ego mass can be considered to include the members of the nuclear family, father-mother-children, and to extend back into the extended family network to include all members of the extended families who still have unresolved emotional dependencies on each other. For example, a grown sibling with an old unresolved dependence on his parents might live far away and have little contact with his parents, but the functioning of parents or sibling is still responsive to events that change the life course of the other. This emotional dependence is considered still active, though quiescent.

For practical purposes the family ego mass is considered to include the family members in active daily living contact with each other. For some families, the members of the household can be considered to be involved in the family ego mass. For others living in separate houses but in daily contact with each other, the family ego mass extends beyond the boundaries of the household.

For clinical purposes, the family ego mass is considered to include those family members most involved in the family emotional interdependence. This always involves the father and mother, maximally and equally. In many families the one child who is most dependent on the parents is as involved in the parental ego mass as the parents. The other children are usually more differentiated. One popular notion is that family psychotherapy includes parents and all the children meeting together to learn to communicate and to verbalize feelings. Some of this is extremely beneficial in relieving symptoms and in creating a temporary better feeling and attitude in the family, but I have not found it helpful in a continuing family psychotherapy effort designed to resolve deep problems.

As a principle, this method of family psychotherapy is directed to the family ego mass, but the goal is to bring about the most rapid possible change, and I direct my effort to that portion of the family ego mass most capable of change. This might be both parents if they are capable of working together as a team, or the one most motivated parent until the other expresses a wish to join the effort. I usually avoid a relationship with the family member already designated "sick" or "patient" by the family process. The stronger side of the family ego plays an important part in creating and maintaining the "sickness" in the weak side. For the therapist to become directly responsible for the "sick" family member is to miss the part played by the rest of the family and to permit a continuation of the process. The goal is to help the stronger side of the family to assume responsibility for the weaker side.

Family members involved in the family ego mass are bogged down in an emotional morass of interdependence, each too dependent on the other to risk becoming a clear self. Spouses become so involved in being the way the other wants them to be to improve the functioning of the other, and demanding that the other be different to enhance the functioning of self, that neither is responsible for self. When either spouse is able to define and maintain a more definite identity from this amorphous feeling mass, the first step in the recovery process is under way. This involves maintaining a self in the face of emotional pressure from the other, and maintaining responsibility for self without so much emotional demand on the other. An over-all goal of family psychotherapy is to help the involved family members to differentiate clearly defined "selfs" from the undifferentiated ego mass. There are times when this differentiating process is facilitated by working with family members alone, or with various combinations of family members, shifting from one side of the family ego to another, as the differentiating process proceeds. The final stages, with those who go on to fairly complete resolution of the problem, invariably involve the two spouses working together in analysis of deeper intrapsychic problems in each.

When the presenting problem is a conflictive marriage, the usual approach is to work with one alone or each separately until they begin calmly working together. If the symptomatic spouse seeks help for self, the most profitable approach has been to work with this one alone until the "sick" one is able to maintain a "self," with both working together on the problem.

When the patient is a child, the best one can hope for is to reach a stage when the two parents can work together on their part of the family problem without involving the child. When the parents can follow this course, the child will automatically improve without participation in the family psychotherapy. When the child has a very serious problem— borderline psychosis, psychosis, or severe character defect—so much of the parental self is invested in the child that it is difficult for the parents to proceed without the child. In these instances, I shift about, utilizing any available family strength, until a more stable family structure is possible. In many of these it has been profitable to work with each parent alone to help each maintain a more definite position in relating to the child. Several of these families have proceeded on to an orderly analysis of the parental problem.

Family psychotherapy provides the greatest flexibility and the best results of any psychotherapeutic method in my experience. A wide range of problems resistive to individual psychotherapy become fluid and workable when the therapist is able to shift about, utilizing family strength wherever it appears. With all the psychotherapeutic advantages, I expect one of the greatest dividends from "the family" may be the new insights it provides in understanding the human phenomenon.

Notes

1. Conducted at the Clinical Center, National Institute of Mental Health, Bethesda, Maryland, 1954-1959.

2. Department of Psychiatry, Georgetown University Medical Center, Washington, D.C.

Chapter 8

Family Psychotherapy with Schizophrenia in the Hospital and Private Practice

The specific method of family psychotherapy in the treatment of schizophrenia which will be described here was developed as an integral part of a theoretical premise about the nature and origin of schizophrenia. The theoretical premise was later extended to "a family concept of schizophrenia," and more recently to "a family theory of emotional illness." Much of the theoretical and background material has been reported in Bowen et al. (1957); Bowen (1959a); and Bowen, Dysinger and Basamania (1959). The family concept of schizophrenia is discussed in Bowen (1960) and family psychotherapy with schizophrenia in Bowen (1961).

Presented here is a series of sections beginning with broad theoretical concepts and proceeding through more specific theory and clinical application of the theory to a clinical description of family psychotherapy. Considerable emphasis is placed on the theoretical orientation. The psychotherapist establishes and controls the milieu in which the psychotherapy takes place, and his theoretical thinking about the nature of the problem to be treated determines his approach to the problem, the procedures he will use, the observations he will make and the way he will respond and react as the therapy proceeds. Thus, it is profitable to know the therapist's specific theoretical emphasis in any description of a method of psychotherapy.

The specific order of this presentation is as follows: The first section is a brief review of important steps in the development of the family theory. This is presented to clarify differences between family theory and individual theory which conceives of emotional illness as a psychopathology confined within the person of the patient. It is difficult to communicate a family orientation to those whose thinking and perceptual systems operate in terms of individual theory. Differences between individual and family theory are repeated in a different context in each section of this chapter. The second section is a specific consideration of important points in the theoretical orientation. The third section is a brief summary of the family theory of emotional illness. Schizophrenia is seen as a part of the total spectrum of human adaptation. An understanding of less severe types of emotional illness has much to contribute to the understanding of schizophrenia. The fourth section is a description of the family projection process by which a parental problem is transmitted to a child, a process especially important in schizophrenia. The fifth section is a description of a clinical program designed to modify the family projection process in the hospital and in private practice. The sixth section deals with specific principles and techniques in the use of this method of family psychotherapy. The last section is an estimation of the current status of the method of family psychotherapy being presented.

Background Information

In the development of the family theory of emotional illness, the initial work was based on previous experience with individual psychotherapy in schizophrenia. It began with a five-year clinical study[1] in which various members of the patients' families, as well as the patients, were treated in individual psychotherapy. As the emphais shifted to include family members, the relationship system between family members came into prominence. Attention was focused on the symbiotic attachment between mothers and patients. Of particular interest was the cyclical nature of the symbiotic relationship in which each pair of mothers and patients could at times be so close that they were "emotional Siamese twins" or, at other times, so distant and hostile they repelled each other. Characteristics of the symbiotic relationship were incorporated into a detailed hypothesis concerning the etiology of schizophrenia.

The most important steps in the development of the family theory were made during a formal family research study[2] in which schizophrenic patients and their families lived in residence on a psychiatric ward. At the beginning of the research the hypothesis from the previous work was incorporated into a research plan for mothers to live on the ward with the schizophrenic patients. The research revealed striking "new" characteristics of the mother-patient relationship not clearly "seen" in the previous work. These characteristics will be described in the next section. Why had these observations been obscured in the previous work? The hypothesis was the same and the families had the same kinds of clinical problems. Two factors seemed to account for the change. One factor was the close living situation in which the relationship actions and responses were more intense, but the most important factor seemed to be "observational blindness" in the investigators. Man can fail to see what is before his eyes unless it fits into his theoretical frame of reference. For instance, man had been looking at the bones of prehistoric animals for centuries without really "seeing them"; he believed the earth had been created exactly as it is now, and he could not "see" the bones until there was a theory of evolution. The initial work with families was based on individual theory, which is so focused on the patient that it was not possible to really "see" the family. The shift to the hypothesis about the symbiotic relationship was a move toward a family orientation. I believe the specific shift was determined more by limitations in theoretical thinking than by the accuracy of the concept in describing the family phenomenon. The symbiotic relationship had been described in the literature; it was a compatible extension of individual theory, and it accurately described one area of the family phenomenon. Only the mother-patient relationship came into focus because the remainder of the phenomenon was obscured by "observational blindness." The "living together" research was another move toward a family orientation. Although the hypothesis was still stated exactly as in the informal study, the attitude behind the living together situation helped set the stage to "see" the family better. Increasing ability to "see" the family, plus the increased intensity of the relationship characteristics, were sufficient for the new observations to break through. Once seen, the new relationship phenomenon was so forcefully present that it pervaded the entire operation. It was then possible to see the phenomenon clearly in concurrent work with out-patient families in which the phenomenon was less intense in its manifestations.

The most important step in the development of the family theory was based on the "new" observations and was made late in the first year of the research study. The hypothesis was extended to include the entire family in the theoretical premise, the research design was modified to permit both parents and other family members to live on the ward with the patient, and the psychotherapy was changed from individual to family psychotherapy. During the last four years of the research study, the theoretical premise was further defined and extended into a family concept of schizophrenia, and the family psychotherapy was developed as an integrated part of the family concept. Concurrently with the live-in research study, an increasing number of out-patient families were treated in out-patient family psychotherapy. Since 1959, the author's work in family psychotherapy has been confined to out-patient work and to private practice.

The most recent steps in the development of the family theory were based on experience with family psychotherapy for families with problems less severe than schizophrenia. This includes some 250 families with problems ranging from simple neuroses to those of near psychotic degree. It was surprising to find that all the family dynamisms so striking in schizophrenia were also present in families with the least severe problems and even in "normal" or asymptomatic families. Experience supports the view that the difference between schizophrenia and less severe psychopathology is one of degree. Changes during family psychotherapy are important in understanding the family phenomenon, and the rapid changes in families with neurotic problems provided a range of observations not possible with the slow, indefinite changes in schizophrenia. Experience with less severe problems provided the observations for expansion of the family concept of schizophrenia into the family theory of emotional illness. The present theory conceives the entire range of human adjustment to be on a single scale, with the highest range of human adjustment to be on a single scale, with the highest levels of maturity at one end of the scale and the lowest forms of maladaptations and emotional illness at the other end of the scale.

Theoretical background. Important differences between individual and family theory were brought into sharp focus at the end of the first year of the research by the decision to change from an individual to a family orientation. The first year the theoretical orientation was based on *individual* theory; each patient and each mother had *individual* psychotherapy, and the research was directed at defining the interlocking of *individual* pathologies. The change was based on the newly observed characteristics of the mother-patient relationship. The mother-patient symbiosis was much more intense and extensive in actuality than had been postulated in the hypothesis. The symbiotic "emotional oneness" was not an entity in itself but a fragment of a larger family "emotional oneness." Concurrent observations of out-patient families suggested that fathers were as involved as the mothers in the emotional oneness and that other family members were also involved. Family relationships alternated between overcloseness and overdistance. In the emotional closeness phases, the intrapsychic systems of involved family members were so intimately fused that differentiation of one from the other was impossible. The fusion involved the entire range of ego functioning. One ego could function for that of another. One family member could accurately know the thoughts, fantasies, feelings, and dreams of the other. One family member could become physically ill in response to an emotional stress in another. Every detail of a patient's psychosis could have its mirror image in the mother. There were examples in which the patient's psychosis acted out the mother's unconscious. In the angry distance phases, family members could "fuse" with other family members, or certain nonrelatives, such as members of the hospital staff, and the other person would also "fuse" into the family problem. Another manifestation of the family oneness was the spontaneous, fluid shifting of ego strengths and weaknesses from one family member to another. Part of a "pathology" could be in one family member and other parts in other family members. It suggested a family jigsaw puzzle of strengths and weaknesses, with each family member holding pieces of the same puzzle and with considerable trading of pieces. These observations suggested the concept, "the family as the unit of illness." A part of the total problem was not possible from examination of the parts separately. In some families, individual psychotherapy with a single family member would tone down the emotional process in the entire family for varying periods of time. Research observations suggested that the larger family emotional oneness had the same basic characteristics as the mother-patient symbiosis. Terms such as *emotional fusion, emotional connectedness, emotional stuck-togetherness*, and *ego fusion* all accurately describe the phenomenon. The "symbiotic" hypothesis was discarded and thinking was directed to a larger family phenomenon.

There were critical practical and theoretical issues in the decision to change to a family orientation. Practical considerations favored individual theory and individual psychotherapy, both within "known" areas of theory and practice, but the observations suggested the family phenomenon was more complex than the interlocking of individual pathologies. Strict theoretical thinking favored a complete change to a family orientation but the initial "family" hypothesis was poorly developed and family psychotherapy seemed incomprehensible. Various combinations of individual and family orientation were considered but any combination plan contained drawbacks. For instance, experience suggested that any individual psychotherapy might obscure "family" observations. After much deliberation, and in spite of doubts that it could be successful, a decision was made to put the entire effort into family research observations, into extension of the family hypothesis, and into an attempt to develop a method of family psychotherapy and give it a fair trial "before returning to the individual orientation." Clinically, the idea was to include sufficient family members in the study to have the essential parts of the "family jigsaw puzzle" together at the same time and to attempt psychotherapy with all the "puzzle parts" present. The most serious doubts concerned the family psychotherapy. Because of orientation in psychoanalysis and individual psychotherapy, I believed the only way toward emotional maturity was careful analysis of the transference relationship between patient and therapist, and I assumed that the proposed "family psychotherapy" could be no more than preparation for eventual individual psychotherapy for each family member. Nevertheless, it was decided to discontinue all individual psychotherapy, and a method of family psychotherapy was devised to fit the clinical problem as defined by the theoretical premise.

The shift to the family orientation constituted a turning point that might not have been possible without the "total commitment" to the family. The family theoretical premise made it possible to "see" an exciting new dimension of clinical observations that had been obscured by individual theory. After a brief time it became evident that family psychotherapy had promising possibilities for the future. Some of the difficulties in the operation of a family orientation in an "individual" environment will be discussed later. This method of family psychotherapy has now been used for eight years with over 300 families. There have been 63 families with a schizophrenic family member in family psychotherapy for periods ranging from seven weeks to over seven years. This includes 51 families with one severely impaired adult schizophrenic offspring, ten families with a psychotic spouse, and two families with severely impaired young children diagnosed as suffering from autism or childhood schizophrenia.

Family Theory of Emotional Illness

It is difficult to conceptualize a family emotional oneness and even more difficult to communicate the idea to those whose focus on the individual makes it difficult for them really to "see" the family. I have used the term "undifferentiated family ego mass" to refer to the family emotional oneness. The term has certain inaccuracies but it aptly describes the over-all family dynamics, and no other term has been as effective in communicating the concept to others. I conceive of a fused cluster of egos of individual family members with a common ego boundary. Some egos are more completely fused into the mass than others. Certain egos are intensely involved in the family mass during emotional stress and are relatively detached at other times. The father and mother are always maximally involved. At times the ego mass may include only a small group of the most involved family members. At other times the active fusion may include members of the extended family network and even nonrelatives and pets. Live-in servants are often more "fused" into the family ego mass than certain blood relatives who are more differentiated. Sonne and Speck (1961) have included pets in family psychotherapy. The ego fusion is most intense in the least mature families. In a family with a schizophrenic family member, the fusion between father, mother, and child approaches maximum intensity. Theoretically, the fusion is present to some degree in all families except those in which family members have attained complete emotional maturity. In mature families, individual family members are contained emotional units who do not become involved in emotional fusions with others.

Clinically, the undifferentiated family ego mass is considered equivalent to a single ego. The family psychotherapy is directed to the family ego mass, without specific regard for the individuals involved in it at the time. The psychotherapist relates himself to the family ego mass in the same way that he relates himself to an individual ego in individual psychotherapy. The family members who are included in the family psychotherapy at any one time depend on the dynamics in the family ego mass and the immediate therapeutic goal. The therapist may approach the family ego mass with all involved family members present, with any combination of family members present, or with only one family member present. Family psychotherapy with a single family member is difficult to explain to those who use a different theoretical orientation. The family psychotherapist who relates to the family ego mass *through* a single family member employs a psychotherapeutic principle similar to that used in individual psychotherapy when the therapist relates himself to the "intact portion of the patient's ego" or to the "mature side of the ego." Since the two spouses (or parents) are the two family members most involved in the family ego mass, the most rapid family change occurs when the spouses are able to work as a team in family psychotherapy. The final stage of successful family psychotherapy includes the two spouses working together on their individual and joint problems.

According to the family theory of emotional illness, children grow up to achieve varying levels of differentiation of "self" from the undifferentiated family ego mass. Some achieve almost complete differentiation to become clearly defined individuals with well-defined ego boundaries. This is equivalent to our familiar concept of a mature person. These individuals are contained emotional units. Once differentiated, they can be emotionally close to their own family members, or to any other person, without fusing into new emotional oneness: People tend to marry spouses who have identical levels of differentiation of self. When the well-differentiated person marries a spouse with an equally high level of identity, the spouses are able to maintain clear individuality and at the same time to have an intense, mature, nonthreatening emotional closeness. These spouses do not become involved in the fusion of "selfs" that occur in marriages of less differentiated spouses.

If the entire range of differentiation of self is considered on a single scale, with the highest level of differentiation of self and theoretical complete emotional maturity at the top and the lowest level of maladaptation and the severest forms of emotional illness at the bottom, the following would be the relative scale positions of the diagnostic categories that are pertinent to this presentation. The person who later develops a neurosis belongs somewhere in the middle of the scale, the person who later becomes the parent of a schizophrenic offspring belongs toward the lower end of the scale, and the person who later becomes schizophrenic belongs at the lower end as a "no self" who functions on a "self" borrowed from others.

People who become parents of a schizophrenic offspring illustrate an important facet of the theory. These are people with very low levels of differentiation of self who somehow manage to function fairly well in their life adjustments. As children, they do not begin the steady process of "growing away from their parents" as do their more differentiated siblings. Instead, they remain emotionally undifferentiated in the ego mass with their parents. After adolescence, in an effort to function without their parents, they "tear themselves away" to establish "pseudo-selfs" with a "pseudo-separation" from the parental ego mass. This may be achieved by denial while still living at home or it may be reinforced by physical distance. The young adult who runs away never to see his parents again may have more basic attachment to his parents than siblings who continue to live with the parents. The Achilles' heel of these people is a close emotional relationship. They may function successfully in business or a profession as long as they keep relationships casual and brief, but in a marriage to a spouse with equally poor differentiation of self, they become overly involved emotionally. The new spouses fuse together into a new family ego mass in which the tenuous ego boundaries are obliterated. This is a replica of their former emotional fusions with their parents. This same process, on a less intense level, occurs in spouses with higher levels of differentiation of self, but the process is most striking in people who become parents of a schizophrenic offspring.

People who later become schizophrenic will illustrate one of the lowest levels of differentiation of self. The main difference here is that these people are never able to "tear themselves away" to achieve an adequate level of "pseudo-self." They continue to function as dependent appendages of the family ego mass. Some achieve so little self that they collapse into psychosis during their first efforts to function independently of the parents. Some achieve sufficient "pseudo-self" to function for brief periods alone, but any long-term separation from parents is accomplished only by finding a new family ego mass to which they can append themselves. Their life adjustment depends on the all-important attachment to others who will guide and advise them and from whom they can borrow enough self to function. They may make it through life without serious trouble but they are extremely vulnerable to the loss of the important other, and they can collapse into psychotic nothingness in the face of life events that threaten or disrupt their dependent attachments.

An important point in family theory is the fusion that takes places in a newly married husband and wife into a new family ego mass. This is most intense in spouses with low levels of differentiation of self. Both spouses long for closeness but closeness results in fusion of the two "pseudo-selfs" into a "common self," with obliteration of ego boundaries between them and loss of individuality to the "common self." To avoid the anxiety of fusion, they keep sufficient emotional distance, called the "emotional divorce," for each to maintain as much "pseudo-self" as possible. In general, the course of the new family ego mass is determined by (1) the pattern of dynamics within the ego mass and by (2) relationships to those outside the ego mass. Dynamics *within the ego mass* are determined by the way the spouses fight for, or share, the ego strength available to them. One spouse usually functions with a dominant share of the ego strength. At one end of the scale are marriages in which both spouses "fight for their rights." A conflictual marriage results. The conflict subsides when either "gives in." In the middle group are the marriages in which differences are resolved by one spouse who reluctantly "gives in." The spouse who gives in "loses strength" to the other who "gains strength." At the other end of the scale are the marriages in which one spouse works actively to be the dependent one who gives in, becoming a "no-self" who supports the strengthened self of the other. A spouse who habitually "gives in" can reach a state of sufficient "no-self" to become incapacitated with (a) physical illness, (b) emotional illness or (c) social dysfunction, such as work inefficiency, drinking, or social irresponsibility. A marriage might become permanently stabilized with the "no-self" spouse disabled with a chronic illness.

Relationships to those outside the family ego mass determine the intensity and extensiveness of the emotional phenomenon within the family ego mass. The important outside relationships are usually to relatives in the extended family network, but nonrelatives can serve the same function. When outside relationships are not too intense, the emotional intensity within the ego mass is toned down. When outside relationships become intense, the problems within the ego mass are "transmitted" to the outside person who then becomes fused into the family ego mass. Spouses may maintain their most important relationships to the past generation, their parents; to the present generation, their siblings; or to the future generation, their children. A small percentage of spouses keep their problems almost completely contained within a small area. For example, there are marriages with intense problems almost completely contained between the spouses, and with little or no involvement of their children. There are also marriages in which the full weight of the parental problem is transmitted to a single, maximally impaired child, leaving the parental relationship calm and harmonious. In the average family the spouses maintain important outside relationships in more than one area and the problem is "spread" over a larger area of the family relationship system.

Schizophrenia develops in a family in which the parents have a low level of differentiation of self and in which a high level of the parental impairment is transmitted to one or more of their children. The important variables in the process are (1) the severity of the problem in the parental ego mass and (2) the degree to which the parental impairment is transmitted to a single child or is "spread" to multiple children or to other relationships in the extended family. For instance, a less severe parental problem transmitted to a single child would produce more severe schizophrenia than a very severe parental problem "spread" to multiple children. Schizophrenia is viewed as the product of a family process in which a child in each generation is more impaired than the parents (children less involved in the process may have higher levels of differentiation of self than the parents). The process repeats for several generations until there is an offspring with a low level of differentiation of self, who, in a marriage, will have sufficient impairment in the parental ego mass to produce schizophrenia in a child. In a previous paper (Bowen 1960), I hypothesized that it requires three or more generations for schizophrenia to develop. That hypothesis, based on the family concept of schizophrenia, considered that the three-generation process can proceed from fairly well-adjusted parents in the first generation to schizophrenia in the third generation if the parents transmit a major part of the parental problem to a single child in each generation. In most situations there are varying degrees of "spread" in the transmission process, which requires more than three generations for the development of schizophrenia. In this presentation it is not possible to consider variables in families with multiple psychotic offspring, nor the variables operative in divorce, death, and other serious family disruptions.

The Family Projection Process
in Schizophrenia

This section will be devoted to the predominant mechanism in schizophrenia, the mechanism through which the parental problem is transmitted to the child. The process can begin long before the child is conceived, when the mother's thoughts, feelings, and fantasies first begin to prepare a place in her life for the child. We can wonder if the pattern of the mother's thinking and fantasies came from her own mother! The process takes a definite form during the mother's pregnancy and it continues through the years with different manifestations in different life stages. The child functions as a stabilizer for the parents, converting the unstable father-mother ego mass into a more stable triad. Parental stability depends on the child functioning as the "triadic one."[3] The child needs parents as stable as possible. His existence is so involved in "being for the parents" that he has no "self" of his own. The parents are made anxious by events that threaten to remove the child from his stabilizing function in the triad, such as "growing away" or "moving away." The triadic emotional process is adaptive and it can reestablish itself after most threats. One of the greatest threats is the psychotic collapse which prevents the usual functioning of the triadic one, but the process can even survive this threat and continue with the parents living at home and the triadic one institutionalized as a permanent ward of the state.

The term "family projection process" refers to the mechanisms that operate as the parents and the child play active parts in the transmission of the parental problem to the child. To account for the process with individual theory, it would be necessary to postulate "projection" by the parents and "introjection" by the child. The parents may force the projection against resistance until the child finally accepts the projection, but most often the parents initiate the projection and the child accepts it. Or the child may initiate the projection and coerce the parents to agree that he is the cause of the family problem. The terms "blamer" and "self-blamer" describe one aspect of the projection process. On one axis of functioning, people divide themselves into "blamers" and "self-blamers."

In a tension situation, both look for causes to explain the situation. The blamer looks outside of self; his perceptual system is attuned to finding the causes in the other or in the environment, and he is incapable of looking inside of self. The self-blamer accurately perceives causes in self but he is as impaired at looking outside himself as the blamer is at looking inside of self.

The *real* cause of any situation is probably a combination of internal and external factors. Theoretically, a mature person can objectively evaluate both the internal and external factors and *be responsible for the part self plays.* The more immature the people, the more intense the blaming and self-blaming. The following example illustrates one aspect of the projection process. Persons A and B are equally responsible for an embarrassing situation. Person A begins thinking, "If I had not been so awkward, this would not have happened." At the very same moment, B is thinking, "Look at the mess caused by A's awkwardness." The process is completed without a word being exchanged. Both blame A, both are blind to the part played by B, and both act as if their diagnosis is accurate. Under certain circumstances the blamer can become self-blamer and the self-blamer a vehement blamer. He can even feel himself to be the cause of floods, storms, and earthquakes. When he reaches an overload of self-blaming he can erupt into blaming. The self-blamer is as irresponsible as the blamer in assuming responsibility for self.

The parental problem is most often projected to the child by the mother, with the father supporting her viewpoint. She is an immature person with deep feelings of inadequacy who looks outside herself for the cause of her anxiety. The projection goes into fears and worries about the health and adequacy of the child. The projection searches out small inadequacies, defects, and functional failures in the child, focuses on them, and enlarges and exaggerates them into major deficiencies. There are three main steps in each episode in the projection process. These steps are important in the later treatment of schizophrenia. The first is a *feeling-thinking* step. It begins with a *feeling* in the mother which merges into *thinking* about defects in the child. The second is the *examining-labeling* step in which she searches for and diagnoses a defect in the child that best fits her feeling state. This is the "clinical examination-diagnosis" step. The third step is the *treating* step in which she acts toward and treats the child as though her diagnosis is accurate. The projection system can create its own defects. For instance, the mother *feels* and *thinks* about the child as a baby (there is an infantile self in the most mature of us), she *calls* him a baby and she *treats* him as though he is a baby. When the child accepts the projection, he *becomes* more infantile. The projection is fed by the mother's anxiety. When the cause for her anxiety is located outside of the mother, the anxiety subsides. For the child, accepting the projection as a reality is a small price to pay for a calmer mother. Now the child *is* a little more adequate. Each time he accepts another projection, he adds to his increasing state of functional inadequacy.

The projection system can also utilize existing minor defects. Some of these require an examination and diagnosis by an expert to confirm the presence of the defect. Parents can go from one physician to another until the "feared" defect is finally confirmed by diagnosis. Any defect discovered in physical examinations, laboratory tests, and psychological tests can also facilitate the projection process. The family projection can pour into a newly discovered innocuous congenital anomaly and convert it to a disability. The important function of the process is to locate and confirm that the "cause" is outside the mother. One need listen to such a mother only a few minutes to hear her invoke outside opinions, diagnoses, and tests to validate the projection.

The projection process reaches a critical stage when the triadic one collapses into psychosis and can no longer function as the absorber of the family projection. Family anxiety is usually high. It is not the psychosis itself that causes the family anxiety but the inability of this triadic one to continue his usual function in the triad. Family anxiety is less intense when the psychosis develops slowly or the psychotic one is quiet and cooperative and continues to serve the purposes of parental projection. Parents may not even seek help for the quiet psychotic one unless urged by some outside person or agency. The intense anxiety occurs when the psychotic collapse is sudden and the psychotic one not only rebels against accepting the projection but turns into a vehement "blamer" who denies the existence of a problem, while, in addition, causing problems with irresponsible behavior.

The three steps of the family projection process can come into prominence when the family seeks psychiatric help for the psychotic collapse. Parental anxiety motivates an increased drive to call the triadic one "sick," to confirm the sickness with a diagnosis, and to start a treatment program. When the diagnosis is confirmed and the triadic one becomes a "patient," another family projection is completed and parental anxiety subsides. *The step into mental illness is probably the most critical in the long series of family projection crises.* One of the most important theoretical and psychotherapeutic propositions of the family theory revolves around this point. The usual psychiatric approach is to examine the patient, confirm the presence of the pathology with a diagnosis, and recommend appropriate treatment. The psychiatric consultation fits, step by step, with the family projection process. Thus, a time-proven principle of good medical practice serves to support the parental projection process in the family, to crystallize and fix emotional illness in the patient, and to help make the illness chronic and irreversible. A therapeutic approach to this dilemma, based on the family theory of emotional illness, is described in the next section of this chapter.

Many years of successful parental projection precede the step into mental illness. In some families the groundwork is so complete and the family members are so fixed in their functioning positions[4] that "the step" does little more than officially note what has already come to be. In these families the triadic one readily accepts the projection and the new designation "patient" and the working contract between family and psychiatrist is one in which the psychiatrist assumes responsibility for the end product of the long family projection process. The chances of modifying the family process are remote. In other families "the step" is bigger, the triadic one opposes the diagnosis and the designation "patient," and, if the psychiatrist avoids supporting the parental side of the projection, the prognosis for modifying the family process is better. Functionally, "the step" is one in which the family problem is projected into the triadic one and fixed there with a diagnosis. When the psychiatrist accepts the responsibility for treating the illness in "the patient," he condones the externalization of the parental problem to the patient, assumes responsibility for the patient (the family problem separated from the family), and permits the parents to continue projecting onto the patient, without holding the parents responsible and accountable for the consequences of their projection. The parents often become students of emotional illness and use psychiatric terms and concepts to better facilitate the projection to the patient. Thus, our usual psychiatric approach to the treatment of the psychoses is one in which the family, the patient, the psychiatrist, and society all play a part in "acting out" and perpetuating the family projection, in turning the problem in the patient into a chronic one, and in creating a situation which permits the family projection to continue long after the patient has become the permanent responsibility of the state. There are outpatient situations in which the psychiatrist is even more effective in facilitating the family projection process. For instance, individual psychotherapy with a "patient" still living with his parents may support the patient sufficiently for him to continue as an unusually effective absorber of the parental projection.

A final clinical characteristic of the family projection process that is important to this presentation is the lack of responsibility for "self" in those who participate in the projection process. A "blamer" who projects his problem to others is not responsible for self. The "self-blamer" is equally irresponsible. He blames himself to relieve anxiety and not to assume responsibility for himself. Our concept "disease" and "illness" conceives of the problem as a dysfunction determined by forces beyond the control or the responsibility of the family.

Clinical Efforts to Modify the Family Projection Process in the Hospital and in Private Practice

The ward milieu program and the family psychotherapy were both designed to modify the family projection process. This section is devoted to clinical management of the three steps in the family projection process: (1) *thinking* of the triadic one as sick, (2) *diagnosing* the triadic one and designating him "patient," and (3) *treating* the "patient" as a sick person. Also included in this section will be a clinical discussion of *responsibility*. The clinical effort was to *think* and *act* toward the families according to the family orientation. This meant avoiding the concepts "sick," "illness," and "patient" and avoiding the use of diagnoses and treating the triadic one (or any other family member) as a sick person. It was not possible to achieve more than partial success with the live-in families, but the effort provided much knowledge about schizophrenia and the experience has been invaluable in subsequent family psychotherapy. A review of the clinical effort with the live-in families will provide another view of the differences between individual and family theory and a glimpse of the depth of change involved in a shift to family theory and family psychotherapy.

Social custom, laws governing sickness and mental illness, and our most basic, time-proven principles of medical practice are all oriented around the individual theory of disease. Medical practice and hospital structure adhere strictly to "sickness-patient-diagnosis-treatment" principles. Any small deviation from standard procedure can cause a reaction within a medical or hospital organization. In this study, which was carried out in a research hospital, permitting some flexibility in operation not possible in a strict medical service institution, an effort was made to anticipate the issues that would arise in the research and to arrange as much "research freedom" as possible from the enforced use of individual principles and procedures. The hospital administration was interested in helping to facilitate the research, but when issues were better defined, it became clear that a medical administrator can "interpret" but not change medical structure. Other than the flexibility permitted for any research, and certain favorable interpretations by the hospital administration, the research operated according to routine medical structure. I, as project administrator, was responsible and accountable to the hospital for every item of individual procedure. Within the confines of the ward, a different milieu was established. Numerous people have said that this research should not have been done in a hospital because of the traditional attitudes of hospitals about sickness. On the other hand, the very same issues are involved even in the private practice of family psychotherapy through a similar attitude to illness on the part of the legal and medical institutions of society. For example, dangerous acting out by one psychotic family member can threaten the therapist with medical-legal breach of responsibility; the charge may be made that the psychotic should have been considered a patient requiring hospitalization.

Some problems were encountered during the first year before the family orientation was started. Three mothers and three patients participated in the study. The mothers were permitted either to room with the patient, or to live outside and spend daytime hours with the patient. One mother chose to room with her daughter; the other two chose to live outside. Emphasis was placed on the "presence" of the mothers. They were not required to function as mothers. The live-in mother was required to fulfill the administrative requirements for "patients," and though she was diagnosed "Normal Control" and her patient status was toned down, she was still a "patient." The other mothers had privileges to eat on the ward and to participate in hospital activities. They were expected to assume some responsibility for the care of the patient but these mothers were never responsibly involved in the study. The staff was responsible for the patients and the mothers were privileged "visitors." The system actually permitted the mothers an ideal situation for carefree projection of their problems to the patients; they could be irresponsible in upsetting the patient and return home, telling the nurse, "*Your* patient is upset." The treatment results were rather good by usual individual standards but individual psychotherapy kept the family problems divided. Critical issues could be avoided by each expecting the other to deal with the issue, and no family went beyond the passive attitude of cooperating while waiting to be changed.

With the shift to the family orientation, all family members were required to live in. The parents and normal siblings were diagnosed "Normal Control" and the psychotic family members "Schizophrenia." Family members had all the records and routine procedures required for "patients." Freedom for fathers to continue their regular work and for other family members to participate in outside activity was permitted by routine 72-hour "patient" passes. Absences over 72 hours required a discharge and a new admission. The maintenance of the project in a hospital required innumerable admissions, discharges, physical examinations, and routine laboratory studies to meet the requirements of good medical care for patients. The administrative structure permitted short cuts in administrative steps but it did not permit elimination of steps.

An important part of the clinical program to deal with the family projection process was the requirement that the parents be responsible for the psychotic family member. The doctors and nursing staff would be available to help the parents but not to assume direct responsibility for the "patients." One parent was required to be with the "patient" at all times. When both parents were away from the ward at the same time they would ask the nurses to be responsible for the "patients." It was almost two years before the staff achieved a reasonable working version of the clinical program. There were three main areas of difficulty in implementing the plan.

The first area of difficulty had to do with the individual medical orientation of the staff. It was second nature for staff members to think in terms of the individual, to "assume responsibility for the patient," and to "feel with" the patient and be angry at the parents. It required time and intimate exposure to the families for the staff to *know* the family orientation. Early efforts to change concepts and terms were no more than "play acting." Shortly after the staff began to avoid the use of the word "patient," the head nurse protested the emptiness of changing words; three years later she wrote a paper, "The Patient Is the Family" (Kvarnes 1959). Among the terms that replaced "sick," "illness," and "schizophrenia," were "dysfunction," "incapacity," and "functional collapse." Among the terms that replaced "patient" were "impaired one," "disabled one," "collapsed one," and "triadic one." In due time, the family orientation became almost as comfortable as the old, especially when families began to respond favorably to the family approach.

The second area of difficulty was intimately connected with the first. The hospital administration required an individual orientation, in conflict with the policy of the research ward administration. The staff complied with the minimal individual requirements of the hospital, but within the ward the staff attempted to think and act the family orientation. The hospital designated each family member a "patient" and required the physicians to be responsible for "patients" under their care. Within the ward there were "family members" instead of "patients" and parents were required to be responsible for all members of their families. The families understood the two orientations and they became students of the fine points of difference between them.

The third area of difficulty was within the families. The family projection process is forceful. It has an amazing capacity to utilize existing structure to project the problem to the triadic one and to make the environment responsible for the externalized problem. When the staff no longer accepted as much responsibility for emotional functioning in the families, the family process found new ways to make the staff responsible. Since the physician was responsible for the physical health of his "patients," an increasing number of family problems became manifested as physical illness, and families overused the ward physician and medical structure to make the staff responsible. Finally the staff developed a system equivalent to a physician in private practice. A "clinic" with regular office hours was established on the ward, and for routine problems, the families made clinic appointments. The family living quarters (twin bedrooms on the ward) were equivalent to private homes. Family members went to the "clinic" for consultation and returned to the "home" where they were responsible for following the recommended treatment. Families were provided with supplies of most drugs to be kept in their "homes." This kind of an arrangement would not have been possible in any but a research setting.

One series of events will convey much about the "responsibility" problem. Parents were free to take the "patients" into the community "when they were capable of controlling the psychotic behavior." They could ask a staff person to accompany them if they doubted their ability to manage the situation. There were frequent complaints from merchants, local citizens, and from other departments in the hospital reporting disturbing behavior. Each incident was discussed with the families. The families would "explain away" the incidents by calling them fusses or disagreements; by blaming the public's lack of understanding about emotional illness; by diagnosing the complainant as an upset, touchy, neurotic person; or by a discussion of whether or not the complaint was justified. The families would promise to try harder. The staff went through a period of being overhelpful to the families in specifying off-limits areas and in helping them to understand and deal with disturbed behavior. The frequency of incidents remained the same except that they occurred in unusual places or in circumstances that "you did not tell us about." Finally came the awareness that the staff attitude played a part in the problem. In providing help and instruction, the staff doubted the parents' ability to find their own solutions. The families had been scolded for their mistakes but they had not been told exactly what was required.

When we became aware of this, the families were told that the research project required the parents to assume responsibility for the disturbed family members and that they had considerable freedom to go and come in the community as long as they could control the behavior of disturbed family members. They were reminded that we lived in a community where people had the same fears and concerns about mental illness as people everywhere, that we had a responsibility to the community, and that the goal was the prevention of complaints, whether justified or unjustified. The families were told that they were held responsible for learning the rules of the community and the hospital and that there be no complaints about disturbed behavior off the ward. Complaints from the hospital and the community stopped. The formerly irresponsible parents became overly responsible. When the disturbed family members became upset, the parents initiated their own systems of control. When an upset became too great, the family might ask permission of the other families to lock the ward for a few days until the upset subsided. This experience, now confirmed by other subsequent experiences, provided evidence that the parents of a schizophrenic offspring, who commonly function as helpless and irresponsible people, have the capacity to function responsibly when it is required. My own functioning as project director played an important part. I had assumed responsibility, with the hospital administration, for stopping the incidents, and when I functioned more responsibly, it was possible to require families to be responsible. Interestingly, it was during the periods when the parents were functioning responsibly that families made the most progress in the daily family psychotherapy meetings.

The live-in families provided a unique and rewarding research experience but a live-in environment is not the most favorable for change in family psychotherapy. It was possible for families to assume a fairly good level of responsibility for the psychotic family member but the parents became overdependent on the hospital resources available to them, which precluded development of their own resources. Family psychotherapy has been more successful with families responsible for the care of the psychotic one in the home.

Clinical results in dealing with the family projection process have been best in outpatient work and private practice. The process that drives toward "sickness-patient-diagnostic-treatment" issues is fed by anxiety. In the early clinical efforts I too often found myself opposing the projection process. The most profitable approach has been to avoid becoming entangled in the issues of the family projection process and to direct attention to the parental anxiety that feeds the projection. A few hours spent with one or both parents is often enough to relieve the immediate anxiety and convert the situation into a calm, productive, family psychotherapeutic effort. When family anxiety is very high and it is not possible to avoid the sickness-diagnosis issues of the projection process, I state my theoretical position as clearly as possible and quietly refuse to participate in action designed to fix the problem in the patient, or I refuse to continue working with the family unless parents are willing to assume some responsibility for their part in the problem.

The issues in the family projection process come into clear focus with the proposed first hospitalization for an acute psychotic disturbance, especially when the psychotic person is protesting that he is not sick and the projection process is insisting on a diagnosis and hospitalization. Much is gained if a diagnosis and hospitalization can be avoided and the projection process can be modified before the family takes this additional major step in confirming emotional illness. If hospitalization is necessary, I prefer that it be for reasons other than "sickness." The following describes my current approach to the situation in outpatient work and private practice. There are three main reasons for hospitalization: (1) The family demands it because the family has reached a tolerance for the disturbance in the home. (2) The community demands it because of offenses to the community. (3) The disturbed person requests it for himself. The first reason is the important one for this presentation. When hospitalization is the issue, the family expects the psychiatrist to use illness as the reason for hospitalization. With this approach, the patient is told that he is sick and he must be hospitalized for treatment. With the psychiatrist responsible for the hospitalization, the family tells the patient, "We are sorry you are sick and have to go to the hospital. You will get good treatment there. When you are well, we want you home." According to a family approach, this sequence contains reality distortions. The first is the concept "sick" and "hospital." The degree of "sickness" is not the real reason for hospitalization. Families keep severe degrees of "sickness" at home as long as the person behaves himself. The real reason is that the family wants the disturbing behavior removed from the home. Hospitalization is more for the family than the patient. Another distortion is, "When you are *well*." This really means, "When you no longer disturb the family."

An impaired ego can deal with hard facts of misbehavior, but it has more difficulty with the reality distortions in "sickness" reasons. A resisting person's ego does not perceive "sickness" with his own perceptual system, and he is at a disadvantage when hospitalized for a reason he cannot perceive within himself. If he insists on his own perception that he is not "sick," he is uncooperative and in conflict with his environment. If he accepts the "sickness" reason, he agrees to something he cannot perceive within himself and he becomes dependent on the environment to teach him about "sickness." There have been amazing benefits when the family assumes responsibility for hospitalization and uses "behavior" as the reason. If the situation permits, I will spend days or weeks on this one point before I will hospitalize a person for "sickness." To illustrate, one psychotic son had been resisting hospitalization for several weeks. The effort was directed at helping the parents use "the family" as the reason. When the mother finally said, "Will you go for us, to give us some relief?" the son calmly replied, "That's the first fair proposition I've heard. I am ready to sign myself in any time." The family can use force, such as, "We are sending you to the hospital because we are fed up with your behavior and the problems you create at home," without the complications and penalties that can come from using "sickness" as the reason. In these circumstances the patients approach the hospital differently, their progress is usually rapid, and hospital stays are brief. A clinical case illustrating some of these points is presented in the next section.

The principles that apply to the "sickness" concept are applicable in many areas not specifically related to the family projection process. The following example is from a situation that did not involve a family. A recovering hospitalized patient was permitted his first pass into town. As he started to step into the bus to return to the hospital, he became immobilized, for voices threatened dire consequences if he stepped on the bus. He was delaying the bus in heavy traffic, and the bus company complained to the hospital about "patients too sick to go to town." His doctor restricted him to the hospital because of "behavior" instead of "sickness." He was told that he was restricted because of his "behavior" at the bus stop, and when he was able to behave in a way that did not call attention to himself or interfere with others, he could try again. Within a week he had another town pass and shortly thereafter he was discharged to return to his job. Later in his psychotherapy he reconstructed the series of events. After his restriction, he spent days practicing ways to behave normally in spite of the voices. He became so successful at this that he returned to work while the voices were still present. The restriction for behavior provided him with something he could understand, that he could work on, and that he could change. If restricted for "sickness," over which he had no control, he might have had no choice but to wait and hope the sickness would go away.

Much effort has gone into avoiding the concepts of "sick" and "patient" and the use of "diagnoses," although this effort may seem unrealistic when the triadic one is so disabled and impaired. How valid is the effort and what are the results? I have not yet seen a family projection process completely resolved in a family with severe schizophrenia. When the family is calm, the process can disappear from view, but if anxiety builds up again, the process appears again. Occasionally, parents can be successful in controlling their side of the process, only to have the triadic one begin acting inadequate and impaired in a way that forces them to recognize his "petition for sickness." The schizophrenic person is not oriented to becoming "normal" and he plays an important part in perpetuating the status quo. Mendell (1958) has used a different approach to the dilemma of diagnosing only the patient. He does psychological tests on all key family members which are then used as authoritative evidence to substantiate a diagnosis on all family members. Each "sick" person is then treated in group psychotherapy but with each family member in a different group.

It is with problems less severe than schizophrenia that avoiding "sick-patient-diagnoses" is of direct benefit in helping the family ego mass toward a higher level of differentiation of self. When the family achieves a higher level of differentiation, the projection process disappears permanently. The following is one of innumerable such examples. A husband in his mid-thirties had four years of fairly successful psychoanalysis for paralyzing obsessions and phobias that had forced him to give up his work. During his analysis, his wife had a period of psychotherapy. The husband returned to work and became fairly successful but he was a "compensated neurotic" with his sickness under control. The wife was the adequate one who protected him from upsetting situations. In a later period of marital conflict, the wife sought further psychiatric help. The husband refused to participate and the wife began family psychotherapy alone. Her thinking-feeling system was totally occupied with the husband's "neurosis." Early in the family psychotherapy, she was asked if she could stop thinking of him as a neurotic, stop calling him neurotic, and stop treating him as an impaired person. She responded, "Okay, but what other term do I use? Do you have a better term?" It was suggested that she "play like" he was not sick, or weak, or neurotic. The suggestion seemed to have missed its mark. About two months later she said, "I have been working on that idea. I no longer call him neurotic or treat him like a neurotic, but for the life of me I cannot stop thinking of him as neurotic." The husband responded to her change with a campaign to act helpless, to call himself neurotic, and to plead with her to mother his helplessness. She refused to give in to his demands. He became angry, accused her of not loving him, and went into a week of individualistic, "I do not need you." Then he joined her in the family psychotherapy and they went on to a good resolution of their problem. From the beginning of their marriage, the husband had been either a potential "patient," an actual "patient," or a compensated "patient," and the wife had been a "mother" to his varying degrees of incapacity. Now for the first time, they were free of the problem and able to be two adult people in their marriage.

Principles and Techniques of Family Psychotherapy

The first structured family psychotherapy was with the live-in families in the research study. Both parents, the schizophrenic offspring, and the normal siblings attended the psychotherapy hours together. This was a nondirective psychotherapy in which the family members "worked together on the family problem." The therapist functioned as a catalyst to facilitate the working together and as a participant observer who was sufficiently detached to observe objectively and interpret the family process. The psychotherapy followed a definite course. The normal siblings soon found reason to separate themselves from the family effort, leaving the father, mother, and psychotic one interlocked in an intense emotional interdependence, which I have called the "interdependent triad." Change within the triad was slow and it appeared to go toward differentiation into three distinct selfs. One parent would pull up to a more confident level of functioning and appear to develop a better defined self with a higher level of identity. Then the other parent would go through the same process, and then the triadic one would appear to "grow up a little." These cycles could take as long as a year. It was hoped the cyclical course would continue until all three emerged as well-differentiated individuals. This did not occur. Some families would continue through a few cycles and stop the psychotherapy during an asymptomatic period or use an angry family incident as a reason to stop. Some families would progress very rapidly for a few months and stop suddenly when symptoms were less troublesome.

A series of experiences led to a modification of the effort to follow the triad through to differentiation. The following is a good example: The daughter, in her late twenties, had spent most of the previous six years in institutions. The father, mother, and daughter attended psychotherapy hours together. Progress was rapid. Within six months the daughter was working and within a year she was on as high a level of confident, adequate functioning as I have ever seen in recovery from schizophrenia. She was free of guilt and defensiveness about the psychotic period. The intensity of the parental relationship pattern (aggressive, anxious mother and compliant father) had receded into the background and the parents were calm and productive. The daughter talked of moving from the parental home to her own apartment and the parents "agreed" with the idea. The daughter asked about "individual" psychotherapy for herself but the plan implied that the parents would stop their participation and the therapist discouraged it. All three continued the psychotherapy together. The day the daughter announced definite plans to move, the formerly calm parents became anxious, pleading, attacking, and helpless, and the old family projection process was back in its full intensity. The daughter decided to "give up her own life goals" for a time "to help her parents." Slowly the daughter's functioning began to fail and within six months she had lost her job and was back in another severe regression. After another ten months she was returned to an institution. This is an example of family reaction when the triadic one attempts to separate self from the parents. Confronted by the parental anxiety, the budding self of the triadic one rushed back into the family ego mass "to save the parents." In recent years, the psychotherapy has been modified to help the family through this separation crisis. As soon as parents and triadic one are aware of the part that each plays in the family process, the parents are seen together with the explicit goal of helping them to separate their lives from the triadic one, and the triadic one is seen alone with the explicit goal of helping him to function without the parents and to resist his automatic emotional "reflex" to "save the parents" (to become the parental projection object) when they are anxious. Results have been better with this approach but it involves a more "supportive" relationship to each side of the family and the basic level of differentiation of self does not change.

The family ego mass in severe schizophrenia is not only an "undifferentiated" family ego mass but in my experience it is "undifferentiatable." I have not yet seen a reasonable resolution of the basic problem in a family with severe schizophrenia. The emotional oneness in schizophrenia is over and beyond other emotional ties. The child is emotionally "welded" into the ego mass with the parents, where he functions as an "ego nothing" which permits the parents to be an "ego something." These three people can be physically separated but it appears impossible for any one to differentiate a "self" from the other two. With the triadic one living away from home in dependent attachments that do not involve the parents, all three members of the triad are more comfortable. The parents function by "borrowing self" from outside themselves and by "projecting their inadequacies" to others. In this situation, the parents perceive no problem within themselves and they have no motivation for family psychotherapy. If the threesome is reunited, the old emotional fusion of the triad is immediately operative again.

The orderly "differentiation of self" from the family ego mass does occur in a wide range of problems less severe than schizophrenia. The differentiation process is most rapid with problems of neurotic degree. The parents can proceed to differentiate selfs from their children (with spontaneous change in the children), from their parents, and from each other; they can attain high levels of identity. The more severe the family problem, the more likely the family to terminate the psychotherapy after symptomatic improvement, as occurs in families with schizophrenia. However, there have been families with transient or borderline psychotic problems in a family member in which family psychotherapy has continued to "differentiation of selfs" from the family ego mass. My goal has been to find a way for complete resolution of the underlying problem in severe schizophrenia. Some families have continued in family psychotherapy for five to seven years with reasonably symptom-free adjustments but no change in the basic problem. In the past three years there has been an effort to involve certain key members of the extended family in the family psychotherapy to add more "strength" to the family ego mass. This effort is too new to report here but initial reports appear promising.

Although family psychotherapy has not been successful in resolving the underlying problem in severe schizophrenia, it has been effective in helping families achieve asymptomatic adjustments without changing the underlying problem. The following is an example of a good asymptomatic adjustment with brief family psychotherapy: A 45-year-old mother was in her second acute psychotic episode. For the first episode she had been hospitalized for a year, given electroshock therapy and psychotherapy, and then received two years of outpatient psychotherapy. The second psychotic episode occurred three years later. The husband was anxious and solicitous in relating to the wife's overactive and bizarre thinking and behavior. The wife reacted to his reactions with an increase in psychotic symptoms. The husband agreed to try family psychotherapy with the wife living at home. The husband worked to make the wife's illness the responsibility of the therapist, while he continued to project his anxiety onto her. My effort was to focus on the husband's anxiety, to avoid direct responsibility for the wife's illness, and to hold the husband responsible for the family problem. He did have considerable responsibility with the wife at home, and after two weeks he asked that she be hospitalized because she was "too sick" to remain at home. I maintained the position that home was best for the wife but that he could go toward hospitalization if he had reached his tolerance for the stress at home. He asked a relative to help him supervise the wife's behavior. When the relative became "fed up" with the situation, he asked if I would give the wife "shock treatment." I refused to participate in "shock treatment," and there was an exchange about what kind of "shock" he meant. On his own initiatve, he began a very firm management program in which the wife's "privileges" were determined by her ability to control her own behavior. Within ten days the psychotic symptoms had disappeared, and the "perfect result," which the family praises highly, has continued five years. The family had fourteen hours of family psychotherapy over a period of seven weeks.

The following family, who fell within the range of impairment in which complete differentiation of self is possible, illustrates several important principles and techniques of family psychotherapy. In this case the family projection process was countered by avoiding hospitalization. Another important principle is illustrated by the technique of conducting family therapy by temporarily seeing only one family member. This was a family with an acutely disturbed seventeen-year-old son with a problem of borderline psychotic degree who had been an increasing behavior problem since adolescence. His school adjustment had always been poor and the schools had long been involved in diagnosing and understanding the problem, in arranging special programs, and in several recommendations for psychotherapy. The parents attempted to deal with the behavior problems with "discipline," which was really angry retaliation against misbehavior. The son reacted to this with violent, angry outbursts which frightened the parents. The son opposed the parental projection by calling the parents "sick." The psychotherapy efforts had never gone beyond psychiatric consulation because the son insisted he was not "sick" and the parents were immobilized because the son would not cooperate.

In the weeks before the referral, the son's anxiety had increased until he was aloof from the family and was spending afternoons and nights wandering in the community. He was unkempt, his behavior and dress were bizarre, he appeared to be hallucinating, and he was less able to follow simple school routines. He frightened some teachers and certain people in the community. When the school suggested that he be hospitalized, the father sought help in arranging hospitalization. I did not agree with the plan for immediate hospitalization and instead offered family psychotherapy evaluation interviews. The son insisted that his only problem was his parents and he had no need for a psychiatrist. The parents were extremely anxious but they were willing to proceed with family psychotherapy for themselves and to leave the son out of the family effort until he expressed a positive wish for psychotherapy. The son's acting out at school and in the community did not appear too great to risk a family psychotherapy effort. The school agreed to "wait and see" what happened, misinterpreting the therapist's recommendation that the boy not be hospitalized to mean that he should remain in school.

A few days later the school reported that some teachers were frightened by the boy's behavior. The school had long followed the usual steps in the family projection process of *thinking* about, *diagnosing*, and *treating* the son as "sick." The school was reminded that the therapist did not recommend that the boy remain in school and was urged to make decisions on the basis of behavior instead of "sickness," sending the boy home if his behavior did not meet school rules. Some teachers feared it would "hurt" the son to make him deal with reality; they preferred excusing his behavior on the basis that it was "sick." Other teachers, pleased with permission to deal with behavior instead of worrying about "sickness," took firmer reality stands, with considerable benefit to the situation.

The parents made little progress in their first family psychotherapy hours together. Their anxiety was high and thoughts went only to inadequacies in the son. In spite of this, the son's anxiety subsided and within two weeks there were no further complaints from the school or the community. The son expressed pleasure that the parents were finally working on their problem. In the psychotherapy, the parents were in so much basic disagreement about the son that their "selfs" neutralized each other. Their effort ended in the same "selfless" lack of direction that characterized the home environment. It was suggested that one parent try the psychotherapy alone and that they decide which one it should be. During the next six months, the mother was the only family member to attend the family psychotherapy hours. Since the effort in these situations is to help one parent work toward a higher level of identity, the mother was encouraged to define a "self," to become clear about her own beliefs and convictions, and especially to maintain a stand on important family issues without losing "self" in the family emotional field. The mother did well at this, and one fairly definite "self" began to emerge from the "selfless mass" of the family. For the first time the mother began to deal with distraught family situations by controlling her own "self" instead of trying to change the "self" of others.

Within a few months the son's behavior was "almost normal" at school and in the community, but his problem was being acted out within the family. Generally, it is a hopeful sign when acting out in the community shifts back within the family. While the mother was more occupied with her own problem and was less involved in family problems, the father began to "feel with" the son's problems. There was a brief period of closeness between father and son, followed by conflict. The father became a strict "disciplinarian," to which the son reacted with aggressive acting out directed specifically at the father.

The next phase of the psychotherapy began some eight months after the start of the family psychotherapy when the exasperated father demanded the family psychotherapy time for himself. He reported that the family situation was worse than it had ever been, but after a few hours he began to define a "self" and a position for himself in the family.

He made more rapid progress than the mother. After a brief period, his thoughts, feelings, and actions were directed more to the mother than the son. About three months after he started, there was a period of overt conflict between the parents. The parents quickly joined forces and began another period of projection of the family problem to the son. The parental conflict subsided and the son went into another period of regression and irresponsible behavior confined within the family. The parents became angry at the son who was still calling them "sick" and who made no effort to help solve the family problem. The son asked for psychotherapy time for himself, the first time he had been seen since the evaluation almost a year before.

The next phase of the family psychotherapy was one in which the son was seen alone in addition to the weekly family appointments which the parents attended together. The son made some progress but soon it became clear that he was "going through the motions" of psychotherapy because the parents insisted. The parents were making little progress on their part of the problem. In these situations, it is common for parental motivation to subside and for parents to depend on the triadic one to solve the entire problem. After two months the son stopped his regular appointments, saying he would return later when he felt the need for psychotherapy. The parents again began projection to the son, who began to act out within the family. The parents, with the tangible problem provided by the son's acting out, were able to focus on a family problem and then to begin the first working together on their own problem.

This family has now had seventy-two hours of family psychotherapy over a period of eighteen months. The son has been able to make passing grades in school for the first time in years, and he was motivated to get a part-time job, but his academic deficit is great and he still has at least another year of high school. The parents continue the focus on their own problem in family psychotherapy but they proceed much more cautiously and slowly at investigation of their own intrapsychic problems than would be characteristic of parents in less impaired families. The family has a higher level of differentiation of self than a family with severe schizophrenia in the triadic one. The ability of the son to oppose the family projection process and the ability of the parents to achieve a reasonable effective level of "self" in acute situations is more "self" than is found with severe schizophrenia. In most families with this level of impairment, the parents find reason to terminate the psychotherapy with some level of symptomatic improvement. The current motivation of the parents to continue suggests that they may be among those to go on to a reasonable resolution of the underlying problem.

Present Status of Family Psychotherapy

It is striking that this method of family psychotherapy, which had its beginnings in the study of schizophrenia, has proven to be effective in resolving the underlying problem in less severe emotional illnesses and ineffective in resolving the underlying family problem in schizophrenia. There are practical and theoretical implications in this. On the practical side, I no longer approach schizophrenia with the expectation that the basic process will be changed by the present techniques of family psychotherapy. In the beginning there was an expectation that the father-mother-patient triad would constitute an autonomous, contained unit within which the problem could be resolved without giving support to each separate individual. But the triad did not prove to be autonomous. I now approach schizophrenia with the expectation that some emotional "support" of the family ego mass by the therapist is necessary, but it makes theoretical and practical sense to direct at least part of the "support" to the parental side of the triad, rather than to the patient alone.

Theoretically, the experience with families adds increasing conviction to the belief that schizophrenia will eventually be explained as an emotional phenomenon if we conceive of an emotional process involving multiple generations. Schizophrenia is as fixed and rigid in the father-mother-patient triad as in the patient, but there is evidence to indicate that the process can be reversed in the family ego mass in which the parents grew up if members of the family of origin are available for therapy.

I view the family projection process as a natural phenomenon that develops as any phenomenon in nature when conditions are favorable for it. At the same time, I believe the "favorable conditions" can be controlled and modified by man if we can be more aware of the way the process operates. Implicit in the family psychotherapy is the assumption that the family projection process does not have to be and that the parents can be responsible for self when it is required, but since the parents of a schizophrenic person grew up as triadic recipients of similar but less intense family projection processes in their own families in which responsibility for self was not possible, it is difficult for such parents to assume more than sporadic periods of responsibility for self. Furthermore, on a practical level, it is easier and more expedient for medicine and society to assume responsibility for the projected family problem (the psychotic patient) than to attempt to hold the parents responsible. The family's use of medical structure of "examination-diagnosis and treatment" to further the cause of the family projection process is a monumental problem for which there are no easy answers. If the medical structure did not exist, the families could find other means to make the environment responsible. There is considerable therapeutic advantage when the therapist can deal with the family projection process without diagnosing sickness in the impaired family member.

Notes

1. Conducted at the Menninger Clinic and Shawnee Guidance Center, Topeka, Kansas, 1949-1954.

2. Conducted at the Clinical Center, National Institute of Mental Health, Bethesda, Maryland, 1954-1959.

3. The one who develops schizophrenia is conventionally referred to as "the psychotic one," "the schizophrenic one," or "the patient." I prefer to use the term "triadic one" because it designates one component part of the family ego mass.

4. The term "role" as defined by Spiegel (1957) might be more accurate than "functioning positions" but I have not been able consistently to adapt role concepts to this work. Rather than permit loose and inconsistent use of role theory, other descriptive terms have been used.

Chapter 9

The Use of Family Theory
in Clinical Practice

In little more than one decade, family psychiatry has evolved from the relative unknown to a position of recognized importance on the psychiatric scene. The term *family therapy*, or some variation of it, is known to the informed lay person. What is the origin and current status of the "family movement"? I believe it is a "movement," which I shall attempt to convey in this paper. Since there is disagreement even among leaders of the family movement about some of the critical theoretical and therapeutic issues, any attempt to explain or describe the family movement will represent the bias and viewpoint of the author. In this paper I shall present some of my ideas about circumstances that gave rise to the family movement and some ideas about the current status and future potential of the movement. The main body of the paper will be a presentation of my own theoretical orientation, which provides a blueprint for the clinical use of family psychotherapy.

I believe that the family movement began in the early and mid 1950s and that it grew out of an effort to find more effective treatment methods for the more severe emotional problems. In a broad sense, I believe it developed as an extension of psychoanalysis which had finally achieved general acceptance as a treatment method during the 1930s. Psychoanalysis provided useful concepts and procedures for the mass need of World War II, and a "new" era in psychiatry began. Within the course of a few years psychiatry became a hopeful, promising specialty for thousands of young physicians. Membership in the American Psychiatric Association increased from 3684 in 1945 to 8534 in 1955. Psychoanalytic theory had explanations for the total range of emotional problems, but standard psychoanalytic treatment techniques were not effective with the more severe emotional problems. Eager young psychiatrists began experimenting with numerous variations in the treatment method. I believe the study of the family was one of these new areas of interest.

There are those who say the family movement is not new and that it goes back twenty-five years or more. There is some evidence to support the thesis that current family emphasis evolved slowly as the early psychoanalytic formulations about the family were put into clinical practice. In 1909 Freud reported the treatment of "Little Hans," in which he worked with the father instead of the child. In 1921 Flugel published his well-known book, *The Psycho-Analytic Study of the Family*. There was the development of child analysis and the beginning of the child guidance movement in which it became standard procedure for a social worker or second therapist to work with parents in addition to the primary psychotherapy with the child. Later, the child guidance principles were adapted to work with adults, both in in-patient and out-patient settings, in which a social worker or second therapist worked with relatives to supplement the primary psychotherapy with the patient. With these early theoretical and clinical awarenesses of the importance of the family, there is accuracy to the statement that "family" is not new. However, I believe that the current family direction is sufficiently important, new, and different to be viewed as a movement. I shall review some of the theoretical and clinical issues that seem important in this development.

Psychoanalytic theory was formulated from a detailed study of the individual patient. Concepts about the family were derived more from the patient's perceptions than from direct observation of the family. From this theoretical position, the focus was on the patient and the family was outside the immediate field of theoretical and therapeutic interest. Individual theory was built on a medical model with its concepts of etiology, the diagnosis of pathology in the patient, and treatment of the sickness in the individual. Also inherent in the model are the subtle implications that the patient is the helpless victim of a disease or malevolent forces outside his control. A conceptual dilemma was posed when the most important person in a patient's life was considered to be the cause of his illness, and pathogenic to him. Psychiatrists were aware that the model did not quite fit and there were attempts to tone down the implicit starkness of the concepts, but the basic model remained. For instance, the concept of the unconscious postulated that the parent could be unconsciously hurtful while trying to help the child. This was different from what it would be if the hurt had been intentional or an irresponsible act of omission, but it still left the parent as "pathogenic." There were efforts to modify diagnostic labels and there were even suggestions that labels be discarded, but a *patient* requires a *diagnosis* for his *illness* and psychiatry still operates with a medical model.

One of the most significant developments in the family movement, which distinguishes it from previous "family" work, is a change in the basic treatment process. Since the beginning of psychoanalysis, the analysis and resolution of the transference has been viewed as the primary therapeutic force for the treatment of emotional illness. Though modified by different "schools," the "therapeutic relationship" is the basic therapeutic modality used by most psychiatrists. The confidential, personal, and private nature of the relationship is considered essential for good therapy. Over the years there have been methods, rules, and even laws to guard this privacy. Since the beginning of the child guidance movement there have been efforts to involve the family in "treatment," but the "therapeutic" patient-therapist relationship was protected against intrusion and the family assigned secondary importance. Among those who initiated the current family movement were psychiatrists who, in addition to the patient's dilemma, began to pay more attention to the family side of the problem.

I believe the current family movement was started by several different investigators, each working independently, who began with either a theoretical or clinical notion that the family was important. As the focus shifted from the individual to the family, each was confronted with the dilemma of describing and conceptualizing the family relationship system. Individual theory did not have a conceptual model for a relationship system. Each investigator was "on his own" in conceptualizing his observations. One of the interesting developments has been the way investigators first conceptualized the system and the ways these concepts have been modified in the past ten years. There were terms for the distortion and rigidity, the reciprocal functioning, and the "interlocking," "binding," "stuck togetherness" of the system. The following illustrates some of the terms used by a few of the early investigators. Lidz et al. (1957) used the concept "schism and skew," and Wynne and his co-workers (1958) used the concept "pseudomutuality." Ackerman, one of the earliest workers in the field, presented a conceptual model in his 1956 paper, "Interlocking Pathology in Family Relationships." He also developed a therapeutic method which he calls "Family Therapy," which might be described as observing, demonstrating, and interpreting the "interlocking" to the family as it occurs in the family sessions. Jackson and his co-workers (Bateson et al. 1956) used a different model with the concept of the "double bind." As I perceived his original position, he used communication theory to account for the relationship system and individual theory to account for functioning in the individual. His "conjoint family therapy," which I interpret as the joining of individuals in family therapy, would be consistent with his conceptual scheme. I conceived of a preexisting emotional "stuck togetherness," the "undifferentiated family ego mass," and developed a therapeutic method for which I have used the term *family psychotherapy*, which is designed to help individuals differentiate themselves from the "mass." Other investigators used a spectrum of slightly different terms to describe and conceptualize the same family phenomenon. As the years pass, the original concepts tend to be less "different."

Current Status and Possible Future
of the Family Movement

The family movement is currently in what I have called a "healthy, unstructured state of chaos." The early investigators arrived at "family therapy" after preliminary clinical investigation and research. There may have been one exception to this general statement, recounted by Bell (1961), one of earliest workers in the field. He misinterpreted a statement about psychotherapy for the family, following which he worked out his own plan to begin seeing family members together. After the idea of "family therapy" was introduced, the number of family therapists began to multiply each year. Most went directly into family therapy from their orientation in individual theory. Group therapists modified group therapy for work with families. As a result, the term *family therapy* is being used to refer to such a variety of different methods, procedures, and techniques that the term is meaningless without further description or definition. I consider this "healthy," because once a therapist begins seeing multiple family members together, he is confronted with new clinical phenomena not explained by individual theory, he finds that many previous concepts have become superfluous, and he is forced to find new theoretical concepts and new therapeutic techniques. The increasing number of family conferences become forums for discussion of experiences and acquiring new ways to conceptualize the family phenomenon.

A high percentage of therapists are using the term *family* to designate therapy methods in which two or more generations (usually parents and children) attend the sessions together, the term *marital therapy* when two spouses are seen together, and *individual therapy* when only one family member is seen by the therapist. The one most widely held concept of "family therapy," both within the profession and by the public, is that of entire families (usually parents and children) meeting together with the therapist while the family acquires the ability to verbalize and communicate thoughts and feelings to each other, with the therapist sitting alongside to facilitate the process and to make observations and interpretations. This I have called *family group therapy*. In my experience, this can be amazingly effective as a short-term process for improving family communication. Even a slight improvement in communication can produce dramatic shifts in the feeling system, and even a period of exhilaration. I have not been able to use this as a long-term method for resolving underlying problems.

Although the family movement may continue to focus on "therapy" for many years to come, I believe the greatest contribution of "family" will come from the theoretical. I think the family movement rests on solid ground, that we have hardly scratched the surface in family research, and that "family" will grow in importance with each passing generation. The study of the family provides a completely new order of theoretical models for thinking about man and his relationship to nature and the universe. Man's family is a *system* which I believe follows the laws of natural systems. I believe knowledge about the family system may provide the pathway for getting beyond static concepts and into the functional concepts of systems. I believe that family can provide answers to the medical model dilemma of psychiatry, that family concepts may eventually become the basis for a new and different theory about emotional illness, and that this in turn will make its contribution to medical science and practice.

Theoretical and Clinical Orientation of the Author

The primary goal of this presentation is to describe a specific theoretical and therapeutic system in which family theory serves as a blueprint for the therapist in doing family psychotherapy and also as a useful theoretical framework for a variety of clinical problems. A family orientation is so different from the familiar individual orientation that it has to be experienced to be appreciated. It is difficult for a person who thinks in terms of individual theory, and who has not had clinical experience with families, to "hear" family concepts. Some are better able to hear abstract theoretical ideas while others hear simple clinical examples. The first part of this selection is designed as a bridge between individual and family orientations. To provide a variety of bridges, it will include a spectrum of clinical observations, broad abstract ideas, theoretical concepts, and some of my experiences as I shifted from an individual to a family frame of reference.

My family experience covers twelve years and over 10,000 hours of observing families in family psychotherapy. For the first five years of family practice I also did some individual psychotherapy and I had a few patients in psychoanalysis. The term *family psychotherapy* was reserved for the process when two or more family members were seen together. The technical effort was to analyze the already existing emotional process between the family members and toward keeping myself emotionally disengaged, which I called "staying out of the transference." This will be discussed later. During those years I used the term *individual psychotherapy* for the process when only one family person was seen. I had not dealt with my own emotional functioning sufficiently nor developed techniques to avoid a transference and there was the "either-or" distinction between family and individual psychotherapy. I considered it *family* when the emotional process could be contained within the family, and *individual* when this was not possible. During those years, another evolutionary process was taking place. After having spent thousands of hours sitting with families, it became increasingly impossible to see a single person without "seeing" his total family sitting like phantoms alongside him. This perception of one person as a segment of the larger family system had governed the way I thought about and responded to the individual, and it had changed my basic approach to psychotherapy. For the past seven years my practice has been devoted entirely to "family" psychotherapy, although about one-third of the hours are spent with only one member of a family. The volume of clinical experience has been in private practice where an average clinical load of forty families are seen with a maximum of thirty hours per week. In past years only a few families have been seen more than once a week, and an increasing number do as well with less frequent appointments. It has been difficult to communicate the notion of avoiding a transference and "family" psychotherapy with only one family member. It is my hope that this can be better clarified in this paper.

A number of facets of the human phenomenon come into view in observing family members together that are obscured with any composite of individual interviews. Any person who exposes himself to daily observations of families as they "relate to" and "interact with" each other is confronted with a whole new world of clinical data that do not fit individual conceptual models. I use the terms "relate to" and "interact with" because these are a few of the inadequate terms that have been used to describe the family phenomenon. Actually, family members are *being*, and *doing*, and *acting*, and *interacting*, and *transacting*, and *communicating*, and *pretending*, and *posturing* in such a variety of ways that structure and order are hard to see. There is something wrong with any single term that has been used. To this point, family research has gone toward selecting certain areas for detailed, controlled study. In 1957 one of my research associates (Dysinger) did a study called "The Action Dialogue in an Intense Relationship," which was an attempt to blank out words and do a coherent "dialogue" from one period of gross action between a mother and daughter. Birdwhistell (1952) and Scheflen (1964) have made a significant contribution in their precise definition of "kinesics," a "body language" system, automatic in all relationships. One of the popular areas for study has been "communication," which on the simplest level is verbal communication. There have been the linguistic studies and the different communications that are conveyed by nuances in tone of voice, inflection, and ways of speaking—communications that each person learns in infancy and uses without "knowing" he knows it. Bateson and Jackson and co-workers, from analysis of verbal communication, developed their concept of the "double bind," which has to do with conflicting messages in the same statement. There is also the area of nonverbal communication and extrasensory perception which operates with fair accuracy in some families. There is an advantage in using terms such as "communication" or "transactional" system in that each lends itself to more precise research analysis. The disadvantage is in the narrowness of the concept and the necessity of using a broad interpretation of the concept. For instance, under "communication" theory it becomes necessary to assume the full range of verbal, action, nonverbal, extrasensory, and feeling communication, plus other modalities such as a visceral response in one family member to anxiety or a mood shift in another. However one approaches the family, each investigator has to choose his own way of conceptualizing the family phenomenon.

One striking group of clinical patterns, present to some degree in all families, will provide a brief view of the family relationship system. These follow the general pattern of the family process that diagnoses, classifies, and assigns characteristics to certain family members. Observations may prove reasonably consistent, periodically consistent, or inconsistent with the family pronouncements about the situation. The "family projection process" by which a family problem is transmitted to one family member by years of nagging pronouncements, and then fixed there with a diagnosis, has been discussed in detail in another paper

(1965a). Family assignments that overvalue are as unrealistic as those that devalue, though the ones that devalue are more likely to come within the province of the psychiatrist. The diagnosed one may resist the family pronouncement and precipitate a family debate; or he may alternately resist and accept; or he may invite it, at which time the assigned characteristic becomes an operational *fact.* Family debates on subjects such as "rejection," "love," and "hostility" will force the therapist to reevaluate his own use of such terms. As I see "rejection," it is one of the most useful mechanisms for maintaining equilibrium in a relationship system. It goes on constantly between people, usually unmentioned. At one point in the family process someone makes a fuss about "rejection" and the debate starts. At a point when rejection is present throughout the family, the one who claims "rejection" is usually more rejecting of the other, rather than the obverse being true. Positive statements about the presence or absence of "love," with reactions and counterreactions, can occupy the scene while there is no objective evidence of change in "love" within the family. Whatever love *is,* it is factual that many family members react strongly to statements about it. The misuse and overuse of the concept "hostility" is another in the same category. The same can apply to terms such as "masculine," "feminine," "aggressive," "passive," "homosexual," and "alcoholic."

The use of the term *alcoholic* provides a good example. In one family, two generations of descendants referred to a grandfather as alcoholic. He had been successful and fairly responsible except to his wife, who was a very anxious woman. He found reason to stay away from her and he did drink moderately. The wife's label was accepted by the children and transmitted to the grandchildren. A recent consultation with another family illustrates another aspect of the problem. A wife had presented the details of her husband's alcoholism. I asked for the husband's view of the problem. He agreed he had a real drinking problem. When asked how much he drank, he flared with, "Listen Buster! When I tell you I have a drinking problem, I mean it!" When asked how many days he had lost from work because of drinking, he said, "One! But I really hung one on that time." It can be grossly inaccurate to assign *fact* to statements such as, "He was an alcoholic." It can be accurate and also convey a *fact* about the relationship system if such statements are heard as, "One family member *said* another was an alcoholic." This applies to the entire spectrum of terms used in the family relationship system.

I would like to present the concept of the family as a system. For the moment I shall not attempt to say what kind of system. There is no single word or term that would be accurate without further qualification, and qualification would distort the *system* concept. The family *is* a system in that a change in one part of the system is followed by compensatory change in other parts of the system. I prefer to think of the family as a variety of systems and subsystems. Systems function at all levels of efficiency from optimum functioning to total dysfunction and failure. It is necessary also to think in terms of overfunction, which can range from compensated overfunction to decompensated overfunction. An example of this would be the tachycardia (overfunctioning heart) of an athlete in strenuous physical activity, to tachycardia that precedes total heart failure and death. The functioning of any system is dependent on the functioning of the larger systems of which it is a part, and also on its subsystems. On a broad level, the solar system is a subsystem of the larger system, the universe. The molecule is one of the smallest defined subsystems. On another level, the process of evolution is a system that operates slowly over long periods of time. There is sufficient knowledge about evolution to recognize the general patterns of its function, but there is much less knowledge about the larger systems of which evolution is a subsystem. We can look back and make postulations about the factors that influenced past evolutionary change, but our lack of knowledge about the larger systems reduces us to guessing about the future course of evolution.

From observing families I have attempted to define and conceptualize some of the larger and smaller family functioning patterns as they repeat and repeat, and as old patterns tone down and new ones become more prominent. The research started with schizophrenia in which one family member was in a state of total dysfunction and collapse, and the patterns so intense they could not be missed, but it required work with the entire range of human dysfunction to see the patterns in broader perspective. One of the most important aspects of family dysfunction is an equal degree of overfunction in another part of the family system. It is factual that dysfunctioning and overfunctioning exist together. On one level this is a smooth working, flexible, reciprocating mechanism in which one member automatically overfunctions to compensate for the dysfunction of the other who is temporarily ill. Then there are the more chronic and fixed states of overfunctioning and dysfunction in which flexibility is lost. An example would be the dominating (overfunctioning) mother and passive father. The overfunctioning one routinely sees this as necessary to compensate for the poor functioning of the other. This might be valid in the case of temporary illness in one spouse, but in the chronic states there is evidence that the dysfunction appears later to compensate for overfunction in the other. However it develops, the overfunction-dysfunction is a reciprocating mechanism. In previous papers (Bowen

1960), I called this the "overadequate-inadequate reciprocity." Symptoms develop when the dysfunction approaches nonfunctioning. Families often do not seek help until flexibility of the system is lost and the functioning of one member is severely impaired. When the mechanism advances beyond a certain point, anxiety drives the mechanism toward panic and rapid increase in both overfunction and dysfunction. The increased pressure can "jam the circuits" of the disabled one into paralyzed collapse. Even at this point, recovery can begin with the slightest decrease of the overfunctioning, or a slight decrease in the dysfunction.

Some of the main functional patterns observed in families have been formulated into component concepts that comprise the family theory of emotional illness. It would be more accurate to say "family dysfunction." The broad family patterns of emotional illness are also present in physical illness and social dysfunction such as irresponsible behavior and delinquency. The component concepts (subsystems) are among those I believe to be the most critical variables in human dysfunction. Symptoms in any part of the family are viewed as evidence of dysfunction, whether the symptoms be emotional, physical, conflictual, or social. There have been most promising results from the effort to view all emotional symptoms as evidence of family dysfunction rather than as intrapsychic phenomena.

The "therapist" also fits into this concept of the family as a system. This is a combination theoretical-therapeutic system in which theory determines therapy, and observations from therapy can in turn modify the theory. The original design, reported in another paper (Bowen 1961), has been continued, although both the theory and therapy have been constantly modified. From the early days of the research there was increasing emotional detachment from the families. The more one observes families, the easier it is to detach from the narrow conceptual boundaries of individual theory; and the more one detaches from individual theory, the easier it is to see family patterns. The early family psychotherapy was predominantly observational, with questions to elicit more information about the observations. Over the years, "research" families have done better in family psychotherapy than those for whom the primary goal was "therapy." This helped establish a kind of orientation which has made all families into "research" families. It has been my experience that the more a therapist learns about a family, the more the family learns about itself; and the more the family learns, the more the therapist learns, in a cycle which continues. In the observational process with early families, some were able to restore family functioning without much "therapeutic intervention." The most successful families followed remarkably consistent courses in accomplishing this. Thereafter, it was possible to "intervene" and tell new families about successes and failures of former families and to save the new families endless hours and months of "trial and error" experimentation. In broad terms, the therapist became a kind of "expert" in understanding family systems and an "engineer" in helping the family restore itself to functioning equilibrium.

The over-all goal was to help family members become "system experts" who could know the family system so well that the family could readjust itself without the help of an outside expert, if and when the family system was again stressed. It is optimum when the family system can begin a shift toward recovery with the important members of the family attending the hours. There were those in which the family became "worse" during the therapy, the "helpless one" becoming more helpless in response to the overfunctioning of the other. Some would struggle through this period and then move toward recovery; others would terminate. In these situations, it was found to be more profitable to work with one side of the reciprocity until the family was able to work together without increasing the "bind." It is far easier for the overfunctioning one to "tone down" the overfunctioning than for the poorly functioning one to "pull up." If the overfunctioning one is motivated, I see this one alone for a period of "family" psychotherpay in which the goal is to free the immobilized system and restore enough flexibility for the family to work together. From my orientation, a theoretical system that "thinks" in terms of family and works toward improving the family system *is* family psychotherapy.

With this theoretical-therapeutic system, there is always the initial problem of the therapist establishing the orientation of the system. Most families are referred with a diagnosis for the dysfunction. They think in terms of the medical model and expect that the therapist is going to change the diagnosed family member, or the parents may expect the therapist to show or tell them how to change the child without understanding and modifying their part in the family system. With many families, it is surprisingly easy for the therapist to establish this family orientation in which he stands alongside to help them understand and take steps to modify the system. To help establish this orientation, I avoid the diagnosis of any family member and other medical model concepts such as "sick" or "patient." I persistently oppose the tendency of the family to view me as a "therapist." Instead, I work toward establishing myself as a "consultant" in family problems for the initial interviews, and as a "supervisor" of the family effort for the long-term process. When the therapist allows himself to become a "healer" or "repairman," the family goes into dysfunction to wait for the therapist to accomplish his work.

From this discussion of the family as a system, I have avoided saying what kind of a "system." The family *is* a number of different kinds of systems. It can accurately be designated a social system, a cultural system, a games system, a communication system, a biological system, or any of several other designations. For the purposes of this theoretical-therapeutic system, I think of the family as a combination of "emotional" and "relationship" systems. The term *emotional* refers to the force that motivates the system and "relationship" to the ways it is expressed. Under relationship would be subsumed communication, interaction, and other relationship modalities.

There were some basic assumptions about man and the nature of emotional illness, partially formulated before the family research, that governed the theoretical thinking and the choice of the various theoretical concepts, including the notion of an "emotional" system. Man is viewed as an evolutionary assemblage of cells who has arrived at his present state from hundreds of millions of years of evolutionary adaptation and maladaptation, and who is evolving on to other changes. In this sense, man is related directly to all living matter. In choosing theoretical concepts, an attempt was made to keep them in harmony with man as a protoplasmic being. Man is different from other animals in the size of his brain and his ability to reason and think. With his intellectual ability he has devoted a major effort to emphasizing his uniqueness and the "differences" that set him apart from other forms of life, and he has devoted comparatively little effort to understanding his relatedness to other forms of life. A basic premise is that what man thinks about himself, and what he says about himself, is different in many important ways from what he *is*. Emotional illness is seen as a disorder of man's emotional system, and man's emotional system is seen as basically related to man's protoplasmic being. I view emotional illness as a much deeper phenomenon than that conceptualized by current psychological theory. There are emotional mechanisms as automatic as a reflex and that occur as predictably as the force that causes the sunflower to keep its face toward the sun. I believe that the laws that govern man's emotional functioning are as orderly as those that govern other natural systems and that the difficulty in understanding the system is governed more by man's reasoning that denies its existence than by the complexity of the system. In the literature there are discrepant views about the definition of and the relatedness between *emotion* and *feelings*. Operationally I regard an emotional system as something deep that is in contact with cellular and somatic processes, and a feeling system as a bridge that is in contact with parts of the emotional system on one side and with the intellectual system on the other. In clinical practice, I have made a clear distinction between feelings, which have to do with subjective awareness, and opinions, which have to do with logic and reasoning of the intellectual system. The degree to which people say, "I feel that . . ." when they mean, "I believe that . . ." is so commonplace that many use the two words synonymously. However valid the ideas behind the selection of these concepts, they did play a major part in the choice of concepts.

An attempt has been made to keep terminology as simple and descriptive as possible. Several factors have governed this. The effort to think of the family as a fluid, ever-changing, functional system was impaired by the use of the static, fixed concepts conveyed by much of conventional psychiatric terminology. Early in family research, the loose use of psychiatric terms, such as "depressed," "hysterical," and "compulsive," interfered with accurate description and communication. An effort was made to prohibit the use of psychiatric jargon within the research staff and to use simple descriptive words. This was a worthwhile discipline. It is difficult to communicate with colleagues without using familiar terms. An effort was made to bridge this gap by the sparing use of familiar terms. In the early years I worked toward some kind of correlation of family concepts with psychoanalytic theory. In writing and professional communication, the use of certain familiar terms would evoke vigorous discussion about the proper definition and use of terms. When the discussion went beyond productive exchanges of views and into nonproductive cyclical debates that consumed both time and energy, I elected to describe the family phenomenon in terms that did not stir up debates, to advance the research as far as possible, and to leave integration of individual and family concepts for some future generation. Although there are inaccuracies in the use of the term "family psychotherapy," I have retained it as the best working compromise between the theory and the practice, and for describing it to the professions to which it is related.

The Family Theory

The central concept in this theory is the "undifferentiated family ego mass." This is a conglomerate emotional oneness that exists in all levels of intensity—from the family in which it is most intense, to the family in which it is almost imperceptible. The symbiotic relationship between a mother and child is an example of a fragment of one of the most intense versions. The father is equally involved with the mother and child, and other children are involved with varying lesser degrees of intensity. The basic notion to be conveyed at this moment is that of an emotional process that shifts about within the nuclear family (father, mother, and children) ego mass in definite patterns of emotional responsiveness. The degree to which any one family member may be involved depends on his basic level of involvement in the family ego mass. The number of family members involved depends on the intensity of the process and the functional state of individual relationships to the central "mass" at that moment. In periods of stress, the process can involve the entire nuclear family, a whole spectrum of more peripheral family members, and even nonrelatives and representatives of social agencies, clinics, schools, and courts. In periods of calm, the process can remain relatively contained within a small segment of the family, such as the symbiotic relationship in which the emotional process plays back and forth between mother and child with the father isolated from the intense twosome.

The term *undifferentiated family ego mass* has been more utilitarian than accurate. Precisely defined, the four words do not belong together, but this term has been the most effective of all in communicating the concept so that others might "hear." Also, the four words, each conveying an essential part of the concept, have provided latitude in theoretical extension of the idea. Clinically, the best examples of the relationship system within the undifferentiated family ego mass are conveyed by the more intense versions of it, such as the symbiotic relationship or the "folie à deux" phenomenon. The emotional closeness can be so intense that family members know each other's feelings, thoughts, fantasies, and dreams. The relationships are cyclical. There is one phase of calm, comfortable closeness. This can shift to anxious, uncomfortable overcloseness with the incorporation of the "self" of one by the "self" of the other. Then there is the phase of distant rejection in which the two can literally repel each other. In some families, the relationship can cycle through the phases at frequent intervals. In other families the cycle can stay relatively fixed for long periods, such as the angry rejection phase in which two people can repulse each other for years, or for life. In the rejection phase, each can *refuse* into a similar emotional involvement with another family member or with certain other people outside the family. Within the family emotional system, the emotional tensions shift about in an orderly series of emotional alliances and rejections. The basic building block of any emotional system is the triangle. In calm periods, two members of the triangle have a comfortable emotional alliance, and the third, in the unfavored "outsider" position, moves either toward winning the favor of one of the others or toward rejection, which may be planned as winning favor. In tension situations, the "outsider" is in the favored position and both of the emotionally overinvolved ones will predictably make efforts to involve the third in the conflict. When tension increases, it will involve increasing outside members, the emotional circuits running on a series of interlocking emotional triangles. In the least involved situations, the emotional process shifts about in a subtle process of emotional responsiveness, which might be compared to an emotional chain reaction. These mechanisms can be defined in the later stages of family psychotherapy in which it is possible to analyze the family emotional system. For instance, a smile in one family member might initiate an action response in another, and this initiate a reverie about a dream in another, which is followed by a "change the subject" joke in another.

There are three major theoretical concepts in the theory. The first has to do with the degree of "differentiation of self" in a person. The opposite of differentiation is the degree of "undifferentiation" or "ego fusion." An attempt has been made to classify all levels of human functioning on a single continuum. At one end of the scale is the most intense version of the undifferentiated family ego mass in which "undifferentiation" and "ego fusion" dominate the field and there is little "differentiation of self." The symbiotic relationship and the "folie à deux" phenomenon are examples of clinical states with intense ego fusion. At the other end of the scale the "differentiation of self" dominates the field and there is little overt evidence of ego fusion. People at this end of the scale represent the highest levels of human functioning. Another concept has to do with the relationship system *within* the nuclear family ego mass and the *outside* emotional forces from the extended family emotional system and from the emotional systems of work and social situations that influence the course of the process within the family ego mass. Important in this concept is the "family projection process" by which parental problems are transmitted to their children. The patterns of this process have been incorporated into a third concept which deals with the multigenerational interlocking of emotional fields and parental transmission of varying degrees of "maturity" or "immaturity" over multiple generations. For practical purposes, the term *family ego mass* refers to the nuclear family which includes the father, mother, and children of the present and future generations. The term "extended family" refers to the entire network of living relatives, though in the everyday clinical situation this usually refers to the three-generation system involving grandparents, parents, and children. The term *emotional field* refers to the emotional process in any area being considered at the moment.

The Differentiation of Self Scale is an attempt to conceptualize all human functioning on the same continuum. This theory does not have a concept of "normal." It has been relatively easy to define "normal" measurements for all areas of man's physical functioning, but attempts to establish a "normal" for emotional functioning have been elusive. As a baseline for this theoretical system, a detailed profile of "complete differentiation of self," which would be equivalent to complete emotional maturity, has been assigned a value of 100 on a scale from 0 to 100. The lowest level of "no-self," or the highest level of "undifferentiation," is at the bottom of the scale. Some of the broad general characteristics of people at the various levels of the scale will be presented.

People in the lowest quarter of the scale (0 to 25) are those with the most intense degree of "ego fusion" and with little "differentiation of self." They live in a "feeling" world, if they are not so miserable that they have lost the capacity to "feel." They are dependent on the feelings of those about them. So much of life energy goes into maintaining the relationship system about them—into "loving" or "being loved" or reaction against the failure to get love, or into getting more comfortable—that there is no life energy for anything else. They cannot differentiate between a "feeling" system and an "intellectual" system. Major life decisions are based on what "feels" right or simply on getting comfortable. They are incapable of using the "differentiated I" (I am—I believe—I will do—I will not do) in their relationships with others. Their use of "I" is confined to the narcissistic, "I want—I am hurt—I want my rights." They grew up as dependent appendages of their parental ego masses and in their life course they attempt to find other dependent attachments from which they can borrow enough strength to function. Some are able to maintain a sufficient system of dependent attachments to function through life without symptoms. This is more possible for those in the upper part of this group. A "no-self" who is sufficiently adept at pleasing his boss might be considered a better employee than if he had some "self." This scale has nothing to do with diagnostic categories. All in the group have tenuous adjustments, they are easily stressed into emotional disequilibrium, and dysfunction can be long or permanent. The group includes those who manage marginal adjustments and those whose efforts failed. At the extreme lower end are those who cannot exist outside the protective walls of an institution. It includes the "dead enders" of society, many of the lower socioeconomic group, and those from higher socioeconomic groups with intense ego fusions. I would see the hard core schizophrenic person at 10 or below on the scale, and his parents at no more than 20. In family psychotherapy, I have yet to see a person in this group attain a higher "basic" level of differentiation of self. Many attain reasonable alleviation of symptoms, but life energy goes into getting comfortable. If they can gain some symptom relief and a dependent attachment from which they can borrow strength, they are satisfied with the result.

People in the second quarter of the scale (25 to 50) are those with less intense ego fusions and with either a poorly defined self or a budding capacity to differentiate a self. This has to be in general terms because a person in the 30 range has many of the characteristics of "lower scale" people, and those between 40 and 50 have more characteristics of a higher scale. This scale provides an opportunity to describe "feeling" people. From 50 down it is increasingly a *feeling* world except for those at the extreme lower end who can be too miserable to feel. A typical *feeling* person is one who is responsive to emotional harmony or disharmony about him. Feelings can soar to heights with praise or approval or be dashed to nothingness by disapproval. So much life energy goes into "loving" and seeking "love" and approval that there is little energy left for self-determined, goal-directed activity. Important life decisions are based on what feels right. Success in business or professional pursuits is determined more by approval from superiors and from the relationship system than the inherent value of their work. People in this group do have some awareness of opinions and beliefs from the intellectual system but the budding "self" is usually so fused with feelings that it is expressed in dogmatic authoritativeness, in the compliance of a disciple, or in the opposition of a rebel. A conviction can be so fused with feeling that it becomes a "cause." In the lower part of this group are some fairly typical "no-selfs." They are transilient personalities who, lacking beliefs and convictions of their own, adapt quickly to the prevailing ideology. They usually go along with the system that best complements their emotional system. To avoid upsetting the emotional system, they use outside authority to support their position in life. They may use cultural values, religion, philosophy, the law, rule books, science, the physician, or other such sources. Instead of using the "I believe" of the more differentiated person, they may say, "Science has shown . . ." and it is possible to take science, or religion, or philosophy out of context and "prove" anything. It is misleading to correlate this scale with clinical categories, but people in the lower part of this segment of the scale, under stress, will develop transient psychotic episodes, delinquency problems, and other symptoms of that intensity. Those in the upper range of the scale will develop neurotic problems. The main difference between this segment and the lower quarter of the scale is that these people have some capacity for the differentiation of selfs. I have had a few families in the 25 to 30 range who have gone on to fairly high levels of differentiation. It is a situation of *possibility* but *low probability*. Most in this range will lose motivation when the emotional equilibrium is restored and symptoms disappear. The *probability* for differentiation is much higher in the 35 to 50 range.

People in the third quarter of the scale (50 to 75) are those with higher levels of differentiation and much lower degrees of ego fusions. Those in this group have fairly well-defined opinions and beliefs on most essential issues, but pressure for conformity is great, and under sufficient stress they can compromise principle and make feeling decisions rather than risk the displeasure of others by standing on their convictions. They often remain silent and avoid stating opinions that might put them out of step with the crowd and disturb the emotional equilibrium. People in this group have more energy for goaldirected activity and less energy tied up in keeping the emotional system in equilibrium. Under sufficient stress they can develop fairly severe emotional or physical symptoms, but symptoms are more episodic and recovery is much faster.

People in the upper quarter of the scale (75 to 100) are those I have never seen in my clinical work and that I rarely meet in social and professional relationships. In considering the over-all scale, it is essentially impossible for anyone to have *all* the characteristics I would assign to 100. In this group I shall consider those that fall in the 85 to 95 range which will include most of the characteristics of a "differentiated" person. These are principle-oriented, goal-directed people who have many of the qualities that have been called "inner directed." They begin "growing away" from their parents in infancy. They are always sure of their beliefs and convictions but are never dogmatic or fixed in thinking. They can hear and evaluate the viewpoints of others and discard old beliefs in favor of new. They are sufficiently secure within themselves that functioning is not affected by either praise or criticism from others. They can respect the self and the identity of another without becoming critical or becoming emotionally involved in trying to modify the life course of another. They assume total responsibility for self and are sure of their responsibility for family and society. They are realistically aware of their dependence on their fellow man. With the ability to keep emotional functioning contained within the boundaries of self, they are free to move about in any relationship system and engage in a whole spectrum of intense relationships without a "need" for the other that can impair functioning. The "other" in such a relationship does not feel "used." They marry spouses with equal levels of differentiation. With each a well-defined self, there are no questions or doubts about masculinity and femininity. Each can respect the self and identity of the other. They can maintain well-defined selfs and engage in intense emotional relationships at the same time. They are free to relax ego boundaries for the pleasurable sharing of "selfs" in sexuality or other intense emotional experience without reservation and with the full assurance that either can disengage from this kind of emotional fusion and proceed on a self-directed course at will.

These brief characterizations of broad segments of the scale will convey an over-all view of the theoretical system that conceives all human functioning on the same continuum. The scale has to do with *basic* levels of differentiation. Another important aspect has to do with *functional* levels of differentiation which is so marked in the lower half of the scale that the concept of *basic* levels can be misleading. The more intense the degree of ego fusion, the more the "borrowing" and "lending" and "giving" and "sharing" of self within the family ego mass. The more the shifting of "strength" within the ego mass, the more likely the marked discrepancies in functional levels of self. The occasional brief shifts are striking. One of the best examples of this is that of the regressed schizophrenic person who pulls up to resourceful functioning when his parents are sick, only to fall back when they have recovered. Other shifts are so fixed that people wonder how one spouse so strong would marry another so weak. A striking example of this is the overadequate husband who might function well in his work at perhaps 55 on strength from a wife housebound with phobias, excessive drinking, or arthritis and a functioning level of 15. In this situation, the basic level would be about 35. Fluctuations in the upper half of the scale are present but less marked and it is easier to estimate basic levels. People high on the scale have almost no functional shifts. Other characteristics apply to the entire scale. The lower the person on the scale, the more he holds onto religious dogma, cultural values, superstition, and outmoded beliefs, and the less able he is to discard the rigidly held ideas. The lower a person on the scale, the more he makes a "federal case" of rejection, lack of love, and injustice, and the more he demands recompense for his hurts. The lower he is on the scale, the more he holds the other responsible for his self and happiness. The lower he is on the scale, the more intense the ego fusions, and the more extreme the mechanisms such as emotional distance, isolation, conflict, violence, and physical illness to control the emotion of "too much closeness." The more intense the ego fusions, the higher the incidence of being in touch with the intrapsychic of the other, and the greater the chance that he can intuitively know what the other thinks and feels. In general, the lower the person on the scale, the more the impairment in meaningful communication.

Relationship system in the nuclear family ego mass. An example of a marriage with spouses in the 30 to 35 range will convey an idea of several concepts in this theoretical system. As children, both spouses were dependently attached to parents. After adolescence, in an effort to function autonomously, they either denied the dependence while still living at home, or they used separation and physical distance to achieve autonomy. Both can function relatively well as long as they keep relationships distant or casual. Both are vulnerable to the closeness of an intense emotional relationship. Both long for closeness but both are "allergic" to it. The marriage for each duplicates essential characteristics of former ego masses. They fuse together into a "new family ego mass" with obliteration of ego boundaries and incorporation of the two "pseudo-selfs" into a "common self." Each uses mechanisms, previously used in their families of origin, in dealing with the other. For instance, the one who ran away from his own family will tend to run away in the marriage. The most common mechanism is the use of sufficient emotional distance for each to function with a reasonable level of "pseudo-self." The future course of this new family ego mass will depend on a spectrum of mechanisms that operate *within* the family ego mass, and others that operate *outside* in their relationships within the extended family system.

Within the family ego mass, spouses use three major mechanisms to control the intensity of the ego fusion. (1) *Marital conflict* in which each spouse fights for an equal share of the common self and neither gives in to the other. (2) *Dysfunction in one spouse.* A common pattern is a brief period of conflict followed by one spouse who reluctantly "gives in" to relieve the conflict. Both spouses usually see self as "giving in," but there is one who does more of it. In another pattern, one spouse volunteers to be the "no-self" in support of the other on whom they become dependent. The spouse who "loses self" in this mechanism may come to function at such a low level that they become candidates for physical, emotional, or social illness. There are some marriages that continue for years with one functioning well and the other chronically ill. (3) *Transmission of the problem to one or more children.* This is one of the most common mechanisms for dealing with family ego mass problems. There are a few families in which ego mass problems are relatively contained within one of the three areas. There are a few with severe marital conflict but no impairment of either spouse and no transmission to the children. There are also a few with no marital conflict, no dysfunction in either spouse and in which the entire weight of the marital problem goes into one child. There may be no significant symptoms until after adolescence, when the child collapses in psychotic dysfunction or other dysfunction of comparable degree. In most families, the problem between the spouses will be "spread" to all three areas. The few families in which the problem remains contained in one area are important theoretically. The fact that there are some families with intense marital conflict and no impairment of children is evidence that marital conflict does not, within itself, cause problems in children. The fact that serious impairment of children can develop in calm, harmonious marriages is further evidence that impairment of children can occur without conflict. The degree of the problem between the spouses can be assigned quantitative measures. The system operates as if there is a certain amount of "immaturity" to be absorbed by the system. Large quantities of this may be "bound" by serious dysfunction in one family member. One chronically ill parent can be a kind of "protection" against serious impairment of children. In the area of transmission to children, the family projection process focuses on certain children and leaves others relatively uninvolved. There are, of course, families in which the "quantity" of immaturity is so great that there is maximum marital conflict, severe dysfunction in one spouse, maximum involvement of children, conflict with families of origin, and still free-floating "immaturity."

The mechanisms that operate *outside* the nuclear family ego mass are important in determining the course and intensity of the process *within* the nuclear family. When there is a significant degree of ego fusion, there is also a borrowing and sharing of ego strength between the nuclear family and the family of origin. In periods of stress the nuclear family can be stabilized by emotional contact with a family of origin, just as the nuclear family can also be disturbed by stress in the family of origin. In general, the intensity of the process in a nuclear family is attenuated by active contacts with the families of origin. There is one striking pattern illustrated by the following example: the father separated himself from his family when he left for college. There was no further contact except infrequent, brief visits and occasional letters and Christmas cards. He married a wife who maintained close contact with her family, including frequent exchanges of letters and gifts, regular family reunions, and visits with scattered members of the clan. Five out of six of the father's siblings followed the same pattern of separating from the family of origin. The mother was one of five siblings, all of whom married spouses who were brought into the emotional orbit of her family. This pattern is so common that I have called these *exploding* and *cohesive* families. The spouse who separates from his family of origin does not resolve the emotional attachment. The old relationship remains "latent" and can be revived with emotional contact. Through the "active" relationship with the cohesive family, the nuclear family system is responsive to emotional events within the cohesive extended family. There are other nuclear families in which both spouses detach themselves from families of origin. In these the spouses are usually much more dependent on each other, and the emotional process in the family tends to be more intense. The average family in which both spouses are emotionally separated from families of origin tend to become more invested in the emotional systems of work and social situations. An example is a family in which the principal outside emotional tie was the father's long-term emotional dependence on his boss at work. Within weeks after the sudden death of the father's boss, a teen-aged son was in serious dysfunction with a behavior problem. A brief period of "family" psychotherapy with the father alone restored the family emotional equilibrium sufficiently for the parents to work productively together toward resolution of the parental interdependence. Knowledge of the relationship patterns in the extended family system is important in understanding the over-all problem and in devising a family psychotherapy program.

Multigenerational transmission process. One of the important concepts of this theoretical system is the pattern that emerges over the generations as parents transmit varying levels of their immaturity to their children. In most families the parents transmit part of their immaturity to one or more children. To illustrate this multigenerational pattern in its most graphic and extreme form, I shall start with parents with an average level of differentiation and assume that in each generation the parents project a major portion of their immaturity to only one child, thereby creating maximum impairment in one child in each generation. I shall also assume that in each generation one child grows up relatively outside the emotional demands and pressures of the family ego mass and attains the highest level of differentiation possible in that situation. It would be essentially impossible for this pattern to occur generation after generation, but it does illustrate the pattern. The example starts with parents at 50 on the scale. They have three children. The most involved child emerges at 35 on the scale, much lower than the basic level of the parents and a faily maximum degree of impairment for one generation. Another child emerges with 50, the same basic level of the parents. A third grows up relatively outside the problems of the family ego mass and emerges with a level of 60, much higher than the parents. In considering the child at 35 who marries a spouse in the 35 range, the personality characteristics of this marriage would vary according to the way this family ego mass handles its problems. A maximum projection family would have a calm marriage and almost total preoccupation with the health, welfare, and achievement of the most involved child, who could emerge with a level as low as 20. They could have another who grew up outside the family ego mass with a level of 45, much higher than the parents. To have two children, one at 20 and another at 45, is hardly probable. The child at 20 is already in the danger zone and vulnerable to a whole spectrum of human problems. In his early years he might be an overachiever in school, and then in the postadolescent years go into an emotional collapse. With special help he might eventually finish school, spend a few aimless years, and then find a spouse whose "needs" for another are as great as his. At this level of ego fusion the problems are too great to be contained in one area. They will probably have a variety of marital, health, and social problems, and the problem will be too great for projection to only one child. They might have one child at 10, another at 15, and another who grows up outside the family mass to a level of 30, much above the basic level of the parents. The ones at 10 and 15 are good candidates for total functional collapse into states such as schizophrenia or criminal behavior. This illustrates former statements that it requires at least three generations for a person to acquire the level of "no-self" for a later collapse into schizophrenia. In the average situation the immaturity would progress at a much slower rate. Also, in every generation there are children who progress up the scale, and in the average family the upward progression is much slower than illustrated in this example.

It is emphasized that the scale level figures used in the preceding examples are to illustrate the broad principles of the theoretical system. The shift in functional levels in the lower half of the scale is so responsive to such a variety of hour-to-hour and week-to-week shifts, through good years and bad, that approximate levels can be established only after having awareness of the particular variables most operative over a period of time for a given family. It is the general level and the pattern that are most important in the clinical situation. The levels in the multigenerational concept are strictly schematic and for illustrative purposes only. The postulations for this concept were derived from historical material covering three to four generations on approximately 100 families, and ten or more generations on eight families.

There is one other theoretical concept that I have combined with my own work that is used with every family in psychotherapy. These are the personality profiles of the various sibling positions as presented by Toman (1961) in *Family Constellation*. I consider his work one of the significant contributions to family knowledge in recent years. He presents the thesis that personality characteristics are determined by the sibling position and the family constellation in which one grows up. I have found his personality profiles to be remarkably accurate, especially for people in the mid-scale range of my Differentiation of Self Scale. Of course, he did his study on "normal" families and made no attempt to estimate other variables. He also did not consider the personality alterations of the child who was the object of the family projection process. An example of the shift is a family of two daughters. The older, the one most involved in the family emotional system, emerged with the profile of a younger "baby." The younger daughter, who was less involved in the emotional system with the parents, emerged with more of the characteristics of an older daughter. Most of his profiles contain a mixture of the adult and the infantile characteristics. The higher a person on the scale, the more the adult qualities predominate; the obverse is also true.

Clinical Use of Family Psychotherapy

I hope that the theoretical concepts help the reader think more in terms of family systems rather than diagnostic categories and individual dynamics. Each point in the theory has application in clinical evaluation and in family psychotherapy. This section will be presented in three main parts: (1) survey of the family fields, (2) the process of "differentiation of self" in family psychotherapy, and (3) family psychotherapy principles and techniques.

Survey of the family fields. This is a term used to designate a family "evaluation" process used in the initial interview with every family I see. It is designed to get a volume of factual information in a brief time. The information is used with the family theory for a formulation about the over-all patterns of functioning in the family ego mass for at least two generations. The formulation is used in planning the psychotherapy. Initially, it required a number of hours to get this information. With practice, and the careful structuring of the interview, and an average uncomplicated family, it is possible to do a survey adequately for planning the psychotherapy in one hour. This is different from the kind of "evaluation" in which the therapist may spend several hours with all family members together to observe the workings of the family relationship system. In the training of young therapists, considerable experience in observing multiple family members together is essential. It is not possible to *know* family without direct clinical observation, and it is not advisable to work with segments of families until one has a working knowledge of the whole. For the average family, the initial interview is with both parents, who can usually provide more information than one. In addition, it provides a working view of the marital relationship. If there is evidence that marital discord might interfere with the fact gathering, I often ask to see the one parent who has the most knowledge about the family. Some interesting developments come from this. Most families seek help when there is dysfunction in one or more of the three main stress areas of the nuclear family system: (1) marital conflict, (2) dysfunction in a spouse, or (3) dysfunction in a child. To illustrate this survey, I shall use a family referred for a behavior problem in a teenage child.

In surveying the family fields, I first want to know about the functioning in the nuclear family field and then how the functioning of the extended family field intergears with the nuclear field. A good starting point is a chronological review of the symptom development in the teenage child, with specific dates and circumstances at the time of each symptom eruption. Many symptomatic eruptions can be timed exactly with other events in the nuclear and extended family fields. The parents might report the child first played hooky from school "in the eighth grade," but it would convey much about the family system if one knew the day he played hooky was the day his maternal grandmother was hospitalized for tests for a feared cancer. Information about feeling and fantasy systems of other family members on that day would be helpful if it could be obtained.

The second area of investigation is the functioning of the parental ego mass since marriage. This emotional unit has its own system of internal dynamics that change as it moves through the years. The internal system also responds to the emotional fields of the extended families and to the reality stresses of life. The goal is to get a brief chronological view of the internal system as it has interresponded with outside forces. This might be compared to two constantly changing magnetic fields that influence each other. The internal functioning is influenced by events such as closeness or distance and emotional contact with extended families, changes in residence, the purchase of a home, and occupational success or failure. Major events that influence both emotional fields are births within the central ego mass and serious illness or death in the extended family. Functioning within the ego mass can be estimated with a few questions about the stress areas, which are marital conflict, illness or other dysfunction, and projection to a child. A change in stress symptoms might be related to internal dynamics or external events. The dates of changes are important. A change from a calm to a conflictual relationship might be explained by the wife as, "The time I began to stand up to him," when it would in fact be timed exactly with a disturbance in an extended family.

Important ego mass changes accompany the birth of children. The birth of the first child changes the family from a two-person to a three-person system. At an important event such as this, it is desirable to do a "fix" on the entire family system, including place, date, ages of each person in the household and the functioning of each, and a check on the realities in the extended families. It is desirable to get readings on the feeling-fantasy systems of various family members at stress points, if this is possible. A check on the family projection process is often easy by asking about the mother's fantasy system before and after the birth of the child. If it is a significant projection process, her worries and concerns have fixed on the child since the pregnancy, her relationship with this one has been "different," she has long worried about it, and she is eager to talk about it. An intense, long-term, projection process is evidence of a deeper and more serious problem in the child. A projection process that started later, perhaps following the death of an important family member, is much less serious and much easier handled in family psychotherapy. A projection process, usually between mother and child, *changes* the internal functioning of the family system. This much psychic energy from mother to child will change the psychic energy system in the family. It might serve to reduce marital conflict, but it might also disturb the husband to the point he would start spending longer hours at work, or he might begin drinking, or have an affair, or become emotionally closer to his parents. This survey is followed to the onset of symptoms in the child for which there are already nodal points that may be connected with dates and events in the parental relationship. The survey provides a picture of general functioning levels, responsiveness to stress, and evidence about the flexibility or rigidity of the entire system. It also provides a notion about the more adaptive spouse who is usually the more passive. The adaptive one is much more than one who "gives in" on a controlled surface level. This involves the entire fantasy, feeling, and action system. A spouse who develops physical symptoms in response to an emotional field is in a "cell to cell" adaptiveness that is deep.

The next area of investigation is the two extended family fields in either order the therapist chooses. This is similar to the nuclear family survey except it focuses on over-all patterns. Exact dates, ages, and places are very important. The occupation of the grandfather and a note about the marital relationship and the health of each grandparent provides key clues to that family ego mass. Information about each sibling includes birth order, exact dates of birth, occupation, place of residence, a few words about spouse and children, a note about over-all life course, and frequency and nature of contact with other family members. From this brief information, which can be obtained in five or ten minutes, it is possible to assemble a fairly accurate working notion about the family ego mass, and how the nuclear parent functioned in the group. Siblings who do best are usually least involved in the family emotional system. Those who do poorly are usually most involved. Distance from other family members and quality of emotional contacts with family provides clues about the way the person handles all emotional relationships and whether this tends toward an "exploding" or "cohesive" family. A high incidence of physical illness often occurs in those with low levels of differentiation of self. The sibling position is one of the most important bits of information. This, plus the general level of family functioning, makes it possible to postulate a reasonably accurate personality profile to be checked later. In general, a life style developed in the family of origin will operate in the nuclear family and also in family psychotherapy.

Surveys of the family fields follow the same pattern for other problems, except for different emphases. Certain areas may require detailed exploration. It is always helpful to go back as many generations as possible. The over-all goal is to follow the total family through time with a focus on related events in interlocking fields. The lower the general level of differentiation in a family, the greater the frequency and intensity of the related events. A secondary dividend of a family field survey is the family's beginning intellectual awareness of related events. The family emotional system operates always to obscure and misremember and to treat such events as coincidental. Family replies to an effort to get specific dates might go, "That was when he was about . . . eleven or twelve years old," and, "He must have been in the fifth grade," or "It was about five or six years ago." It requires persistent questioning and mathematical computation to get specific information. The obscuring process is illustrated by a family in family psychotherapy. Ten days after the wife returned from her mother's funeral, her daughter developed nephritis. Some weeks later the wife was insisting that the daughter's illness preceded her mother's death. The husband's memory and my notes were accurate. In theoretical thinking, I have never been willing to postulate causality or go beyond noting that such events have a striking time sequence. I believe it may have to do with man's denial of dependence on his fellow man. I avoid glib dynamic speculations and record the family explanations as, "The family member *said*. . . . " I have never been able to use the related events early in psychotherapy. Early in family psychotherapy there was the temptation to show this to the family after the initial interview. Some families found reason to never return. My goal is to keep asking questions and let the calendar "speak" when others are able to "hear."

The family field survey is primarily for the therapist in knowing the family and how it operates, and in planning the psychotherapy. If the symptoms develop slowly in the nuclear family, it is likely to be the product of a slow buildup in the nuclear family. If the symptoms develop more quickly, the situation deserves a thorough exploration for disturbance in the extended family. If it is a response to the extended family, it can be regarded as an "acute" situation and it is fairly easy to restore the family functioning. The following is an example of multiple acute problems following a disturbance in the extended family.

A 40-year-old woman was referred for a depression for which hospitalization had been suggested. Her husband belonged to a "cohesive" family of six siblings, all of whom lived within a few hundred miles of their parents. Two months before, his 65-year-old mother had a radical mastectomy of breast cancer. Two weeks after the operation, one of the husband's sisters had a serious automobile accident which required months of hospitalization. Six weeks after the operation, one of the husband's brothers had a son arrested for a series of delinquent acts, the first of which had occurred two weeks after the operation. After an initial interview with the depressed wife alone, the husband and wife were seen together. A few hours with the process focused on feelings about the mother brought rapid relief of the depression and set the stage for long-term family psychotherapy with both together.

The process of differentiation of a self. The basic effort of this therapeutic system is to help *individual* family members toward a higher level of differentiation of self. An emotional system operates with a delicately balanced equilibrium in which each devotes a certain amount of being and self to the welfare and well-being of the others. In a state of disequilibrium, the family system operates automatically to restore the former togetherness equilibrium, though this be at the expense of some. When an individual moves toward a higher level of differentiation of self, it disturbs the equilibrium and the togetherness forces oppose with vigor. In larger emotional systems, an individual may seek an ally or group to help oppose the forces of the system, only to find self in a new undifferentiated oneness with his allies (even a sect or minority group within the larger system) from which it is harder to differentiate than from the original oneness. Any successful effort toward differentiation is for the individual alone. Some of the forces that oppose the "differentiation of self" will be described later. When the individual can maintain his "differentiation" stand in spite of opposition, the family later applauds.

One of the important concepts in this theoretical system has to do with "triangles." It was not included with the other concepts because it has more to do with therapy than the basic theory. The basic building block of any emotional system is the "triangle." When emotional tension in a two-person system exceeds a certain level, it "triangles" a third person, permitting the tension to shift about within the triangle. Any two in the original triangle can add a new triangle. An emotional system is composed of a series of interlocking triangles. The emotional tension system can shift to any of the old preestablished circuits. It is a clinical fact that the original two-person tension system will resolve itself automatically when contained within a three-person system, one of whom remains emotionally detached. This will be discussed under "detriangling the triangle."

From experience with this therapeutic system, there are two main avenues toward a higher level of "differentiation of self." (1) The optimum is differentiation of a self *from* one's spouse, as a cooperative effort, in the presence of a potential "triangle" (therapist) who can remain emotionally detached. To me, this is the "magic" of family psychotherapy. They must be sufficiently involved with each other to stand the stress of "differentiation" and sufficiently uncomfortable to motivate the effort. One, and then the other, moves forward in small steps until motivation stops. (2) Start the differentiation alone, under the guidance of a supervisor, as a preliminary step to the main effort of differentiating a self *from* the important other person. This second avenue is a model for family psychotherapy with one family member. A third avenue is less effective: (3) the entire process under the guidance of a supervisor who coaches from the sidelines. Direct use of the "triangle" is lost, the process is generally slower, and the chances of an impasse are greater. As a general comment about "differentiation," the highest level of differentiation that is possible for a family is the highest level that any family member can attain and maintain against the emotional opposition of the family unit in which he lives.

Family psychotherapy principles and technique. My optimum approach to any family problem, whether marital conflict, dysfunction in a spouse, or dysfunction in a child, is to start with husband and wife together and to continue with both for the entire period of family psychotherapy. In most families, this "optimum" course is not possible. Some 30 to 40 percent of "family" hours are spent with one family member, mostly for situations in which one spouse is antagonistic or poorly motivated, or when progress with both is too slow. The method of helping one family member to "differentiate a self" will be discussed later. The method of working with the two parents evolved from several years of experience in which both parents and symptomatic child (usually postadolescent behavior and neurotic problems) attended all sessions together. An average course would continue a year or more. Family communication improved, symptoms disappeared, and the families would terminate, much pleased with the result. There was no basic change in the pattern of the parental relationship, postulated to be fundamental in the origin of the problem. On the premise that the entire family system would change if the parental relationship changed, I began asking such parents to leave the child at home and to focus on their own problems. These have been the most satisfying results in my experience. Many of the children who initiated the family effort were never seen, and others were seen only once. The parents who achieved the best results would continue about four years at once a week for a total of 175 to 200 hours with better results than could be achieved with any other psychotherapeutic method in my experience. The children were usually symptom free in a few weeks or months, and changes have gone far beyond the nuclear family into the extended family system. The time has been so consistently in the four-year range that I believe it might require this amount of time for significant differentiation of self. Some people can spend a lifetime without defining themselves on numerous life issues. I am now experimenting with less frequent appointments to reduce the total amount of time.

The basic process of working with husbands and wives together has remained very much the same over the years with some different emphases and modifications in theoretical concepts. In the past I stressed the communication of feelings and the analysis of the unconscious through dreams. More recently, it has been a process of watching the step by step process of externalizing and separating out their fantasy, feeling, thinking systems. It is a process of knowing one's own self, and also the self of the other. There have been comments such as, "I never knew you had such thoughts!" and the counterresponse, "I never dared tell anyone before, most especially *you*!"

The following is an example of two small "differentiation" steps with the emotional response of the other. One wife, after many hours of private thinking, announced, "I have decided to take all the thoughts, time, and energy that I have devoted to trying to make you happy and to put it into trying to make myself into a more responsible woman and mother. Nothing I tried really worked anyway. I have thought it out and I have a plan." The husband reacted with the usual emotional reaction to an "I" position by the other. He was angry and hurt. He ended with, "If I had realized it would come to this after fifteen years, I can tell you one thing, there never would have been a wedding!" Within a week he was happy with his "new" wife. Some weeks later, after much thinking by the husband, he announced, "I have been trying to think through my responsibilities to my family and to work. I have never been clear about this. If I worked overtime, I felt I was neglecting my family. If I spent extra time with the family, I would feel I was neglecting my work. Here is my plan." The wife reacted with emotion about his real selfish lack of concern finally showing its true color. Within a week that had subsided.

As spouses change in relation to each other, they disturb the emotional equilibrium in families of origin where there are the same emotional reactions and resolutions as between themselves. Most of these spouses have become the most responsible and respected in both extended family systems. The emotional opposition to change also occurs in social and work emotional systems. The main point to be communicated here is t. at a change in "self" disturbs the emotional equilibrium and evokes emotional opposing forces in all interlocking emotional systems. If two spouses can make the primary changes in relation to each other, it is relatively easy to deal with the other systems.

One of the most important processes in this method of psychotherapy is the therapist's continuing attention to defining his "self" to the families. This begins from the first contact which defines this theoretical and therapeutic system and its differences from others. It proceeds in almost every session around all kinds of life issues. Of importance are the "action" stands which have to do with "what I will do and will not do." I believe a therapist is in poor position to ask a family to do something he does not do. When the family goes slowly at defining self, I begin to wonder if there is some vague ambiguous area of importance about which I failed to define myself.

At this point, I shall describe *family* psychotherapy with one family member. The basic notion of this has to do with finding a way to start some change in the deadlocked family; with finding a way to get into contact with family resourcefulness and strength and to get out of contact with the sickness morass; and with getting some differentiation to rise out of the family quagmire. Actually, if it is possible to get some differentiation started in one family member, it can loosen up the entire family system. Communication of this idea has been difficult. To those who use a medical model and consider the therapeutic relationship the basic healing force in emotional illness, the idea is erroneous. I have used several different concepts in trying to write about the idea and a number of different angles in trying to teach it. There are those who heard it as "treating the healthiest family member instead of the patient, on the grounds that the healthiest is more capable of modifying behavior." This is an accurate description of the goal but it uses a "health" concept in the place of "sickness," which is still a medical model. A therapist who attempts to "treat" the healthiest with his medical orientation could either drive him away or make him into a "patient."

The conflictual marriage provides one of the best examples of working with one spouse. This is a clinical situation in which the emotional system is already fairly well locked in dysfunction before they seek help. A fair level of overt conflict is "normal" and it has to reach a relative state of dysfunction before they seek help. The marriage began with an almost idyllic model in which each devoted a high percentage of "self" to the happiness and well-being of the other. This I have called a "fraudulent" emotional contract in which it was realistically impossible for either to live up to the agreement. With this arrangement, the functioning of self *is* dependent on the other and, in that sense, any failure in happiness or functioning *is* the fault of the other. The emotional investment in each other continues; only it shifts into negative energy that accuses, indicts, and diagnoses. I believe the conflictual marriage is an enduring one because of the energy investment. The amount of *thinking* time that goes into the other is probably greater than calm marriages. With the intensity of emotional interdependence and the ability to utilize conflict, the conflictual spouses usually do not seek help until adaptive mechanisms are jammed. In a high percentage of conflictual marriages, I see one spouse alone for a few months to a year before calm working together is possible. Choice about the one to see first is easy when one is motivated and the other antagonistic. It is a little different when both are seen together and the repetitious "accuse the other—excuse self" continues in the interview. If they have any capacity to stop the cycle and look at the pattern, I continue with both together. If a vigorous effort to help them contain the cycle is not successful, I say that I consider this cyclical and nonproductive, that I am not willing to spend time this way, and that I want to see the healthiest, best-integrated one alone for a period of time to help this one gain some objectivity and emotional control. A request for the "healthiest" establishes a different orientation and changes their long-term diagnosing, "You are the sick one who needs a psychiatrist." I do not see spouses alternately. It invites "triangling," neither really works at the problem, each expects the other to do it, and each tends to justify self to the therapist. My "I" stands, all based on experience, are in terms of what I will do and will not do, and are never in terms of "what is best."

Since the process of working with one family member alone is similar in all situations, I shall describe the effort with the conflictual spouse in some detail. The early sessions go into a detailed communication of an orientation with the use of clinical examples and a blackboard for diagrams. In broad terms, the concept is one of withdrawing psychic energy from the other and investing it in the poorly defined ego boundaries. It involves the idea of "getting off the back" of the other by reducing the "other directed" thinking, verbal, action energy which is designed to attack and change the other, and directing that energy to the changing of self. The changing of "self" involves finding a way to listen to the attacks of the other without responding, of finding a way to live with "what is" without trying to change it, of defining one's own beliefs and convictions without attacking those of the other, and in observing the part that self plays in the situation. Much time is devoted to establishing the therapist's self in relation to the one spouse. These ideas are passed along for their possible use in defining a "self." They are told that others have found some of them helpful, that the effort will fail if they try them without incorporating them into "self" as their own beliefs, that they would be unrealistic to try something they could not really believe in, and it will be their responsibility to find other ideas and principles if these do not fit with their own "selfs." They are assigned the task of becoming "research observers" and told that a major part of each hour will go into their report on their efforts to see self. I tell them about the predictable stages they can expect if their efforts are successful in defining "self" and containing the critical actions, words, and thoughts that have been trying to direct the life of their spouse. If they are successful at this, the first reaction will be a version of, "You are mean, selfish and vicious; you do not understand, you do not love, and you are trying to hurt the other." When they can listen to the expected attack without reacting, a milestone will have been passed. Then they can expect a withdrawal from the other which emphasizes, "To heck with you. I do not need you." This will be the most difficult stage. They might get depressed and confused and develop a whole spectrum of physical symptoms. This is the reaction of one's psyche and soma as it cries out for the old dependence and togetherness. If they can live with the symptoms without reacting, they can expect the other to make a new and different bid for affection on a higher level of maturity. It is usually not many days after that before the other spouse asks to take the therapy hour, and often not many hours before they can finally work together.

The life style of this low level of "differentiation" is the investment of psychic energy in the "self" of another. When this happens in the therapy, it is transference. A goal of this therapy is to help the other person make a research project out of life. It is important to keep "self" contained with the therapist as the other spouse. If the person understands the life-goal nature of the effort and that progress will slow down or stop with energy invested in the "self" of the therapist, he is in a better position to help keep the energy focused on the goal. If progress does stop, the family psychotherapy is shifted to a similar effort with the other spouse. It is not possible to use this "differentiation of a self" approach with two spouses. It results in intense "triangling."

Work with one sick spouse depends on the problem and which one seeks help. If the well one seeks help, the "sick" one is near collapse. With these I work toward avoiding a relationship with the sick side of the family, and work toward relating to the well one about his problems with the sick one. Some of these families achieve remarkable symptom relief with a few appointments, but these people are not motivated for more than symptom relief. When the "sick" one seeks help, I maintain a detached, "Let's examine this and understand your part in the family problem." The cells of the "sick" spouse literally go into dysfunction in the presence of the other spouse, especially in those with severe introjective and somatic dysfunctions. If the other spouse is brought in too early, the therapy effort may terminate within a few hours. A goal is to propose "family" early and wait until the "self" of the sick one can operate in the presence of the other without going into dysfunction. There have been some excellent long-term results which include about six months with the sick one and some two years with both. Problems such as impotence and frigidity belong more in the area of relationship functioning. These can usually be converted to "family" within a few hours and the response has been good. Impotence often disappears within a few weeks and frigidity is rarely mentioned after a few months. Most of these go on with long-term family therapy for two years or more.

The problem of the "triangled" child presents one of the most difficult problems in family psychotherapy. From the initial family survey can come a fair estimate of the intensity of the process. If it is not too severe, the parents can focus on their own problems immediately, they almost forget about the child and, suddenly, he is symptom free. Even with severe "triangling," I do a "trial run" with both parents together to test the flexibility in the parental relationship. In the severe "triangling" or projection of the parental problem to the child, the parents are not able to leave the child out of their feelings, thoughts, and actions. There are the less severe versions in which parents try hard to work on their problem but the relationship between them is dull and lifeless. Life and self is invested in the child. The "gut reaction," in which a parent's "insides tie into knots" in response to discomfort in the child, is common. After several years of symptom-relieving methods, including working with various combinations of family members, I began what I have called "detriangling the triangle." This is too complex for brief discussion but it involves helping one parent to establish an "I" position and to "differentiate a self" in the relationship *with the child*. If there is another "magic" in family psychotherapy, it is the family response when one parent can begin to "differentiate a self" from the amorphous "we-ness" of the intense undifferentiated family ego mass. One bit of clearly defined "self" in this area of amorphousness can bring a period of amazing calm. The calm may quickly shift to other issues, but the family *is* different. The other parent and child fuse together into a more intense oneness that alternately attacks and pleads with the "differentiating parent" to rejoin the oneness. If the differentiating one can maintain a reasonable "I" for even a few days, there is an automatic decrease in the intensity of the attachment between the other two and a permanent decrease in the intensity of the triangle. The second step involves a

similar effort by the other parent to "differentiate a self." Now the
parental relationship has come a little more to life. Then there is another
cycle with each parent separately, and then still more life and zest
between the parents. Differentiation proceeds slowly at this level of ego
fusion, but there has been a few of these families that have gone on to
reasonable levels of differentiation.

There are several other configurations of family psychotherapy with
one family member, but this provides a brief description of the basic
principles. It is used when the family system is so stalled that efforts to
work with multiple family members increases the dysfunction, or when
work with multiple members reaches a cyclical impasse. The effort is to
help one family member to a higher level of functioning which, if
possible, can restore function to the family system.

Summary. Presented here is a family theory of emotional illness and its
component system of family psychotherapy, which is one of several
different theoretical approaches to the family, and one of many different
kinds of "family therapy" that have come on the psychiatric scene in little
more than one decade. A brief review of the family movement attempts
to put this system into a kind of perspective with the over-all family
movement. Since this system places maximum emphasis on "family" as a
theoretical system, the theory has been presented in some detail. The
shorter section of family psychotherapy presents both broad principles
and specific details about the usefulness of family concepts in clinical
practice.

Chapter 10

Family Therapy and
Family Group Therapy

Introduction

The frequent and confident use of such terms as *family therapy, family psychotherapy* and *family group therapy* implies that they refer to well-defined, standardized procedures. Actually, they are used to refer to such a wide variety of principles, methods, and techniques—all based on such a conglomerate of vague theoretical notions—that the terms are misleading without further clarification. This situation is linked with a similar situation in the more conventional areas of psychiatric theory and practice. Even the oldest and most accepted conventional theories are based on a complex of theoretical assumptions. Theoreticians and early clinicians were aware of the assumptions, but recent generations of clinicians have come to regard the assumptions as fact. When family therapists create new concepts from pieces of preexisting theory, an interesting theoretical maze results.

The family field is too new to have a body of knowledge about which there is general agreement. Each investigator is so immersed in his own thinking system that it is difficult for any to really hear and know the work of others. A few authors have attempted to survey the field, but each evaluation has been based on the theoretical bias of the author, and others have not agreed with his conclusions.

With the premise that the dilemma will be more quickly resolved if each investigator presents his own thinking as clearly as possible, with the understanding that anything the author says about the work of others will be based on his own theoretical orientation, and with awareness of the inaccuracy entailed in comparing the work of one with another, the author here presents his own theory and method of family psychotherapy in detail and presents some ideas about the work of others that highlight the wide range of theory and practice in the family field.

History

Antecedents

Family movement refers to the new emphasis on family theory and family therapy that began in the mid 1950s. Some say the family movement is not new, and they refer to family methods used in child guidance clinics and in marriage counseling as early as the 1920s. There is some accuracy to the early claims, but there is probably more accuracy to the thesis that the family movement developed as an evolutionary process, with some early antecedents of family methods discovered in retrospect after the family movement started. A strict historian might validate the thesis that the family movement began when man became literate and recognized the importance of his family in his own life.

On a practical level, the family movement probably began with the development of psychoanalysis, which has concepts about the ways one life influences another. However, the psychoanalytic forcus was on the patient, and the basic concepts were developed from the patient's retroactive memories about his family, as remembered in the transference. The pathogenic family was outside the immediate field of interest. Freud's 1909 paper on the treatment of Little Hans is unique. His work with the father instead of the child is consistent with present family methods in which the designated patient is not a part of the psychotherapy. In 1921 Flugel's book *The Psycho-Analytic Study of the Family* presented individual psychoanalytic formulations about different family members.

The child guidance movement passed very close to present family concepts without seeing them. The focus was on diagnosis and treatment of the sick child. Parents were seen separately to facilitate treatment of the child. Psychiatric social workers came into prominence for casework with parents whose child was in child therapy. By the late 1940s the child guidance model was adopted by adult clinics, with the increasing use of casework for the relatives of adult patients in individual psychotherapy.

Thus, some valid antecedents of the family movement preceded the family movement by some forty years. However, these developments were not recognized until after the family movement was under way. Not to be ignored is the fact that sociologists and anthropologists were studying the family and contributing to the literature long before the family movement in psychiatry. Also to be remembered is the fact that general systems thinking began in the 1930s, long before there was much recognizable connection between it and psychiatric theory.

Early History

The family movement actually began in the mid 1950s, when the movement surfaced after it had been operating underground in several places for a number of years. There were too many small roots, each growing independently, for any to say which was first. It was an evolutionary development that suddenly burst into the open when the psychiatric world was ready for it.

Various investigators, each working independently, began to hear about the work of others. Mittelman in 1948 reported on the concurrent analysis of married couples. Middelfort began experimenting with a form of family therapy during his psychiatric training, but did not report on his work for several years. Early work and late reporting was also characteristic of Bell, who in 1951 misheard a comment about individual psychotherapy for family members while visiting a clinic in England. Enroute home, he devised a method that he put into clinical operation. Ackerman, who had been thinking family for several years, began writing in the mid 1950s. Several investigators started family research from previous work with schizophrenia. Among these were Lidz, who started in Baltimore in the early 1950s and continued with his co-workers in New Haven; Jackson and his co-workers in Palo Alto; and Bowen and his co-workers in Bethesda. The formation of the Committee on the Family of the Group for the Advancement of Psychiatry in 1950 was another important event in the early days of the family movement. The Committee was formed at the suggestion of William C. Menninger, who considered the family an important area for study. The Committee worked several years without much knowledge of the field until after the family movement appeared openly. In 1962 two writers visited various family centers, investigating the origin and status of the family movement. Their report, published in *The Saturday Evening Post*, noted that the movement began with several different investigators, including one in Europe—each working without knowledge of the others.

Why did the family movement begin in this way at this time? Most of the originators came from psychoanalytic backgrounds, and the family concepts had been available for years. Why did not the family movement evolve from the child guidance movement a decade or two before? Almost no child psychiatrists have been associated with the family movement.

The family movement seems to be related to the development of psychoanalysis, which gained increasing acceptance in psychiatry during the 1930s, provided concepts for mass use in World War II, and then contributed to the popularity of psychiatry as a specialty after the war. Psychoanalytic theory had explanations for all emotional problems, but treatment techniques had not been developed for the more severe problems. Hundreds of eager psychiatrists began experimenting with modifications of psychoanalytic treatment for the more difficult problems. Those who began family research appear to have been motivated by a search for more effective treatment methods. The strict admonition against contaminating the transference relationship may have accounted for the isolation of the early work and the slowness to report this supposedly unacceptable practice in the literature.

Clinical observations of the entire family together provided a whole new spectrum of clinical patterns never really seen before. Each investigator was on his own in reporting and conceptualizing his observations. Some of the concepts from the early research have remained or have been further developed into the most useful concepts in the field today.

Growth of the Movement

After the family movement was in the open, family sections were held at national professional meetings. The annual meeting of the American Orthopsychiatric Association had a section for family papers in March 1957, and the American Psychiatric Association had a similar section in May 1957. All the papers at both meetings were on research; clinical observation and family psychotherapy were only mentioned. News about family therapy spread rapidly. Beginning in 1958, swarms of therapists crowded the family sections at national meetings. Many therapists soon left the field, but new ones have continued to come in great numbers.

The early workers had arrived at the notion of family therapy as the logical method for the problem as conceptualized by research. The new workers grasped the promise of family therapy without hearing the family orientation on which it was based, which began the widespread empirical use of family therapy as a technique by therapists whose theoretical orientation was in individual theory. Meanwhile, group therapists adapted conventional group therapy to family group therapy.

The rapid increase in therapists was the beginning of a healthy unstructured state of chaos in the family movement. The new therapists, trained in conventional individual theory, stampeded into therapy with a wide spectrum of intuitive feeling techniques based on a conglomerate of discordant partial theories and philosophical principles. Theory was largely ignored, and most therapists operated with the basic assumptions of individual theory, which were quoted as scientific fact. It is difficult to find structure in a field that is exploding with intuitive techniques and when therapists have lost contact with the basic assumptions from which they operate. But this trend had a healthy aspect because conceptual dilemmas come into focus when family members are seen together. The more therapists are exposed to this dilemma, the more some are motivated to find new theoretical concepts and new psychotherapeutic techniques. During the late 1960s, the chaos began to subside as a larger segment of the field became interested in theory and structure and a smaller segment continued the spiral into intuitive techniques.

Current State

In 1970 the Committee on the Family of the Group for the Advancement of Psychiatry completed a report on the family movement. The basis for the study was a long, detailed questionnaire completed by more than 300 family therapists, who represented a cross section of family therapists from all the professional disciplines and with all levels of experience. The questions concerned details of theoretical thinking and clinical practice. The questionnaires, completed in the fall of 1966, covered such a wide range of theory and practice that it was difficult to report the results. Finally, a scheme was devised to designate therapists on a scale from A to Z.

The A therapists are those whose theory and practice is the same as individual psychotherapists. They use family therapy as a technique to supplement individual psychotherapy or as the main technique for a few families. The A therapists are individual therapists who use a little family in their practices. They are usually young or have just started experimenting with family techniques.

The therapists toward the Z end of the scale use theory and techniques that are quite different from individual psychotherapy. They think in terms of systems and emotional fields and relationships. They tend to think family for all emotional problems, and they usually see a number of family members in the treatment of any problem. The Z therapists are the ones who came into the family movement through research or who have been practicing family therapy for a long time.

The overwhelming majority of practicing family therapists are far toward the A end of the scale, with relatively few therapists toward the Z end of the scale. Therapists seem to move from the A end toward the Z end in direct proportion to their experience with family therapy. The A therapist thinks in terms of individual psychopathology and of the therapeutic relationship as the modality for emotional growth; he sees family therapy as a technique to facilitate individual psychotherapy. The Z therapist thinks of symptoms in terms of disordered family relationships and of therapy as a way to help the family restore relationships and achieve better communication or a higher level of differentiation.

The A therapist thinks of several different kinds of family techniques. Designation of the kind of family therapy is determined more by who attends the family sessions than by theory and method. Most family therapists think of individual therapy when one family member attends the sessions, of couples therapy when both spouses are present, of family therapy or conjoint family therapy for parents and child, and of family group therapy when the entire family is present. Therapists toward the Z end of the scale use terminology determined more by theory than by technique.

Theoretical Aspects

An Evolution from Individual to Family Theory

Family theory is so different from conventional individual theory that it is difficult to conceptualize and communicate the nuances of difference. Common denominators appear in all systems of family thinking, but to list these misses the clinical rationale for a different approach. In order to present the reasons for a different way of thinking, the author here discusses some of the theoretical nodal points in his experience as he moved from an orientation in psychoanalysis to family theory.

Early work with families. The author had considerable early experience with hospitalized patients and a special interest in psychoanalytic psychotherapy with schizophrenic patients. He became interested in the intensity of the emotional attachment between patients and relatives, which could be either an intense, overt overdependence or an equally intense rejection of each by the other.

Hospital treatment and psychotherapy were more orderly when contact between the family and the patient was limited, but the therapist and the hospital staff tended to perceive the patient as the hapless victim of a pathological family, reintegration of the patient into the family was prolonged, and the relatives could remove the patient from treatment just as he appeared to be making progress. With more involvement of the family, therapy went faster, and results appeared to be better, but there were also more emotional upheavals, and some families still terminated treatment prematurely.

A program was started to find better ways to involve the family in the treatment. A special study was made of the intense relationship between parents and young psychotic patients. In addition to providing therapy to the patient, therapists gave the parents a type of supportive information-getting psychotherapy. Progress depended on maintaining a good psychotherapy relationship with the patient and on keeping the parents sufficiently calm so that they did not upset the patient and the patient did not upset them.

At best, even when the patient had one therapist and the parents another, the staff was caught in the intense emotional field between the patient and the parents, trying to manage the parents' relationship with the patient and to protect the patient from parents seen as hurtful. This approach was more successful than previous approaches, but there were still the unexpected failures, too often blamed on pathological parents. During this period the author did enough psychotherapy with parents to recover somewhat from the hate-the-parents syndrome and to begin concurrent psychotherapy with the parents in addition to the patient, rather than the previous procedure which required one therapist to see the parents and another therapist to see the patient. This experience led to a hypothesis about the mother-patient relationship, which later became the basis for a formal research study started in 1954 at the National Institute of Mental Health in Bethesda, Maryland.

Research study. As part of the study, mothers lived on the ward with the patients. The original hypothesis excluded fathers, who are usually much less active than mothers in these relationships. After a few months, the hypothesis was extended to include fathers. Within the year, both parents and the normal siblings were included in the live-in study with the patients.

Assumptions. Some important basic assumptions went into the design of the research. In the background was the assumption, derived from psychoanalysis, that emotional growth could take place only in the careful analysis of the patient's relationship with the therapist. An important assumption in the foreground considered the mother's incomplete self to have incorporated the self of the developing fetus and to have been emotionally unable to give up the child in later years. This one child might fulfill the mother's emotional needs sufficiently so that her other children would not be as incorporated. This emotional stuck-togetherness was considered a primary phenomenon of almost biological proportions. Other phenomena—such as maternal deprivation, hostility, rejection, seductiveness, and castration—were considered to be secondary manifestations of this intense relationship rather than causal factors. The relationship was hypothesized as a locked-in emotional responsiveness that required the complete submission of one for the comfort of the other and that neither one liked or wanted, a self-perpetuating enigma in which either could block the other's effort to free himself. The hypothesis further stated that the patient's life-growth force had been blunted in this intense relationship and that the growth force could be freed in a specific therapeutic milieu that toned down the emotional tugging between mother and patient.

This hypothesis was designed to help the therapist understand the mother-patient relationship as a natural phenomenon for which no one is blamed, not even by inference. Systems thinking was not understood at the time, but the hypothesis represented a significant unplanned step into systems thinking. It explained the two-person system as a single unit, and it bypassed large areas of causality formulations necessary in individual theory.

The assumptions implicit in this hypothesis constituted such a departure from the cause-and-effect formulations of individual theory that the implications may not be readily appreciated. Individual theory may assume, with some accuracy, that Event D caused Event E, which followed it. This is a frozen-section assumption that blames D. This assumption could be followed by other assumptions that blame C for causing D or that blame Event E for causing Event F. Systems thinking attempts to conceptualize the total chain of events as a predictable phenomenon, and it obviates the use of the unconscious to postulate a cause.

The clinical operation of the research study was based on the theoretical assumption that the mother and the patient could resolve the emotional attachment if both were together in a specific supportive milieu in which no one would take sides emotionally or take action for either one against the other in the intense emotional field between the two. It was hypothesized that these two people had lived with each other for years, that each knew the other well, that each had built-in mechanisms to control the other, and that neither had ever seriously hurt the other. The likelihood that either would hurt the other during the clinical research was insignificant enough to take the chance. This one principle remained an unaltered core principle of the research, and it is still a core concept in the family theory developed after the initial research. The concept—a tension system between two people will resolve itself in the presence of a third person who can avoid emotional participation with either while still relating actively to both—is so accurate that it can be predictably repeated in family psychotherapy with less severe emotional problems.

The design in 1954 was to permit the mother to leave the ward at will if tensions between her and her child became too great and to provide each with individual psychotherapy designed to support each without taking sides against the other. The patients and mothers did not begin to grow away from each other, as had been hypothesized. Symptoms subsided rather quickly, but, after the relationship was fairly calm, neither mothers nor patients were motivated to disturb the basic intensity of the interdependence.

Nonparticipation. The staff and therapists found it difficult to acquire more than nominal ability at emotional nonparticipation in family emotions during the early years of the research. Families had many subtle ways to force staff into emotional participation, and personality characteristics in staff members made it automatic for them to feel with the victim or victor. It was commonplace for the staff to maintain a posture of nonparticipation while intimately involved on a deeper feeling level, which families recognized immediately. A cool, aloof, distant posture that feigns nonparticipation and prevents the staff person from relating freely to the family fools no one. Sometimes a family member assumed and acted on the misperception that a staff member was on his side when the staff member was actually neutral.

An incident early in the research study illustrates another facet of the problem. A daughter pushed her mother to the floor. The nurse, acting with a principle of nonparticipation, was in a dilemma. The nurse finally restrained the daughter, after which the nursing staff made a rule of nonparticipation except in situations of physical violence. Thereafter, the families had an automatic mechanism to force the nurses into emotional participation: A family member need only slap or hit another to involve the nurses.

It is difficult to train psychiatrists and psychotherapists to become nonparticipant observers and to regard the family as a phenomenon. Members of the mental health professions, perhaps because of their own early life experiences, are oriented toward understanding and helping the sick and the unfortunate. Individual psychiatric theory, which explains the mechanisms by which the fortunate victimize the oppressed, further fixes the psychiatrist's orientation. Formal training in psychotherapy trains the therapist to hear, to understand, to identify with, to put himself into the patient's situation, and to form a therapeutic alliance with the patient. This alliance is at the core of the therapeutic relationship, the main treatment modality of relationship therapy. The principle of emotional nonparticipation goes against the grain of conventional psychotherapy, but a therapist can be trained to gain this level of functioning if he is willing to work toward that end.

Emotional nonparticipation or staying out of the family emotional system does not mean the therapist is cold, distant, and aloof. Instead, it requires the therapist to recognize his own emotional involvement when it does occur, to gain sufficient control over his emotional system to avoid emotional side-taking with any family member, to observe the family as a phenomenon, and to be able to relate freely to any family member at any time.

Most therapists find it easier to attain a reasonable level of emotional nonparticipation if they are exposed over and over to the conflicting forces within a family. This exposure helps to force the therapist to a more observational overview of the family in order to maintain his own emotional equilibrium. Psychiatric residents in family psychotherapy training find it easier to attain emotional nonparticipation than do older psychiatrists, for whom the therapeutic relationship has become second nature. But when a resident who is being trained in family and in individual psychotherapy concurrently begins to develop competence at staying out of the emotional system, his supervisors of individual psychotherapy often begin to evaluate him as having a rigid personality with neurotic defensiveness against a warm relationship with his patient.

The author has placed more emphasis on emotional nonparticipation than have other family therapists. But to do successful family therapy, any therapist must gain some control over taking sides with any family faction. Older successful therapists have developed intuitive ways to do what this method attempts to structure and to specify.

One of the important dividends of emotional nonparticipation has to do with more accurate research observations. When the family can function as an emotional unit, the relationship patterns are definite, orderly, and predictable. When an important other person becomes fused into the family emotional system or is removed from the system, the relationship patterns become atypical and important nuances of the relationships are obscured. Family relationship patterns become atypical when a therapist becomes emotionally fused into the family.

The greatest dividend of emotional nonparticipation is in family psychotherapy. Long-term results are far superior, progress is more orderly and consistent, and unresolvable therapeutic impasses are less likely when the therapist can remain relatively outside the system, with freedom to move about and relate to any family member at any time. When the therapist can remain emotionally free while still in contact with any member of the family, the family system becomes calmer and more flexible, and family members become freer within the family. The therapist can use his knowledge of family systems to guide his effort with the family. When family relationship patterns become atypical, progress slows down, or the family becomes passive and waits for the therapist to solve the problem, the signs indicate that the therapist has become fused into the family emotional system, and he needs to devote attention to his own emotional functioning.

Clinical Experiences. The early research families were not motivated to go beyond symptom relief in individual psychotherapy. Parents neglected to take up significant issues in their psychotherapy, expecting the patient to deal with the issues; and patients neglected issues, expecting the parents to do it. Family psychotherapy was the next logical step.

The theoretical thinking and the research design considered the mother-patient relationship as a unit, and the staff began thinking about psychotherapy for the unit within a few months after the research started. After a year, all families were started in family psychotherapy, the only form of therapy for newly admitted families. The old families continued their already-established individual therapy and began going to family psychotherapy sessions, too. Family therapy for the new families was alive and fast-moving, and progress was more rapid than with any other therapy. The other families were not making progress in either individual or family psychotherapy. In family sessions their attitude was, "I'll take up my problems with *my* therapist." But their individual therapy was also slow, both patients and parents expecting the other to deal with significant issues. After a few months, all individual psychotherapy was discontinued.

In the beginning, family psychotherapy was considered a profitable initial procedure to deal with intense issues until family members were seriously motivated for individual psychotherapy, which was still considered the only modality for significant personality growth. After a relatively brief period with family therapy, therapists saw that this method could do anything that was possible with individual therapy, plus much more. If the goal was to analyze the transference, then every nuance that might come to light in the transference was vividly present in living detail in already-existing family relationships. If the goal was to get at a family member's intrapsychic process through dreams, then one had only to analyze the dreams of that family member—and obtain the added dividend of the thoughts and fantasy reactions of the other family members to the dream.

It was a shaking experience for one long-schooled in psychoanalytic theory to become aware that all he had held to be factual and irrevocable was no more than another theoretical assumption and that psychoanalytic therapy was no longer *the* therapy but simply another method. It was even more shaking when the family investigator reported his findings, expecting that some therapists might hear and become interested, only to have old friends and colleagues listen but continue on in the unshaken belief that psychoanalysis was the one proved theory and that psychoanalytic therapy was the ultimate in therapy. Then the investigator had a choice of going on alone or of giving up the effort.

The type of family psychotherapy started in the research study in 1955 would now be called family group therapy. Any family member could speak at any time and the therapist could ask the silent ones to speak. The method used group therapy techniques, but with a different goal about issues to be defined. There was also multiple-family group therapy, attended by all members of the live-in families (three to five families), and large multiple-group therapy sessions attended by all the members of all the families and the staff. The multiple-family group meetings were useful for communicating feelings and for promoting calmness but not for defining issues in a single family. It was slow plodding for any family member to establish a self in that setting. The large multiple-family groups were discontinued and were not resumed until ten years later, when their principles were incorporated into network therapy.

The patterns seen in the live-in families had always been present between schizophrenic patients and their parents. Why had the patterns never really been seen before? The main reason seems to be that the research study had a broad theoretical frame of reference, which opened minds to new data. Other factors facilitating the observations could have been the intensity of the patterns in this live-in project and of the effort to stay outside the family emotional system.

After the patterns were seen in the research families, it was inescapable to see the very same patterns in all degrees of lesser intensity in all other people. Patterns originally thought to be characteristic of schizophrenia were also present in families with less severe problems and even in normal families. To the author this was evidence that schizophrenia and all other forms of emotional illness belong on a continuum, the difference between schizophrenia and the neuroses being one of degree of impairment rather than a qualitative difference. This finding was the beginning of a long effort to classify all levels of human adaptation, from the lowest to the highest possible levels, on a single scale.

The opportunity to observe the same family relationship patterns in all degrees of emotional illness provided an added dimension for the research. Schizophrenia is a relatively fixed state in which change is confined to regression, remission, and changes that evolve over time. The same mechanisms in less severe emotional illness are much more flexible and amenable to significant change in psychotherapy. The same mechanisms in borderline emotional impairment can change slowly, especially under ideal conditions. The opportunity to observe the full spectrum helps to put the human phenomenon in better perspective.

Private practice. A few months after family group therapy was started for the research study, the method was started with the entire spectrum of emotional problems encountered in a busy private practice, providing an invaluable contrast with the more severe schizophrenic level problems encountered in the research study. The first psychoanalytic patient was changed to family psychotherapy about four months after the method was developed.

This patient was a bright young husband with a phobic reaction in a compulsive personality who was making steady progress after six months of psychoanalysis for four hours a week. The dilemma was discussed with the project consultant, who was a senior psychoanalyst. The therapist said:

This man has a good chance for one of the better psychoanalytic results in three to four years with a total of 600 to 700 hours. There is also a good chance his wife will develop enough problems in about two years to refer her to another analyst for three to four years. About six years from now, after 1,000 or more combined psychoanalytic hours, they should have their lives in reasonable order. How can I in good conscience continue this long and expensive course when I know within me that I can accomplish far more in less time with different approach? On the other hand, how can I in good conscience take a chance and suggest something new and untried when I know the chances are good with the proved psychoanalytic method?

The consultant mused about analysts who hold onto patients too long and wondered how the husband and wife could react to the questions. The issue was discussed with the patient, and one week later his wife accompanied him to her first session. The clinical method used was analysis of the intrapsychic process in one and then the analysis of the corresponding emotional reaction in the other. They continued the family therapy sessions three times a week for 18 months for a total of 203 hours. The result was far better than would ordinarily be expected with 600 hours of psychoanalysis for each. This family has been followed periodically by letter and telephone during the 12 years since the therapy was terminated, and their life course has been ideal.

Hypotheses

The various early family research studies provided a completely new order of observations never previously recognized or reported. Each investigator was observing the same phenomena, but each was using different conceptual models to describe observations. There were models from psychology, sociology, mythology, biology, physics, mathematics, and chemistry. There were descriptions of seesaws, reciprocities, complementarities, chemical bonds, magnetic fields, rubber fences, and hydraulic and electrical energy systems—all interwoven with concepts from individual theory. Psychoanalytic theory, on which most of the psychotherapies are based, describes a fairly predictable system of dynamisms, but there has never been a solid connection between psychoanalysis and the accepted sciences. Family research had a potential for an eventual new theory of emotional illness. A plan was devised to make the most of new clues.

A hypothesis is necessary for research. Without it, one is confronted with too much data to be sorted or conceptualized, and there is the ever-present problem of losing direction in pursuit of irrelevant interesting details. A specific hypothesis predicts what will be found, but it limits the researcher's ability to see other data that may be important.

Two orders of hypotheses were developed. One was the short-term hypothesis for each substudy in the total research. An effort was made to use similar conceptual models, each consistent with the others and all of them consistent with the other hypothesis—a broad, long-term hypothesis to govern the total study over the years.

The long-term hypothesis had several advantages. It provided a source of models for new short-term hypotheses. Most important, it provided predictions for new observations that might otherwise be missed. Most of the observers had been trained in psychoanalysis, and they tended to see only what they had been trained to see. It was hoped that the long-term hypothesis would open thinking to new kinds of observations.

The long-term hypothesis was based on the original concepts about the mother-child relationship, which had proved to be surprisingly accurate in the research study; on observations about the father and other family members, which made them an integral part of the total family system; on observations about the total family system; and on some new hunches and beliefs about the basic nature of emotional illness. There were consistent observations to suggest that emotional illness is a far deeper process than can be explained by emotional trauma in a single generation. The parents of a schizophrenic patient have almost as much basic impairment as the patient. They manage to function at the expense of the patient, who functions poorly. The pattern is one in which children become more impaired than their parents through several generations until the impairment is great enough to make the patient vulnerable to schizophrenia. Symptoms erupt when the emotionally and somatically impaired person is exposed to critical stress. In an opposite process, children can become better integrated than their parents through successive generations. These observations resulted in the concept of the multiple-generation transmission process.

Observations about the difference between feeling and thinking led to concepts central to the theory and to the psychotherapy. Emotionally impaired people do not distinguish between the subjective feeling process and the intellectual thinking process. Their intellectual processes are so flooded with feeling that they are incapable of thinking that is separate from feelings. They routinely say, "I feel that . . ." when it would be more accurate to say, "I think" or "I believe" or "It is my opinion." They consider it truthful and honest to speak in terms of feelings and insincere and false to speak of thinking, beliefs, and opinions. They work always for togetherness and agreement in relationship to others and avoid statements that would establish one person as different from another. Better integrated people can distinguish between the feeling and thinking processes, but they usually use, "I feel that . . ." when communicating with others. The best integrated people distinguish between the two processes, and they are much more accurate in their use of the terms.

Much study and work with families, from the most impaired to the best integrated, went into the effort to clarify feeling-thinking issues. The interplay between feeling and thinking is considered one of the best common denominators for judging levels of emotional integration. The world literature is vague in distinguishing between feelings and emotion, and there is lack of clarity with terms such as philosophies, beliefs, opinions, convictions, and impressions. The literature makes little distinction between the subjectivity of truth and the objectivity of fact. Lacking other than dictionary guidelines, some hypotheses about the terms were made for the purposes of the research.

The long-term hypothesis about the nature of emotional illness considered it to be a disorder of the emotional system, which is an intimate part of man's phylogenetic past, which he shares with lower forms of life, and which is governed by the same laws that govern all other living things. Man's ability to think, his intellectual system, is a function of his newly added cerebral cortex, which was developed last in his evolution and which is the main difference between man and the lower forms of life. The emotional and intellectual systems have different functions, but they are interconnected, each influencing the other. The important connection for this hypothesis is the feeling system, through which certain influences from the upper strata of the emotional system are perceived by the cerebral cortex as feelings.

The literature refers to emotions as much more than states of contentment, agitation, fear, weeping, and laughing. It refers also to states in animals—including contentment after feeding, sleep, and mating and agitation states in fight, flight, and the search for food. One might consider an emotional system present in all forms with an autonomic nervous system, but why exclude states of contentment and agitation in one-cell forms, in which stimuli could be more biochemical in nature? When one considers emotion on this level, it becomes synonymous with instinct which governs the life process of all living things. Emotional illness is viewed as a deep phenomenon that is much more than a disorder of the mind. The term *mental illness*, connoting a disorder of thinking, has been discontinued in favor of the term *emotional illness*.

Man's brain is part of his protoplasmic totality, but, through the functioning of his brain, he has been able to do wondrous things. His intellect does best when devoted to subjects outside himself. He has created the sciences, through which he has learned many of the secrets of the universe; he has created technology for modification of his environment; and he has gained control over all lower forms of life. He has even controlled evolution in lower forms within controlled environments. Man has done less well when his intellect is directed at himself. Though related intimately to all living things, he has done far better at defining the ways he is different from lower forms than in defining his kinship with them.

This hypothesis says that the emotional system runs a course as predictable as any natural phenomenon, that emotional illness surfaces in a variety of different ways when the emotional system goes into states of dysfunction, and that the main problem in learning the secrets of emotional illness lies more in the way man denies and rationalizes and thinks about emotional illness than in the nature of emotional illness. Man can do far better than he has done thus far in defining the predictable natural course of emotional illness. Once he knows the secrets, he is in a better position to modify the process.

Family Systems Theory

The triangle. The theory considers the triangle—a three-person system—as the molecule of any emotional system, whether it exists in a family or in a social system. The term *triangle* is used instead of the more familiar term *triad*, which has come to have fixed connotations that do not apply to this concept. The triangle is the smallest stable relationship system. A two-person system is an unstable system that immediately forms a series of interlocking triangles. The triangle has definite relationship patterns that predictably repeat in periods of stress and calm.

In periods of calm, the triangle is made up of a comfortably close twosome and a less comfortable outsider. The twosome works to preserve the togetherness, lest one become uncomfortable and form a better togetherness elsewhere. The outsider seeks to form a togetherness with one of the others, and there are numerous well-known moves to accomplish this. The emotional forces within the triangle are constantly in motion from moment to moment, even in periods of calm. Moderate tension states in the twosome are characteristically felt by one while the other is oblivious. It is the uncomfortable one who initiates a new equilibrium toward more comfortable togetherness for self.

In periods of stress, the outside position is the most comfortable and most desired position. In stress, each works to get the outside position to escape tension in the twosome. When it is not possible to shift forces in the triangle, one of the involved twosome triangles in a fourth person, leaving the former third person aside for reinvolvement later. The emotional forces duplicate the exact patterns in the new triangle. Over time, the emotional forces continue to move from one active triangle to another, really remaining mostly in one triangle as long as the total system is fairly calm.

When tensions are very high in families and available family triangles are exhausted, the family system triangles in people from outside the family, such as police and social agencies. A successful externalization of the tension occurs when outside workers are in conflict about the family while the family is calmer. In emotional systems such as an office staff, the tensions between the two highest administrators can be triangled and retriangled until conflict is acted out between two who are low in the administrative hierarchy. Administrators often settle this conflict by firing or removing one of the conflictual twosome, after which the conflict erupts in another twosome.

A triangle in moderate tension characteristically has two comfortable sides and one side in conflict. As patterns repeat and repeat in a triangle, the people come to have fixed roles in relation to each other. The best example of this is the father- mother-child triangle. Patterns vary, but one of the most common is basic tension between the parents, with the father gaining the outside position—often being called passive, weak, and distant—leaving the conflict between mother and child. The mother—often called aggressive, dominating, and castrating—wins over the child, who moves another step toward chronic functional impairment. This pattern is described as the family projection process. Families replay the same triangular game over and over for years, as though the winner were in doubt, but the final result is always the same. Over the years the child accepts the always-lose outcome more easily, even to volunteering for this position. A variation is the pattern in which the father finally attacks the mother, leaving the child in the outside position. This child then learns the techniques of gaining the outside position by playing the parents off against each other.

Each of the structured patterns in triangles is available for predictable moves and predictable outcomes in families and social systems. A knowledge of triangles provides a far more exact way of understanding the father-mother-child triangle than do the traditional oedipal complex explanations. And triangles provide several times more flexibility in dealing with such problems therapeutically.

Differentiation of Self Scale. This scale is a way of evaluating all people on a single continuum, from the lowest to the highest possible level of human functioning. The scale ranges from 0 to 100. It is comparable to a scale of emotional maturity except that this theory does not use the concept of maturity or immaturity.

At the lowest point on the scale is the lowest possible level of self or the greatest degree of no-self or undifferentiation. At the highest point on the scale is a postulated level of complete differentiation of perfect self, which man has not yet achieved. The level of differentiation is the degree to which one self fuses or merges into another self in a close emotional relationship. The scale eliminates the concept of normal, which has been elusive for psychiatry.

The scale has nothing to do with emotional illness or psychopathology. There are low-scale people who manage to keep their lives in emotional equilibrium without developing emotional illness, and there are higher-scale people who can develop severe symptoms under great stress. However, lower-scale people are vulnerable to stress and are much more prone to illness, including physical and social illness, and their dynsunction is more likely to become chronic when it does occur. Higher-scale people can recover emotional equilibrium quickly after the stress passes.

Two levels of self have been postulated. One is solid self, made up of firmly held convictions and beliefs. It is formed slowly and can be changed from within self, but it is never changed by coercion or persuasion by others. The other level of self is the pseudo-self, made up of knowledge incorporated by the intellect and of principles and beliefs acquired from others. The pseudo-self is acquired from others, and it is negotiable in relationship with others. It can be changed by emotional pressure to enhance one's image with others or to oppose the other.

In the average person, the level of solid self is relatively low in comparison with the level of pseudo-self. A pseudo-self can function well in most relationships; but in an intense emotional relationship, such as marriage, the pseudo-self of one merges with the pseudo-self of the other. One becomes the functional self and the other a functional no-self. The emotional interplay in fusion states, the undifferentiated family ego mass, is the subject of much of the dynamics in a family emotional system.

Low-scale people live in a feeling world in which they cannot distinguish feeling from fact. So much life energy goes into seeking love or approval or in attacking the other for not providing it that there is no energy for developing a self or for goal-directed activity. The lives of low-scale people are totally relationship-oriented. Major life decisions are based on what feels right. A low-scale person with a life in reasonable asymptomatic adjustment is one who is able to keep the feeling system in equilibrium by giving and receiving love and by the sharing of self with others. Low-scale people do so much borrowing and trading of self and show such wide fluctuations in their functioning levels of self that it is difficult to estimate their basic levels of self except over long periods of time.

As a group, low-scale people have a high incidence of human problems. Relationships are tenuous, and a new problem can arise in an unsuspected area even while they are trying to deal with the previous problem. When the relationship equilibrium fails, the family goes into functional collapse, with illness or other problems. They can be too numb to feel, and there is no longer any energy to seek love and approval. So much energy is devoted to the discomfort of the moment that they live from day to day. At the very lowest point on the scale are those too impaired to live outside an institution.

People in the 25-to-50 segment of the scale also live in a feeling-dominated world, but the fusion of selfs is less intense, and there is increasing capacity to differentiate a self. Major life decisions are based on what feels right rather than on principle, much life energy goes into seeking love and approval, and there is little energy for goal-directed activity.

Those in the 35-to-40 range present some of the best examples of a feeling-oriented life. They are removed from the impairment and life paralysis that characterize the lower-scale people, and the feeling orientation is more clearly seen. They are sensitized to emotional disharmony, to the opinions of others, and to creating a good impressions. They are apt students of facial expressions, gestures, tones of voice, and actions that may mean approval or disapproval. Success in school or at work is determined more by approval from important others than by the basic value of the work. Their spirits can soar with expressions of love and approval or be dashed by the lack of it. These are people with low levels of solid self but reasonable levels of pseudo-self, which is obtained from and is negotiable in the relationship system.

People in the upper part of the 25-to-50 segment of the scale have some awareness of intellectual principles, but the system is still so fused with feeling that the budding self is expressed in dogmatic authoritativeness, in the compliance of a disciple, or in the opposition of a rebel. Some of those in this group use intellect in the service of the relationship system. As children, their academic prowess won them approval. They lack their own convictions and beliefs, but they are quick to know the thoughts and feelings of others, and their knowledge provides them with a facile pseudo-self. If the relationship system approves, they can be brilliant students and disciples. If their expectations are not met, they assemble a pseudo-self in point by point opposition to the established order.

People in the 50-to-60 segment of the scale are aware of the difference between feelings and intellectual principle, but they are still so responsive to the relationship system that they hesitate to say what they believe, lest they offend the listener.

People still higher on the scale are operationally clear about the differences between feelings and intellect, and they are free to state beliefs calmly, without attacking the beliefs of others for the enhancement of self and without having to defend themselves against the attacks of others. They are sufficiently free of the control of the feeling system to have a choice between intimate emotional closeness and goal-directed activity, and they can derive satisfaction and pleasure from either. They have a realistic appraisal of self to others, in contrast to lower-scale people, who feel self to be the center of the universe and who either overvalue or devalue self.

The differentiation of self scale is important as a theoretical concept for viewing the total human phenomenon in perspective. It is valuable in estimating the over-all potential of people and in making predictions about the general pattern of their lives. But it is not useful in making month to month or even year to year evaluations of scale levels. There is so much trading and borrowing and negotiating for pseudo-self in the relationship system, especially in the lower half of the scale, and such wide functional shifts in the level of self that it is difficult to estimate scale levels on short-term information.

Most people spend their lives at the same basic level they had when they left their parental families. They consolidate this level in a marriage, after which there are few life experiences that change this basic level. Many life experiences automatically raise or lower the functioning levels of self, but this shift can be as easily lost as gained. There are calculated ways to raise the basic level of self, but doing so is a monumental life task, and it is easy for one to say that the possible gain is not worth the effort. The method of psychotherapy described here is directed at helping families differentiate a few points higher on the scale.

Nuclear family emotional system. The term *undifferentiated family ego mass* was originally used to refer to the emotional system in the nuclear family—father, mother, children. The emotional process has the same basic pattern in extended families and social relationship systems. The original term is still as accurate as ever when applied to the nuclear family, but it is less apt when applied to the extended families, and it is awkward when applied to social systems. Now the terms *nuclear family emotional system, extended family emotional system*, and *social system* are used to describe the same emotional process in different areas.

A rough estimate of the spouses' level of differentiation of self conveys an idea about the quantity of undifferentiation potentially present for future trouble in the nuclear family. The greater the undifferentiation, the greater the potential problems. People pick spouses who have equivalent levels of differentiation of self. The life styles of people at one point on the scale are so different from others a few points removed that they consider themselves to be incompatible.

Many spouses experience the closest and most open relationship in their adult lives during courtship. In the commitment of each to the other in the marriage, the two pseudo-selfs fuse into a new emotional oneness. The mechanisms they use in dealing with the emotional fusion, which becomes a kind of life style for them, help to determine the kinds of problems they will encounter in the future. Most spouses use some degree of emotional distance from each other to control the symptoms of fusion. The patterns of relationships back to their families of origin help determine the intensity of nuclear family problems. The more open the relationships to families of origin, the less the tension in the nuclear family.

The undifferentiation in the marriage focuses on three areas. It is as if there is a quantitative amount of undifferentiation to be absorbed, and it may be focused largely in one area or mostly in one area and less in others or distributed evenly in all three areas. If the amount is great enough, it can fill all areas and spill outside to the extended family and social systems. The areas are marital conflict, dysfunction in one spouse, and impairment of one or more children. Families with symptoms in all three areas do best in family psychotherapy. Families with symptoms largely in one area are resistent to change other than symptomatic relief.

Marital conflict. The basic pattern in conflictual marriages is one in which neither gives in to the other on major issues. These marriages are intense in terms of the amount of emotional energy each invests in the other. The energy may be thinking or action energy, either positive or negative, but the self of each is focused intensely on the self of the other. The relationship cycles through intense closeness, conflict that provides a period of emotional distance, the makeup, and another period of intense closeness. Marital conflict does not in itself harm children unless the parents feel guilt and fear that it will hurt the children. The amount of psychic energy that each invests in the other protects children from emotional overinvolvement. The amount of undifferentiation absorbed by marital conflict reduces the amount to be absorbed elsewhere.

Dysfunction in one spouse. This is the pattern in which one spouse becomes the adaptive or the submissive one, and the other spouse becomes the dominant one. The pseudo-self of the adaptive one merges into the pseudo-self of the other, and the dominant one becomes responsible for the twosome. In such a marriage each spouse sees self as adapting to the other, but it is the one who adapts the most who becomes a no-self, dependent on the other to think and act and be for the twosome. The one who remains in the adaptive position is vulnerable to dysfunction, which can be physical illness, emotional illness, or social dysfunction—such as drinking, acting-out behavior, loss of motivation, irresponsible behavior. These illnesses tend to become chronic, and they are hard to reverse. The marriage between one overadequate spouse and a chronically ill spouse is enduring. Chronic illness—such as arthritis, stomach ulcers, or depression—can absorb great quantities of the undifferentiation in a nuclear family and can protect other areas from symptoms.

Impairment of one or more children. This is the pattern in which parents operate as a "we-ness" to project their undifferentiation to one or more children. This mechanism is so important that in this family theory it has been included as a separate concept, family projection process.

Family projection process. This is the basic process by which parental problems are projected to children. It is present in the full range of problems from the mildest to the most severe, such as hard-core schizophrenia and autism. The basic pattern involves a mother whose emotional system is more focused on children than on her husband and a father who is sensitive to his wife's anxiety and who supports her emotional involvement with the children.

The mother has varying degrees of emotional fusion with each child. Most mothers work hard to treat all their children the same, but the average mother has one child with whom the fusion is far more intense. The intensely fused child may be one who has a positive attachment to the mother, one who was considered strange or different from infancy, or one whom the mother repulsed from birth—and vice versa.

Anxiety in the mother is quickly felt in that extension of herself, the most fused child. The mother's sympathetic, oversolicitous, overprotective energy goes into allaying the anxiety in the child instead of in herself, which establishes a self-perpetuating cycle, with the mother infantilizing and the child gradually becoming more impaired. A moderately severe example is one in which the relationship is a positive overattachment in infancy, gradually increasing evidence of behavior problems or internalized problems as the child approaches adolescence, and a rapid development of severe problems in adolescence, when the relationship with the mother becomes negative. During this period the father either agrees and tries to support the mother or withdraws when he does not agree. The same basic pattern applies to the child who later develops schizophrenia or other severe impairments except that the process is much more intense and additional mechanisms are used to deal with complications of the basic process.

The family projection process is selective in that it typically focuses on the child first. The mother's involvement with this child may so fulfill the deficit in her own self that the other children are relatively uninvolved. The amount of undifferentiation can be so great that it involves more than one child. Among the factors that influence the selection of the child to be fused are sibling position, the mother's preference for boys or girls, and the mother's level of anxiety at the time the child was conceived and born. Among the most vulnerable for the projection process are oldest children, the oldest boy or oldest girl, an only boy or only girl, a child born when anxiety is high, and a child born with a defect.

The family projection process is universal in that it exists in all families to some degree. It alleviates the anxiety of undifferentiation in the present generation at the expense of the next generation. The same process by which the group functions better at the expense of one is present in all emotional systems.

Multigenerational transmission process. This concept defines the principle of projection of varying degrees of immaturity (undifferentiation) to different children when the process is repeated over a number of generations. If the process begins with parents with low-level differentiation and the family is one that focuses maximal maturity on one child in several generations, it will eventually produce a child so impaired, both physically and emotionally, that he will collapse into dysfunction, such as schizophrenia, at any effort to survive outside the family.

In any one generation the family projection process involves each child with a different level of intensity. The maximally incolved child emerges with a lower level of self than the parents. Minimally involved children may emerge with about the same level as the parents. Children relatively out of the process may emerge with higher levels of self. When each child marries at about the level from which he emerges from the nuclear family, some descendants in the family do better with life than their parents did, and others do less well. The multigenerational process provides a base from which to make predictions in the present generation and gives an overview of what to expect in coming generations.

Personality profiles of sibling positions. Toman's personality profiles of sibling positions are remarkably consistent with the author's own observations except that he does not consider children who are the object of the family projection process. Toman's basic thesis is that important personality characteristics are determined by the family configuration in which the child grows up. With his ten detailed personality profiles of sibling positions, one can determine the profile of all sibling positions. The profiles are so accurate that they can be used to reconstruct the family emotional process of past generations, to understand the emotional process in the present nuclear and extended family, and to make postulations about the future.

Toman studied only normal families, and he made no effort to study the ways a profile can be altered by the family projection process. For instance, if an oldest child is the object of a moderately severe family projection process, he is likely to become helpless and complaining and to marry an equally impaired spouse who overfunctions as the protective mothering one. In this family, the second child in the sibling order is likely to have the characteristics of an oldest child.

Theoretical Trends

The one major theoretical effort since the beginning of the family movement has been to find a way to integrate family concepts with psychoanalytic theory. There have been no major gains in this area, but the effort has resulted in a much more detailed definition of the relationship system between family members.

The one most consistent change in family concepts in the past ten years has been toward systems thinking. The relationships between family members constitute a system in the sense that a reaction in one family member is followed by a predictable reaction in another, and that reaction is followed by a predictable reaction in another and then another in a chain-reaction pattern. Jackson and his co-workers were among those who moved far toward systems thinking before his death in 1968. They were originally impressed by distortions in verbal messages and by the breakdown in communication in disturbed families. Their focus was on communication theory and restoration of communication in conjoint family therapy. In their first paper they presented the concept of the double-bind, which has since become one of the most-used terms in the family field. As with any initial concept, it was not sufficiently broad to conceptualize the total phenomenon, and theorists had to add new concepts to enlarge the system. The communication concept was extended to include nonverbal communication, in which the other comes to act and be through modalities and influences. Still later, the theoretical thinking moved into systems thinking with the *quid quo pro,* which conceptualized a chain-reaction phenomenon. In the past several years, a number of family therapists have made an increasing effort to use general systems theory to conceptualize family relationships.

Concepts from outside the family field have also been adopted for understanding family relationships. Games theory provides one of the most flexible ways for describing the constantly moving, predictable, repeating patterns of family relationships. New games can be defined as needed for accurately describing the complexity of the patterns. Some family therapists have tried to help the family recognize the game, as a step toward modifying the pattern. The kinesics research of Birdwhistell and Scheflen has provided new knowledge about unconscious body action language, which also functions in a systematic chain-reaction pattern between family members. This communication system operates without words—a characteristic of much that is communicated in a family. Some therapists use kinesics concepts in family therapy; the goal is to help make families aware of the kinesics language in the hope that they will modify the pattern. Neither games theory nor knowledge of kinesics lends itself to theoretical concepts, but the use of these concepts is evidence of a search for different kinds of concepts.

Most of the early family investigators were first impressed by the emotional stuck-togetherness of nuclear family members. Later they began to see varying degrees of the same phenomenon in other areas of the family. Ackerman, who had been thinking family before his published papers began in the mid-1950s, was one of the first, with he concept of interlocking psychopathologies, and he has continued to refine and extend his concepts. In the early 1960s Boszormenyi-Nagy developed the concepts of pathological-need complementarity. He and his co-workers are among those who have worked at defining both a relationship system and a personality structure. Their therapeutic system includes family therapy—with co-therapists—for the relationship system and individual psychotherapy for certain family members.

Numerous partial concepts exist more as rationales for family therapy than as theoretical concepts. Sources such as the Group for the Advancement of Psychiatry survey (1970) indicate that a majority of family therapists use individual theory for conceptualizing the psychopathology and group therapy methods for working out the problem in group process. The therapy is directed at such issues as lack of communication, perceptual distortions, increasing awareness of feelings in self and others, and the open communication of feelings in family therapy meetings. The therapist serves as a catalyst, directing attention to issues he considers important and facilitating group process.

With the increasing use of family group therapy, therapists tend to use group theory as families go through variations of the same stages characteristic of groups of nonrelated people. And as experience with families has increased, thinking about the nature of emotional problems has gradually shifted. Therapists tend to think less about psychopathology and more about relationships, and they tend to be more aware of a spectrum of patterns not observable in groups of nonrelated people. For instance, a therapist may become aware of passivity as a reciprocal function of activity or aggressiveness in another family member. When he begins to think about passivity-activity as a single pattern, his therapy changes, and the family is less pathology-oriented.

Clinical Aspects

Background Issues

The process of seeing a number of family members together, with any method of any technique, poses a spectrum of questions and issues not encountered in other forms of psychotherapy. These issues evolve from the premise that the emotional problem involves the entire family, not just the sick patient. One group of issues revolves around the traditional posture of medicine toward disease, which is to examine, diagnose, and treat the sick patient. This medical model is deeply ingrained in society in the form of customs, laws, and social institutions that require medical examination and health reports. Implicit in the doctor-patient relationship is the image of the physician as the healer and of the good patient as one who places himself under the care of the physician and follows instructions. Only when the family therapist attempts to focus on the family does he become aware of the ramifications of the medical orientation he had hardly noticed before.

Another group of issues involves the family projection process, through which the family creates the patient. This powerful emotional force, driven by anxiety, can be very intense when anxiety is high or can be toned-down and reasonable when anxiety is low. When anxiety is high, family members can be dogmatic in insisting that it is the patient who is sick and in resisting efforts to involve them in the therapy. When anxiety is low, the family rapidly becomes amenable to a family approach. It is usual for one part of the family or one parent to accept the idea of family therapy and for the other to oppose it. The opposing one may compliantly attend sessions without really participating. Another variation is one in which the family neither accepts nor rejects the family approach. They retain the idea that it is the patient who is sick, and they attend the sessions as co-therapists to help the therapist treat the patient. The goal in therapy with these tenuous situations is to focus on the process that creates the polarized issues rather than to be drawn into debate about the merits of any position.

A third group of issues that govern the situation is the orientation of the therapist. He participated in a family projection process in his own family of origin, and he participates in varying degrees in the family projection process that operates constantly in the setting in which he lives and works. If the therapist is dogmatic, either in diagnosing the patient or in fighting against the forces that would diagnose, he is probably emotionally polarized in his own personal life, and his intellectual beliefs are probably determined more by emotions than by objectivity.

The complex emotional forces in the administrative environment, in the family, and in the therapist's own personal situation all govern the establishment of a setting in which family therapy takes place. In any emotional system, the usual automatic response to an emotional issue is an emotional counterresponse which leads to escalation of the emotional process and to an increase in symptoms in some member of the system. The goal in dealing with an anxious situation is to get the emotional forces as much into neutral as possible. The therapist is the key to the emotional tension when a family first contacts him. He must have a working plan for dealing with operating principles and anxiety in his administrative and professional environment before he can start clinical work in family psychotherapy. Once this plan is established, the therapist can begin to deal with anxiety in the family. If he really believes in a family orientation and if he is not emotionally polarized in debates that argue the virtues of one therapy principle against another, the family is amazingly receptive to and even enthusiastic about the notion of family psychotherapy.

The therapist can start family therapy even when the family is in the process of hospitalizing one member; he can so neutralize family anxiety that hospitalization is avoided and the patient is permitted to remain at home with the family. This is the principle in crisis intervention therapy, which is coming into wide use in community mental health centers. The family problem is resolved much more rapidly and the final result is far better if hospitalization is avoided. The act of hospitalization helps to confirm both to the family and to the patient that he is sick. A fluid family projection process can be made more fixed and irreversible by this action. The organization and function of a psychiatric hospital confirm the belief that the patient is the sick one. Verbal statements that deny the family projection process have limited effect when the environment repeatedly takes action to confirm it. There are situations in which hospitalization cannot be avoided. In these cases, the family projection process becomes increasingly difficult to neutralize. Softening the impact of hospitalization on a family requires a knowledge of the family projection process and considerable skill in clinical management.

Once the therapist has established a workable initial family orientation with a family, repeating crises during therapy stir family anxiety and reactivate an intense wave of the family projection process, which focuses on sickness in the patient and absolves the family of responsibility and participation in the therapy. The family stops the effort to work at change within the family and begins to blame the therapist for lack of progress. If the therapy is in a psychiatric center, the family is aware of the difference between family theory and conventional psychiatry. In periods of anxiety, family members complain to the therapist's supervisor or the center administrator, who may agree emotionally with the complaint and take administrative action that defeats the family therapy. If the family members are also involved with school or juvenile court authorities, they may complain there and invoke another kind of outside pressure that agrees with the complaint and impedes or disrupts the family psychotherapy. Even when the therapist is successful in keeping his balance on the tightrope of emotional neutrality in most of these outside emotional forces, other reality issues interfere with maintaining the family premise. The writing of a prescription for a single family member or the diagnosis of a single family member or an insurance form or other medical report acts to confirm sickness in the patient.

Each therapist has to find his own ways to establish and maintain a family orientation. The more successful he is, the more likely the family is to continue the therapy to a favorable result.

The question of diagnosing the patient is an important issue. At one end of the scale are therapists who vigorously oppose the family pressure for an explanation and diagnosis of the patient's illness. There are problems with this approach when the symptomatic one is in a state of collapse that could be accurately diagnosed by the average lay person. At the other end of the scale are therapists who do psychological tests on all family members in order to diagnosis each of them. This approach successfully neutralizes the pressure within the family, but resourceful family members may take the helpless posture of a patient in their effort to change the family. In the middle of the scale are the therapists who attempt to focus on issues that feed into the family projection process. This approach avoids polarized positions and attempts to work out the issues in family therapy.

Therapists also use a variety of ways in dealing with drug prescriptions. Most therapists minimize or avoid the use of drugs. But with nonmedical therapists, families easily assume he would prescribe drugs if he were a physician.

The author attempts to stay as close to the midline as possible in each of these areas. He communicates to families that medical institutions, courts, insurance companies, and social institutions have to operate on policies defined by accepted professional practice. In all matters that have to do with medical reports, he interprets the situation as closely as possible to conventional practice and makes diagnoses and opinions conform to accepted practice. But in dealing with the family, he maintains the family orientation as strictly as possible. Young family therapists usually do not appreciate the structure within which social institutions must operate. Enthusiastic about their results with family therapy, they attempt to explain their family orientation, certain that they will persuade an insurance company, for instance, to make a policy change recognizing their work. Eventually, they become aware that insurance companies change rules in response to the practice of all psychiatrists and not in response to family therapists alone.

Clinical results are several times more effective with a family orientation than with conventional psychotherapy. To facilitate a family orientation, terms that connote a patient-sickness-treatment orientation have been replaced by terms more consistent with a family orientation. In the beginning the new terms seem odd and strange, but, after they are used for a time, the conventional terminology seems odd and out of place. Conventional terminology is retained for communicating with the medical community. In professional writing an effort is made to avoid use of the new words, but conventional terms are used sparingly. Conventional terms are used when it would be awkward to use "symptomatic one" or "impaired one" or the "one in dysfunction" rather than "patient." An effort has been made to discard the term *therapy*. The therapist can establish himself as a coach in working with families, but the term *family psychotherapy* is retained as the best working compromise between the method and the usual practice in the field. The term *designated patient* has come into common usage in family clinics to mean the one initially designated as the patient by the family.

Family Group Therapy

This method of family therapy or some extension of it is used by an overwhelming majority of family therapists, and it has led to more technical variations than have other methods. The theory and practice of family group therapy vary from therapist to therapist, but some common denominators apply to the entire field. The basic theoretical formulations are derived largely from conventional individual theory, and the practice is based largely on established principles and techniques from group therapy. The widespread use of the method helps to determine the definition of family therapy more by who attends the sessions than by the method employed. The method is usually called individual psychotherapy when one family member is present, couples therapy or marital therapy when both spouses or both parents attend the sessions, and family therapy only when at least two generations—parents and child—attend the sessions. In the author's method, however, the term is defined by the theory, and the therapy is designed to facilitate change in the family, whether the change is brought about through one or more family members.

Family group therapy is the method of choice for the beginning family therapist. He can use his existing knowledge of individual dynamics and group process to get started. It is difficult to learn about family emotional patterns except in the clinical situation. Once the therapist has started, he has an opportunity to observe the entire family as they relate to each other and to appreciate the fact that family members are not the same in relation to each other as they are in any other setting or as they appear to be from secondhand reports about them. Most psychotherapists with reasonable experience in psychotherapy and group process can do an acceptable professional level of family group therapy without previous experience in family emotional systems.

The greatest advantage of family group therapy is the fact that it can be used as a short-term process. It reaches its highest efficiency when therapist and family have a specific goal in mind, such as improving family communication or understanding the plight of a single family member. A few family group meetings can bring amazing relief in a symptomatic child, in a parent who is feeling frustrated and overburdened, or in a family reacting to a death or some other misfortune.

Family group therapy is effective with all levels of family problems, but it requires much more skill and activity when the family is potentially explosive. Uncontrolled feeling can result in emotional outbursts, disruption of the therapy, and symptomatic repercussions in other family members. Family group therapy can be effective as a long-term method for a certain range of moderately severe problems in which the feeling system is not rigidly controlled or so lacking in control that emotional issues can result in serious acting out.

Family group therapy lends itself well to the use of co-therapists; the second therapist can help if the first therapist becomes emotionally overinvolved. Some of the most experienced family therapists routinely work with co-therapists in a coordinated team approach. And some experienced family therapists routinely operate as male-female teams with the theoretical premise that the co-therapy team serves as a father-mother model.

The average family group therapy includes parents and all children who can thoughtfully participate, plus other family members who are available for the sessions. Most therapists want at least one meeting with all family members so that they get to know the total family system. But very young children react to family anxiety, and repeated sessions with them present are not profitable. Most therapists try to include available grandparents for a few sessions.

The therapist serves as chairman of the sessions and as a catalyst to facilitate communication in the family or whatever is his goal. The therapist should have a goal, lest the sessions start nondirected wandering. Some amazing things can happen when the therapist's goal is to reestablish family communication. Therapist and family are fascinated by the astute observations children make about the families, the child is grateful for the opportunity to formulate and express his ideas and for the forum where his thoughts are valued, and the children benefit from hearing the parents' calm expression of viewpoints. The family is so pleased by such a session that they eagerly look forward to more meetings. This process can reach a point of calm exhilaration, with the parents increasingly aware of the children and the children pleasantly surprised at seeing the human side of parental foibles. The symptoms in family members subside, and the family exhibits more togetherness and understanding.

When this process goes beyond a short-term goal, the parents begin to depend on the more adequate children to assume responsibility for the family problem. The children begin to find repetitive issues boring, and they find reasons to avoid the sessions. If forced to attend, the formerly talkative children became reluctant to speak. The therapist can shield the resourceful child from parental helplessness in the sessions but not at home. The maximal benefit from family group therapy sessions is usually achieved in twelve to twenty sessions, after which the family group diminishes to parents and the most involved child.

Family group therapy for both parents and one symptomatic child presents some formidable therapeutic blocks when used as a long-term method and involves the most intense triangle in the nuclear family. The parents continue to project their problem to the child even in the therapy hours.

The average problem is a moderate-level neurotic or behavior problem in a postadolescent child. The parents' thoughts and feelings are so invested in the child that it is difficult for them to focus on themselves. When the therapist finally focuses on an issue between the parents, the most anxious parent criticizes the child, or the child does something to draw parental attention, and the focus goes back to the child. The average good result comes after about a year—thirty-five to forty-five sessions. By that time, the passive father is a little less passive, the nagging mother is calmer, and the child's symptoms are reduced to an acceptable level for the family or for school. The family is usually pleased with the result on termination of therapy, but the therapist may see no basic change in the family pattern.

As a therapy variation, the therapist may schedule separate sessions for the parents together and for the child alone if the child is motivated. The results with this approach have been found to be less satisfactory. The parents tend to go through the motions of therapy without engaging the problem, expecting the therapy with the child to change the problem.

Another technique has been used for more than ten years with only minor changes: The parents begin therapy with the premise that this is a family problem, that the total family can change if the parents change, and that the family therapy will be directed to the parents without involving the child. This approach puts the responsibility for change on the parents, relieves the child of responsibility for change, and permits the child to have an occasional session alone if he is interested. Some of the most striking changes in family psychotherapy have been in families in which the child was never involved in the family therapy. Schools and courts that had recommended psychotherapy for the child were briefly critical when they discovered that the child did not attend the sessions, but this criticism disappeared when the child's symptoms subsided, which usually occurred much sooner than with other approaches.

One of the early techniques of family group therapy encouraged the expression of feeling between family members and offered psychoanalytic interpretations to explain intrapsychic functioning in individual family members. But many families overreacted to feeling expression and suddenly terminated therapy after a few sessions. The interpretations were eagerly awaited by families as authoritative statements of fact, and families were less motivated to seek their own answers.

The plan that finally worked best came after the observation that research families changed more than therapy families. The therapist put himself in the role of a research investigator, asking the families hundreds of questions about the family system and avoiding interpretations. Those were the years when the family theory was being formulated, and there were endless questions. With this technique, the families made faster progress, stayed in therapy longer, and achieved better final results than did previous families studies. Also, they expressed feelings more spontaneously than those who had been encouraged to express feeling.

On a theoretical descriptive level, family group therapy restores emotional harmony in the undifferentiated family ego mass. Open communication and the sharing of feelings seem to spread the family problem more evenly among all family members. Family group therapy works best when the family problem is already fairly evenly distributed between marital conflict, dysfunction in a spouse, and projection to several children. It is far less effective when a major part of the problem is projected to only one area, such as serious impairment of one child. Family group therapy provides an effective short-term method of symptom relief, but it does not provide the structure for a higher level of differentiation of self.

Multiple-family group therapy. In this extension of family group therapy, members of a number of families meet together. The method has come into increased use, especially for hospitalized patients and their families and by community mental health centers. There are many variations in technique, but in the basic method any family can present its problem, and any member of any family can respond to it. Theoretically, the method permits emotional fusion between the families, which prohibits the differentiation of self, but this is essentially impossible with any method. If groups using this method continue indefinitely, permitting families to attend or not attend for long periods, they should do much to provide a wider relationship system, reasonable alleviation of symptoms, and a more comfortable life adjustment. This is a promising method for mass use with severely impaired people.

Network therapy. This method, devised by Speck in the mid-1960s, is one of the most exciting new extensions of family group therapy in recent years. Many people—relatives and friends of the designated patient—meet in the community to discuss all levels of personal problems. Both family relationships and friendships are utilized, and the method appears to include many essential elements of small-town relationship systems, in which people share problems and help each other in crisis.

Theoretically, this method probably has the highest potential of the new method in helping the community to help itself and in providing help for the masses. Practically, the method takes much energy to keep the networks motivated, it requires a full evening of the therapist's time, network members tend to go back to their urban isolation, and most therapists tend to permit the networks to dwindle to termination. Still, this method is worthy of careful research and experimentation.

Family Psychotherapy

The author's theory postulates the triangle as the molecule of any emotional system and the total emotional system as a network of interlocking triangles. The psychotherapy is directed at changing a central triangle, through which all other triangles change automatically. A central concept is the undifferentiated family ego mass. The specific therapy technique is to create a situation through which the central triangle can attain a higher level of differentiation of self. The differentiating force is opposed by emotional forces for togetherness that successfully block any move toward differentiation in any family member.

Responses to differentiation. When any family member makes a move toward differentiating a self, the family emotional system communicates a three-stage verbal and nonverbal message: (1) You are wrong. (2) Change back. (3) If you do not, these are the consequences. Generally, the messages contain a mixture of subtle sulks, hurt feelings, and angry exchanges, but some communicate all three stages in words. The differentiating one responds in two ways. The first kind of response is within self and can include almost any emotional or psychological symptom or even symptoms of physical illness. The second kind of response is to the family. A high percentage of differentiating ones merge back into the family togetherness within hours. The merger may be to allay one's own distress, or it may come in response to a family accusation of indifference or of not loving. Or the differentiating one may fight back, which is still part of the family reaction-response system. The family emotional system has an automatic response for any emotional stimulus. The differentiating one may react with silence and withdrawal, another emotional reaction to which the family has the balancing response. A family member may run away, never to return— another emotional reaction. Predictably, the member then fuses into another receptive family and duplicates old patterns in the new emotional field. This emotional complex is much deeper than superficial angry retaliation. If one can conceive of the emotional triangle in constant balancing motion, interlocked with a complex of other triangles in the family and with still others in the extended family and social network, with the balances operating within each person and between each one and all the others, it is easier to conceptualize the total system in which each is dependent on the others, and the variety of gyroscopic balancing always operates to maintain emotional equilibrium.

This therapeutic system defines an Achilles' heel of the emotional system and provides one predictable answer to breaking through the emotional barrier toward differentiation. There is one major secret: an emotional system responds to emotional stimuli. If any member can control his emotional response, it interrupts the chain reaction. The most important factors in successful differentiation are a knowledge of triangles and the ability to observe and predict the chain-reaction events in the family. This knowledge and ability provide some help in controlling one's own responses in the system. The next important factor is an ability to maintain reasonable emotional control in one's responses to the family and within self during the hours or days of the family's attack and rejection—while remaining in constant emotional contact with the family. This last point is important. Silence or withdrawal from the emotional field is a signal of emotional reaction to the others.

In broad terms, a differentiating step requires long and careful deliberation to define a life principle secure enough to become a firm belief that can be stated as such without anger or debate or attack—all of which are emotional stimuli. The life energy that goes into defining a principle for self goes in a self-determined direction, which detracts from the former energy devoted to the system, especially to the important other. When this self-determined position is presented, the system reacts emotionally to win back the differentiating one into the togetherness. The family uses any mechanism to achieve this. There are calm arguments to favor the rightness of togetherness, fervent pleading, accusations, solicitousness, and threats of the consequences in terms of hurt to the family and the family's rejection if this course is continued. A high percentage of differentiating ones, fairly sure of beliefs and principles, can go into a session with the family, be won over by the logical argument of the family, and forget the principles that were carefully thought out before the session. Most people require several attempts to get through the first step.

The therapist can help the differentiating one when family pressure is great. He must do this without being perceived as against the family. At moments when the differentiating one develops such symptoms as stomach distress, the therapist may help with a comment such as: "You may have convinced your head to stand for what you believe, but you have not yet convinced your stomach."

When the differentiating one can finally control self throughout the step without fighting back or withdrawing, the family usually reaches a final showdown session with maximal attack and feelings. If the differentiating one can maintain a calm stand through this, the family anxiety suddenly subsides into a new and different level of closeness, with open appreciation and a higher regard for the differentiating one as a person. This step is usually followed by a calm period, until the other spouse or another family member starts on a similar step of defining self, which repeats the same pattern as the first. The process goes back and forth between the spouses in successive small steps. If one person in a family system can achieve a higher level of functioning and he stays in emotional contact with the others, another family member and another and another will take similar steps. This chain reaction is the basis for the principle that change in a central triangle is followed by automatic change throughout the family system. The change in all the others takes place automatically in the living situations of everyday life. Change is most rapid when the initial triangle involves the most important people in the system.

Togetherness force. In broad terms, the togetherness force defines family members as being alike in terms of important beliefs, philosophies, life principles, and feelings. It uses the personal pronoun "we" to define what "We feel or think," or it defines the self of another—"My husband thinks that . . ."—or it uses the indefinite "it" to represent common values—"It is wrong" or "It is the thing to do." In addition, emotional forces overlap and bind together, assigning positive values to thinking about the other before self, being for the other, sacrificing for others, considering others, feeling responsible for the comfort and well-being of others, and showing love and devotion and compassion for others. The togetherness force assumes responsibility for the happiness, comfort, and well-being of others; it feels guilty and asks, "What have I done to cause this?" when the other is unhappy or uncomfortable; and it blames the others for lack of happiness or for failure in self.

Differentiating force. The differentiating force place the same kind of emphasis on "I" in defining the above characteristics. It has been called the "I position," which defines principle and the taking of action in terms such as, "This is what I think or feel or stand for" and "This is what I will do or not do." This is the responsible "I", which assumes responsibility for one's own happiness and comfort and well-being. It avoids thinking that tends to blame one's own unhappiness, discomfort, or failure on the other. The responsible "I" also avoids the posture of the irresponsible or narcissistic "I", which makes demands on others with "I want or deserve" or "This is my right or my privilege."

Case History

The husband and wife had a sufficient level of pseudo-self to illustrate a fairly intense level of fusion and togetherness early in the marriage, and they also had sufficient solid self to motivate them to go beyond symptom relief in family psychotherapy. Many families with this much initial impairment either stop therapy when the symptoms subside or work at differentiation without the success that was achieved here.

The husband and wife, each thirty years old, had been married at twenty-two, when he began his career in accounting. She was the younger of two daughters. Relationships with her family, living in the same city, had been formal and pleasant. He was the oldest of three, with a younger brother and sister. His family lived 200 miles away. The husband and wife had two children, a son of five and a daughter of three, who were minimally involved in the family problem.

There had been an increasing level of turmoil in the marriage for five years, with moderate dysfunction in the wife. Their selfs were completely invested in each other from the time of marriage until after their first child was born, some three years after the marriage. They had close agreement on most life issues and principles, the agreement achieved by the adaptiveness of the wife, who blindly accepted her husband's operating beliefs and who did not seriously think about such issues. The self of each was highly invested in the happiness, comfort, and well-being of the others. As with most such marital fusions, happiness was stated as their primary goal in life.

More differentiated spouses state their primary goals in terms of the most important individual life goals. When each is in a satisfying pursuit of individual goals, happiness usually evolves as a dividend. As a result of seeing families with varying levels of differentiation and varying goals, the author believes that happiness as a primary goal is unattainable.

The two spouses in this clinical example achieved a near-perfect state of happiness and nirvana-like marital bliss early in the marriage. Their lives were financially secure, there were no traumatic events in their extended families, and they managed to keep the emotional system between them in almost perfect equilibrium. An excellent sexual adjustment was added evidence of the calm emotional equilibrium.

They paid close attention to expressions of what the other liked and disliked, and each attempted to provide what the other liked. The husband, for example, would make a mental note about the wife's preference in color and about items she would like, and at the first opportunity he would buy her a present that fitted her wishes. The wife matched the husband's reactions and listened for his comments at dinner to determine his food preferences and dislikes. She spent much time preparing the food he liked. She made note of his comments about women's hair styles and clothing in an effort to wear her hair and dress to please her husband. This pattern of being, acting, and doing for the other included innumerable items in their relationship. The pattern was most pervasive in the wife, who was the most adaptive in acting on what she knew or assumed to be her husband's wishes.

Later, in family psychotherapy, she was asked to estimate her percentage of success in knowing and guessing her husband's wishes. She estimated it to be about 75 percent. Her husband estimated her percentage of success as no more than half of that figure because he was aware of her effort to please him and he acted pleased in order to please her. She was also asked what percentage of her effort went into being the kind of wife her husband wanted her to be, and what percentage went into being the kind of wife she wanted to be. She quickly responded: "More than 90 percent! No, it was about 90 percent to please him and 3 percent to please me, and the rest was in the middle."

It is amazing how people with this life orientation can quickly assign percentage figures when asked this question.

The idyllic marriage continued until the two-person system became a three-person system, and less of the wife's energy was available for her husband. The harmonious two-person system is unstable, since it does not stand the stress of others in the emotional field.

The marital adjustment was less satisfactory after the birth of the first child and even worst after the second child was born, two years later. The wife became more involved with the children, and the husband devoted more time to his work. As is predictable, the wife, the more adaptive one, began to develop symptoms of dysfunction. She fatigued easily, her mood was depressed, and she spent more time in bed, trying to rest. At first, the husband tried to function for the wife, another predictable characteristic of emotional systems in which one functions for another within the limits of reality. The husband helped with the children in the mornings and evenings, and on weekends he initiated a thorough cleaning of the house. As the husband began to father in his overfunctioning, the wife's mother became more active in trying to help with the children, and there was increasing conflict between the wife and her mother. The husband gained the outside position in this triangle. He began to work later, and he either fell asleep after dinner or went out with men friends in the evening. On weekends he went to ballgames.

The situation reached a breaking point after eight years of marriage. There was increased conflict between the wife and her mother. The wife was angry with the absent husband, who "demanded everything and gave nothing." The husband was angry with the wife, who was "so demanding no one could please her," and was bothered by her nagging, by her constant complaining, and by the dirty house.

After a series of angry arguments with threats of divorce, they sought the help of a marriage counselor, who considered the problem to be the result of a meddlesome mother-in-law, On his advice, the couple terminated contact with the wife's mother. He diagnosed the marital problem as "failure to recognize and meet the needs of the other." Then the husband and wife each made monumental efforts to be more considerate and loving toward the other, but each effort produced no more than transient relief. The wife felt, that no matter how hard she tried, her husband went back to staying away from home, and the husband felt that no amount of loving would stop the wife's nagging, to which he was very sensitive. The counselor advised more time to talk out the problem, but each effort to talk resulted in long angry outbursts. The couple terminated with the marriage counselor, considering their problem insoluble. The husband moved out to live separately and prepare for a divorce. At this time, the wife heard about family therapy and sought an appointment.

According to family systems theory, and contrary to what the counselor said, the wife's mother had relieved the problem more than she had hurt it. Her additional functioning added something to an already foundering unit and postponed the collapse. Tension within the emotional unit actually decreases when there are open relationships with more family members and friends. Rather than cutting off the relationship with the wife's mother, the spouses were encouraged to enlarge the relationship system. The tension system had increased when the wife's mother was excluded. These two people had already put maximal effort into maintaining emotional harmony within the emotional fusion, and the system had lost flexibility. Rather than encouraging each to work harder at meeting the needs of the other, which would increase the fusion, the effort went to work at being a more contained and responsible self, to meet one's own needs as much as possible and to contain as many more needs as possible, to decrease the demands on each other, to gain control over automatic responsiveness to the demands of the other, and to reduce efforts to communicate at home until they could do so without angry outbursts.

These people continued during three years of twice-a-month appointments to gain a rather good result. The first fifteen to twenty sessions went to improving the communication between them. When the conflict disappeared, they had what most would consider to be a happy, normal adjustment. The wife's appearance changed soon after hearing that the husband would really prefer her to choose her own hair style and to dress the way she wished.

A fair percentage of families terminate therapy once emotional harmony is restored. But these spouses were motivated to continue. The differentiation of selfs is a long, slow process made up of many small steps, each accompanied by controlled emotional crises. These crises are different from crises that go with emotional regression, since the involved ones continue to engage each other without threats of action such as divorce.

The husband was the first to take a step. He devoted weeks to thinking through his professional goals and future. His life energy went to individual goals rather than the previous goal of happiness. As his life energy was directed more to the responsible functioning of self, the wife pleaded, accused, attacked, and alternated over interest in sex and withdrawal of sex—all favoring a return to togetherness. He stayed fairly well on course, with only minor relapses in response to accusations that he was a terrible father, that his children were being harmed by his lack of interest, that he was not capable of a close family relationship or an adequate sexual relationship.

The process reached a breakthrough during a noisy emotional outburst from the wife in which he maintained his calm and was able to stay close. The following day the relationship was calm. The wife said: "One part of me approved of what you were doing, but somehow I had to do what I did. Even when I was most excited and angry, I was hoping you would not let that change you. I am so glad you did not give in."

There were a few weeks of calm before the wife started on a self-determined course. Then the husband was the petulant, demanding one. It was as though he had lost the gain from his previous effort. Then came another emotional breakthrough and new levels of differentiation for both. This pattern, in which one and then the other changed, continued in several definite cycles over the three years. Meanwhile, each was changing in relationship to families of origin, working through in crises similar to the crises between the spouses. Also, the husband began to find differences in his work situation that were resolved with a new and better job.

In the course of psychotherapy, the couple began to find old friends less attractive. They no longer liked the old social gatherings with gossip, the berating of other people, the intense emotional reactiveness between spouses in the group, and the bias and prejudice in those who crusaded against bias and prejudice. This reaction follows the predictable pattern of people choosing friends from among others with equivalent levels of differentiation. They found new friends with a different orientation to life while maintaining casual, pleasant, infrequent contact with the old friends.

The process of differentiation is never complete. A goal of psychotherapy is that the family members learn the nature of the problem and decide when they are ready to discontinue the formal effort. These two spouses achieved sufficient levels of differentiation for each to stand above the togetherness forces without losing self in fusions. In the marriage relationship they could stand close and function better as a team. The relationship lost the intense nirvana-like emotional ecstasy of the early marriage, but it also lost the conflict and distance of fusion. They described the final relationship this way:

"We are much less close than we were before, but we are also much closer. It is hard to describe."

Comment. This is an ideal rather than an average clinical course. The time, the situation, the extended family configuration, and the endowment and motivation of the spouses favored the rapid course. Others with less motivation, more demands, and more pressure from extended families, plus other possible variables, may spend years without developing the emotional stamina to get solidly through the first differentiation step.

Family psychotherapy with low-scale people. Some families are so low on the differentiation scale that a higher level of differentiation is beyond expectation. And some families are so fragmented that there are not enough motivated members to form a single viable triangle. In these situations the various group therapy methods directed at symptom relief and support have much more to offer than does any other kind of psychotherapy. The various group methods are used in any combination that best meets the motivation and needs of the families. A major problem in these families is a lack of motivation for any kind of psychotherapy. The new methods of network therapy and other forms of community therapy have much more potential than does further refinement of most of the present conventional types of psychotherapy.

Clinical Approaches
to Differentiation of Self

Three main clinical approaches have been the most effective in family psychotherapy in which the differentiation of self is the goal: psychotherapy with both parents or both spouses, psychotherapy with one family member, and psychotherapy with one spouse in preparation for a long-term effort with both spouses. The choice depends on the family configuration and motivation.

Family psychotherapy with both parents or both spouses. This, the most effective of all approaches, accomplishes the most in the least time. It involves the two most important people in the family and the therapist as a potential triangle.

There has been much experience with both parents and one child—one complete triangle from the family. In this therapy situation, the family emotional patterns run their repetitive circuits with little tendency to involve the therapist or to be influenced by him. When the child is removed and the therapist becomes the third side of a potential triangle, the parents attempt to use him as a triangle person for issues between them. If the therapist can remain operationally outside the emotional system between the parents while actively relating to each, the parents begin differentiating selfs from each other. This is part of a central concept about triangles: Conflict between two people will resolve automatically if both remain in emotional contact with a third person who can relate actively to both without taking sides with either. This reaction is so predictable that it can be used in other areas of the family system and in social systems. The resolution of the problems between the spouses proceeds more rapidly if the therapist has knowledge about triangles, but the concept is so accurate that resolutions between the two would probably proceed with any third person who fulfilled the requirement of emotional contact without taking sides, no matter what the subject matter for discussion, as long as discussion touched emotional issues.

There is another advantage in having both parents or both spouses present. The differentiation of a self does not take place in a vacuum. It involves the definition of self in relation to other selfs about important life issues important to self. The other spouse is one of the best other people for the introduction of important issues.

Since the goal is to modify the most important triangle in any emotional system, this approach is used with all forms of emotional illness in which it is possible to get both parents or both spouses into a working relationship with the therapist. The basic triangular pattern is the same whether symptoms eventually come to focus between the parents, as a dysfunction in one spouse (if both spouses are dysfunctional, it is a collapsed family), or in a child. There have been spectacular results in which the child is excluded from therapy responsibility and in which the symptomatic child is never seen. In several dozen families, the symptoms have focused in a college student who was never seen by the therapist. The student had no psychiatric help, and the only contact between the parents and the student was the usual contact parents have with college students. The results were characteristically excellent.

Techniques. During the first several years of family therapy, the technique of working with two spouses was changed several times. The present technique, in use more than five years, has been constantly refined and is the most effective approach found thus far. The first format placed strong emphasis on the intrapsychic process in each spouse. There was a focus on dreams and on the emotional reaction in the other spouse. In a later working format, the goal was to reach the point where either spouse could communicate to the other anything that self thought or felt about the other and anything thought or felt about self. This approach focused more on the relationship system. Considerable emphasis was placed on careful discrimination between feelings and thoughts. This was a profitable approach, but the spouses tended to overreact to the communication of feeling. In early approaches there was an emphasis on spouses talking to each other in the sessions, which resulted in emotional reactiveness without either really hearing the other. The present approach involves constant activity by the therapist, who asks questions of one spouse, defocusing feelings, while the other spouse listens. Then the questions shift to the other spouse. With this format, the spouses can hear each other, and the feeling process becomes more spontaneous.

Using the present approach, the therapist maintains the role of an interested clinical investigator with thousands of questions to ask about the details of the problem in the family. In the first interview, he asks each family member how he understands the problem. The responses are usually fumbling generalizations, and the therapist's list of questions grows instead of diminishing. He leaves the impression that, if these questions are to be answered, someone in the family will have to become a better observer. The focus is always on questions. There are no interpretations in the usual sense and only an occasional statement about past experiences with other families that might be considered an interpretation. About a fourth of the comments by the therapist are designed to detriangle the situation when a family member invokes the emotional process in a session. In the background are questions about events since the last session.

One parent usually spends much time thinking about the family problem, and the other has thought little about it. The therapist is always interested in who has been thinking, how much he has thought, what was the pattern of the thoughts, and what kinds of working conclusions came from the thinking. The therapist implies with questions that it is the family's problem to solve. He asks if they have made progress, what is blocking their progress, if they have any ideas about how to get past the block, if they have any plans to speed up progress, and many other questions of this nature.

The opening subject of a session may be left to the family, or the therapist may ask one spouse what he has in mind for this session. Once under way, the working format is to help that spouse express a clear piece of thinking, then to ask the other spouse for a response to what has been said, and back to the first spouse for a response to the second—going back and forth the entire session when possible. A clean session is one in which the therapist says nothing except to direct questions from one spouse to the other. When the first spouse makes minimal comments, the therapist asks him to elaborate and amplify his comment into a word picture to which the other can respond.

Questions range all the way from asking for very intellectual responses to asking for feeling responses, with more than 95 percent of the questions far to the intellectual end of the scale. For instance, the therapist might ask the wife: "What were you thinking while your husband was talking?" Or the question might move slightly toward feelings: "What is your reaction? What is your impression about this situation?'

When the situation is calm and the second spouse appears to have a mild emotional reaction, the question might be: "Can you give a reading on what you were feeling inside yourself the past few minutes?"

The over-all plan is to keep the sessions active with clearly expressed thoughts, always keeping questions calm and low-keyed. If a spouse—it is usually the wife—becomes tearful or shows overt feelings, the immediate goal is to get someone to thinking about the feeling rather than expressing it. The question to the wife might be: "Can you tell us the thought that ticked off the feeling?" Or to the husband: "Did you notice your wife's tears? What did you think when you saw them?"

Results with this toned-down, intellectual, conceptualizing approach in families have far surpassed results when the emphasis is on the therapeutic externalization of feelings. Family members begin to express feelings more spontaneously and openly and to do so faster than with any other approach. There are frequent exchanges similar to the following after about ten family sessions.

The wife began:
"I can't wait to come to these appointments. They are wonderful!"
The therapist asked what was so wonderful about problems. The wife said:
"I am fascinated by the way my husband thinks."
The therapist asked how she explained living with him for ten years without knowing what he thought. She finally concluded that she could listen to him and really hear what he said when he talked to

the therapist, and that had never been possible when he talked directly to her. After a year of rather good progress, the husband was explaining the progress on his learning what went on in his wife. He had been in the dark for twenty years, and it was good to finally know the other side of what had been going on.

Some version of this development occurs in a high percentage of families. One wife watched her husband with intense interest while he talked. When asked what she thought when she looked at him like that, she said:

"I am liking him more every time I hear him talk. I never knew he thought like that."

Most spouses are caught in feeling worlds in which they react and respond to the feeling complex in the other, without ever really knowing the other. Most spouses probably have the most open relationships in their adult lives during the courtship. After marriage, each quickly begins to learn the subjects that make the other anxious. To avoid the discomfort in self when the other is anxious, each avoids anxious issues, and an increasing number of subjects become taboo for discussion in the marriage. This breakdown in communication is present to some degree in most marriages.

Experience with various psychotherapy approaches is consistent with the concept of an intellectual system so interwoven with the submerged in the feeling system that primary attention to expression of feeling increases the fusion and delays or blocks forces toward differentiation. The present psychotherapy approach, which is directed at distinguishing between intellect and feeling, and at verbalization of intellectual ideas and thoughts in the presence of the other spouse, is the most efficient method thus far found for the rapid establishment of communication between spouses. The opening of communication is accompanied by positive reactions of the spouses to each other.

The communication of intellectual thoughts and ideas also sets the stage for beginning differentiation of self. Each spouse begins to know the other and to know self in a way that was not possible before, and to become aware of differences in thinking and acting and being. A line of demarcation begins developing between the spouses as they clarify the beliefs and principles that differ one from the other. The point at which one begins to take action stands based on principles and beliefs is the point where they encounter the emotional reactions that go with the steps in differentiation of self. The emotion that accompanies differentiation is contained within the twosome, it is cohesive rather than disruptive, and it is followed by a new level of more mature togetherness.

Special attention goes to defining the details of a system of minor-appearing stimuli that trigger intense emotional responses in the other spouse. Both the stimulus and the response operate more out of awareness than in awareness. There are hundreds and perhaps thousands of these stimuli in any intense emotional interdependence. The responses are more numerous, more intense, and more life-influencing in people with intense emotional fusions and are correspondingly less so in people with better levels of differentiation. The goal is to define the stimulus-response system in a step by step sequence to help spouses gain some control over it.

Some responses are unpleasant. Examples are feelings of revulsion in response to habits and mannerisms in the other, reactions in which one's flesh crawls, and jarring emotional responses to sensory stimuli. An equal number of responses range from mildly to hurtfully pleasurable. For example, a wife felt strong sexual attraction at a look of helplessness on her husband's face. The stimuli may involve any of the five senses. There surely must be responses in which one kills in response to the stimulus.

Most of the stimulus-response situations in a marriage are out of conscious intellectual awareness, but they are an intimate part of an automatic relationship system, and they profoundly affect the relationship. The following is an example of a stimulus-response reaction that was out of awareness.

In a conflictual marriage, the husband would slug his wife with his fist in response to a trigger stimulus. Several efforts to discover the stimulus failed. The physical violence usually occurred in a flooded emotional field, and there appeared to be no specific stimulus. Then, in a situation without words, he hit her in response to "that look of hatred in her eyes." That was the last time he hit her. He gained some control by looking away in periods of critical emotional tension, and she gained some control over the looks.

Other common types of stimuli are "that cold icy stare," "that tone of voice," and "that sneer of contempt." The goal in working with spouses is to isolate and define several of the more prominent stimulus-response mechanisms and to teach the spouses to be observers. Knowledge that the mechanism exists gives them some control, and any additional conscious control over the reactiveness may add up to enough emotional control to facilitate a step toward differentiation.

Each therapist must define his own way of remaining relatively free of the intense emotional field between the spouses while he helps each spouse in turn to express a piece of thinking for the other spouse. The following is a brief description of the author's way of doing this.

Though the spouses and therapist may be sitting so close that their knees almost touch, as occasionally happens in demonstration and videotaped interviews, the goal is to back up emotionally to the point where the spouses are sufficiently distant to watch the ebb and flow of the emotional process between them while always thinking family systems. The technique is similar to changing from a high-power to a low-power lens while still the same distance from the subject. The therapist's goal is to focus on the chain reaction between the two spouses or on the process or on the flow of events between the spouses and to keep self out of the flow.

The human phenomenon is serious and tragic, but, at the very same time, there is a comical or humorous aspect to most serious situations. If the therapist is too close to the family, he can become entangled in the seriousness. If he is too distant, he is not in effective contact. The right emotional distance for the author is a point between seriousness and humor, where he can shift either way to facilitate the process in the family. This is part of the basic principle: The emotional problem between two people will resolve automatically if they remain in contact with a third person who can remain free of the emotional field between the two while actively relating to each.

The spouses predictably use triangling moves to involve the therapist in the emotional process between he two. Triangling moves are more frequent when tension in the twosome is high. The therapeutic principle is to keep tension low. Tension can build up as one spouse tells a story with emotional overtones. The therapist is extremely vulnerable to becoming part of the triangle when he listens to the content of such a story. Focusing on process rather than on content helps the therapist keep his perspective. If the spouse continues emotional involvement in the story, a reversal or comment that focuses on the opposite side of the issue or that picks up the humorous side of the situation can decompress the mounting tension.

A wife was becoming more and more emotionally involved in describing her nagging, meddlesome mother. There were several valid opposite sides to this image, but the therapist chose a reversal that effectively decompressed the tension. He asked:

How do you account for your lack of appreciation for your mother's life-long effort to make you turn out right?

The spouses laughed, and the tension was lowered.

No one can teach a therapist what to do or say in such situations. If he is sufficiently distant to see the process and to see the humorous side, he will automatically make an effective comment. If the therapist is already emotionally involved, any effort to reverse the emotional process will be heard as sarcastic and mean.

One of the common examples of mounting tension occurs when one spouse interrupts the conversation between the other spouse and the therapist, ignores the therapist, and emotionally rebuts the first spouse directly. If their talk continues for many exchanges, the locked emotional responsiveness between the spouses increases while the silent and involved therapist watches. The therapeutic goal is to maintain the structure of having each spouse talk to the therapist and to increase the calm intellectual questions to a level that excludes the other spouse. The percentage of success with conflictual spouses has been higher with this approach than with any other approach thus far tried.

One of the therapist's other functions in this method of family psychotherapy is to continually demonstrate the taking of the "I" position. When one member of a family can calmly state his own beliefs and convictions and can take action based on his convictions without criticism of the beliefs of others and without becoming involved in emotional debate, then other family members start the same process of becoming more sure of self and more accepting of the beliefs of others. When the therapist can find occasions to define his own beliefs and principles in the course of the psychotherapy, the spouses begin to do the same in relation to each other.

There are numerous detailed techniques in this method of family psychotherapy with both spouses. Most involve shifting from individual dynamics to systems thinking and avoiding emotional fusion into the family emotional system. When the therapy loses its orderly structure, the problem is usually caused by a lapse back into individual dynamics or by the therapist's becoming fused into the family emotional system. Getting beyond the vestiges of individual dynamics requires long disciplined work by the therapist. When he begins to think in terms of individual dynamics, he is vulnerable to taking sides in the family emotional process.

A good example of the differences between individual theory and systems theory is illustrated by sexual disharmony. Individual theory has well-defined postulations about impotence in the male and frigidity in the female. Individual psychotherapy has well-defined techniques for examining the dynamics in the context of the transference. Family systems theory sees sexual inadequacy in the male as occurring in the man whose pseudo-self fuses into the pseudo-self of his wife in close emotional relationships and sees frigidity as occurring in the wife whose self fuses into her husband's self. Systems theory sees the sexual disharmony as part of the relationship between the spouses. When the therapist continually thinks of sexual disharmony as a symptom of the relationship, he is much less likely to think in terms of individual dynamics, to become entangled in the family emotional system, and to work toward defining the problem in only one family member. Sexual symptoms resolve much faster when viewed as a relationship problem than when viewed as a crystallized problem in one family member.

The same pattern applies to the entire spectrum of emotional symptoms that tend to become fixed in one family member. For instance, when one spouse has a drinking problem, system thinking focuses on the disfunction of that spouse in relation to the family rather than on the individual dynamics. Among the most difficult symptoms to view in a family systems context are serious physical illnesses, such as asthma and ulcerative colitis, in which flare-ups of the illness occur in emotional response to the family emotional system. The therapeutic response is more rapid if the physical illness is regarded as another type of dysfunction in the family system, which avoids glib formulations about individual dynamics. It is easy to lose the total family perspective when initial attention goes to dynamics in one family member. The individual dynamics can be considered much later.

Finally, there is a teaching aspect in family psychotherapy. The therapist communicates important principles of systems theory and makes indirect suggestions about directions the family may find profitable in resolving problems. In order to remain outside the family emotional field, the therapist must make sure that these communications are not perceived by the family as telling them what to do or as taking sides in the controversy between the spouses. When there is tension in the family, the spouses routinely hear the therapist's communication differently. They often debate the issue at home and then return to ask the therapist to clarify his statement. At that point the therapist's immediate goal is to detriangle himself from involvement in the family emotional system rather than to clarify his statement, which would only involve him more deeply in the emotional system. Optimally, the teaching communications come when the family tension system is low and they are presented in a way that does not involve the therapist in the family emotional system.

Many comments are made from the "I" position, in which the therapist presents his views, beliefs, and operating principles in such a way that they can be accepted or rejected by the family. The therapist has much knowledge that can help the family find solutions. The goal is to find a neutral way to present the knowledge. The following framework has been successful in most situations:

I have some experience from work with other families that you may find helpful in planning a course of action. If any of the ideas make sense and if you can incorporate and use them as your own ideas, there is a fair chance your effort will succeed. If the ideas do not make sense, then you are in the position of using someone else's ideas, and the chances of failure are very high.

The suggestions about working out relationships in the extended family are presented in the same way—as detailed as necessary to make a point but with freedom and deliberation in acceptance of the viewpoint.

Multiple-Family Therapy. The method and techniques of family therapy with a single family—both spouses—were adapted for use with a number of families in the mid-1960s. Early experiences with multiple-family group therapy and later experiences with single families were incorporated into the method.

The goal was to keep each family unit a contained triangle, to work on the emotional process between the spouses, and to avoid emotional communication between families. From past experience, the theorists believed that the emotional exchange between families encouraged a fusion of all the families into a large undifferentiated ego mass, which made if difficult to focus on details within a single family and made the differentiation process difficult in any family. The theorists believed that each family could learn much from the close observation of other families and that the effects of teaching communications might be cumulative and save time.

Families were chosen who did not know each other, and they were asked not to have social contact with each other outside the sessions. The therapist, one side of a potential triangle with each family, approached each family the same as he would if working with only that family while the other families observed. Then the process was repeated with each of the other families. Any family could talk to the therapist about another family but they could not talk directly to the other family.

This method of multiple-family therapy has been so successful in keeping the emotional process contained within each family, in facilitating differentiation in each family, and in bringing profits from observational exposure to other families that the author has converted much of his own practice to this method, and the method has been adopted widely by others. The average family progresses about one and a half times faster than similar families do in single-family therapy. Family members say it is easier to see one's own problem when it is present in another family than when the problem involves self. Families learn from others in their search for solutions to problems.

The optimal number of families is three to five for each multiple-family group. With only two families, the group tends toward emotional fusion between the families, which requires much therapeutic agility to control. Having more than five families in a group reduces the amount of the time available for each family. Families become restless and inattentive in sessions of more than two hours. The most effective format is one in which the available time is divided equally between the families at each session. Including families with varying levels of problems in the same group is workable, but families have done best with others who have the same kind of problems. Families in multiple-family therapy have done as well on infrequent appointments as single families have on weekly appointments. The average multiple-family group is seen every two weeks, but some are on monthly schedules, which reduces the number of sessions in the total course of family therapy.

Family psychotherapy with one family member. This is a teaching-supervising method throughout the entire course. The first several sessions are for teaching one motivated family member about the functioning of family systems. The next sessions are devoted to formulations about the part the family member plays in his own family. The family member is encouraged to visit his family as often as possible to observe, to check the accuracy of previous formulations, and to test his own ability to relate within his family. Later appointments are devoted to supervising the family member's effort with his own family. The family member is encouraged to do a multigenerational study of his own family. Supervisory sessions may be as often as every two weeks or as infrequent as every few months, depending on the number of visits with his family and the amount of work done between appointments.

This method involves learning about triangles, keeping an active emtoional relationship with important members of the family, and developing an ability to control emotional reactiveness and to stay emotional relationship with important members of the family, and for the family member is to stay emotionally outside the triangles, just as was described for the therapist in family psychotherapy with both spouses.

The initial sessions with the family member are devoted to didactic teaching about triangles and the functioning of emotional systems. The following sessions are devoted to presenting postulations about the part the family member plays in his own family, instructions about developing the ability to observe his family and himself, and suggestions about ways to stay in emotional contact with the family without taking polarized sides on any issue. Once the effort is under way, the sessions are devoted to supervision of the family member's effort. He reports his experiences with his family and any new observations that may lead to new postulations, and the therapist suggests new techniques that might be tried. The details of the instruction depend on whether it is for a short-term goal or for a long-term definitive effort. The system of triangles is so predictable that any failure to achieve a result can be considered a failure in emotional control rather than an error in the system.

This approach is often used for one motivated spouse when the other spouse is antagonistic to family psychotherapy. Since this is a short-term goal, the instruction is not very detailed. An immediate goal is to reduce the emotional reactiveness to the point where the antagonistic spouse is willing to participate in the family psychotherapy. Understanding the family with systems concepts helps to reduce the diagnosing and the blaming of the other. A little knowledge about broad principles of emotional systems can help the motivated one reach a calmer and more contained level of functioning. For instance, family members are dependent on other family members to fulfill certain functions. When the functioning of one fails, the failure impairs the functioning of others. The system tends to blame the one who failed and to exert pressure on that one to resume functioning.

The effort to change the other is best illustrated in a marital interdependency in which the functioning of self depends on the other to meet a variety of needs. When the other's functioning fails, that failure results in distress and impairment in self. The other is often seen as the cause of the problem and is blamed for the problem in self. The effort to change the other can range from a direct assault to subtle efforts, such as giving more love as an inducement to change. In mild states of distress, this effort to change the other can be successful within narrow limits, but in chronic states in which there is no adaptive flexibility in the system, the effort to change the other predictably makes the situation worse. If the motivated one can know intellectually that the effort to change the other is one of the basic forces that creates and intensifies triangles and that this effort is doomed to failure by basic characteristics of emotional systems, the motivated one can then create a formula for reducing the tension. Any effort toward assuming responsibility for one's own distress, toward containing one's own needs a little better, toward blaming the other less, or toward controlling one's emotional responsiveness to the other is a step toward reduction in family tension.

Family psychotherapy with one parent is used occasionally to control explosive behavior problems in a teenage offspring. These are rare situations when control of the acting-out child is sufficiently critical to take precedence over long-term work with both parents. In most situations the symptoms in the child subside when the parents are productively working on their relationship. However, when the primary focus is the child, one parent can gain control much more rapidly than can both parents working together. Parents always disagree on the management of such a child and usually alternate between permissiveness and angry retaliatory punitiveness.

Parents can maintain complete order in their homes by always controlling self and never punishing or controlling the child or doing anything to the child. To act in this way, the motivated parent must carefully define his responsibility for self in his family, the operating rules and principles within the area of his responsibility, and what he will and will not do in relation to those who go beyond the rules. The rules, like laws, are never made in anger, nor are they personalized to deal with a single situation. Those who live under their jurisdiction have a choice of living within the rule or of risking automatic consequences, which have been previously defined.

The important principle is that the parent calmly defines self and rules and consequences, communicates them when he is sure of them, and is prepared to stand on the consequences of broken rules if need be. Such a system by a calm parent who does not act in anger can bring chaotic behavior problems under control rather quickly, provided the other parent does not interfere. If the family situation is chaotic enough, the other parent will not interfere until after the critical situation is past. Ultimately, the motivated parent has to deal with the disagreements with the other parent, which invokes a triangle between parents and child.

Family psychotherapy with one family member is used frequently with young, single, self-supporting adult children. This approach is best described as coaching the young adult in differentiating a self from his family of origin. The total process continues about the same length of time that would be required for intensive individual psychotherapy, but the total number of appointments is a fraction of the number required for individual psychotherapy, and the results are far-reaching.

Motivation for this kind of effort is highest in oldest sons and daughters and in others who feel a responsibility for family problems and who still maintain reasonable contact with their families. This approach has never been successful with a young adult still financially dependent on his family. They have the aptitude for quickly understanding family emotional systems, but they lack the courage to risk family displeasure in the differentiation process. The effort takes longer in younger children, who are more inclined to expect the environment to change for them and who are slower to grasp the idea that they have the capacity to change family patterns if they so desire.

Primary emphasis goes to differentiating a self in the triangle of self and both parents, but, because of the interlocking of triangles, it is necessary to include a number of peripheral family members in the effort. If the family member can work toward an open relationship system with every member of his extended family system, the result is highly rewarding. Through such a differentiating process in self, change can occur throughout the entire family system if the family can continue to maintain emotional contact with the various members without taking sides in any of the emotional issues that develop. The process goes better if the family of origin lives a sufficient distance to be outside the immediate emotional field but sufficiently close for frequent visits. The differentiating process may be slowed if parents live in the same town and are in daily contact by telephone or in person. Results have been good with some extended families who live a thousand or more miles away, provided the members make a few personal visits a year and maintain an active emotional interchange through letters and telephone calls.

The basic process for differentiating a self from a family of origin involves establishing a person-to-person relationship with each parent. In the extended family this process is equivalent to establishing personal communication between two spouses. The person-to-person relationship is one in which it is possible to talk about self as a person to the parent as a person. Most people are not capable of more than a few minutes of a person-to-person relationship before one becomes anxious, goes silent or begins to talk about external things, or invokes a triangle and talks about a third person who is absent. Many people have relatively free-talking relationships with one parent and relatively formal and distant relationships with the other parent. Achieving a person-to-person relationship with either parent is a major undertaking, but, if the differentiating person is aware that the result is highly desirable and of great potential benefit to self, he has a long-term assignment at which he can work constantly in his own way. The average young adult who applies self to this effort is able to get a rather good result in about three years with a total of fifty to seventy-five psychotherapy hours.

Variations of this approach are possible when one or both parents are dead. But then the young adult needs to make more of an effort to relate to a spectrum of other important extended-family members.

A surprising extension of family therapy with one family member has evolved during the past few years. During the past decade, family psychotherapy for family therapists and their spouses has come to replace psychoanalysis as a method for resolving emotional problems in the therapist. Now there has been an experience with a group of young therapists who devoted their primary energy to defining a self in their families of origin. They had more motiviation than average for this effort. Supervision was provided as part of the training program. These young therapists began to develop unusual ability in their clinical work. They were unusually versatile in relating freely to all family members without emotional involvement with the families. After a year or two, they found that they had also changed in relation to their wives and children. They progressed as much in their nuclear families as had other trainees who had been seen in family psychotherapy with their spouses for the same length of time. This development in a number of trainees at the same time was a pleasant surprise. The approach is now the subject of study in other training programs with larger groups of trainees.

This experience suggests that psychotherapy, as it has been known in the past, may one day be considered superfluous for those motivated for the effort in the extended family. The course here suggests that the less intense emotional process in parental families made it easier to observe and define patterns and to take appropriate action stands more quickly than is possible with a spouse, in whom emotional needs are more intimately interwoven. Differentiation of self gains made in peripheral emotional systems may be automatically manifested in the nuclear family.

Family psychotherapy with one spouse in preparation for a long-term effort with both spouses. In many families, one spouse is too antagonistic to participate in family psychotherapy. In this situation, the motivated spouse is seen alone until the other spouse is willing to become part of the long-term effort.

This approach is included as a separate method because it provides a technique of family psychotherapy for many people who ordinarily would have no option except individual psychotherapy. Many of these people have already had long periods of individual psychotherapy with little benefit.

The initial phase of the family therapy is similar to that used in family psychotherapy with a single family member. The goal is to teach the family member about the functioning of emotional systems, to discover the part that self plays in the system and especially toward the other spouse, and to modify the system by controlling the part that self plays. If the motivated spouse is successful in toning down emotional reactiveness, the antagonistic spouse often asks to participate in the sessions, after which the method is identical to that already described for both spouses.

Progress with this method depends on the therapist's remaining outside the emotional system when working with one spouse and avoiding the use of sessions for emotional support. This method has been used successfully with a spectrum of difficult disruptive families, including a number in which the spouses have lived separately for long periods. More than half of the antagonistic spouses have entered family therapy within periods of a few months to a year or so.

Clinical Triangle Patterns

The following are clinical examples of predictable change when one motivated family member is finally able to control his emotional responsiveness.

1. An explosive father developed the persistent pattern of hitting a preadolescent son for poor table manners at dinner. The mother routinely intervened in the child's behalf, after which the conflict would continue between the parents. After months of coaching, the mother was finally able to control her feelings sufficiently to deal adequately with the pattern.

The therapist told them that a child is capable of dealing with a single parent but that he is forced to extreme measures in dealing with both at the same time. The son played his part in this pattern. He knew well the things that would trigger the father's anger and the things that would please the father, and he had some kind of choice about whether or not he angered the father. If the mother really had confidence that the son could manage the father alone, if she communicated this confidence to the son ahead of time, and if she controlled her sympathy for the son, good things would predictably happen. But unless the mother communicated her intention before taking action, the father and son could misinterpret her silence and escalate the conflict to force her to intervene.

One afternoon the mother told the son of her intentions: if he angered the father, he would have to find his own way to deal with the father. The dinner table conflict started earlier than usual that evening. The mother had difficulty in controlling her reactiveness, but she did not take action. One time she left the room briefly to regain her emotional composure. The son handled his own conflict with the father. When she put the son to bed later in the evening, he said, "Thanks, Mom, for what you did tonight." That was the last dinner table conflict between father and son.

2. Another mother, in frequent verbal and physical conflict with her children, was a strong advocate of the notion that it was the father's responsibility to maintain discipline and punish the children. Through the years he was confronted with repeating conflictual situations between the mother and a child. He followed the predictable triangle

pattern of trying to calm the conflictual twosome, but there was no satisfactory solution. The mother could move him toward punishment by saying that he was a poor father or that he was not a man. The pattern became more intense as the children grew larger than the mother, and there were physical fights between the mother and a child when the father was present.

After the therapist talked about triangles and the ability of either parent to manage his relationship with the children, the father decided to stay out of the conflict, but his feelings still participated, and the conflict escalated until he was forced to intervene. As he gained more control, he told the mother that he was going to manage his own relationships with the children and leave her to settle the conflicts she started. In the midst of the next fight, he was able to chuckle slightly at the sequence of events, and he asked the child, "Are you going to let your mother push you around?" The mother ran to the bedroom, slammed the door, and stayed there for an hour. That was the last of the serious conflictual scenes. The father had found a way to stay detached from the mother-child conflict. Thereafter, the mother-child conflicts never went beyond mild words.

3. Another woman, an only child, was close to her mother and negative and distant with her father. As a child, she and her mother had long confidential talks, in which the mother communicated details about the father's many faults. The woman grew up accepting her mother's views of the family situation. When the woman married and left home, she moved far away, and her return visits were brief and infrequent.

During family therapy the woman found it difficult to develop an open relationship with her father. It became easier when she began to realize that her father was not as terrible as she had believed. Her goal was to detach herself from the emotional dependence on her mother and to foster a situation in which the parents could fulfill the needs of each other.

The breakthrough came when she no longer wished to keep her mother's secrets. In the next meeting with her father she said:

"Daddy, do you know what Mother told me about you? I wonder why she tells me these things instead of telling you?"

A new flexibility developed in the family emotional system. Later, the father attempted to tell the woman some stories about the mother, which she reported to the mother, the woman recovered much self from the fixed parental triangle in which she grew up. The change in her parental family was only a side dividend of changes in other areas in her life. She developed an open relationship with each parent; visits with her parents were so pleasurable that they visited often, and her parents were closer than they had ever been.

Conclusion

The family movement will play an increasingly important role as psychiatry goes into the 1970s. Family psychiatry has changed rapidly in the fifteen years since the family movement suddenly evolved as a recognized entity. There is evidence that therapists have hardly scratched the surface of its potential. The movement may eventually have more to offer as a different way of thinking about the human phenomenon than as a therapeutic method.

Chapter 11

Principles and Techniques
of Multiple Family Therapy

The method of multiple family therapy described here was developed as part of a clinical research study at Georgetown University Medical Center. The method, already successfully used by an increasing number of family therapists for a wide range of clinical problems, takes less of the therapist's time than more conventional methods, and is quite different from other methods of multiple family therapy. It was developed as an extension of my own theoretical-therapeutic system, and combines clinical observations from family research with developments in family systems theory and practice. First I shall deal with observations from the early family research which are important to the rationale for this method. Then I shall review some important changes in theory and therapy after the original research; describe my method of family psychotherapy for a single family; and finally deal with principles and techniques involved in adapting this method for use with multiple families.

Background Observations

Details about the early family research have been presented in other papers (Bowen 1960, 1961), describing a five-year research project in which entire families lived on the research ward with their schizophrenic son or daughter for periods as long as thirty months. The number of families living in at any one time varied from three to five. This was determined by the size of the families and available room space. The project ran five years. The first year the focus was on mothers and patients. Each mother and each patient had individual psychotherapy. During that year the research hypothesis was modified to consider schizophrenia a process that involved the entire family.

At the beginning of the second year, fathers were required to live on the ward with the families, and "family psychotherapy" was started. All available family members attended the psychotherapy sessions. One goal in the use of the term "family psychotherapy" was to emphasize and complement the companion theoretical concept which considered "the family as the unit of illness." During the first year, with parents and patients in individual psychotherapy with separate therapists, family problems were diffuse and compartmentalized, and difficult to define for research or therapy. After that, all individual psychotherapy was discontinued and family psychotherapy became the only treatment modality.

The initial family sessions were for the families only, but there were major emotional problems in every segment of the operation. In addition there was an over-all policy toward openness and moving meetings from behind closed doors into the open. Very soon the daily psychotherapy meetings included all the members of the families and all available staff members. The four therapists functioned as co-therapists, and focused on any issue whether it be between members of the same family, between one family and another, between staff members and the group of families, or between individual staff members. In the effort to achieve a completely open communication system, family members were free to read any records written about them and to attend any clinical, administrative, or research meeting. Initially there was a large family attendance, but the families did not have the time or the interest to continue the meetings, or to consistently send family delegates to the more important meetings. What was important was that the system was open and they could attend if they wished.

In retrospect, those early meetings would more accurately be called "multiple family-therapeutic milieu network therapy." The meetings were so important to the total operation that the project might not have survived those early months without the open communication policy and the open meetings for the entire group. The basic therapeutic method employed during that period was group therapy, although the meetings were called "family psychotherapy" to emphasice the primary focus on the family, and to establish a clear delineation between this and conventional group therapy. The meetings resulted in a kind of therapeutic honeymoon for the families, and enthusiasm in the staff. The conversion of the small closed system operation into an open system probably accounted for much of this. The symptoms decreased in most of the families, and there were fairly well sustained periods of enthusiasm and near exhilaration in some.

The honeymoon ended after about a year, and the family psychotherapy meetings became repetitive and less productive. The therapists had specific issues for focus within the families, but all too often the focus was lost in a group therapy type of feeling exchange between family members and the ward staff. The first major change in the structure of the meetings came when members of the ward staff attended the sessions as silent observers rather than participants. There were well-established administrative policies for dealing with such issues, and family members could no longer use the meetings to externalize intrafamily anxiety into conflict with the ward staff. This was the beginning of a period in which the active participants consisted of all the members of the families and four therapists. Anyone could speak at any time. This is not a place to evaluate co-therapists or multiple therapists, but in addition to the positive values, there were negative aspects. One therapist might start to define a specific point, and before he could finish, another therapist could interrupt and focus on a completely different issue. More and more time was spent on therapists trying to define issues between themselves. Most important, the families began to use this channel for externalizing intrafamily anxiety into differences between the therapists.

Eventually the therapists' roles were more clearly defined, and the structure of the meetings was changed so that a single therapist was in charge of each session. The therapist in charge could ask another therapist for an opinion, or another therapist could intervene if he had a compelling reason; but ordinarily the therapist in charge directed that session with little participation from the other therapists. This resulted in a structure in which the active participants consisted of all the members of all the families and the therapist who was designated to run the meeting for that day. Any member of any family could speak at any time. Just as the therapist was successfully working toward a definition of an issue in one family, some anxious member from another family would interrupt and change the subject to another issue in another family. It was extremely difficult to keep the issue in a single family in focus, when any member of another family could interrupt the process.

Finally, during the last year of the research project, there was the most important change in the structure of the family psychotherapy sessions.

Each family session was designated for a single family, while the other families attended as silent auditors. For the first time in the entire course of the research project, it was possible to work through to clearly define intrafamily emotional issues. From the standpoint of the families, they made much more progress in this period than any other. Some families said they often obtained more benefit from auditing, when they were free to listen and to really "hear," than when they spent time preparing their next comment. The therapy-research staff members considered this year their most productive. This was the final structure of the family psychotherapy sessions when the formal research was terminated in 1959.

Changes in Theory and
Therapy After the Early Research

The significant evolutionary changes in the development of this theoretical-therapeutic system have been presented in reasonable detail in other papers (Bowen 1965, 1966, 1971). One of the main efforts over the years has been to further define the systems concepts, and to replace conventional theory with new systems concepts.

A major change in practice occurred early in 1960, when the problem child for whom the parents had originally sought psychiatric help was excluded from ongoing family psychotherapy sessions with the parents. This was the result of mediocre results with some twenty-five of these children in the period between about 1957 and 1960. Though the formal research study from 1954-1959 had been devoted exclusively to families with a severely impaired schizophrenic son or daughter, there was a simultaneous clinical operation in progress for a wide range of less severe emotional problems. The children in this group varied in age from preadolescent to midteen years, and had been referred by the Juvenile Court, or by the school, for behavior problems or academic difficulty. Both of the parents and the child were routinely seen together at weekly intervals. In the sessions the parents would focus so much on details about the child's problem that it was difficult to maintain sufficient focus on the parental relationship to foster change in the parents. The average "good" result with these families was one in which they would attend the sessions about a year and then terminate at a point when the child's symptoms had decreased, the mother's "domination" had subsided, and the father's "passivity" had decreased. The family would leave with glowing praise about the success of the therapy, while I considered them to have attained little or none of the basic change of which they were capable.

Rather than continue this mediocre operation, I began to see the parents alone in the first interview to state my conviction that the basic problem lay in the relationship between the parents, and if the parents could define and modify their relationship, the children's problems would automatically disappear. A high percentage of parents readily accepted this working premise. Most of these family therapy sessions were lively and profitable instead of dull and nonproductive as they had been with the child present; most of the children became free of symptoms, so that the average "bad" result was better than the "good" results with the former approach. Since 1960 I have not seen children as part of family psychotherapy sessions, although I occasionally see the children for special reasons.

In the early 1960s I began defining my theoretical concept of "triangles," which provides a flexible and predictable way to conceptualize and modify the family emotional system. This concept has been described in detail in other papers (1966, 1971). The triangle is the basic building block of an emotional system. A system that includes four or more people consists of a series of interlocking triangles. The characteristics of all triangles are the same, whether in a family system, an emotional system at work, a social system, or elsewhere. A triangle is in constant motion with moves that operate automatically like emotional reflexes, and that are so predictable that one can precisely predict the next move in the system. If one can modify the functioning of a single triangle in an emotional system, and the members of that triangle stay in emotional contact with the larger system, the whole system is modified. Gross behavior in an emotional system may appear too random and strange to describe or classify; but beneath the gross behavior is the constant, predictable microfunctioning of triangles.

On a practical level, there are two major ways to modify the functioning of a triangle. One way is to put two people from a familiar emotional system into contact with a third person who knows and understands triangles, and who does not play into the emotional moves of the familiar twosome. If the third person can continue to stay in contact with the twosome without playing the familiar game of the twosome, the functioning in the twosome will automatically be modified

Consider the father-mother-child triangle. When these three people are together, the triangle operates automatically on its already built-in circuits. Put a stranger into the system in place of the child; after a brief time he will either become programmed into the familiar patterns of the triangle, or he will withdraw—also a predictable response to triangles. Put a family therapist with knowledge of triangles into the triangle in the place of the child. The parents will make predictable moves designed to involve the therapist into the triangle with them. If the therapist can avoid becoming "triangled," and still remain in constant emotional contact with them over a period of time, the relationship between the parents will begin to change. This is the theoretical and practical basis for much of the family psychotherapy in this theoretical-therapeutic system, in which a family is considered to consist of the two most important people in the family, together with the therapist who constitutes a potential triangle person.

Theoretically, a family system can be changed if any triangle in the family is changed, and if that triangle can stay in meaningful emotional contact with the others. Practically, the two spouses are usually the only ones who are important enough to the rest of the family and who have the motivation and dedication for this kind of an effort.

The second way to modify a triangle is through one family member. If one member of a triangle can change, the triangle will predictably change; and if one triangle can change, an entire extended family can change. Thus, an entire family can be changed through one family member, if this motivated family member has sufficient dedication and life energy to work toward his goal in spite of all obstacles. The "change" mentioned here is not some superficial change in role or posture, but is deeper and more far-reaching than the change generally associated with most therapeutic systems. An entire family can be changed through the effort of one person. This "family psychotherapy with one family member" involves teaching the motivated person the predictable characteristics of triangles and emotional systems, and then coaching and supervising his efforts as he returns to his family to better observe and learn about them, and as he gains increasing ability to control his own emotional reactiveness to his family. The basic goal has to be to change and improve self, which then secondarily affects the others. This method can be used in families in which one spouse is motivated to work on a family problem and the other is antagonistic, or with young unmarried adults.

With experience, I discovered that research families did better in psychotherapy than families seen only for psychotherapy, and since then I have worked to make every family into a research family. Subtle and important things take place when the therapist functions as a "therapist" or a healer, and the family functions passively, waiting for the therapist to work his magic. Equally subtle and important factors are involved in getting a therapist out of his healing or helping position and getting the family into position to accept responsibility for its own change.

This theoretical-therapeutic system has thus evolved through several major changes and through constant minor change and modification. It began with the relatively simple theoretical notion that the problem involves the entire family; the relatively simple therapeutic method was to get the family together to talk about it. It has arrived at a much better defined and precise systems theory, composed of several interlocking theoretical concepts and at a therapeutic system in which the therapy is usually with the two most responsible family members, or the one most responsible family member.

Family Psychotherapy With Both Spouses

Since the principles and techniques of working with families in a multiple family setting are exactly the same as working with a single family, I will first describe the process as it applies to a single family. For therapy purposes, this theoretical approach considers a "family" to be the two most responsible family members (both spouses) with the therapist as a potential triangle person.

The technique of working with both spouses has been modifed several times, especially in the early years of family practive. From about 1956 to 1960 there was strong emphasis on analyzing the intrapsychic process in each spouse in the presence of the other spouse. There was a strong focus on dreams, which provided an opportunity to analyze the process in the dreamer, and also to analyze the simultaneous emotional response in the other spouse. By 1960 the primary emphasis was on the relationship system between the spouses, with far less emphasis on the intrapsychic process in each. One goal in that period was that spouses reach the point at which each could communicate to the other anything they thought or felt about the other, or anything they thought or felt about self. The spouses were encouraged to speak directly to each other rather than to the therapist, and there was emphasis on the careful discrimination between thoughts and feelings, and the direct expression of feeling to each other. The present method started about 1962, after the triangle concept was suffiently developed to be put into clinical operation. It developed rather rapidly until about 1964, since which time there have been fewer changes in technique and more emphasis on the differentiation of self in the therapist.

With this method of family psychotherapy, the therapist has four main functions: (1) Defining and clarifying the relationship between the spouses; (2) Keeping self detriangled from the family emotional system; (3) Teaching the functioning of emotional systems; and (4) Demonstrating differentiation by taking "I position" stands during the course of the therapy.

Defining and clarifying the relationship between the spouses. To some degree, all spouses are caught in feeling worlds, in which they react and respond to the emotional complex in the other without really *knowing* the other. This exists to a significant degree in a majority of spouses, and there is a very large group in which it exists to a paralyzing degree. Most people probably have the most open relationships in their adult lives during courtship, in common-law relationships, or in other fairly intimate relationships that are not permanent. After marriage, each quickly begins to learn the subjects that make the other anxious. To avoid the discomfort in self when the other is anxious, each avoids the subjects that make the other anxious; an increasing number of subjects thus become taboo for discussion. Most spouses attempt to resolve the communication gap by "talking it out," with less than satisfactory results. All too often the attempt to communicate only stirs up emotional reactiveness and drives then farther apart. Very early in my family psychotherapy I discouraged spouses from attempting to talk more at home; and after about 1962, I stopped suggesting that they talk directly to each other in the family therapy sessions.

In this format, I control the interchange. Each spouse talks directly to me in the calmest, low-keyed, most objective possible way. In this situation, the other spouse is often able to listen and to "really hear," without reacting emotionally, for the first time in their lives together.

A typical session might go as follows. I open by asking the husband what kind of progress he has made since the last session, and ask him to give me his most objective report. If his report has reasonable content, I then turn to the wife and ask for her *thoughts* while he was talking. Early in the course of therapy, my questions are designed to elicit the intellectual process by asking for thoughts, opinions, or ideas. In other situations I ask for her response or reaction, which is a little less intellectual. Only much later in therapy, and in special situations do I ask for a reading from her subjective, inner feelings. After the wife has spoken, a question may be directed to the husband, such as, "What was going on in your thoughts while she was talking?"

There are occasional "clean" sessions, in which the therapist does nothing more than direct questions from one to the other. There are situations in which the husband's comments are too minimal for an adequate response from the wife; then I ask sufficient questions to get him to elaborate his ideas before asking the wife for her thoughts. If the wife responds with minimal comments, there are more questions to get her to elaborate before I turn to the husband again. If feelings build up and one responds emotionally and directly to the other without waiting for my questions, I increase the directness and tempo of the questions so as to return the process to me. I am always dozens of questions ahead of them. There is always a backlog of theoretical assumptions about the family about which I have questions. During sessions when there is a lull, I make notes about new areas for questions. During sessions when there is a lull, I make notes about new areas for questions. When obvious feelings are stirred up during a session, the goal is to get them *talking about* the feeling, rather than expressing it. For instance, if the wife suddenly becomes tearful, I may ask her husband if he noticed the tears; or ask him what was going on in his thoughts when he saw the tears. An over-all goal for the questions is to touch on areas known to be emotionally important for them, and to get calm, low-keyed responses.

Results of this calm, intellectual, conceptual approach with families have been much more successful than emphasizing the "therapeutic" expression of feelings. The spontaneous, free, open expression of feelings comes automatically and much faster than when therapy is directed at the feelings. One great dividend is that for the first time each spouse finally hears and knows the other. In one session, for instance, which came after about ten family sessions, the wife said she could not wait to come to the sessions because they were so wonderful. The therapist asked what was so wonderful about family problems. She answered that in the process of listening to her husband talk to the therapist, she had learned more about him than during ten years of marriage. A husband, summarizing progress after twelve monthly sessions, said the greatest value to him had been learning what went on inside his wife after having been in the dark for twenty years. Another wife, watching her husband with fixed adoration while he talked, was asked what she thought while she looked at him like that. She said she was absolutely fascinated by the way his mind worked, and that she never had any idea he thought like that.

Special attention goes to defining the system of automatic emotional responses in every marriage that operate largely out of awareness. They are so numerous that one could probably spend a lifetime and never define all of them. In general, they consist of minor emotional stimuli in one that trigger major emotional responses in the other. The response may involve any of the five senses, but most relate to visual or auditory stimuli. The stimulus may be so revulsive that the responder would do almost anything to avoid it, or so pleasurable he would work hard to elicit it. Among the negative stimuli are mannerisms, gestures, facial expressions, and tones of voice that stir jarring emotional responses in the other, or that can make the other's "flesh crawl." As one example, a husband was so attracted by, and so emotionally dependent on his wife for, a certain smile that he spent a sizable segment of his life trying to evoke it, while she was generally turned off by his efforts.

Emotional responsiveness can profoundly affect the course of a relationship. A goal in therapy is to be aware of such mechanisms, to define them in as much detail as possible, and to help the spouses become better observers in an effort to define more and more of them. Often the careful definition of the mechanism is enough to defuse it. For instance, on one conflictual marriage, the husband would slug his wife in response to a trigger stimulus. Several attempts to find the stimulus had failed. He did not hit her often, but when he did it was in the midst of noisy argument, and there appeared to be no specific stimulus. Finally, a situation without words arose when he hit her in response to "that look of hatred in her eyes." That was the last time he ever hit her. He was immensely pleased with the discovery and with his control. Thereafter when tension was high, he avoided looking at her face; she also had some control over "the look." Other stimuli that caused acting-out responsiveness have been identified as "that cold icy stare," "that sneer of contempt," and "that awful snarl in his voice." This level of emotional responsiveness in a marriage has been described as part of the emotional interdependence, and also as part of the family emotional process.

Keeping self detriangled from the family emotional system. If the therapist is to develop the capacity to stay relatively outside the family emotional system in his clinical work, it is essential that he devote a continuing effort to differentiate his own self from the emotional system of his own family, and also from the emotional system in which he works. Said in another way, it is necessary that he learn about triangles, and that he use his knowledge successfully in the emotional systems most important to him. However, there are some rules and principles that are important in the clinical situation. It is essential that he always stay focused on process, and that he defocus the content of what is being said.

It is absolutely predictable that each spouse will use mechanisms with which each is most familiar and at which each is most adept to involve the therapist in the family emotional system. The first move is usually to cause the therapist to take sides with one or the other; but the therapist is as effectively triangled when angry as he is if charmed. To judge effective emotional distance for myself even though I may be sitting physically close, as occasionally happens in videotaped interviews, I attempt to back out emotionally to the point where I can watch the ebb and flow of the emotional process while always "thinking process," and without getting caught in the flow. Furthermore, there is usually a humorous or comical side to most serious situations. If I am too close, I can get caught in the seriousness of the situation. If I am too distant, I am not effectively in contact with them. The "right" point for me is one between seriousness and humor, when I can make either a serious or a humorous response to facilitate the process in the family.

A basic principle in this theoretical-therapeutic system is that the emotional problem between two people will resolve automatically if they remain in contact with a third person who can remain free of the emotional field between them, *while actively relating to each.* It is essential for the therapist to keep talking, especially in response to a triangling move. If he has the right degree of emotional distance—emotional contact, it is almost automatic for him to say and do the right thing. If he becomes silent and cannot think of a response, he is too emotionally involved. The spouses are continually misperceiving the therapist's involvement, or lack of it, or misperceiving him to either be for or against them. Casual comments are effective messages that he is not overinvolved. A "reversal," which is a comment that focuses on the unobvious or the opposite side of an issue, or that picks up the casual or slightly humorous aspect, is a most effective way of decompressing an overserious situation. One wife, for example, became more emotionally uptight in describing her dominating, nagging mother. I made a casual comment about her lack of appreciation for her mother's lifelong effort to make her be a good daughter; the spouses laughed, the tension was decompressed, and I had communicated awareness that there was another side to the issue.

When the therapist can remain casual about such serious situations, it is usually not long before the spouses can begin to get outside themselves to a more objective view of the situanion. No one can tell a therapist what to say in such situations. If the therapist is already emotionally involved, his effort to reverse the emotional process will be heard as sarcastic and mean. Knowledge of triangles is the most effective way I know for understanding emotional systems and keeping self in meaningful emotional contact without becoming emotionally overinvolved.

Teaching the functioning of emotional systems. Some teaching or instruction is necessary with any kind of psychotherapy. With family systems theory and therapy, which explains the human phenomenon in special terms, and which utilizes intellectual concepts to guide the effort to modify emotional systems, teaching is even more necessary. There are hazards to emotional systems in talking *about* emotional systems. When family tension is moderately high, the therapist is vulnerable to being triangled into the family system if he tries to instruct or direct them away from a direction that appears unprofitable. Each spouse interprets the communication differently; then, after debating the issue at home, they return to ask the therapist for the correct interpretation. At that point the therapist's goal is to detriangle himself rather than explain, because that would involve him more deeply in the family system. Over the years I have worked out a plan which works fairly well in teaching the family about emotional systems. Communication is made in a neutral way that is not perceived as authoritative, and at a time when family anxiety is lowest. Early in therapy, when family anxiety is often high, instructional communications are put in terms of the "I position," which is explained below. Later, when anxiety is lower, teaching is done by parables, illustrated by successful clinical solutions of similar problems in other families. Still later, when there is little anxiety, the teaching can successfully be quite didactic.

Taking "I position" stands. When one member of a family can calmly state his own convictions and beliefs, and take action on his convictions without criticism of the beliefs of others and without becoming involved in emotional debate, than other family members will start the same process of becoming more sure of self and more accepting of others. The "I position" is very useful early in therapy as an operating position in relation to the family. It is advantageous to use it whenever possible through therapy. The more the therapist can clearly define himself in relation to the families, the easier it is for family members to define themselves to each other.

A goal of this method of family psychotherapy is to provide a structure in which spouses can proceed as far toward the differentiation of self as the situation and their motivation can take them, and as rapidly as is possible for them. The therapist makes a continuing effort to challenge them to maximum effort, and to help them through the predictable episodes of anxiety that occur. They are free to stop at any point, and the therapist is free to exercise his "I position" to define his part in the effort. A high percentage of the families have what is conventionally defined as moderate to severe neurotic problems; only a few are borderline or mildly psychotic. The average family starts with a significant degree of ego fusion or undifferentiation. This has evolved over the years to the point of acute dysfunction in a spouse (usually emotional illness, somatic illness, or social dysfunction such as drinking), to marital disharmony and conflict, or to a behavior problem or life failure problem in a child. A significant number of the families have had long exposure to other forms of psychiatric treatment. The approach for all families is to involve both spouses in this method of family psychotherapy.

The therapy proceeds through several distinct phases. One of the significant early phases is the stage through which they each come to "know" each other better. In some this is slow and gradual; in others it can be a rapid and almost exhilarating experience. Some are so pleased with the decrease in symptoms and increase in togetherness in the marriage that they are ready to terminate. There have been a number of striking early "cures" in a relatively few sessions, such as a seven-session "cure" of fairly severe fridigity in a wife.

For those motivated to proceed, the process helps each spouse to gradually begin to differentiate a self from the other spouse. Characteristically, one spouse begins to focus on self while the other pleads for togetherness. It is common for the differentiating one to yield to the togetherness pressure at least once before proceeding on a self-determined course in spite of the opposition. This results in a brief emotional reaction in the other, following which they both arrive at a new and slightly higher basic level of differentiation. This is usually followed by another fairly calm period, after which the other spouse focuses on self and takes the same steps toward differentiation while the former opposes with togetherness pressure. Thus, differentiation proceeds in small alternating steps. Each new step stirs emotional disharmony in extended families and other interlocking emotional systems, which is generally easier to handle than the disharmony between the spouses. As early as possible the therapist begins to coach spouses in differentiating a self in their families of origin. When a motivated spouse is successful at this, the total process proceeds more rapidly without the alternating pattern that occurs when there is less attention to families of origin.

This is in my experience the most successful and efficient method of family psychotherapy. The family can stop at the point of symptom relief, or they can continue toward a more satisfying, deeper resolution. If the family is well motivated, and the therapist has been relatively successful at keeping himself out of the emotional system with the family, it is usual for the family to find more and more to work on and to resolve. Abrupt termination after fairly brief therapy is often the result of the therapist's emotional involvement in the family emotional system. As the family proceeds through the nodal points of differentiation, it is common for the togetherness-oriented spouse to become negative and disenchanted with the therapy effort. The other is usually pleased and wishes to continue. It is usually fairly easy to help them through these nodal anxiety periods.

There are situations in which a fairly sudden and abrupt termination can occur at a nodal point of change. This happens when the opposing spouse demanding togetherness can stir enough momentum to overcome the more positive forces in the other. I have had experience with over twenty-five families in which a togetherness-oriented husband at such a nodal point suddenly left on a business assignment in another city or overseas, which terminated the therapy effort. An orderly termination is reached when both have achieved a reasonable level of differentiation of self from each other, and from their families of origin; when they know enough about families systems so that one or the other of them has developed the capacity to handle crises; and when they have some kind of reasonable plan and motivation to continue working toward differentiation in the years ahead.

Multiple Family Therapy

The theory and technique for multiple family therapy had been developed in detail for about two years before it was actually put into operation as a clinical research experiment. Two main ideas motivated the effort. The method of family psychotherapy just described was in successful operation both in private practice and also in my various teaching and supervision programs. The clinical results were excellent with a variety of single families; in some of these families both spouses attended sessions regularly; in some large blocks of sessions were with one spouse alone; in others the total course was with a single family member.

In all areas, the family psychotherapy efforts were going well; but in going from one session to another, I found myself teaching the same principles in session after session. I began thinking of the time that could be saved, and the advantages of covering the material in more detail to many families at the same time. I heard about the striking experiences in each of the families as they worked toward the differentiation of self, but then I had to assimilate these experiences into my own experience and communicate that to others. In thinking about some kind of a structure that would bring a number of families together, yet that would avoid the social and emotional togetherness of groups, and preserve the emotional separateness between families necessary for working out the nuances of emotional interdependence and family process between the spouses, I remembered the structure my staff and I had developed for the live-in families in 1958 and 1959. Using that as a basic structure, I added the details that would be necessary for this new clinical effort.

In the following few years I made some unsuccessful efforts to start this method of multiple family therapy, starting with about three or four new families, each with neurotic level problems of about the same intensity. I spoke to a clinic about finding such families; but most of the "good" families of this type were referred for individual psychotherapy, and those referred to me were too severely impaired and fragmented and too poorly motivated for this effort. I tried to save up enough of these families to start in my private practice, but there were not enough referrals at about the same time to get started. Finally, in 1965, there was an admissions social worker who did understand what I wanted. Within a short time she had found three families applying for family therapy at about the same time that perfectly met the criteria. The families were interviewed, all agreed to participate, and we quickly worked out a relatively simple research plan for observation and the recording of sessions.

The therapy was started with families sitting in a semicircle facing the therapist, and a variety of research observers sitting in the back. The early operating rules were more strict than they have been since. The focus was to be on the emotional interdependence between the spouses in each family, with the other families as silent observers. Elaborate precautions were taken to keep the families emotionally isolated from each other, and to prevent the families from emotionally merging into one large undifferentiated family ego mass which could inundate the family process in each family. The families were all unknown to each other before the start of the project. The purpose and technique of the study was explained to each, and they agreed to avoid social contact with each other outside the sessions, and in case they might later find they had mutual friends, to not mention the other families in any of their social contacts. They had no contact with each other outside the sessions except for meeting in the hallways and elevators as they assembled or left the sessions. In the sessions, each husband and wife sat beside each other, slightly separated from the next two spouses.

The weekly sessions were planned for one and a half hours each, with no fixed rules about the amount of time with each family, and with one half-hour research summary at the end of each session. Originally I had planned a very flexible format which might allow most of the time for a single family, and little or none with the others until the following week, but very quickly we began to divide available time about equally between the families. Too often a silent family would have problems of an urgent nature with too little time. It did not work well to skip any family at any session. Too much could take place in their thinking-feeling systems in that period of time without the therapist's awareness. Originally we planned to build up the group to many more than the original three families, but this was not feasible if the therapist was to do even a brief check on each family each week. Two hours was about the maximum time that families could keep their attention on the sessions without fatigue, and four families was the optimum number for this format. Five families made the schedule too rushed and pressured.

Two major findings of this research effort had not been accurately predicted. (1) The larger group did not facilitate advantageous use of teaching time. It was even easier for the therapist to become emotionally triangled into the families' emotional systems in this setting than in dealing with individual families. (2) The surprise was the unusually rapid progress of the families. This was estimated to be about 50 percent faster than comparable clinical problems in other families. When we asked about this, we usually got the same reason given by people starting group therapy: "It is reassuring to know that other people have the same kinds of problems." Apparently, it is easier to really see and know your own problem when you watch it in other people than when you only know about it in relation to yourself. Families learn from each other. If one family made a breakthrough in an area, within a week or two other spouses would be trying some version of that in their own families.

The rapid progress of families in the multiple family sessions led to my establishing the first multiple family group in my practice about eight months after the start of this project. This led to the establishment of more and more multiple family groups as fast as schedules could be arranged, until a major portion of my practice, in terms of number of families, is now this method of multiple family therapy. The same has been true of other research observers, and this method of multiple family therapy, which began as a pilot research study at Georgetown University Hospital, is now being widely used in the Washington area.

Another dividend of the research project was the development of a more detailed formal research study on the question of change in psychotherapy. In professional practice, the concept of change or improvement is applied to things as elusive as feeling better, or disappearance of presenting symptom. The research staff on this project has tried hard to define *change* in a way that can be measured and quantified.

The pilot research study has also affected the practice of family psychotherapy. Until this project was over two years old, it was generally accepted that families should be seen once a week in family psychotherapy. This once a week format had generally evolved over the past ten years to replace the two or three appointments per week common in the late 1950s. A year and a half after the start of this project, I began an ongoing multiple family therapy group on videotape in another medical school. My schedule allowed no more than one session every four weeks. There were many reservations about holding multiple family therapy sessions only once a month. One of the wives for the proposed venture, who had been hospitalized several times, was very anxious. She said, "With appointments that far apart, I could get into the hospital and out again between appointments." However, the outstanding success of the multiple family therapy group was responsible for my changing my practice of all kinds of family psychotherapy to monthly appointments, and families have made as much, and possibly even more, progress than equivalent families seen in other multiple family groups that have met weekly.

Considering all the ideas and the explanations offered by the families and the observers, the best explanation for the remarkable progress with the monthly sessions seems to be that families are more on their own, made to be more resourceful and less dependent on therapy to provide working solutions. This also fits with my conviction that it takes a certain amount of time on the calendar for families to change, and the length of time necessary for change is not decreased by increasing the frequency of appointments. (*Change* here refers to change as it is considered at this Center, and not to superficial manifestations of change.) The favorable experience with the monthly appointments has led me to reduce the frequency of appointments with all families, whether therapy with multiple families or single families, to once every two weeks. An increasing number are seen once a month, and a small experimental group of families are being seen once every three months.

From the perspective of this experience, my answer to the often asked, impossible question, "How long does family therapy take?" is now that some families, because of the intensity of their ingrained life patterns and their initial basic level of differentiation of self, will never be able to change significantly. Almost all people in the mental health professions, with whom most of the research has been involved, have so much deep resistance to learning about and getting to know the people in their extended families that they literally have to force themselves to work at it. Even while they are searching for data and going to see distant relatives, this resistance is working to oppose the success of their efforts. This emotional revulsion is very strong in some people, and operates to deny them meaningful contact with the past. There is some indirect evidence that the people who do best at the differentiation of a self in family psychotherapy have some of the same qualities of people who do well in searching out and getting to know people in their extended families. This example may convey some idea of the forces that permit people to do well in family psychotherapy or that prevent them from significant change. As far as upper middle class families who are motivated to continue working until they have achieved significant change in family psychotherapy are concerned, the average family continues for about four years, whether appointments are once a month or twice a month.

One last word. As should be obvious, it is inaccurate to refer to the clinical method described here as "psychotherapy." I would like to drop the entire concept of "psychotherapy," but there is no accurate and acceptable word to replace it. As we move more and more into systems thinking, we will have to find new terms to describe what we are doing, for conventional terms simply no longer apply.

Chapter 12

Alcoholism and the Family

Family systems theory is relatively new as applied to emotional problems. This paper will outline some over-all principles of family systems theory, the ways that alcoholism can be conceptualized as a symptom of the larger family or social unit, and ways in which family systems therapy can be used to alleviate the problem.

Systems theory assumes that all important people in the family unit play a part in the way family members function in relation to each other and in the way the symptom finally erupts. The part that each person plays comes about by each "being himself." The symptom of excessive drinking occurs when family anxiety is high. The appearance of the symptom stirs even higher anxiety in those dependent on the one who drinks. The higher the anxiety, the more other family members react by anxiously doing more of what they are already doing. The process of drinking to relieve anxiety, and increased family anxiety in response to drinking, can spiral into a functional collapse or the process can become a chronic pattern.

Before going into systems theory, some explanation of terminology is in order. Family therapy is well known, but it is far from being a standardized method. There are a few well developed methods, but a majority of family therapists use the term to indicate that multiple family members attend the sessions, without regard for method or technique. About ten years ago the term "system" was introduced from family research, after it became clear that the same patterns that exist in families are present also in social and work relationships, and that relationship patterns have the quality of "systems." Now the term "system" is used loosely, and it is often associated with general systems theory, which has not been clearly defined for relationships. In this paper I will describe my family systems theory, which was developed from family research, and a method of family systems therapy, which is based on the theory. The terms systems theory and systems therapy are really more accurate, especially in referring to relationships outside the family.

The family *is* a system in that a change in the functioning of one family member is automatically followed by a compensatory change in another family member. Systems theory focused on the *functioning* of a system and its component parts. Almost any natural or man-made "system" can be used to illustrate systems concepts, but I have chosen a biological system, the human body, to illustrate the ideas. The total organism is made up of numerous different organ systems. An intricate set of automatic mechanisms controls the smooth reciprocal operation of vital functions such as heart rate, temperature, respiration, digestion, reflexes, and locomotion. Systems function at all levels of efficiency, from robust health to total failure. There are healthy compensated functioning states in which an organ can increase its functioning to handle an increased work load. There are decompensated states in which the organ loses the capacity to increase functioning. These are situations in which one organ increases its function to compensate for the poor functioning of another organ. There are states of dysfunction that range from the short-term dysfunctions of acute illness, through the long-term dysfunctions of chronic illness, to permanent dysfunction in an organ system. An organ that functions for another for long periods of time does not return to normal so easily. There are situations of decompensated overfunctioning in which a failing organ works faster and faster in a futile effort to overcome a work overload. An example is the racing of a worn-out heart as it approaches total failure. The same patterns of function, overfunction, and dysfunction are present in the way people relate to each other in families and small social systems. For instance, the underfunctioning of a family member who is temporarily ill will be automatically compensated by other family members who overfunction until the sick one recovers. If the sick member becomes chronically or permanently disabled, the overfunctioning of the others becomes a long-term imbalance in the family. Certainly the overfunctioning of some family members will result in underfunctioning in others. In the case of an anxious mother and a small child, the underfunctioning of the child can become a permanent functional impairment. Another functional imbalance in family systems can occur when family members pretend disability.

Family systems theory was developed during the course of family research for emotional problems. Part of the effort was directed at extracting *facts* from the morass of subjectivity, discrepant explanations, and verbal dialogue that is common in psychiatric research. Eventually the research included the approach that is described here.

Systems theory attempts to focus on the functional *facts* of relationships. It focuses on what happened, how it happened, and when and where it happened, insofar as these observations are based on fact. It carefully avoids man's automatic preoccupation with why it happened. This is one of the main differences between conventional and systems theory. Conventional theory places much emphasis on the *why* of human behavior. All members of the mental health professions are familiar with *why* explanations. *Why* thinking has also been a part of cause-and-effect thinking because ever since man first became a thinking being he began to look around for causes to explain events that affected him. In reviewing the thinking of primitive man, we are amused at the various evil forces he blamed for his misfortunes, or the benevolent forces he credited for his good fortunes. We can chuckle at the causality that man in later centuries assigned to illness before he knew about germs and microorganisms. We can smugly assure ourselves that scientific knowledge and logical reasoning have now enabled man to go beyond the erroneous assumptions and false deductions of past centuries and that we now assign accurate causes for most of man's problems. However, an assumption behind systems theory is that man's cause-and effect thinking is still a major *problem* in explaining his dysfunctions and behavior. A major effort in systems theory is to get beyond cause-and-effect thinking and to concentrate on facts, which are the basis for systems thinking. There were practical reasons for his disciplined effort. Part of man's cause-and-effect thinking is to blame his fellow man for his own problems. Blaming others for one's own failures is present in all of us to some degree. The greater the degree of anxiety in a family, the greater the tendency for even the most reasonable person to resort to blaming others for his own problems. Further, there is the predictable discrepancy between what man does and what he *says* he does. So, systems research moved into trying to isolate observable facts about man and his relationships, and to carefully avoid verbal dialogue and *why* explanations. The approach also requires the researcher to lay aside his own *why* assumptions. Efforts have been made to discover formulas for converting subjective observations into objective and measurable facts. For example, when applied to dreams, the formula says, "That man dreams is a scientific fact, but what he dreams is not necessarily a fact." The same formula can be applied to a whole range of subjective concepts, such as, "That man feels (or thinks or talks) is a scientific fact, but what he feels (or thinks or says) is not necessarily a fact." The entire spectrum of subjective states, even of the intensity of love and hate, can similarly be stated as functional facts.

Why bother to try to convert human relationship concepts into the functional facts of systems theory? One primary reason was to facilitate research. Focusing on one small aspect of relationship eliminated a complex mass of uncontrolled research data. The theory that evolved from the research resulted in a different kind of therapy. Then it was discovered that a system of therapy based on systems theory and functional facts was far superior to conventional therapy. However, a shift from conventional to systems theory is difficult and the superior results are not possible until the therapist is able to get reasonably beyond his "second nature" cause-and-effect thinking. A "little systems theory" mixed with conventional theory is not enough. Even the most experienced and disciplined systems thinker will automatically revert to cause-and-effect thinking when anxiety is high. The main thesis presented here is that systems theory and systems therapy provide a different approach to emotional problems. Therapists with the motivation and discipline to work towards systems thinking can reasonably expect a different order of therapeutic results as they are more successful in shifting to systems thinking.

How does alcoholism fit into systems concepts? From a systems viewpoint, alcoholism is one of the common human dysfunctions. As a dysfunction, it exists in the context of an imbalance in functioning in the total family system. From a theoretical viewpoint, every important family member plays a part in the dysfunction of the dysfunctional member. The theory provides a way for conceptualizing the part that each member plays. From a systems therapy viewpoint, the therapy is directed at helping the family to modify its patterns of functioning. The therapy is directed at the family member, or members, with the most resourcefulness, who have the most potential for modifying his or her own functioning. When it is possible to modify the family relationship system, the alcoholic dysfunction is alleviated, even though the dysfunctional one may not have been part of the therapy.

Theoretical Concepts

Family systems theory is made up of several different theoretical concepts. Some of the central concepts will be summarized briefly to convey a notion of how drinking dysfunctions fit into the total theory. An important theoretical concept is the degree of "differentiation of self" of the person. It is the degree to which the person has a "solid self" or solidly held principles by which he lives his life. This is in contrast to a "pseudo-self" made up of inconsistent life principles that can be corrupted by coercion for the gain of the moment. The differentiation of self is roughly equivalent to the concept of emotional maturity. The level of differentiation of a person is determined by the level of differentiation of one's parents, by the type of relationship the child has with the parents, and the way one's unresolved emotional attachment to his parents is handled in young adulthood. People marry spouses who have equal basic levels of differentiation of self. These various factors predict the degree of undifferentiation or immaturity to be absorbed in the new nuclear family (this includes, father, mother, and children). It is common for young people to get into marriage blaming their parents for past unhappiness, and expecting to find perfect harmony in the marriage. The two pseudo-selfs "fuse" into the emotional "we-ness" of marriage, which has a high potential for impairing the functioning of one spouse. The discomfort of fusion is handled in one of several ways. Almost universal is some degree of emotional distance in the marriage, which helps each to be a more definite self than would otherwise be possible. Then there is the conflictual marriage in which neither "gives in" to the other. The conflict provides good reason for them to keep the emotional distance and the "make-up" between conflicts provides intervals of intense closeness. The most frequent pattern for handling emotional fusion is one in which the spouse becomes the dominant one, and the other the adaptive one, who is "programmed" to support the more dominant decision-making spouse. The adaptive spouse becomes a functional "no-self." If this pattern is continued long enough, the adaptive one is vulnerable to some kind of chronic dysfunction, which can be physical illness, emotional illness, or a social dysfunction such as drinking, the use of drugs, or irresponsible behavior. The other pattern is one in which parents project their immaturity to one or more of their children. There are some parents who use one pattern predominantly. Most use a combination of all three patterns.

There is a range of adaptive patterns available in the nuclear family. In periods of calm, the adaptive patterns can function without symptoms arising in any family member. As anxiety and tension increase, the adaptive patterns lose flexibility and symptoms erupt. The family does not have conscious choice about the selection of adaptive patterns. These were "programmed" into the spouses in their own parental families. In general, there is more adaptability in families with a spectrum of patterns than in a family with fewer patterns. Another most important variable has to do with the quality and the degree of emotional contact each spouse has with their families of origin. Here again, there is a spectrum of ways that people handle the relationships to their parental families. Some can distance themselves emotionally while living close by; others maintain emotional closeness while living far apart. Emotional closeness or distance to parental families is determined by a combination of physical distance and quality of relationship. A common pattern in our society is the emotionally distant relationship with parental families, with brief, formal, superficial "duty" visits. In general, the more a nuclear family is emotionally cut off from parental families, the higher its incidence of problems and symtoms. Details about the theory have been presented in other papers (Bowen 1966, 1971).

Clinical Patterns

In general, the person who later becomes an alcoholic is one who handles the emotional attachment to his parents, and especially to his mother, by denial of the attachment and by a super-independent posture which says, "I do not need you. I can do it myself." The level of emotional attachment is fairly intense, but it is no greater than exists in a fair spectrum of all people. It is the way the attachment is handled rather than the intensity that is important. There are a variety of outcomes to his life posture. At one extreme is the person who can make this pseudo-independent attitude work for long periods. He might be a dynamo in his profession or business and appear to be doing well with his immediate family. Such a person usually has an exaggerated sense of responsibility for others. He tries hard to live up to this responsibility, but since it is ultimately unattainable, the outcome is irresponsibility and broken promises. This person has the same "I can do it myself" posture to wife and children, who participate in his over-responsible posture by expecting him to always function at this level. This person's life is burdened by his high self-expectations and unrealistic sense of responsibility. His Achilles' heel is the denial of his need for others, and his super-independent posture, which is in turn reinforced by his spouse and children. The harder he works, the more he becomes emotionally isolated. When he feels most burdened and the isolation is most intense, he often finds relief from alcohol, thus initiating a well known drinking pattern.

At the other extreme is the person who is so attached to his parents, and especially to his mother, that he is never able to manage a productive life. He was "de-selfed" in the emotional fusion with his poorly differentiated mother. The mechanism of denial permits him to keep his distance from the realization of his need for his mother and from all subsequent such relationships in which need would have to be acknowledged. He collapses into drinking early in life, while loudly affirming his independence and his continuing, "I can do it myself" posture. These are the people who become social outcasts: those whose need for emotional closeness is so great, yet who have to go to such extremes to deny it. From a systems theory viewpoint, they are dysfunctional refugees from the family relationship system. Most of the people with drinking problems fall somewhere between the two extremes presented here. A high percentage of adult alcoholism is in people who are married, and who have the same kind of emotional attachment in marriage that they had in their parental families. They are emotionally isolated from their spouses, who play the reciprocal role in the drinking dysfunction.

People marry spouses with equal levels of differentiation of self, although they usually appear to have opposite ways of dealing with stress. They commonly have a combination of the three patterns for dealing with the marital fusion. They have some degree of marital disharmony, some degree of the adaptive spouse being "de-selfed" in the marital fusion, and some degree of projection of the problem to their children. The pattern of one spouse adapting or giving in to the other spouse is the important pattern in drinking problems. The adaptive spouse pattern is rarely a simple issue. Each spouse sees himself or herself as giving in to the other. It is the one who gives in the most who later becomes "de-selfed," and then becomes vulnerable to development of a drinking problem. The following is a clinical example of one common pattern. The wife was a productive professional woman before marriage. She was also an adaptive person, dedicated to the notion of agreeableness, emotional togetherness, and marital harmony. She voluntarily devoted herself to supporting the career of her husband, who was a striving business man. She prided herself in having the perfect marriage in which she and the husband thought alike on all important issues. She gradually became "de-selfed" by her husband, who gained functional strength at her expense. As he made more and more decisions for the two of them, she gradually became less capable of making decisions. This is the familiar pattern of the dominant spouse overfunctioning, and the adaptive spouse going into an equal degree of dysfunction. It became harder for her to find energy for the home and children. She began taking drinks during the day to help her through the chores, taking the usual precautions to hide the drinking from her husband, and to be ready for the ideal togetherness when he returned home from work. Although he was an integral part of the problem, the husband had the usual degree of "blindness" to his wife's increasing dysfunction. He even overlooked the situation when he brought business associates home for dinner and found the wife "passed out" on the living room couch with no dinner prepared. He took the associates out for dinner and never mentioned the incident. The alcoholism was "discovered" later in another incident in which his wife passed out and was hospitalized for a "surgical emergency." There was fairly prompt relief from the drinking symptom during the course of family therapy for the husband and wife together since the therapy sessions reduced the emotional isolation between them. In the recovery process, as she regained more of her functioning self, they went through a period of fairly intense marital conflict. She discovered that their "thinking alike" had been her failure to think for herself.

The following is an example of another common pattern with an opposite manifestation of symptoms. The wife was a "no-self" adaptive person and the husband a super-functioner. He gained in emotional functioning from the wife's dysfunction, which she was able to maintain at a marginal level through an emotional overinvolvement with their children. The husband assumed overfunctioning responsibility for the full range of decisions for the emotional cocoon of the nuclear family. Both spouses were cut off from meaningful emotional contact with their parental families, and both were isolated from each other. As the husband became more and more burdened by his responsibility at work and by his responsibility for the wife and children, he began to increase and to extend his "social" drinking by excessive drinking in the evening and over weekends. There are thousands, and perhaps millions, of such families in which the family system continues to function on a marginal level, in which the husband's regular consumption of alcohol at home is excessive, and in which he is able to manage a reasonable level of functioning at work. Such a family is motivated for professional help when there is a breakdown in adaptive patterns and symptoms erupt. The family in this example was motivated to seek professional help when there was a breakdown in the emotional cocoon of mother and children. A child developed behavior problems, the wife collapsed into dysfunction in relation to the child's problem, and the husband was then motivated to be part of the therapy effort.

Family and Sytems Therapy

Alcoholism has always been one of the most difficult of all emotional dysfunctions to modify regardless of the therapeutic method. Family systems therapy offers no magic solution for the total problem, but the theory does provide a different way to conceptualize the problem, and the therapy provides a number of approaches to the problem that are not available with conventional theory and therapy. The therapeutic principles are derived directly from the theory. The following is a brief summary of the way the various principles are applied.

I have found it helpful to think of the degree of impairment in the person who develops drinking problems. The basic strength or level of differentiation of self, rather than the intensity of the alcoholism, is a rather good predictor of the outcome of any effort at therapy. In the Clinical Patterns section I mentioned two profiles at each extreme of the spectrum. The closer a person is to the upper end of the spectrum, even though alcohol consumption may be high and consistent, the greater the basic strength and the more likely a favorable clinical result. The closer a person is to the "social outcast" end of the spectrum, even though alcohol consumption is lower, the less likely there will be any change with any therapy effort.

First, attention is given to the over-all level of anxiety. Those family members who are most dependent on the drinking person are more overtly anxious than is the one who drinks. This says much about the nature of the problem. The more the family is threatened, the more anxious they get, the more they become critical, the greater the emotional isolation, the more the alcoholic drinks, the higher the anxiety, the greater the criticism and emotional distance, the more the drinking, et cetera, in an emotional escalation that makes the problem worse and both sides more rigidly self-righteous. Anything that can interrupt the spiraling anxiety will be helpful. Any one significant family member who can "cool" the anxious response, or control one's own anxiety, can make a step toward de-escalation. I have had a number of complete "cures" of serious drinking problems in husbands, in which the husbands steadfastly refused to attend sessions and the total time was spent with the wives. In these situations the time was spent in teaching the wives about the way family systems work, and in helping them to control their reciprocal role in the problem. I have seen two families with alcoholism in a parent, in which neither parent would have anything to do with "therapy." In both cases the total time was spent with a motivated oldest daughter, and the outcome was favorable. In one family, it was the father who was alcoholic, and in the other family it was the mother. It is far more usual to have the drinking person attend at least part of the sessions.

Knowledge of the "I'll do it myself" posture as well as of the emotional isolation from the parental family in the past generation and from the spouse in the present generation provides a number of clues to helpful techniques in therapy. The alcoholic person operates on a narrow margin between too much closeness and too much emotional isolation. When he is drinking, he is emotionally isolated. Frequently, it takes only a slight decrease in the emotional isolation to stop the drinking and get the therapy on a more constructive level. Frequently it is possible to "coach" the family to reestablish more meaningful emotional contact with a parental family. The immediate results can be striking in situations in which the relationships with parents can improve only slightly.

There is one basic principle that applies in any family in which one significant family member is in a marked overfunctioning position, and the other in a marked dysfunctioning position: It is far easier to help the overfunctioning person to tone down the overfunctioning than it is to help the dysfunctional one to increase the functioning. In any situation in which there is an either/or choice on where to put the focus in therapy sessions, it is with the overfunctioning family member. There are numerous reasons for this, which are too detailed for this presentation.

Finally, there are situations in which one spouse is an alcoholic and both spouses are willing and eager to attend the sessions. In general, these are the families that do best. Most of the time can be devoted to defining the emotional interdependence from the beginning. Results are less favorable when one spouse is reluctant to attend. In these families, I now tend to look for one member who is motivated to work on the total problem alone, until both are willing to be involved together. Family therapy with two spouses is one of the high roads to successful family therapy.

Summary

Family systems theory provides a different framework for conceptualizing alcoholism, and family systems therapy provides a spectrum of effective ways for modification of the family relationship patterns.

Chapter 13

Societal Regression as Viewed Through Family Systems Theory

This paper represents one nodal point in a long term effort to systematically correlate emotional forces in the family with emotional forces in society. My earliest interest in societal issues began in the 1940s. A new interest began early in my family research with the awareness that the study of the family provided a completely new theoretical dimension for conceptualizing the total human phenomenon. There was an impulse to go exploring, and look at many things through this new theoretical perspective, but the research was focused on schizophrenia and that had priority. Also I wanted to avoid making sweeping assumptions from minimal facts, which has been a weakness of most of our theories about society. I purposely avoided any except private thinking and observations about society.

Over the years, there has been a slow extension of concepts about the family, into larger social systems. In the period around 1960 there were several conferences in which I was one who expressed the belief that the greatest gain from the family movement would come, not from family therapy, but as the basis of new theories about man and his efforts to adapt. Through the 1960s, there were comments about emotional patterns in society being the same as emotional patterns in the family. This seemed logical and right, but specific connecting facts were elusive. Then came my emphasis on triangles that operate the same in society as in the family. Gradually came the use of the term *systems* to replace older terms. Even though the term *systems* has been overused and misused, the concept has helped to broaden the field of vision.

And so, the part-time informal thinking about society and broader systems concepts continued some eighteen years, without a formal effort to integrate some of the partial concepts. The impetus for the new effort came in 1972–1973 with an invitation to do a formal paper about man's predictable reaction to crisis, and specifically to the crises over which the new Environmental Protection Agency had been assigned governmental responsibility. This will be the first time that some of the material from that effort will be presented to a national meeting of "family" people. I have been waiting for this Memorial Meeting to Nathan Ackerman to begin discussion of these issues. If I know Nat, he would like this for his memorial meeting.

Background Information

One basic view that has influenced my thinking since the 1940s is that man is an evolving form of life, that he is more related to lower forms of life than he is different from them, that most psychological theories focus on the uniqueness of man rather than his relatedness to the biological world, and that the instinctual forces that govern all animal and protoplasmic behavior are more basic in human behavior than most theories recognize. Over the years I have probably spent more time reading Darwin than reading Freud, and more time on the work of biologists, ethologists, and natural scientsits than on the work of psychologists and sociologists. It is not that any field is exclusive or inclusive but I have carefully avoided the use of theoretical concepts that are not in basic accord with man as a biological-instinctual animal. It is difficult to convey this notion to people who have some isolated knowledge of natural sciences but who use a different framework in thinking about man.

Fairly serious thinking and observations about social unrest and societal regression began about 1955. At that time, society appeared more restless, more selfish, more immature, more lawless, and more irresponsible than in previous years. How could one be sure about this? There was the notion that the media focused on the bad things about society, and we did not hear about the good. At almost any period in history, there are those who have described the situation as the worst it has ever been, and throughout history there have been those who predicted doomsday as just around the corner. I have been fascinated by writings from hundreds of years ago that perfectly described the social or political situation of the hour. However, most of the evidence seemed to indicate there is such a thing as social regression. Much has been written about the rise and fall of the Roman Empire, and the decadence that preceded its final deterioration. There were those who suggested that cultures have fairly predictable life courses, followed by decline and deterioration. Biblical history contains accounts of the more wicked and sinful periods, and the good and righteous periods in man's existence. Popular explanations for societal anxiety are numerous and varied. In the decade after World War II, it was popular to cite anxiety as related to fear of the atomic bomb, or that the cold war would become another fighting war. There were those who suggested that sweeping societal change was to be expected after World War II, or that a decay in values is predictable during good times or periods of affluence. My part-time interest in this led to the conclusion that fluctuations in social adaptation are cyclical, that they have been present through the centuries, that man's long-term history on earth has been good, and it would be interesting to watch his recovery from the regression. My own thinking tended to favor the hypothesis that societal anxiety was related to post-war recovery, and to the sweeping advances in technology, and the changes that went with that.

There were problems in finding some kind of baseline to make judgments about the presence or absence of societal regression. One can collect statistics about the increasing divorce rate, or increasing crime rate, but what does one do with this material? Clinical work with families provided evidence that anxiety, and the accompanying behavior symptoms, can occur with change that represents progress. How is one to know the difference between social symptoms that go with progress, and those that go with regression? I believe that some method similar to my "differentiation of self scale" is essential for this kind of study. It is necessary to have some reasonably accurate baseline for evaluating the functioning of people, for comparing them with each other, and for evaluating change over time. The differentiation of self scale was developed in 1960 and it has been used long enough, with enough people, to make it a reasonably accurate method in the hands of those experienced in the variables.

A number of hypotheses were considered, and later discarded, in the search for a working explanation of the forces that triggered societal regression. Here was evidence of increasing societal anxiety during one of the most secure periods in man's history. Man has overcome many of the forces that threatened his existence in former centuries. His life span has been increased by medical science, his technology has advanced rapidly, he has become increasingly more in control of his environment which has been his adversary, and a higher percentage of the world's population have more economic security and creature comforts than at any time during man's history on earth. A brief paper does not permit a review of the various hypotheses and their ramifications. During the 1960s it was difficult to get beyond the war in Vietnam. A large segment of the population saw it as causing societal unrest, but there was much evidence to support the thesis that it was a symptom of a preexisting tension. By the late 1960s, there was a hypothesis that has not only held up for several years, but that has also been strengthened by new evidence, and the work of others. The hypothesis postulates that man's increasing anxiety is a product of population explosion, the disappearance of new habitable land to colonize, the approaching depletion of raw materials necessary to sustain life, and growing awareness that "spaceship earth" cannot indefinitely support human life in the style to which man and his technology have become accustomed. Man is a territorial animal who reacts to being "hemmed in" with the same basic patterns as lower forms of life. Man tells himself other reasons to explain his behavior while important life patterns are the same as non-thinking animals. Man has always used "getting away from the crowd" as a way of allaying anxiety and stabilizing his adjustment. The thesis here is that man became increasingly aware of the disappearance of frontiers, more through his "instinctual radar" than by logical thinking. Man has become increasingly aware that his world is limited in size through rapid communication and television, and rapid travel. When animals are confined to a limited space, and their numbers are increasing, they test the limits of the compound, there is more mobility and moving around, and they finally come to live more in piles than spread evenly over existing space. Man has become more mobile the past twenty-five years, more people move more often, and a higher percentage of the population is coming to live in the large metropolitan centers.

Another theoretical notion is important to this background thinking; it is another predictable characteristic of man. With his logical thinking and knowledge, he could have known decades ago that he was on a collision course with his environment. His emotional reactiveness and its cause-and-effect thinking prevent him from really "knowing" what he could know. He has been a cause-and-effect thinker since he first began to look for reasons to explain the world and his part in it. We can review his thinking in previous centuries and be amused at the spectrum of evil forces he blamed for his misfortune, and benevolent forces he credited with good fortune. Science has enabled man to get beyond cause-and-effect thinking in many areas of life. He was first able to use systems in astronomy, far removed from him personally. Later he was able to think "systems" about the physical sciences, and later in the natural sciences. In the past decades he has had some notion that systems thinking also applies to himself and his own emotional functioning, but in an emotional field, even the most disciplined systems thinker reverts to cause-and-effect thinking and to taking action based more on emotional reactiveness than objective thinking. This phenomenon plays an important part in man's decisions and actions about societal problems. There is evidence that the political-legislative process is more emotional reactiveness than logical thinking, and that much legislation is more a "band-aid" type of legislation directed at symptom relief than at underlying factors. Society's emotional reactiveness in dealing with societal problems is similar to the years of slow build-up of an emotional breakdown in a family. When the first symptom appears, the family either ignores it or does enough to relieve the immediate symptom, considering the problem to be solved. Then they continue the usual course until another more serious symptom, which is followed by another superficial effort to relieve the symptom. The process keeps repeating until the final breakdown, which is seen as having developed unexpectedly.

Comparison of Family and Societal Patterns

The more detailed clinical part of this study involved a comparison between the way "permissive" parents deal with delinquency and behavior problems in their teenage children, and the way society deals with the same problems. This is the one emotional problem in which the therapist and the representative of society have intimate, different, and separate relationships with the same problem at the same time. It has become one of the commonest problems of our time. Primary emphasis is on the way parents and society think about, act and react, or fail to act and react, in relating to the problem. Secondary attention goes to the symptom in the youngster. From long clinical experience, one comes to know the problem rather well. A brief clinical evaluation of the way the parents function in relation to their extended families, to each other, and to their children makes it possible to make reasonable predictions of those who will do well in "therapy," those who will slow progress over a long period, and those that do not change or get worse. Over the years, I have assigned "differentiation scale" estimates, (estimating functional strength) from single interviews, from several interviews in a "trial" at therapy, and at the end of the therapy effort. There has been experience

with all socioeconomic groups. In the beginning there were many errors
in scale estimates. With increasing experience, the method has become
sufficiently accurate to make it a valid clinical approach. One of the best
indices has been the type and quality of the mother's relationship with
her mother, and the maternal grandmother's relationship with her
mother. Estimating the functional strength of a family involves
knowledge of family emotional forces and judgment in evaluating the
multiple interlocking emotional forces. It is not the concise and simple
procedure that non-systems therapists would like it to be. The important
part of this communication is that it has been possible, from estimating
family backgrounds, to do fairly reliable comparisons of the various
levels of behavior problems with each other, and with the average of
society.

Delinquency and behavior problems are not new. They have always
been present in a percentage of families and they are well known to
clinicians and to the social agencies that deal with them. In the past
decades there would appear to be a marked increase in the percentage of
the problems. From a clinical practice, this has been an overwhelming
increase. Part of the increase appears to be in youngsters whose tensions
would previously have been expressed more as internalized problems
than as behavior problems. It is a clinical fact that insecure and
permissive parents, in situations that require parental control, will
automatically shift to a degree of authoritative cruelty that is equal to the
unsure permissiveness on the other side. The past few decades, society
has put more emphasis on understanding children than on former social
attitudes that demanded obedience and conformity. The authoritative
cruelty and permissiveness are seen as different expressions of equal
levels of immaturity. The study suggests that changing societal attitudes
creates an environment that encourages behavior problems that would
not have previously been symptomatic. Said in another way, a regression
increases the incidence of human problems.

The following are some of the characteristics of overly permissive
parents that I consider most important. Most of the parents are devoted
to doing the best for their children. From the child's infancy, the mothers
have high levels of investment of her self in the child. This is determined
by the mother's basic level of differentiation attained in her family of
origin, the degree of anxiety in the mother during conception,
pregnancy, and the childhood of the child; and the degree to which her
anxiety goes into caring for the child. The degree and intensity of the
mother's anxiety is different for each of her children, there is often a
difference in her attitude toward boys and girls, and mothers usually

have one child most involved in the process. Much of the mother's thinking, worry, feeling energy goes into "giving attention" to the child, to which the child responds by "giving" an equal amount of self to the mother. This is in contrast to the better differentiated mother whose giving to the child is determined by the child's need, and not the mother's anxiety. The amount of mother's "giving of self" to the child constitutes a programmed "need for love" in the child, that will be manifested in the child's future relationships. This amount of "need for love" tends to remain fixed for life. The amount of reciprocal "giving and receiving" in the early mother-child relationship provides the first clue of the future level of "differentiation of self" for the child. The parent-child relationship may stay in fairly calm equilibrium until adolescence when the dependently attached child attempts to break away from parents and form peer relationships. People choose their closest personal friends from those with equal "needs for love." Current teenage peer relationships tend toward groups made up on an interlocking network of "closest friends." There is a separate group for different levels of differentiation. The lower the level of the group, the more intense its antifamily and antiestablishment posture. It is considered grown-up, or courageous, or "cool" to "stand up to" parents and society. At this level of differentiation, to "stand up to" means to attack and shock the other with language and behavior, and to get away with breaking rules. In relationship with the parents, the youngster is driven by anxiety in demanding rights and freedom, and the material advantages of being grown up. Initially, the parents are against the youngster but without clear convictions of their own. In the emotional field with the youngster, they may be partially "sold" on the youngster's argument, and give in to the demands to allay the anxiety of the moment, hoping this will solve the problem. This sets the stage for new and greater demands and threats. The process can keep repeating until the parents have exceeded their ability to provide material demands, and the youngster's misbehavior has become a social problem. These youngsters are masters in knowing the weaknesses of parents and society and in presenting willful arguments in favor of "rights." At this level of differentiation the concept of responsibility is lost, both in the parents and in the youngster.

The study of the way society deals with behavior problems provided the first solid clues to extending knowledge about the family into social systems. In the past twenty years, the full range of public officials who represent society in dealing with behavior problems have also become increasingly "permissive." This includes public officials at local, state, and national levels. Operationally, the vocal segment of society is in the position of the anxious teenager who is driven by anxiety and who is demanding rights, and the public official is in the position of the unsure parent who give in to allay the anxiety of the moment. The public officials include those in education, including teachers, counselors, principals, superintendents, and college presidents; those in charge of judicial and law enforcement functions, including police, judges, courts, and others; and the full spectrum of those who establish policy and pass laws. Societal pressure is directed first at those who are most unsure of self, and most vulnerable to pressure. Then it extends to others. There have been those in office the full twenty years who have changed their operating decisions in response to pressure. People such as teachers and police tend to change in response to the more permissive policy of the chief, the principal, or the superintendent. Newly elected officials are more likely to conform to the more permissive policy than the outgoing incumbent. There are those who are better differentiated who still maintain a reasonable level of self determined self, and who still manage to function in society, but they are more the exception than the rule. These judgments are made from personal knowledge of public officials in my local area; from following the national scene closely for many years, through newspapers, magazines, and the literature; and from keeping a file on landmark decisions and cases in which there was enough information on the principal people to make a valid estimation. There has been enough experience with families to know the characteristics of different scale levels. The operating positions of society on critical issues were compared to know levels in families. The average functioning level of society has regressed a full ten points on my scale in twenty-five years. The comparison was based on issues known to influence regression in families, and small social groups. It excluded change that might have direct connection with the sweeping progressive change in society. The evaluation also has no direct connection with the polarized issues that are called liberal and conservative forces. The regressive curve has had up and down swings throughout the entire period, but there was an over-all slow downward curve from the late 1940s until about 1960, a more marked downward curve from about 1960 to 1964, a sharp downward curve from about 1964 to 1969 (as great in the last half of the 1960s as the previous fifteen years), and then a gradual upward curve through about 1972. Since then the curve has fluctuated too much to establish a definite curve. The degree of the regression was a surprise when it was charted. Considering that most of the population falls within about fifty points on the scale, the regression constitutes about twenty percent in percentage figures.

Emotional Process and Regression

There are striking analogies between regression in a family and regression in larger social groups and society. Regression occurs in response to chronic sustained anxiety, and not in response to acute anxiety. If there is regression with acute anxiety, it disappears when the anxiety subsides. Regression occurs when the family, or society, begins to make important decisions to allay the anxiety of the moment.

Togetherness-individuality forces. A critical index of the functioning of an emotional system is the balance of the togetherness-individuality forces. The two forces exactly balance each other. In a period of calm, the two forces operate as a friendly team, largely out of sight. The togetherness forces are derived from the universal need for "love," approval, emotional closeness, and agreement. The individuality force is derived from the drive to be a productive, autonomous individual, as defined by self rather than the dictates of the group. Any emotional system has an amount of togetherness forces, and a reciprocal amount of individuality forces, which constitute a life style or "norm" for that group at the point in time. Optimum functioning would be somewhere near a fifty-fifty balance, with neither force overriding the other and the system sufficiently flexible to adapt to change. In an anxiety field, the group moves toward more togetherness to relieve the anxiety, and a new balance would be established at perhaps fifty-five or even sixty on the togetherness side, and a reciprocal forty-five or forty on the individuality side, which becomes the new "norm" for the group at that period. These figures are used to illustrate the principle and they do not have specific meaning other than to clarify the point.

These two forces are in such a sensitive balance that a small increase in either results in deep emotional rumblings as the two forces work toward the new balance. The presence of rumblings can provide a clue that a shift is in progress even before overt symptoms are present. The balance is sensitive to anxiety. A shift toward togetherness of a family level can be illustrated by the anxious teenager who demands rights and freedom. The insecure parents object, and then go along with the demands to relieve the anxiety of the moment. Now the system is in balance at a slightly increased level of regression. On a societal level, the anxious vocal segment begins a plea for peace, harmony, togetherness, caring for others, more rights, and for decisions that provide this. The individuality forces oppose and plead for principle, the autonomy of self, and staying on a predetermined course in spite of anxiety. The togetherness forces can counter the individuality position as irrational, uncaring, disloyal, and hurtful, and the individuality forces counter with the rights of an individual to determine his own course. If the togetherness forces win out, the individuality forces give up the opposition and now the system is back in emotional harmony with a new "norm" of increased togetherness and less individuality and a slight increase in regression. If the anxiety continues, the togetherness forces will begin a new surge of pressure, and the cycle repeats. In calmer periods the shift can go back and forth, with neither overriding for long periods. To illustrate the process, I will assume a situation in which togetherness forces prevail through repeated steps until togetherness seriously overrides individuality. As the new "norms" are established after each step, the style of life changes to fit the new togetherness, and regression symptoms predominate. The togetherness forces keep pressing to influence elections and selection of public officials, individuality is submerged, decision-making ability is lost, viable members desert the group, and there is overwhelming emotional reactivity, violence, and chaos. The endpoint of too much togetherness comes with viable members leaving to join other groups, and the others huddled in impotent fear, so close they live in "piles" and so alienated they still clamor for togetherness which further increases the alienation, or they become violent and start destroying each other.

The togetherness-individuality balance is also disturbed by an increase in individuality. A shift toward individuality on a family level can be illustrated by a single responsible family member who proceeds on an individually determined course. For example, it could be a father who has been trying to be the kind of husband and father his family wanted him to be, and who has promised to try harder, and has failed. If he reaches the point of defining himself as the kind of husband and father he responsibly wants to be, and he makes a move in that direction, he meets immediate emotional opposition that he is selfish and mean and does not love the others. At this point, it would be usual for him to start defending his actions, or counterattacking, or become silent, any of which would pull him back into the old togetherness. Increasing individuation is slow and difficult and it takes place only with a disciplined decision to stay on a principled course in spite of the urge to return to the togetherness. A successful attempt usually comes after several failures. When he is finally able to maintain his course without getting angry at the opposition, the opposition does a final intense emotional attack. If he remains calm with this, the opposition becomes calm and pulls up to his level of individuality. Now the family is balanced in emotional harmony with a bit more of individuality. When one family member successfully makes such an individuality move, then another, and another will do the same. In a small or large social system, the move toward individuality is initiated by a single, strong leader with the courage of his conviction who can assemble a team, and who has clearly defined principles on which he can base his decisions when the emotional opposition becomes intense. The large social system goes through the same small steps with rebalancing the togetherness-individuality forces after each step. There is never a threat of too much individuality. The human need for togetherness prevents going beyond a critical point. A society with higher levels of individuality provides great growth for individuals in the group, it handles anxiety well, decisions are based on principle and are easy, and the group is attractive to new members. This was characteristic of the United States for most of its history. The founder of the nation were strong on principles that provided flexible guarantees for individual rights, and were attractive to immigrants from everywhere. The breakdown in individuality starts when leaders become lax in maintaining principles. When the next anxiety episode occurs, the leaders are sufficiently unsure of principles to begin making decisions based on the anxiety of the moment, and the togetherness forces again become dominant.

Manifestations of Regression

A regressive process is made up of such a complex group of forces it is not yet possible to know which is first or which is most important. The over-all process is set in motion when man is exposed to a certain kind of sustained anxiety. Man is still an emotional reactive product of nature, and he is responsive to nature, in spite of protestations to the contrary. The anxiety that starts regression appears to be related more to a disharmony between man and nature than to disharmony between man and his fellow man, such as war.

It is possible to identify some of the manifestations of regression. Togetherness forces begin to override individuality, there is an increase in decisions designed to allay the anxiety of the moment, an increase in cause-and-effect thinking, a focus on "rights" to the exclusion of "responsibility," and a decrease in the over-all level of responsibility. There is a paradox in the rights-responsibility issue. The greater the anxiety, the greater the focus on "rights" that submerge "responsibility." There can be no rights without a responsible majority to guarantee the rights. The more a person focuses on rights for himself, the less he is aware of the rights of others, and the more he becomes irresponsible in violating the rights of others. The focus on rights destroys the goal it was designed to attain.

There is another paradox in the focus on togetherness. The more man anxiously strives for togetherness, the more he loses what he strives for. Man needs human closeness but he is allergic to too much of it. As anxiety increases, more and more move into the concentrations of people in the metropolitan centers. He withdraws emotionally from the togetherness, which increases his alienation, which increases the need for togetherness, which stirs up the anxiety of too much closeness, which results in more withdrawal and alienation. Man responds to alienation in the "human pile" in a combination of ways. Some withdraw into lonely isolation in the middle of the "pile." Others, unable to achieve closeness with those important to them, go into frenetic socializing and the seeking of brief, or transient, or infrequent closeness with outsiders and relative strangers.

Sexuality is one of the prominent mechanisms for achieving closeness. As anxiety, regression, and the need for closeness increase, and it is impossible to achieve closeness in their own families, more and more seek closeness through sexual activity outside their families. The incidence of sex outside of marriage has increased and the divorce rate has steadily increased. Active sexuality begins for an increasing number of teenagers as early as junior high school. Withdrawn people whose sexuality is confined more to fantasy, have pornography and sex movies readily available. Forms of sexuality, previously disapproved and called perverse by society, have now become more accepted. Communal living arrangements, long present on social experiment levels, have become a common way of life for the most anxious and least stable segment of young people. The sexual revolution, in all its many forms, is seen as a product of the regression. Another manifestation of the anxiety and regression has been the overuse of drugs in all its manifestations, which is part of the total picture. Still another product of the regression is violence, which is an integral part of the anxiety-regression complex. An increase in violence, in all its myriad forms, predictably follows an increase in the togetherness forces. A regressed society cannot substantially reduce the crime which is part of the total complex, without first reducing the regression. In a regression, the "norm" of society in business, the professions, in government, and social institutions, gradually falls to levels that match the regression.

As regression increases through successive stages, new "norms" of behavior are established throughout society. The cycle operates as has been described in more detail for the behavior problem teenager. The vocal segment of society begins pressuring public officials to conform. Some of these issues reach the Supreme Court for reinterpretations of law that more nearly fit the new level of regression. The togetherness forces also seek professional and scientific approval for the new "norms."

One of the most interesting areas has to do with professional approval for the new sexuality of the sexual revolution. Almost all of the professional papers thus far have viewed the sexual revolution as evolutionary progress toward a new and more objective sexuality, and a new freedom from sexual repression. Actually, the main impetus for the sexual revolution began in the mid 1960s. It is not possible for *progressive* change of this magnitude to occur this rapidly. Those who call the sexual revolution "progressive" point to the slow change in this direction that has been in progress for decades. While there are some facts to support this, the thesis here is that change of this magnitude can only occur in a regression.

In a regression, time honored principles that have been cornerstones of our democratic society are also misused to promote the regression. The principle of "rights" has been mentioned. Others include the principles of "free speech" and "freedom of the press."

Future of the Regression

A regression stops when anxiety subsides or when the complications of the regression are greater than the anxiety that feeds the regression. Man is not willing to give up the easy life as long as there is a way to "have his cake and eat it too." If my hypothesis about societal anxiety is reasonably accurate, the crises of society will recur and recur, with increasing intensity for decades to come. Man created the environmental crisis by being the kind of a creature he is. The environment is part of man, change will require a change in the basic nature of man, and man's track record for that kind of change has not been good. Man is a versatile animal and perhaps he will be able to change faster when confronted with the alternatives. I believe man is moving into crises of unparalleled proportions, that the crises will be different than those he has faced before, that they will come with increasing frequency for several decades, that he will go as far as he can in dealing symptomatically with each crisis, and that a final major crisis will come as soon as the middle of the next century. The type of man who survives that will be one who can live in better harmony with nature. This prediction is based on knowledge about the nature of man as an instinctual being, and on stretching existing thinking as far as it can go. There are many questions about what man can do about his environmental crisis. The thesis here is that he might modify his future course if he can gain some control over his reaction to anxiety and his "instinctual" emotional reactiveness, and begin taking constructive action based on his fund of knowledge and on logical thinking.

Summary

    The main goal of this paper is to present a beginning effort to correlate knowledge gained from the study of the family with broad societal patterns. A comparison between the ways that parents deal with delinquency and behavior problems in their teenage children, and the ways that representatives of society deal with the same problem, provided the first data on which to base such a bridge. Whether or not this particular effort eventually proves reliable is of less importance than the fact that knowledge gained from study of the family is of critical importance to the total human phenomenon.

III
The Bowen Theory

Chapter 14

Family Therapy
After Twenty Years

Family therapy came on the psychiatric scene in the mid 1950s. It had been developing in the private work of a few investigators for some years prior to that. The growth and development of family therapy has paralleled the ferment and change in psychiatry during the same period. There are psychiatrists who consider family therapy to be a superficial counseling method. A majority think of family therapy as a treatment method based on conventional psychiatric theory. A small percentage of family therapists think of family research as providing new dimensions for thinking about human adaptation and family therapy as pointing the way toward more effective ways of dealing with human problems. All three views are probably accurate, depending on the way the person thinks about the nature and origin of human maladaptation. In this chapter the author will present his view of how the family movement began, how it has developed during its first two decades of existence, and how this has been related to the changing psychiatric scene. There are many differences in method and thchnique in family therapy, based on a variety of theoretical premises. Each therapist is emotionally invested in his own approach and therefore has some degree of bias in the way he views the total field. With awareness of the differences, the author will present one version of the way the field has evolved in the past two decades. The author was one of the originators of the family movement and has continued to be active in the field. He began his family explorations in the late 1940s from a psychoanalytic orientation. He has moved from psychoanalytic thinking toward a systems theory and systems therapy.

History of the Family Movement

The family movement in psychiatry began in the late 1940s and early 1950s with several widely separated investigators who worked privately without knowledge of each other. The movement suddenly erupted into the open in the 1955-1956 period when the investigators began to hear about each other and they began to communicate and to meet together. Growth and development was rapid after the family idea had come to the surface. After family therapy was well known, there were those who said it was not new and that it had developed from what child psychiatrists, or social workers, or marriage counselors had been doing for several decades. There is some evidence to support the thesis that the family focus evolved slowly as early psychoanalytic theory was put into practice. Freud's (1909) treatment of Little Hans in 1909 through work with the father was consistent with methods later developed from family therapy. Flugel's (1921) book, *The Psycho-Analytic Study of the Family*, conveyed an awareness of the family but the focus was on the psychopathology of each family member. The child guidance movement passed close to some current family concepts without seeing them. The focus on pathology in the child prevented a view of the family. Psychiatric social workers came on the scene in the 1930s and 1940s but their work with families was oriented around the illness in the patient. Sociologists and anthropologists were studying families and contributing to the literature but their work had no direct application to psychiatry. Marriage counseling began its growth in the 1930s but the dynamic formulations came from conventional psychiatry. Also, general systems theory had its beginnings in the 1930s before there was recognizable connection between it and psychiatric theory. There is little evidence that these forces played more than an indirect role in ushering in the family movement.

Most of the evidence favors the thesis that the family movement developed within psychiatry, that it was an outgrowth of psychoanalytic theory, and it was part of the sequence of events after World War II. Psychoanalysis had finally become the most accepted of the psychological theories. It had theoretical postulations about the full range of emotional problems, but psychoanalytic treatment was not clearly defined for the more severe emotional problems. After World War II, psychiatry suddenly became popular as a medical specialty and hundreds of young psychiatrists began experimenting in an effort to extend psychoanalytic treatment to the full range of emotional problems. This includes those who began experimenting with families. A psychoanalytic principle may have accounted for the family movement remaining underground for some years. There were rules to safeguard the personal privacy of the patient-therapist relationship and to prevent contamination of the transference by contact with the patient's relatives. Some hospitals had a therapist to deal with the carefully protected intrapsychic process, another psychiatrist to handle reality matters and administrative procedures, and a social worker to talk to relatives. In those years this principle was a cornerstone of good psychotherapy. Failure to observe the principle was considered inept psychotherapy. Finally it became acceptable to see families together in the context of "research."

The investigators who started family research with schizophrenia were prominent in starting the family movement. This included Lidz in Baltimore and New Haven (Lidz, Fleck, and Cornelison 1965), Jackson in Palo Alto (Bateson et al. 1956), and Bowen (1960) in Topeka and Bethesda. Family therapy was so associated with schizophrenia in the early years that some did not think of it as separate from schizophrenia until the early 1960s. Ackerman (1958) developed his early family ideas from work with psychiatric social workers. Satir (1964), a psychiatric social worker, had developed her family thinking through work with psychiatrists in a state hospital. Bell (1961) and Middlefort (1957) were examples of people who started their work very early and who did not write about it until the family movement was well under way. The pattern suggests there were others who never reported their work and who were not identified with the family movement. The formation of the Committee on the Family, Group for the Advancement of Psychiatry, provides other evidence (1970) about the early years of the family movement. The Committee was formed in 1950 at the suggestion of William C. Menninger who considered the family to be important for psychiatric study. The Committee was not able to find psychiatrists working in the field until the family investigators began to hear about each other in the 1955-1956 period.

Spiegel, chairman of the Committee on the Family, helped organize the first national meeting for psychiatrists doing family research. It was a section meeting at the annual meeting of the American Orthopsychiatric Association in March 1957. It was a quiet meeting. All the papers were on family research but the notion of "family therapy" or "family psychotherapy" was discussed. Some investigators had been working toward methods of family therapy for several years but I believe this was the first time it was discussed as a definite method at a national meeting. That was the beginning of family *therapy* on a national level. Dozens of new people, attracted by the promise of therapy, and with little knowledge of the family research that had led to the development of family therapy, rushed into the field and began their own versions of family therapy. Another section meeting for family papers at the American Psychiatric Association annual meeting in May 1957, helped amplify the process set in motion two months before. All the papers were on research but the meeting was crowded and there was more audience urgency to talk about family therapy. The national meetings in the spring of 1958 were dominated by new therapists eager to report experiences with family therapy. Family research and theoretical thinking that had given birth to family therapy were lost in the new rush to do therapy. New therapists entered the field in numbers. Many dropped out after initial therapeutic failure, but there was a rapid net gain in the total field. The 1957-1958 period was important in determining the future course of the family movement. In that year, family research became known nationally, and in the same year the new family therapists began what the author has called the "healthy unstructured state of chaos." It was considered healthy on the premise that clinical experience would bring an awareness of the theoretical dilemma implicit in family therapy, and awareness would result in efforts to clarify the dilemma. This has not evolved to the degree it was predicted. Some of the newer generations of family therapists have worked toward establishing some theoretical order and structure to the field. A majority of family therapists see family therapy as a method based on conventional individual theory or as an intuitive, experiential method conducted by therapists who are guided by their own feelings and subjective awareness toward the "use of self" in therapy. Others fall between the two extremes. The range of clinical methods and techniques will be discussed later.

There is suggestive evidence that family therapists come largely from childhood situations in which they had more than average awareness of relationship disharmony, some ability to see both sides of an issue, and some motivation to modify the situation. The author uses the term "family movement" in psychiatry to include the theoretical thinking, the family research, and family therapy as they have evolved together and as they continue to grow in psychiatric thinking and practice. This is in contrast to the more popular use of the term "family therapy" as it is used to connote a treatment method.

Common Differences Between Individual
and Family Theory and Therapy

The one main difference between an individual and a family approach is a shift of focus from the individual to the family. The nuances of difference between the two approaches are more subtle and far-reaching than is evident on the surface. The total fabric of society, as it pertains to human illness, dysfunction, and misbehavior, is organized around the concept of man as an autonomous individual who controls his own destiny. When the observing lens is opened to include the entire family field, there is increasing evidence that man is not as separate from his family, from those about him, and from his multigenerational past as he has fancied himself to be. This in no way changes what man is or has always been. He is as autonomous as he has always been, and he is as "locked in" to those about him as he has always been. The family focus merely points to ways that his life is governed by those about him. It is simple enough to say that the family therapist considers the illness in the patient to be a product of a total family problem, but when this simple concept is extended to its ultimate, then all mankind becomes responsible for the ills of all mankind. It is easy to say this in a philosophical, detached kind of way, but man becomes anxious about the notion of changing himself to help modify the ills of mankind. It is easier for man to fight his wars, inflation, social ills, and pay his money for noneffective corrective action, than to contemplate changing himself. From family therapy, we know it is relatively easy for family members to modify their part in the creation of emotional illness once they clearly see what has to be done, but this does not decrease initial anxiety and evasive action at the mere contemplation of it. This section of the chapter is not designed as a theoretical treatise on the ultimate implications of family theory but it is to indicate that the deeper implications are there, and they are more far reaching than is easily realized. The following differences between individual and family theory point up a few of the more obvious examples of the differences.

The medical model. This cornerstone of sound medical practice requires the physician to examine, diagnose, and treat the pathology in the patient. The medical model also applies to conventional psychiatry and the social institutions that deal with human dysfunction, including courts, social agencies, and insurance companies. There is an emotional process in the family through which the family helps to create and maintain the "illness" in the "patient." The process is more intense when anxiety is high. The process also operates in the family therapy sessions.

The family members point to the sickness in the patient and try to confirm this by getting the therapist to label the patient as the sick one. The therapist tries to avoid diagnosing the patient, and to focus on the family emotional process that creates the patient. The family problem is intensified when the medical records and insurance companies require a diagnosis to comply with the medical model. Each therapist has to find his own way to oppose, or neutralize, or deflect the intensity of family emotional process. The situation is usually less dramatic than presented here but this illustrates the counterforces as the therapist tries to change the family process and also meet the minimal requirements of the institutions. Some therapists explain the situation to the family that medical model principles are necessary for records but a different orientation is used for the therapy. Also, the institutions are a bit less strict in requiring adherence to the medical model. Therapists have come to use the terms "designated patient" or "identified patient" to refer to the symptomatic family member. The mere use of the term implies an awareness of the basic process in the family, in the therapy, and in society. The issues that go around the medical model have ramifications that involve the lives of all the people connected with the problem.

Clinical responsibility. Members of the mental health professions have second nature awareness of the nuances of clinical responsibility for a single "patient." The welfare of the patient comes first and the welfare of the family is outside the realm of direct responsibility. The principles of medical responsibility are changed when the focus is on the entire family instead of the patient. There are situations in which an improvement in the former "patient" is followed by serious symptoms in another family member. A conventional therapist might send the second family member to another therapist. A family therapist would operate with the premise that the best interests of the family would be served with a single therapist who could deal with the total family problem. There are other similar situations. A conventional therapist could more easily conclude the patient should be separated from the family which he considers innately pathogenic to the patient. A family therapist would believe the total family situation would be advanced if the patient were kept at home while he attempted to deal with the over-all family anxiety. Family therapists are less likely to consider family members hurtful to each other. They have experience to support the premise that family members want to be responsible and helpful to each other and that it often requires very little help to shift the family climate from a hurtful to a helpful one. The general direction of family therapy is toward helping the family to be responsible for its own, including the "sick" one. It is far more difficult for the impaired family member to begin to assume responsibility than it is for healthier family members. In an effort to more quickly work toward family responsibility, the author developed an approach to work with the "healthiest family member" and to exclude the "sick" family member from the therapy. It has been possible to do an entire course of family therapy with the focus on family health without ever seeing the "sick" family member.

Confidentiality and secrets. A basic principle of medicine and individual psychotherapy requires that the physician and psychotherapist not divulge confidential information. Family therapists are forced to reevaluate this principle. There are situations in which keeping the confidence of one family member can be detrimental to the total family. From family research we have learned that the higher the level of anxiety and symptoms in a family, the more the family members are emotionally isolated from each other. The greater the isolation, the lower the level of responsible communication between family members, and the higher the level of irresponsible underground gossip about each other in the family, and the confiding of secrets to those outside the family. Through pledging a confidence, a person becomes part of the emotional network around the family problem. The basic problem is the relationship pattern in the family rather than the subject matter of the secrets and confidences. A goal in family therapy is to reduce the level of anxiety, to improve the level of responsible open communication within the family, and to reduce the irresponsible, underground communication of secrets and gossip to others. When a family therapist becomes entangled in the secrets and confidences, he becomes part of the emotional webwork and his effectiveness as a therapist is lost. Each family therapist has to find his own way of dealing with confidences within the family without becoming part of the emotional entanglements. Most family therapists employ some kind of working rule about not keeping secrets, and they find ways to communicate secrets in the family sessions, rather than err on the side of becoming a part of the family intrigue. From family therapy experience, we know it can be as detrimental on the one side to blindly keep individual secrets as it is detrimental on the other side for the therapist to gossip to outsiders about private matters in a family. The goal of a family therapist is to be a responsible person who knows the difference between underground secrets and valid, responsible, private communication and who respects this difference.

From family therapy we have learned much about the function of secret communication in situations that range from the avowed privacy of the individual psychotherapy hour to the function of secrets and gossip in society. The higher the avowed intent of secrecy in individual psychotherapy, the greater the chance the patient will gossip to others about the therapist, or the therapist will gossip to others about the patient, all done in strictest confidence. In larger social systems, a "gossip" is one who came from an anxious gossipy family. The higher the level of anxiety in a social system, the lower the level of responsible communication to each other, and the higher the level of irresponsible gossip and the keeping of irresponsible secret files about each other. Family therapy research, with its emphasis on open communication within the family, has been the most observed, audiotaped, filmed, and videotaped of all the psychotherapies. The research points up the emotional problems in rigid adherence to conventional rules about confidentiality and the responsibility in respecting essential private communication.

The spectrum of methods and techniques in family therapy. The best survey of the family field thus far is *The Field of Family Therapy*, a report by the Committee on the Family, Group for the Advancement of Psychiatry, published in March 1970. It was based on the analysis of a detailed questionnaire completed by some 300 family therapists from all the professional disciplines and all levels of experience. Experience since 1970 indicates that the basic pattern of theory and practice is still very much as it was then. The questionnaire responses represented such wide diversity in theory and practice that it was difficult to find a format to report the results. Finally, a scheme was devised to characterize therapists on a scale from A to Z.

Therapists toward the A end of the scale are those whose theory and practice is the same as individual psychotherapists. They use family therapy as a technique to supplement individual psychotherapy or as the main technique for a few families. The A therapists are usually young or they have just started experimenting with family techniques. The overwhelming majority of family therapists are toward the A end of the scale. The A therapist thinks in terms of individual psychopathology and the therapeutic relationship between the therapist and patient as the modality for emotional growth. He sees family therapy as a technique to facilitate his psychotherapy with the patient, and he speaks of indications and contraindications for family therapy. It is impossible to know how many individual therapists now do occasional family interviews. They characteristically do not do formal reports about their work.

Therapists toward the Z end of the scale use theory and techniques that are quite different. They think in terms of systems, relationships, emotional fields, and breakdown in communication. They tend to "think family" for all emotional problems and they usually end up seeing a number of family members even if the initial problem in the patient is one for which others would clearly recommend individual psychotherapy. The therapy of a Z scale therapist is directed toward restoring communication, improving relationships in the family, and toward helping family members toward higher levels of differentiation. There are few therapists toward the Z end of the scale. They are the ones more oriented to research and theory or who have been in practice a long time.

Between the two extremes are therapists with theoretical orientations made of a mixture of individual and family concepts and with a wide variety of techniques. The place of therapists on the scale seems to be determined by the therapists' motivation for theory and research and the professional environment in which he works. The research oriented therapist is guided more by theory than approval from the professional environment. He usually moves steadily toward the Z end of the scale. The therapy-oriented therapist is more sensitive to the approval of colleagues. He is guided toward a philosophy of treatment that includes a mix of individual and family concepts. When he finds the best "fit" between himself and the professional environment, and between himself and the clinical problem, there is little movement on the scale. The therapy-oriented therapist tends more to try to "sell" his viewpoint and to be critical of others with another viewpoint.

Popular terminology in the field is determined by popular usage of terms by a majority of therapists. Most therapists are toward the A end of the scale. They tend to think of family therapy as a method and technique for the application of individual theory. Designations of the type of therapy is determined more by the configuration of family members who attend the sessions than by the theory. The term *family therapy* popularly refers to any psychotherapy session attended by multiple family members. The terms *couples therapy* or *marital therapy* are used when most sessions are attended by both spouses. The term *individual therapy* is used to designate sessions with only one family member. Some use the term *conjoint family therapy* for psychotherapy sessions attended by family members from two or more generations. It often refers to parents and child together. From this orientation it would be possible for a single family to have individual therapy for the patient, couples therapy for the two parents, and conjoint therapy for parents and patient. The author is at the extreme Z end of the scale. For him the terminology is based on the theory. The term *family therapy* is used for the effort to modify the family relationship system, whether that effort is with one or with multiple family members. Since 1960 he has spoken of "family therapy with one family member," which is consistent with his orientation but can be considered inaccurate by most family therapists. The author objected to the title "The Field of

Family Therapy," for the 1970 survey of the family field on the grounds that it did not recognize the thinking and research that helped create the field. A majority of the Committee members insisted on this title on the grounds that it best represented the field as it exists.

Specific Methods and Techniques of Family Therapy

The following is a brief summary of some of the most prominent, different methods of family therapy. The list is designed to communicate the author's view of the over-all pattern to the growth and development of family therapy. It is not designed to present the work of any one therapist or any group of therapists. Most therapists tend to use a combination of the methods.

Family group therapy. A high percentage of family therapy should more accurately be called family group therapy since many of the basic principles were adapted from group psychotherapy. It is noteworthy that specialists in group psychotherapy have had no more than secondary interest in family therapy. There were no group psychotherapists among the originators of the family movement. A few group therapists became interested in developing family therapy a few years after family therapy was introduced. That group has grown gradually, but it has been relatively separated from the main body of family therapists. The group therapists doing family therapy attend the group therapy meetings and they publish in group therapy journals with relatively little overlap between the groups. If one can consider this as a fact without value judgment about why it came to be, it can say something about the nature of the family movement.

Most of the influence of group psychotherapy on family therapy has come from people who had some early professional training in group psychotherapy but who did not consider themselves to be group therapists. In 1957, when new therapists began developing their own version of family therapy, without much knowledge of family research, the already defined methods of group psychotherapy offered more guidelines than any of the other existing methods. In addition, the psychodynamic formulations of group psychotherapy were reasonably consistent with training in individual psychotherapy. I believe this may account for the heavy influence of group psychotherapy on family therapy.

Methods of family group therapy vary from therapist to therapist but there are some common denominators. The basic theory, the psychodynamic formulations, and the interpretations are reasonably consistent with individual therapy and also with group therapy. The therapeutic method and encouraging family members to talk to each other comes from principles of group therapy. Family group therapy comes closer to the popular stereotype of family therapy than any other. This involves all the family meeting together to discuss problems. Family group therapy is one of the easiest of the methods for the relatively inexperienced therapist. It requires that the therapist develop some facility for relating to multiple people in a group without taking sides and without becoming too entangled in the family emotional system. Beyond this, most professional people can operate on skills learned in training. As a method it yields very high initial results with comparatively little effort by the therapist. Most families with symptoms are out of emotional contact with each other and are not aware of what others are thinking and feeling. The higher the level of anxiety, the more family members are isolated from each other. With a family therapist acting as chairman of the group and the facilitator of calm communication, much can be accomplished in a short time. Parents can profit from hearing the thoughts and feelings of each other. Children can be fascinated at hearing the parental side of issues and learning that parents are human too. Parents can be amazed at the astute observations of their children about the family, and the child is grateful for an opportunity to say what he thinks and for the forum that values his ideas. The family can eagerly look forward to such sessions which they cannot manage at home because of emotion and communication blocks. The process can reach a point of pleasant exhilaration with parents increasingly aware of each other and the children increasingly accepting of the foibles in the parents. When communication increases, family symptoms subside and the family can report much more fun and togetherness. Of course there are situations when the process is not as smooth as described here. These are the very impaired, chaotic families and those in which it is difficult to bring family members together without emotional explosiveness. However, if the therapist is able to keep the communication calm for the volatile family and if he is able to stimulate communication for the more silent family, the net result is on the favorable side.

The main advantage in family group therapy is the striking, short term result. The main disadvantage comes when the family group therapy becomes a longer term process. At this point, the family begins to act out the same problems they had at home. The parents begin to expect the children to assume more responsibility in the family. The more adequate children become bored by the repetition of issues they have heard before and they begin to find reasons not to attend. If forced to attend, the formerly talkative children can become silent. The maximum results with short-term family group therapy come within about ten to twenty sessions, depending on the intensity of the problem and the skill of the therapist.

A fair percentage of families tend to terminate at the point of feeling good about the family. If they terminate before they reach the impasse of longer term therapy, they may terminate feeling that little was accomplished. It is usually not possible for parents and children to continue together beyond a certain point. It often results in the parents and one child or the two parents continuing without the others.

Family group therapy is not as effective for long term family therapy as some of the other methods. The continuation of it as a long term method, to a reasonable resolution of the underlying problem, depends on the intensity of the problem and the skill of the therapist. Very impaired families may continue for a long time, using the therapy much as an individual psychotherapy patient uses therapy for support. Therapists tend to develop other methods and techniques if the goal is to get through the emotional impasses.

Couples therapy or marital therapy. These terms help to point up the ambiguity in the field. Specifically, the terms imply that the spouses are in some kind of therapy in which the focus is on two people and their relationship. The terms convey nothing about the problem for which the therapy is used, or the theory or method of therapy. Some therapists restrict use of the terms for problems in the marital relationship, such as marital conflict or marital disharmony. A high percentage of marriages have some degree of conflict or disharmony. Other therapists have a broader view of marital problems and use marital therapy for an additional range of problems, such as impotence and frigidity. From experience, the focus on the relationship aspects of such problems can more quickly resolve the problems than focusing on the individual aspects of the problems. Others use marital therapy for problems outside the marital relationship, such as problems in a child. Such considerations say nothing about the theory, the method, or the technique of therapy. In general, theory is determined by the way the therapist thinks about the nature of the family problem; method is determined by broad principles for implementing the theory into a therapeutic approach; and techniques are the specific ways or strategies for implementing the method. Therapists trained in individual theory, and who accept the assumptions of individual theory as fact, are usually not much aware of theory. Terms such as *theory, hypothesis, assumption, formulation,* and *concept* are used loosely and inaccurately. It is not uncommon to hear someone say, "I have a theory," when it would be more accurate to say, "I have an idea." It would be improbable that anyone could have a theory about marital relationships that is not part of a larger theory. Marital therapy might accurately apply to a method if it is based on a theory about the nature of the problem to be modified. The general use of the terms, *couples therapy* or *marital therapy*, implies merely that both spouses attend the sessions together. The use of the terms is a good example of the wide divergence of practice in the family field.

Psychoanalytic marital therapy. This term has not been used widely. If it were generally used, it would be one of the more specific terms in the family field. The theory would be consistent with psychoanalytic theory, the method would be reasonably consistent with the theory, and therapy techniques would have a reasonable resemblance to psychoanalytic techniques. This is a method used frequently by family therapists who formerly practiced psychoanalysis. One of the main differences in techniques would be the analysis of the relationship between the spouses, rather than the transference relationship with the therapist. This method involves the process of learning more about the intrapsychic process in each spouse, in the presence of the other spouse, with access to the emotional reactiveness of each spouse to the other. The approach provides access to the unconscious through the use of dreams. A new dimension is added when spouses can analyze the dreams of each other. Readings on the intrapsychic process in each are obtained through simultaneous dreams. This is one of the most effective long term methods of family therapy. It works best when the initial problem was in one spouse or the marital relationship. The author used it a number of years before moving to a systems approach to the entire family relationship system.

Child-focused family. This term refers to a well defined family problem rather than a therapy approach, but it is used frequently enough to warrant discussion here. The child-focused family is one in which sufficient family anxiety is focused on one or more children to result in serious impairment in a child. The child focused energy is deeply imbedded, and it includes the full range of emotional involvements from the most positive to the most negative. The higher the anxiety in the parents, the more intense the process. For instance, a mother in her calmer periods can *know* that nagging makes the child's problem worse. She may resolve to stop the nagging, only to have it recur automatically when anxiety rises. The usual approach in family therapy is to soften the intensity of the focus on the child and to gradually shift the emotional focus to the parents, or between parents and families of origin. This might be relatively easy if the problem is not intense, or it can be so intense that little is accomplished beyond symptomatic relief and easing the pressure for the child. There are differences about what to do with the child. Child psychiatrists tend to focus major attention on the child and supportive attention on the parents. Family therapists tend to focus on the emotional process in the family with parents and child together. This approach may bring good initial results, but there are difficulties when it becomes a long-term process. Some family therapists will see the child separately or have someone else see the child. This can result in parents becoming complacent, expecting the problem to be solved in the child's "therapy." There is no single high-road to success in these families. Finding a way through the problem depends on the therapist's concept of the problem and his skill in keeping the family motivated. My own approach is to defocus the child as quickly as possible, to remove the child from the therapy sessions as early as possible, and to give technical priority to getting the focus on the relationship between the parents, at the risk of a temporary increase in the child's symptoms. This broad spectrum of differences around a single clinical problem conveys some idea of the differences in the field, and this does not even touch the differences about what goes in the individual sessions.

Transactional analysis, games theory, and gestalt theory. These three theoretical concepts are grouped together because all three, though each different in its own right, occupy similar positions in the total scheme of family therapy as it is practiced. These concepts and the therapeutic approaches that go with them were either developed before family therapy or they were developed independent of family therapy. These approaches are not incompatible with individual theory, they provide ingenious ways of conceptualizing relationship systems, and they represent a step toward systems theory. For the therapist attempting to extend his knowledge of family process, these concepts provide ready-made concepts that are more precise for understanding the family and for improvements in therapy. Success with these therapy methods, as with most other methods, depends on the skill of the therapist.

Behavior modification therapy. Almost every experienced family therapist has done some version of behavior modification therapy, which has now become a well defined method. The family presents a near perfect model of a "system" in operation. The family is a system in that each member of the system, on cue, says his assigned lines, takes his assigned posture, and plays his assigned role in the family drama as it repeats hour by hour and day by day. This process operates without intellectual awareness. When any central member of the family can observe and come to know his own part in the family, and he can purposely change his part, the others will immediately change in relation to it. Family members who can become adept at knowing their roles can bring about predictable change in the action-behavior patterns in others. The disadvantage is in the short-term nature of the change. There are two main variables that limit the long-term result. First, the other family members rather quickly catch on and they start their own versions of adapting to it, or they initiate their own changes. Then the process can become "game playing." Secondly, the whole system of reacting and counter-reacting is imbedded in the emotional system, and the initiator has to keep on consciously and purposely initiating the change. When the effort lapses, the family system returns to its former level. Long-term change requires a modification in the intensity of the emotional level, at which time changes can become permanent.

Co-therapist therapy. The use of two therapists, or multiple therapists, began very early in the family movement. A high percentage of family therapists have had some experience with it. Originally, it was used to help the therapist become aware of his own emotional overinvolvement with family members. Whitaker (1967) routinely used a co-therapist in psychotherapy with schizophrenia long before he started family therapy. He also has become well known for using co-therapists in his long career in family therapy. Others have developed it as a method for including both male and female therapists who serve as a model for the family. Boszormenyi-Nagy (1973) is one who has been prominent in perfecting this model in his method of therapy. Still another use of co-therapists is the team approach in which several therapists, representing the various members of the mental health professions, work together as a team. MacGregor (1964) and his group made a major effort to perfect this during his work in Galveston in the early 1960s. He now teaches and trains family therapists with the team approach. Some version of the family therapy team approach is now used in most centers that do family therapy. In the broad spectrum of family therapy, co-therapist therapy exists as one of the major innovations and developments in family therapy. It is used both as a method and technique.

Sculpting and simulated families. These two innovations are the modern day descendants of drama therapy. Sculpting is listed first because it has more application to therapy. The simulated family was developed in the early 1960s, more for teaching than for therapy. In teaching, it involves professional people who play-act hypothetical family situations. Role playing helps family process become more real to the participants. In therapy, one or more members of a real family have outside people to role play the parts of absent family members. People who participate in simulated families discover an uncanny sense of realness to the role played situation. Sculpting was developed in the late 1960s to help family members become more aware of self in relation to their own families. The therapist helps the family members decide on the functioning position of each family member in relation to the others, following which the family members are put into physical apposition. The sculpting sessions in which family members debate the position of each, plus the living sculpture in which they assume positions such as bossy, meek, clinging, and distant provides both a cognitive and feeling experience that is one of the more rapid ways of helping family members become aware of each other. The sculpting may be repeated during therapy for awareness of change and progress. These two methods are examples of other innovative developments in the field.

Multiple family therapy. The most popular version of this was developed by Lacqueur et al. (1964) for multiple members of multiple families who meet together in a form of family group therapy for discussion of individual and joint problems. It is most useful for severely impaired or fragmented families. Multiple family groups have been started around groups of inpatients and families on visiting days at mental hospitals, around families and patients attached to mental health centers, and families and patients discharged from mental hospitals. This method provides a unique and effective method of support and a relationship system that enables patients to be discharged earlier and to be maintained at home and in the community. New families can replace those who discontinue, while the group continues to serve an ongoing resource for former families who wish to return. This method has also been used with less impaired people with excellent results. This method is least effective in helping individual family members toward defining a self. The author has devised a method of multiple family therapy specifically designed to help individual family members toward higher levels of functioning. The therapist works with each family separately, dividing the time between the three or four families and avoiding communication or emotional exchange between the families. The focus on the family emotional process in each family can permit beginning individuation in that family. Emotional exchange between the families encourages group process, which overshadows family process, and individuation is impaired or blocked. Advantages of the method are faster progress in each family from observing the others and a net saving in time. Disadvantages are additional work in scheduling and the energy required of the therapist in maintaining structure.

Network therapy. This method was devised by Speck (1973) in the mid-1960s. It was designed to help "create" families for fragmented, disorganized families. The goal is to include people from the friendship network in addition to relatives. The isolated family may have few available relatives and few close friends. The therapist encourages the family to invite relatives and close friends, and friends of friends, and friends of friends, etc. The meetings often include 15 to 40 people, but Speck has had meetings with up to 200 people. Meetings are held in homes or in other appropriate places in the neighborhood. The therapist begins with discussion about the problem in the central family, but discussions shift to other problems in the network. Theoretical premises about networks are that people have distorted ideas about problems in others, that distortions are often worse than reality, that friends become distant during stress, and open discussion of problems can stimulate more real relationship activity and helpfulness to network members. Experience with networks tends to support the premises. Some remain to talk for hours after meetings have ended, some do become more helpful around the central problem, and network attitudes about the central problem are modified. When regular network meetings continue, a fair percentage lose interest, attendance at meetings dwindles, and continuation requires enthusiasm by the therapist and those who organize the network. On the negative side, the logistical problems of organizing time consuming evening meetings, and the clinical expertise necessary for managing large meetings with divergent emotional forces, makes this into a difficult therapeutic method. The network idea has a potential both for the understanding of social networks and the development of therapeutic methods. In practice, the network has come to be a short-term method, or one to achieve a specific goal. One successful application (Kelly and Hollister 1971) has been for new admissions to mental hospitals. One or two meetings are held to include the family, friends, and people who had contact with the patient before admission. Meetings ease the impact of admission and facilitate discharge. Additional meetings may be called at nodal points during hospitalization.

Encounters, marathons, and sensitivity groups. These methods are examples of a trend that has increased in the past decade. Therapists who practice the method say it lends itself to unstructured use by people with little training. The methods are short-term and are based on partial theoretical notions that suppressed feelings are responsible for symptoms, and that awareness of feelings and the expression of feelings in relation to others are therapeutic. For some, the methods can result in temporary periods of good feeling and exhilaration, which are called growth. For others, the sessions are followed by increased disharmony. This movement is antithetical to the efforts of the majority of family therapists.

Experiential and Structured Family Therapy

An increasing number of family therapists are beginning to classify the various family therapy methods into experiential and structured methods. This is a modification of the A to Z scale in "The Field of Family Therapy." The experiential approaches put a high premium on becoming aware of feelings, in being able to express feelings directly to others, and in becoming more spontaneous in relationship systems. Most therapists agree that a spontaneous, open relationship system is a desirable result for family therapy, but there is disagreement about the best way to help families achieve this. The structured approach uses theoretical concepts about the nature of the family problem and a therapeutic method that is based on the theory. The method contains a built-in blueprint to guide the course of the therapy. The method knows the problems to be encountered during therapy, it has a methodology for getting through the difficult areas, and the method knows when it approaches its goal. This is in contrast to the experiential approaches that emphasize the subjective experience of therapy, that rely on the subjective awareness and intuition of the therapist to guide the therapy, and that considers a development of more open spontaneity in relationships to be the goal. A structure-oriented therapist makes decisions based on theory and he stays on course in spite of his feelings that might oppose it. An experiential therapist uses feelings and intuitive, subjective awareness to make his decisions. If all approaches are put on a continuum, the encounter-marathon approaches would be at one extreme end of the continuum. Farther along the continuum would be approaches that offer more and more structure, with less and less emphasis on the expression of feelings as a guiding principle. There is no such thing as an all-feeling situation, or an all-structured situation. The human animal is a feeling being, and any approach has to somehow deal with feelings and, also, the realities of relationships with others. The type of approach is not a positive index of success in therapy. There are Indian scouts better qualified to lead an expedition through the wilderness than inexperienced novices with scientific instruments. The structure-oriented therapists believe that knowledge and structure, in addition to experience, will eventually produce a better result. To summarize this point, the experiential orientation says, "Know and express your feelings and the process will break down the unhealthy structure that interferes with your life." The structured orientation says, "Problems are the result of a poorly structured life. The surest approach is the modification of the structure which will automatically result in free and spontaneous relationships."

The following are some examples of therapists who have worked toward theoretical structures that are different from conventional individual theory. Jackson began working on communication theory in the 1950s (Jackson and Lederer 1969). Before his death he had extended his thinking into well defined systems concepts that clustered around his communication model. His therapy reflected his theoretical thinking. In more recent years, Minuchin (1974) in association with Haley who formerly worked with Jackson, has developed a structured approach with theoretical concepts so well formulated that he has automatic therapeutic moves for any clinical situation. His theoretical concepts view man and his intrapsychic self in the context of the relationship system around him. Through his relationships, man influences those about him, and man in turn is influenced by those about him. His therapeutic approach, consistent with his theory, is designed to modify the feedback system of the relationship system through which the whole family is modified. His therapy specifically avoids a focus on the intrapsychic forces. The author has worked toward a family systems theory of human adaptation and a method of therapy designed to modify the relationship system by modifying the part the individual plays in the relationship system. The therapy also avoids focus on the intrapsychic forces. No one is ever really accurate in describing the work of another.

The author's approach will be presented in more detail later.

Summary

This survey represents one view of the diversity in theory and practice as it has evolved in the family field the past two decades. In 1960, the author used the analogy of the six blind men and the elephant to describe a similar situation in the family field. Each blind man felt a different part of the elephant and the assumption of each was accurate within one frame of reference. The same analogy is accurate today as different family therapists view the family through different frames of reference. The family is a complex organization that remains relatively constant no matter who observes and defines it. At the same time, there can be a wide variety of different concepts that accurately describe the family. Early in the family movement, most therapists viewed the family through familiar theories about intrapsychic forces within the individual. This was accurate within limits, but the theory was awkward and inaccurate for conceptualizing the relationship patterns through which the intrapsychic forces in one person were interlocked with the intrapsychic forces in others. Family therapists began using a variety of different concepts to account for the interpersonal forces. This resulted in one theory for the intrapsychic forces and another for the interpersonal forces. A majority of therapists still use this combination of theories, each finding the most compatible combination for himself. There are problems in using two different kinds of theories for the same over-all phenomenon. Most of the relationship theories used the functional concepts of systems theory. In the past decade, the term "systems" has been misused to the point of simplistic meaninglessness, but the trend toward systems thinking points a definite direction. The world of systems thinking has sent men to the moon and back, but systems concepts are poorly defined in areas that apply to man and his functioning. Systems thinking has a tremendous potential for the future, but the "elephant" of systems thinking is far bigger and more complex than the simpler "elephants" of the past. The author's effort at developing a systems theory represents the serious effort of another "blind man." It is presented in the following sections of this chapter.

A Systems Theory of Emotional Functioning

The main problem in defining a systems theory is in finding a workable collection of functions that can be integrated into a functional whole. The number of choices in the selection of pieces for such a theory is almost infinite. Selection is governed by some over-all framework. It is easier to do a theory about a small area of functioning than a large area. Without a framework, one can emerge with multiple concepts, each accurate within itself, that do not fit together. The universe is our largest conceptualized system. From a systems model, we know there are logical connections between the atom and the organization of the universe and between the smallest cell and the largest known collection of cells, but the development of workable theories are still far in the future. Large areas of specific knowledge are lacking. The conceptual integration of new knowledge can take longer than the original scientific discovery. Into the far distant future, man must be content with his lack of knowledge and discrepant, partial theories.

The following are some of the basic notions about the nature of man that guided the selection of the various concepts in this systems theory. Man is conceived as the most complex form of life that evolved from the lower forms and is intimately connected with all living things. The most important difference between man and the lower forms is his cerebral cortex and his ability to think and reason. Intellectual functioning is regarded as distinctly different from emotional functioning, which man shares with the lower forms. Emotional functioning includes the automatic forces that govern protoplasmic life. It includes the force that biology defines as instinct, reproduction, the automatic activity controlled by the automatic nervous system, subjective emotional and feeling states, and the forces that govern relationship systems. There are varying degrees of overlap between emotional and intellectual functioning. In broad terms, the emotional system governs the "dance of life" in all living things. It is deep in the phylogenetic past and is much older than the intellectual system. A "feeling" is considered the derivative of a deeper emotional state as it is registered on a screen within the intellectual system. The theory postulates that far more human activity is governed by man's emotional system than he has been willing to admit, and there is far more similarity than dissimilarity between the "dance of life" in lower forms and the "dance of life" in human forms. Emotional illness is postulated as a dysfunction of the emotional system. In the more severe forms of emotional illness, the emotions can flood the intellect and impair intellectual functioning but the intellect is not primarily involved in emotional dysfunction. There are varying degrees of "fusion" between the emotional and intellectual systems in the human. The greater the fusion, the more the life is governed by automatic emotional forces that operate, despite man's intellectual verbalization to the contrary. The greater the fusion between the emotion and intellect, the more the individual is fused into the emotional fusions of people around him. The greater the fusion, the more man is vulnerable to physical illness, emotional illness, and social illness, and the less he is able to consciously control his own life. It is possible for man to discrimate between the emotions and the intellect and to slowly gain more conscious control of emotional functioning. The biofeedback phenomenon is an example of conscious control over automatic functioning.

A major concept in this systems theory is developed around the notion of fusion between the emotions and the intellect. The degree of fusion in people is variable and discernable. The amount of fusion in a person can be used as a predictor of the pattern of life in that person. In developing any systems theory, it is not possible to develop concepts to cover each piece of the total puzzle. In developing this theory, an effort has been made to make each concept harmonious with overall view of man described here, and above all to avoid concepts that are discrepant with the over-all view.

The Theoretical Concepts

The theory is made up of a number of interlocking concepts. A theory of behavior is an abstracted version of what has been observed. If it is accurate, it should be able to predict what will be observed in other similar situations. It should be able to account for discrepancies not included in the formulations. Each concept describes a separate facet of the total system. One may have as many different concepts as desired to describe smaller facets of the system. These concepts describe some over-all characteristics of human relationships, the functioning within the nuclear family system (parents and children), the way emotional problems are transmitted to the next generation, and the transmission patterns over multiple generations. Other concepts about details in the extended family and the ways family patterns are interlinked with larger social systems will be added to the theory at a later time. Since the total theory has been described in other publications (Bowen 1966, 1971) the concepts will not be described in detail here.

Differentiation of self scale. This concept is a cornerstone of the theory. It includes principles for estimating the degree of fusion between the intellect and emotions. The term *scale* conveys the notion that people are different from each other and that this difference can be estimated from clinical information. It is not a scale to be used as a psychological instrument by people not familiar with the theory and the variables in a relationship system. The scale refers to the level of solid self which is within self, which is stable under stress, and which remains uninfluenced by the relationship system. The solid self is easily confused by the pseudo-self, which is determined by the relationship system and which can fluctuate from day to day, or year to year. The pseudo-self can be increased by a congenial relationship and emotional approval and decreased by a negative relationship or disapproval. An index of pseudo-self is the degree to which people act, pretend, and use external appearance to influence others and to feign postures that make them appear more or less adequate or important than they really are. The degree of pseudo-self varies so much it is not possible to make a valid estimate of solid self except from estimating the life patterns over long periods of time. Some people are able to maintain fairly even levels of pseudo-self for several decades. With all the variables, it is possible to do a reasonably accurate estimate of the degree of differentiation of self from the fusion patterns in past generations and from the over-all course of a life in the present. Estimates of scale levels provide important clues for family therapy and for predicting, within broad limits, the future adaptive patterns of family members.

Triangles. This concept describes the way any three people relate to each other and involve others in the emotional issues between them. The triangle appears so basic that it probably also operates in animal societies. The concept postulates the triangle, or three person system, as the molecule or building block of any relationship system. A two person system is basically unstable. In a tension field, the two people predictably involve a third person to make a triangle. If it involves four or more people, the system becomes a series of interlocking triangles. In a multiple person system, the emotional issues may be acted out between three people, with the others relatively uninvolved, or multiple people clump themselves on the poles of the emotional triangle. Psychoanalytic theory, without specifically naming it, postulates the oedipal triangle between both parents and child, but the concept deals primarily with sexual issues, and it is awkward and inaccurate to extend this narrow concept into a broad one. There are two important variables in triangles. One deals with the level of "differentiation of self." The other variable deals with the level of anxiety or emotional tension in the system. The higher the anxiety, the more intense the automatic triangling in the system. The lower the level of differentiation in the involved people, the more intense the triangling. The higher the level of differentiation, the more the people have control over the emotional process. In periods of low anxiety, the triangling may be so toned down it is not clinically present. In calm periods, the triangle consists of a two-person togetherness and an outsider. The togetherness is the preferred position. The triangle is rarely in a state of optimum emotional comfort for all three. The most uncomfortable one makes a move to improve his optimum level of emotional closeness-distance. This upsets the equilibrium of another who attempts to adjust his optimum level. The triangle is in a constant state of motion. In tension states, the outside position is preferred, and the triangle moves are directed at escaping the tension field and achieving and holding the outside position. The predictable moves in a triangle have been used to develop a system of therapy designed to modify the triangular emotional system. The moves in a triangle are automatic and without intellectual awareness. The therapy focuses on the most important triangle in the family. It is designed to help one or more family members to become aware of the part self plays in the automatic emotional responsiveness, to control the part that self plays, and to avoid participation in the triangle moves. When one person in the triangle can control self while still remaining in emotional contact with the other two, the tension between the other two subsides. When it is possible to modify the central triangle in a family, the other family triangles are automatically modified without involving other family members in therapy. The therapy also involves a slow process of differentiation between emotional and intellectual functioning and slowly increasing intellectual control over automatic emotional processes.

Nuclear family emotional system. This concept describes the range of relationship patterns in the system between parents and children. Depending on the relationship patterns each spouse developed in their families of origin and the patterns they continue in marriage, the adaptive patterns in the nuclear family will go toward marital conflict; toward physical or emotional or social dysfunction in one spouse; toward projection of the parental problems to one or more children; or to a combination of all three patterns.

Family projection process. This concept describes the patterns through which parents project their problems to the children. This is part of the nuclear family process, but it is so important that an entire concept is devoted to it. The family projection process exists to some degree in all families.

Multiple generation transmission process. This concept describes the over-all pattern of the family projection process as it involves certain children and avoids others and as it proceeds over multiple generations.

Sibling position. This concept is an extension and modification of sibling position profiles as orginally defined by Toman (1961). The original profiles were developed from the study of "normal" families. They are remarkably close to the observations in this research, except Toman did not include the predictable ways that profiles are skewed by the family projection process. Knowledge gained from Toman, as modified in this concept, provides important clues in predicting areas of family strength and weakness for family therapy. This is so important it has been included as a separate concept.

Background for Family Systems Therapy

This method of therapy evolved as the theoretical concepts were developed and extended. During the late 1950s, the term *family therapy* was used for the method when two or more family members were present. The deciding factor revolved around the therapeutic relationship when only one family member was present. In the years prior to family research, the author had operated on the premise that the more reliable method for emotional growth was the working out of psychopathology as it was expressed in the relationship with the therapist. Now this basic premise was changed. The new effort was to work out problems in the already existing intense relationships within the family and to specifically avoid actions and techniques that facilitate and encourage the therapeutic relationship with the therapist. A change of this magnitude, for one trained in psychoanalysis, is so great that many say it is impossible. The first few years it was difficult to avoid a therapeutic relationship with only one family member, and the designation *individual therapy* was accurate for that situation. Gradually, it became impossible to see one family member without automatically thinking about the part played by other family members in this person's life. Transference issues, formerly considered critical for resolution of problems, were avoided until more family members could join the sessions. By 1960, the technique of working with one family member was sufficiently refined so that it was accurate to begin to talk about family therapy with one family member.

Family therapy for both parents and one child together will illustrate another nodal point in the development of this theory and method. These were families with adolescent behavior problems and school problems in the youngster. Most of the parental anxiety is focused on the sympton in the child. In the family therapy sessions, in the physical presence of the child, it was difficult to get the parents to focus on themselves. The average good outcome of such therapy would come in about twenty-five to forty appointments that covered about a year, with the aggressive mother becoming less aggressive, the passive father less passive, and the child's symptoms much improved. The family would terminate with high praise for family therapy but with no basic change in the family problem. This experience led to rethinking the theory and new techniques to get the focus on the hypothesized problem between the spouses. The triangle concept was partially developed. Now parents were asked to accept the premise that the basic problem was between them, to leave the child out of the sessions, and to try to focus on themselves. The results were excellent and this technique has been continued since 1960. Some of the best results have come when the symptomatic child was never seen by the therapist. In other situations, the child is seen occasionally to get the child's view of the family, but not for "therapy." The child's symptoms subside faster when the child is not present in the therapy, and parents are better motivated to work on their own problems. This experience led to the present standard method of family therapy, in the triangle consisting of the two parents and the therapist.

Another effort began early in the family movement. This was directed at neutralizing the family emotional process to create the "sick patient," and to make the therapist responsible for treating the patient. Terms such as *people*, *person*, and *family member* replaced the term *patient*. Diagnoses were avoided, even in the therapist's private thinking. It has been more difficult to replace the concepts of "treatment," "therapy," and "therapist" and to modify the omnipotent position of the therapist to the patient. Most of these changes have to occur within the therapist. Changing the terms does not change the situation, but it is a step in an over-all direction. When the therapist has changed himself, the old terms begin to seem odd and out of place. There is the continuing problem of using an appropriate mix of old terms and new terms in relating to the medical and social institutions and in writing. It has been most difficult to find concepts to replace the terms *therapy* and *therapist* in work with the families and to retain them for relating to the profession. I have found terms such as *supervisor, teacher,* and *coach* to be the best. The *coach* is probably the best in conveying the connotation of an active expert coaching both individual players and the team to the best of their abilities.

One of the most difficult changes has been in finding ways to relate to the healthy side of the family instead of the weak side. It is a slow, laborious task to improve the functioning of the weakest family member. It is many times more effective to work through the healthy side of the family. Opposing this are the family forces to create the patient and the popular notion that psychiatrists are to treat mental illness. One example from a period in the early 1960s will illustrate the point. This came from therapy with conflictual marriages in which each spouse would continue the cyclical, nonproductive report about what was wrong with the other, each trying to prove it was the other who needed to see a psychiatrist. It was effective for the therapist to say he would not continue the cyclical process, that they should decide who was healthiest, and he would do the next sessions with the healthiest alone. The focus on both parents, no matter the location of the problem in the family, is a step toward work with the healthy side of the family. The search for the most responsible, most resourceful, and most motivated part of the family can be elusive. It is best determined from knowledge of the family emotional process and the functioning patterns in the past and present generations, in collaboration with the family. The potential source of family strength can be submerged in an emotional impasse with a nonproductive family member. More details about working with a single, motivated family member will be presented later.

With this theoretical-therapeutic system, the term *family therapy* is derived from the way the therapist thinks about the family. It refers to the effort to modify the family relationship system, whether the effort is with multiple family members, the two spouses together, or only one family member. The term *family systems therapy* began after the theoretical concepts were better defined. It is more accurate than previous terms, but it is not well understood by those not familiar with systems concepts. The term *systems therapy* is now used more often to refer to the process either in the family or in social systems.

Family Systems Therapy with Two People

This method is a standard approach for therapists who use this theoretical-therapeutic system. The concept about modifying the entire family in the triangle of the two most important family members and the therapist was well formulated by the mid 1960s. The method has had wide clinical use on several thousand families by the staff and trainees in a large family training center. It has been used alongside other methods in the effort to find the most productive therapy with the least professional time. The major changes since the mid 1960s have been in the better understanding of triangles, clearer definition of the therapist's functioning in the triangle, and minor changes in techniques. The method was designed as one that would be effective for short-term therapy and that could also go on to long-term therapy. It works best for people who are capable of calm reflection. It is for two people in the same generation with a life commitment to each other. For practical purposes, this means husbands and wives. Other twosomes, such as parent and child, two siblings living together, man and woman living together, or homosexual pairs, are not motivated for significant change in the relationship.

Theoretical issues. A relationship system is kept in equilibrium by two powerful emotional forces that balance each other. In periods of calm, the forces operate as a friendly team, largely out of sight. One is the force for togetherness powered by the universal need for emotional closeness, love, and approval. The other is the force for individuality, powered by the drive to be a productive, autonomous individual, as determined by self rather than the dictates of the group. People have varying degrees of need for togetherness, which constitutes the life style (level of differentiation of self) for that person. The greater the need for togetherness, the less the drive for individuality. The mix of togetherness and individuality into which the person was programmed in early life becomes a "norm" for that person. People marry spouses who have identical life styles in terms of togetherness-individuality.

People with lower levels of differentiation of self have greater needs for togetherness and less drive for individuality. The greater the need for togetherness, the harder it is to keep togetherness forces in equilibrium without depriving certain family members. Discomfort and symptoms develop when togetherness needs are not met. The automatic response to anxiety and discomfort is to strive for more togetherness. When this effort fails repeatedly, the family member reacts in ways characteristic for that person. The reactions include dependent clinging, seductiveness, pleading, acting helpless, denial of need, acting strong, dictatorial postures, arguing, fighting, conflict, sexual acting out, rejection of others, drug and alcohol abuse, running away from the family, involving children in the problem, and all the other reactions to the failure to achieve togetherness.

When a family seeks psychiatric help, they have already exhausted their own automatic mechanisms for achieving more togetherness. Most family therapy methods put emphasis on the family need for understanding and togetherness. The therapist tries to help the family toward more love, consideration, and togetherness by discarding counterproductive mechanisms. These methods are effective in achieving symptom relief and a more comfortable life adjustment, but they are less effective in modifying the life style of family members.

This method is designed to help the family move as rapidly as possible toward better levels of differentiation. It proceeds on the assumption that the forces of individuality are present beneath the emotional reactiveness around togetherness, that the individuality forces will slowly emerge in the favorable emotional climate of the therapy triangle, and that togetherness forces will automatically readjust on a higher level of adaptation with each new gain in individuality.

Therapeutic method. The method was developed from experience with emotional forces in a triangle. Emotional tension in a two-person system immediately results in the twosome involving a vulnerable third person in the emotional issues of the twosome. From earlier family therapy with three family members present, the emotional issues cycled between the family members and evaded the therapist's efforts to interrupt the cycles. This method is designed to put the two most important family members into therapy with the therapist, which makes the therapist a target for family efforts to involve a third person. Progress in therapy depends on the therapist's ability to relate meaningfully to the family without becoming emotionally entangled in the family system.

At the beginning of therapy, the two family members are involved in an emotional fusion manifested by a "we," "us," and "our" clinging together, or by an opposite version of the same thing which is an antagonistic posture against the other. If the therapist can relate to the family over time, without becoming too entangled in emotional issues, and if he can recognize and deal with his entanglements when they do occur, it is possible for two separate selfs to slowly emerge from the emotional fusion. As this occurs, the emotional closeness in the marriage automatically occurs, and the entire family system begins to change in relation to the change in the spouses.

Therapeutic techniques. The most important aspect of the therapy depends on the therapist's emotional functioning, his ability to stay neutral in an emotional field, and his knowledge of triangles. Each therapist has to find his own way to maintain emtoional neutrality in the therapy situation. My best operating emotional distance from the family, even when sitting physically close, is the point I can "see" the emotional process flowing back and forth between them. The human phenomenon is usually as humorous and comical as it is serious and tragic. The right distance is the point it is possible to see either the serious or the humorous side. If the family goes too serious, I have an appropriate humorous remark to defuse the seriousness. If the family starts to kid and joke, I have an appropriate serious remark to restore neutrality. An example was a wife going into detail about her critical, nagging, bossy mother. The husband was indicating his agreement. If the therapist permitted them to believe he also agreed, he would be in the emotional process with them. His comment, "I thought you appreciated your mother's devotion to you," was enough to change the seriousness to a chuckle and defuse the emtoional tension. A calm tone of voice and a focus on facts rather than feelings is helpful in keeping an even emotional climate. Moves toward differentiation of self are usually not possible in a tension field.

It is necessary for the therapist to keep his focus on the process between the two. If he finds himself focusing on the content of what is being said, it is evidence that he has lost sight of the process and he is emotionally entangled on a content issue. It is necessary to listen to content in order to follow process but to keep the focus on process. The greater the tension in the family, the more it is necessary for the therapist to stay constantly active to affirm his neutral position. If he cannot think of anything to say, he is emotionally entangled. Within narrow limits, the therapist may use learned comments for emotional situations. If he is only moderately involved, the comment may be effective. Over the years, the "reversal" or "paradoxical comment" has come into use to defuse emotional situations. The "reversal" is a technique of picking up the opposite side of the emotional issue for a neutralizing comment. If the therapist is deeply involved in the family emotional system, the "reversal" is heard as sarcasm or hostility and the effort fails.

The principal technique of this method is a structure for each spouse talking directly to the therapist in a factual, calm voice. It is talking about emotional process, rather than the communication of emotional process. The therapist avoids a structure in which family members talk directly to each other. Even when the emotional climate is calm, direct communication can increase the emotional tension. This one technique is a major change from earlier methods in which emotionally distant family members were encouraged to talk directly to each other.

A typical session might begin with a comment from the husband to the therapist. To respond directly to the husband involves risk in triangling with the husband. Instead, the therapist asks the wife what she was thinking when she heard this. Then he turns to the husband and asks what was going through his thoughs while the wife was talking. This kind of interchange might go back and forth for an entire session. More frequently the husband's comment is too minimal for the clear presentation of an idea. The therapist then asks the husband as many questions as necessary to elaborate his thinking into a clearer presentation. Then the therapist turns to the wife for her thoughts while the husband was talking. If her comments are minimal, the therapist might ask a series of questions to more clearly express the wife's views. Then he turns to the husband for his response to the wife's comments. There are numerous other techniques for getting to the private thinking world of each, and getting it expressed to the therapist in the presence of the other spouse. For instance, the therapist might ask for a summary of private thoughts about the family situation since the last session, or ask for the most recent thinking about a particular family situation. The therapist asks for thoughts, ideas, and opinions, and avoids asking for feelings or subjective responses. In my opinion, this process of externalizing the thinking of each spouse in the presence of the other is the epitome of the "magic of family therapy." Therapists accustomed to emotional exchanges can find these sessions dull and uninteresting, but the families are interested and motivated to attend the sessions. It is common for spouses to say how much they look forward to the sessions and how they are fascinated to hear how the other thinks. When asked how they could live with each other so many years without knowing what the other thought, they say they can listen and hear when the other spouse talks to the therapist in a way they could never listen when talking to each other. It is common to hear these comments about increasing fascination at discovering what goes on in the other after having been in the dark so long. Spouses experience a challenge in being as expressive and articulate as possible. People who have formerly been nontalkers gradually become talkers. Expressions of emotional closeness and increasing affection for each other occur at home. This occurs faster than when the effort is directed at emotional expression in the sessions. Other reports about new abilities at home include the ability to deal calmly with children, the ability to listen to others for the first time, and new experiences about being able to work together calmly.

When tears or emotion erupts suddenly in a session, the therapist stays calmly on course, asking what was the thought that stimulated the tears, or asking the other what they were thinking when the feeling started. If feeling mounts and the other spouse responds directly to the first spouse, it is evidence of building emotional tension. The therapist increases the calm questions to defuse the emotion and to focus the issue back to him. The therapist is always in control of the sessions, asking hundreds of questions and avoiding interpretations. By considering each new family as a research project, the therapist always has so many questions there is never time to ask more than a fraction of them. Occasionally, there might be indication for the therapist to guess what might be going on in the family, following which he would ask questions to get family ideas about his guess. He might tell the family he thinks a particular area of investigation might be helpful, as a way of telling the family what he is thinking and a way of enlisting their effort in the exploration.

A fair percentage of the therapist's time may go to keeping himself emotionally disentangled from the family emotional process. The families use their automatic mechanisms in the effort to involve others in the triangle. This is more intense early in the therapy and at periods when anxiety is higher than usual. When the therapist knows the characteristics of triangles, and he is alert, he can often anticipate the triangling move before it occurs. There are situations in which a spouse erroneously assumes the therapist has taken sides with an issue. The process of keeping the therapist emotionally neutral gets first priority in the therapy. The goal of the therapist is to keep active and to make statements or take actions that affirm his neutrality and to avoid transference type interpretations to the family about it. Systems theory assumes that the triangling move is an automatic emotional response of the people involved, and it is not personally directed as it might be interpreted to be in an individual relationship therapy. The casual comment or a calm "reversal" is effective in helping the therapist maintain his neutral position.

After the family anxiety subsides and the spouses are more capable of reflection, individuality forces begin to surface in one spouse. This occurs as the spouse begins to focus more on the part that self plays in the relationship problems, to decrease blaming of the other for one's own discomfort and unhappiness, and to accept responsibility for changing self. The other spouse increases the pressure on togetherness demands, which commonly results in the first spouse falling back into the old togetherness. This process proceeds through a number of false starts, with the differentiating one gradually gaining more strength and the other increasing the tempo of the togetherness pleas. The togetherness pressure includes accusations of lack of love, indifference, not caring, and lack of appreciation. When the differentiating one is sure enough of self to proceed calmly on course, in spite of the togetherness pleading in the other, without defending self or counterattacking, and without withdrawing, the attack subsides and the differentiating process passes through its first major nodal point. It may require a year or two for the first spouse to reach this point. This is followed by a period of calm and a new, higher level of adjustment in both. Then the second spouse begins a similar differentiating effort to change self, and the first spouse becomes the promoter of togetherness. New cycles usually take less time and the steps are not as clearly defined as in the first step.

The individuality force emerges slowly at first and it takes very little togetherness force to drive it back underground for fairly long periods. An average life course of people is one that keeps the togetherness-individuality forces in neutralizing balance. The therapist can facilitate the differentiating process by focusing questions on this new area of family issues, by focusing on responsibility for self, and by avoiding any connotation that he is siding with the more righteous sounding togetherness pleading.

Teaching in family systems therapy. Some kind of didactic teaching is necessary for families who go on to long-term therapy with this method. This kind of knowledge provides the family with a way of understanding the problem, an awareness they are responsible for progress, and a framework in which they can direct their energy on their behalf. A very anxious family is unable to "hear" didactic explanations, and the therapist who attempts such explanations becomes deeply entangled in the family emotional system with inevitable distortions and impasses in the therapy. Teaching statements are used cautiously until after the family is calm. This applies to the rationale for sending spouses home for frequent visits with their families of origin, which is part of the effort of encouraging them to "differentiate a self" in their extended families. In the later stages of therapy, all kinds of conferences and didactic sessions can be helpful.

Summary. This method is effective as a short-term, middle-term, or long-term process. The length of the therapy is determined by the family. There have been a fair percentage of striking "cures" in five to ten sessions, usually for symptoms that erupted from an overintense relationship. An example was a seven-session "cure" of severe frigidity in a young wife. Middle-term good results often come in twenty to forty sessions when symptoms have subsided and the togetherness-oriented spouse exerts pressure to discontinue. No other approach has been as effective as this in producing good long-term results. In 1966, this method was adapted for multiple family therapy. The therapist does thirty minute mini-sessions with each of four families while the other families are nonparticipant observers. The average family makes a little faster progress than those in one-hour sessions for single families. The difference appears related to the ability to "hear" and learn from the other families without reacting emotionally and to learn. When the differentiation of self is the goal, it appears to take a certain amount of time, on the calendar, for motivated people to modify their life styles. There have been experiments to spread a given amount of therapy time over longer periods of time with less frequent appointments. A majority of multiple family therapy sessions are now held monthly, with results as good, or better, than with more frequent sessions. The families are able to accept responsibility for their own progress and to use the sessions for the therapist to supervise their efforts. Long-term families continue for an average of five years, which include about sixty multiple family sessions and about thirty hours of direct time with the therapist.

Toward the differentiation of self in one's own family. The turning point in the method came in 1967 after an anonymous paper on the differentiation of self in one's own family at a national meeting (Anonymous 1972). The method involved a detailed family history for multiple generations in the past and developing a personal relationship with all important living relatives. This activates old family relationships grown latent with neglect. Then, with the advantage of objectivity and the knowledge of triangles, the task is to detriangle old family triangles as they come to life.

In the spring of 1967, I began using material from that conference in teaching family therapy to psychiatric residents and other mental health professionals. They began to see themselves in their own families and to go home to secretly try out the knowledge on their families. This was followed by reports of inevitable emotional impasses and further conference discussion to help understand the problem and make suggestions for the next trip home.

Also in 1967, the residents were better than previous residents as clinicians in family therapy. At first, I thought this was related to the quality of residents that year, but the residents said it was experience with their own families that made the difference. There were comments, such as, "Family theory is just another theory until you see it work with your own family."

The next awareness came in 1968. The residents were doing so well in their clinical work that no attention had been devoted to personal problems with their spouses and children. The effort had been to train family therapists. There had been no mention of problems in their nuclear families. In 1968, I discovered that these residents had made as much progress with spouses and children as similar residents in formal weekly family therapy with their spouses. There was a good sample for comparison. Since the early 1960s, I had been suggesting family therapy for residents and their spouses instead of individual psychotherapy or psychoanalysis for personal problems. There was a volume of clinical experience with formal weekly family therapy for psychiatric residents, to compare with residents who were going home to visit their families of origin and who were not in any type of formal psychotherapy. This professional experience with psychiatric residents and other mental health professionals was the beginning of a new era in my own professional orientation.

There are some speculations about the more rapid change in working with the extended families than with the nuclear family. It is easier to "see" self and modify one's self in triangles a bit outside the immediate living situation than in the nuclear family in which one lives. In the years since 1968, this method of work with the extended family has been used in all kinds of conferences and teaching situations and, also, in private practice type "coaching." A person working actively can utilize "coaching" sessions about once a month. Some who have access to teaching sessions do not need private sessions, or they need them less often. Some who live at a distance are seen three or four times a year or as infrequently as once a year. This approach is so different it is hard to compare results with other approaches. It bypasses the nuclear family and the infinite emotional detail in close-up relationships. It appears to produce better results than the more conventional family therapies.

This method has been used largely for those in training to be family therapists, but it has been used with a growing number of others who hear about it and request it. Results are the same, except there are few other people who seek family therapy until they have symptoms. Once a family starts formal family therapy sessions, it is harder to find motivation for serious work with the families of origin.

The method of defining a self in the extended family has been used as the only method of therapy for a broad spectrum of mental health professionals, and for nonprofessional people who hear about the method and request it. Work with the extended family is urged for all families in other types of family therapy, but extended family concepts make little sense when people are anxious. After symptoms subside, it is harder for people to find motivation for serious work with their extended families. Any gain from the extended family is immediately translated into automatic gain with spouses and children. Success in working toward defining self in the family of origin depends on motivation and the family situation. It is easiest with highly motivated people with intact families that have drifted apart. At the other extreme are those who are repulsed with the idea of contacting extended family and those whose families are extremely negative. In between are all different levels of motivation and families with varying degrees of fragmentation and distance. There is not a serious problem when parents are dead if there are other surviving relatives. Reasonable results are possible with those who believe they have no living relatives.

Unique experiences with change in extended families are commonplace. This is in addition to change in the nuclear family. In a course in family therapy for freshman medical students and their spouses, there was a student whose father had been in a state hospital for about twenty years. The hospital was near his home town, several hundred miles away. The family had been visiting the father about once a year. I suggested that the student visit his father alone, any time he was home, and that he try to relate through the psychosis to the man beneath the symptoms. I was guessing that the father might be able to leave the hospital by the time the son graduated from medical school. He visited the father about four times that year. The following year, about nine months after the course started, the father visited the son while on a furlough from the hospital. Exactly twelve months after the course started, as the son was starting his sophomore year, the father had been discharged from the hospital and was visiting the son. The father attended the twenty-second meeting of that class in family therapy. After having been in a state institution from the age of thirty to about fifty, he was having adjustment and employment problems but the son, the father, and the family had come far in only one year.

Systems Theory and Societal Problems

The emotional forces in a triangle operate the same in society as in the family. Family therapists have been aware of this for a number of years, but the specific mechanisms involved in this have been elusive and hard to define. The author has made one serious effort at this (Bowen 1974a). The larger societal field, with its multiple emotional forces, is a challenge for the concepts of systems theory. Sometime within the next decade, systems theory has promise for some contributions in this new area.

Summary

This chapter presents an over-all view of family therapy as it began almost twenty years ago and as it has developed as part of the changing psychiatric scene. An effort has been made to identify some of the forces that seem to have determined the direction of the growth of family therapy. Family therapists represent such a diversity in theory and therapeutic method that it is difficult to find a frame of reference for either the common denominators or differences in the field. An effort has been made to focus on broad direction rather than attempting to categorize the work of well known people in the field. It is factual that the greatest number of family therapists operate from psychiatric theory learned in training and that they use family therapy as a technique. Another large group of family therapists use conventional theory for thinking about emotional forces in the individual and another theoretical scheme for thinking about the relationship system between family members. A smaller group of family therapists have moved into completely different theories for conceptualizing and working with families. These differences in theory do not have common denominators in the practice of family therapy. There are skillful therapists who would be masters with any therapeutic method. In this sense, family therapy is still more of an art than a science.

Presented here is the thesis that the study of the family opened the door for the study of relationships between people. There was not a ready-made, conceptual scheme for understanding relationships. We are living in the computer age in which systems thinking influences the world about us, but systems concepts are poorly developed in thinking about man and his functioning. Most of the family therapists who have worked on relationships have developed systems concepts for under-standing the subtle and powerful ways that people are influenced by their own families, by the totality of society, and by the past generations from which they descended. Those who have developed the most complete systems concepts have developed therapeutic methods that bypass individual theory and practice, not because one is considered better than the other, but to experiment with possible new potentials. The author is among those who have worked toward developing systems concepts for understanding emotional illness in the broader family framework. He has presented his theoretical-therapeutic system as one of the many ways that family and social systems may be conceptualized, and to provide the reader with the broadest possible view of the diversity in the practice of family therapy. If the present trend in systems thinking continues, we can reasonably expect even more striking developments in the field in the next decade.

Chapter 15

Family Reaction to Death

Direct thinking about death, or indirect thinking about staying alive and avoiding death, occupies more of man's time than any other subject. Man is an instinctual animal with the same instinctual awareness of death as the lower forms of life. He follows the same predictable instinctual life pattern of all living things. He is born, he grows to maturity, he reproduces, his life force runs out, and he dies. In addition, he is a thinking animal with a brain that enables him to reason, reflect, and think abstractly. With his intellect he has devised philosophies and beliefs about the meaning of life and death that tend to deny his place in nature's plan. Each individual has to define his own place in the total scheme and accept the fact that he will die and be replaced by succeeding generations. His difficulty in finding a life plan for himself is complicated by the fact that his life is intimately interwoven with the lives about him. This presentation is directed to death as a part of the total family in which he lives.

There are no simple ways to describe man as part of the relationship around him. In another chapter in this volume, I have presented my own way of conceiving of the human as an individual and, also, as part of the emotional-social amalgam in which he lives. According to my theory, a high percentage of human relationship behavior is directed more by automatic instinctual emotional forces than by intellect. Much intellectual activity goes to explain away and justify behavior being directed by the instinctual-emotional-feeling complex. Death is a biological event that terminates a life. No life event can stir more emotionally directed thinking in the individual and more emotional reactiveness in those about him. I have chosen the concept of "open" and "closed" relationship systems as an effective way to describe death as a family phenomenon.

An "open" relationship system is one in which an individual is free to communicate a high percentage of inner thoughts, feelings, and fantasies to another who can reciprocate. No one ever has a completely open relationship with another, but it is a healthy state when a person can have one relationship in which a reasonable degree of openness is possible. A fair percentage of children have a reasonable version of this with a parent. The most open relationship that most people have in their adult lives is in a courtship. After marriage, in the emotional interdependence of living together, each spouse becomes sensitive to subjects that upsets the other. They instinctively avoid the sensitive subjects and the relationship shifts toward a more "closed" system. The closed communication system is an automatic emotional reflex to protect self from the anxiety in the other person, though most people say they avoid the taboo subjects to keep from upsetting the other person. If people could follow intellectual knowledge instead of the automatic reflex, and they could gain some control over their own reactiveness to anxiety in the other, they would be able to talk about taboo subjects in spite of the anxiety, and the relationship would move toward a more healthy openness. But people are human, the emotional reactiveness operates like a reflex, and, by the time the average person recognizes the problem, it can be impossible for two spouses to reverse the process themselves. This is the point at which a trained professional can function as a third person to work the magic of family therapy toward opening a closed relationship.

Chief among all taboo subjects is death. A high percentage of people die alone, locked into their own thoughts which they cannot communicate to others. There are at least two processes in operation. One is the intrapsychic process in self which always involves some denial of death. The other is the closed relationship system. People cannot communicate the thoughts they do have, lest they upset the family or others. There are usually at least three closed systems operating around the terminally ill person. One operates within the patient. From experience, every terminally ill patient has some awareness of impending death and a high percentage have an extensive amount of private knowledge they do not communicate to anyone. Another closed system is the family. The family gets its basic information from the physician, which is supplemented by bits of information from other sources and is then amplified, distorted, and reinterpreted in conversations at home. The family has its own carefully planned and edited medical communiqué for the patient. It is based on the family interpretation of the reports and modified to avoid the patient's reactiveness to anxiety. Other versions of the communiqué are whispered within the hearing of the patient when the family thinks the patient is sleeping or unconscious. Patients are often alert to whispered communications. The physician and the medical staff have another closed system of communication, supposedly based on medical facts, which is influenced by emotional reactivity to the family and within the staff. Physicians attempt to do factual reports to the family which are distorted by the medical emotionality and the effort to put the correct emphasis on the "bad news" or "good news." The more reactive the physician, the more likely he is to put in medical jargon the family does not hear or to become too simplistic in his efforts to communicate in lay language. The more anxious the physician, the more likely he is to do too much speechmaking and too little listening, and to end up with a vague and distorted message and little awareness of the family misperception of his message. The more anxious the physician, the more the family asks for specific details the physician cannot answer. Physicians commonly reply to specific questions with overgeneralizations that miss the point. The physician has another level of communication to the patient. Even the physician who agrees with the principle of telling the patient "facts" can communicate them with so much anxiety that the patient is responding to the physician instead of the content of what is being said. Problems occur when the closed communication system of medicine meets the age-old closed system between the patient and the family, and anxiety is heightened by the threat of terminal illness.

My clinical experience with death goes back some thirty years to detailed discussions about death with suicidal patients. They were eager to talk to an unbiased listener who did not have to correct their way of thinking. Then I discovered that all seriously ill people, and even those who are not sick, are grateful for an opportunity to talk about death. Over the years I have tried to do such discussions with seriously ill people in my practice, with friends and people I have known socially, and with members of my extended families. I have never seen a terminally ill person who was not strengthened by such a talk. This contradicts former beliefs about the ego being too fragile for this in certain situations. I have even done this with a spectrum of comatose patients. Terminally ill people often permit themselves to slip into coma. A fair percentage can pull themselves out of the coma for important communications. I have had such people come out long enough to talk and express their thanks for the help and immediately slip back. Until the mid 1960s, a majority of physicians were opposed to telling patients they had a terminal illness. In the past decade the prevailing medical dictum about this has changed a great deal, but medical practice has not kept pace with the changed attitude. The poor communications between the physician and the patient, and between the physician and the family, and between the family and the patient are still very much as they were before. The basic problem is an emotional one, and a change in rules does not automatically change the emotional reactivity. The physician can believe he gave factual information to the patient, but in the emotion of the moment, the abruptness and vagueness in the communication, and the emotional process in the patient, the patient failed to "hear." The patient and the family can pretend they have dealt clearly with each other without either being heard through the emotionality. In my family therapy practice within a medical center, I am frequently in contact with both the patient and the family, and to a lesser extent with the physicians. The closed system between the patient and the family is great enough, at best. I believe the poor communication between the physician and the family and between the physician and the patient is the greatest problem. There have been repeated situations in which the physicians thought they were communicating clearly, but the family either misperceived or distorted the messages, and the family thinking would be working itself toward malpractice anger at the physician. In all of these, the surgical and medical procedures were adequate, and the family was reacting to terse, brief speeches by the physician who thought he was communicating adequately. In these, it is fairly easy to do simple interpretations of the physician's statements and avert the malpractice thinking. I believe the trend toward telling patients about incurable illness is one of the healthy changes in medicine, but closed systems do not become open when the surgeon hurriedly blurts out tense speeches about the situation. Experience indicates that physicians and surgeons have either to learn the fundamentals of closed system emotionality in the physician-family-patient triangle, or they might avail themselves of professional expertise in family therapy if they lack the time and motivation to master this for themselves. A clinical example of closed system emotionality will be presented later.

Family Emotional Equilibrium and The Emotional Shock Wave

This section will deal with an order of events within the family that is not directly related to open and closed system communications. Death, or threatened death, is only one of many events that can disturb a family. A family unit is in functional equilibrium when it is calm and each member is functioning at reasonable efficiency for that period. The equilibrium of the unit is disturbed by either the addition of a new member or the loss of a member. The intensity of the emotional reaction is governed by the functioning level of emotional integration in the family at the time, or by the functional importance of the one who is added to the family or lost to the family. For instance, the birth of a child can disturb the emotional balance until family members can realign themselves around the child. A grandparent who comes for a visit may shift family emotional forces briefly, but a grandparent who comes to live in a home can change the family emotional balance for a long period. Losses that can disturb the family equilibrium are physical losses, such as a child who goes away to college or an adult child who marries and leaves the home. There are functional losses, such as a key family member who becomes incapacitated with a long-term illness or injury which prevents his doing the work on which the family depends. There are emotional losses, such as the absence of a light-hearted person who can lighten the mood in a family. A group that changes from light-hearted laughter to seriousness becomes a different kind of organism. The length of time required for the family to establish a new emotional equilibrium depends on the emotional integration in the family and the intensity of the disturbance. A well integrated family may show more overt reactiveness at the moment of change but adapt to it rather quickly. A less integrated family may show little reaction at the time and respond later with symptoms of physical illness, emotional illness, or social misbehavior. An attempt to get the family to express feelings at the moment of change does not necessarily increase the level of emotional integration.

The "Emotional Shock Wave" is a network of underground "after-shocks" of serious life events that can occur anywhere in the extended family system in the months or years following serious emotional events in a family. It occurs most often after the death or the threatened death of a significant family member, but it can occur following losses of other types. It is not directly related to the usual grief or mourning reactions of people close to the one who died. It operates on an underground network of emotional dependence of family members on each other. The emotional dependence is denied, the serious life events appear to be unrelated, the family attempts to camouflage any connectedness between the events, and there is a vigorous emotional denial reaction, when anyone attempts to relate the events to each other. It occurs most often in families with a significant degree of denied emotional "fusion" in which the families have been able to maintain a fair degree of asymptomatic emotional balance in the family system. The basic family process has been described in another chapter in this volume.

The "Emotional Shock Wave" was first encountered in the author's family research in the late 1950s. It has been mentioned in papers and lectures, but it has not been adequately described in the literature. It was first noticed in the course of multigenerational family research with the discovery that a series of major life events occurred in multiple, separate members of the extended family in the time interval after the serious illness and death of a significant family member. At first, this appeared to be coincidence. Then it was discovered that some version of this phenomenon appeared in a sufficiently high percentage of all families, and a check for the "shock wave" is done routinely in all family histories. The symptoms in a shock wave can be any human problem. Symptoms can include the entire spectrum of physical illness from an increased incidence of colds and respiratory infections to the first appearance of chronic conditions, such as diabetes or allergies to acute medical and surgical illnesses. It is as if the shock wave is the stimulus that can trigger the physical process into activity. The symptoms can also include the full range of emotional symptoms from mild depression, to phobias, to psychotic episodes. The social dysfunctions can include drinking, failures in school or business, abortions and illegitimate births, an increase in accidents, and the full range of behavior disorders. Knowledge of the presence of the shock wave provides the physician or therapist with vital knowledge in treatment. Without such knowledge, the sequence of events is treated as separate, unrelated events.

Some examples of the shock wave will illustrate the process. It occurs most often after the death of a significant family member, but it can be almost as severe after a threatened death. An example was a grandmother in her early sixties who had a radical mastectomy for cancer. Within the following two years, there was a chain of serious reactions in her children and their families. One son began drinking for the first time in his life, the wife of another son had a serious depression, a daughter's husband failed in business, and another daughter's children became involved in automobile accidents and delinquency. Some symptoms were continuing five years later when the grandmother's cancer was pronounced cured. A more common example of the shock wave follows the death of an important grandparent, with symptoms appearing in a spectrum of children and grandchildren. The grandchild is often one who had little direct emotional attachment to the grandparents. An example: after the death of a grandmother, a daughter appeared to have no more than the usual grief reaction to the death but reacted in some deep way, transmitting her disturbance to a son who had never been close to the grandmother but who reacted to the mother with delinquency behavior. The family so camouflages the connectedness of these events that family members will further camouflage the sequence of events if they become aware the therapist is seeking some connectedness. Families are extremely reactive to any effort to approach the denial directly. There was a son in his mid-thirties who made a plane trip to see his mother who had had a stroke and who was aphasic. Before that time, his wife and children were leading an orderly life, and his business was going well. His effort to communicate with his mother, who could not speak, was a trying experience. Enroute home on the plane, he met a young woman with whom he began the first extramarital affair in his life. During the subsequent two years, he began living a double life, his business was failing, and his children began doing poorly in school. He made a good start in family therapy which continued for six sessions when I made a premature connection between his mother's stroke and the affair. He cancelled the subsequent appointment and never returned. The nature of the human phenomenon is such that it reacts vigorously to any such implications of the dependence of one life on another. Other families are less reactive and they can be more interested in the phenomenon than reactive to it. I have seen only one family who had made an automatic connection between such events before seeking therapy. This was a father who said, "My family was calm and healthy until two years ago when my daughter was married. Since then, it has been one trouble after another, and the doctor bills have become exorbitant. My wife had a gall bladder operation. After that, she found something wrong with each house where we lived. We have broken three leases and moved four times. Then she developed a back problem and had a spinal fusion. My son had been a good student before my daughter married. Last year, his school work went down and this year he dropped out of college. In the midst of this, I had a heart attack." I would see this as a family with tenuously balanced emotional equilibrium in which the mother's functioning was dependent on her relationship with the daughter. Most of the subsequent dysfunction was in the mother, but the son and father were sufficiently dependent on the mother that they too developed symptoms. The incidence of the emotional shock wave is sufficiently prevalent that the Georgetown Family Section does a routine historical check for it in every family history.

Knowledge of the emotional shock wave is important in dealing with families on death issues. Not all deaths have the same importance to a family. There are some in which there is a fair chance the death will be followed by a shock wave. Other deaths are more neutral and are usually followed by no more than the usual grief and mourning reactions. Other deaths are a relief to the family and are usually followed by a period of better functioning. If the therapist can know ahead of time about the possibility of an emotional shock wave, he can take some steps toward its prevention. Among the deaths most likely to be followed by a serious and prolonged shock wave are the deaths of either parent when the family is young. This not only disturbs the emotional equilibrium, but it removes the function of the breadwinner or the mother at a time when these functions are most important. The death of an important child can shake the family equilibrium for years. The death of the "head of the clan" is another that can be followed by a long-term underground disturbance. It can be a grandfather who may have been partially disabled but who continued some kind of decision-making function in family affairs. The grandmothers in these families usually lived in the shadow of their husbands, and their deaths were less important. The family reaction can be intense following the death of a grandmother who was a central figure in the emotional life and stability of the family. The "head of the clan" can also be the most important sibling in the present generation. There is another group of family members whose deaths may result in no more than the usual period of grief and mourning. They may have been well liked, but they played peripheral roles in family affairs. They are the neutral ones who were neither "famous nor infamous." Their deaths are not likely to influence future family functioning. Finally, there are the family members whose deaths are a relief to the family. This includes the people whose functioning was never critical to the family, and who may have been a burden in their final illness. Their deaths may be followed by a brief period of grief and mourning, which is then followed by improved family functioning. A shock wave rarely follows the death of a dysfunctional family member unless that dysfunction played a critical role in maintaining family emotional equilibrium. Suicides are commonly followed by prolonged grief and mourning reactions, but the shock wave is usually minor unless the suicide was an abdication of an essential functional role.

Therapy At The Time Of Death

Knowledge of the total family configuration, the functioning position of the dying person in the family, and the overall level of life adaptation are important for anyone who attempts to help a family before, during, or after a death. To attempt to treat all deaths as the same can miss the mark. Some well functioning families are able to adapt to approaching death before it occurs. To assume that such families need help can be an inept intrusion. Physicians and hospitals have left much of the problems about death to chaplains and ministers with the expectation they know what to do. There are exceptional clergymen who intuitively know what to do. However, many young chaplains or clergymen tend to treat all death as the same. They operate with their theology, a theory about death that does not go beyond the familiar concepts of grief and mourning, and they tend to aim their help at the overt expression of grief. This may provide superficial help to a majority of people, but it misses the deeper process. The popular notion that expression of grief through crying may be helpful to most complicates the situation for others. It is important for the physician or therapist to know the situation, to have his own emotional life under reasonable control without the use of too much denial, or other extreme mechanisms, and to respect the denial that operates in the family. In my work with families, I carefully use direct words, such as death, die, and bury, and I carefully avoid the use of less direct words, such as passed on, deceased, and expired. A direct word signals to the other that I am comfortable with the subject, and it enables others to also be comfortable. A tangential word may appear to soften the fact of death; but it invites the family to respond with tangential words, and the conversation soon reaches the point that one wonders if we are talking about death at all. The use of direct words helps to open a closed emotional system. I believe it provides a different dimension in helping the family to be comfortable within themselves.

The following is a clinical example that illustrates an effort to open the communication with a terminally ill patient, her family, and the medical staff. As a visiting professor in another medical center, I was scheduled to do a demonstration interview with the parents of an emotionally disturbed daughter. Enroute to the interview room, I learned the mother had a terminal cancer, that the surgeon had told the father, and the father had told the family therapist, but that the mother did not know about it. In my own practice, it would have been automatic to discuss this issue with the family, but I was reluctant to take this course when follow-up interviews would not be possible. A large group of professional people and trainees observed the interview. I elected to avoid the critical issue. The beginning of the interview was awkward, difficult, and sticky. I decided the cancer issue had to be discussed. About ten minutes out, I asked the mother why she thought her surgeon, her family, and the others had not told her about her cancer. Without the slightest hesitation, she said she thought they were afraid to tell her. She calmly said, "I know I have cancer. I have known it for some time. Before that, I was afraid of it, but they told me it was not cancer. I believed them for a time, thinking it was my imagination. Now I know it is cancer. When I ask them and they say 'No,' what does it mean? It either means they are liars or I am crazy, and I know I am not crazy." Then she went into detail about her feelings, with some moderate tears, but with full control of herself. She said that she was not afraid to die for herself, but she would like to live long enough to see the daughter have a life for herself. She hated the responsibility of leaving the daughter the responsibility of the father. She spoke with deep feeling but few tears. She and I were the calmest people in the room. Her therapist wiped away tears. The father reacted by joking and kidding about the mother's vivid imagination. To prevent his reaction from silencing her, I made a few comments to suggest he not interfere with his wife's serious thoughts. She was able to continue, "This is the loneliest life in the world. Here I am, knowing I am going to die, and not knowing how much time I have left. I can't talk to anyone. When I talk to my surgeon, he says it is not a cancer. When I try to talk to my husband, he makes jokes about it. I come here to talk about my daughter and not about myself. I am cut off from everyone. When I get up in the morning, I feel terrible. I look at my eyes in the mirror to see if they are jaundiced and the cancer has spread to my liver. I try to act cheerful until my husband goes to work, because I don't want to upset him. Then I am alone all day with my thoughts, just crying and thinking. Before my husband returns from work, I try to pull myself together for his sake. I wish I could die soon and not have to pretend any longer." Then she went into some background thoughts about death. As a little girl she felt hurt when people walked on graves. She had always wished she could be buried above ground in a mausoleum, so people would not walk on her grave. "But," she said, "we are poor people. We can't afford a mausoleum. When I die, I will be buried in a grave just like everyone else." The technical problem in this single interview was to permit the mother to talk, to keep the father's anxiety from silencing her, and to hope the regular therapist could continue the process later. It is impossible to do much toward opening an emotionally closed relationship of this intensity in a single session, although the father said he would try to listen and understand. The patient was relieved to be partially out of the closed system in which she had lived. The therapist said she had known about the cancer but had been waiting for the mother to bring it up. This is a common posture for mental health professionals. The therapist's own emotionality had prevented the wife from talking. At the end of the interview, the mother said, smiling through her tears, "We have sure spent an hour walking around on my grave, haven't we?" As I said goodbye to them in the hall, the mother said, "When you go home tonight, thank Washington for sending you here today." The less expressive father said, "We are both grateful." There were a few minutes with the audience who had observed the interview. Part of the group had been moved to tears, most were silent and serious, and a few were critical. The criticism was expressed by a young physician who spoke of hurting the wife and having taken away her hope. I was pleased at having decided to take up this issue in this single demonstration interview. Enroute home, my thoughts went to the differences in audience response and the problems of training young professional people to contain their own emotionality sufficiently to become more objective about death. I guessed it would be easier to train those who cried than those who intellectualized their feelings. This is an example of a good result in a single session. It illustrates the intensity of a closed relationship system between the patient, the family, and the medical staff.

The Function Of Funerals

Some twenty-five years ago, I had a clinical experience that illustrates the central point of the next section of this chapter. A young woman began psychoanalysis with, "Let me bury my mother before we go to other things." Her mother had been dead six years. She cried for weeks. At that time, I was practicing within the framework of transference and intrapsychic dynamics. The patient's statement was used later as a way of describing systems theory about the unresolved emotional attachments between people that remain viable for life, that attach to significant future relationships, and that continue to direct the course of a life. There is a way to utilize the funeral to more completely "bury the dead at the time of death." Few human events provide as much emotional impact as serious illness and death in resolving unresolved emotional attachments.

The funeral ritual has existed in some form since man became a civilized being. I believe it serves a common function of bringing survivors into intimate contact with the dead and with important friends, and it helps survivors and friends to terminate their relationship with the dead and to move forward with life. I think the best function of a funeral is served when it brings relatives and friends into the best possible functional contact with the harsh fact of death and with each other at this time of high emotionality. I believe funerals were probably more effective when people died at home with the family present, and when family and friends made the coffin and did the burial themselves. Society no longer permits this, but there are ways to bring about a reasonable level of personal contact with the dead body and the survivors.

There are numerous present-day funeral customs that function to deny death and to perpetuate the unresolved emotional attachments between the dead and the living. It is most intense in people who are anxious about death and who use the present form and content of funerals to avoid the anxiety. There are those who refuse to look at a dead body because, "I want to remember them as I knew them." There is the anxious segment of society that refers to funerals as pagan rituals. Funeral custom makes it possible for the body to be disposed of from the hospital without the family ever having personal contact with it. Children are commonly excluded from funerals to avoid upsetting them. This can result in a lifetime of unrealistic and distorted fantasies and images that may never be corrected. The private funeral is another custom that avoids the emotionality of death. It is motivated by family anxiety to avoid contact with emotionality in others. It prevents the friendship system an opportunity to terminate their relationship with the dead, and it deprives the family of the supportive relationships from friends.

I believe that professional support to a family at the time of death can help the family members toward a more helpful funeral than would be possible if they listened to advice from anxious relatives and friends. In twenty years of family practice, I have had contact with several thousand families, and I have been in the background "coaching" families through hundreds of deaths and funerals. I urge family members to visit dying family members whenever possible and to find some way to include children if the situation permits. I have never seen a child hurt by exposure to death. They are "hurt" only by the anxiety of survivors. I encourage involvement of the largest possible group of extended family members, an open casket, and the most personal contact that is possible between the dead and the living, prompt obituary notices, and the notification of relatives and friends, a public funeral with the body present, and the most personal funeral service that is possible. Some funeral services are highly ritualized but it is possible to personalize even the most ritualized service. The goal is to bring the entire family system into the closest possible contact with death in the presence of the total friendship system and to lend a helping hand to the anxious people who would rather run than face a funeral.

The following is an example of coaching friends from the background. It involved neighbors rather than people in my professional practice. The young parents in their early thirties and their three children ages ten, eight, and five, had come to live with her widowed mother in preparation for the husband's going overseas on a prolonged assignment. On a Sunday one month before his scheduled departure, the young mother died suddenly of a heart attack. The entire community was shocked. That evening, I spent some three hours with the father. He and the wife had been very close. He had dozens of questions about how to handle the present emergency, the funeral, the future of the children, and his own life. He wondered if the children should go to school the next day, what he should tell the teachers, and if he should seek release from his overseas work. In the afternoon, he had tried to tell the children about the mother's death, but he started to cry and the children responded, "Please don't cry, Daddy." He said he simply had to have another mother for the children, but he felt guilty saying this only eight hours after his wife had died. During the visit, I outlined what I would consider to be the ideal course of action for him. I suggested he take as many of the ideas as were consistent with himself, and if they made sense to him, to use them as far as he could go. I suggested that the ability of children to deal with death depends on the adults, and the future would be best served if the death could be presented in terms the children could understand and they could be realistically involved in the funeral. I warned him of adverse emotional reactions of friends and to be prepared for criticism if he decided to involve the children. In the first hours after the death, the children had been responding to his emotionality rather than to the fact of the mother's death. In this kind of a situation, it is common for the children to stop talking and deny the death. I suggested that he get through this block by mentioning the death at frequent intervals during the coming days, and, if he started to cry, to reassure the children that he was all right and not to worry about him. I wanted to keep the channel open for any and all questions they might have. I suggested that the children decide whether or not they wished to go to school the next day. On the issue of involving the children with the dead mother, I suggested that he arrange a time before the funeral to take the children to the funeral home, to remove all other people from the room, and for him and the children to have a private session with their dead mother. I reasoned that this would help the children adapt to the reality of the mother's death, and that it could work if anxious members of the extended family were excluded. On Tuesday evening, I spent an hour in the bedroom, with the father in a chair and the three children in his lap. He could cry, and they could cry, and the children were free to ask questions. He told them about the plan to go to the funeral home the following afternoon. The five-year-old son asked if he could kiss Mommie. The father looked to me for an answer. I suggested that would be between the son and his mother. Later, in the living room, I announced to the relatives and friends that the father would take the children to the funeral home the next afternoon, that it was to be private, and that no one else could be present. Privately, I considered it unwise to expose the children to the emotionality in that family. The father's mother said, "Son, that will be too hard on you." The father replied, "Mother, shut up. I can do it." On Wednesday evening, I visited the funeral home. The entire family-friendship system was present. The maternal grandmother, who had been calm through these days, said, "Thank you very much for your help." The father did a detailed account of the children's visit in the afternoon. The children went up to the casket and felt their mother. The five-year-old son said, "If I kissed her, she could not kiss back." All three spent some time inspecting everything, even looking under the casket. The eight-year-old son got under the casket and prayed that his mother could hold him in her arms again in heaven. Some family friends came while the father and children were in the room. The father and children withdrew to the lobby while the friends went into the room. In the lobby, the youngest son found some polished pebbles in a planter. He was the one who found objects to give his mother as "presents." He took a small pebble into the room and placed it in his mother's hand. The other children also got pebbles and put them into their mother's hand. Then they announced, "We can go now, Daddy." The father was much relieved at the outcome of the visit. He said, "A thousand tons were lifted from this family today." The following day I attended the funeral. The children did well. The ten-year-old daughter and eight-year-old son were calm. During the service, the eight-year-old whispered to the father, "Daddy, I sure am going to miss Mommie." The five-year-old clung to the father with some tearfulness.

There was some criticism about the father involving the children in the funeral, but he did well with it and the criticism turned to admiration after the funeral home visit. I was in close contact with the family the following year. The father continued to mention the mother's death. Within a week the children were talking about the mother in the past tense. The children stayed with their grandmother. There were none of the usual complications usually seen after a death of this kind. The father took an assignment closer to home, so he could return if he was needed. The following year, the father remarried and took the children with him and his new wife to another city. It has now been twelve years since the death and the family adjustment has been perfect. I am still in periodic contact with the family, which now includes three grown children from the first marriage and younger children from the second marriage. Some years after the death, the father wrote his version of the experience when the first wife died, entitled, "My God, My Wife is Dead." He described his initial shock, his efforts to get beyond self-pity, his resolution to make his own decisions when anxiety was high, and the emotional courage that went into his plan in the critical days before the funeral and burial. This illustrates what I would consider an optimum result from a traumatic death that could have had lifelong sequelae; but this father had more inner strength than any other relative I have seen under stress of this intensity.

Summary

Family systems theory provides a broader perspective of death than is possible with conventional psychiatric theory, which focuses on death as a process within the individual. The first part of this chapter deals with the closed relationship system between the patient, the family, and physicians, and family therapy methods that have been helpful in overcoming some of the anxiety that creates the closed system communication. The second section deals with the "Emotional Shock Wave" that is present to some degree in a significant percentage of families. Knowledge of this, which is the direct result of family research, provides the professional person with a different dimension for understanding emotional interdependence and the long-term complications of death in a family. The final section deals with the emotional impact of funerals and ways the professional person can help surviving relatives to achieve a better level of emotional functioning by calmly facing the anxiety of death.

Chapter 16

Theory in the
Practice of Psychotherapy

There are striking discrepancies between theory and practice in psychotherapy. The therapist's theoretical assumptions about the nature and origin of emotional illness serve as a blueprint that guides his thinking and actions during psychotherapy. This has always been so, even though "theory" and "therapeutic method" have not always been clearly defined. Primitive medicine men who believed that emotional illness was the result of evil spirits had some kind of theoretical notions about the evil spirits that guided their therapeutic method as they attempted to free the person of the spirits. I believe that theory is important now even though it might be difficult to define the specific connections between theory and practice.

I have spent almost three decades on clinical research in psychotherapy. A major part of my effort has gone toward clarifying theory and also toward developing therapeutic approaches consistent with the theory. I did this in the belief it would add to knowledge and provide better structure for research. A secondary gain has been an improvement in the predictability and outcome of therapy as the therapeutic method has come into closer proximity with the theory. Here I shall first present ideas about the lack of clarity between theory and practice in all kinds of psychotherapy; in the second section I will deal specifically with family therapy. In discussing my own Family Systems theory, certain parts will be presented almost as previously published (1966, 1971). Other parts will be modified slightly, and some new concepts will be added.

Background To Theory
In Psychotherapy

Twentieth-century psychotherapy probably has its origin in Freud, who developed a completely new theory about the nature and origin of emotional illness. Before him, mental illness was generally considered the result of some unidentified brain pathology, based on the structured model used by medicine to conceptualize all disease. Freud introduced the new dimension of functional illness which dealt with the function of the mind, rather than brain pathology. His theory was derived largely from patients as they remembered details of early life experiences and as they communicated this detail in the context of an intense emotional relationship with the analyst. In the course of the analysis it was discovered that the patients improved, and that the patient's relationship with the analyst went through definite, predictable stages toward a better life adjustment. Freud and the early analysts made two monumental contributions. One was a new theory about the origin and nature of emotional illness. The other was the first clearly defined theory about the transference relationship and the therapeutic value of a talking relationship. Although counseling and "talking about problems" may have existed before, it was psychoanalysis that gave conceptual structure to the "therapeutic relationship," and that gave birth to the profession of psychotherapy.

Few events in history have influenced man's thinking more than psychoanalysis. This new knowledge about human behavior was gradually incorporated into psychiatry, psychology, sociology, anthropology, and the other professional disciplines that deal with human behavior, and into poetry, novels, plays, and other artistic works. Psychoanalytic concepts came to be regarded as basic truths. Along with the acceptance there were some long-term complications in the integration of psychoanalysis with other knowledge. Freud had been trained as a neurologist. He was clear that he was operating with theoretical assumptions, and that his concepts had no logical connection with medicine or the accepted sciences. His concept of "psycho" pathology, patterned after medicine, left us with a conceptual dilemma not yet resolved. He searched for a conceptual connection with medicine, but never found it. Meanwhile, he used inconsistent models to conceptualize his other findings. His broad knowledge of literature and the arts served as other models. A striking example was the oedipal conflict, which came from literature. His models accurately portrayed his clinical observations and represented a microcosm of human nature; nonetheless, his theoretical concepts came from discrepant sources. This made it difficult for his successors to think in concepts synonymous with medicine or the accepted sciences. In essence, he conceptualized a revolutionary new body of knowledge about human functioning that came to exist in its own compartment, without logical connection with medicine or any of the accepted sciences. The knowledge was popularized by the social sciences and the artistic world, but few of the concepts found their way into the more basic sciences. This further separated psychoanalysis from the sciences.

There have been some clear evolutionary developments in psychoanalytic theory and practice during the twentieth century. Successors to Freud have been more disciples than scientists. They lost contact with the fact that his theory is based on theoretical assumption, and they have tended to regard it as established fact. The more it is considered to be fact, the less it has been possible to question the theoretical base on which it rests. Very early the disciples began to disagree with certain details of the theory (predictable in human relationship systems), and to develop different "theories," concepts, and "schools of thought" based on the differences. They have made such an issue over "differences" that they have lost sight of the fact that they all follow Freud's broad assumptions. The different branches of the tree spend their lives debating the proclaimed "differences," unaware that all spring from the same basic roots. As time passes and the number of branches increase, so do the differences.

The number of differences about the therapeutic relationship are even greater. Freud defined a basic theory about the therapeutic relationship. Beyond that, each practitioner is on his own in developing methods and techniques for applying the theory. There is more flexibility for developing "differences" about therapeutic method and techniques than about theory. Psychoanalysts maintain a strict interpretation of the "transference," which is considered to be different from the popular notion of the therapeutic relationship. There are differences, but the focus on differences obscures the common denominators. Group therapy is a good illustration of the trend. It sprang primarily from theory about the therapeutic relationship, and secondarily from basic psychoanalytic theory about the nature of emotional illness. The growing multitudes of mental health professionals who use all the different theories and therapies still follow two of the basic concepts of psychoanalysis. One is that emotional illness is developed in relationship with others. The second is that the therapeutic relationship is the universal "treatment" for emotional illness.

There are other evolutionary trends that illustrate the separation of theory and practice. It has to do with psychological research. The basic sciences have long been critical of psychoanalysis and psychological theory as nonscientific and based on shifting hypotheses that defy critical scientific study. There is validity to this criticism. The psychoanalysts and psychologists have countered that the field is different, and the same rules do not apply. They have coined the term social "sciences," and much research has gone into proving that they are scientific. There is some support for the proposition that social sciences are scientific. The major change has been in the development of the scientific method designed to study random and discrepant data in a scientific way. If the scientific method is pursued long enough, it should eventually produce the data and facts that are acceptable to the basic sciences. This has not occurred. The debate has gone through the century with the psychologists accepting psychoanalytic assumptions as fact and believing that the scientific method makes the field into a science, while workers in the basic sciences are still unconvinced. This is where research in the mental health field is today. The directors of research and experts who control the funds for research are schooled in the scientific method, which tends to perpetuate fixed postures. My own position on this is that, "There is no way to chi square a feeling and make it qualify as a scientific fact." This is based on the belief that human behavior is a part of all nature, so that it is as knowable and predictable and reproducible as other phenomena in nature; but I believe that research should be directed at making theoretical contact with other fields, rather than applying the scientific method to subjective human data. This has been a long-term conflict I have had with research in mental illness. To summarize, I believe that research in emotional illness has helped to contribute to the separation of theory and practice, and to the notion that psychological theory is based on proven fact.

There are trends in the training of mental health professionals that support the separation of theory and practice. Early in the twentieth century the popularity of psychoanalysis was increasing, but over-all, psychiatry, and also the public, was still negative about it. By the 1940s and 1950s, psychoanalytic theory had become *the* predominant theory. By that time the psychoanalysts had developed so many superficial "differences" among themselves that the new trainees of the 1940s and 1950s were confronted with a spectrum of different "theories" all based on basic psychoanalytic concepts. They learned psychoanalytic theory as proven fact and the therapeutic relationship as *the* treatment for emotional illness. The trainees from that period are now the senior teachers in the field. The number of superficial "differences" have increased. Starting in the 1950s and increasing into the 1960s, we have heard much antipsychoanalytic talk by people who use basic psychoanalytic concepts in theory and practice. In the present era we have the "eclectic," who tells us that there is no single theory adequate for all situations and he chooses the best parts of all the theories to best fit the clinical situation of the moment.

I believe that all the differences belong within the basic framework of psychoanalysis, and that the eclectic shifting may be more for the needs of therapist than the patient. The average training programs for mental health professionals contain a few didactic lectures on theory appended to the basic training. An overwhelming amount of time goes to tutorial training, which emphasizes the therapeutic relationship, learning about one's own emotional problems, and the management of self in relation to the patient. This produces professionals who are oriented around the therapeutic relationship, who assume they know the nature and origin of emotional illness, who are unable to question the theoretical base on which the field rests, and who assume the therapeutic relationship is the basic treatment for emotional problems. Society, insurance companies, and the licensing bodies have come to accept this theoretical and therapeutic position, and have become more lenient about providing payment for psychotherapeutic services. Counselors, teachers, police, courts, and all the social agencies that deal with human problems have also come to accept the basic assumptions about theory and therapy.

Mental health professionals relate to theory in a spectrum. At one extreme are the few who are serious students of theory. A larger group can state theoretical positions in detail, but they have developed therapeutic approaches discrepant with the theory. A still larger group treats theory as proven fact. These last are similar to the medicine men who *knew* that illness was caused by evil spirits. Professional expertise becomes a matter of finding more ingenious techniques for externalizing the bad spirits. At the other extreme are the therapists who contend there is no such thing as theory, that theoretical efforts are post hoc explanations for the therapist's intuitive actions in the therapeutic relationship, and that the best therapy is possible when the therapist learns to be a "real self" in relation to the patient.

In presenting these ideas about the separation of theory and therapy in the mental health professions, I have inevitably overstated to clarify the issues. I believe that psychoanalytic theory, which includes the theory of the transference and talking therapy, is still the one major theory to explain the nature and origin of emotional illness, and that the numerous different theories are based more on minor differences than on differences with basic concepts. I believe Freud's use of discrepant theoretical models helped make psychoanalysis into a compartmental-ized body of knowledge that prevented successors from finding conceptual bridges with the more accepted sciences. Psychoanalysis attracted followers who were more disciples than scholars and scientists. It has evolved into more of a dogma or religion than a science, with its own "scientific" method to help perpetuate the cycle. I believe it has enough new knowledge to be part of the sciences, but the professionals who practice psychoanalysis have evolved into an emotional ingroup, like a family or a religion. Members of an emotional ingroup devote energy to defining their "differences" with each other and defending dogma that needs no defense. They are so caught up with the ingroup process that they cannot generate new knowledge from within, nor permit the admission of knowledge from without that might threaten the dogma. The result has been a splintering and resplintering, with a new generation of eclectics who attempt to survive the splintering with their eclecticism.

The Therapeutic Relationship
In Broader Perspective

Family research has identified some characteristics of emotional systems that put the therapeutic relationship into broader perspective. An emotional system is usually the family, but it can be a larger work group or a social group. The major characteristic to be examined here is that *the successful introduction of a significant other person into an anxious or disturbed relationship system has the capacity to modify relationships within the system.* There is another characteristic of opposite emotional forces, which is that the higher the level of tension or anxiety within an emotional system, the more the members of the system tend to withdraw from outside relationships and to compartmentalize themselves with each other. There are a number of variables that revolve around the characteristic in focus. The first variables have to do with the *significant other*. Other variables have to do with what is meant by *successful* introduction. Other variables have to do with the *introduction* of the significant other and how long he remains a member of the system. I have chosen the term *modify* in order to avoid the use of *change,* which has come to have so many different meanings in psychotherapy.

An individually-oriented psychotherapist is a common *significant other.* If he can manage a viable and moderately intense therapeutic relationship with the patient, and the patient remains in viable contact with the family, it can calm and modify relationships within the family. It is as though the therapeutic relationship drains the tension from the family and the family can appear to be different. When the therapist and patient become more intensely involved with each other, the patient withdraws from emotional contact with the family and the family becomes more disturbed. Therapists have intuitive ways of dealing with this situation. Some choose to intensify the relationship into a therapeutic alliance, and to encourage the patient to challenge the family. Others are content with a supportive relationship. There are a number of other outside relationships that can accomplish the same thing. A significant new relationship with a friend, minister, or teacher can be effective if the right conditions are met. The right degree of an outside sexual relationship can calm a family as much as individual psychotherapy. When the affair is kept at the right emotional level, the family system can be calm and blind to evidences of the affair. The moment the outside affair becomes emotionally overinvested, it tends to alienate the involved person from the family and increase tension within the family. At this point the other spouse becomes a suspicious detective, alert to all the evidence previously ignored. This phenomenon, which has to do with the balance of relationships in a family, applies to a broad spectrum of relationships.

A set of variables revolve around the qualities that go into a significant other relationship. One variable deals with the importance of the family member to the rest of the family. The family would respond quickly to the outside emotional involvement of an important family member who is relating actively to the others. It would respond slowly to a withdrawn and inactive family member unless the outside relationship was fairly intense. The most important variable has to do with the assumed, assigned, or actual importance of the significant other person. At one extreme is the significant other who assumes or is assigned magical or supernatural importance. This includes voodoo experts, leaders of cults, great healers, and charismatic leaders of spiritual movements. The significant other can pretend to represent the diety and to have supernatural power. He pleads for the other to "believe in me, trust me, have confidence in me." The assuming of great importance and the assigning of importance is usually a bilateral operation, but there probably could be situations in which the importance is largely assigned, and significant other goes along with it. These relationships operate on high emotionality and minimal reality. When successful, the change can come rapidly or with instantaneous conversion.

At the other extreme are the situations in which the evaluation of the significant other is based largely on reality, with little pretense, and with little of the intense relationship phenomenon. The principal ingredient is knowledge or skill. Examples of this might be a genetic counselor, an estate planner, or a successful professor who has the ability to inspire students in his subject, more through knowledge than relationship. In between these two extremes are relationships with healers, ministers, counselors, physicians, therapists of all kinds, and people in the helping professions who either assume or are assigned an importance they do not have. The assuming and assigning of importance is clearest in its extreme forms in which the pretending of importance is sufficiently grotesque for anyone to notice. Actually, the assigning and assuming of importance, or unimportance, is present to some degree in all relationships, and present enough to be detectable in most relationships on careful observation. A clear example is a love relationship in which each has an overvalued image of the other. It is also easy to recognize the change in a person who is in love. Over-all, the degree of assigning and assuming overimportance in the therapeutic relationship is on the high side. Psychoanalysis has subtle techniques to encourage the development of a transference, which is then dealt with in the therapy. Other methods do even more of this, and efforts to correct the distortion are even less.

Another set of variables revolve around the way the significant other is introduced into the system. At one extreme, the significant other pleads, exhorts, advertises, evangelizes, and makes promises of the great things if he is invited in. At the other extreme, the significant other enters the system only on unsolicited invitation and with a contract either verbal or written that comes closer to defining the reality of the situation. The rest fall somewhere between these two extremes. Other variables have to do with the length of time the significant other is involved in the system. The successful involvement depends on whether or not the relationship works. This involves the family member devoting a reasonable amount of thinking-feeling energy to the relationship without becoming too emotionally preoccupied.

An important set of variables revolves around what it means to modify relationships within the family. I avoid using *change* here because of the loose way this word is used within the profession. Some speak of an emotional conversion, a shift in mood, a shift in attitude, or a shift from feeling sad to happy as being "change" or emotional "growth." The word *growth* has been so misused during the past decade, that it has become meaningless. In contrast, other people do not consider change to have taken place without basic, documentable, structural alteration in the underlying situation that gave rise to the symptoms. Between these two lie all the other manifestations of change. It is common for mental health professionals to consider the disappearance of symptoms as evidence of change.

The more the relationship with the significant other person is endowed with high emotionality, messianic qualities, exaggerated promises, and evangelism, the more the change can be sudden and magical, and the less likely it is to be long term. The lower the emotionality and the more the relationship deals in reality, the more likely the change is to come slowly and to be solid and long lasting. There is some degree of emotionality in any relationship, especially in the helping professions where the principal ingredient is services rather than materials, but it is also present around those who deal in materials, such as supersalesmen. The emotionality can exist around the charismatic person who attracts the assignment of importance from others. Emotionality may be hard to evaluate with public figures who attain their positions from superior skill and knowledge, in which emotionality is low, and who then operate on reputation, in which assigned importance is high. The doctor-patient relationship encompasses a wide range of emotionality. At one extreme it can be almost all service and little relationship, and at the other extreme the emotional component is high. The physician who operates with a posture which says, "Have no fear, the doctor is here," is assuming great importance, and also using it to calm anxiety. The physician who says, "If doctors could only be half as important as their patients think they are," is operating with awareness and less assumption of importance. Emotionality is sufficiently high in medicine that the placebo effect is routinely built into responsible research to check the emotional factor.

Psychotherapy is a service that deals in a higher level of emotionality than the average doctor-patient relationship. The level of assumed and assigned importance is on the high side. The well-trained therapist has techniques to encourage the patient to assign him an overimportance which he interprets to the patient as part of the therapy. He is aware of transference "cures," and of the unhealthy aspects of countertransference when he becomes emotionally overinvolved with the patient. He may have operating rules to govern the right kind of therapeutic relationship: trying to match the patient with the therapist's personality, avoiding working with a patient he does not "like," or recommending a male or female therapist for particular kinds of problems. The psychotherapist does not get into emotionality that is in the spiritual range, but he deals constantly in a high level of emotionality. The well-trained therapist does well with these emotional forces, but the rapidly enlarging field of psychotherapy includes many who do not have this expertise. The training of therapists may involve the selection of trainees who have the right personality for a good "therapeutic relationship." The level of emotionality in the field makes it difficult to evaluate the results of psychotherapy.

I go into this much detail about the therapeutic relationship because concepts about the therapeutic relationship and the notion that

psychotherapy is *the* treatment for emotional illness are basic teachings in
the training of mental health professionals. The orientation is probably
greater for nonmedical people who do not have to learn the medical part
of psychiatry. Mental health professionals are so indoctrinated in these
basic concepts they have difficulty hearing another way of thinking. That
is why my own theory is incomprehensible to those who cannot think
through their early basic teaching and practice. Early in my professional
career I was a serious student of the therapeutic relationship. In the
psychotherapy of schizophrenia much effort went into eliminating the
assumed and assigned importance from the therapeutic relationship. The
more I was successful at this, the more I could get good results after
others had failed. It was usual for others to consider these good results as
related to some undefined personality characteristic in me, or to
coincidence. A good result could be followed by a comment such as,
"Some schizophrenics come out of their regression automatically."
Successfully managing the transference in schizophrenia made it easy to
automatically manage the milder transference in the neuroses. The
change to family research provided a new dimension for dealing with the
therapeutic relationship. It became theoretically possible to leave the
intensity of the relationship between the original family members, and
bypass some of the time-consuming detail. I began to work toward
avoiding the transference. When I started to talk about "staying out of
the transference," the usual response was, "You don't mean you stay out
of the transference; you mean you handle it well." That is, my statement
was countered by another even more dogmatic, and pursuit of the issue
only resulted in polarized emotional debate.

The prevailing opinion of therapists who operate with the therapeutic
relationship is that I handle the transference well. However, a therapist
with knowledge of the facts inherent in systems theory, and especially a
knowledge of triangles (discussed below) can deal largely in reality and
facts and eliminate much of the emotional process that usually goes into a
transference. Indeed, it is possible to routinely reproduce an operational
version of the same expertise in a good percentage of professional
trainees. This is in contrast to usual training methods in which the result
of training depends more on the intuitive and intangible qualities in the
trainee than on knowledge. One never reaches the point of not being
vulnerable to automatically falling back into the emotionality of
transference. I still use mechanisms to reduce the assumed and assigned
overimportance that can get into any relationship. When one acquires a
reputation in any field, one also acquires an aura of assigned
overimportance that goes beyond reality. Among the ways I have dealt

with this is by charging average fees, which helps avoid the emotional pitfalls inherent in charging high fees. The therapeutic effort is so different from conventional therapy that I have developed other terms to refer to the therapy process; for instance I speak of "supervising" the effort the family makes on its own behalf, and "coaching" a family member in working with his own family. It is accurate to say there is some emotionality in any relationship, but it is also accurate to say that the emotionality can be reduced to a low level through knowledge about emotional systems.

The Therapeutic Relationship
In Family Therapy

The separation between theory and therapy in most family therapy is far greater than with individual therapy. The vast majority of family therapists started from a previous orientation in individual or group therapy. Their family therapy descends almost directly from group therapy, which came out of psychoanalytic theory with an emphasis on the theory of the transference. Group therapy led to far more differences in method and technique than individual therapy, and family therapy lends itself to more differences than group therapy. I have referred to this as the "unstructured state of chaos" in family therapy.

Family therapists deal with the therapeutic relationship in a variety of ways. Some great family therapists, who were adept at dealing with transference in individual or group therapy, continue their adeptness in family therapy. They use psychoanalytic theory for thinking about problems in the individual, and transference theory for thinking about relationships. There are those who speak of "getting into and getting out of" intense relationships with individual family members. They are confident in their skill and ability to operate freely within the family. They operate more on intuition than any special body of knowledge. Their therapy is difficult for trainees to imitate and reproduce. Most therapists use some version of group therapy in their effort to keep relationships "spread out" and manageable. Another group uses co-therapists, usually of the opposite sex; their rationale is derived from psychoanalytic theory that this provides a male-female model for the family. The co-therapist functions to keep some degree of objectivity when the other therapist becomes emotionally entangled in the family.

Others use a team approach in which an entire mental health team meets with a family or group of families in a problem-focused group therapy method. The team, or "therapeutic group," is composed of members of the various mental health professions. The team-group meetings are commonly used for "training" inexperienced professional people who learn by participation in the team meetings, and who can rather quickly gain the status of "family therapist." Trainees begin by observing, following which they are encouraged to become part of the group by expressing their "feelings" in the therapy meetings. These are people who have never had much training in theory, or in the emotional discipline of learning the intricacies of transference and countertransference. Theory is usually not explicit, but the implicit format conveys that emotional illness is the product of suppressed feeling and poor communication, that treatment is the free expression of feelings and open communication, and that a competent therapist is one who can facilitate the process. Family therapy has also attracted therapists who were never successful at individual therapy, but who find a place in one of the numerous kinds of group therapy methods being used in family therapy. These admitted overstatements convey some idea of the many kinds of family therapy methods and techniques that are in use.

Group therapy has long acted as though it did not have a theory. I believe the reasons for this are that family therapy for the most part is a decendant of group therapy, that family therapy has started variations in method and technique that were not possible in group therapy, and that the separation between theory and practice is greater in family therapy than any of the other therapies. All these circumstances may account for the fact that few family therapists have much awareness of theory.

My approach differs from the mainstream of family therapy. I have learned more about the intricacies of the therapeutic relationship from family research than from psychoanalysis or the psychotherapy of schizophrenia. Most of this was learned from the study of triangles. The automatic emotional responsiveness that operates constantly in all relationships is the same as the therapeutic relationship. As soon as a vulnerable outside person comes into viable emotional contact with the family, he becomes part of it, no matter how much he protests the opposite. The emotional system operates through all five senses, and most often through visual and auditory stimuli. In addition, there is a sixth sense that can include extrasensory perception. All living things learn to process this data very early and to use it in relation to others. In addition, the human has a sophisticated verbal language which is as often used to deny the automatic emotional process as to confirm it. I believe the automatic emotional process is far more important in establishing and maintaining relationships than verbal language. The concept of triangles provides a way of reading the automatic emotional responsiveness so as to control one's own automatic emotional participation in the emotional process. This control I have called detriangling. No one ever stays outside, but a knowledge of triangles makes it possible to get outside on one's own initiative while staying emotionally in contact with the family. Most important, family members can learn to observe themselves and their families, and to control themselves while on stage with the family without having to withdraw. A family member who is motivated to learn and control his own responsiveness can influence relationships in the entire family system.

The effort of being outside the family emotional system, or remaining workably objective in an intense emotional field, has many applications. Family relationships are remarkably different when an outsider is introduced into the system. A disturbed family is always looking for a vulnerable outsider. It would be healtheir if they worked it out among themselves, but the emotional process reaches out for others. For a quarter of a century there has been a debate in family research about ways to do objective observations of the family, free from outside influences. Well-known research investigators such as Erving Goffman and Jules Henry have insisted that objective observations be made in the family's native habitat, the home, by a neutral observer. Based on my experience with emotional systems, I am sure any such observers were fused with the family as soon as they entered the home, that the family automatically became different, and that their belief they were being objective was erroneous. Complete objectivity is impossible; but I believe the best version of objectivity is possible with significant others who know triangles. There was a recently publicized movie-television study of a family done by a movie crew who went into the home to film the family as it really was. From my viewpoint, the movie crew automatically became a significant other which helped propel the parents toward divorce. This situation might have found another triangle that would have served the same triangle force.

Theory In The Development
Of Family Therapy

The family movement in psychiatry was started in the mid 1950s by several different psychiatrists who worked independently for several years before they began to hear about each other. I have described my version of that in other papers (1966, 1971, 1975). Among those who started with family research on schizophrenia was Lidz and his group at Johns Hopkins and Yale (Lidz, Fleck and Cornelison 1965), Jackson and his group in Palo Alto (Bateson et al. 1956), and Bowen and his group in Bethesda (1960, 1961). The psychoanalytic principle of protecting the privacy of the patient-therapist relationship may account for the family movement's remaining underground for some years. There were strict rules against the therapist's contaminating the transference by seeing other members of the same family: the early family work was done privately, probably to avoid critical colleagues who might consider this irresponsible until it was legitimized in the name of research. I began formal research in 1954 after several years of preliminary work. During 1955 and 1956 we each began to hear about the others and to meet. Ackerman (1958) had been thinking and working toward family concepts in social service agencies and clinics. Bell, who remained separate from the group for some years, had a different beginning. His first paper (1961) was written some seven or eight years after he started. There were others mentioned in the earlier summaries.

For me, 1955 to 1956 was a period of elation and enthusiasm. Observing entire families living together on a research ward provided a completely new order of clinical data never before recorded in the literature. Only those who were there could appreciate the impact of the new observations on psychiatry. Other family researchers were observing the same things, but were using different conceptual models to describe their findings. Why had these findings, now so commonplace, been obscured in previous observations? I believe two factors to account for this observational blindness. One was a shift in the observing lens from the individual to the family. The other is man's failure to see what is in front of him unless it fits his theoretical frame of reference. Before Darwin, man considered the earth to have been created as it appeared before his eyes. He had stumbled over the bones of prehistoric animals for centuries without seeing them, until Darwin's theory permitted him to begin seeing what had been there all the time.

For years I had pondered the discrepancies in psychoanalytic theory without finding new clues. Now I had a wealth of new clues that could lead to a completely different theory about emotional illness. Jackson was the other of the early workers who shared the theoretical potential. Lidz was more established in his psychoanalytic practice than Jackson and I, and he was more interested in an accurate description of his findings than in theory. Ackerman was also established in psychoanalytic practice and training, and his interest lay in developing therapy and not theory. I had built a method of individual therapy into my research design for studying the families. Within six months there was evidence that some method of therapy for family members together was indicated. I had never heard of family therapy. Against the strong theoretical and clinical admonitions of the time, I followed the dictates of the research evidence and after much careful planning started my first method of family psychotherapy. Later, I heard that others had also thought of family therapy. Jackson had been approaching on one level and Ackerman was approaching on another. In 1956 I heard that Bell had been doing something called family therapy, but I did not meet him until 1958.

The first family section at a national meeting was organized by Spiegel at the American Orthopsychiatric meeting in Chicago in March 1957. He was Chairman of the Committee on the Family of the Group for the Advancement of Psychiatry and he had just heard about the family work in progress. That was a small and quiet meeting. There were papers on research by Spiegel, Mendell, Lidz, and Bowen. In my paper I referred to the "family psychotherapy" used in my research since late 1955. I believe that may have been the first time the term was used in a national meeting. However it happened, I would date the family therapy explosion to March 1957. In May 1957, there was a family section at the American Psychiatric meeting, also in Chicago. In the two months since the previous meeting, there had been an increasing fervor about family therapy. Ackerman was secretary of the meeting, and Jackson was also present. Family ideas generated there led to Jackson's book, *The Etiology of Schizophrenia,* finally published in 1960. At the national meetings in 1958, the family sessions were dominated by dozens of new therapists eager to report their family therapy of the past year. That was the beginning of the family therapy that was quite different from the family research of previous years. The new people, attracted by the idea of family therapy, had been developing empirical methods and techniques based on the psychoanalytic theory of individual and group psychotherapy. The family research and the theoretical thinking that gave birth to family therapy were lost in the rush.

The rush into family therapy in 1957 and 1958 produced a wild kind of therapy which I called a "healthy, unstructured state of chaos." There were almost as many different methods and techniques as there were new therapists. I considered the trend healthy in the belief the new therapists would discover the discrepancies in conventional theory, and that the conceptual dilemma posed by family therapy would lead to new concepts and ultimately to a new theory. This did not occur. I did not realize the degree of therapeutic zeal that makes psychiatrists oblivious to theory. Family therapy became a therapeutic method engrafted onto the basic concepts of psychoanalysis, and especially the theory of the transference. New therapists tended toward therapeutic evangelism, and they trained generations of new therapists who also tended toward simplistic views of the human dilemma and family therapy as a panacea for treatment. Family therapy not only inherited the vagueness and lack of theoretical clarity from conventional psychiatry, but it added new dimensions of its own. The number of minor differences and schools of thought are greater in family therapy than in individual therapy, and it now has its own group of eclectics who solve the problem through eclecticism.

Jackson and I were the only two from the original family researchers with a significant interest in theory. Jackson's group included Bateson, Haley, and Weakland. They began with a simple communication model of human relationships, but soon expanded the concept to include the total of human interaction in the concept. By the time Jackson died in 1968, he had moved toward a rather sophisticated systems model. I believe my theory had a sounder base to connect it with an instinctual motor; Jackson was operating more on phenomenology, but he was moving toward a distinctly different theory. One can only guess where he would have emerged had he lived.

In the past decade, there has been the slow emergence of a few new theoretical trends. It is not possible to stay on a broad conceptual level and do justice to the work of individuals, and at this point it is not possible to do more than survey the field in broad concepts. The notion of systems theory started gaining popularity in the mid 1960s, but the use of systems in psychiatry is still in a primitive state. On one level, it is no more than the use of one word to replace another. On another level, it has the same meaning as a transportation system or circulatory system. On a more sophisticated level, it refers to a relationship system, which is a system in human behavior. On a broad level, people believe that "system" is derived from general systems theory, which is a system of thinking about existing knowledge. In my opinion, the attempt to apply general systems theory to psychiatry, as psychiatry is presently conceptualized, is equivalent to the effort to apply the scientific method to psychoanalysis. It has a potential, long-term gain if things work out right. However, the slow emergence of something that goes in a systems direction is one of the new evolutions in the family field. There have been some fascinating innovations in concepts that still retain much basic psychoanalytic theory. Among these is Paul's (1975) concept concerning unresolved grief reactions which has a therapeutic method that fits the theoretical concept, and effectively taps the basic emotional process. Boszormenyi-Nagy (1973) is one of the theoretical scholars in the field. He has a rather complete set of theoretical abstractions that may one day provide a theoretical bridge between psychoanalysis and a different family theory. One of the more unique new orientations is Minuchin's (1974). He carefully avoids the complex concepts of theory, but he uses the term *Structural Family Therapy* for a therapeutic method designed to change the family through modification of the feedback system in relationships. His focus is more on therapy than on theory.

Family Systems Theory

The evolution of my own theoretical thinking began in the decade before I started family research. There were many questions concerning generally accepted explanations about emotional illness. Efforts to find logical answers resulted in more unanswerable questions. One simple example is the notion that mental illness is the result of maternal deprivation. The idea seemed to fit the clinical case of the moment, but not the large number of normal people who, as far as could be determined, had been exposed to more maternal deprivation than those who were sick. There was also the issue of the schizophrenogenic mother. There were detailed descriptions of schizophrenogenic parents, but little to explain how the same parents could have other children who were not only normal, but who appeared supernormal. There were lesser discrepancies in popular hypotheses that linked emotional symptoms to a single traumatic event in the past. This again appeared logical in specific cases, but did not explain the large number of people who had suffered trauma without developing symptoms. There was a tendency to create special hypotheses for individual cases. The whole body of diagnostic nomenclature was based on symptom description, except for the small percentage of cases in which symptoms could be connected to actual pathology. Psychiatry acted as if it knew the answers, but it had not been able to develop diagnoses consistent with etiology. Psychoanalytic theory tended to define emotional illness as the product of a process between parents and child in a single generation, and there was little to explain how severe problems could be created so rapidly. The basic sciences were critical of psychiatric explanations that eluded scientific study. If the body of knowledge was reasonably factual, why could we not be more scientific about it? There were assumptions that emotional illness was the product of forces of socialization, even though the same basic emotional illness was present in all cultures. Most of the assumptions considered emotional illness as specific to humans, when there was evidence that a similar process was also present in lower forms of life. These and many other questions led me to extensive reading in evolution, biology, and the natural sciences as part of a search for clues that could lead to a broader theoretical frame of reference. My hunch was that emotional illness comes from that part of man that he shares with the lower forms of life.

My inital family research was based on an extension of theoretical formulations about the mother-child symbiosis. The hypothesis considered emotional illness in the child to be a product of a less severe problem in the mother. The hypothesis described the balancing forces that kept the relationship in equilibrium. It was a good example of what is now called a system. Very quickly it became apparent that the mother-child relationship was a dependent fragment of the larger family unit. The research design was modified for fathers and normal siblings to live on the ward with mothers and the schizophrenic patients. This resulted in a completely new order of observations. Other researchers were observing the same things, but they were using a variety of different models to conceptualize findings, including models from psychoanalysis, psychology, mythology, physics, chemistry, and mathematics. There were some common denominators that clustered around the "stuck togetherness," bonds, binds, and interlocking of family members with each other. There were other concepts for the balancing forces, such as complementarity, reciprocity, magnetic fields, and hydraulic and electrical forces. Accurate as each concept might be descriptively, the investigators were using discrepant models.

Early in the research, I made some decisions based on previous thinking about theory. Family research was producing a completely new order of observations. There was a wealth of new theoretical clues. On the premise that psychiatry might eventually become a recognized science, perhaps a generation or two in the future, and being aware of the past conceptual problems of psychoanalysis, I chose to use only concepts that would be consistent with a recognized science. This was done in the hope that investigators of the future would more easily be able to see connections between human behavior and the accepted sciences than we can. I therefore chose to use concepts that would be consistent with biology and the natural sciences. It was easy to think in terms of the familiar concepts of chemistry, physics, and mathematics, but I carefully excluded all concepts that dealt with inanimate things, and studied the literature for concepts that dealt with inanimate things, and studied the literature for concepts synonymous with biology—that is, I used biological concepts to describe human behavior. The concept of symbiosis, originally from psychiatry, would have been discarded except for its use in biology where the word has a specific meaning. The concept of differentiation was chosen because it has specific meanings in the biological sciences. When we speak of the "differentiation of self," we mean a process similar to the differentiation of cells from each other. The same applies to the term *fusion*. *Instinctual* is used exactly as it is used in biology, rather than in the restricted, special meaning of its use in psychoanalysis. There are a few minor exceptions to this over-all plan, which will be mentioned later. In the period when I was reading biology, a close psychoanalyst friend advised me to give up "holistic" thinking before I got "too far out."

Another long-term plan was directed at the research staff, and was based on the notion that the clues for important discoveries are right in front of our eyes, if we can only develop the ability to see what we have never seen before. Research observers can see only what they have been trained to see through their theoretical orientations. The research staff had been trained in psychoanalysis, and they tended to see confirmation or extensions of psychoanalysis. On the premise there was far more to be seen if they could get beyond their theoretical blindness, I devised a plan to help us all open our eyes to new observations. One long-term exercise required investigators to avoid the use of conventional psychiatric terminology and to replace it with simple descriptive words. It was quite an exercise to use simple language instead of terms such as "schizophrenic-obsessive-compulsive-depressed-hysterical-patient." The over-all goal was to help observers clear their heads of preexisting ideas and see in a new way. Although much of this could be classified as an exercise or a game in semantics, it did contribute to a broader viewpoint. The research team developed a new language. Then came the complications of communication with colleagues, and the necessity of translating our new language back into terminology others could understand. It was awkward to use ten words to describe "a patient," when everyone else knew the correct meaning of "patient." We were criticized for coining new terms when old ones would be better, but during the exercise we had discovered the degree to which well-trained professional people use the same terms differently, while assuming that everyone understands them the same way.

The core of my theory has to do with the degree to which people are able to distinguish between the *feeling* process and the *intellectual* process. Early in the research, we found that the parents of schizophrenic people, who appear on the surface to function well, have difficulty distinguishing between the subjective feeling process and the more objective thinking process. This is most marked in a close personal relationship. This led to investigation of the same phenomenon in all levels of families from the most impaired, to normal, to the highest functioning people we could find. We found that there are differences between the ways feelings and intellect are either fused or differentiated from each other, and this led us to develop the concept of differentiation of self. People with the greatest fusion between feeling and thinking function the poorest. They inherit a high percentage of life's problems. Those with the most ability to distinguish between feeling and thinking, or who have the most differentiation of self, have the most flexibility and adaptability in coping with life stresses, and the most freedom from problems of all kinds. Other people fall between the two extremes, both in the interplay between feeling and thinking and in their life adjustments.

Feeling and emotion are used almost synonymously in popular usage and also in the literature. Also, little distinction is made between the subjectivity of truth and the objectivity of fact. The lower the level of differentiation, the more a person is not able to distinguish between the two. The literature does not clearly distinguish between *philosophy, belief, opinion, conviction,* and *impression.* Lacking guidelines from the literature, we used dictionary definitions to clarify these for our theoretical purposes.

The theoretical assumption considers emotional illness to be a disorder of the *emotional system,* an intimate part of man's phylogenetic past which he shares with all lower forms of life, and which is governed by the same laws that govern all living things. The literature refers to emotions as much more than states of contentment, agitation, fear, weeping, and laughing, although it also refers to these states in the lower forms of life—contentment after feeding, sleep, and mating, and states of agitation in fight, flight, and the search for food. For the purposes of this theory, the emotional system is considered to include all the above functions, plus all the automatic functions that govern the autonomic nervous system, and to be synonymous with instinct that governs the life process in all living things. The term *emotional illness* is used to replace former terms, such as mental illness and psychological illness. Emotional illness is considered a deep process involving the basic life process of the organism.

The *intellectual system* is a function of the cerebral cortex which appeared last in man's evolutionary development, and is the main difference between man and the lower forms of life. The cerebral cortex involves the ability to think, reason, and reflect, and enables man to govern his life, in certain areas, according to logic, intellect, and reason. The more experience I have had, the more I am convinced that far more of life is governed by automatic emotional forces than man is willing to acknowledge. The *feeling system* is postulated as a link between the emotional and intellectual systems through which certain emotional states are represented in conscious awareness. Man's brain is part of his protoplasmic totality. Through the function of his brain, he has learned many of the secrets of the universe; he has also learned to create technology to modify his environment, and to gain control over most of the lower forms of life. Man has done less well in using his brain to study his own emotional functioning.

Much of the early family research was done with schizophrenia. Since the clinical observations from those studies had not been previously described in the literature, it was first thought that the relationship patterns were typical of schizophrenia. Then it was discovered that the very same patterns were also present in families with neurotic level problems, and even in normal families. Gradually, it became clear that the relationship patterns, so clear in families with schizophrenia, were present in all people to some degree and that the intensity of the patterns being observed was related more to the anxiety of the moment than the severity of the emotional illness being studied. This fact about the early days of family research conveys some notion of the state of psychological theory twenty years ago that is not appreciated by those who were not part of the scene at that time. The family studies in schizophrenia were so important that they stimulated several research studies of normal families in the late 1950s and early 1960s. The influence of the schizophrenia research on family therapy was so important that family therapy was still being considered to be a form of therapy for schizophrenia as much as ten years after the family movement started. The results of the early studies on normal families might be summarized by saying that the patterns originally thought to be typical of schizophrenia are present in all families some of the time and in some families most of the time.

My work toward a different theory began as soon as the relationship patterns were seen to repeat over and over, and we had achieved some notion about the conditions under which they repeated. The early papers were devoted mostly to clinical description of the patterns. By 1957, the relationship patterns in the nuclear family were sufficiently defined that I was willing to call a major paper, "A Family *Concept* of Schizophrenia." Jackson, who was reasonably accurate in his use of the word *theory*, had coauthored a paper in 1956 called, "Toward a Theory of Schizophrenia" (Bateson et al.). He urged me to use the term *theory* in the 1957 paper, which was finally published in 1960, but I refused on the basis that it was no more than a concept in a much larger field, and I wanted to avoid using *theory* for a partial theory or a concept. The situation in the late 1950s was an absolute delight for me. It satisfied my theoretical curiosity that schizophrenia and the psychoses were part of the same continuum with neurotic problems, and that the differences between schizophrenia and the neuroses were quantitative rather than qualitative. Psychoanalysis and the other theoretical systems viewed psychosis as the product of one emotional process, and the neuroses as the product of another emotional process. Even today a majority of people in psychiatry probably still hold the viewpoint that schizophrenia and the neuroses are qualitatively different. It is usual for mental health professionals to speak of schizophrenia as one thing, and the neuroses as another type of problem; they also still speak of "normal" families. However, I *know* they are all part of the total human dimension, all the way from the lowest possible level of human functioning to the highest. I believe that those who assume a difference between schizophrenia, the neuroses, and the normal are operating from basic psychoanalytic theory without being specifically aware of it, and that they base the difference on therapeutic response rather than on systems theory. I believe psychiatry will some day come to see all these conditions as parts of the same continuum.

The main part of this family systems theory evolved rather rapidly over a period of about six years, between 1957 and 1963. No one part was first. A concept about the nuclear family emotional system and another about the family projection process had both been started in the early descriptive papers. They were both reasonably clear by the time it was possible to compare the patterns in schizophrenia with the total range of human problems. The notion that all human problems exist on a single continuum gave rise by the early 1960s, to the concept of differentiation of self. The notion of triangles, one of the basic concepts in the total theory, had been started in 1957 when it was called the "interdependent triad." The concept was sufficiently developed to be used in therapy by about 1961. The concept of multigenerational transmission process started as a research hypothesis as early as 1955, but the research that brought it to reasonable clarification had to wait till 1959 to 1960, when there was a larger volume of families for study. The concept of sibling position had been poorly defined since the late 1950s, but it had to wait until Toman's *Family Constellation* (1961) provided structure. By 1963, these six interlocking concepts were sufficiently defined that I was willing to put all six together into family systems theory, which satisfied a fairly strict definition of theory. It was not included in *Intensive Family Therapy* by Boszormenyi-Nagy and Framo (1965), which was published in 1965, because they had specifically asked for a chapter on schizophrenia. The six concepts were finally published as a coherent, theoretical system in 1966. After 1966, there were numerous changes in therapy, but the theory as presented in 1966 has remained very much as it is today, with some extensions and refinements. Finally, in 1975, two new concepts were added. The first, the emotional cutoff, was merely a refinement and a new emphasis of former theoretical principles. The last and eighth concept, societal regression, had been rather well defined by 1972, and was finally added as a separate concept in 1975. Also, the name *family systems theory* was formally changed to *the Bowen theory* in 1975.

Any relationship with balancing forces and counterforces in constant operation is a system. The notion of *dynamics* is simply not adequate to describe the idea of a *system*. By 1963, when the six interlocking concepts were defined, I was using the concept of system as a shorthand way to describe the complex balancing of family relationships. This idea was finally presented in some detail in the 1966 paper on theory. By the mid 1960s, the term *systems* was being used more frequently; some therapists picked it up from my writings, and others picked it up from general systems theory, which was first defined in the 1930s. In the past decade, the term has become popularized and overused to the point of being meaningless. Family systems theory has been confused with general systems theory, which has a much broader frame of reference and no specific application to emotional functioning. It is very difficult to apply general systems concepts to emotional functioning except in a broad, general way. My family systems theory is a specific theory about the functional facts of emotional functioning.

It is grossly inaccurate to consider family systems theory as synonymous with general systems, although it is accurate to think of family systems theory as somehow fitting into the broad framework of general systems theory. There are those who believe family systems theory was developed from general systems theory, in spite of my explanations to the contrary. At the time my theory was developed, I knew nothing about general systems theory. Back in the 1940s, I attended one lecture by Bertalanffy, which I did not understand, and another by Norbert Wiener which was perhaps a little more understandable. Both dealt in systems *of* thinking. The degree to which I heard something in those lectures that influenced my later thinking is debatable. In those years, I was strongly influenced by reading and lectures in aspects of evolution, biology, the balance of nature, and the natural sciences. I was trying to view man as a part of nature rather than separate from nature. It is likely that my systems orientation was patterned after the systems in nature, and unlikely that systems of thinking played any part in the theory. However it developed, family systems theory as I have defined it is a specific theory about human relationship functioning that has now become confused with general systems theory and the popular, nonspecific use of the word *systems*. I have long opposed the use of proper names in terminology, but in order to denote the specificity that is built into this family systems theory, I am now calling it the Bowen theory.

Emotionality, feelings, and subjectivity are the principal commodities which the theoretician has to conceptualize, which the researcher has to organize into some kind of structure, and which the clinician has to deal with in his practice. It is difficult to find verifiable facts in the world of

subjectivity. Conventional psychiatric theory forcuses on the why of
human behavior. All members of the mental health professions are
familiar with why explanations. The search for why reasons has been
part of man's cause and effect thinking since he became a thinking being.
Once the researcher starts asking why, he is confronted by a complex
mass of variables. It was the search for reliable facts about emotional
functioning that led toward systems thinking early in the family
research. From this effort came a method of separating the functional
facts from the subjectivity of emotional systems. Systems thinking
focused on what happened, and how, when, and where it happened,
insofar as these observations could be based on observable facts. The
method carefully avoids why explanations and the discrepant reasoning
that follows. Some fairly efficient formulas were developed for
converting subjectivity into observable and verifiable research facts. For
example, one such formula might be, "That man dreams is a scientific
fact, but what he dreams is not necessarily a fact," or, "That man talks is a
scientific fact, but what he says is not necessarily factual." The same
formula can be applied to almost the whole range of subjective concepts,
such as, "That man thinks (or feels) is a scientific fact, but what he thinks
(or feels) is not necessarily factual." The formula is a little more difficult
to apply in the intense feeling states, such as love and hate, but as long as
the researcher stays on the facts of loving and hating and avoids the
content of these intense emotions, he is working toward systems
thinking.

The effort to focus on the functional facts of relationship systems is a
difficult and disciplined task. It is easy to lose sight of the fact and become
emotionally involved in the content of the communication. The main
reason for making this effort was for research purposes. The main
concepts in the Bowen theory were developed from the functional facts
of relationship systems. In this disciplined research effort, it was
discovered that a method of therapy based on the functional facts was
superior to conventional therapy. It is so difficult for most therapists to
shift from conventional therapy to this method of family systems
therapy that no one ever achieves more than partial success at it. When
anxiety is high, even the most disciplined systems thinker will
automatically revert to cause and effect thinking and why explanations.
However, it is possible for therapists to keep perfecting their ability to
think in systems concepts. The more I have been able to shift to thinking
systems, the better my therapy has become. The shift to systems
thinking requires the therapist to give up many of his old concepts. A
recent exchange with a therapist involved in psychoanalytic research
illustrates the dilemma in making such a shift. He said he could hear the

notion of trying to find facts in subjectivity, but he simply could not give up the therapeutic contributions of dreams and analyzing the unconscious. I replied that I could respect his conviction if he could respect mine about the ultimate advantage of a total systems approach. A major advantage of systems theory and systems therapy is that it offers options not previously available. The young professional has the choice of continuing conventional theory and therapy, or of incorporating a few systems concepts, or of trying to go all the way toward systems thinking. I believe a few systems concepts are better than none.

The Bowen theory contains no ideas that have not been a part of human experience through the centuries. The theory operates on an order of facts so simple and obvious that everyone knew them all the time. The uniqueness of the theory has to do with the facts that are included, and the concepts that are specifically excluded. Said in another way, the theory listens to a distant drumbeat that people have always heard. This distant drumbeat is often obscured by the noisy insistence of the foreground drumbeat, but it is always there, and it tells its own clear story to those who can tune out the noise and keep focused on the distant drumbeat. The Bowen theory specifically excludes certain items from individual theory that are equivalent to the foreground drumbeat. The concepts we learned in individual theory all have their accuracy within one frame of reference, but they tend to nullify the unique effectiveness of the simple story told by a broad systems perspective. The Bowen theory is very simple to those who can hear, and the simple approach to therapy is determined by the theory.

The Bowen Theory

The Bowen theory involves two main variables. One is the degree of anxiety, and the other is the degree of integration of self. There are several variables having to do with anxiety or emotional tension. Among these are intensity, duration, and different kinds of anxiety. There are far more variables that have to do with the level of integration of the differentiation of self. This is the principal subject of this theory. All organisms are reasonably adaptable to acute anxiety. The organism has built-in mechanisms to deal with short bursts of anxiety. It is sustained or chronic anxiety that is most useful in determining the differentiation of self. If anxiety is sufficiently low, almost any organism can appear normal in the sense that it is symptom free. When anxiety increases and remains chronic for a certain period, the organism develops tension, either within itself or in the relationship system, and the tension results in symptoms or dysfunction or sickness. The tension may result in physiological symptoms or physical illness, in emotional dysfunction, in social illness characterized by impulsiveness or withdrawal, or by social misbehavior. There is also the phenomenon of the infectiousness of anxiety, through which anxiety can spread rapidly through the family, or through society. There is a kind of average level of differentiation for the family which has certain minor levels of difference in individuals within the family. I shall leave it to the reader to keep in mind there is always the variable of the degree of chronic anxiety which can result in anyone appearing normal at one level of anxiety, and abnormal at another higher level.

Three of the theory's eight concepts apply to over-all characteristics of the family. The other five focus on details within certain areas of the family.

Differentiation of self. This concept is a cornerstone of the theory, and if my discussion becomes repetitive, I beg the reader's indulgence. The concept defines people according to the degree of *fusion,* or *differentiation,* between emotional and intellectual functioning. This characteristic is so universal it can be used as a way of categorizing all people on a single continuum. At the low extreme are those whose emotions and intellect are so fused that their lives are dominated by the automatic emotional system. Whatever intellect they have is dominated by the emotional system. These are the people who are less flexible, less adaptable, and more emotionally dependent on those about them. They are easily stressed into dysfunction, and it is difficult for them to recover from dysfunction. They inherit a high percentage of all human problems. At the other extreme are those who are more differentiated. It is impossible for there to be more than relative separation between emotional and intellectual functioning, but those whose intellectual functioning can retain relative autonomy in periods of stress are more flexible, more adaptable, and more independent of the emotionality about them. They cope better with life stresses, their life courses are more orderly and successful, and they are remarkably free of human problems. In between the two extremes is an infinite number of mixes between emotional and intellectual functioning.

The concept eliminates the concept of *normal,* which psychiatry has never successfully defined. It is not possible to define *normal* when the thing to be measured is constantly changing. Operationally, psychiatry has called people normal when they are free of emotional symptoms and behavior is within average range. The concept of differentiation has no direct connection with the presence or absence of symptoms. People with the most fusion have most of the human problems, and those with the most differentiation, the fewest; but there can be people with intense fusion who manage to keep their relationships in balance, who are never subjected to severe stress, who never develop symptoms, and who appear normal. However, their life adjustments are tenuous, and, if they are stressed into dysfunction, the impairment can be chronic or permanent. There are also fairly well-differentiated people who can be stressed into dysfunction, but they recover rapidly.

At the fusion end of the spectrum, the intellect is so flooded by emotionality that the total life course is determined by the emotional process and by what "feels right," rather than by beliefs or opinions. The intellect exists as an appendage of the feeling system. It may function reasonably well in mathematics or physics, or in impersonal areas, but on personal subjects its functioning is controlled by the emotions. The emotional system is hypothesized to be part of the instinctual forces that govern automatic functions. The human is adept at explanations to emphasize that he is different from lower forms of life, and at denying his relation with nature. The emotional system operates with predictable, knowable stimuli that govern the instinctual behavior in all forms of life. The more a life is governed by the emotional system, the more it follows the course of all instinctual behavior, in spite of intellectualized explanations to the contrary. At higher levels of differentiation, the function of the emotional and intellectual systems are more clearly distinguishable. There are the same automatic emotional forces that govern instinctual behavior, but intellect is sufficiently autonomous for logical reasoning and decisions based on thinking. When I first began to present this concept, I used the term *undifferentiated family ego mass* to describe the emotional "stuck togetherness" in families. Although this phrase was an assemblage of words from conventional theory, and thus did not conform to the plan to use concepts consistent with biology, it fairly accurately described emotional fusion. I used it for a few years because more people were able to hear the concept when it was put into words they understood.

As I began to present the concept of a well-differentiated person as one whose intellect could function separately from the emotional system, it was common for mental health professionals to hear the intellectual system as equivalent to intellectuality which is used as a defense against emotionality in psychiatric patients. The most common criticism was that a differentiated person appeared to be cold, distant, rigid, and nonfeeling. It is difficult for professional people to grasp the notion of differentiation when they have spent their working lives believing that the free expression of feelings represents a high level of functioning and intellectualization represents an unhealthy defense against it. A poorly

THERAPY IN CLINICAL PRACTICE

differentiated person is trapped within a feeling world. His effort to gain the comfort of emotional closeness can increase the fusion, which can increase his alienation from others. There is a lifelong effort to get the emotional life into livable equilibrium. A segment of these emotionally trapped people use random, inconsistent, intellectual-sounding verbalization to explain away their plight. A more differentiated person can participate freely in the emotional sphere without the fear of becoming too fused with others. He is also free to shift to calm, logical reasoning for decisions that govern his life. The logical intellectual process is quite different from the inconsistent, intellectualized verbalizations of the emotionally fused person.

In earlier papers, I presented this as a "differentiation of self scale." I did that to convey the idea that people have all gradations of differentiation of self, and that people at one level have remarkably different life styles from those at other levels. Schematically, I presented a scale from 0 to 100, with 0 representing the lowest possible level of human functioning and 100 representing a hypothetical notion of perfection to which man might evolve if his evolutionary change goes in that direction. I wanted a spectrum broad enough to cover all possible degrees of human functioning. To clarify the fact that people are different from each other in terms of emotional-intellectual functioning, I did profiles of people in the 0 to 25, the 25 to 50, the 50 to 75, and the 75 to 100 ranges. Those profiles are still amazingly accurate ten years later. In that first paper, I also presented the notion of functional levels of differentiation that can shift from moment to moment, or remain fairly constant for most of a life. Some of the major variables that govern the shifting were presented as a way of clarifying the concept and categorizing the apparent complexity of human functioning into a more knowable framework. The schematic framework and the use of the term *scale* resulted in hundreds of letters requesting copies of "the scale." Most who wrote had not grasped the concept nor the variables that govern the functional levels of differentiations. The letters slowed down my effort to develop a more definite scale that could be used clinically. The theoretical concept is most important. It eliminates the barriers between schizophrenia, neurosis, and normal; it also transcends categories such as genius, social class, and cultural-ethnic differences. It applies to all human forms of life. It might even apply to subhuman forms if we only knew enough. Knowledge of the concept permits the easy development of all kinds of research instruments, but to attempt to use the scale without knowledge of the concept can result in chaos.

Another important part of the differentiation of self has to do with the levels of *solid self* and *pseudo-self* in a person. In periods of emotional intimacy, two pseudo-selfs will fuse into each other, one losing self to the other, who gains self. The solid self does not participate in the fusion phenomenon. The solid self says, "This is who I am, what I believe, what I stand for, and what I will do or will not do," in a given situation. The solid self is made up of clearly defined beliefs, opinions, convictions, and life principles. These are incorporated into self from one's own life experiences, by a process of intellectual reasoning and the careful consideration of the alternatives involved in the choice. In making the choice, one becomes responsible for self and the consequences. Each belief and life principle is consistent with all the others, and self will take action on the principles even in situations of high anxiety and duress.

The pseudo-self is created by emotional pressure, and it can be modified by emotional pressure. Every emotional unit, whether it be the family or the total of society, exerts pressure on group members to conform to the ideals and principles of the group. The pseudo-self is composed of a vast assortment of principles, beliefs, philosophies, and knowledge acquired because it is required or considered right by the group. Since the principles are acquired under pressure, they are random and inconsistent with one another, without the individual's being aware of the discrepancy. Pseudo-self is appended onto the self, in contrast to solid self which is incorporated into self after careful, logical reasoning. The pseudo-self is a "pretend" self. It was acquired to conform to the environment, and it contains discrepant and assorted principles that pretend to be in emotional harmony with a variety of social groups, institutions, businesses, political parties, and religious groups, without self's being aware that the groups are inconsistent with each other. The joining of groups is motivated more by the relationship system than the principle involved. The person may "feel" there is something wrong with some of the groups, but he is not intellectually aware. The solid self is intellectually aware of the inconsistency between the groups, and the decision to join or reject membership is an intellectual process based on careful weighing of the advantages and disadvantages.

The pseudo-self is an actor and can be many different selfs. The list of pretends is extensive. He can pretend to be more important or less important, stronger or weaker, or more attractive, or less attractive than is realistic. It is easy for most people to detect gross examples of pretense, but there is enough of the impostor in all of us so that it is difficult to detect lesser degrees of the impostor in others. On the other hand, a good actor can appear so much for real that it can be difficult for the actor or for others without detailed knowledge of how emotional systems function to know the dividing line between solid self and pseudo-self. This also applies to therapists, mental health professionals, and researchers who may attempt to estimate the level of differentiation in themselves or in others. The level of solid self is stable. The pseudo-self is unstable, and it responds to a variety of social pressures and stimuli. The pseudo-self was acquired at the behest of the relationship system, and it is negotiable in the relationship system.

Based on my experience with this concept, I believe that the level of solid self is lower, and of the pseudo-self is much higher in all of us than most are aware. It is the pseudo-self that is involved in fusion and the many ways of giving, receiving, lending, borrowing, trading, and exchanging of self. In any exchange, one gives up a little self to the other, who gains an equal amount. The best example is a love relationship when each is trying to be the way the other wants self to be, and each in turn makes demands on the other to be different. This is pretending and trading in pseudo-self. In a marriage, two pseudo-selfs fuse into a we-ness in which one becomes the dominant decision maker or the most active in taking initiative for the we-ness. The dominant one gains self at the expense of the other, who loses it. The adaptive one may volunteer to give up self to the dominant one, who accepts it; or the exchange may be worked out after bargaining. The more that the spouses can alternate these roles, the healthier the marriage. The exchanging of selfs may be on a short or long-term basis. The borrowing and trading of selfs may take place automatically in a work group in which the emotional process ends up with one employee in the one-down or de-selfed position, while the others gain self. This exchanging of pseudo-self is an automatic emotional process that occurs as people manipulate each other in subtle life postures. The exchanges can be brief—for instance, criticism that makes one feel bad for a few days; or it can be a long-term process in which the adaptive spouse becomes so de-selfed, he or she is no longer able to make decisions and collapses in selfless dysfunction—psychosis or chronic physical illness. These mechanisms are much less intense in better levels of differentiation or when anxiety is low, but the process of people losing and gaining self in an emotional network is so complex and the degree of shifts so great that it is impossible to estimate functional levels of differentiation except from following a life pattern over long periods.

Profile of low levels of differentiation. This is the group I previously described as 0 to 25, the lowest level of differentiation. The emotional fusion is so intense that the variables extend beyond the undifferentiated family ego mass into the undifferentiated societal ego mass. The intricacies of fusion and differentiation are much clearer in people with moderate levels of fusion in whom the various processes are more easily defined. There are some striking over-all characteristics of the low levels of differentiation. People at the lowest level live in a feeling-dominated world in which it is impossible to distinguish feeling from fact. They are totally relationship oriented. So much energy goes into seeking love and approval and keeping the relationship in some kind of harmony, there is no energy for life-directed goals. Failing to achieve approval, they can spend their lives in withdrawal or fighting the relationship system from which they fail to win approval. Intellectual functioning is so submerged that they cannot say, "I think that . . ." or, "I believe. . . ." Instead, they say, "I feel that . . ." when it would be accurate to express an opinion or belief. They consider it truthful and sincere to say, "I feel," and false and insincere to express an opinion from themselves. Important life decisions are made on the basis of what feels right. They spend their lives in a day to day struggle to keep the relationship system in balance, or in an effort to achieve some degree of comfort and freedom from anxiety. They are incapable of making long-term goals except in vague general terms, such as, "I want to be successful, or happy, or have a good job, or have security." They grow up as dependent appendages of their parents, following which they seek other equally dependent relationships in which they can borrow enough strength to function. A no-self person who is adept at pleasing his boss may make a better employee than one who has a self. This group is made up of people preoccupied with keeping their dependent relationships in harmony, people who have failed and who go from one symptomatic crisis to another, and people who have given up in the futile effort to adapt. At the lowest level are those who cannot live outside the protective walls of an institution. This group inherits a major portion of the world's serious health, financial, and social problems. Life adjustments are tenuous at best, and when they fall into dysfunction, the illness or "bad luck" can be chronic or permanent. They tend to be satisfied with the result if a therapy effort brings a modicum of comfort.

Profile of moderate levels of differentiation of self. This is the group previously presented as 25 to 50. There is some beginning differentiation between the emotional and intellectual systems, with most of the self expressed as pseudo-self. Lives are still guided by the emotional system, but the life styles are more flexible than the lower levels of differentiation. The flexibility provides a better view of the interplay between emotionality and intellect. When anxiety is low, functioning can resemble good levels of differentiation. When anxiety is high, functioning can resemble that of low levels of differentiation. Lives are relationship oriented, and major life energy goes to loving and being loved, and seeking approval from others. Feelings are more openly expressed than in lower-level people. Life energy is directed more to what others think and to winning friends and approval than to goal-directed activity. Self-esteem is dependent on others. It can soar to heights with a compliment or be crushed by criticism. Success in school is oriented more to learning the system and to pleasing the teacher than to the primary goal of learning. Success in business or in social life depends more on pleasing the boss or the social leader, and more on who one knows and gaining relationship status than in the inherent value of their work. Their pseudo-selves are assembled from an assortment of discrepant principles, beliefs, philosophies, and ideologies that are used in pretend postures to blend with different relationship systems. Lacking solid self, they habitually use, "I feel that . . ." when expressing their pseudo-self philosophies; they avoid, "I think," or "I believe," positions by using another person or body of knowledge as their authority when making statements. Lacking a solid self-conviction about the world's knowledge, they use pseudo-self statements, such as, "The rule says . . ." or "Science has proved . . ." taking information out of context to make their points. They may have enough free-functioning intellect to have mastered academic knowledge about impersonal things; they use this knowledge in the relationship system. However, intellect about personal matters is lacking, and their personal lives are in chaos.

The pseudo-self may be a conforming disciple who pretends to be in harmony with a particular philosophy or set of principles, or, when frustrated, he can assume the opposite posture as a rebel or revolutionary person. The rebel is lacking a self of his own. His pseudo-self posture is merely the exact opposite of the majority viewpoint. The revolutionary person is against the prevailing system, but he has nothing to offer in its place. The sameness of polarized opposites in emotional situations has led me to define revolution as a convulsion that prevents change. It is relationship-oriented energy that goes back and forth on the same points, the issue on each side being determined by the position of the other; neither is capable of a position not determined by the other.

People in the moderate range of differentiation have the most intense versions of overt feeling. The relationship orientation makes them sensitive to others and to the direct action expression of feelings. They are in a lifelong quest for the ideal relationship with emotional closeness to others and direct, open communication of feelings. In their overt emotional dependence on others, they are sensitized to reading the moods, expressions, and postures of the other, and to responding openly with direct expression of feeling or impulsive action. They are in a lifelong pursuit of the ideal close relationship. When closeness is achieved, it increases the emotional fusion to which they react with distance and alienation, which can then timulate another closeness cycle. Failing to achieve closeness, they may go to withdrawal and depression, or to pursuit of closeness in another relationship. Symptoms and human problems erupt when the relationship system is unbalanced. People in this group develop a high percentage of human problems, including the full range of physical illness, emotional illness, and social dysfunctions. Their emotional illness includes neurotic-level internalized problems, depression, and behavior and character disorder type problems; they get involved in the increasing use of alcohol and drugs to relieve the anxiety of the moment. Their social disorders include all levels of impulsive and irresponsible behavior.

Profile of moderate to good differentiation of self. This is the group in the 50 to 75 range. These are the people with enough basic differentiation between the emotional and intellectual systems for the two systems to function alongside each other as a cooperative team. The intellectual system is sufficiently developed so that it can hold its own and function autonomously without being dominated by the emotional system when anxiety increases. In people below 50, the emotional system tells the intellectual system what to think and say, and which decisions to make in critical situations. The intellect is a pretend intellect. The emotional system permits the intellect to go off into a corner and think about distant things as long as it does not interfere in joint decisions that affect the total life course. Above 50, the intellectual system is sufficiently developed to begin making a few decisions of its own. It has learned that the emotional system runs an effective life course in most areas of functioning, but in critical situations the automatic emotional decisions create long-term complications for the total organism. The intellect learns that it requires a bit of discipline to overrule the emotional system, but the long-term gain is worth the effort. People above 50 have developed a reasonable level of solid self on most of the essential issues in life. In periods of calm, they have employed logical reasoning to develop beliefs, principles, and convictions that they use to overrule the emotional system in situations of anxiety and panic. Differentiation between the emotions and the intellect exists in subtle gradations. People at the lower part of this group are those who *know* there is a better way; but intellect is poorly formed, and they end up following life courses similar to those below 50.

People in the upper part of this group are those in which there is more solid self. Persons with a functional intellectual system are no longer a prisoner of the emotional-feeling world. They are able to life more freely and to have more satisfying emotional lives within the emotional system. They can participate fully in emotional events knowing that they can extricate themselves with logical reasoning when the need arises. There may be periods of laxness in which they permit the automatic pilot of the emotional system to have full control, but when trouble develops they can take over, calm the anxiety, and avoid a life crisis. People with better levels of differentiation are less relationship directed and more able to follow independent life goals. They are not unaware of the relationship system, but their life courses can be determined more from within themselves than from what others think. They are more clear about the differences between emotion and intellect, and they are better able to state their own convictions and beliefs calmly without attacking the beliefs of others or without having to defend their own. They are better able to accurately evaluate themselves in relation to others without the pretend postures that result in overvaluing or undervaluing themselves. They marry spouses with equal levels of differentiation. The lifestyle of a spouse at another level would be sufficiently different to be considered emotionally incompatible. The marriage is a functioning partnership. The spouses can enjoy the full range of emotional intimacy without either being de-selfed by the other. They can be autonomous selfs together or alone. The wife is able to function more fully as a female and the husband more fully as a male without either having to debate the advantages or disadvantages of biological and social roles. Spouses who are more differentiated can permit their children to grow and develop their own autonomous selfs without undue anxiety or without trying to fashion their children in their own images. The spouses and the children are each more responsible for themselves, and do not have to blame others for failures or credit anyone else for their successes. People with better levels of differentiation are able to function well with other people, or alone, as the situation may require. Their lives are more orderly, they are able to cope successfully with a broader range of human situations, and they are remarkably free from the full range of human problems.

In previous papers I have described a level of 75 to 100, which is more hypothetical than real, and which conveys an erroneous impression of the human phenomenon to concretistic thinkers who are searching for another instrument to measure human functioning. Rather than pursue the hypothesis about the upper extremes of differentiation, I shall instead make some general comments about differentiation. A common mistake is to equate the better differentiated person with a "rugged individualist." I consider rugged individualism to be the exaggerated pretend posture of a person struggling against emotional fusion. The differentiated person is always aware of others and the relationship system around him. There are so many forces and counterforces and details in differentiation that one has to get a broad panoramic view of the total human phenomenon in order to be able to see differentiation.

Once it is possible to see the phenomenon, there it is, operating in full view, right in front of our eyes. Once it is possible to see the phenomenon, it is then possible to apply the concept to hundreds of different human situations. To try to apply it without knowing it is an exercise in futility.

The therapy based on differentiation is no longer therapy in the usual sense. The therapy is as different from the conventional therapy as the theory is different from conventional theory. The over-all goal is to help individual family members to rise up out of the emotional togetherness that binds us all. The instinctual force toward differentiation is built into the organism, just as are the emotional forces that oppose it. The goal is to help the motivated family member to take a microscopic step toward a better level of differentiation, in spite of the togetherness forces that oppose. When one family member can finally master this, then other family members automatically take similar steps. The togetherness forces are so strong in maintaining the status quo that any small step toward differentiation is met with vigorous disapproval of the group. This is the point at which a therapist or guide can be most helpful. Without help, the differentiating one will fall back into the togetherness to get emotional harmony for the moment. Conventional therapy is designed to resolve, or talk out, conflict. This does accomplish the goal of reducing the conflict of that moment, but it can also rob the individual of his budding effort to achieve a bit more differentiation from the family togetherness. There are many pitfalls in the effort toward differentiation. If the individual attempts it without some conviction of his own, he is blindly following the advice of his therapist and is caught in a self-defeating togetherness with the therapist. I believe that the level of differentiation of a person is largely determined by the time he leaves the parental family and he attempts a life of his own. Thereafter, he tends to replicate the lifestyle from the parental family in all future relationships. It is not possible ever to make more than minor changes in one's basic level of self; but from clinical experience I can say it is possible to make slow changes, and each small change results in the new world of a different lifestyle. As I see it now, the critical stage is passed when the individual can begin to know the difference between emotional functioning and intellectual functioning, and when he has developed ways for using the knowledge for solving future problems in a lifelong effort of his own. It is difficult to assess differentiation during calm periods in a life. Clinically, I make estimates from the average functional level of self as it operates through periods of stress and calm. The real test of the stability of differentiation comes when the person is again subjected to chronic severe stress.

It is reasonably accurate to compare the functioning of the emotional and intellectual systems to the structure and function of the brain. I conceive of one brain center that controls emotions and another that controls intellectual functions. The fusion suggests centers that are side by side with some degree of fusion, or grown togetherness. Anatomically, it would be more accurate to think of the two as being connected by nerve tracts. In poorly functioning people, the two centers are intimately fused, with the emotional center having almost total dominance over the intellectual center. In better functioning people, there is more functional separateness between the centers. The more the separateness between the centers, the more the intellectual center is able to block, or screen out, a spectrum of stimuli from the emotional center, and to function autonomously. The screening process, which might be biochemical, operates best when anxiety is low. The emotional center controls the autonomic nervous system and all other automatic functions. The intellectual center is the seat of intellect and reasoning. The emotional center handles the myriads of sensory stimuli from the digestive, circulatory, respiratory, and all the other organ systems within the body, as well as stimuli from all the sensing organs that perceive the environment and relationships with others. In periods of calm, when the emotional center is receiving fewer stimuli from its sensing network, the intellectual center is more free to function autonomously. When the emotional center is flooded by stimuli, there is little intellectual functioning that is not governed by the emotional center. In some areas, the intellect operates in the service of the emotional center.

There are many clinical examples that illustrate emotional dominance over the intellect in determining a life course. The intellectual center is either appended to, or is directed by, the emotional center. In the various psychotic and neurotic states, the intellect is either obliterated or distorted by emotionality. There may be an occasional situation in which there is an island of reasonably intact intellectual activity, such as in the psychotic person with a computer mind. In the various neurotic states the intellect is directed by emotionality. There is the intellectualizing person whose apparent intellect is directed by the emotional process. There are the behavior problems in which automatic impulsive action is directed by emotionality, and the intellect attempts to explain or justify it after the action. This can vary from childish misbehavior to criminal action. The parents and the social system ask why, pretending there is a logical answer. The organism responds with an instant excuse that appears most acceptable to self and others. In the same category falls the mass of emotional center-dominated behavior that is often called self-destructive. This behavior is designed to relieve anxiety of the moment, and the impulse for immediate relief overrules awareness of long-term complications. It is at its worst in alcohol and drug abuse. There are situations in which the intellect aids emotionally-directed behavior—as, for instance, intellectual planning that helps emotionally directed crime. A large group of people choose their philosophies and ideologies because of emotional system pressure. In another group, a section of the intellect functions well on impersonal subjects; they can be brilliant academically, while their emotionally-directed personal lives are chaotic. Even in people who exhibit some degree of separation between emotion and intellect, and in whom the intellect can hold its own with the emotional system in certain areas most of the time, there are periods of chronic stress in which the emotional system is dominant.

Triangles. I began work on this basic concept in 1955. By 1956 the research group was thinking and talking about "triads." As the concept evolved, it came to include much more than the meaning of the conventional term *triad,* and we therefore had a problem communicating with those who assumed they knew the meaning of triad. I chose *triangle* in order to convey that this concept has specific meaning beyond that implied in triad. The theory states that the triangle, a three-person emotional configuration, is the molecule or the basic building block of any emotional system, whether it is in the family or any other group. The triangle is the smallest stable relationship system. A two-person system may be stable as long as it is calm, but when anxiety increases, it immediately involves the most vulnerable other person to become a triangle. When tension in the triangle is too great for the threesome, it involves others to become a series of interlocking triangles.

In periods of calm, the triangle is made up of a comfortably close twosome and a less comfortable outsider. The twosome works to preserve the togetherness, lest one become uncomfortable and form a better togetherness elsewhere. The outsider seeks to form a togetherness with one of the twosome, and there are numerous well-known moves to accomplish this. The emotional forces within the triangle are constantly in motion from moment to moment, even in periods of calm. Moderate tension states in the twosome are characteristically felt by one, while the other is oblivious. It is the uncomfortable one who initiates a new equilibrium toward more comfortable togetherness for self.

In periods of stress, the outside position is the most comfortable and most desired position. In stress, each works to get the outside position to escape tension in the twosome. When it is not possible to shift forces in the triangle, one of the involved twosome triangles in a fourth person, leaving the former third person aside for reinvolvement later. The emotional forces duplicate the exact patterns in the new triangle. Over time, the emotional forces continue to move from one active triangle to another, finally remaining mostly in one triangle as long as the total system is fairly calm.

When tensions are very high in families and available family triangles are exhausted, the family system triangles in people from outside the family, such as police and social agencies. A successful externalization of the tension occurs when outside workers are in conflict about the family while the family is calmer. In emotional systems such as an office staff, the tensions between the two highest administrators can be triangled and retriangled until conflict is acted out between two who are low in the administrative hierarchy. Administrators often settle this conflict by firing or removing one of the conflictual twosome, after which the conflict erupts in another twosome.

A triangle in moderate tension characteristically has two comfortable sides and one side in conflict. Since patterns repeat and repeat in a triangle, the people come to have fixed roles in relation to each other. The best example of this is the father-mother-child triangle. Patterns vary, but one of the most common is basic tension between the parents, with the father's gaining the outside position—often being called passive, weak, and distant—leaving the conflict between mother and child. The mother—often called aggressive, dominating, and castrating—wins over the child, who moves another step toward chronic functional impairment. This pattern is described as the family projection process. Families replay the same triangular game over and over for years, as though the winner were in doubt, but the final result is always the same. Over the years the child accepts the always-lose outcome more easily, even to volunteering for this position. A variation is the pattern in which the father finally attacks the mother, leaving the child in the outside position. This child then learns the techniques of gaining the outside position by playing the parents off against each other.

Each of the structured patterns in triangles is available for predictable moves and predictable outcomes in families and social systems. A knowledge of triangles provides a far more exact way of understanding the father-mother-child triangle than do the traditional oedipal complex explanations. Triangles provide several times more flexibility in dealing with such problems therapeutically.

Knowledge of triangles helps provide the theoretical perspective between individual therapy and this method of family therapy. An emotionally involved relationship is unavoidable in the average two-person, patient-therapist relationship. Theoretically, family therapy provides a situation in which intense relationships can remain within the family and the therapist can be relatively outside the emotional complex.

This is a good theoretical premise that is hard to achieve in practice. Without some special effort, it is easy for the family to wrap itself around the therapist emotionally, install the therapist in an all-important position, hold the therapist responsible for success or failure, and passively wait for the therapist to change the family. I have already discussed ways other therapists have dealt with the therapeutic relationship, as well as my continuing effort to operate from outside the family emotional system. Initially that included making the family members responsible for each other, avoiding the family tendency to assign importance to me, and promising no benefits except from the family's own effort to learn about itself and change itself. Most important was a long-term effort to attain and maintain emotional neutrality with individual family members. There are many subtleties to this. Beyond this effort, it was knowledge of triangles that provided the important breakthrough in the effort to stay outside the emotional complex.

One experience, above all others, was important in learning about triangles. That was a period in which much of my family therapy was with both parents and behavior problem adolescent child. It was possible to see the workings of the triangle between parents and child in microscopic detail. The more I could stay outside the triangle, the more clearly it was possible to see the family emotional system as it operated on well-defined emotional circuits between father, mother, and child. Therapeutically, the family did not change its original patterns. The passive father became less passive, the aggressive mother less aggressive, and the symptomatic child would become asymptomatic. The average, motivated family would continue for thirty to forty weekly appointments and terminate with great praise for the "good result." In my opinion, the family had not changed, but I had learned a lot about triangles. It was possible to observe a family and know the next move in the family before it occurred.

From the knowledge of triangles, I hypothesized the situation would be different by excluding the child and limiting the therapy to the two parents and the therapist. Rather than dealing in generalities about staying out of the family emotional system, I was then armed with specific knowledge about the parents' triangling moves to involve the therapist. Therapeutically, the results were far superior to anything before that time. This has remained the one basic therapeutic method since the early 1960s. On a broad theoretical-therapeutic level, if the therapist can stay in viable emotional contact with the two most significant family members, usually the two parents or two spouses, and he can be relatively outside the emotional activity in this central triangle, the age-old fusion between the family members will slowly begin to resolve, and all other family members will automatically change in relation to the two parents in the home setting. This is basic theory and basic method. The process can proceed regardless of content or subject matter discussed. The critical issue is the emotional reactiveness between the spouses, and the ability of the therapist to keep self relatively detriangled from the emotionality. The process can proceed with any third person who can keep self detriangled, but it would be difficult to find such an outside relationship. The method is as successful as other methods in short-term crisis situations. In the early years, I was active in engaging the family emotionally in consultations and short-term crisis situations. A calm, low-keyed, detriangling approach is more effective with a single appointment or with many.

Nuclear family emotional system. This concept describes the patterns of emotional functioning in a family in a single generation. Certain basic patterns between the father, mother, and children are replicas of the past generations and will be repeated in the generations to follow. There are several rather clear variables that determine the way the family functions in the present generation, which can be measured and validated by direct observation. From a careful history, in connection with knowledge of the details in the present generation, it is possible to do a rather remarkable reconstruction of the way the process operated in past generations. From knowledge about the transmission of family patterns over multiple generations, it is possible to project the same process into future generations, and, within limits, do some reasonably accurate predictions about future generations. No one person lives long enough to check the accuracy of predictions into the future, but there is enough detailed knowledge about some families in history to do a reasonable check on the predictive process. Based on experience in family research, the predicitions of ten to twenty years ago have been rather accurate.

The beginning of a nuclear family, in the average situation, is a marriage. There are exceptions to this, just as there have always been exceptions, which is all part of the total theory. The basic process in exceptional situations is similar to the more chaotic pattern in poorly differentiated people. The two spouses begin a marriage with lifestyle patterns and levels of differentiation developed in their families of origin. Mating, marriage, and reproduction are governed to a significant degree by emotional-instinctual forces. The way the spouses handle them in dating and courtship and in timing and planning the marriage provides one of the best views of the level of differentiation of the spouses. The lower the level of differentiation, the greater the potential problems for the future. People pick spouses who have the same levels of differentiation. Most spouses can have the closest and most open relationships in their adult lives during courtship. The fusion of the two pseudo-selfs into a common self occurs at the time they commit themselves to each other permanently, whether it be the time of engagement, the wedding itself, or the time they establish their first home together. It is common for living together relationships to be harmonious, and for fusion symptoms to develop when they finally get married. It is as if the fusion does not develop as long as they still have an option to terminate the relationship.

The lower the level of differentiation, the more intense the emotional fusion of marriage. One spouse becomes more the dominant decision maker for the common self, while the other adapts to the situation. This is one of the best examples in the borrowing and trading of self in a close relationship. One may assume the dominant role and force the other to be adaptive, or one may assume the adaptive role and force the other to be dominant. Both may try for the dominant role, which results in conflict; or both may try for the adaptive role, which results in decision paralysis. The dominant one gains self at the expense of the more adaptive one, who loses self. More differentiated spouses have lesser degrees of fusion, and fewer of the complications. The dominant and adaptive positions are *not* directly related to the sex of the spouse. They are determined by the position that each had in their families of origin. From my experience, there are as many dominant females as males, and as many adaptive males as females. These characteristics played a major role in their original choice of each other as partners. The fusion results in anxiety for one or both of the spouses. There is a spectrum of ways spouses deal with fusion symptoms. The most universal mechanism is emotional distance from each other. It is present in all marriages to some degree, and in a high percentage of marriages to a major degree.

Other than the emotional distance, there are three major areas in which the amout of undifferentiation in the marriage comes to be manifested in symptoms. The three areas are marital conflict; sickness or dysfunction in one spouse; and projection of the problems to children. It is as if there is a quantitative amount of undifferentiation to be absorbed in the nuclear family, which may be focused largely in one area or distributed in varying amounts to all three areas. The various patterns for handling the undifferentiation comes from patterns in their families of origin, and the variables involved in the mix in the common self. Following are general characteristics of each of the three areas.

Marital conflict. The basic pattern in conflictual marriages is one in which neither gives in to the other or in which neither is capable of an adaptive role. These marriages are intense in the amount of emotional energy each invests in the other. The energy may be thinking or action energy, either positive or negative, but the self of each is focused mostly on the other. The relationship cycles through periods of intense closeness, conflict that provides a period of emotional distance, and making up, which starts another cycle of intense closeness. Conflictual spouses probably have the most overtly intense of all relationships. The intensity of the anger and negative feeling in the conflict is as intense as the positive feeling. They are thinking of each other even when they are distant. Marital conflict does not in itself harm children. There are marriages in which most of the undifferentiation goes into marital conflict. The spouses are so invested in each other that the children are largely outside the emotional process. When marital conflict and projection of the problem to children are both present, it is the projection process that is hurtful to children. The quantitative amount of marital conflict that is present reduces the amount of undifferentiation that is focused elsewhere.

Dysfunction in one spouse. This is the result when a significant amount of undifferentiation is absorbed in the adaptive posture of one spouse. The pseudo-self of the adaptive one merges into the pseudo-self of the dominant one, who assumes more and more responsibility for the twosome. The degree of adaptiveness in one spouse is determined from the long-term functioning posture of each to the other, rather than from verbal reports. Each does some adapting to the other, and it is usual for each to believe that he or she gives in more than the other. The one who functions for long periods in the adaptive position gradually loses the ability to function and make decisions for self. At that point, it requires no more than a moderate increase in stress to trigger the adaptive one into dysfunction, which can be physical illness, emotional illness, or social illness, such as drinking, acting out, and irresponsible behavior. These illnesses tend to become chronic, and they are hard to reverse.

The pattern of the overfunctioning spouse in relation to the underfunctioning spouse exists in all degrees of intensity. It can exist as an episodic phenomenon in families who use a mixture of all three mechanisms. When used as the principal means of controlling undifferentiation, the illnesses can be chronic and most difficult to reverse. The sick or invalided one is too impaired to begin to regain function with an overfunctioning spouse on whom he or she is dependent. This mechanism is amazingly effective in absorbing the undifferentiation. The only disadvantage is the dysfunction in one, which is compensated for by the other spouse. The children can be almost unaffected by having one dysfunctional parent as long as there is someone else to function instead. The main problem in the children is inheriting a life pattern as caretaker of the sick parent, which will project into the future. These marriages are enduring. Chronic illness and invalidism, whether physical or emotional, can be the only manisfestation of the intensity of the undifferentiation. The underfunctioning one is grateful for the care and attention, and the overfunctioning one does not complain. Divorce is almost impossible in these marriages unless the dysfunction is also mixed with marital conflict. There have been families in which the overfunctioning one has died unexpectedly and the disabled one has miraculously regained functioning. If there is a subsequent marriage, it follows the pattern of the previous one.

Impairment of one or more children. This is the pattern in which parents operate as a we-ness to project the undifferentiation to one or more children. This mechanism is so important in the total human problem it has been described as a separate concept, the family projection process.

There are two main variables that govern the intensity of this process in the nuclear family. The first is the degree of the emotional isolation, or cutoff, from the extended family, or from others important in the relationship system. I will discuss this below. The second important variable has to do with the level of anxiety. Any of the symptoms in the nuclear family, whether they be marital conflict, dysfunction in a spouse, or symptoms in a child, are less intense when anxiety is low and more intense when anxiety is high. Some of the most important family therapy efforts are directed at decreasing anxiety and opening the relationship cutoff.

Family projection process. The process through which parental undifferentiation impairs one or more children operates within the father-mother-child triangle. It revolves around the mother, who is the key figure in reproduction and who is usually the principal caretaker for the infant. It results in primary emotional impairment of the child; or, it can superimpose itself on some defect or on some chronic physical illness or disability. It exists in all gradations of intensity, from those in which impairment is minimal to those in which the child is seriously impaired for life. The process is so universal it is present to some degree in all families.

A composite of families with moderately severe versions of the projection process will provide the best view of the way the process works. It is as if there is a definite amount of undifferentiation to be absorbed by marital conflict, sickness in a spouse, and projection to the children. The amount absorbed in conflict or sickness in a spouse reduces the amount that will be directed to the children. There are a few families in which most of the undifferentiation goes into marital conflict, essentially none to sickness in a spouse, and relatively small amounts to the children. The most striking examples of this have been in families with autistic, or severely impaired, children in which there is little marital conflict, both spouses are healthy, and the full weight on the undifferentiation is directed to a single, maximally impaired child. I have never seen a family in which there was not some projection to a child. Most families use a combination of all three mechanisms. The more the problem shifts from one area to another the less chance the process will be crippling in any single area.

There are definite patterns in the way the undifferentiation is distributed to children. It focuses first on one child. If the amount is too great for that child, the process will select others for lesser degrees of involvement. There are families in which the amount of undifferentiation is so great it can seriously impair most of the children, and leave one or two relatively out of the emotional process. There is so much disorder and chaos in these families, it is difficult to see the orderly steps in the process. I have never seen a family in which children were equally involved in the family emotional process. There may be some exceptions to the process described here, but the over-all patterns are clear, and the theory accounts for the exceptions. There are suggestions about the way children become the objects of the projection process. On a simplistic level, it is related to the degree of emotional turn on or turn off (both equal in emotional systems terms) the mother feels for the child. This is an automatic emotional process that is not changed by acting the opposite. On a more specific level, it is related to the level of undifferentiation in the parents, the amount of anxiety at the time of conception and birth, and the orientation of the parents toward marriage and children.

The early thoughts about marriage and children are more prominent in the female than the male. They begin to take an orderly form before adolescence. A female who thinks primarily of the husband she will marry tends to have marriages in which she focuses most of her emotional energy on the husband, and he focuses on her, and symptoms tend to focus more in marital conflict and sickness in a spouse. Those females whose early thoughts and fantasies go more to the children they will have than the man they will marry, tend to become the mothers of impaired children. The process can be so intense in some women that the husband is incidental to the process. Spouses from lower levels of differentiation are less specific about marriage and children. The children selected for the family projection process are those conceived and born during stress in the mother's life; the first child, the oldest son or oldest daughter, an only child of either sex, one who is emotionally special to the mother, or one the mother believes to be special to the father. Among common special children are only children, an oldest child, a single child of one sex among several of the opposite sex, or a child with some defect. Also important are the special children who were fretful, colicky, rigid, and nonresponsive to the mother from the beginning. The amount of initial special emotional investment in such children is great. A good percentage of mothers have a basic preference for boys or girls, depending upon their orientation in the family of origin. It is impossible for mothers to have equal emotional investment in any two children, no matter how much they try to protest equality for all.

On a more detailed level, the projection process revolves around maternal instinct, and the way anxiety permits it to function during reproduction and the infancy of the child. The father usually plays a support role to the projection process. He is sensitive to the mother's anxiety, and he tends to support her view and help her implement her anxious efforts at mothering. The process begins with anxiety in the mother. The child responds anxiously to mother, which she misperceives as a problem in the child. The anxious parental effort goes into sympathetic, solicitous, overprotective energy, which is directed more by the mother's anxiety than the reality needs of the child. It establishes a pattern of infantilizing the child, who gradually becomes more impaired and more demanding. Once the process has started, it can be motivated either by anxiety in the mother, or anxiety in the child. In the average situation, there may be symptomatic episodes at stressful periods during childhood which gradually increase to major symptoms during or after adolescence; intense emotional fusion between mother and child may exist in which the mother-child relationship remains in positive, symptom-free equilibrium until the adolescent period, when the child attempts to function on his own. At that point, the child's relationship with the mother, or with both parents, can become negative and the child develop severe symptoms. The more intense forms of the mother-child fusion may remain relatively asymptomatic until young adulthood and the child can collapse in psychosis when he attempts to function away from the parents.

The basic pattern of the family projection is the same, except for minor variations in form and intensity, whether the eventual impairment in the child be one that leads to serious lifelong dysfunction, or one that never develops serious symptoms and is never diagnosed. The greatest number of people impaired by the projection process are those who do less well with life and who have lower levels of differentiation than their siblings, and who may go for a few generations before producing a child who becomes seriously impaired symptomatically. This theory considers schizophrenia to be the product of several generations of increasing symptomatic impairment, with lower and lower levels of differentiation, until there is a generation that produces schizophrenia. In clinical work, we have come to use the term *the triangled child* to refer to the one who was the main focus of the family projection process. Almost every family has one child who was more triangled than the others, and whose life adjustment is less good than the others. In doing multigenerational family histories, it is relatively easy to estimate the family projection process and identify the triangled child by securing historical data about the life adjustments of each sibling.

Emotional cutoff. This concept was added to the theory in 1975 after having been a poorly defined extension of other concepts for several years. It was accorded the status of a separate concept to include details not stated elsewhere, and to have a separate concept for emotional process between the generations. The life pattern of cutoffs is determined by the way people handle their unresolved emotional attachments to their parents. All people have some degree of unresolved emotional attachment to their parents. The lower the level of differentiation, the more intense the unresolved attachment. The concept deals with the way people separate themselves from the past in order to start their lives in the present generation. Much thought went into the selection of a term to best describe this process of separation, isolation, withdrawal, running away, or denying the importance of the parental family. However much *cutoff* may sound like informal slang, I could find no other term as accurate for describing the process. The therapeutic effort is to convert the cutoff into an orderly differentiation of a self from the extended family.

The degree of unresolved emotional attachment to the parents is equivalent to the degree of undifferentiation that must somehow be handled in the person's own life and in future generations. The unresolved attachment is handled by the intrapsychic process of denial and isolation of self while living close to the parents; or by physically running away; or by a combination of emotional isolation and physical distance. The more intense the cutoff with the past, the more likely the individual to have an exaggerated version of his parental family problem in his own marriage, and the more likely his own children to do a more intense cutoff with him in the next generation. There are many variations in the intensity of the basic process and in the way the cutoff is handled.

The person who runs away from his family of origin is as emotionally dependent as the one who never leaves home. They both need emotional closeness, but they are allergic to it. The one who remains on the scene and handles the attachment by intrapsychic mechanisms tends to have some degree of supportive contact with the parents, to have a less intense over-all process, and to develop more internalized symptoms under stress, such as physical illness and depression. An exaggerated version of this is the severely impaired person who can collapse into psychosis, isolating himself intrapsychically while living with the parents. The one who runs away geographically is more inclined to impulsive behavior. He tends to see the problem as being in the parents and running away as a method of gaining independence from the parents. The more intense the cutoff, the more he is vulnerable to duplicating the pattern with the parents with the first available other person. He can get into an impulsive marriage. When problems develop in the marriage, he tends also to run away from that. He can continue through multiple marriages, and finally resort to more temporary living together relationships. Exaggerated versions of this occur in relationship nomads, vagabonds, and hermits who either have superficial relationships or give up and live alone.

In recent years, as the age-old cutoff process became more pronounced as a result of societal anxiety, the emotional cutoff has been called the generation gap. The higher the level of anxiety, the greater the degree of generation gap in poorly differentiated people. There has been an increase in the percentage of those who run away, and who become involved in living together arrangements and communal living situations. These substitute families are very unstable. They are made up of people who ran away from their own families; when tension builds up in the substitute family, they cutoff from that and move on to another. Under the best conditions, the substitute family and outside relationships are poor substitutes for original families.

There are all gradations of the emotional cutoff. An average family situation in our society today is one in which people maintain a distant and formal relationship with the families of origin, returning home for duty visits at infrequent intervals. The more a nuclear family maintains some kind of viable emotional contact with the past generations, the more orderly and asymptomatic the life process in both generations. Compare two families with identical levels of differentiation. One family remains in contact with the parental family and remains relatively free of symptoms for life, and the level of differentiation does not change much in the next generation. The other family cuts off with the past, develops symptoms and dysfunction, and a lower level of differentiation in the succeeding generation. The symptomatic nuclear family that is emotionally cut off from the family of origin can get into cyclical, long-term family therapy without improvement. If one or both parents can reestablish emotional contact with their families of origin, the anxiety level subsides, the symptoms become softer and more manageable, and family therapy can become productive. Merely telling a family to go back to the family of origin is of little help. Some people are very anxious about returning to their families. Without systems coaching, they can make the problem worse. Others can return, continue the same emotional isolation they used when they were in the family, and accomplish nothing. Techniques for helping families to reestablish contact have been sufficiently developed so that it is now a family therapy method in its own right. This differentiation of a self in one's own family has been presented in another paper (1974b). It is based on the experience that a spouse who can do a reasonable job at differentiating self in his parental family will have accomplished more than if he was involved in regular family therapy with self and his spouse.

Multigenerational transmission process. The family projection process continues through multiple generations. In any nuclear family, there is one child who is the primary object of the family projection process. This child emerges with a lower level of differentiation than the parents and does less well in life. Other children, who are minimally involved with the parents, emerge with about the same levels of differentiation as the parents. Those who grow up relatively outside the family emotional process develop better levels of differentiation than the parents. If we follow the most impaired child through successive generations, we will see one line of descent producing individuals with lower and lower levels of differentiation. The process may go rapidly a few generations, remain static for a generation or so, and then speed up again. Once I said it required at least three generations to produce a child so impaired he would collapse into schizophrenia. That was based on the notion of a starting point with fairly good surface functioning and a process that proceeded at maximum speed through the generations. However, since I now know the process can slow down or stay static a generation or two, I would now say that it would require perhaps eight to ten generations to produce the level of impairment that goes with schizophrenia. This is the process that produces the poorly functioning people who make up most of the lower social classes. If a family encounters severe stress in perhaps the fifth or sixth generation of a ten-generation process, it may produce a social failure who is less impaired than the schizophrenic person. The degree of impairment in schizophrenia comes from those poorly differentiated people who are able to keep the relationship system in relatively symptom-free equilibrium for several more generations.

If we followed the line through the children who emerge with about the same levels of differentiation, we see a remarkable consistency of family functioning through the generations. History speaks of family traditions, family ideals, and so on. If we follow the multigenerational lineage of those who emerge with higher levels of differentiation, we will see a line of highly functioning and very successful people. A family at a highest level of differentiation can have one child who starts down the scale. A family at the lowest level can have a child who starts up the scale. Many years ago I described schizophrenia from a phenomenological standpoint as a natural process that helps to keep the race strong. The weakness from the family is fixed in one person who is less likely to marry and reproduce and more likely to die young.

Sibling position. This concept is an adaptation of Toman's work on the personality profiles of each sibling position. His first book in 1961 was remarkably close to the direction of some of my research. He had worked from an individual frame of reference and only with normal families, but he had ordered his data in a way no one else had done, and it was easy to incorporate them into the differentiation of self and the family projection process. His basic thesis is that important personality characteristics fit with the sibling position in which a person grew up. His ten basic sibling profiles automatically permit one to know the profile of any sibling position, and, *all things being equal,* to have a whole body of presumptive knowledge about anyone. His ideas provided a new dimension toward understanding how a particular child is chosen as the object of the family projection process. The degree to which a personality profile fits with normal provides a way to understand the level of differentiation and the direction of the projection process from generation to generation. For instance, if an oldest turns out to be more like a youngest, that is strong evidence that he was the most triangled child. If an oldest is an autocrat, that is strong evidence of a moderate level of impaired functioning. An oldest who functions calmly and responsibly is good evidence of a better level of differentiation. The use of Toman's profiles, together with differentiation and projection, make it possible to assemble reliable presumptive personality profiles on people in past generations on whom verifiable facts are missing. Knowing the degree to which people fit the profiles provides predictive data about how spouses will handle the mix in a marriage, and how they will handle their effort in family therapy. Based on my research and therapy, I believe that no single piece of data is more important than knowing the sibling position of people in the present and past generations.

Societal regression. This eighth and last of the concepts in the Bowen theory was first defined in 1972, and formally added to the theory in 1975. I have always been interested in understanding societal problems, but the tendency of psychiatrists and social scientists to make sweeping generalizations from a minimal number of specific facts resulted in my interest remaining peripheral except for personal reading. Family research added a new order of facts about human functioning, but I avoided the seductive urge to generalize from them. In the 1960s, there was growing evidence that the emotional problem in society was similar to the emotional problem in the family. The triangle exists in all relationships, and that was a small clue. In 1972 the Environmental Protection Agency invited me to do a paper on human reaction to environmental problems. I anticipated doing a paper on assorted facts acquired from years of experience with people relating to larger societal issues. That paper led to a year of research, and a return to old files for confirmation of data. Finally I identified a link between the family and society that was sufficiently trustworthy for me to extend the basic theory about the family into the larger societal arena. the link had to do, first, with the delinquent teenage youngster, who is a responsibility for both the parents and society, and secondly, with changes in the way the parents and the agents of society deal with the same problem

It has not yet been possible to write this up in detail, but the over-all structure of the concept was presented in outline form (1974a). The concept states that when a family is subjected to chronic, sustained anxiety, the family begins to lose contact with its intellectually determined principles, and to resort more and more to emotionally determined decisions to allay the anxiety of the moment. The results of the process are symptoms and eventually regression to a lower level of functioning. The societal concept postulates that the same process is evolving in society; that we are in a period of increasing chronic societal anxiety; that society responds to this with emotionally determined decisions to allay the anxiety of the moment; that this results in symptoms of dysfunction; that the efforts to relieve the symptoms result in more emotional band-aid legislation, which increased the problem; and that the cycle keeps repeating, just as the family goes through similar cycles to the states we call emotional illness. In the early years of my interest in societal problems, I thought that all societies go through good periods and bad, that they always go through a rise and fall, and that the cyclical phenomenon of the 1950s was a part of another cycle. As societal unrest appeared to move toward intensification of the problems through the 1960s, I began to look for ways to explain the chronic anxiety. I was looking for concepts consistent with man as an instinctual being, rather than man as a social being. My current postulation considers the chronic anxiety as the product of the population explosion, decreasing supplies of food and raw materials necessary to maintain man's way of life on earth, and the pollution of the environment which is slowly threatening the balance of life necessary for human survival.

This concept proceeds in logical steps from the family to larger and larger social groups, to the total of society. It is too complex for detailed presentation here. I outline it here to indicate that the theoretical concepts of the Bowen theory do permit logical extension into a beginning theory about society as an emotional system.

Summary

Most members of the mental health professions have little interest in, or awareness of, theory about the nature of emotional illness. I have developed a family systems theory of emotional functioning. For some ten years I have been trying to present the theory as clearly as it is possible for me to define it. Only a small percentage of people are really able to hear it. In the early years, I considered most of the problem to be my difficulty in communicating the ideas in ways others could hear. As the years have passed, I have come to consider that the major difficulty is the inability of people to detach themselves sufficiently from conventional theory to be able to hear systems concepts. In each presentation, I learn a little more about which points people fail to hear. I have devoted almost half of this presentation to some broad background issues which I hoped would set the stage for people to hear more than they had heard before, and to clarify some of the issues between my family systems theory and general systems theory.

I have never been happy about my efforts to present my own theory. I can be perfectly clear in my own mind, but there is always the problem of restating it so others can hear. If it gets too brief, people hear the theory as too static and too simplistic. If I try to fill out the concepts with more detail, it tends to get wordy and repetitive. Ultimately, I hope to present it so that each theoretical concept is illustrated with a clinical example, but that is a long and complex book. I believe that some systems theory will provide a bright new promise for comprehending emotional illness. Whether the ultimate systems theory is this one or another remains to be seen. After some twenty years of experience with this theory, I have great confidence in it. It does mean that the therapist must keep the whole spectrum of variables in his head at once; but, after some experience, knowing the variables well enough to know when one is out of balance becomes automatic.

Chapter 17

An Interview With
Murray Bowen

Berenson: The first time I heard Murray Bowen speak, I was not sure what he was talking about. I knew it had something to do with not blaming your family for how you got to be the way you are and with accepting responsibility for yourself. I was pretty scared by what he said, and it took me about two years before I was prepared to take a closer look. I finally heard him, and I'm now in the fortunate, or unfortunate, position of seeing that all those confusing ideas Dr. Bowen has been presenting are absolutely obvious and clear.

Others seem to have had a similar experience. Dr. Bowen, people are no longer so shocked by what you are saying and you are getting downright respectable. Are there any drawbacks connected with being accepted?

Bowen: Not for me personally. I am pleased when thinking people really come to know the theory and they can accept it for its accuracy rather than from blind belief.

Berenson: What about the fact that people are beginning not only to accept what you are saying, but are beginning to treat it a little bit like dogma?

Bowen: I have now spent over twenty years trying to build a theory that is a factual representation of the human phenomenon, that can remain open to new knowledge from the accepted sciences, and that can rise above dogma. I do not like it when people treat it as dogma, but it is fact of life that a percentage of people will continue to do it.

Berenson: Is there any danger now of people accepting the body of knowledge without criticism? Have you run into the situation where people will believe anything you say and yet don't understand it?

Bowen: Yes, indeed. From the beginning I have been concerned about people who become disciples and who accept the theory without thinking for themselves. Over the years I have tried very hard to work against this, with relative success. One variable is the degree to which my theory, or any theory, is a closed belief system. Another variable is the degree to which people erroneously treat it as a closed system. For instance, I think psychoanalysis is a closed system of beliefs such as a philosophy, or religion, or dogma. There is a considerable danger that my theory will also become a closed system of beliefs. I think I have a way to eventually avoid this, if it works out the way I hope it does.

Let me back up a bit and try to explain what I mean. Early in my psychiatric career I began to question some inconsistencies in psychoanalytic theory and to doubt conventional explanations for human motivation and behavior. The basic pattern of inconsistency suggested a problem in basic assumptions rather than a failure to define details. This led to wide reading in the social sciences and also in evolution, biology, and the natural sciences. It seemed to me that emotional illness is a deeper phenomenon than can be explained by disturbed relationships in a single generation. I had a hunch that emotional illness is somehow related to that part of man he shares with the other forms of life, rather than a phenomenon peculiar to man. There were no solid clues to support this notion and it remained in the distant background for most of a decade. During the same period I was also trying to understand the failure of psychiatry in becoming a science and what it would take for it to become a science.

Now let me move to some ideas about psychoanalysis that influenced future decisions. I believe that Freud's discovery of psychoanalysis is one of the most significant discoveries of the past century. He developed a completely new theory about the nature and origin of emotional illness. Basically he considered emotional illness to be the product of disturbed early life relationships. The theory was developed as patients remembered early life experiences, and as they communicated this material in the context of an intense emotional relationship with the analyst. In the course of the analysis it was discovered that patients improved, and that the relationship went through definite predictable stages toward a better life adjustment. However much "talking about problems" had existed in previous centuries, it was Freud who gave conceptual structure to the therapeutic relationship, which I believe gave birth to the profession of psychotherapy. I consider Freud and the early psychoanalysts to have made two monumental contributions. One was the theory that defined emotional illness as the product of disturbed relationships with others. The second was the discovery and conceptualization of the therapeutic relationship, which has since come to be regarded as a near universal treatment for emotional illness.

I believe that Freud's main weakness, if we can call it a weakness for the time in which he lived, was the way he conceptualized his findings. He was dealing with *functional* illness long before there was a concept of illness without structural etiology. He had been trained as a neurologist. To describe his findings, he used the medical disease model as far as it would go. His concept of *psycho*pathology is an example of that. Then he used a mixture of other models to describe additional observations, including models from the arts and literature. An example is the oedipal conflict from literature. He discovered a significant new body of *facts* about human functioning. His findings were substantial enough that they were eventually incorporated into the theoretical foundations of psychiatry and the social sciences that deal with human motivation and behavior. Psychoanalytic thinking also had a strong appeal in the arts. This was reflected by the early appearance of psychoanalytic themes in literature and artistic productions. To summarize this point, psychoanalysis came into existence as a substantial new body of facts about human functioning that was framed in a conceptual dilemma. It was a compartmentalized body of knowledge that was out of conceptual contact with medicine or with any of the accepted sciences. The successors to Freud accepted the concepts as "basic truths" which further prevented contact with the sciences and the utilization of new scientific discoveries in extending and modifying the theory. Functionally, it was a closed belief system equivalent to the religions, the philosophies, and the dogmas that are used on *truth* but which are unable to generate new knowledge from within nor permit new knowledge from without.

In my opinion, one of the major problems was Freud's use of discrepant theoretical models which made it difficult for his successors to *think toward* medicine or any of the accepted sciences. The twentieth century has been involved in a debate about whether psychoanalysis is a science. It *is* a science in the sense that it defines a body of facts about human functioning never previously described. It is *not* a science in the sense that it has never been able to make contact with, nor be accepted by the known sciences. The use of the scientific method has lulled psychoanalysis and psychiatry into believing it can someday become a science. The scientific method is a way of ordering random and discrepant data in a scientific way in the search for common denominators and scientific fact. Researchers have spent decades studying and restudying facts within psychoanalysis, discovering some new bits of information within the closed compartment, but they have not been able to make contact with the accepted sciences. Use of the scientific method does not make a body of knowledge into a science.

Recent knowledge from systems theory adds support to the conviction that psychoanalysis is a closed belief system. As time passes and the emotional tension within a closed system increases, the people in the system begin to disagree with each other, to split off and separate from each other, and to form different sects, denominations, and schools of thought. They become so emotionally embroiled with their differences they can no longer see they came from the same basic roots. No one needs be reminded of the family of different schools of thought in psychoanalysis and psychiatry in the past fifty years. A good example is the debate about differences between transference and the other forms of the therapeutic relationship. A psychoanalyst can debate at length about the finer points of difference. There certainly are documentable differences, but in the debate about differences both sides lose contact with the fact they both sprang from common roots. There are dozens of minor differences in psychoanalysis and psychiatry. The focus on the differences is a closed process. In the process the practitioners lose contact with the broader theoretical picture, basic assumptions come to be regarded as truth and proven fact, the thinking shifts from theory to dogma, and practitioners are no longer able to question basic assumptions nor look at new facts that do not fit the belief system. The debate about differences between psychiatry and psychoanalysis is a popular one. In the last fifty years psychiatry has incorporated the basic concepts of psychoanalysis. Now psychiatry and psychoanalysis are pretty much the same except for the minor differences. The increasing number of schools of thought has led to the age of eclecticism. New people entering the field are not able to conceptualize the many differences. More and more profess to be eclectics, which means they choose the ideas that best fit their personalities rather than choosing those that best fit the clinical problems. The differences in group therapy are interesting. I believe that group therapy, with all of its modifications and ramifications, sprang directly from Freud's original theory about the therapeutic relationship. Group therapists focus on concepts derived from the theory of the therapeutic relationship but the main body of psychoanalytic theory is in the background of their thinking. It is my conviction that the basic thinking in psychiatry and all the social sciences is rooted in the two basic concepts of psychoanalysis.

I believe that theory is far more important than is generally recognized. There was a period when the early medicine men believed the problem was the result of evil spirits. As long as they held that basic belief, the therapeutic efforts were directed at freeing the person of the evil spirits. The same principle applies today. Theory defines the thinking about the nature and origin of the problem. Though the practitioner may have lost contact with the basic theory, it still governs the choice of therapeutic methods and societal efforts to modify the problem.

Berenson: Are you saying that most mental health professionals are not aware of the theory from which they operate?

Bowen: That's right. A high percentage of mental health professionals have little awareness of theory. I think it may be part of the process as time has passed and so much of psychoanalytic theory has come to be accepted as truth. Most mental health professionals can quote a little theory but it is not part of them. It is as if they are reciting something they were required to learn in the early months of their professional training. If one takes a very broad theoretical view, without becoming embroiled in the emotional debate about minor differences, we have all descended from psychoanalytic theory about the nature of emotional illness and from the theory about the therapeutic relationship.

Berenson: Including yourself?

Bowen: Including me. Psychoanalytic thinking goes far beyond psychiatry and psychotherapy. It is the prevailing way that all people think about human problems. It is part of the warp and woof of society. It determines the rules and laws that govern the courts, schools, welfare agencies, and all our other social institutions. Considered on this level, it is not only the truth, but it is also the law. The acceptance of the theory by society helps make it into a dogma. I have been thinking theory almost thirty years and working toward a different theory since starting formal family research in 1954. It is not possible to quickly discard one way of thinking and adopt another way of thinking, especially when the new way is poorly defined.

Berenson: When you were developing a new theory, was there a time when you were still trying to fit it into the former way of thinking, the psychoanalytic orientation? How long did it take you to realize it would not fit?

Bowen: About six years. In the beginning I was working with schizophrenia and I was deeply invested in psychoanalysis. I thought the family research might eventually make a contribution to psychoanalytic theory as it applies to schizophrenia. I had no idea the research would take the direction it did. These are not simple issues with simple one-factor answers. The changes were part of an evolutionary process with multiple determinants. I will try to touch briefly on some of the main trends. For instance, since the late 1940s I had a background hunch that emotional illness is somehow related to that part of man he shares with the lower forms of life, but I could find no way to implement this idea and it did not play a part in the early family research. A fundamental order of change was taking place in me, and the others who started family research, in the years before the research started. The big changes began soon after the research began. The early family researchers of the 1954-1956 period were describing a completely new order of observations never previously described in the literature. I think it was related to the ability to finally shift thinking from an individual to a family frame of reference. People who were not there, and who were not aware of theory, can have little appreciation of the impact of family research on theory and therapy. In my research the change came as a sudden insight shortly after schizophrenic patients and their entire families were living together on the research ward. Then it was possible to really see the family phenomenon for the first time. After it was possible to see this phenomenon in schizophrenia, it was then automatic to see varying degrees of the same thing in all people. Why had this important observation been delayed this long? I had been working with the same kinds of patients and their families for a number of years without seeing. Part of this was surely related to the intensity of the emotional process in schizophrenia and the staff's close relationship with the families. I believe the major factor was "theoretical blindness" which had prevented me from seeing what had been there all the time. During the previous months and years my theoretical orientation had gradually shifted toward a family orientation. When the thinking had shifted far enough, and the observational stimuli were great enough, it was finally possible to see a whole new vista previously obscured by conventional thinking. I have used the example of Darwin and his theory of evolution to illustrate this point. The evidence for evolution had been there all the time but no one had been able to see it. Family research with schizophrenia played a major role in starting the family movement, the development of family therapy, and the evolution of theory. In 1957 the notion of family *therapy* began to attract hundreds of new therapists. Each began his own method of therapy superimposed on previous theoretical thinking. I called it a "healthy unstructured state of chaos." I considered it "healthy" in the belief that continued exposure to families would soon enable them to see the family phenomenon, and this would result in new theoretical developments. This did not occur. After almost twenty years, only a few have been able to see and become interested in theory. Considering the total field, family therapy is still an empirical method engrafted onto the old way of thinking. This is too complex a story for discussion here.

For me, the 1954-1956 period was one of theoretical exhilaration. Before the family research, I had spent years searching for theoretical clues with minimal success. Suddenly there was such a wealth of clues it was impossible to know which was most important or which deserved highest research priority. I believed that from this wealth of clues there would eventually come a completely different theory of human adaptation, if the clues could be structured in an orderly way. One other early family researcher also held this view about the potential for a new theory. He was Don Jackson who had also spent years working with schizophrenia before he started his family research. From then until his death in 1968 he worked steadily toward a systems theory based on communication concepts. Lidz was one of the major contributors to the field from the early 1950s until the mid 1960s. He was a practicing psychoanalyst before he started family research and his theoretical thinking remained in that field. Ackerman was a training psychoanalyst and one of the most gifted and innovative of all therapists before he developed his own intuitive method of family therapy. He was one of the great pioneers in family therapy but his theoretical thinking remained psychoanalytic. Bell developed one of the very early methods of family group therapy based on group therapy theory which came from psychoanalysis. The family therapists who entered the field after 1957 tended to develop therapy methods based on psychoanalytic theory. A few are now moving toward systems theory.

I made some disciplined decisions early in the family research that have influenced the course of my theoretical thinking. The early family researchers began using a variety of discrepant theoretical models to describe their observations. There were fairly simple mechanical models such as "seesaw," "interlocking gears," "interfaces," and "rubber fences" to describe over-all patterns, and more complex energy models from physics to describe forces that attract and repel at the same time, or forces that complement or oppose each other. There were also models from mathematics, chemistry, literature, and mythology. Research observers automatically think with models from the field of knowledge with which they are most familiar. It might be equally effective to compare a piece of human behavior with the theme from an opera, with animal behavior, with electronic circuits, with mathematical concepts, or with the psychic events when one looks at his image in the mirror, but the thinking sequence stimulated in the listener or reader is different with each model. For my research I made some decisions based on thinking about the use of discrepant models, and on the background hunch that emotional illness is related to the part of man he shares with the lower forms of life. I chose to use consistent models from the biological-natural sciences, and to exclude models from the arts and literature and also models from the sciences of inanimate things. This was based on the belief that if psychiatry is ever to make conceptual contact with the accepted sciences, it will be with the sciences that deal with living things. I was hoping the use of consistent biology oriented models would help researchers to think toward the sciences, and a few generations in the future it would be easier for researchers to make viable contact with the accepted sciences and to raise psychiatry to the status of an accepted science. This decisions governed nothing except the background thinking of the research staff. This effort is producing faster results than I expected. In less than twenty years my assistants are finding analogies between my theory and biology, cell biology, immunology, and virology. A simple analogy is not viable conceptual contact but I believe the thinking direction is healthy.

Another decision was directed at the "theoretical blindness" of the research observers. They came from psychoanalytic backgrounds and all they could see in the families was confirmation of psychoanalytic theory. I assumed there was much to be seen if they could clear their heads of theoretical bias and really see what was taking place. I believe this applies to all of us, all of the time. How does one go about clearing heads of theoretical bias? One long-term exercise was directed at the use of psychiatric jargon in research reports. Observers were asked to translate psychiatric terms into simple descriptive language. One can appreciate the magnitude of this by trying to eliminate one simple word such as *patient*. Most of the staff was challenged by this exercise to eliminate words such as *depressed, schizophrenia, sick, hysterical, obsessive, paranoid, catatonic, unconscious, ego, id, superego, passive father, dominating mother*, and all the rest. Some complained, "You are playing a a game in semantics. He is still a schizophrenic no matter what you call him." In many ways it was a game in semantics but it did help people to think and to see. In the beginning it seemed odd and out of place to avoid a word such as "patient." Eventually it became natural and right to avoid the term, and out of place to use it. In time we developed a new and more accurate language. This became a problem later in writing papers and presenting to outside people who did not understand our language. It was odd and awkward to use half a dozen simple words to avoid a well-known term. It was necessary to translate back into language an editor or audience would understand. For this we developed a mid-ground language with the sparing use of conventional terms, often modified with adjectives to make them slightly more accurate. It is hard to assess the long-term result of this exercise. It probably was most useful in helping me and my staff toward a different way of thinking.

There is one more point before I make this into a monologue. From 1948 to 1960 I was a candidate in psychoanalytic institutes, with certain phases of training interrupted by a move and by research activities. Every small point in theory was debated at length even before the move to Washington in 1954. I learned more psychoanalytic theory from debating about the research than from taking courses in the institute. An occasional psychoanalytic theorist would see the point but have no ideas about how to proceed. The main problem was not in the theory but in those who practiced the theory, who could not see beyond the dogma. The debates became cyclical and nonproductive and they used time needed for the research. My membership in the group became an issue between those who supported me and those who opposed. Supporters wanted me to accept membership and then follow the research. One senior analyst said, "I give up my concern about you and psychoanalysis. It now needs you more than you need it." Finally a supporter asked me to do one more round of debates. I agreed. The following day he called to release me from the promise. The following day I submitted my resignation. This phase took about six years. I could have spent an entire lifetime within psychoanalysis with minimal progress. I decided to leave the problem to future generations to incorporate new facts into psychoanalysis, if that eventually becomes productive. I have worked hard to stay on my own systems course and to avoid an "anti" position. An "anti" psychoanalytic theory *is* psychoanalytic in that it takes its point of reference from psychoanalysis. I have done well in avoiding an "anti" position but it has not prevented psychoanalysts from perceiving me as "anti" psychoanalytic. This is part of emotional systems polarization which assumes, "If you are not for me, it means you are against me."

Berenson: This question needs to be modified about as follows: Would your term *undifferentiated family ego mass* be an example of translating back into traditional language? I notice you do not use it much anymore.

Bowen: In one sense it was. I first used it at a meeting in an attempt to communicate the idea to an audience. It was an assemblage of words from conventional theory that people heard and liked. It became popular and I continued to use it for a time. More recently I have avoided it because it is conceptually inaccurate. Years later there was an interesting episode concerning this term. A psychology class asked to be excused to hear me lecture on the "undifferentiated family ego mass." The professor said he would not excuse anyone to attend a lecture on psychoanalysis.

There is another common misconception that should be mentioned. Many believe that family systems theory, as I have developed it, came from general systems theory. That is totally inaccurate. I knew nothing about general systems theory when I started my research. It is a way of "thinking about thinking" which occupies the same position to divergent theories that the scientific method occupies in relation to divergent and discrepant facts. In the 1940s I attended one lecture by von Berfalanffy of which I remembered nothing, and one lecture by Norbert Wiener of which I remembered very little. Whether anything from those lectures found its way into my thinking is a matter for conjecture. I did extensive reading in biology, evolution, and the national sciences, which I believe led to my formulation of emotional systems theory on the model of "systems" in nature.

Let me return to some thinking about psychiatry and science. Psychiatry, the social sciences, and the behavioral sciences that deal with human behavior, are far from becoming accepted sciences. There are definable, predictable, and reproducible facts about human behavior and, insofar as there are facts, it is potentially possible to expand a body of facts into science. Periodically psychiatrists admonish each other to "become more scientific" which means to return to medical science as it pertains to the science of the body. They do not conceive of human behavior becoming a science. When man starts thinking about his own behavior he introduces subjectivity, motivation, feelings, free will, and other intangibles into the mixture with the facts. My long-term goal has been to work toward a theory based on knowable facts about human behavior and to later build on that. The hunch about the biological part of man was no more than an educated guess. The choice of biological conceptual models was in support of the educated guess. I am merely trying to say what I have tried to do, without saying this should be done.

The concepts *differentiation* and *fusion* are general terms that also have specific use and meaning in biology. I originally used the concept *symbiosis* as it has been used in psychiatry to refer to the intense mother-child interdependency. During the research I considered dropping the term until I became aware of its very specific meaning in biology. Since then we have used it exactly as it is used in biology which has refined over thirty separate stages between parasitism and symbiosis. In parasitism one form lives entirely on the other and contributes nothing to the host. This proceeds through many stages to symbiosis in which the two forms complement each other. The term *instinct* has a special meaning in psychoanalysis which equates it with primal force of the libido. In this theory I have used *instinct* and *instinctual* exactly as used in biology and the natural sciences. Some terms are simply descriptive without connations for any special body of knowledge. Examples are the family projection process and the multigenerational transmission process, implying a natural process.

Berenson: Where did you get triangles? That does not fit easily into biology. It sounds almost mathematical.

Bowen: You are correct. It may be my most unfortunate term. Many people think geometry when they hear it. The thinking about this started in 1956 with the use of the term *interdependent triad* to describe the emotional "stuck togetherness" between father, mother, and schizophrenic offspring. The term *triad* was well defined in the literature and was within the bounds of an acceptable term for the research. We continue to use *triad* about two years. Work on this concept proceeded rapidly as we watched family members, and the ward staff, form themselves into configurations and disrupt and reform into new configurations. In the therapy situation I found that the groupings were different when the therapist was not a part of the emotional responsiveness. Then came the notion of using knowledge from research observations in the therapy. We had quickly gone beyond the meaning of *triad* as defined in the literature into using it as a precision therapeutic technique. People responded to our use of *triad* as if they knew what it meant. In the meantime we had been reading the literature for a more precise term to describe these cyclical emotional forces as they operated in a relationship system. We did not find it. There is the microscopic motion in Brownian movement and all kinds of motion in one-cell animals and larger forms but nothing seemed to fit. Finally I replaced the term *triad* with *triangle* to convey there was an important difference. If I had it to do over again, I probably would have found another term, but I still do not know what it would be. The triangle concept came from watching people as they go through a dance or drill or fixed pattern of movement. It continues until the anxiety builds up, or decreases. Suddenly, on an observable cue, they go into counter marching or another fixed pattern. This is all observable, knowable, and predictable. It is so precise the therapist can introduce the correct emotional cue to start the next sequence in the counter marching. From the early research days I have said that if one's observations were sufficiently accurate, and he really knew the system, and he could control his own emotional inputs, he could control the system. In the world of "triangles" this is as predictably precise as the system is precise. I cannot substantiate it but I believe that "triangle" emotional forces must apply to all forms of life. The protoplasmic dance is too precise for it to be otherwise. When I began thinking "triangles," I was thinking of emotional flow and counter-flow. I did not anticipate that many would hear it as geometry.

Berenson: Let's stay with "triangles." In your writings I am never clear on one point. You sometimes talk about dyadic interaction sometimes leading to triangulation. At other times you postulate the triangle as the basic building block of the family. I sometimes get confused about whether the triangle is a "natural way of being" or whether it is a failure of dyadic interaction.

Bowen: A "triangle" is a "natural way of being" for people. It is not inaccurate to think of the triangle as a failure in a two person relationship, but that is a narrow view of the larger relationship system. When anxiety is low and external conditions are ideal, the back and forth flow of emotion in a twosome can be calm and comfortable. One could refer to this as the ideal or the "normal" state for a two person relationship. However, the human situation does not remain ideal for long, even under the best conditions when both people are fairly stable. The two person relationship is unstable in that it has a low tolerance for anxiety and it is easily disturbed by emotional forces within the twosome and by relationship forces from outside the twosome. When anxiety increases, the emotional flow in a twosome intensifies and the relationship becomes uncomfortable. When the intensity reaches a certain level the twosome predictably and automatically involves a vulnerable third person in the emotional issue. The twosome might "reach out" and pull in the other person, the emotions might "overflow" to the third person, or the third person might be emotionally programmed to initiate the involvement. With involvement of the third person, the anxiety level decreases. It is as if the anxiety is diluted as it shifts from one to another of the three relationships in a triangle. The triangle is more stable and flexible than the twosome. It has a much higher tolerance for anxiety and is capable of handling a fair percentage of life stresses. When anxiety in the triangle subsides, the emotional configuration returns to a calm twosome and an outsider. Anxiety may even subside to the point there are three separate functional individuals. Anxiety can increase beyond the ability of the triangle to handle it. At this point, one of the people involves another outsider. Now the emotional forces follow the same triangle patterns between two of the original people and the outsider. The other member of the original triangle becomes emotionally inactive. If anxiety remains high, the emotional process may involve still another outsider, or it may shift back to the original triangle. If anxiety continues to increase, the triangular spread can go outside the family to involve neighbors, friends, and people in the schools, social agencies, and courts. When the anxiety subsides it goes back to the original triangle.

On a broad descriptive level, a two person relationship is emotionally unstable, with limited adaptability for dealing with anxiety and life stresses. It automatically becomes a triangular emotional system with a much higher level of flexibility and adaptability with which to tolerate and deal with anxiety. When anxiety involves more than three people, the configuration spreads in a series of interlocking triangles. When a large group or crowd is involved in an active emotional issue, multiple people append themselves to each corner of the triangle and the emotional forces continue the basic triangle patterns. I think a bona fide two person relationship is one in which two people are primarily invested in each other. These are relatively rare and it is a difficult balancing act to keep them in emotional equilibrium. Most so-called two person relationships are the calm side of an already functioning triangle in which the calmness is maintained at the expense of a negative relationship with the other corner of the triangle.

Berenson: Some people say you use a triangular concept because it is simpler for your own head. What you are saying here is this is the way people really operate.

Bowen: There are also a few people who say the entire theory is a product of my imagination. I hope I have already responded to most of this kind of comment. I am always amazed at how little people know about theory and how they misuse the term. There are those who say, "I have a theory" when it would be accurate to say, "I have an idea." The main criticisms about the total theory come from those who regard psychoanalysis as truth and who cannot comprehend another way of thinking. A valid theory is an abstract conceptual formulation about verifiable natural events. A theorist cannot use all the facts in this theory. He develops hypotheses and assumptions to help him choose the facts that will go together to make up the mosaic of his theory. There are exceptions to any theory. For a theory to be valid, the theory must also be able to account for the exceptions. The person who says the triangle concept is a product of my thinking is one who cannot see triangles. We live our lives in networks of emotional forces that follow triangle patterns. There are two main reasons for people being unable to see the traingles. The first reason is that the system is calm and the triangles inoperative. The more likely reason for the failure to see triangles is that people are so emotionally involved in the automatic "dance of life" they cannot see. One has to become an observer before it is possible to see. The inability to see is fairly common in new trainees who have not been able to master their own emotionality enough to observe and who cannot see a triangle unless it jumps out and hits them. I remember one young trainee who said, "I think I have found a triangle in my family."

Berenson: There is one part of your theory that people seem to have difficulty with, and they end up either rejecting it or overaccepting it. That is the "differentiation of self scale." People don't understand it, and they write to ask for a copy of it. I wonder if you could clarify that for us.

Bowen: This concept is the heart of the theory and also one often misinterpreted. In the early years I assumed it had been my failure in communicating clearly when others failed to understand. Later I learned that much of the failure was in the thinking bias of the listener or reader. In an effort to communicate more clearly, I became over-simplistic in presenting it as the differentiation of self *scale*. I was merely trying to communicate that people are definably different from each other in the way they handle the mix between emotional and cognitive functioning, and that the difference was on a continuum from its most intense to its least intense form. I used the term *scale* to illustrate a continuum from 0 to 100. At the lower end of the continuum were the most undifferentiated people and at the other end the most differentiated. There were four detailed profiles to describe people in each segment of the scale. In that paper I was careful to point out the subtle differences between basic and functional levels of differentiation and the inaccuracy in trying to estimate a level of differentiation except by evaluating the life over long periods of time, or even for an entire lifetime. People responded to the term *scale*. I began to get letters asking for a copy of the scale. It was clear they either had not read the original paper, or they had not understood it. A few letters would have gone unnoticed but the number kept increasing. I was not aware of the degree to which our society is oriented to the use of "scales" and "instruments" to judge and categorize others. Graduate students, urged on by faculty advisors, are constantly on the prowl for research "instruments." The students are not reluctant to demand material and time. One group of letters is illustrated by a college student who wanted to "administer the scale" to the patients on the chronic ward of a state hospital to determine how much they improved during a summer of social activity. A school psychologist wanted to use the scale on parents of problem students to determine if their level of "differentiation" matched the child's behavior. Another group of letters is illustrated by a director of psychiatric research who was collecting a file of "instruments" for measuring maturity and who wanted a copy of my "scale" for his files. A large group of letters were from graduate students who wanted an "instrument" for their research. A majority of these showed no grasp of the concept. I suspect some librarian had put my scale on a computer with the list of other "instruments" and the students found the list. Another group of students gave evidence of having read and understood parts of the paper and they asked reasonably intelligent questions. The simplistic letters I answered briefly. To the more thoughtful inquiries, I often sent a reprint or a copy of a paper. A few of those wrote again for more detail. To those who asked knowledgeable questions, I did knowledgeable replies. A few of those are now doing family systems therapy. At the time the letters started, I had already done considerable work toward identifying various levels of differentiation. It would be chaos to put an "instrument" in the hands of people who do not know the theory. I stopped work directed at defining various scale levels, and I dropped the word *scale* from the concept. Recent efforts have gone toward a more careful description of the concept. Communicating the concept is difficult enough with people who are fairly knowledgeable and who are trying to understand. The misinterpretation of "differentiation" is so great I often wish I had never heard of the term, but the problem is with the emotional process the term defines and not with the term.

A basic premise behind this concept is that neurosis and schizophrenia, and all other variations in human adaptation, can be put on the same continuum. The difference between the neuroses and the psychoses is a key issue among mental health professionals. A majority still support the premise these are basically different processes. The majority determines the policy of the professional associations, the attitude of society, and the allocation of research funds. Psychoanalysis defines a basic difference between the neuroses and schizophrenia but it also has a method of psychoanalytic psychotherapy for schizophrenia. There are many shadings of gray between the deteriorated symptom state clearly known as schizophrenia and the mild symptom state clearly defined as neurosis. There were people in the neurotic range who became psychotic and people who appeared to have severe schizophrenia who recovered promptly. Since the early days there has been much work on the "gray areas," mostly aimed at developing new diagnostic categories and the skill to know one state from another. There were terms such as *incipient schizophrenia, latent schizophrenia*, and the more popular term *borderline states*. The less severe psychoses were also subdivided into new categories. Psychiatrists became experts at careful diagnosis, and a group of psychologists became experts in detecting small points of difference from psychological tests.

Berenson: And also based on whether or not you liked the person.

Bowen: That was in it too. Even before the family research I believed the difference was in varying levels of intensity in the same basic process. The family research added a new dimension, with its focus on the entire family instead of the patient. I was elated at the new order of observations from the family research, and at the automatic ability to then see the same relationship patterns, in varying degrees of lesser intensity, in all families. This was sufficient evidence for me that schizophrenia and the neuroses all belonged on the same continuum. I no longer had to be concerned about how schizophrenia is different from the neuroses, or how the neuroses are different from "normal." Other professional people reacted differently. At one extreme was a nationally known expert in schizophrenia research who had been impressed with my research until we found these new findings were also present in families without schizophrenia. He suggested the schizophrenia research be terminated because the findings were not specific for schizophrenia. Others were stimulated to do research on "normal" families to verify if the relationship patterns were also there. The new result of the various studies was that the patterns were also present in "normal" families. Psychiatry has never adequately defined the concept "normal." It is usually defined as freedom from symptoms, or success at life goals, or some mixture of the two. It is difficult for researchers to study "normal" without focusing on what is "sick" about the person. I think it is impossible to define "normal" with a conventional conceptual framework.

There was one finding from my schizophrenia research that later became the core of the differentiation concept. It was a finding that probably would have been missed had it not been possible to first see it in its most intense form in schizophrenia. It had to do with the degree to which the family is involved in the intensity of the feeling process which is centered in the patient. The family lives in a feeling dominated world. It is difficult to impossible for them to make principled determined decisions that oppose the feelings. They make life decisions to relieve the anxiety of the moment when they could know, if they could think at the time, that serious life complications would result from the decisions. Family life becomes a mass of complications from years of feeling determined decisions. After the research with schizophrenia was under way, I began studying families with all degrees of lesser problems, "normal" families, and the best integrated families I could find. People are remarkably different from each other in the way their feeling-thinking functions are fused or are relatively differentiated. At one end of the spectrum are those whose thinking functioning is largely obliterated by the emotional process which governs their lives. Some in this category lead symptom free lives but adjustments are tenuous and they are easily triggered into dysfunction. Poorly differentiated people have a high percentage of all of life's problems including emotional and physical illness, social maladaptation, and failures. At the other end of the spectrum are those whose thinking-feeling functions are more differentiated and autonomous. They have more freedom both in emotional and intellectual functioning. They are more successful in life, they have far fewer life problems, there is more energy to devote to their own life courses, and their emotional relationships are more free and intimate. The rest of us fit between these two extremes. When I started the "scale" idea, the goal was to conceptualize the total range of human functioning from the lowest possible level to the highest level of perfection, on a single continuum. The three lower profiles were taken from direct observation, from a volume practice in family therapy with all levels of problems, and from research with "normal" people and others with the highest functioning I could find. The fourth profile for those with the highest levels of differentiation was an hypothesized projection of known characteristics from the other profiles. Complete "differentiation" is practically and theoretically impossible but I wanted the upper profile to complete the total concept.

There have been some problems in conceptualizing the differentiation of self concept, and with people who attempt to learn it, to use it, and to communicate about it to others. On the positive side it has more breadth for thinking about the total human phenomenon than anything else I know. In the beginning I expected that the total population might be distributed more evenly along the scale. This has not evolved. From experience, about 90 percent of the population fits into the lower half of the scale and no more than about 10 percent of the population into the third segment. Thus far I do not see enough disadvantage to try to modify the "scale." The biggest single problem for me has been shifting from conventional to systems thinking. Ten years ago I believed I had mastered a fair degree of systems thinking. Changes since then have indicated there is still much more to be mastered. The main problem in communicating and teaching this theory has been the other person's automatic tendency to think in conventional theory, and to mix systems concepts with old concepts. This theory contains no new ideas. It operates on an order of facts so simple that everyone knew them all the time. The uniqueness of the theory has to do with the facts that are included, and those that are specifically excluded. I have compared the theory to a distant "drumbeat" that people have always heard. The distant drumbeat is often obscured by a noisy foreground drumbeat, but it is always there and it tells its own single story to those who can keep the focus on the distant drumbeat and tune out the noisy insistence of the foreground. This theory specifically excludes certain items from conventional theory that are equivalent to the foreground drumbeat. It is easy for new people to start listening to the foreground noise and believe they are still within the systems framework. Conventional theoretical concepts have their own relevance but they tend to nullify the unique effectiveness of the simple story told by the broad systems perspective. People always have a choice of mixing concepts but a fascinating new world of theory and therapy is available to those with the motivation and discipline to finally see for themselves.

The main problem in conceptualizing the human phenomenon with a differentiation of self concept is the wide shifts in functional levels of self. New people tend to be concretistic in trying to estimate "differentiation" in themselves and others. they mistake functional shifts for basic change. I have used the terms *solid self* and *pseudo-self* to convey one important variable. The solid self is made up of clearly defined beliefs, convictions, opinions, and life principles. Each is incorporated into self, from one's own life experience, after careful intellectual reasoning and weighing the alternatives and accepting responsibility for his own choice. Each belief and principle is consistent with the others and self will take responsible action on the principles even in situations of high anxiety. The pseudo-self is acquired under emotional pressure and it can be changed by emotional pressure. It is made up of random and discrepant beliefs and principles, acquired because they were required, or it is the right things to believe and do, or to enhance the self image in the social amalgam. The solid self is aware of inconsistency in beliefs but the pseudo-self is not aware. The solid self is incorporated into self in contrast to the pseudo-self which is appended to self. The pseudo-self is a "pretend" self. It was acquired to conform to the environment, or to fight it, and it pretends to be in harmony with all kinds of discrepant groups, beliefs, and social institutions. The list of "pretends" is extensive. One can pretend to be more important or less important, stronger or weaker, or more attractive or less attractive than is consistent or realistic. It is easy to detect gross examples of pretense but there is enough of the pretender in all of us to make it difficult to detect lesser degrees of the imposter in others. From experience with this concept, the level of solid self is much lower, and the level of pseudo-self much higher in all of us than any of us can easily accept. It is the pseudo-self that is involved in emotional fusion with others, with the loss or gain in "functional" self in the transaction. It is the pseudo-self that is involved in the giving, receiving, lending, borrowing, trading, and bargaining about self with others to gain an advantage; and that uses subtle maneuvering, manipulating, scheming, and plotting to gain a self advantage at the expense of another. It is the pseudo-self activity that results in false readings when one attempts to estimate levels of differentiation. It is possible to do fairly accurate estimations by evaluating a life course over long periods of time, or for a lifetime, if it is considered in the context of the past generations and others in the present generation.

There is another set of variables in my theory that is hard for some to grasp. On a broad level, there are two major variables in the theory. One has to do with the level of integration of self in a person. This has to do with the differentiation of self concept. The other variable is the level of anxiety. The lower the level of self, the more reactive the person to anxiety. A poorly differentiated person can appear "normal" in an anxiety-free field, but he is the first to develop his usual symptoms when the anxiety increases. Those with the best levels of differentiation are among the least reactive to anxiety and the least likely to develop symptoms in an anxiety field. Knowledge about reactiveness to anxiety provides information in evaluating the functioning of a person, and clues that are useful in therapy.

In this discussion I have tried to talk about theory without describing it in more broad principles. The details are in the literature. I would like to return to the question we started with, which has to do with the theory becoming a closed belief system or dogma. I have tried to point the theory in the direction of the sciences, hoping that future generations can keep going on basic research which will eventually make enough contact with the sciences to use new discoveries from the sciences in extending and refining the theory. I believe that basic research, directed toward the accepted sciences will keep it "open" for a long time to come. If it ever makes viable contact with the sciences, it will then be able to share knowledge with the sciences, and contribute to the other sciences, and it will have become a science. To this point, most of the people who have learned the theory and are practicing it, still rely on my formulation of the theory as their source of knowledge. If this should continue into the future, then this theory will also have become another closed belief system.

Berenson: There is one last question. A stereotype that people get is that Bowen's differentiation of self scale, with feeling at one end and thinking at the other, results in people who think all the time and who are unfeeling, cold, and unemotional. I know this is not what you are saying, and I would like you to clarify that point again.

Bowen: This has been the most frequent criticixm of the theory and the method of therapy. I began hearing it in the early 1960s when the differentiation concept was sufficiently structured to begin talking about it. On a theoretical level, the question comes from a person whose thinking is psychoanalytic and who views the therapeutic relationship as the treatment for all emotional problems. It comes from a person who has not heard the theory and who is deeply involved in the feeling system with the patient. The person hears my concept of the "intellect" as similar to the familiar concept of "intellectualization" from psychoanalysis which is defined as a mechanism of defense against feelings. In that orientation, the expression of feelings is viewed as healthy and intellectualization is the unhealthy defense. The intellectual system as I have defined it is quite different from the defense mechanism called intellectualization. As long as that person remains in that theoretical orientation, there is no way for them to hear this point. It is interesting that this perennial question, which is asked in the context of theory, is usually based on therapy technique. I have no easy answers to this question. I think the basic problem is that some of my theoretical assumptions are at odds with basic truths held by the questioners and there can be no conceptual contact until the questioners can either hear my assumptions or accept the fact their truths are no more than assumptions. I have never found it productive to discuss this point around the issue as it is presented. I do my explanation and the questioner stops asking questions but it does not change their thinking.

Berenson: There is a great deal more I wanted to get into, including the extended family process and the three generational process. Right now we will take about five minutes or so of questions from the audience.

Question: Dr. Bowen has been talking about symptomatology. What about the etiology of neurosis and psychosis?

Bowen: The question of etiology comes from a psychoanalytic frame of reference. You are on one wave length, and I am on another. There is no way to deal with this in a few minutes.

Question: Would you equate increasing level of differentiation of self with power?

Bowen: No, they are not in the same ballpark. The idea of "power" is one to which I have devoted much thinking the past twenty years. The notion of "power" is usually used in a relationship sense, having to do with other people, and specifically with exerting control and domination over others. It is a relationship term which has to do with other people. The concept of differentiation has to do with self and not with others. Differentiation deals with working on one's own self, with controlling self, with becoming a more responsible person, and permitting others to be themselves.

Question: Why are some people more differentiated than others?

Bowen: One simple answer would be, "Because that is the way the human has evolved as a form of life." On another level it would be accurate to say your differentiation level is determined by the differentiation level in your parents at the time you were born, your sex and how that fitted into the family plan, your sibling position, the normality or lack of it in your genetic composition, the emotional climate in each of your parents and in their marriage before and after your birth, the quality of the relationship each of your parents had with their parental families, the number of reality problems in your parents' lives in the period before your birth and the years after your birth, your parents' ability to cope with the emotional and reality problems of their time, and other details that apply to the broad configuration. In addition, the level of differentiation in each of your parents was determined by the very same order of factors in the situation into which they were born and grew up, and the levels of differentiation in each grandparent was determined by the same factors in their families of origin, and on back through the generations. As I see it now, the biological, genetic, and emotional programming that goes into reproduction and birth is a remarkably stable process, but it is influenced to some degree by the fortunes, misfortunes, and fortuitous circumstances when things go wrong. All things being equal, you emerge with about the same basic level of differentiation your parents had. This is determined by the process before your birth and the situation during infancy and early childhood. This is then modified to some degree by the fortunes and misfortunes during later childhood and adolescence. All things equal, the basic level of differentiation is finally established about the time the young adult establishes self separately from his family of origin. I am talking about basic levels of differentiation that proceed through the generations as a stable process. Above and beyond that are the many functional levels of differentiation that are superimposed on the basic level. The lower the basic level of differentiation, the more marked the functional adaptations. The functional level of differentiation is influenced by numerous factors we have come to know in some detail, which result in wide fluctuation in the functional level. In systems therapy we speak of increasing the level of differentiation. Most of the time this refers to the functional levels of differentiation. If we can control the anxiety, and the reactiveness to anxiety, the functional level will improve. Beyond that I believe it is possible, over a long period of time, to increase the basic level to some degree. Systems therapy cannot remake that which nature created, but through learning how the organism operates, controlling anxiety, and learning to better adapt to the fortunes and misfortunes of life, it can give nature a better chance.

Question: What has this to do with genetics?

Bowen: In a strict sense, it has nothing to do with genetics. My concept, multigenerational transmission process, defines a very broad pattern in which certain children emerge with lower levels of differentiation than the parents, and others emerge with higher levels of differentiation, while most continue at about the same level as the parents. Those who emerge with lower levels have been exposed to more than an average number of life's misfortunes, and those who emerge with higher levels have had more of life's good fortunes. The fortunes and misfortunes are defined more by the family emotional process than by the usual advantages and disadvantages as defined by society. From a strict definition of genetics, this process follows a genetic-like pattern but it has nothing to do with genes as they are currently defined. In the past decade some different views of genes have emerged. The new medical specialty, genetic counseling, is one evidence of change in the field. In the past decade the sociobiologists have been referring to programmed animal behavior which is transmitted from generation to generation, as genetically determined. Over the years I have used the term "programmed behavior" for such phenomena. Now the sociobiologists are using a "genetic" concept for the same thing. This does not mean they have discovered and identified new genes. It means they are postulating genes as the determiner of this behavior. Now there is disagreement about this in the field of genetics. What this means to me is that scientists in the biological and natural sciences are working to expand their bodies of knowledge, and they are working in the direction of several of the concepts I have defined in my theory. The multigenerational transmission process is one of the concepts on which I have done the least detailed work, and one that needs the most attention. I am looking for a family therapist-researcher for my Georgetown program who has enough interest in genetics to learn it, and who can devise family research that can "reach toward" some of the new developments in genetics. This is what I talked about before. If we can keep reaching toward the sciences, perhaps we will someday make solid conceptual contact with the known sciences, and then psychiatry will have become a science. Thus far our theories of human behavior have not been able to get beyond the status of closed belief systems. At this period in time, I can do no more than say that the levels of differentiation are transmitted from generation to generation in a genitic-like pattern which has nothing to do with genetics as genetics is currently defined.

Chapter 18

Society, Crisis, and
Systems Theory

This is a slightly modified version of my first paper about emotional process in society. In 1972 I was invited by the Environmental Protection Agency to do a paper entitled "Cultural Myths and Realities of Problem Solving" for a symposium on the environmental crisis. The symposium included scientists from a number of different fields directly involved in environmental problems. The others did papers on population explosion, the energy crisis, pollution of the air and water, and the problems of providing food for a burgeoning population. I was asked to do a paper on specifying predictable human reactions to crisis situations. I had many discrepant ideas on the subject but they were not organized into an orderly conceptual framework. I had planned to organize the paper around the disconnected ideas. The writing of the paper catapulted me into an area of thinking which I had long avoided because of the complexity and enormity of the task.

For many years I had been sufficiently interested in societal issues to keep files of professional and popular articles on the subject. I believed that systems thinking would one day provide a new way to societal problems but I never seemed to have sufficient data and I wanted to avoid the pitfall of making sweeping generalizations from minimal data. I believe this was the main defect in the many efforts to apply psychoanalytic theory to societal problems. This paper occupied my total thinking time for months. There were multiple different drafts of the paper. Each draft contained glaring conceptual errors that probably would have made little difference to the environmental symposium but they were not acceptable to me. I went back to old files in search of clues to resolve discrepancies. In the process of going back and forth between the writing and old charts and clinical material, I discovered a missing link which made it possible to do a logical conceptual bridge between emotional process in the family and emotional process in society. The link came from the study of clinical notes from families with delinquent teenaged children. A delinquency problem begins as a multigenerational family problem which can progress to involve schools, social agencies, the police, courts, the judicial process, and the entire fabric of society that deals with human problems. The clinical notes covered a period of sixteen years. In that period there had been a marked change in the way the family, and the total of society, had conceptualized and dealt with transgressions against society. Here was factual evidence of a changing process in the family and complementary change in society. I was elated at finding one missing link between emotional process in the family and society, but the deadline for the paper was approaching. I was deeply involved in thinking that required a detailed knowledge of family systems theory and the paper was designed for people who would have difficulty understanding the theoretical premises of system theory. In the last two weeks before the deadline, I did another draft of the paper which focused on broad theoretical issues that would establish a conceptual baseline between conventional theory and systems theory. My ideas about emotional reactiveness were based on a different way of thinking and I wanted to convey the logical thinking of systems theory, without which the conclusions would not fit. The final draft of "Cultural Myths and the Realities of Problem Solving" was marginally successful. It was more of a success for me than the purpose for which it was written. There was a misfit between the title and the content. I was surprised to find that scientists could hear systems thinking better than mental health professionals. For the audience there was too much detail about emotional problems in the family and too little about societal issues. For me, it was one of the most important papers in my career. It had helped me get clear about a bridge between emotional process in the family and society but I was not as successful as I wanted to be in conveying this.

In the months after the Environmental Protection Agency experience, much time went to clarifying issues I called "Societal Regression." At the 1973 Annual Georgetown Family Symposium I did my first presentation on this subject to mental health professionals. The presentation was too brief and the audience not as sophisticated about systems theory as I had expected. People reacted emotionally to the notion of "regression" which made it impossible for them to really hear.

In 1975 as we approached publication of the Symposium papers for 1973 and 1974, I attempted to write the societal paper in sufficient detail to be understandable by anyone with moderate knowledge of systems theory. It was inaccurate to think of societal regression without the opposite process which is societal progression. The title was changed to "Emotional Process in Society." The manuscript became as detailed as a book and there was not enough time to finish it. After the publication deadline had passed, I was deeply involved in planning and starting our new Georgetown Family Center and the manuscript was set aside for most of a year. In 1976 there was an attempt to shorten the manuscript and still make it comprehensible but there was not enough time to achieve my goal and another deadline passed. In 1977 I have been too involved with papers on schizophrenia and the differentiation of self in one's family of origin to devote much time to emotional process in society. It is not possible for me to deal adequately with the complexity of societal issues without a block of time with freedom from all other pressures. My goal is to present the concept of Emotional Process in Society as accurately as possible, with knowledge as it now exists, and then move on to other areas that demand attention.

In order to go on and publish the volume of symposium papers that should have been published in 1975, without further delay to other authors whose papers are in that volume, I have agreed to publish this early version of the paper written early in 1973. It was never published in more than an abstract form, it was never made available to the mental health professions, and it goes into considerable detail about basic concepts of family systems theory on which the concept of societal process is based.

A systems view of man represents a different order of thinking than is represented in our conventional theories. First I will present some of the major differences between systems and conventional thinking. It is difficult for man to shift from conventional *toward* systems thinking. I am not sure he can ever shift *to* systems thinking, when he is thinking about himself. In an effort to make the clearest possible presentation of the differences between conventional and systems thinking, I will present some personal experiences in my effort to shift toward systems theory. Then I will present the key theoretical concepts that interlock to make up this total family systems theory. Then, to bring the theory a bit more to life, there will be some clinical profiles to illustrate the theory. This will be followed by some of the numerous relationship patterns in society that parallel family relationship patterns. Finally, there will be a summary of man's predictable emotional reactions to crisis situations, the difficulty in finding solutions that are not emotionally determined, the tendency of emotionally determined solutions to merely preserve the status quo, and ways emotionally determined solutions can intensify the problem. Systems thinking provides no magical answers, but it does provide a different way of conceptualizing human problems. It offers a more realistic evaluation of the difficulty in changing the basic patterns in any human dilemma, and it suggests ways to avoid some of the pitfalls of conventional thinking, and to institute progress toward long term goals.

Differences Between Conventional and Systems Thinking

The goal of this section is to introduce the reader to some of the broad concepts on which systems thinking is based. This theory focuses on the *facts of functioning* in human relationships systems. It focuses on *what* happened, and on *how* and *when* and *where* it happened, insofar as observations are based on *fact*. It carefully avoids man's automatic preoccupation with *why* it happened. The conclusion of *why* thinking into systems theory automatically results in a reversion to conventional theory, and the loss of the unique advantage in systems concepts. Systems theory focuses on what man does and not on his verbal explanations about why he does it.

My concerted effort toward a different theory of emotional illness began almost twenty years ago in family research with maximally impaired, institutionalized, young schizophrenic patients in which the patient and his entire family lived on a research ward together for indefinite periods of time. This living together experience revealed a fascinating new world of clinical observations never previously reported in the literature. Existing literature was based on the study of a single person and it did not account for the relationship phenomena. A few other centers were doing different versions of family research. The investigators in this new field tended to report findings as extensions of existing theory, or to report them descriptively. For a number of years prior to the research, I had been reading extensively in all the sciences, and especially in evolution, biology, and the natural sciences, in an unsuccessful search for some clue that might provide psychiatry with solid membership among the accepted sciences. Current theories have used scientific models to conceptualize psychic and emotional functioning in the effort toward scientific objectivity, and the medical sciences have tried to extend neurophysiology to conceptualize emotional functions, but a solid bridge between the fields does not exist. Theories about emotional illness still describe a body of knowledge separate from the other sciences. In the hope that these fascinating new observations might provide some clue that would eventually help psychiatry become an accepted science, and to help broaden the perspective of the research observers, some broad assumptions about the nature of emotional illness were made to guide the over-all research. The observers had all been trained in conventional psychiatric theory and they tended to see only what theory had taught them to see. It was hoped that the broad assumptions might help observers see through a wider lens and to "see" other phenomena that were right before their eyes. The remainder of this section will be devoted to some of the broad background assumptions and hypotheses.

Background Assumptions and Hypotheses

The first of these assumptions was worked out early in the research. It came from previous study and experience and was based on the notion that emotional illness is deeper than a one generation product of parent-child relationships; that it has about the same incidence in different cultures with widely different child rearing practices, if there is allowance for the ways different cultures deal with emotionally impaired people; that there are suggestions it might even exist in wild animals; and it would be profitable to have this broad assumption in the background. The other assumptions were also defined as broadly as possible, but they were more directly related to early observations in the research. The earliest research models about relationships were based on systems thinking but there was not specific awareness of this at the time. As time passed, the term *systems* was spontaneously used to refer to the automatic predictable behavior between family members.

1. That emotional illness is directly related to the biological part of men. This was based on the assumption that man is more intimately related to the lower forms of life than is generally recognized, and that emotional illness is a dysfunction of that part of man which he shares with lower forms. Before Darwin, man operated with the notion that the earth was created exactly as it is now and all theoretical thinking was based on man's uniqueness. Darwin presented his work just over a century ago and it was over sixty years before man could hear it, and take it seriously. The estimates of the amount of time involved since the earth was formed, and in the evolutionary process, are different, and they are constantly being revised, but any timetable is so vast that figures are beyond ordinary comprehension. It is easy to believe that evolution is a

slow process, but it has occurred rapidly if one looks at the total timetable. If the earth was formed perhaps 4,000 million years ago, and if life first appeared on earth some 500 million years ago, then the earth went seven-eights of its present existence without life. If the first man to walk upright evolved about 750,000 years ago, and if man became a thinking being about 200,000 years ago, and if man became a thinking being about 200,000 years ago, and a "civilized" being about 20,000 years ago, and he learned to read and write about 10,000 years ago, and if the earth still has 10 to 15 billion years before it becomes a dead planet, we are faced with awesome percentages. If we computed the 4 billion year time span into a century, a unit of time we can more reasonably comprehend, it would mean that the earth was formed 100 years ago, that the first primitive life appeared about 12 years ago, that a man that walked upright appeared 7 days ago, that he became a thinking being about 4 days ago, that he showed evidences of civilization about 4 hours ago, that he learned to read and write about 2 hours ago, that Christ lived for a fraction of a second only 24 minutes ago, that Columbus discovered America 6 minutes ago, and that the earth still has 350 years before it becomes a dead planet.

Man is one of the most highly developed forms of life thus far. His most rapid evolution is the rapid increase in the size of his brain. The hypothesis about overspecialization postulates that it is the most highly developed forms that become extinct the fastest. Twenty years ago, when I devoted more study to this, I was postulating that man's brain, an overspecialized development of the special protoplasm we call brain cells, would be the evolutionary development that leads to man's extinction. Obviously I did not agree with some of the popular theories of that time which postulated that since man had unlocked so many secrets of nature, he would be able to gain mastery over his environment and be able to perpetuate himself. Twenty years ago, population overgrowth was not one of the variables considered in these postulations. These ideas about evolution are presented, not because they have any direct relation to this paper or to systems theory, but to communicate that this systems theory has made a continuing effort to view man as an evolving integral part of life on earth.

2. That emotional illness is a multigenerational process. There were early experiences and observations to support this working general assumption. This was later defined in detail and incorporated as one of the theoretical concepts in the total theory. This postulated that the problem in the patient is a product of imperfections in the parents, and the parents a product of imperfections in the grandparents, continuing back for multiple generations, and that each generation was doing the best it could considering stresses and available resources. The most

important function of this postulation was to help observers escape from the narrow limits of individual theory which blames parents for the child's problem, and to gain a more objective over-all perspective.

3. That there is a wide discrepancy between what man does and what he says he does. The beginnings of this were based on early research observations. This was another guiding principle that permitted observers to gain some distance and begin to see some order to the multiplicity of messages and actions that are part of the hour to hour observations. The second year a member of the research team did a paper, "The Action Dialogue in an Intense Relationship," which told a story based on action alone, that appeared to have more validity than verbal dialogue.

4. Structuring "hard to define" concepts into functional facts. This was part of an effort to find some structure and *fact* in the shifting, subjective world of human experience. It is difficult enough to conceptualize subjectivity in dealing with one person. In a family relationship system it is far more complex. Over a period of time, we began developing a formula which helped to move more rapidly into systems thinking and which made research observations more objective and measurable. The incorporation of functional concepts into therapy has resulted in therapeutic results that are far superior to conventional therapy. For instance, one concept would say, "That man dreams is a scientific fact, but what he dreams is not necessarily a fact." The same formula was applied to a wide range of functional concepts, such as "That man feels (or thinks, or talks) is a scientific fact, but what he feels (or thinks or says) is not necessarily fact." This same formula produced interesting results when applied to love, and also to hate. People speak glibly of love as if it is a well defined entity. It is more accurately a subjective feeling state that occurs in response to a variety of stimuli, that is experienced in a spectrum of ways, and in a scale of intensity, and that also operates in the relationship system. After much experience with family members, as they used the term and reacted to it, I arrived at the following functional definition of love as a relationship fact. It was, "I am not able to accurately define love, but it is a fact that statements to another important person about the presence or absence of love in self, or in the other, predictably results in an emotional reaction in the relationship."

5. Cause-and-effect thinking. Man has been a cause-and-effect thinker since he first became a thinking being and he began to look for causes to explain events in his life. We can review the thinking of primitive man and be amused at the evil and malevolent forces blamed for his misfortunes, or we can review the history of recent centuries and chuckle at the errors in the assignment of blame that resulted from lack

of scientific knowledge, while we smugly assure ourselves that new scientific breakthroughs and logical reasoning now enables us to assign accurate *causes* for most of man's problems.

Systems thinking, which this research has tried to implement in human relationships, is directed at getting behind cause-and-effect thinking and into a systems view of the human phenomenon. In the course of trying to implement systems theory and systems therapy, we have encountered the intensity and rigidity of cause-and-effect thinking in the medical sciences and in all our social systems. Man is deeply fixed in cause-and-effect thinking in all areas that have to do with himself and society. Systems thinking is not new to man. He first began to use it in theories of the universe. Much later he started thinking systems in the natural sciences, and also in the physical sciences. There was a rapid increase in systems thinking with the beginning of the computer age, until now we hear about efforts to implement systems thinking in many new areas of the applied sciences. The medical model has been one of the proven cornerstones of good medical practice. It is based on cause-and-effect thinking and the principles of careful examination, the establishment of etiology (cause), making an accurate diagnosis, and specific treatment directed at the etiology. The medical model has served medicine and society well for all diseases within the person of the patient. The theory and practice of psychiatry also employs the medical model, and cause-and-effect thinking. The theory, based on the study of the individual, postulates an illness in the patient developed in relationship with the parents or other close family members. It requires a diagnosis, and treatment is directed to the patient. The model "blames" the parents for the illness, even though the psychiatrist may deny that he blames the parents, and the model excludes other family members from the treatment process. And so, the medical model created a dilemma when applied to emotional (functional) illness. Family research was directed at trying to find an answer to this dilemma. The development of systems theory and therapy has been superior in treating emotional problems but it is conceptually and therapeutically out of step with medicine and conventional psychiatry. The medical centers in which a family orientation has been most successful are those in which conventional psychiatry has not been too strict in enforcing the medical model and family therapists have not tried to oversell their viewpoint.

Emotional reactiveness in a family, or other group that lives or works together, goes from one family member to another in a chain reaction pattern. The total pattern is similar to electronic circuits in which each person is "wired" or connected by radio, to all the other people with whom he has relationships. Each person then becomes a nodal point or an electronic center through which impulses pass in rapid succession, or even multiple impulses at the same time. One important variable has to do with different kinds of impulses, and each kind exists in a wide spectrum of intensity, and in degree of importance. A more important set of variables has to do with the way each nodal point, or person, functions in the system. Each person is programmed from birth to serve a certain set of functions and each "senses" what is required or expected, more from the way the system functions around him than from verbal messages that he is free to function as he pleases. Each person, or nodal point, has varying degrees of ability for handling impulses (native ability), styles for handling impulses (personality characteristics), a narrow range of choice in rejecting or transmitting impulses, and an intellectual awareness (intelligence) for understanding the operation of the system. There is another important set of variables that have to do with the way the family unit functions together. Each person becomes aware of his dependence on all the other nodal points. To be remembered is that each nodal point is "wired" to the others with two-way circuitry. There is a wide variety of subtle alliances for helping each other, refusing to help, or hurting the other. The larger unit can punish a single member, and a single member in a key position can hurt the whole unit. Another predictable pattern is the placing of "blame" for failure to function (cause-and-effect thinking) and the pattern of either blaming the other or blaming self. Under tension, every person tends either to place the "blame" outside of self (blamer), or within self (self-blamer), or alternate between the two, which is the pattern of cause and effect thinking. If the head of the family unit is calm, the entire family unit can be calm and the electronic system operates smoothly. When the head goes into panic and transmits panic impulse, the others send back panic messages which further panics the head, in a mounting cycle of panic, with poor handling of messages, disorderly and conflicting messages, and increasing paralysis of functioning. Any unit can recover from periodic panic or overloads, but when the panic becomes chronic one or more of the individual units can collapse (become sick), and there are several variables for handling that. There is another set of very important variables having to do with the way the family unit is wired into other families and larger social systems, and into the total system of all society.

The electronic model appears to have the potential and the flexibility to accurately account for *almost* every item of human relationships that can be structured as facts of functioning, *except for that which is determined by biology and reproduction and evolution.* I believe this may have been the point computer scientists reached a decade or two ago in theorizing about the construction of the human brain. This family systems theory postulates that all of the characteristics described under "emotional reactiveness,"

including all those "choices" man appears to have, are all part of that part
of man he shares with lower forms of live. All of these items can be
understood as facts of functioning and put into the electronic model. He
does have one ability beyond *other* protoplasmic life, and that is his ability
to observe, think, abstract, and see the natural order, to understand the
secrets of nature, and to govern himself a bit differently. However, an
inordinately high percentage of brains are so imbedded in the emotional
system that their thinking is mostly governed by emotionality. Even the
most objective of all thinking is done with brain cells that are
protoplasmic outgrowths of all protoplasm, it is impossible for man to
ever become completely objective, and the future of the brain will
ultimately be determined by the natural order.

What is "emotional reactiveness" and how does it operate? I have used
the term *emotional reflex* which is accurate and which makes it a little
more synonymous with biology. It is easiest to observe emotional
reflexes in an intense emotional twosome, such as a marriage, in which
they operate mostly within the twosome, without the introduction of
variables from the larger system. The reflexes are most observable in
moderate levels of tension. In low tension they are not observable, and in
high tension, the reflexes are too chaotic to see much order. The term
reflex is accurate in that it occurs automatically and out of awareness, but
like a reflex can be brought within limited observation and under limited
conscious control just as one can control a knee jerk with specific energy.
The reflexes operate with antennae like extensions of all sensory
modalities, but a high percentage operates from visual and auditory
stimuli. For example, one spouse may return from work with a higher
than average tension level, reflected in a glum "look," which raises
tension in the other and which is reflected in an octave or two increase in
the verbal response. The first is sensitized to sounds which results in a
higher tension, etc. Systems therapy directed at helping spouses discover
the reflexes can give each a bit of control over the automatic emotional
reactiveness. The ability to observe and "see" emotional reflexes is
dependent on the level of emotional tension. A molecular scientist who
knows systems in his work, and who is beyond cause-and-effect thinking
there, will lose all objectivity and revert to cause-and-effect thinking in
emotional systems. A family systems therapist who knows emotional
systems fairly well may be able to remain objective, without "blaming" as
long as emotional tension is within ordinary limits, but will immediately
revert to his former cause-and-effect thinking in higher levels of tension.

Though man may have gained some knowledge about systems
thinking from the sciences, he is still a cause-and-effect thinker on all
things that involve his emotional system. The thesis communicated here

is that, insofar as man is a cause-and-effect thinker, which is most of the time in calm periods and all of the time in tense periods, he is still as inaccurate, unrealistic, irrational, and overly righteous in his assignment of causality for his problems as were his ancestors who pursued a different kind of evil influence, who eliminated different kinds of witches and dragons, and who built different kinds of temples to influence benevolent spirits.

Theoretical Concepts

Some background about the theory will help in understanding the separate concepts. This is a theory about the functioning of the emotional system in man. In broad terms, the *emotional system* is conceived to be the function of the life forces inherited from his phylogenetic past, that he shares with the lower forms, and that governs the subhuman part of man. It would be synonymous with instinct, if instinct is considered to include forces that operate automatically. The *intellectual system* is conceived to be the function of his highly developed cerebral cortex. The emotional and *feeling systems* are interconnected, each influencing the other. The *feeling system* is a bridge between the emotional and intellectual systems through which subjective states from the upper levels of the emotional system are registered in the cerebral cortex. This theory postulates that more of man's life and behavior is governed by automatic emotional forces than he can easily admit.

Some observations about feeling and thinking in the early research families were later extended to a central concept in the theory. Those emotionally impaired people did not distinguish between the subjective feeling process and the intellectual thinking process. It is as if their intellect was so flooded with feeling that they were incapable of thinking that was separate from feelings. They routinely said, "I feel that . . ." when it would have been more accurate to say, "I think," or, "I believe," or, "It is my opinion." They absorbed their governing life principles from those about them which were expressed as "feelings" in disciple like agreement or in angry disagreement to manage relationships with others. They considered it truthful and honest to speak of feelings, and insincere and dishonest to speak of thoughts, beliefs, and convictions. They worked always for togetherness in relationships with others and avoided "I position" statements that would establish themselves as separate from another. This was especially striking in the parents of the impaired patients who were "no-selfs" in terms of their own beliefs and convictions but were so adept at getting along with others that they were successful in their businesses, in their professions, and in social lives. This experience led to the careful study of these characteristics in the total range of families with less severe emotional problems and in normal families. This led to the development of the differentiation of self scale as an important concept in this theory. It scales people according to the degree their selfs fuse into each other in close relationships, or the degrees that can function separately from the emotional system even in intense feeling states. In therapy, primary effort goes to helping people distinguish feeling states from intellectual functioning and helping them dare to develop firmer opinions, beliefs and convictions, in spite of pressure from the relationship system to retain the former level of amorphous "no-self."

The theory postulates two opposing basic life forces. One is a built-in life growth force toward individuality and the differentiation of a separate "self," and the other an equally intense emotional closeness.

The family systems theory is made up of six separate interlocking theoretical concepts, each dealing with characteristics that apply to the whole system, or to separate segments of the system. The concepts most important to social systems are presented in more detail.

1. Differentiation of self. This concept is a cornerstone of the theory. It defines all people, from the lowest to the highest possible level of human functioning, according to a single common denominator. This has to do with the way the human handles the intermix between emotional and intellectual functioning. At the highest level are those with most "differentiation" between emotional and intellectual functioning. They are more free to live their emotional lives to the fullest, or they have the capacity to make decisions based on intellect and reasoning when confronted with reality issues. People at the lower levels have emotion and intellect so "fused" that intellectual functioning is submerged in emotionality that their lives are dictated by emotionality. They may be able to "think" about issues outside themselves, or think about themselves when anxiety is low but under stress their thinking is replaced by automatic emotional reactiveness. There are relatively fixed levels of differentiation called "solid self" determined by forces from within self, and tremendous areas of "pseudo-self" or functional self which is determined by relationship forces. It is possible to assign a functional level of self for an individual, for an entire family which is determined by the level of self in the head of the family, or in the total of society which is determined by prevailing environmental forces.

2. Triangles. This is a key concept which describes the predictable pattern of emotional forces between any three people. A triangle, the smallest stable emotional unit, has been called the molecule of emotional systems. A two person relationship is unstable in that it automatically

becomes a three person system under stress. When stress increases, and it involves additional people, the emotional forces continue the action between three poles in the system. An emotional system is in a constant state of movement as the most uncomfortable one attempts to establish a more comfortable state of emotional closeness-distance. When the uncomfortable one achieves equilibrium, it disturbs the balance between the other two and the subtle activity shifts to the other most uncomfortable one. The term *triangle* defines the fact that emotional forces flow back and forth between three poles. The movement repeats and repeats and repeats in moves so precise and predictable that one who knows triangles can predict the next move before it occurs. Knowledge of triangles has been used to develop a method of therapy as predictable as triangles are predictable. The therapist can use his knowledge to introduce emotional cues, which result in predictable shifts in emotional flow. These emotional forces, which operate automatically and out of awareness, have been incorporated into a theoretical concept which describes the microscopic organization of emotional systems. In very large groups, or the total of society, the same automatic emotional forces operate with large numbers of people siding with each emotional issue.

3. Nuclear family emotional system. This concept describes the pattern of emotional forces as they operate over the years in the nuclear family. The intensity of the process is governed by the degree of undifferentiation, by the degree of emotional cutoff with families of origin, and the degree of stress in the system. Over time, the emotional problem becomes manifest as (a) emotional distance between the spouses; (b) dysfunction in one spouse which is manifested as physical illness, emotional illness, or social illness; (c) marital conflict; or (d) projection of the problem to one or more children. The projection of the family problem to children is so important it has been accorded a position as a separate theoretical concept.

4. Family projection process. This concept describes the details of the process by which parental problems are projected to one or more children. As a part of the total theory, this concept describes the most important way family emotional process is transmitted from one generation to the next.

5. Multigeneration transmission process. This concept describes the pattern as family emotional process is transmitted through multiple generations. In each generation the most emotionally involved child moves toward a lower level of differentiation of self and the least involved child toward a better level of differentiation.

6. Sibling position. This concept consists of modifications of Toman's basic work on the personality profiles of children who grow up in

different sibling position. Unless there are variables to prevent the process, children develop certain fixed personality characteristics determined by the sibling position in which they grew up. Knowledge of these characteristics is important in determining the part a child will play in the family emotional process, in predicting family patterns in the next generation, and in helping a family to reconstitute itself in therapy.

Two additional concepts were officially added to the theory in 1975. One was (7) *emotional cutoff,* which describes the most prominent mechanism involved in emotional process between the generations. This was formerly included partly in the nuclear family emotional process, and partly in the family projection process. It was considered important enough to have a separate concept. The last concept, (8) *emotional process in society,* describes the ideas partially presented in this paper. It describes the extension of family emotional process into larger social systems and to the totality of society.

Clinical Profiles and Examples

Clinical profile of a family. These clinical examples are presented to help illustrate the value of the differentiation of self scale in estimating present problems and predicting future problems in a family. It is impossible to do scale values for any month or year but it is possible to do estimates of the general levels of differentiation over a period of years, and from this one can do fairly accurate predictions of things to come. I will start with a mother with two young children, one that grows up with a poor level of differentiation and another with a good level of differentiation. The same mother can have two children that are quite different. The differences will be exaggerated here to illustrate the point.

The mother's first child was conceived when her life was unsettled and anxious. Anxiety and marital disharmony decreased during the pregnancy. (This is good evidence a family projection process is already in progress.) The child, a girl, was tense and fretful and required more than average mothering attention. A second child was born eighteen months later. The pregnancy was uneventful except for the mother's worry about the older child's reaction to a sibling. She wondered if she could provide adequate care for the baby without "hurting" the older one. (This is more evidence of a projection process.) The mother was aware of something different. She mentioned it to her pediatrician and friends who assured her this was not unusual for first babies. She concluded the problem would disappear if she could be a calm, patient, "giving" mother. (Projection of mother's anxiety to the child, and treating it as a problem in the child, helps perpetuate the problem in the child. A better approach would be to work on her relationship with her husband, or with her own mother.) The second child, a son, was an easy baby. (Indication that most of the basic problem was being "absorbed" by the oldest.) The mother kept trying to resolve the clinging attachment of the first child.

An example from the preschool years will illustrate critical qualities of the mother's relationship with each child. In dressing the children to play outside, the younger one was eager to dress and get started, while the older one was a dawdling problem. Outside, the younger one ran ahead to explore and play alone. The older child's attention was too preoccupied with mother to have energy for play. The mother tried to help the girl get started in play. It worked well as long as mother was there. When mother tried to sneak away, the girl stopped the play and ran to mother. The older child, with as much investment of self in the mother as the mother had in the child, was able to "read" mother's facial expressions, tone of voice, body posture, and footsteps. (These are examples of a goal-directed child and a relationship-oriented child.)

The first nodal point came when the children started school. The older child had a moderate "school phobia." She was fearful about school, with many questions about what would happen in school. The mother tried to prepare her by walking her to school to show her the building and grounds. When school started, the tearful, anxious parting was finally accomplished by a teacher who permitted mother to sit in the room a few days while the teacher devoted extra attention to the child. Mother was pleased when the mission was accomplished. At home, mother's thoughts still went to the child. She was encouraged by her frequent telephone conversations and conferences with the teacher, and overjoyed at the good reports. The younger child had no anxiety as he reached school age. He was interested in when he would finally be able to go and when he could learn to read and write. He had the same "understanding" teacher as his older sister. The teacher and the mother had a good relationship from conferences about the daughter. The mother credited the teacher's counseling for help in solving the older child's problem. The teacher reported the younger child was "no problem. He is more interested in learning than in me."

For the older child, this was a smooth transition from home to school. The child developed the same relationship pattern with the teacher as she had with her mother. The teacher was a shy woman with a poor level of differentiation who was relationship-oriented in her own life. She was said to have "a way" with shy children. Of the older child she said, "I do well with children like this. I can bring them out. I *give something to them*, and *they give me something in return*, and we do well." The child was attached to the teacher and the teacher helped place the child with other "understanding" teachers as the child progressed through the six years in that school. In their meetings at PTA and school functions, the teacher always inquired about the older child, but never about the younger child who was self-motivated and who did well academically and socially. He had numerous friends among the other boys and he was an achiever in the boy scouts. The older child also did well academically, but she was less consistent. When she was with a teacher she "liked" she worked hard at pleasing the teacher and was at the top of the class. When the teachers who gave her less attention (less of the relationship-oriented "giving and receiving" to each other), she did less well in school, she was often absent from school because of illness, she complained about the teacher, she was more dependent on her mother, and school performance fell. The mother blamed the bad years on time lost because of illness and teachers who were too "hard on her." This child found it easier to relate to adults than to other children in the grade school years (a common characteristic of children overattached to parents). The mother was concerned and became a girl scout leader to help her cultivate friends among the other girls. She compliantly participated when her mother was present for girl scout activities, but found reasons not to participate when her mother was not there.

The first major change in the girl's life came rather suddenly in the seventh grade, the first year of junior high school. The problem surfaced at mid-year, about the time of her thirteenth birthday. Two developments appeared about the same time. Since childhood, the mother had an "open" and honest relationship with the girl, who told the mother "everything" in a "giving and receiving" relationship that both enjoyed. Early in the seventh grade, the girl began to confide less and less. Mother missed these heart-to-heart talks, and in addition, she wondered what was going on in the girl. Mother's anxiety increased and the more she pushed for information, the more the child gave brief answers and withdrew to her room. The mother tried to be calm, telling herself the girl had never told her a lie, that this was a phase, and it would pass. The second development came with a poor report card. The mother resumed her push to know what was happening, and for the first time they had an angry exchange of words. The girl withdrew more and more and began long telephone talks with friends. This was the beginning of overt conflict between mother and daughter. The mother was afraid to ask too many questions lest she start a fight. Mother contained her anxiety as much as possible, but she was also good at reading the daughter's facial expressions, tones of voice, and actions, and when she "felt" the daughter was upset or anxious, she would again press for explanations. The daughter learned to be evasive and distant, and that "white lies" would settle mother's immediate anxiety. The girl's school record was erratic, but with a little effort before exams, she could manage average grades in most subjects. Socially the girl became part of a group of "fast" girls who the mother blamed for the daughter's behavior that became increasingly more extreme and antifamily. Periodically, at the time of an anxiety episode, the mother would seek information and counsel from school but there was no longer a single teacher and the school counselor, who had little direct contact with the girl, first reassured mother that this was normal and then later suggested psychiatric help. When the mother mentioned this to the girl, it elicited the angriest response of all. The mother herself saw a psychiatrist who explained the adolescent rebellion and adolescent sex conflict and who suggested an evaluation and possible psychotherapy for the mother to help her find answers in herself. The girl's refusal to have anything to do with a "shrink" terminated that effort.

The adolescent period is fast moving and difficult for such a relationship-oriented child. The girl started life with a moderately intense fusion of self with mother. Much of mother's psychic energy, which included worry, concern, "love," and anger, etc., were invested in the girl, and the girl invested an equal amount of herself in the mother. This investment of self, or fusion, exists in all levels of intensity that parallel levels of differentiation of self on the scale. Once a child is "programmed" to a certain level of "giving and receiving," with mother, this level remains relatively fixed throughout life. The child can have an "open and loving" relationship only when conditions for that level of investment of self in each other are met. There are certain variables that govern the "conditions" that are discussed elsewhere. The mother's degree of undifferentiation that fuses with the child is determined by her total amount of undifferentiation and by the amount absorbed elsewhere. If the mother's undifferentiation is absorbed in this child, her relationships with her other children will be more normal. Mother had no excessive worry or concern about the other child. There is a spectrum of families in which other children "grow up" outside the parental fusion with the involved child and they are free to grow toward goal-directed lives.

This mother was "successful" in managing a fairly calm relationship with the girl throughout childhood. She found a school situation that was extremely favorable for keeping the child free of symptoms. The teacher had a similar low level of differentiation herself and she fitted well as a relationship figure the next six years. A less favorable "fit" would have resulted in more symptoms early in school, and probably more symptoms as the child moved through elementary school years. The child managed to do better than average in school work. A better school adjustment would have been one in which the child would have been an overachiever who put in sufficient work to excel academically in order to "receive" approval from teachers and parents. Another child of about the same level of differentiation and a little less free intellect to apply to school could become an underachiever to relieve the pressure of academic success, and still receive an acceptable amount of psychic energy directed to the poor school record. The problems with poorly differentiated youngsters who are academically brilliant will be discussed elsewhere in this paper. The difficulty that such a child has in relating to other children is familiar. The average small child is not capable of relating to other children and an impaired child has little energy outside the adult "giving and receiving" sources. The breakdown in the successful school adjustment period came at the beginning of junior high school, which is a common breakdown point for impaired children. There is no longer a single room and single teacher. The children move from room to room with a different teacher for each subject. The system works well for better integrated children, but chances are not too good for an impaired child finding an efficient "giving and receiving" relationship with a teacher. Children are also maturing physically, which moves them away from parents.

The combination of age and circumstance brings the students into the first "natural selection" process for the choosing of personal friends. Here is a large group and a high percentage have a significant dependent attachment to their parents which they handle by turning away from the parents. They form themselves into groups determined by the lifestyle of "giving and receiving" into which they were programmed by their mothers. Those with the lowest level of functional self do the greatest rejection of the parents, and therefore have the most emotional "needs" to be met in the group. There are other groups made up of successive better levels of integration. Groups are organized around "leaders" and "best friend" principles. The group quickly becomes an active network of triangles. All the students have been well schooled in relationship-oriented experience, and seeking and giving "love" and approval. They put as much energy into the relationships in the group as they formerly devoted to their mothers, with primary energy into the current "best friend," with whom there is frequent contact and endless telephone calls. In general, the groups are "anti-parent" and "secret" and each has its own specified type of activity determined by intensity of the negative "cut-off" with parents. The group prescribes language, dress, and behavior. A minimal amount of excessive behavior is necessary to be accepted, but the most approved member is one that shows the most "cool" in taking chances at getting caught. There is a premium on "standing up" to parents and authorities, and standing up to someone means doing or saying something that will "get a reaction" from the parent. There is satisfaction from shocking and getting reactions from parents, not because they enjoy hurting (as is commonly assumed), but from the satisfaction of "being a grown-up self." This is the level of thinking for someone with this level of undifferentiation.

There is one important aspect of teenage groups which has to do with relationships with parents at home. They are still *financially dependent on parents* and the parents are *emotionally dependent* on the youngsters, who still have the ability to dissolve the selfs of the parents. It is easy for parents to yield to meeting excessive demands for money and privileges, in the hope the youngster has finally changed.

The daughter in this clinical profile belonged to one of the middle range "groups" in her school. There were antiestablishment things her group would not do that was commonplace for lower level groups. There were activities in her group that better integrated groups would not do. In the junior high years her activities included staying out late, staying overnight with her "best friend" without telling the parents, "cool" parties, shoplifting, and the use of four-letter words that would shock others. The group placed high approval on those who reported escapades on beer, and wine, and marijuana, and who were most successful in "making out" with boys. In high school her dress became more extreme, and involvement with sex, drug use, and the use of obscene language was routine. She had run away to live with her boy friend so many times, after fights with her mother, that the family hardly reacted to it. She was moderately addicted to hard drugs supplied by her boy friend. She had hepatitis from drug injections, and she was in two serious car wrecks. She and the boy friend were living together when she managed to graduate from high school. She tried college but dropped out and then moved across country with her boy friend where they have a car, an apartment, and they manage to live without working except for part-time jobs in antiestablishment activity.

In the meantime, the goal-directed younger son has led an orderly life. He was an honor graduate in high school and he was not functionally affected by his sister's erratic course. He maintained close contact with his parents without being affected by their emotional involvement with his sister. He is now nearing the end of college which will be followed by graduate school. He has a long-time girl friend from high school days who went to another college, and they plan to marry when the reality of education and finances permit.

One last item is important in this clinical profile. The daughter's boy friend, also a refugee from his parental family, has the exact pattern of investment of self in the other as the daughter had originally with her mother, and as she has had in subsequent relationships. They can "read" each other's feelings from facial expressions, voice, and movement; each feels pity for the other at any sign of inner pain, and they somehow are able to keep the intense "giving to each other" in equilibrium as long as neither works and they devote self fully to the other. From observing their relationship in the past, neither is able to cope with serious illness, injury, or other serious reality need, and either will run away from the disabled one. Their emotional cocoon can continue fairly stable as long as they can keep the total investment in each other, and as long as neither works and the cocoon is not threatened by inner or outer forces. This girl could have been a periodically hospitalized, marginally adjusted mental patient if she had been born a generation earlier.

Life patterns predictable with systems theory. A significant range of life patterns comes within reasonable predictability with knowledge currently available from systems theory. There is evidence that the scope and accuracy of predictability can be greatly extended with relatively little research. The more man knows about the human phenomenon, the more he should be able to ultimately use it in the monumental problems that rob him of conscious choice in decisions that affect him and his environment.

· The patterns predictable about the future course of a family, from information available when two people are married, will convey some notion of the possibilities, and the current trends in society. The one most important information would be a reasonably accurate estimate of the levels of differentiation of self in each spouse. The second most important information would be an accurate estimate of emotional functioning in the families of origin of each spouse, the function that each had in that family, and efficiency with which he or she functioned. The next information would be the over-all functioning patterns within each spouse. The difficulty comes from getting reasonably accurate estimates. It is impossible to do a differentiation of self estimate except over a period of years or an entire segment of a life. There are too many different functional levels of self in which self functions better than the basic level or less than the basic level. The functional shifts of those with lower levels of self are so great, and they operate for such long periods of time, it is hard to find an average baseline. Function shifts include appending one self onto another, or permitting other selfs to append themselves to one's own self. However, the estimates of average functioning levels, over long periods of time, are accurate for most clinical and theoretical purposes.

One of the most important functional patterns in a family has to do with the intensity of the unresolved emotional attachment to parents, most frequently to the mother for both men and women, and the way the individual handles the attachment. All people have an emotional attachment to their parents that is more intense than most permit themselves to believe. At one extreme are those who continue to live within the parental emotional field. There are those who deny the attachment while living near the parents and who do more definite "cutoffs" from parents than others who live at a distance. At the other extreme are those who cut off from parents and leave home and never return nor communicate with them again. There are those who cut off from their own parents and append themselves to the families of their spouses. The most common pattern is the partial cutoff in which the nuclear family lives away and maintains a token contact with parents. However the issue is handled, *the denied emotional attachment to the past replicates itself with one's spouse and one's children.* This can be said another way: *The more one denies the attachment to the past, the less choice one has in determining the pattern with his own wife and children* (as if he has much to begin with). It can also be accurately said that a divorce or threatened divorce, or an emotional problem in a child, is implicit evidence of an unresolved emotional attachment to the parental families.

There are over-all patterns in a family that can be predicted before marriage. The degree of undifferentiation in the spouses will predict the degree of the emotional fusion early in the marriage, when the two "pseudo-selfs" fuse into a "we-ness." The symptoms from fusion come at marriage or shortly after. There is one way that almost all use to one degree or another. This is *emotional distance* from each other, which is hard to maintain over time. There are three important patterns to deal with this. One is *marital conflict* which permits them to keep reasonable emotional distance most of the time and intense closeness during "make-ups." Another pattern is the *continuation of the fusion.* One spouse either volunteers or is coerced into the dependent or "number two position," leaving the other as the functional decision maker for the "we-ness." The one in the dependent position may be fairly comfortable as a no-self beginning, but if continued for long periods, the dependent one will become dysfunctional with physical illness, emotional illness, or a social dysfunction such as drinking or irresponsible behavior. The third pattern is *transmission of the problem to the child.* This will be the next section because it is important in the family and society. All of these patterns are ways man has to deal with overcloseness. All have to do with the way the family impinges other family members in an effort to maintain living space for self. Denying and cutting off emotional contact with parental and extended families increases the intensity of symptoms in a family. Opening up meaningful relationships with the parental and extended families automatically reduces the tension and symptoms in the entire nuclear family. This has implications for man and his living space in society.

Family protection process. The goal here is to elaborate on the more theoretical description in the last section. Descriptively, the family projection process is a triangular emotional process through which two powerful people in the triangle reduce their own anxiety and insecurity by picking a defect in the third person, diagnosing and confirming the defect as pitiful and in need of benevolent attention, and then ministering to the pitiful helpless one, which results in the weak becoming weaker and the strong becoming stronger. It is present in all people to some degree, and by overcompassion in poorly integrated, over-emotional people, powered by benevolent overhelpfulness that benefits the stronger one more than the recipient, and is justified in the name of goodness and self-sacrificing righteousness. The prevalence of the process in society would suggest that more hurtfulness to others is done in the service of pious helpfulness than in the name of malevolent intent.

This is a process through which most parents permanently impair one or more of their children to some degree. Specifically, it begins with an overanxious mother devoted to being the best possible mother and having the most wonderful child. The child becomes anxious in response to the mother's anxiety. Instead of controlling her own anxiety, she anxiously tries to relieve the child's anxiety by more anxious mothering, which makes the child more anxious, which further drives her anxious mothering, etc. She can never slow down to see her own part. Instead, she seeks for causes for the problem in the child and goes to physicians seeking a positive diagnosis and a new avenue through which to structure and focus the mothering. In periods of calm, she might neglect reality needs of the child. The process continues through the years until the child is functionally impaired. This is most intense in the child who later develops schizophrenia, the most severe form of mental illness. Eventually she seeks the help of a psychiatrist who, in the implementation of sound principles of medicine, examines the patient, diagnoses his illness, and agrees to treat the illness as a pathology in the patient. The medical model reenacts another step in the family projection process. An essential ingredient in the process is the mother's perception of the child as pitiful. By the time this severe process has reached an advanced stage, the patient is so functionally impaired and so programmed to act the part of the pitiful one that the process is irreversible. The father plays a passive role in the mother-child relationships, adding his approval of her actions. In the beginning, the process is a triangle which consists in mother as one strong person soliciting and getting approval of the other strong person to take definitive action about the third. In the process of commitment, it is the two parents acting as one agent, soliciting and getting approval of another, the psychiatrist and legal commitment procedure, to take the action about the patient.

There are many less severe family projection processes in which a child is less severely impaired. In these, it is a relatively simple process to remove the child from the projection process by asking the parents to assume the working premise that the problem is in the parents and not in the child, in which the child is never seen as a "patient." In the act of seeing the child, there is some degree of automatic confirmation that the child is "sick." Though this working approach is criticized by conventional psychiatry, it has been the repeating experience with systems therapy that results are better and faster if the child is never involved in any process designed to modify the parents.

The force that drives the family projection process is intense. It is an automatic emotional force that functions to keep the patient sick. The full power of the force is most clearly seen in "action language" in families with severely impaired patients, when family anxiety is high. The family will overextend itself to do anything for the patient as long as treatment is for the patient. It has been a common experience in expensive private mental hospitals to have families exhaust their financial reserves in futile efforts for improvement in the patient. There are many who never complain about cost and who are complimentary of the hospital's efforts as long as the patients do not improve. The same families can become disgruntled and remove the patient from the hospital if the patient does improve. The process can be aptly described by the following analogy. The family approaches the psychiatrist with a problem in one family member that, from a systems viewpoint, is the product of years of "sinning" throughout the family. The group is adamant in its demands that the product of the "sinning" be removed without doing anything to disturb family patterns.

The same projection process operates in psychiatry. There have been reports about family therapy in the literature for almost twenty years. One of the best family research studies in the past decade was designed to keep mental patients out of hospitals. It was carefully designed and controlled, and it demonstrated that about eighty percent of patients already approved for admission to a public mental hospital could be kept at home and treated with a fraction of the professional personnel and time and expense that was required for the control group, and that the end result after a five year follow-up was much superior to the conventionally treated group. The scientific reports about it appeared periodically until the final book report five years ago. Reviews of the work in professional journals described the work as "interesting and worthy of further study," etc. One could say that innovations in thinking and procedure require time for acceptance. There is evidence that this force in psychiatry is part of the same force in all families, and also in society. Society probably spends more time and energy in futile attempts to remove the products of "sinning" than in trying to stop the "sinning."

Clinical patterns during therapy. The changes that occur in successful therapy are essential for understanding the full range of functioning in emotional systems. When any key member of an emotional system can control his own emotional reactiveness and accurately observe the functioning of the system and his part in it, and he can avoid counterattacking when he is provoked, and when he can maintain an active relationship with the other key members without withdrawing or becoming silent, the entire system will change in a series of predictable steps. This is the essence of change in emotional systems, which is proving even more effective than working with multiple family members at the same time. This is a method of teaching one person the predictable functioning of systems and supervising his effort to modify his functioning in ongoing relationships. It is not "therapy" in the usual sense. These basic principles have been successfully used in a variety of small social systems.

In general, all the patterns in a system are more pronounced when anxiety is high. This involves every pattern, including the more microscopic triangle patterns, to the larger ones that result in emotional outbreaks and symptoms, to the broader ones involved in the projection process. By the same token, any process that lowers the anxiety reduces the intensity of the patterns. For instance, the functioning of the triangle patterns is not observable in a completely calm system. One of the most effective ways of calming a tense system is through a motivated head of the system, usually the one parent who is most motivated. When an unsure, changeable parent can become more sure of his own operating principles, and he can calmly state his position without trying to force others, the calming trend is often dramatic. The same applies to the heads of small social and work groups. An anxious system is one in which members of the group are isolated from each other, and communication between group members is in underground gossip. Anything that improves open communication will reduce the tension, as an initial step to more definitive efforts to modify the system.

One principle about differentiating change is probably more important than all the others. Differentiation begins when one family member begins to more clearly define and openly state his own inner life principles and convictions, and he begins to take responsible action based on convictions. This is in contrast to principles derived from the rest of the family. It may require months or longer for this one to become reasonably sure within himself. The remainder of the family opposes this differentiating effort with a powerful emotional counterforce, which goes in successive steps: (1) "You are wrong," with volumes of reason to support this; (2) "Change back and we will accept you again"; and (3) "If you don't these are the consequences," which are then listed. The accusations commonly list indifference, meanness, lack of love, selfishness, coldness, the sadistic disregard for others, etc. When the differentiating one defends himself, or counterattacks, or falls silent, he slips back into the old emotional equilibrium. When he can finally stay on his own calm course, in spite of the togetherness forces, the accusations reach a peak and quickly subside. The opposition then expresses a single statement of appreaciation at the conviction and strength of the differentiating one and the entire group pulls up to the new level attained by the first. Later, another member of the group will start his or her own effort at the better definition of self. The togetherness opposition to individuation, or differentiation, is so predictable that differentiation does not occur without opposition from the togetherness forces.

Overlenient parents. The permissive parent appears to be rapidly replacing the strict disciplinarian parent in our society. Whatever the forces involved, overlenient parents tend to blame society for the misbehavior of their children. This includes blaming schools, blaming authorities for failing to eliminate harmful forces such as drugs, and the failure of helping agencies to change the problem early. Disciplinarian parents tend to blame themselves to each other. The children of permissive parents tend to blame parents for lack of love, and children of disciplinarian parents blame the parents for cruelty. The net result is an increasing trend to blame society for the problem and to expect society to find solutions. These are over-all trends.

The basic pattern in the overlenient family is similar to the one described in the first clinical profile. The average of these parents are intelligent, overdevoted people who have made a life-long project of doing the best for their children. They have studied and read and tried to implement the best child rearing practices. Initially the mothers try to relieve the symptoms of the total giving of love to the child, which is the core of the family projection process. The process has the same pattern whether the end point is psychosis or behavior problems. It is a bit more intense in those who become psychotic. There feelings of deprivation and demands for love are more submerged in the psychosis. The behavior problem child feels deprived if he fails to receive the total love for which he was programmed. The process continues until the family exhausts itself trying to meet demands. The same pattern continues in society with the child "feeling" his attacks as justification for society's failure in meeting his basic "rights." Societal attitudes participate in the process. A parent can declare a child "out of parental control" and the juvenile court relieves the parents of responsibility and continues the focus on the child.

One interesting observation is important theoretically. An occasional overlenient parent, usually the father, will attempt a "firm" stand with a behavior problem child. A person at this level of emotional integration does not comprehend differentiation and goal-directed development of his own life principles. He is a relationship-oriented person who perceives "control" as controlling the life of the other. He attempts to control the child by physical force and becomes as punitive and mean on that side as he had been overlenient on the other. The degree of nonviolent overleniency on one side can shift to the same undifferentiated degree of violent, cruel, meanness on the other side. This is important on a societal level.

Societal Problems from an Emotional Systems View

All of the people who were, or who are, members of families replicate the same emotional patterns in society. Family and societal emotional forces function in reciprocal equilibrium to each other, each influencing the other and being influenced by the other. This section will be devoted to a spectrum of societal patterns.

Functional level of differentiation of self. There are only a few areas in which societal patterns are slightly different from family patterns. Most of these have to do with the ways leaders come into, or are selected, for policy-making responsibility. The past twenty-five years, society appears to have been slipping into a functionally lower level of differentiation, or emotional regression. There have been upswings and slumps with a marked downswing during most of the 1960s, and an apparent upswing in the early 1970s. These observations are based on the same criteria used to estimate family functioning, which is the amount of principle determined "self" in comparison to the "feeling orientation" which strives for an immediate short-term feeling solution to the anxiety of the moment. The over-all mode of operation in the past decade has been similar to the unsure, overlenient "no-self" parent in dealing with the emotional demands of his immature teenage child. The pattern belongs in the mid range between the poorly differentiated family that still operates on a fairly orderly course that is relatively free of symptoms, and the chaotic paralyzed family inundated by feelings and impulse. This mid range pattern is similar to the intense triangle between parents and overwhelmed child who fluctuates between compliant niceness, facile intellectual discourses on his rights, and a medium amount of retaliation and threats. Originally, the fusion operated mostly with mother, with father on the periphery. He originally had a viewpoint different from mother, but his pseudo-principles and ideas about responsibility were not sufficiently firm to stand against the strong emotional forces when he entered the emotional arena on the mother's side. He lost his pseudo-self to the mother in the intense polarization between parents and child. His notions about responsibility were washed out in this more intense emotional field.

The triangling process in a large family will help illustrate the process in society. It may begin with conflict between a parent and child. When another takes sides emotionally, he is potentially triangled. When he talks (to influence others) or he takes action based on feelings, he is actively triangled. Each person who becomes involved can involve others until a fair percentage of the group is actively taking sides. The controversy is defined on "right" and "wrong" issues, and often as victimizer and victim. In societal conflict, those who side with the "victim" are more likely to demonstrate and take activist postures. Those who "feel more responsible" for the total group will side with the parental side. They are more likely to stay silent or to take action in letters to the editor, or to actively counteract the activists. One interesting group of activists is made up of members of professional and scientific organizations who attempt to use knowledge and social status to further entangle the triangular emotional system. To summarize the process, it begins with emotional tension in a bipolar situation, it spreads by involving emotionally vulnerable others, it is fed by emotional reactiveness and response to denial and accusation and it becomes quiescent when emotional energy is exhausted. There are several ways it can be started, intensified, deintensified, or stopped. It can be started by one person who, intentionally or unintentionally, touches an emotional trigger in the second. The triggered person characteristically defends or counterattacks which adds emotional fuel. It can be deintensified or stopped by a calm person who stays in "low key" contact without defending self or counterattacking. The words used in triangular emotional exchange, based on rational thinking, are usually not heard by the other except to defend or prepare a rebuttal. The words can be heard only after the emotion is reduced. The triangle emotional system is most intense when anxiety is high. It disappears when the system is calm.

There is other evidence that the functional level of differentiation in society has been lower the past few decades. It would be the number and intensity of the forms of emotional disruptions, such as major crimes, riots, etc. If the functioning level of differentiation, or maturity, or responsibility is lower, how can we account for it? It is factual that the functioning level of an individual can vary from day to day, or it can be up for most of a life, or down. There is also a functioning level for a family unit that can fluctuate through good periods and bad. There is fair evidence that man functions at his best under adversity or when he is challenged. Until the mid 1960s, I considered society's slump to be functional, and perhaps a cyclical phenomena related to the depression of the 1930s or to World War II, and that after World War II man became lazy and greedy as he luxuriated in the greatest period of material plenty and freedom from want in his existence. I was guessing that he meet another challenge and rise to the occasion. After the mid 1960s there was more evidence of an even lower level of societal functioning. There was more feeling-oriented action and less long-term principle planning, more "rights" thinking and less "responsibility" thinking. The over-all pattern was closer to that of a family with a problem child, giving into emotional demands, hoping the problem would go away.

Society appears to be much more similar to a family with an intense "undifferentiated family ego mass," than the less intense emotional fusion of twenty-five years ago. The members of society are fused into each other and are more emotionally dependent on each other, with less operating autonomy in the individual. Emotional events are more similar to those "within an ego fusion" than to events between relatively autonomous people. A relatively differentiated self can live a more orderly life whether alone, or in the middle of the human pile. A poorly differentiated person is not productive alone. Powerful emotional "togetherness" forces draw him into the discomfort of fusion, with the impingement of self on self and the counter mechanisms to deal with too much closeness. Society has been gravitating into the human piles in large urban centers where the individual may become more alienated from his fellowman than before. Group activity, including encounter groups, and promiscuous sexuality become panicky pretenses to overcome the alienation of too much fusion proximity to others. In the past, man has used physical distance to relieve the tension of emotional fusion. Physical distance is harder to arrange with an exploding population.

I believe a spectrum of problems associated with population explosion play a major role in man's deeper anxieties. There are the obvious spiraling problems of rapidly developing technology, providing more and more people with the high standard of living made possible by the technology, maintaining an economy in which the masses provide the market for the products that keep technology operating, the rapid depletion of world's natural resources that supply the technology, and pollution of the environment with the byproducts of technology and man. The process has proceeded to point that certain natural resources are nearing exhaustion, the balance of nature is being disturbed, and the life of man is approaching jeopardy. These are some of the problems that belong in fields of expertise other than my own.

The main idea presented here is that society appears to be functioning on a less differentiated emotional level than twenty-five years ago, that this may be related to the disappearance of land frontiers. Man has long used physical distance as a way of "getting away from" inner emotional pressures. It was important for him to know there was new land for him, even if he never went to it. The end of World War II was an important nodal point in a process in which the world became functionally smaller at a more rapid rate. That was before man had much awareness of population growth. After the war, the colonial powers began to grant independence to their colonies, and it became more difficult for citizens to get away to a colony. After the war there were the rapid technological advances in instant communication and rapid travel. If it was hard for him to comprehend this one year, he need not wait long for the next advance that could not be ignored. In little more than one decade plane travel developed so fast it was difficult to cross an ocean on a ship and television had brought far away events into his living room.

Man can "know" something intellectually a long time before he "knows" it as part of his total being. The main sensory modalities that operate in the emotional reactiveness of relationships are vision and hearing. It might be that television, which uses both modalities, was the most important factor in making man intellectually and emotionally aware of his earth. It was harder to doubt that his earth was one "colony" after 1969 when his television screen took him on an audiovisual tour of the moon with his planet Earth in the background.

Now, back to man and his emotional reactiveness as he began to "know" the last land frontier was gone and he could no longer "get away from" the old to something new. The concept of differentiation of self is important. At the more differentiated end of the scale is the person who can "know" with his intellect, and who can also "know," or "be aware of," or "feel" the situation with his emotional system. He has reasonable ability to keep an operational differentiation between intellect and emotions and to take action on the fact of intellectual reasoning, that opposes his feelings and the truth of subjectivity. A small percentage of the population has this level of differentiation. An example of a person lower on the differentiation scale will illustrate another functional level. This person has a well functioning intellect but intellect is intimately fused with his emotional system, and a relatively small part of his intellect is operationally differentiated from his emotional system. He can accurately "know" facts that are personally removed, such as mathematics and the physical sciences, but most of his "intellect" is under the operational control of the emotional system, and much of his total knowledge would be more accurately classified as an intellectual emotional "awareness," without much differentiation between intellect and feelings. He may have had some distant intellectual awareness, from school and science exhibits, that the earth is a planet, but his first real "awareness" came when he could "experience" it with his intellect and his total emotional, cellular self, all at the same time, during the Apollo space program. The person at this level of differentiation does not commonly have a clearly formed notion of fact, or differences between truth and fact, or fact and feeling, or theory and philosophy, or rights and responsibility, or other critical differentiations between intellectual and emotional functioning. Personal and social philosophy are based on the truth of subjectivity and life decisions are based more on feelings and maintaining the subjective harmony. A high percentage of the population, probably a majority, are in various subgroups of this broad category. At the lower levels of differentiation are those whose intellect is so submerged in the emotional system that intellect operates more in the service of the emotions than separately. They come nearer "experiencing " the world through the emotional side of their fused intellectual-emotional system than "knowing" through their intellect. They learn best by "experiencing" new situations. They are probably more accurate when they say, "I feel that . . . " about an intellectual opinion or conviction than if they used "I believe that. . . . " They live in subjective worlds in which lives are vulnerable to symptoms when anxiety is high. A high percentage of the population, probably over one-third, is in sub-groups in this category.

When I first developed the differentiation of self scale in the late 1950s, I expected people would group themselves more evenly on the scale than has been the experience. With increasing experience with a wide range of people, there is evidence that most of the population is below 50 on the scale. The population is distributed with most in the 20 to 45 scale range, with a small percentage above 50, and the highest levels in a decreasingly smaller group up to a few in the 65 to 70 range.

The functional level of differentiation in society is lower than twenty-five years ago. It is postulated that it is a "functional" shift related to man's anxiety about the disappearance of land frontiers, gradually brought more into his awareness by the "decreasing size of the earth" and the increasing evidences of population growth. Man's reaction to being trapped on earth is similar to the emotional process of feeling "trapped" in other situations. The emotional closeness of marriage is commonly referred to by terms such as *trapped* or *caught.* There is the common syndrome called "weekend neurosis," "cabin fever," etc., to refer to the discomfort of "too much closeness" between husband and wife. It is common for both to look forward to these periods together, for one to enjoy it and the other be allergic to it, and for the total experience to be uncomfortable. There is a similar experience in larger groups, together for vacations, etc. This might be best described by a comment from a "weathered in" group in a resort hotel. "This has been like the crowd on a cruise ship. There is no way to get away from these people until we reach the next port." In the past twenty-five years man has found other ways to deal with the anxiety of overcloseness. The population has become more mobile. Families now have choices of work that require frequent moves for the entire family, or other jobs that require one spouse to travel most of the time. There is very little opportunity for new "colonies" anywhere on earth.

Societal projection process. The family projection process is as vigorous in society as in the family. The essential ingredients are anxiety and three people. Two people get together and enhance their functioning at the expense of a third, the "scapegoated" one. Social scientists use the word "scapegoat." I prefer the term *projection process* to indicate a reciprocal process in which the twosome can force the third into submission, or the process is more mutual, or the third can force the other two to treat him as inferior. The one biggest group os societal scapegoats is the hundreds of thousands of mental patients in institutions. People can be held there against their wishes, or stay voluntarily, or they can literally force society to keep them there as objects of pity. All society gains something from the benevolent posture to this segment of people. A fair percentage of "inmates" are too impaired to ever exist outside the institution where they will remain for life as permanently impaired objects of the projection process.

One example will illustrate an important principle that can help understand scapegoated people. A hospitalized mental patient was permitted a town pass. En route back to the hospital, hallucinated voices resulted in his becoming immobile as he tried to board a busy bus. The bus company complained about the hospital permitting "sick" patients in town. A usual psychiatric approach would have been to tell the patient he was "too sick" to go to town and passes would be suspended until he was "better." Instead, this patient was told that town passes were being suspended until he learned to behave himself in public. He practiced hard trying to learn to act normally in spite of voices. Within a week he asked for another pass. The town trip was uneventful and within another week he was out of the hospital and back at work supporting his family, with some voices still present. The voices disappeared after a brief period of out-patient therapy. If told the passes were suspended because of "sickness" until he was "better," he would have been confronted with two conditions out of his direct control. When put in terms of "behavior" that offended others, he had a situation he could control, and he did. Confronted with "sickness" and "better," he could have gone into chronic illness, passively waited to get better. A systems approach that avoids diagnosis has been superior in a wide range of problems. Most people are put in mental hospitals because of odd or uncontrollable behavior. Hospitalization has been markedly shorter for those put there for "unacceptable behavior" than similar patients hospitalized for "sickness."

The conventional steps in the examinations, diagnosis, hospitalization, and treatment of "mental patients" are so fixed as a part of medicine, psychiatry, and all interlocking medical, legal, and social systems that change is difficult. There are other projection processes. Society is creating more "patients" of people with functional dysfunctions whose dysfunctions are products of the projection process. Alcoholism is a good example. At the very time alcoholism was being understood as the product of family relationships, the concept of "alcoholism as a disease" finally came into general acceptance. There might be some advantage to treating it as a disease rather than a social offense, but labeling with a diagnosis invokes the ills of the societal projection process, it helps fix the problem in the patient, and it absolves the family and society of their contribution. Other categories of functional dysfunctions are in the process of being called sickness.

The most interesting of the new group of "sick" people are criminals. Society has followed the same course in dealing with people who seriously offend society, as anxious parents in dealing with the difficult teenage child. Like the parents, society (the people who make up society) has an over-all overemotional involvement with impaired children which helps to create the orientation for later criminal behavior. When the first antisocial act occurs, society follows the same feeling oriented, "band-aid" type interim action as parents who hope the problem will go away. The same posture continues through successive offenses, multiple arrests, trials, imprisonment, "rehabilitation programs" that fail, etc. During the past twenty years, an overlenient society has passed laws and made rules that further foster the development and preservation of criminals. The total trend is seen as the product of a lower level of self in society. If, and when, society pulls up to a higher level of functioning such issues will be automatically modified to fit the new level of differentiation. To debate such a specific issue in society, with the amount of intense emotion in the issue, would result in non-productive polarization and further fixation of current policy and procedures.

A universal target of the projection process is the scapegoating of vulnerable minority groups. The necessary ingredients for this are anxiety and people. For over a century, the Negro has been the main object of the projection process to minority groups. Now that this has been greatly modified, the process will find new objects. It would appear that the process will focus on another group of "unfortunates."

The most vulnerable new groups for objects of the projection process are probably welfare recipients and the poor. These groups fit the best criteria for longterm, anxiety relieving projection. They are vulnerable to become the pitiful objects of the benevolent, oversympathetic segment of society that improves its functioning at the expense of the pitiful. Just as the least adequate child in a family can become more impaired when he becomes an object of pity and oversympathetic help from the family, so can the lowest segment of society be chronically impaired by the very attention designed to help. No matter how good the principle behind such programs, it is essentially impossible to implement them without the built-in complications of the projection process. Such programs attract workers who are oversympathetic with less fortunate people. They automatically put the recipients in a "one down" inferior positon, and they either keep them there, or get angry at them.

A recent proposal was considered for legislation which had a potential for continuing a widespread projection process in society. It was a Child Advocacy Act devleoped after long deliberation by child experts, which was the focus of a White House Conference in 1971. It proposed an expensive, wide network of child care and treatment centers to provide the best possible care for the total spectrum of problems in children. It considered every conceivable problem in children, on a high professional level. Its focus ignored the intense child focus of society, which some experts consider a detriment to society. From a systems orientation, it would attempt to diagnose and treat innumerable problems in children that are the product of the family projection process, it would bypass the parents through whom the problems are most reversible, and it had a high potential for replicating the family projection process in society.

Overlenient public officials in society. In general, the percentage of overlenient public officials in society has paralleled the increase in overlenient parents. It includes administrations in schools, colleges, courts, public agencies, etc. These officials approach social problems with the same general relationship feeling orientation as the parents. This raises the question about whether family patterns influence society, or the obverse. One postulation is that society either chooses officials who operate at the same level of society, or society pressures officials to function the way society functions. The college riots in past years are good examples. Most of the presidents were as ineffective in dealing with the crises as overlenient parents in their homes. There is one suggestion that the rioters chose colleges with unsure administrations and that riots could not have occurred in other colleges. Some presidents were tied by overlenient faculty members with tenure. Most of the evidence supports the thesis that the emotional orientation is set by society and such public officials are slowly forced into that mold. There is a group of judges whose decisions routinely are attacked by social forces that demand a more "no-self" feeling orientation. The police occupy a special place in the social system. They are charged with maintaining law and order in a more lawless society. It would require a person with a high level of differentiation to meet requirements of total firm fairness. There would be enough well differentiated people for this only by depriving other professions. A less differentiated person would automatically go either toward leniency or cruelty. It would be impossible for police to operate without some counterreactive cruelty. Society is quick to charge "brutality" and force police into the mold.

Humanitarian, responsive, sensitive. Society now places emphasis on these qualities in public officals. These terms would all apply to the relationship system between a mother and the child with whom she is emotionally overinvolved. It would be considered "humanitarian" to invest so much of self in another person, "responsive" to automatically know the needs of the other, and "sensitive" to be constantly aware of feelings. All are relationship-oriented terms that ignore the field of goal-oriented activity. A well differentiated person would automatically have these qualities, but a focus on them excludes a goal orientation and is more evidence of a lower level of differentiation in society. From long experience with families, the relationship-oriented person, if he continues his course long enough, will eventually meet a crisis in which he operates with a level of punitive cruelty which is the reciprocal opposite of leniency. Perhaps this was part of war crime atrocities.

Summary What kind of evidence is there to support the theoretical notion about differentiation, and to suggest that a higher level of differentiation is better? This systems theory and systems therapy has been used with hundreds of families over a period of twenty years. The no-self parent is a constant phenomenon in any family with emotionally determined major symptoms in any area of the family. Only a fraction of disturbed families are motivated for the emotional stress of moving to higher differentiation. Those who are able to achieve better differentiation come to function far better than the societal level, and to find ways to live calmly and productively in the emotional system of society.

Man and His Environmental Crisis

Systems thinking is not new as applied to astronomy, nature, and the physical sciences, but it is new as applied to man's emotional and relationship functioning. Very few know about this area of systems thinking even though it has been in the professional literature for fifteen years. From long experience in presenting this systems theory to professional audiences, no more than one-third can really "hear." Most of the others react emotionally with doubts or antagonism. So, I approached this presentation with challenge and trepidation. The trepidation comes partially from the difficulty in presenting to any audience, but mostly from the effort to extend systems thinking into societal relationship systems. I have had little direct experience with large social systems and it can be pretentious to even venture into that area. However, I "know" systems thinking applies also to society. The challenge was enough for me to try as hard as possible, in the hope it may stimulate others toward more definitive answers. In the effort to present as clearly as possible to a new audience, I devoted considerable time to background data to provide a base on which the ideas were developed. The main section of the paper may sound like a psychiatric clinical report, but the goal here was to present material from which analogies could be drawn.

This systems approach postulates the environmental problem as having been created by biological man (in contrast to intellectual man) as he has evolved, developed, and propagated; that man has permitted the environmental problem to develop so far he is beginning to threaten his own future existence; that the biological-instinctive-feeling oriented part of man will not provide consistent help in finding solutions; and that constructive solutions to the problem will depend on the highest functioning of intellectual man in directing total man toward solutions. A systems approach strives to view the environmental problem as a functional part of society's other problems, rather than separate from other problems.

In this paper I have presented the working hypothesis that society is in a regression, which may be cyclical in nature but which appears to be in a gradual downward decrease in differentiation of self since World War II. However this low level of functioning came to be, it is a critical factor in any teamwork effort by the total of society.

From a systems standpoint, what are some of the things society might do to modify the environmental problem and what are some reasonable predictable outcomes of the various approaches? Society's most common approach would be emergency, feeling-oriented, fragmented measures directed at a specific symptom. It could even go on to specific legislation "with teeth in it" to apprehend violators. This type of approach would be similar to the distraught family and its crisis-oriented measures to relieve the symptom of the moment. This can lead to the delusion that the problem is solved, a complacency that permits him to continue what he was doing, and then the rude awakening with new and more serious crises, and a basic problem that grows worse. These are some of the characteristics of efforts at corrective measures that make the problem worse and worse. It is easy now to see corrective activity, most of which is good, which attacks a symptom here and another there, which leads people to believe they are working out a solution while the basic problem remains unchanged. The various "ecology" programs to limit the use of pesticides, to control air and water pollution, to recycle waste products, clean up litter, etc., are all positive, but any program directed at symptoms as they surface can well lead to missing more basic issues and a long-term "making the problem worse."

Any approach to the environmental problem must take into account the current lower functioning level of society. Any issues that are settled by public debate and congressional action will automatically reflect the average level of society and emerge with emotionally determined corrective action. Society tends to elect public officials, from local level to congressional level, who reflect the average functioning of society. There are some notable exceptions, but the majority represent the emotionally determined average of society. Whatever happens, any proposed solutions should come from the best brains and the highest levels of technical and emotional functioning in society who can lead and set an example. To expose the critical issues to the emotional average level of society would expose the whole program to a lower level of emotionally determined cause-and-effect thinking. Perhaps an agency similar to the Space Agency could accomplish the mission.

There may be some guidelines from the long-term effort toward differentiation in a family. In the beginning, when symptoms are high, it might be indicated to use anxiety relieving measures, such as meetings with the entire family unit or with the parents, the heads of the unit, to reestablish communication and settle disharmony. If the goal is toward long term stability and the differentiation of self, this eventually becomes the effort of one person who can give primary attention to self. This involves the principle that all family members play a part in everything that goes on in the family. It is never possible to really change another person, but it is possible to change the part that self plays. The modification of self requires that person to be sure of self on all life principles that involve himself and his family, to have the courage to take action on his convictions, and to devote primary attention to becoming the most responsible possible person. Most people operate on poorly defined principles and have never devoted much time to their own beliefs. There are repeated principles that are hard to clarify. At such moments of indecision, it is common for people to discuss issues with spouses or other close family members who use this opportunity to sell their own values, which, if accepted, modifies the self of the differentiating one toward a "family self." At such points, if one is to be successful at differentiation of a self, discussion should be with those emotinoally removed from the family, or he could go to the literature, or go into isolation to work it through for himself. A person working toward responsibility in self is always aware of his responsibility to others. As he devotes primary energy to self, he automatically becomes more responsible toward others, and less irresponsibly overinvolved with others. As the differentiating one moves toward more differentiation, the others go through the brief period of attacking, designed to reestablish the old level of togetherness. When the differentiating one is through his first nodal point, then another, and another, and other family members begin the same kind of effort. Such a family is a far more healthy organism with freedom from old regressive symptoms. The family is calm, with a new, more mature level of togetherness and a new ability to responsibly handle problems as they arise.

A more differentiated society would not have as serious an environmental problem as we now have. If society functioned on a higher level, we would have a higher percentage of people oriented to responsibility for self and others, and for the environment, and a lower percentage focused on rights and force and on legal mechanisms to guarantee rights. A more differentiated society could take the present environmental problem and find better solutions than will be possible in our present less differentiated state.

The differentiation of self on a societal level would be hard to implement. In a family, differentiation begins with one responsible family member in a key position. When this person pulls up to a higher level of functioning, then another, and then others automatically do the same. This family, with each focused on the responsibility for self, is automatically more responsible for others. With each responsible for self, there is no longer the intense emotional triangles that impinge certain family members, nor a family projection process in which the stronger family members improve their functional strength at the expense of the weak who become weaker. In our society, the whole of the middle and upper classes of society spend a fair percentage of their time, energy, and money being concerned about and trying to be helpful to the less fortunate. The effort activates the family projection process and the well-to-do segment of society, through the projection process, further impairs the less fortunate. Man has a responsibility to those less fotunate. Responsible man fulfills such responsibilities automatically. If the most influential segment of society could work toward the differentiation of self, it would automatically spread through the less influential segments and really benefit the less fortunate segment and raise the functional level of all society. The powerful togetherness forces in society oppose any efforts at differentiation of self. The lower the level of differentiation, the harder it is to start a differentiating effort. The togetherness forces at the present are intense. However, any differentiation in any key person in society automatically rubs off on others. Anyone who moves in this direction benefits society.

The population growth is one factor that is of key importance in the environmental problem and one under direct control of man's emotional system. Sex and reproduction is an instinct. This has to be considered in any effort to control population growth. The current decrease in birth rate is interlocked with numerous factors, as are most of the various aspects of environemtal problems.

Finally, I think the word *crisis* should be removed from the term *environmental crisis* and replaced by a term implying a long-term process. Our society is oriented to the use of cause-and-effect thinking and instituting crash solutions directed at symptoms which lull people into the belief the problem is solved. Man's disharmony with his environment is a long-term evolutionary process and if it continues man may exterminate himself. The thesis here is that man is not going to change the environment enough to correct the disharmony, and that the ultimate change will require an order of change in man he is not yet able to contemplate.

IV
Applications

Chapter 19

Problems of Medical Practice Presented by Families With A Schizophrenic Member

By Robert H. Dysinger, M.D.,
and Murray Bowen, M.D.

The practice of general medicine on a special psychiatric ward encountered consistent difficulties which appeared to be manifestations of patterned emotional processes. The medical practice was one part of the clinical services offered a series of family groups with a schizophrenic son or daughter who participated in a project designed to study the emotional problems of the family unit from the vantage point of a long term psychotherapy. The consideration of the difficulties in the medical situation led to an effort to describe and conceptualize characteristic modes of relating of the family members in much the same way that difficulties in psychotherapy are studied as derivatives of emotional processes.

The project of which this work was one part has been described elsewhere (Bowen 1957, 1959, 1960). A series of seven family groups consisting of both parents and a schizophrenic son or daughter participated for periods ranging from four to thirty-three months. The clinical work centered in a psychotherapy designed for the family unit. During the period of treatment the families lived on a special psychiatric ward operated by the project staff.

The medical work was carried out in a ward clinic operated by a psychiatrist on the project staff. This service was supplemented as indicated with consultation and other clinical services easily available in a large medical research center. The clinic was structured to operate as much as possible like an outpatient service. The responsibilities of the clinic were carefully defined to distinguish them from psychiatric functions. When an emotional problem was presented for medical attention, the responsibility of the clinic was considered discharged when the nature of the problem had been recognized. The treatment of emotional problems was a psychiatric responsibility, and many things commonly handled symptomatically in medical practice were, in this situation, matters for attention in psychotherapy. The doctor necessarily dealt with those emotional problems that operated to impair the medical functioning of the clinic. The experience over a three-year period was that intense emotional forces were consistently present which could cause difficulties of this kind.

The total clinical situation afforded continuous direct observation of the functioning of each individual in relation to his family and others both in psychotherapy and on the ward; this provided a view of ongoing family functioning in which the relating in the medical situation could be seen in its current context. It appeared that the turning to and using of medical services was often to a striking extent an enacted emotional process which took the form of an interest in medical diangosis and treatment.

The presence of such a problem was of practical relevance since significant, poorly defined medical problems were not uncommon especially in the parents, and effective medical service was often clearly indicated. The use of the medical setting by the family members for emotional purposes was often so intense as to make it difficult for the doctor to function responsibly as a physician. This was the case whether or not significant medical problems were present, but was minimal on the few occasions of actual medical emergency. The process of settling even trivial medical matters in a satisfactory sensible way was often laborious and difficult. These difficulties were characteristic in the medical work with the parents and the schizophrenic sons or daughters, but were rarely experienced with normal siblings. The histories indicated that the families' use of medical services in the past had been similarly involved in acted out emotional issues.

An example of the problem:

A mother had avoided serious medical consideration of a lower abdominal pain associated with the menses, of gradually increasing intensity over several years' time. She was anxious and tentative in approaching the clinic about it. A consultant in gynecology was asked to examine her. He found a pelvic mass and recommended examination under anesthesia, D&C, and laparotomy if indicated With no mention of it on the ward, the mother consulted practicing gynecologists during visits to the city. One doctor called to describe his experience. He said that the mother had been unwilling to provide a history and asked for his professional opinion on the basis of examination only. He said he had done the best he could for her under difficult circumstances and asked to be informed of the findings if surgery was done in order to check his clinical impression. Later a laparotomy was performed and a rather large fibroid uterus successfully removed.

The numerous difficulties in the medical situation take on some order when seen as manifestations of specific emotional processes. Many observations indicated that the parents and the schizophrenic child discriminated poorly between intense feelings of helplessness and anxiety on the one hand and evidences of medical problems on the other. Much of their functioning appeared to follow from an assumption that feeling helpless was equivalent to being ill, and not feeling helpless was equivalent to being healthy. For example, a person could notice something physical and estimate it to be of no consequence. The estimate might be accurate or not and yet be largely in the service of a denial of feelings of helplessness.

By defining the characteristic ways the family members were dealing with intense feelings of helplessness in the medical situation two general modes of functioning are identified. The first and more common is described as an acting out of feelings of helplessness, the second as an acting out of a denial of such feelings.

The first mode of functioning was characteristic of the mothers and the schizophrenic sons or daughters and was also common for the fathers. It could be gross or so subtle as to masquerade for sensible action. The person related himself at each step of his dealings with the doctor in a way that accented helplessness. The decision to arrange an appointment could be avoided and the doctor's attention sought outside the clinic. This took the form of vague allusions to health matters in the context of a social greeting, acting sick or speaking of symptoms to others in the doctor's presence, and messages about vague ailings that the doctor heard as a rumor from others. The doctor could later discover that his response or lack of it had been given the weight of a professional opinion. Under such circumstances, there was ambiguity about whether or not the person was dealing with the doctor in his professional capacity. This ambiguity was frequently present in clinic appointments also when the person related himself as though he were in a social situation.

In speaking of his problem the person emphasized illness. Physical experiences and incapacity were elaborated beyond the actual difficulty. Medical terms were used authoritatively as though they adequately defined the situation. Past histories were distorted and past medical opinions and diagnoses introduced to document a picture of major illness. The emotional tone was commonly grim, urgent, and serious and could be imperiously demanding, plantive, or simple insistent. This feeling was infectious and could tend to hurry the doctor into a view that the problem was actually an emergency. Medical inquiry about specific points and attempts to confirm impressions often met with obtuseness, vagueness, irrelevant elaboration, helpless unresponsiveness, or pressure for treatment.

When the doctor stated an initial clinical impression, the patient often became more thoughtful and at times decided to postpone medical work. A statement that diagnostic study revealed no evidence of a medical problem was often followed by a critical point in the clinical relationship. When a definite diagnosis was made it tended to be seen as the source of all problems. Medical treatment was often complicated by vagueness about symptoms and pressures to prolong the use of medications. With the completion of treatment, a similar critical point in the clinical relationship was often reached.

At such critical points the person could create an unmistakable impression that he found the doctor unsatisfactory. This operated as an intense pressure to alter medical opinion to accommodate to emotional goals. The doctor seemed to be faced with the choice of losing working contact or compromising his best judgment. When such a point was reached the extent of the emotional use of the medical situation was unequivocally apparent. This anxious encounter between the emotional process and medical judgment could then resolve toward a more adequate recognition of the actual problems.

Throughout the medical relationship, the acted out helplessness appeared to maintain an emotional pressure to induce the doctor to assume a very great responsibility for the intense feelings by virtue of a diagnosis of illness. The person functions as though the action message is—"I feel intensely helpless, therefore I am ill. The doctor must recognize this, and when he has agreed, I then have an answer to my problem." The finding of any physical condition is one of the things that the doctor can do which appears to be taken as at least a token concurrence.

A characteristic example:

A mother in her fifties arranged an appointment several weeks after the family arrived. In the early weeks on the ward she had often commented about a variety of ailments. In the initial appointment she spoke with an urgent plaintiveness of pains in the neck.

Persistence by the doctor developed a reasonable trustworthy history out of much diffuse talk. After a local examination a preliminary clinical impression was conveyed. The mother responded by repeating her own diagnosis as though to ask the doctor's assent. When he replied that his impression was somewhat different, the mother introduced another problem. Further diagnostic study over a number of weeks revealed a minor chronic medical problem which was not responsible for the long standing distresses of which she complained, and supported the view that these were on an emotional basis. The mother's acted out presentation of herself as a chronically ill helpless woman made for difficulty in evaluating her actual medical condition.

A second mode of functioning is described as an acting out of a denial of feelings of helplessness. It was characteristic of the fathers, occurred also in mothers, but was not seen in the son or daughter. Problems were presented in a manner that emphasized the health of the person. Symptoms and incapacity were minimized out of proportion to actual difficulty. Past histories were distorted, the negative findings from previous medical check-ups emphasized, and the value of previous medical efforts minimized to support a picture of physical health. The possibility that a problem was psychological could be given prominence. The emotional tone was commonly casual, friendly, jocular, and appealing, and tended to lull the doctor into a premature view that no problem existed. Medical inquiry encountered vagueness about simple facts, plausible explanations, reassurances that the doctor need not worry, and when anxiety mounted, actual retreating. An opinion that a medical problem existed was the occasion for an anxious point in the clinical relationship. The acted out denial could continue into the treatment situation in the form of a casualness about treatment measures and unreliable reports of progress.

The emotional pressures appear to operate to induce the doctor to assume a responsibility for problems with feelings of helplessness by virtue of a diagnosis of health. The person acts as though he were conveying the message, "I am almost certain that I am not helpless, therefore I am in good health; a doctor must recognize this and when he has agreed I will then be certain of my answer to the problem."

A striking example from the medical history of a father:

After a period of some weeks during which he had noticed difficulties in an important sense organ, he casually mentioned them to a physician friend. His friend apparently sensing that the matter might be of some moment examined him and quickly recognized a serious problem. Appropriate attention from an outstanding specialist was promptly arranged. The indications were that the serious loss of function that resulted was largely a consequence of delay in arranging appropriate medical attention.

On many occasions two or more family members were active about a medical matter. A variation of the acting out of feelings of helplessness could be identified in these situations which differed in that the problem was seen to exist in another rather than in the self. The most common form was a parent's action from concern for the schizophrenic son or daughter, the mother more commonly than the father. The mother's acted out concerns about the father were also significant.

In some situations the concern for the other brought about the medical consultation. In other situations, medical work already initiated by one member could become the focus of the acting out process of a second. The second member might even move to displace the other from his position of dealing with the doctor about his own problem. In a milder form he could simply invite himself to be also present at the other's appointment. The member whose health was being considered might accept the concern of the second member as his own; might go along with it without acceptance; defensively oppose it, or on occasion maintain his own view. The doctor was often looked to for a resolution of the intense differences.

The emotional pressure in this other appeared to operate to induce the doctor to assume a great responsibility for feelings of helplessness by virtue of a diagnosis of illness in the other. The person functions as though he were saying, "I feel helpless, it is because he is ill; a doctor must agree with me, and when he does, I then have an answer to my problem." The most prominent and intense of all the situations involving more than one member were those in which one or both parents acted out intense feelings of helplessness externalized as a medical problem seen in the son or daughter.

Summary and Conclusions

Medical practice with seven families with a schizophrenic son or daughter regularly encountered difficulties in accomplishing medical evaluations and treatment. The use of medical services by the parents and the son or daughter was extensively involved in intense emotional processes. Two modes of relating are described as an acting out of feelings of helplessness and an acting out of a denial of these feelings. A variation is described in which the acting out of feelings of helplessness took the form of a concern about another.

The emotional pressures tended to lead to inaccurate medical overdiagnosis and overtreatment in response to the acted out feelings of helplessness and to inaccurate medical estimates of good health in response to the acted out denial pattern. When medical findings differed from the emotional view, the clinical relationship could reach a difficult point. The problems in the medical experiences appeared to be one clear evidence of general processes pervading the family emotional life.

Chapter 20

Toward the Differentiation of
Self in Administrative Systems

This is a summary of my paper at the 1972 Georgetown Family Symposium. On the program the title was "Toward the Differentiation of Self in the Georgetown 'Family'." A more accurate descriptive title would have been, "My Own Efforts to Practice Principles of the Differentiation of Self in My Administrative Functioning as Head of the Family Faculty and the Family Programs at Georgetown University." I was trying to emphasize the fact that differentiation of self principles apply in all areas of relationships whether it be within the family, or in social or work relationships. I wanted to make this point more by demonstration than by explanation. If a differentiating effort is to be successful, it has to take place in action, as a result of careful private planning, and without previous announcement of one's plan. The subject was timely in 1972. The symposium provided an opportunity to talk about differentiation in administrative systems in general, by talking about my own differentiating efforts from the people associated with me at Georgetown, with my family faculty in the audience of some 1100 people. The over-all result was no more than partially successful. Feelings were high. There had been a high level of overpositive systems therapy enthusiasm at the symposium. I was still trying to shift the feelings toward reality even during my presentation. Some of the audience "heard" the message but most were reacting emotionally without hearing. Now, after two years, I hope that more can hear the subject of that paper.

Basic relationship patterns developed for adapting to the parental family in childhood are used in all other relationships throughout life. The basic patterns in social and work relationships are identical to relationship patterns in the family, except in intensity. Over-all, the emotional process in social and work systems is less intense than in the original family. However, there are exceptions to this in which the intensity of relationships in work systems approximates the intensity in the original family. This is more pronounced in people with lower levels of differentiation who have higher levels of unresolved emotional attachments to their parents. In order to function as adults, people deny the attachments and move toward emotional distance from the parents. The emotional distance is achieved by internal mechanisms while living close to parents, or by physical distance, or by a combination of the two. Those who use physical distance in "cutting-off" from the parents tend to have the most intense relationships with those outside the family. A wide spectrum of people find work relationships to be more useful than social relationships for fulfilling emotional "needs." These intense relationships are often more covert than overt to the casual observer. The better differentiated person has goal directed interests to motivate his life work. A less differentiated person tends to seek relationships at work that satisfy emotional needs. The process of seeking work relationships, in lieu of family relationships, for the fulfillment of emotional needs, is further intensified by administrative policy and by bosses who encourage a "happy family" attitude in the work situation. There are those who refer to the work relationship system as a "family." My thesis is that it might be similar to a family, but it is *not* a family. The tendency to use the term *family* in referring to work systems led to the use of the term *family* in the original title of this paper.

People with better levels of differentiation keep the emotional "needs" of family members sufficiently contained within the family that there is little need to shift emotional needs to relationships outside the family. Parents with better levels of differentiation are more contained people, they are more sure of themselves and clearer about the responsibility of self and responsibility to each other, and important family decisions are based more on the reality of the situation than on the emotion of the moment. These parents handle "administrative" decisions in the family with the same principles used by good administrators in work situations. It is accurate to think of all levels of differentiation of self in work situations just as in families. Less well-differentiated bosses are more inclined to make decisions based on the feeling of the moment than on principle and reality, as it is with less-differentiated parents in the family.

At Georgetown I have utilized knowledge and experience from research, theory, and the practice of family therapy in my effort to function on the best possible level of differentiation. The Georgetown Family Faculty and the various family teaching and training programs have grown slowly around me and my work since 1959. This is the kind of an administrative system that is most vulnerable to becoming involved in all kinds of emotional alliances and intense emotional processes that would make it more like a family. A good percentage of such organizations do not continue for many months or many years before there are major splits and disruptions in the central organization, just as there are in poorly differentiated families. It has been a fascinating challenge to me to find a way toward a reasonable level of differentiation among professional colleagues, who are far more important to me than most employees would be in other situations. I have attempted to use principles, as defined in family systems theory, that I have found useful with families in the clinical situation. The goal is to be as much of a "self" as is possible for me, to always focus as much on me and my functioning as possible, and to permit the others as much latitude as possible toward developing their selfs. In addition to principles that are well known in good administrative functioning, such as clearly defined contracts, there have been some guiding principles from family research back in the 1950s, and from subsequent clinical work in families. In the early stages of family research, a good percentage of my time went into thinking about problems in the staff and in the families, and in offering solutions. This worked very well but everyone was dependent on me for suggesting solutions and the staff was not developing in the direction of assuming responsibility for their own solutions. It was then that I discovered I was being overresponsible for the staff in some areas, and that I was in fact being irresponsible in my own functioning in other areas. My effort went into clarification of my responsibility as head of the research, and functioning responsibly there, without assuming responsibility for others. Very quickly I learned that if there was an emotional issue in the organization, I was playing a part in it, and if I could modify the part I was playing, the others would do the same. This principle has been used through the years in my own family, in my clinical work, and in my administrative functioning. Any time one key member of an organization can be responsibly responsible for self, the problem in the organization will resolve.

A clear-cut issue in the Georgetown Family Faculty will illustrate a way that anxiety in the faculty can be transmitted to trainees. The initial symptom would begin to show when the faculty would become overcritical of trainees in one of the various training programs. The faculty does routine evaluation of the progress of trainees, but when the emotional tension in the system increases, the faculty would tend to become overcritical of the trainees. I often noticed this first when I would tend to become critical of the faculty for being too critical of the trainees, instead of being helpful. At that point my effort would be to restrain my urge to become critical of the faculty, to assume that I was playing a part in the anxiety process, and to devote my time to work on myself. Another way of detecting increasing anxiety in the system is to listen to "the language of the triangles." As tension mounts there is an increasing incidence of emotional issues between people; people tend to withdraw from the group or become silent, or form cliques or alliances between faculty members, or talk or gossip about an absent faculty member. The goal is to listen to the incidence of these phenomena, rather than focusing on the content of what is said. My effort is always to avoid an unwitting focus on the content of issues, and to focus on the process. Sometimes I am able to "catch" myself when I am passing along a bit of news about an absent member. The main goal in these situations is to take stock of my own functioning and to make an effort to modify it. Often I already know the areas in which my functioning has not been as responsible as it should be. Frequently I get so involved with my own work that I tend to lose contact with certain faculty members. Other times I have failed to state my position, or to detriangle myself from some emotional issue between other faculty members. One always has to be aware of emotional issues in the life of an individual faculty member that are being transmitted to the group. Even in those situations, if the faculty is functioning well, it can handle this problem without administrative intervention. One of the biggest hazards in a principle that says, "Be responsible for yourself, and the emotional issue will resolve itself," has to do with the inner orientation of self. It is easy for a person in such a position to say the situation is his "fault" and to accept the "blame" without being responsible. There is a fine line between accepting the responsibility for the part self plays in a situation and accepting the "blame" for it.

The over-all goal of this paper was to indicate that emotional issues in administrative organizations have the same basic patterns as emotional issues in the family, that it is as accurate to think of varying levels of differentiation in work situations as it is in the family, and that the principles toward the differentiation of self in work situations can be as effective as they are in the family. In work situations, the person who works toward the differentiation of self does not have to be the boss or the head of the total organization. His effort can be effective in the area in which he has administrative responsibility. I have outlined some of the basic efforts as I have attempted to use them in the family organization at Georgetown. The result of my effort, in my own family, and at Georgetown, has always left much to be desired. It has been a challenging effort and I am sufficiently satisfied with the result to keep always working on myself. It is accurate to say that if self can do a reasonable job in defining the problem, and if self is able to make some progress in modifying self, the problems within his sphere of responsibility will work toward automatic resolution.

Chapter 21

On the Differentiation of Self

In the months before the Family Research Conference, I had wondered how to do an effective, brief presentation about my family theory and method of family psychotherapy that would be "heard" by more people. My past experience has been that many in my audiences hear the words that go with the theory without really grasping the concepts, and that frequently they perceive the psychoterhapy as an intuitive method that goes with my personality rather than as a method determined by theory. In training family therapists I have found that some trainees quickly grasp the theory, and some never really "know" the theory even after extended periods. I believe a major part of this problem has to do with the theoretical orientation and emotional functioning of the therapists. My theory is best understood if the therapist can listen and observe and function from a position at least partially "outside" the emotional field of the family. Conventional theory and psychotherapy teaches and trains therapists to operate "inside" the emotional field with the patient or the family. In this paper I hope to communicate more clearly my version of what it means to be "inside" or " outside" an emotional system. The Family Research Conference, composed of people important in the family field, was sufficient motivation for me to work at finding a more effective way of presenting my ideas.

In the months preceding the conference, I had been working intensively in a new phase of a long-term effort to differentiate my own "self" from my parental extended family. That effort reached a dramatic breakthrough only a month before the conference. The following week I considered, and then quickly rejected, a presentation about my own family. As the days passed, the factors that favored such a presentation began to outweigh the factors that opposed. The presentation would contain a practical application of the major concepts in my theoretical and therapeutic systems, and, since I know more about my own family than any other family, I decided to use it as an example. I believe and teach that the family therapist usually has the very same problems in his own family that are present in families he sees professionally, and that he has a responsibility to define himself in his own family if he is to function adequately in his professional work. Also, this presentation would be a good example of "family psychotherapy with a single family member." Previous presentations about this subject had only seldom been heard. Another aspect of this enterprise became more appealing as the days passed. For some years I had been aware of the "undifferentiated family ego mass" that exists among the prominent family therapists. The same emotional system exists in the "family" of family therapists that operates in the "sick" families they describe at meetings. In a conference room, talking about relationship patterns in "sick" families, therapists do the same things to each other that members of "sick" families do. They even do the same things to each other while talking about what they do to each other. The final determination of this form of presentation, then, was based on my continuing effort to differentiate my "self" from the "family" of family therapists. I knew, parenthetically, that I would get some of the same reactions from the participants of the conference as I had gotten from my own family members.

In planning the presentation, I had two main goals. The first was to present the clinical material without explanation of theory or the step by step planning that went into it. There was reality to support the plan for this goal. The thirty minutes allowed for the presentation would not permit a review of theory. Though not many participants really "knew" my theory or method of family psychotherapy, I could with good conscience assume they had heard or read my previous papers. Also, I was hoping that clinical material without explanation might bring more indirect awareness of theory than another paper on theory. The second goal was the element of surprise that is essential if a differentiating step is to be successful. Rather than trying to explain that here, I will leave it to the reader to remember as he goes along. The plan was not discussed even with trusted friends. A routine didactic paper about family theory was prepared and the required copies mailed to discussants before the meeting. The stage was set to do either the formal paper or the experience with my own family. I was anxious and sleepless the night before the presentation. Intellect favored the family presentation but feelings demanded that I give up this silly notion and do it the easy way by reading the formal paper. My anxiety would have suffficed to have me abandon the project had I not remembered similar anxiety before each differentiating effort in my own family. Impulses to read the formal paper continued to the very moment of presentation. Even during the presentation I was more anxious than I had anticipated I would be. From past experience, this anxiety was related to the "secret" action move with other family therapists rather than reporting "secrets" about my own family.

There have been special problems in preparing this report for publication. This final version is written in 1970, three years after the conference. The emotional forces that operate at any stage of differentiation have operated in the final step toward publication. These forces will be described in detail later in the paper. On one side has been the anxiety of the original editor and publisher about publishing personal material, and their understandable defensive posture and overconcern about danger. A positive posture that can facilitate further differentiation in me is more important than publication. Anonymous authorship helped to resolve the issues.

Each version of the paper has been a new emotional hurdle for me because I had to respect the realities of publication and at the same time maintain an essential posture for myself. There was a special purpose in presenting the clinical material to the conference without explanation. To publish it as it was presented, to be read by people without knowledge of the special situation, with no awareness of the theory which guided the years of work with my own family, and with a variety of theoretical orientations, would result in the inevitable interpretations and misinterpretations based on each reader's own theoretical bias. The purpose of this written report is to present the theory and the method of psychotherapy based on the theory, and then use the example with my own family to illustrate the clinical application of the theory.

Theoretical Background

Overall description. The total theory is made up of six interrelated concepts, only one of which, the "triangle," will be discussed at this point. One of the basic concepts considers the "triangle" (three-person system) the "molecule" of any emotional system, whether it exists in the family or in a larger social system. The term *triangle* was chosen instead of the more familiar term *triad* which has come to have fixed connotations that do not apply to this concept. The triangle is the smallest stable relationship system. A two-person system is an unstable system that forms a triangle under stress. More than three people form themselves into a series of interlocking triangles. The emotional forces within a triangle are in constant motion, from minute to minute and hour to hour, in a series of chain reaction moves as automatic as emotional reflexes. Knowledge about the functioning of triangles makes it possible to modify the triangle by changing the function of one person in the triangle. The therapeutic system is directed at modifying the functioning of the most important triangle in the family system. If the central triangle changes, and it stays in contact with others, the entire system will automatically change. Acutally, the entire system can change in relation to change in *any* triangle, but it is easier for the system to ignore a more peripheral or less important triangle. The relationship patterns, based on triangles which function through the years in the total family system, are described by other concepts in the theory. Since the clinical example, described in the latter part of this paper, will not be understandable without knowledge of triangles, a later part of this theoretical section will be devoted further to triangles.

Background principles. Some of the basic principles that went into the development of this theory and method of family psychotherapy will help in understanding the theory. My primary effort has gone into making psychotherapy as scientific and predictable as possible. Early in psychiatry I was bothered when "intuition" and "clinical judgment" were used to change the course of a plan of psychotherapy or other forms of psychiatric treatment. Gross examples occur at times of crisis when the staff, reacting emotionally, meets to plan a change in treatment that is based more on "feeling" and "clinical hunches" than on scientific knowledge and theoretical principles. It is commonplace for psychotherapists to make changes based more on feeling perceptions and subjectivity than on clinical fact and objectivity.

The theory was developed in the course of family research. The original focus was on the symbiotic relationship between the mother and the schizophrenic patient. The first research hypothesis, based on the previous years of clinical experience, *knew* the origin and development of schizophrenia as a product of the two-person mother-patient relationship. The hypothesis was elaborated in such detail that it anticipated every relationship problem and every clinical situation that could develop. Psychotherapeutic principles and techniques were developed for each clinical situation. The hypothesis also predicted the changes that would occur with the psychotherapy. When research observations were not consistent with the hypothesis, the hypothesis was modified to fit the new facts, the psychotherapy was modified to fit the hypothesis, and new predictions were made about the results of the psychotherapy.

When an unexpected clinical crisis arose, it was handled on an interim "clinical judgment" basis, but the hypothesis was considered at fault for not "knowing" about the situation ahead of time, and not having a predetermined therapeutic principle. The therapy was never changed to fit the situation except in emergencies. The goal was to change the hypothesis to account for the unexpected crisis, to change the therapy to fit the hypothesis, and to make new predictions about the therapy. Any failure to change in psychotherapy was as much a reason to reexamine and change the hypothesis as any other unpredicted change. Strict adherence to this principle resulted in a theoretical-therapeutic system that was developed as an integrated unit, with psychotherapy determined by the theory. A major advantage was the systematic utilization of change in psychotherapy as a criterion of hypothesis formation. A major disadvantage was that it required a more consistent and higher grade of psychotherapy than is generally available. However, the discipline of the research improved the skill of the therapists. Similar hypotheses and observations were made on the functioning of staff and therapists to the families.

The research plan was designed to fit as closely as possible to other structured research in science. An example would be the principle used in developing the national space program. The first space probe was based on the best scientific knowledge available at that time. The probe brought new scientific facts to be incorporated into the body of knowledge for making the next space probe. This is an example in which science and technology advance in a teamlike manner.

Our original hypothesis about the mother-patient relationship proved to be amazingly accurate in predicting the details of the relationship within this twosome, but it had completely omitted the observations about the way the twosome related to others. An extended hypothesis was developed to include fathers; new families with fathers were admitted to the research, and a method of family psychotherapy was devised to fit the hypothesis. The relationship patterns observed in families with schizophrenia had been hypothesized to be specific for schizophrenia. Once it was possible to finally "see" the patterns in families with schizophrenia, it was possible to see the same patterns in a less intense form in all levels of people with less emotional impairment. We could see the patterns even in "normal" families, and in the staff, and in ourselves. This development constituted a major change in the research, which was then directed away from schizophrenia to all levels of lesser problems and to people without clinical problems. New vistas were opened up for new hypotheses. Since people with lesser problems change more rapidly in family psychotherapy, new observations and further changes in the hypotheses were accelerated. The theory presented here is thus a presentation of the original research hypothesis, modified and extended hundreds of times, with each modification checked many times in and out of the clinical situation. When a body of theoretical thinking is sufficiently accurate so that it no longer requires significant modification, is accurate in describing and predicting the human phenomenon, and can explain discrepancies as well as consistencies, it is called a "concept." The term *theory* has not been used loosely. After there are several consistent concepts, the term is used for the total theoretical system.

The Theoretical Concepts

This family theory is made up of six essential interlocking concepts. All will be described sufficiently so that they can be understood as parts of the total theory. Those that are most important to this presentation will be described in the most detail. The discussion of triangles will be listed last.

Differentiation of self scale. This scale is an effort to classify all levels of human functioning, from the lowest possible levels to the highest potential level, on a single dimension. In broad terms it would be similar to an emotional maturity scale, but it deals with factors that are different from "maturity" concepts. The scale eliminates the need for the concept "normal." It has nothing to do with emotional health or illness or pathology. There are people low on the scale who keep their lives in emotional equilibrium without psychological symptoms, and there are some higher on the scale who develop symptoms under severe stress. However, lower scale people are more vulnerable to stress and, for them, recovery from symptoms can be slow or impossible while higher scale people tend to recover rapidly. The scale has no direct correlation with intelligence or socioeconomic levels. There are intellectually brilliant people far down the scale and less bright ones far up the scale. A majority of the lower socioeconomic group are far down the scale but there are those in the lower social groups who are well up the scale and those from high social groups who are far down the scale.

This is a scale for evaluating the level of "differentiation of self" from the lowest possible level of "undifferentiation," which is at 0 on the scale, to the highest theoretical level of "differentiation," which is at 100 on the scale. The greater the degree of undifferentiation (no-self), the greater the emotional fusion into a common self with others (undifferentiated ego mass). Fusion occurs in the context of a personal or shared relationship with others and it reaches its greatest intensity in the emotional interdependency of a marriage. The life style and thinking and emotional patterns of people at one level of the scale are so different from people at other levels that people choose spouses or close personal friends from those with equal levels of differentiation. In the emotional closeness of marriage the two partial "selfs" fuse into a common "self"; the degree of fusion depends on the basic level of differentiation before the marriage. Both partners want the emotional bliss of fusion but it is extremely difficult to maintain this equilibrium. One of the selfs in the common self becomes dominant and the other submissive or adaptive. Said in another way, the dominant one gains a higher level of functional self and appears "stronger," at the expense of the adaptive one who gave up self and who is functionally "weaker." There is a spectrum of mechanisms that spouses use in adapting to the fusion. These mechanisms will be discussed in the concept that deals with the dynamics of the nuclear family system. The lower the level of differentiation or "basic self" in the spouses the more difficult it is to maintain reasonable emotional equilibrium and the more chronic the disability when adaptive mechanisms fail.

The differentiation of self scale is an effort to assess the basic level of self in a person. The basic self is a definite quality illustrated by such "I position" stances as: "These are my beliefs and convictions. This is what I am, and who I am, and what I will do, or not do." The basic self may be changed from *within* self on the basis of new knowledge and experience. The basic self *is not negotiable in the relationship system* in that it is not changed by coercion or pressure, or to gain approval, or enhance one's stand with others. There is another fluid, shifting level of self, which I call the "pseudo-self," which makes it difficult to assign fixed values to the basic self, and which is best understood with functional concepts. The pseudo-self is made up of a mass of heterogeneous facts, beliefs, and principles acquired through the relationship system in the prevailing emotion. These include facts learned because one is supposed to know them, and beliefs borrowed from others or accepted in order to enhance one's position in relationship to others. *The pseudo-self, acquired under the influence of the relationship system, is negotiable in the relationship system.* The pseudo-self can accept a plausible sounding philosophy under the emotional influence of the moment, or it can just as easily adopt an opposite philosophy to oppose the relationship system. It is the pseudo-self that fuses with others in an intense emotional field. There is so much borrowing and trading of pseudo-self among those in the lower half of the scale that definite scale values can be estimated only from observations that cover months or years, or from a lifetime pattern.

People in the lower half of the scale live in a "feeling" controlled world in which feelings and subjectivity are dominant over the objective reasoning process most of the time. They do not distinguish feeling from fact, and major life decisions are based on what "feels" right. Primary life goals are oriented around love, happiness, comfort, and security; these goals come closest to fulfillment when relationships with others are in equilibrium. So much life energy goes into seeking love and approval, or attacking the other for not providing it, that there is little energy left for self-determined, goal-directed activity. They do not distinguish between "truth" and "fact," and the inner feeling state is the most accurate possible expression of truth. A sincere person is regarded as one who freely communicates the feeling process. An important life principle is "giving and receiving" love, attention, and approval. Life can stay in symptom-free adjustment as long as the relationship system is in comfortable equilibrium. Discomfort and anxiety occur with events that disrupt or threaten the relationship equilibrium. Chronic disruption of the relationship system results in dysfunction and a high incidence of human problems, including physical and emotional illness and social dysfunction. People in the upper half of the scale have an increasingly defined level of basic self and less pseudo-self. Each person is more of an autonomous self: there is less emotional fusion in close relationships, less energy is needed to maintain self in the fusions, more energy is available for goal-directed activity, and more satisfaction is derived from directed activity. Moving into the upper half of the scale one finds people who have an increasing capacity to differentiate between feelings and objective reality. For instance, people in the 50 to 75 range of the scale have increasingly defined convictions and opinions on most essential issues but they are still sensitive to opinions of those about them and some decisions are based on feelings in order not to risk the disapproval of important others.

According to this theory, there is some degree of fusion in close relationships, and some degree of an "undifferentiated family ego mass" at every scale level below 100. When the scale was first devised, the 100 level was reserved for the being who was perfect in all levels of emotional, cellular, and physiological functioning. I expected there might be some unusual figures in history, or possibly some living persons who would fit into the mid-90 range. Increasing experience with the scale indicates that all people have areas of good functioning and essential areas in which life functioning is poor. It has not yet been possible to check the scale on extremely high-level people, but my impression is that 75 is a very high-level person and that those above 60 constitute a small percentage of society.

The characteristics of high-scale people convey an important aspect of the concept. They are operationally clear about the difference between feeling and thinking, and it is as routine for them to make decisions on the basis of thinking as it is for low-level people to operate on feelings. The relative separation of feelings and thinking brings life much more under the control of deliberate thoughts, in contrast to low-scale people whose life is a pawn of the ebb and flow of the emotional process. In relationships with others, high-scale people are free to engage in goal-directed activity, or to lose "self" in the intimacy of a close relationship, in contrast to low-scale people who either have to avoid relationships lest they slip automatically into an uncomfortable fusion, or have no choice but continued pursuit of a close relationship for gratification of emotional "needs." The high-scale person is less reactive to praise or criticism and he has a more realistic evaluation of his own self in contrast to the lower-level person whose evaluation is either far above or far below reality.

The scale is most important as a theoretical concept for understanding the total human phenomenon and as a reliable instrument for making an over-all evaluation of the course of a life, and accurate predictions about the possible future life directions of a person. It is not possible to do day to day or week to week evaluations of scale levels because of the wide shifts in the functional level of pseudo-self in low-scale people. A compliment can raise the functioning level of self and criticism can lower it. It is possible to do reasonably accurate general estimations from information that covers months or years. For instance, a detailed history of functional shifts within a family over a period of years can convey a fairly accurate pattern of the family members in relation to each other. The scale makes it possible to define numerous differences between people at various scale levels. The life style of a person at one level is so different from someone only a few points removed on the scale they do not choose each other for personal relationships. There are many life experiences that can raise or lower the *functioning* levels of self, but few that can change the basic level of differentiation acquired while people are still with their parental families. Unless there is some unusual circumstance, the basic level from their parental family is consolidated in a marriage, following which the only shift is a functional shift. The functional shifts can be striking. For example, a wife who had a functional level at marriage equal to her husband's may become de-selfed to the point of chronic alcoholism. She then functions far below her original level while the husband functions equally far above his original level. Many of these functional levels are sufficiently consolidated so that they can appear much like basic levels to the inexperienced.

Nuclear family emotional system. This developmental concept deals with the emotional patterns that begin with plans for marriage and then follow through the marriage, the types of relationships with families of origin the adjustment of the spouses to each other before children, the addition of the first child, their adjustment as a three-person relationship, and then the addition of subsequent children. The level of differentiation of self of the spouses plays a major part in the intensity of the patterns. I originally used the term *undifferentiated family ego mass* to describe the emotional "stuck togetherness" or fusion in the nuclear family. The term is still accurate when applied to the nuclear family, but the term is less apt in referring to the same phenomenon in the extended families, and the term is awkward when applied to the same phenomenon in emotional systems at work, or in social systems. More recently the term *emotional system* has been used to designate the same triangular emotional patterns that operate in all close relationships, with an additional term to designate the location of the system, for example, a *nuclear family emotional* system.

The level of differentiation of self determines the degree of emotional fusion in spouses. The way the spouses handle the fusion governs the areas in which the undifferentiation will be absorbed and the areas in which symptoms will be expressed under stress. There are three areas within the nuclear family in which symptoms are expressed. These areas are (1) marital conflict, (2) dysfunction in a spouse, and (3) projection to one or more children. There is a quantitative amount of undifferentiation, determined by the level of differentiation in the spouses, to be absorbed by one, or by a combination of the three areas. There are marriages in which a major amount goes to one area, with other areas absorbing the "spill" from the primary area. Most families use a combination of the three areas. Marital conflict occurs when neither spouse will "give in" to the other in the fusion, or when the one who has been giving in or adapting refuses to continue. Conflict absorbs large quantities of the undifferentiation.

One of the commonest mechanisms is one in which the two pseudo-selfs fuse into a common self, one giving up pseudo-self to merger and the other gaining a higher level of functioning self from the merger. This avoids conflict and permits more closeness. The dominant one who gains self is often not aware of the problems of the adaptive one who gives in. The adaptive one is a candidate for dysfunction, which can be physical or emotional illness, or social dysfunction such as drinking or irresponsible behavior. Dysfunction which serves to absorb undifferentiation is difficult to reverse. Dysfunction routinely occurs in one spouse, the other gaining strength in the emotional exchange. Dysfunction in a spouse can absorb large quantities of the undifferentiation, which protects other areas from symptoms.

The third area is the mechanism by which parental undifferentiation is projected to one or more children. I believe this exists in all families to some degree. This mechanism is so important that it is described in the following separate concept. The over-all concept being described here is that of a specific amount of immaturity of undifferentiation to be absorbed within the nuclear family, which is fluid and shifting to some degree, and which increases to a symptomatic level during stress. The borrowing and trading of pseudo-self which goes on with other people at this level of undifferentiation is the point to be emphasized here.

Family projection process. This is the process by which parents project part of their immaturity to one or more children. The most frequent pattern is one which operates through the mother with the mechanism which enables the mother to become less anxious by focusing on the child. The lifestyle of parents, fortuitous circumstances such as traumatic events that disrupt the family during the pregnancy or about the time of birth, and special relationships with sons or daughters are among factors that help determine the "selection" of the child for this process. The most common pattern is one in which one child is the recipient of a major portion of the projection, while other children are relatively less involved. The child who is the object of the projection is the one most emotionally attached to the parents, and the one who ends up with a lower level of differentiation of self. A child who grows up relatively outside the family projection process can emerge with a higher basic level of differentiation than the parents.

Multigenerational transmission process. This concept describes the pattern that develops over multiple generations as children emerge from the parental family with higher, equal, or lower basic levels of differentiation than the parents. When a child emerges with a lower level of self than the parents and marries a spouse with equal differentiation of self, and this marriage produces a child with a lower level who marries another with an equal level, and this next marriage produces one with a lower level who marries at that level, there is a process moving, generation by generation, to lower and lower levels of undifferentiation. According to this theory, the most severe emotional problems, such as hard core schizophrenia, are the product of a process that has been working to lower and lower levels of self over multiple generations. Along with those who fall lower on the differentiation of self scale are those who remain at about the same level and those who progress up the scale.

Sibling position profiles. The personality profiles of each sibling position, as described by Toman (1961), have added an important dimension to this theoretical orientation and the therapeutic system. I have found Toman's profiles to be remarkably consistent with my own observations of "normal" siblings. In his initial work, he did not study the "abnormal" sibling who is the recipient of the family projection process. The more intense the projection process, the more like an infantile youngest child this one becomes, no matter which the sibling position of birth. In evaluating a family, a note about the sibling position of each parent and whether or not the profile of each parent was reasonably typical, conveys invaluable information about the way this family will adapt itself to life, to the emotional forces in the family, and to working on its problem in family psychotherapy. For instance a "fusion of selfs" mix made up of an oldest daughter and youngest son automatically conveys a wealth of information about the family, "all things being equal." In addition, this mix behaves differently in conflict, in the dysfunction of one spouse, and in the family projection process. The many details of this concept are of peripheral interest to this presentation.

Triangles. The concept of triangles provides a theoretical framework for understanding the microscopic functioning of all emotional systems. Most important, the step by step understanding of triangles provides an immediate working answer that can be used by the therapist, or by any family member, for predictably changing the functioning of an emotional system. The pattern of triangle functioning is the same in all emotional systems. The lower the level of differentiation, the more intense the patterns, and the more important the relationship, the more intense the patterns. The very same patterns are less intense at higher levels of differentiation and in relationships that are more peripheral.

A two-person emotional system is unstable in that it forms itself into a three-person system or triangle under stress. A system larger than three persons becomes a series of interlocking triangles. The following are some of the characteristics of functioning of a single triangle. As tension mounts in a two-person system, it is usual for one to be more uncomfortable than the other, and for the uncomfortable one to "triangle in" a third person by telling the second person a story about the triangle one. This relieves the tension between the first two, and shifts the tension between the second and third. A triangle in a state of calm consists of a comfortable twosome and an outsider. The favored position is to be a member of the twosome. If tension arises in the outsider, his next predicatble move is to form a twosome with one of the original members of the twosome, leaving the other one as outsider. So the forces within the triangle shift and move from moment to moment and over longer periods. When the triangle is in a state of tension, the outside position is the preferred position, in a posture that says, "You two fight and leave me out of it." Add this extra dimension of gaining closeness, or escaping tension, and it provides an even more graphic notion of the shifting forces, each one constantly moving to gain a little more close comfort or to withdraw from tension, with each move by one requiring a compensatory move by another. In a state of tension, when it is not possible for the triangle to conveniently shift the forces within the triangle, two members of the original twosome will find another convenient third person (triangle in another person) and now the emotional forces will run the circuits in this new triangle. The circuits in the former triangle are then quiet but available for reuse at any time. In periods of very high tension, a system will triangle in more and more outsiders. A common example is a family in great stress that uses the triangle system to involve neighbors, schools, police, clinics, and a spectrum of outside people as participants in the family problem. The family thus reduces the tension within the inner family, and it can actually create the situation in which the family tension is being fought out by outside people.

Over long periods of time, a triangle will come to have long-term postures and functioning positions to each other. A common pattern is one in which the mother and child form the close twosome and the father is the outsider. In this triangle, the minute to minute process of emotional forces shifts around the triangle, but when forces come to rest, it is always with each in the same position. A triangle characteristically has two positive sides and one negative side. For instance, one member of the close twosome has a positive feeling orientation to the outsider while the other member may feel negative about him. The triangle concept is remarkably more fluid for understanding a three-person system than the more conventional oedipal complex concepts. For instance, conflict between siblings consists almost universally of a triangle between mother and two children in which mother has a positive relationship to each child and the conflict is fought out between the children. The triangle concept provides many more clues about what to do to modify the sibling situation than is provided by oedipal theory. In even the most "fixed" triangle, the positive and negative forces shift back and forth constantly. The term *fixed* refers to the most characteristic position. A three-person system is one triangle, a four-person system is four primary triangles, a five-person system is nine primary triangles, etc. This progression multiplies rapidly as systems get larger. In addition there are a variety of secondary triangles when two or more may band together for one corner of a triangle for one emotional issue, while the configuration shifts on another issue.

There are characteristics of the triangle that lend themselves specifically to psychotherapy, or to any other efforts to modify the triangle. The emotional forces within a triangle operate as predictably as an emotional reflex. The reactiveness operates in a chain reaction fashion, one reaction following another in predictable sequence. The therapetuic system is based on being able to observe accurately to see the part that self plays, and to consciously control this programmed emotional reactiveness. The observation and the control are equally difficult. Observation is not possible until one can control one's reactions sufficiently to be able to observe. The process of observation allows for more control, which in turn, in a series of slow steps, allows for better observation. The process of being able to observe is the slow beginning toward moving one small step toward getting one's self "outside" an emotional system. It is only when one can get a little outside that it is possible to begin to observe and to begin to modify an emotional system. When there is finally one who can control his emotional responsiveness and not take sides with either of the other two, and stay constantly in contact with the other two, the emotional intensity within the twosome will decrease and both will move to a higher level of differentiation. Unless the triangled person can remain in emotional contact, the twosome will triangle in someone else.

The Therapeutic System

A very brief review of the therapeutic system is presented to provide an overall view of the place of the forthcoming clinical presentation in the total theoretical and therapeutic systems. The theoretical system conceives of an undifferentiated family ego mass and the therapeutic system is designed to help one or more family members toward a higher level of differentiation. The concepts of triangles provides another theoretical dimension, which says an emotional system is made up of a series of interlocking triangles. The most important therapeutic principle, which is repeatable in an orderly predictable way, says that when the triangular emotional pattern is modified in a single important triangle in the family, and the members of the triangle remain in emotional contact with the rest of the family, other triangles will automatically change in relation to the first.

Family psychotherapy with both parents or both spouses. This is the main family configuration for family psychotherapy with any family. The therapeutic method employs the concept of differentiation of self, and of the triangle emotional system that operates in the family. The goal is to work toward modification of the most important triangle in the family, and from experience this has been found to stem from the two parents or the two spouses. I have found that the quickest way to modify the central triangle is to constitute a new triangle with the two primary members of the family and the therapist. When the family triangle includes three or more from the natural family, the emotional system runs its own built-in emotional circuits and it requires much more time for the family to observe or modify the triangle patterns. If the family configuration permits, the family psychotherapy is routinely with both spouses or both parents, whether the initial problem be marital conflict, a dysfunction in a spouse, or a problem in a child. If it is possible to modify the emotional patterns in this central triangle, then all other family members automatically change.

The one basic principle in this method of psychotherapy involves the therapist keeping himself "detriangled" or emotionally outside the emotional field that involves the marital twosome. These two people automatically use mechanisms with the therapist that they use in dealing with any third person. If the therapist can remain outside the emotional field and not respond as others do to the emotional twosome, then patterns between them come to be more quickly modified. I believe this method would work no matter what the subject of discussion, as long as the therapist remained relatively "detriangled," and as long as the twosome dealt with issues that revealed critical triangles.

There are four main things I do in a situation with two spouses or both parents. The first is to keep the emotional system between them sufficiently alive to be meaningful and sufficiently toned down for them to deal with it objectively without undue emotional reactiveness. The therapist is active with constant questions, first to one spouse, and then the other, getting the thoughts of one in reaction to what the other had communicated to the therapist. This prevents emotional exchanges between the spouses and enables each to "hear" the other without the automatic emotional bind that develops in exchanges between them. A second function is to keep self "detriangled" from the emotional process between the two family members. There are many details to this function. The third function is to establish what I have called an "I position," which is part of the differentiation of a self. The therapist takes action stands in relation to them, which then permits them to begin to do the same to each other. The fourth function is to teach them how emotional systems operate and to encourage them each to work toward the differentiation of self in relation to their families of origin. This step has many important details. It is necessary that the psychotherapy be done in a way that does not involve the therapist in the emotional system between the spouses. With this method, each can differentiate a self from the other as long as the therapist does not get involved in the process and as long as he can keep the process between them active.

Family psychotherapy with one spouse in preparation for family psychotherapy with both spouses. This method is designed for families in which one spouse is negative and unwilling to be involved in the family psychotherapy. The first part is similar to what will be described in the next section on family psychotherapy with one family member. The goal with this method is to help the motivated spouse to understand the part that self plays in the family system, until the unmotivated spouse is willing to join the therapy as a cooperative effort.

Family psychotherapy with one motivated family member. This method has been in regualr use some eight years. It was designed for unmarried young adults who lived at a distance from parents, or whose parents refused to be a part of the therapy effort. This method is so similar to what will be described with my own family that it will be mentioned only briefly. The initial sessions are spent teaching the characteristics of family systems. Then sessions are devoted to making postulations about the part this single member plays in the total system. Then time is devoted to learning to observe patterns in one's own emotional reactions in the parental system. This plan involves relatively frequent contact with families of origin to check postulations, to seek new observations that will confirm or refute postulations, and to develop ways to modify reactions. It works best with oldest children who usually feel more responsibility for their families and who are more motivated for such an effort. It requires that the single members be self-supporting, else they never develop the emotional courage for change that might threaten the family attitude about them. An optimum distance from extended families is about 200 to 300 miles, which is close enough for frequent contact and far enough away to be outside the immediate emotional sphere of the family. Appointments are spaced farther apart when distance from family does not permit frequent visits. It is also possible to use work and social relationship systems for learning the properties of emotional systems. The average well-motivated young person will spend about 100 hours spread over a period of four or five years at such an effort. More frequent appointments do not increase the capacity to observe and to control emotional responsiveness. The average result with this method has been far superior to results with conventional psychotherapy.

The Clinical Report

The object of this report is a clinical experience that covered a period of a few months in which I achieved a major breakthrough in differentiating a self from my family of origin. That experience was preceded by a twelve-year effort to understand my family within the framework of family theory. There had been an active effort to modify myself in relation to my family during the last seven or eight years of that period. This slow trial and error effort was intertwined with the stages of my professional work in family research, family theory, and family psychotherapy. Since reaching this evolutionary stage with my own family, I have been able to "coach" motivated family therapists toward significant differentiation in their parental families in as little as two or three years. This goal is achieved by helping them focus on the productive areas and avoiding the time-consuming pitfalls. In an effort to help the reader understand the rationale for this effort, the material will be presented in its evolutionary steps, with each step explained in terms of the theory which has already been presented.

Personal background information. There was very little from my conventional psychiatric training that provided a workable understanding of my own family. Most of the useful concepts came from my experience with family research. However, I had some early experiences that may have played a part in the development of my thinking; these will be summarized briefly. Since many ask questions about motivation for working on one's own family, I will begin with some very early trends in my life. During my childhood I possessed two assets that played a part in future choices. One was an unusual ability for solving difficult puzzles and in devising working solutions for insoluble-appearing problems. Another asset was skill in the use of my hands. By the age of twelve I had decided to go into a profession and the choice was equal between law and medicine. After twelve the choice went more toward medicine. At fifteen an incident occurred which resulted in my making a firm decision for medicine. I was an ambulance helper and had to take an unconscious teenage girl to a university hospital. The girl lay unconscious all afternoon and by early evening she was dead. The vivid memory of the emergency room and the doctors who seemed bewildered, unsure, and fumbling incited me to help medicine find better answers. In medical school, my interest automatically gravitated to areas with the most pressing unsolved problems. First there was neurology, then neurosurgery, and then the challenge of differential diagnosis in medicine. The intellectual challenge of the skilled techniques of surgery did not fascinate me until internship. A series of surgical deaths led to my building a crude artificial heart and being accepted for a fellowship in surgery, and, following this, I was in the military service for five years. The extent of psychiatric dysfunction that I observed in Army personnel and the lack of adequate solutions for these problems led to a decision to undertake psychiatric training. I got involved immediately with schizophrenia, and then explored every known theory and treatment of schizophrenia until my interest settled on the family. Hypotheses about the family led to my devoting myself full-time to psychiatric research on the family a few years later.

I was relatively unaware of psychological or psychoanalytic concepts when I went into psychiatry. Superficial knowledge about these concepts had been compartmentalized as applying to those who were "sick." My close, congenial family had been free of conflict, marital problems, drinking problems, or any diagnosable neurotic or behavior problem for every generation of which I had knowledge. My parental family relationships and my marriage relationship were considered happy, normal, and ideal. My first year or two in psychiatry was a period of near exhilaration as I heard those logical-sounding explanations of human behavior. The exhilaration began to disappear with awareness of logical discrepancies in theory that the experts could not explain. Most psychiatrists did not seem bothered by the contradictions which formed the core of my later research.

In essence, those early years in psychiatry, and my own psychoanalysis, helped me to become aware of a fascinating new world of hidden motivation and conflict. I learned the concepts and became adept at applying them to self, staff, friends, family, and even to prominent people in the news I had never met. Everyone was "pathological," and those who denied it were even more "pathological." Thinking about members of my family took the form of analyzing their psychodynamics and diagnosing them. This stance tended to intensify my previous posture to my family of origin. As an oldest son and physician I had long been the wise expert preaching to the unenlightened, even when it was done under the guise of expressing an opinion or giving advice. The family would listen politely and put it aside as "just psychiatry." During my psychoanalysis there was enough emotional pressure to engage my parents in an angry confrontation about childhood grievances that had come to light in the snug harbor of transference. At the time I considered these confrontations to be emotional emancipation. There may have been some short-term gain from knowing my feelings a little better and learning to "sound off" at my parents, but the long-term result was an intensification of previous patterns. The net result was my conviction that my parents had their problems, and I had mine, that *they would never change,* and nothing more could be done. I felt justified in maintaining a formal distance and keeping relationships superficial. I did not attempt to work on relationships in my family of origin until after the development of my new concepts in family research.

One emotional phenomenon from a system outside the family is of special importance to this family concept. I worked in a large, well-known psychiatric clinic where the emotional system in the "family" of staff and employees was identical to the emotional system in any family. The patterns of all emotional systems are the same whether they be family systems, work systems, or social systems, the only difference being one of intensity. The emotional system where I worked provided valuable observations. I noticed that when I was away on trips I was much clearer and more objective about work relationships, and that the objectivity was lost on returning to work. After it was first noticed, I made more careful observations of the phenomenon. The objectivity could come by the time the plane was an hour away. On return, the objectivity would be lost as I went through the front door returning to work. It was as if the emotional system "closed in" as I entered the building. This is the emotional phenomenon I later came to call the "undifferentiated family ego mass." I wondered what it would take to keep emotional objectivity in the midst of the emotional system. A "differentiated self" is one who can maintain emotional objectivity while in the midst of an emotional system in turmoil, yet at the same time actively relate to key people in the system. I made other observations about the emotional system at work. After a trip, when I returned to the city on Saturday, objectivity would hold until returning to work Monday morning. There was one occasion when the objectivity was lost during a telephone conversation with a staff member before returning to work. On other occasions the objectivity would be lost when greeting a staff member in the parking lot before entering the building. This "fusion" into the emotional system operated most intensely with those most involved in the gossip system at work. Gossip is one of the principle mechanisms for "triangling" another into the emotional field between two people. The details of this phenomenon will be discussed elsewhere in this presentation. In that work system much "triangling" took place at coffee breaks, social gatherings, and bull sessions in which the "understanding" ones would "analyze" and talk about those who were not present. This mechanism conveys, "We understand each other perfectly (the togetherness side of the triangle). We are in agreement about that pathological third person." At social gatherings people would clump in small groups, each talking about someone outside that clump, and each apparently unaware that all the clumps were doing the same "triangling" gossip about them.

I consider involvement in that work emotional system to have been one of the fortunate experiences in my life. It just happened to have been of sufficient intensity to afford observations. After having observed the phenomenon there, it was then easier to see the same phenomenon in all other work systems. It provided a kind of "control" for the very same phenomenon in my family or origin. During the years I worked hardest to "differentiate a self" in my family of origin, I would return occasionally to the old work system for a visit. Some of my best friends are still there. On the average visit, though I had been away for two or three years, it would take no more than thirty minutes to meet someone important to the system, and immediately "fuse" into taking sides in the emotional issues of the system. Finally, after I had mastered the experience with my own family that is reported here, I returned to the old work system for a long visit and was able to relate intimately to those important to the system without a single episode of "fusion."

The Family History

My own family of origin is the clinical example of this presentation. I am the oldest of five children of a cohesive, congenial family that has lived in the same small town for several generations. My parents, now quite elderly, are active in community life and both work in the family business. My personality profile is that of an over-responsible oldest son. I am married to the second of three daughters, who functions more as an oldest. We have four children, ranging from age 14 to 20. My first brother, two years younger than myself, is an outgoing, energetic businessman who established himself in another state immediately after college. He married a college classmate who is a socially active only child. They have one daughter. The third child, my second brother, three years younger than my first brother, is head of the family business and functions as head of the clan at home. He married a second child and oldest daughter while he was in the military service. They have two sons and a daughter. The forth child in my family origin, an oldest daughter, is two years younger than the third child. She is the one most emotionally triangled into the family system, the only one who did not go to college, and the one who has made the poorest life adjustment. She married an employee of the family business and they have a daughter and a son. The fifth child is a daughter four years younger than the fourth. After college she worked in another town where she married; she has one daughter. After several years her husband sold his business and they returned to the family hometown where he works in the family business. There have never been any disabling illnesses, accidents, or injuries in any of the five children, in their spouses, or their children.

The step by step sequence of events in this family emotional field covers a period of over fifty years. My father was an only child who has functioned as a responsible oldest. His father died when he was an infant. He was reared by his mother until he was twelve, when she remarried and had other children. He was self-supporting from childhood. My mother was a responsible oldest daughter, seven years older than her brother. Her mother died when she was one year old, following which she and her father returned to live with his parents until she was six, when her father remarried. She lived the next seventeen years with her father, her stepmother, and a half brother born one year later. My parents first knew each other well when they both worked in town. They were married when he was a station agent for the railroad and she worked with her father in the family business, a department store founded by his father. After marriage, my parents lived in their own home in town for the next five years. I was born a year and a half after the marriage and my first brother was born two years later.

A sequence of events which profoundly influenced the future of the family began shortly after the birth of my brother. My mother's brother was in college several hundred miles away. Her father's health began to fail and my father began spending more and more time in the business, in addition to his regular full-time work. My grandfather had been a responsible oldest son in a large family. His death, when my first brother was two years old, was a nodal point in the family history. My father resigned from his previous job, my mother's brother stayed home from college, and my father and uncle became partners in the family business. My parents moved into my mother's parental home where the household consisted of my parents, then in their late twenties, my brother and myself, my grandmother, then in her fifties, and my uncle, then in his early twenties. The personality profiles of the household will convey something of the family emotional field. My father is an action-oriented oldest son and my mother a responsible "doing" oldest daughter. They are among that percentage of "oldests" who make marriage into a smooth-functioning partnership. My grandfather, as an oldest, had married two adaptive young daughters. My grandmother, his second wife, was quiet and supportive. My uncle, a functional only child by virtue of the seven years between him and my mother, was his mother's only child. He emerged with a profile of a bright youngest son. These particular personality profiles made for a congenial household with a low level of conflict.

About five months after the death of her father, my mother became pregnant with her third child, my second brother. A few months later, my uncle was among the first to be drafted for the war, and my father assumed responsibility for the business. My second brother was conceived within months after my grandfather's death, the reorganization of the business, and the merger into a single household. My second brother was born within the month after my uncle left. It was as if he was born to take over the family business. I and my first brother had been born while my parents had their own home, and we are the only two who moved away and who have no connection with the business. There was no particular pressure on anyone to leave or stay. It just evolved that I and my first brother left. My uncle returned from the war almost two years later, about the time mother became pregnant with her fourth child and oldest daughter. Mother had long wanted a daughter and this child became "special" and overprotected, the one most involved in the family emotional process, and the one who was impaired by it. There is one such child in almost every family. Though the impairment in my first sister did not go beyond overall poor functioning in her life course, the emotional pattern is the same as other families in which the most involved child is severely impaired. With less basic differentiation in my parents and more stress in the family emotional system, this daughter could have later developed severe disabling emotional or physical problems. Why did the emotional patterns involve a daughter instead of a son, and why this child? I believe this pattern is predictable in families and, implicit in Toman's work, are suggestions about whether the involved one is likely to be a son or daughter. In my family, there were reality factors that played into the emotional process. My father was the active responsible one in the family business and my mother assumed responsibility for the family operation at home. There were always chores and need for extra help in the home and business and the children all worked as a matter of course. Clear distinctions between men's work and women's work helped keep my sister in a special category. My older sister has remained emotionally dependent on my parents. School was difficult for her and she was the only one who did not go to college. She has the personality profile of a dependent youngest child, which happens with the one most involved in the family emotional process. The fifth child, another daughter, was born four years after the fourth. She grew up more outside the family emotional system and she has the profile of a responsible oldest daughter.

The period after the last child is born, when the family composition is relatively stable, usually provides the best overview of family functioning. The three boys had about equal levels of adjustment. We spent considerable time with my father in work and recreation while my mother provided more of the reminders about hard work, fair play, helping others, and success. My mother was the active, responsible one in the home. My grandmother helped with fixed chores, and she devoted special attention to my uncle. The major triangle in this combination of home and business involved my father, mother, and uncle. Any member of a relatively fixed triangle perceives his self as "caught." My father was caught between his wife and her brother, my uncle between his sister and her husband, and my mother between her husband and her brother. My father was the one most active in the business and also in civic and community activity. In the business he represented expansion and "progress." My uncle represented caution, and he functioned as the loyal opposition that questioned "progress." In calm periods, a triangle functions as a comfortable twosome and an outsider. My uncle was the outside one, which caused no problems for him since he had the close relationship with his mother who was relatively uninvolved in business issues. In stressful periods, a triangle has two positive sides and a negative side. The negative side in this triangle was between my father and uncle in the business, usually expressed as discontent communicated through my mother. The stress, however, rarely reached a point of overt anger between them.

The family triangle illustrates an important difference between family theory and certain conventional psychiatric concepts. There are those who would say that the differences between my father and uncle represented deeply buried hostility controlled by maladaptive suppression, and that healthier adaptation would result from searching out and openly expressing the hostility. Family theory would say that the negative side of the triangle is merely a symptomatic expression of a total family problem and to focus on issues in one relationship is to misidentify the problem, to convey the impression that the problem is in this one relationship, and to make the triangle more fixed and less reversible. There may be transient anxiety relief from direct expression of anger, but to focus on this dimension makes the family maladaptive. The mild symptom expressed only under stress is evidence of a good level of emotional compensation.

The next major shift in the family came as I and my brothers left for college. My grandmother died suddenly a few months before my second brother left for the army. In the following five years there were several changes. My uncle married and established his own home, my parents and two sisters moved to a house in town, and the old family home was rented. My first brother, who was established away from home, married shortly before entering the army. During the war my second brother, and then I, were married while in the army. A few months later my older sister married and joined her husband who was away in war industry. My younger sister was in college during the war. My parents were alone at home. It was difficult to find employees during the war, so my mother devoted full time to helping my father and uncle run the business. There developed a different version of the family triangle, a familiar one in family systems. My uncle and his wife constituted one corner of the triangle, and she tended to verbalize her discontent outside the family.

After the war there was need for young ideas and energy to rebuild the business, which had been merely maintained during the war. My second brother returned with his family to start as an employee with an understanding that he would ultimately have his share of the business. Also, my older sister and her husband returned, and he resumed his employment in the business. A few years later my younger sister and her husband moved back to help in the business. My second brother, as energetic in business and civic activity as our father, was the motivating force in the successful growth of the business. Emotional forces were operating for this brother to become the "head of the clan" and for my younger sister to succeed my mother as the responsible woman in the next generation. Within the family there were a variety of triangles and shifting emotional alignments on lesser issues, but the original triangle pattern continued on major issues. Now the triangle consisted of my father and brother at one corner, my mother and younger sister at another, and my uncle and his wife at the other. During periods of stress the negative issues were expressed between my father and brother on one side and my uncle and his wife on the other. Stress occurred around the issue of expansion of the business and when my brother pressed for his share of the business. Since the family lived in five separate households, there was more of a tendency for family issues to be confided to friends outside the family. With each period of stress there would be discussion about dividing the business, some new recognition of my brother's contribution, and a new period of calm. This sequence continued until the time came when, in a new period of stress, my uncle sold his half to my second brother and retired. The business was reorganized as a corporation, with my brother holding half of the stock and my father and mother each holding one fourth. The family tended to see the new arrangement as the final solution. This is another predictable characteristic of emotional systems: When the focus of the symptom is removed from the system, the system acts as if the problem is solved. If the system could think instead of react, it would know that it would be only a matter of time until the symptom surfaced elsewhere. This event in my family occurred after I had learned much about families from research but before I had begun my active effort to use the knowledge in my family of origin. However, I made some postulations about the next area in which symptoms would develop. The next part of the clinical presentation will deal with the course of events for the ten years after the reorganization of the business.

My posture to my family or origin during this period was one of kidding myself that I was "detached" and "objective" and that I was "staying out of the family problem." This stance is the most common misperception that people have when they first begin to become better observers and to be less emotionally reactive in their own families. Actually, I was almost as emotionally involved as ever, and I was using emotional distance and silence to create an illusion of nonresponsiveness. Distance and silence do not fool an emotional system.

Concepts Important in the Differentiation of a Self

New concepts from family research and family psychotherapy provided exciting new ways for understanding my own family that had never been possible with individual concepts. The new ideas were applied to my own family, and other immediate emotional systems, by the time they were fairly well formulated. Observations and experience from my own living situation also made contributions to the family research. Most of the effort went to my own nuclear family (my wife and children), which is a story all in itself. I considered my family of origin as important in understanding my nuclear family, but less important in helping the nuclear family resolve its problems. Very early in clinical work with families, I tried to correlate each pattern in my nuclear family with similar patterns in family of origin. This effort was followed by a short period of precise focus on my nuclear family, with the premise that focus on the family of origin avoided the most important issues in my nuclear family. Gradually I focused more and more on my family of origin, culminating in the present effort being described here. The following is a series of concepts that were important in the effort to differentiate a self in my own family of origin.

Multigenerational family history. My initial effort in this area was motivated by a research interest. Early in family research I began structured studies to trace the transmission of family characteristics from one generation to another. This was part of the effort to define the "multigenerational transmission process," one of the concepts in the theory. Then I developed a special interest in the transmission of illness patterns from generation to generation. Each facet of the study provided interesting new leads to follow. Thousands of hours went into a microscopic study of a few families, in which I went back as far as 200 or 300 years, and I traced the histories of numerous families back 100 years or more. All families seemed to have the same basic patterns. This work was so time-consuming that I decided it was more sensible to study my own family. My goal was to get factual information in order to understand the emotional forces in each nuclear family, and I went back as many generations as it was possible to go. Until this time I had no special interest in family history or genealogy. In less than ten years, working a few hours a week, I have acquired family tree knowledge about twenty-four families of origin, including detailed knowledge about one that I traced back 300 years, another 250 years, and several that were traced back 150 to 200 years. The effort brought me into contact with genealogists who were surprised that I was as interested in family members who did poorly as those who did well. This is tedious work in the beginning, but a surprising amount of detail can be obtained once the effort is underway.

It is difficult to estimate the direct contribution of family historical information to the understanding of one's family in the present. I believe the indirect contributions are great enough to warrant the effort by anyone who aspires to become à serious student of the family. In only 150 to 200 years an individual is the descendent of 64 to 128 families of origin, each of which has contributed something to one's self. With all the myths and pretense and emotionally biased reports and opinions, it is difficult to ever really know "self" or to know family members in the present or recent past. As one reconstructs facts of a century or two ago, it is easier to get beyond myths and to be factual. To follow a nuclear family of 200 years ago from marriage through the addition of each new child, and then to follow the life course of each child, can provide one with a different view of the human phenomenon than is possible from examining the urgency of the present. It is easier to see the same emotional patterns as they operated then, and one can get a sense of continuity, history, and identity that is not otherwise possible. More knowledge of one's distant families of origin can help one become aware that there are no angels or devils in a family; they were human beings, each with his own strengths and weaknesses, each reacting predictably to the emotional issue of the moment, and each doing the best he could with his life course. My work on multigenerational family history was in progress during most of the period of this report.

Undifferentiated ego mass in family of origin. I have already mentioned early observations about the emotional phenomenon where I worked, which I later came to call the undifferentiated family ego mass. The same mechanism operated on visits to my family of origin. I made increasing observations about the phenomenon but had not clues about effective action for maintaining objectivity while still in contact with the family. I had long since tried the conventional things for dealing with family emotional situations, such as talking openly to family members about problems, both individually and in groups. The model for this method came from the early experience with family psychotherapy in which open discussion about problems seemed to help. Discussions about family

issues seemed to make the family system calmer, but they made the
fusions more intense and it was more difficult to get back to objectivity
later. When the family was calm it was possible to go several hours or a
day before fusing into taking sides on emotional issues. If the family was
tense, the fusion could occur on first contact with a key person in the
family system. Objectivity would usually return within an hour or two
after the visit while en route home. Then came the theoretical notion of
the "undifferentiated family ego mass" and some early principles about
"differentiating a self." These principles will be discussed further later.
From experience I had learned that the effort to define or differentiate a
self is most effective if one is "outside" the emotional system, or before
one becomes fused into the system. Since trips home were infrequent,
the goal was to maintain objectivity as long as possible and to find ways to
extricate myself from the fusion, all during the same visit. One effort
was to leave my wife and children at home while I visited among
extended family in town. When I became "fused" into the system I would
return home and relate intensively to my nuclear family, hoping this
would extricate me from the fusion and permit another period of
objectivity with the extended family. This plan never worked. In
discussions, my wife would communicate some terrible something a
sister or my sister-in-law had said or done, indicating that my nuclear
family had also "fused into the family system," even though it was
relatively isolated from the larger family system. Usually I regained
objectivity within an hour or two after the visit had ended. Based on this
experience, I tried another technique to extricate myself. I planned two-
day visits with the extended family, following which I would "leave" with
my wife and children for a two-day subvacation 100 miles or so away; this
technique was designed to extricate myself from the "fusion" and to
permit another period of objectivity for a second visit. This plan also
never worked. It was as if I could not extricate myself until that visit was
over and I was an hour or so en route home. I made one final effort using
this technique. This one was based on the experience that it was easier
for me to do it alone than with wife and children. When professional trips
permitted, I would visit a day or so with my parental family before the
meeting in some distant state, and then would make a brief visit after the
meeting. This worked somewhat better than the subvacation plan with
my wife and children, but I never really regained objectivity until an hour
or two after the second visit had ended. During the years that I tried
these various techniques, I was also working at "defining a self" by letter
and telephone calls with my family of origin, while I also worked at
"defining a self" in other emotional systems, such as the effort with the
"family" of family therapists. A partial success in a more peripheral

emotional system would contribute something to the effort with my family of origin, but significant success had to wait until I obtained a better mastery of the concept of triangles.

My own experience with fusion into the undifferentiated ego mass of my family of origin is remarkably consistent with what I have observed in a broad spectrum of reasonably well-integrated families with whom I have worked in my teaching and practice. I have never seen a family in which the "emotional fusion" pheonomenon is not present. Theoretically, emotional fusion is universal in all except the completely differentiated person, who has not yet been born. Usually, most people are not aware of the phenomenon. There are those who can become aware if they can learn to observe more and react less to their families. There are others so intensely "fused" they probably can never know the world of emotional objectivity with their parents. Few people can be objective about their parents, see and think about them as people, without either downgrading or upgrading them. Some people are "comfortably" fused and others so "uncomfortably" fused they use hate or a covert negative attitude (either is evidence of fusion) to avoid contact with parents. There are those of "positive fusion" who remain so attached they never leave home. There are also those who kid themselves into believing they have "worked out" the relationship with parents and who make brief formal visits home without personal communication; they use as evidence of maturity that they do not see their parents. In my work with families, the effort is to help people become aware of the phenomenon and then to make brief frequent trips home to observe and work at differentiation. Frequent short visits are many times more effective than infrequent long visits.

The differentiation of a self. Each small step toward the "differentiation" of a self is opposed by emotional forces for "togetherness," which keeps the emotional system in check. The togetherness forces define the family members as alike in terms of important beliefs, philosophies, life principles, and feelings. The forces constantly emphasize the togetherness by using "we" to define what "we think or feel," or the forces define the self of another such as, "My wife thinks that . . . ," or the forces use the indefinite "it" to define common values, as in, "It is wrong" or "It is the thing to do." The togetherness amalgam is bound together by assigning positive value on thinking about the other before self, living for the other, sacrifice for others, love and devotion and compassion for others, and feeling responsible for the comfort and well being of others. If the other is unhappy or uncomfortable, the togetherness force feels guilty and asks, "What have I done to cause this?" and it blames the other for lack of happiness or failure in self.

The differentiating force places emphasis on "I" in defining the foregoing characteristics. The "I position" defines principle and action in terms of, "This is what I think, or believe" and, "This is what I will do or will not do," without impinging one's own values or beliefs on others. It is the "responsible I" which assumes responsibility for one's own happiness and comfort, and it avoids thinking that tends to blame and hold others responsible for one's own unhappiness or failures. The "responsible I" avoids the "irresponsible I" which makes demands on others with, "I want, or I deserve, or this is my right, or my privilege." A reasonably differentiated person is capable of genuine concern for others without expecting something in return, but the togetherness forces treat differentiation as selfish and hostile.

A family system in emotional equilibrium is symptom-free at any level of differentiation. The system is disturbed when any family member moves toward regression. The system will then operate to restore that former symptom-free level of equilibrium, if that is possible. The family system is also disturbed when any family member moves toward a slightly higher level of differentiation, and it will move as automatically to restore the family system to its former equilibrium. Thus, any small step toward differentiation is accompanied by a small emotional upheaval in the family system. This pattern is so predictable that absence of an emotional reaction is good evidence that the differentiating effort was not successful. There are three predictable steps in the family reaction to differentiation. They are: (1) "You are wrong," or some version of that; (2) "Change back," which can be communicated in many different ways; and (3) "If you do not, these are the consequences." If the differentiating one can stay on course without defending self or counterattacking, the emotional reaction is usually brief and the other then expresses appreciation. The clearest examples of the steps in differentiation occur in family psychotherapy with husband and wife. The following is a typical example: One couple in family therapy spent several months on issues about the togetherness in the marriage. They discussed meeting the needs of each other, attaining a warm, loving relationship, the ways each disappointed the other, and the making of joint decisions. They discovered new differences in opinion as the process continued. Then the husband spent a few weeks thinking about himself, his career, and where he stood on some central issues between him and his wife. His focus on himself stirred an emotional reaction in the wife. Her anxiety episode lasted about a week as she begged him to return to the togetherness, and then went into a tearful, angry, emotional attack in which she accused him of being selfish, self-centered, incapable of loving anyone, and an inadequate husband. She was sure the only answer was divorce. He maintained his calm and was able to stay close to her. The following day the relationship was calm. At the next therapy session she said to her husband, "I liked what you were doing but it made me mad. I wanted to control what I was saying but it had to come out. All the time I was watching you, hoping you would not give in. I am so glad you did not let me change you." They were on a new and less intense level of togetherness which was followed by the wife starting on a self-determined course, with the husband then reacting emotionally to her efforts at differentiation.

In this example, the husband's effort represented a small step toward a better level of differentiation. Had he yielded to her demand, or attacked, he would have slipped back to her level. When he held his position, her emotional reaction represented a pull-up to his level. This theoretical orientation considers this sequence a basic increase in bilateral differentiation which can never return to the former level. On the new level they both have different attitudes about togetherness and individuality. They say things like, "We are much more separate but we are closer. The old love is gone. I miss it sometimes but the new love is calmer and better. I know it sounds crazy but that's how it is."

The course of differentiation is not as smooth and orderly when one person attempts it alone in his family of origin. One reason has to do with the diversity of issues about which each can take an "I position." Differentiation cannot take place in a vacuum. It has to take place in relation to others, around issues important to both people. A marriage contains an endless supply of issues important to both spouses if they can disentagle self from the emotional system in order to define the issues. Differentiation also has to be in the context of a meaningful relationship in which the other has to respect the belief and the action stand that affirms it. One who affirms a "self" around issues that can be ignored is quickly labeled a fool. It is more difficult to find meaningful issues in a family of origin when one has little or no contact with its members.

The long-term efforts to define my own self in my family of origin have had significant effects, but the year-to-year results have been disappointing. All too often the family would ignore the effort. However, my attempts did result in principles applied successfully in professional practice that were later used with my family of origin in the clinical example to be discussed later. A family system in quiet emotional equilibrium is less amenable to the discussion of emotional issues, or change, than a family system in tension or stress. My most meaningful visits have been during an illness or hospitalization of a significant family member. In coaching others with their families, I encourage visits when the system is emotionally fluid or during family upsets such as deaths, serious illness, reunions, weddings, or other stressful or significant family events.

The parental we-ness. Until I had experience in family research, I subscribed to the principle that parents should "present a united front to their children." This belief is so common that it has come to be regarded as a basic psychological principle. Certainly I heard this often enough in my own professional training and it is commonly presented as a sound principle in the literature on child rearing. The reasoning states that the united front is necessary to "prevent the child from playing off one parent against the other." Before family research I believed that parents tended to become divided in their approach to children and it was necessary to remind them to discuss differences about the children in private and to present a united front in dealing with the child. With family research I developed the conviction that this dictum is one of the most unsound psychological principles.

All familes with whom I have had experience have arrived at the principle of the united parental front on their own. Most sophisticated families tend to present this dictum as a modern principle of child rearing and less sophisticated families present it as a culture-bound principle about children obeying their parents. There is evidence that parents automatically invoke this principle because it makes the parents more comfortable and not because it is good for the child. There are numerous variations of this principle in the triangle between parents and child, but the most frequent pattern is the one in which mother becomes unsure of herself in relation to the child and seeks the father's approval and support. Observation of families in family psychotherapy indicates that parents tend to develop more individual relationships with the child as the family improves.

This phenomenon can be considered from several different levels. On a clinical level, the "parental we-ness" presents the child with a parental amalgam which is neither masculine nor feminine and it deprives the child of knowing men by having an individual relationship with his father, and knowing women from the relationship with his mother. From the standpoint of triangles, the "parental we-ness" presents the child with a locked-in "two against one" situation which provides no emotional flexibility unless he can somehow manage to force a rift in the other side of the triangle. From a theoretical standpoint, the poorly defined selfs of the parents fuse into a common self and it is this that becomes the "parental we-ness." Early in family psychotherapy I began working toward depveloping an individual relationship between each parent and the child. Nothing but good things have come from this principle. Once the effort goes toward developing an individual relationship between each parent and the child, it is possible to see the intensity of the parental effort to reestablish the "parental we-ness." There are some situations in which the parents fuse into a common self so automatically that it is difficult to establish individual relationships. When it is possible to separate the parental we-ness early, the change in the child is usually rapid and dramatic. Even a very young child is capable of managing a relationship to either parent.

Very soon after working out the principle of each parent having an individual relationship with each child, I began to apply it in my nuclear family. The full implications of this principle, however, were not realized until I knew about the "person-to-person" relationship principle and had more awareness about triangles. The results of these efforts in my family of origin will be presented in another section.

The person-to-person relationship and related principles. The person-to-person relationship will be discussed in conjunction with other principles from which it was derived. Early in family research I observed the striking calm and the rapid change in families when one family member could begin to "differentiate a self" in chaotic, disturbed families. This phenomenon would occur after the anxious family had been submerged in symptoms and paralyzed by the inability to arrive at a joint decision for action. Eventually one member, unable to speak for the whole family, would begin to define where he stood on a issue and what he intended to do and not do. Almost immediately the entire family would become calmer. Then another family member would begin a version of the same process. Those families were too impaired for any member to maintain this operating position over long periods of time, but the observations provided ideas for theory and clinical experimentation in less impaired families. In the midst of these observations on families, I noted chaotic upsets within the research staff; staff members complained about each other and efforts to resolve differences in group discussions were unsuccessful. Using a principle developed from the research, I, the director, set out to define my role, and stated my long-term plans and intentions as clearly as possible. The "togetherness" group meetings were terminated. In the course of this rather exacting self-imposed assignment, I realized the degree to which I had infantilized the staff members by instructing them and even functioning for them, while I had been irresponsible in failing to do other things that came within my own area. Almost immediately the staff tension subsided and then another and another of the staff members began to define their responsibilities. Thereafter there were few staff upsets that could not be settled within hours instead of days. This same principle has been used frequently since then in all kinds of clinical, work, and family situations.

The principle of defining a self was later used in a modified form within my entire extended family network. The various nuclear families in the extended family system tend to group themselves into emotional clumps and the communication is often from "clump to clump' rather than from individual to individual. It was common for letters to be addressed to "Mr. and Mrs.——— and Family," or to "Mr. and Mrs.———," and often each nuclear family had one letter writer who would write for the entire family. I had used carbon copy letters to disseminate family information to multiple family members. This method was used during the period I was working on the multigenerational family history and I had more occasion to write than usual. The new plan was to define myself as a person as much as possible and to communicate individually to a wide spectrum of extended family members; I tried to establish as many individual relationships within the family as possible. Every possible opportunity was used to write personal letters to every niece and nephew. The less differentiated family segments still tended to reply with letters to my entire family, but more and more some began to write personal letters addressed to my office, and since they were addressed to me personally, my family never saw them. The return on this endeavor is like a long-term dividend; it has modified my image within the entire family.

Another project was the development of a "person-to-person" relationship with each of my parents and also with as many people as possible in the extended family. A person-to-person relationship is conceived as an ideal in which two people can communicate freely about the full range of personal issues between them. Most people cannot tolerate more than a few minutes on a personal level. When either party becomes anxious, he begins talking about a third person (triangles in another person), or the communication becomes impersonal and they talk about things. My immediate goal was to work toward a person-to-person relationship with each parent. Although I made some effort to develop this type of relationship with extended family members by writing letters to individuals, my effort with my parents was more intensive. In such an effort, one encounters every rejection, alliance, and resistance that are present in emotional systems everywhere. In disciplining the self to do this, one develops versatility and emotional courage in all relationships, one learns more about people than in most endeavors, and the family profits too. In some family situations the positive results are sweeping, both for the family and the one who initiated the effort. These experiences were used in clinical practice, which in turn made contributions to the effort with my own family. Most of the patterns in my family are present in all families to some degree. In practice, for instance, a nuclear family out of meaningful emotional contact with families of origin is more vulnerable to intense symptoms, and the problems tend to be more chronic than in families that maintain contact with parental families. The nuclear family is usually reluctant to face the emotional forces that led to isolation, but if they can know that successful establishment of meaningful emotional contact (an infrequent duty visit is not meaningful contact) usually decreases tension in the nuclear family, they are more motivated to make the effort. Progress is several times faster in the nuclear family that is in contact with families of origin than in the nuclear family that is isolated.

Person-to person relationships in the parental triangle. In clinical work with other families, I discovered that the pattern in my own family is the most common one in all families. My mother was the most active parent on most issues that had to do with her children. She made it her business to know what went on everywhere with the children. My father played a more peripheral role except on certain issues that came within his sphere of activity. He had to do with money issues, though it was within the rules of the system to speak to my mother before speaking to my father. He always made himself part of the action when anxiety issues developed between my mother and the children, and he made effective comments and actions to allay my mother's anxiety. From early childhood I participated in special activities with my father that did not include my mother. Much was oriented around work chores, but there were also frequent hunting and fishing trips, and in my teen years I took frequent business trips by car with him. We had long conversations about issues of special interest, but a smaller amount of time was spent on personal issues. He had boundless knowledge about nature and observations about wildlife, too little of which has been remembered in my years of urban living. Mother was the letter writer. My father's letters were usually brief and to the point, usually centered around money matters while I was in college. After I left college his letters to me were less frequent. My mother usually wrote for the family and signed her name, and my letters to my parents were addressed to "Mr. and Mrs."

It was a theoretical idea, rather than personal experience, that directed my effort over many years to differentiate myself from my family of origin, and to use the person-to-person relationship for a central part of the effort. At that time I knew a little about "triangles" but I did not have many techniques for using the knowledge to extricate myself from the emotional system. It took much more than the person-to-person relationship to get free of the emotional binds of the triangle, but that will be described later. My first effort with my parents consisted of writing individual letters to each of them. This method did not change the basic pattern. My mother still wrote for both even though her letters became a bit more personal. Then I made an effort utilizing telephone calls. When I telephoned, the usual sequence was one in which my father would answer and within seconds he would call my mother who would do most of the talking from an extension. My goal was to engage him in conversation longer, but this never worked. I rehearsed dialogue designed to talk straight to him but very soon he would either refer the issue to her for comment, or she would cut in and talk for him. If I asked him to silence her so we could talk, she would start a dialogue about that. I have never been effective in using the telephone for this effort. There was always the problem of others on extensions and I could not develop effective feedback.

Time with each parent alone is essential for establishing an individual relationship, but mere private talk with a single parent can accomplish little. One has to be aware that one was "programmed" into the system long ago and it is automatic for both parties to fall back on familiar patterns. An optimum condition for such a relationship is to find a subject of interest to both that does not involve the rest of the family. Each person has his own built-it resistance to working at such a relationship. I have sent people on special missions to parental families and have then had them report that it was impossible to get parents separated, or that there was not an "ideal time" for talking, or that they had postponed the effort until the last few hours, when the effort turned out to be inept. The experience with my parents paralleled that of many. With my father, it was hard to find personal subjects and difficult to keep a conversation alive. When I did introduce a personal subject, he would invoke the parental we-ness and respond with, "Mother thinks . . ." With my mother it was easy to keep conversation alive, but she would invoke triangles by talking about other people and it was just as difficult to keep the discussion on a person-to-person level. My over-all aim was to keep the conversation alive with my father, and to eliminate the triangles with my mother. With my father, I tried to prepare long lists of subjects ahead of time, but this was not the answer. To many issues he would respond with minimal comment, the list would be exhausted, and again there would be the uncomfortable silence.

There were some special occasions when I made more progress on the person-to-person relationships than all other times together. Two of these occurred at times of sickness. The first occasion occurred when my father was in the hospital after a moderately severe heart attack. This occasion provided the opportunity to talk about his fears of death, his philosophy of life, and the life goals and aspirations he may not have expressed otherwise. Another occasion occurred when my mother had major elective surgery. There were days with her in the hospital and evenings with my father at home alone. It was there also that I discovered the value of past history as a subject for personal communication. Most people are eager to talk about their own early life experiences to those interested in listening. I was working on the multigenerational family history at that time and I was eager for all that could be remembered. The next opportunity came a year or two later with my mother. In my work on past generations I had discovered a whole segment of her side of the family that she did not know existed. It covered a period from 1720 to 1850 when this segment had moved west. The family name was well-recorded in the area and there were cemeteries where they were buried, churches where they worshipped, lands they had owned, houses they had built, and other items of personal and family interest. I arranged a week-long automobile trip with her to visit all these places. That was a solid week of intense person-to-person contact with very little talking about others. This trip with my mother will be mentioned in the personal experience to be reported later.

In addition to the effort to develop a person-to-person relationship with my parents, I had also continued the effort to "detriangle" myself from the parental triangle. Since the "detriangling" was much more prominent in later family events, the description of that process will be only briefly described. The process of "differentiating a self" from a parental family involves two major steps. The first step is to develop the person-to-person relationships. This step helps to bring relationships more alive, it helps one to recognize old patterns that may have faded from view, and most of all, it results in livelier family response to the effort to "detriangle" or change the old patterns. A parental family can ignore such detriangling moves if relationships are distant. In this report, I have put more emphasis on the person-to-person relationship in relation to triangles than I do in my current work in "coaching" others with their families. There are two reasons for this emphasis. The first is the importance of the person-to-person relationship as a part of the total scheme. The second is that the person-to-person relationship method was in use before the detriangling process was well understood.

Up to this point in my family effort, I had incorrectly assumed that I could differentiate a self from my family of origin by differentiating a self from my parents. I believed that if I accomplished this step well I would not have to bother with all the other triangles in which my parents were imbedded. The notion about interlocking triangles had been in use almost ten years but I had not integrated this aspect of the theory into the work with my own family. As I developed increasing facility with triangles, and as the expected result had not been achieved, it became clear that some kind of a different effort was in order.

The original observation about the undifferentiated ego mass of my family of origin was always an over-all guide. My over-all goal, it will be recalled, was to be able to have an entire visit with the family without becoming fused into the emotional system. Though the result from all my various efforts with the family had been satisfying, especially the effort at developing person-to-person relationships, I still had not significantly increased the length of time before I would become "fused" into the family system when I visited, nor had I found a way to extricate myself before the visit had ended. The remainder of this report represents a new era in the family effort.

The Family History—Continued

After the reorganization of the family business, there was no obvious disharmony in the primary triangle of my father, mother, and second brother. My original postulation was that the negative side of the triangle would have to occur between my brother and mother, but this prediction was based entirely on theory and knowledge about triangles and not on experience from the past nor anything observed in the family. The relationship between my father, mother, and second brother had always been such a congenial one that it would be hard to conceive of friction between them. Even though I had become enough of a specialist to be a part-time consultant in organizational problems in business, and even with my relatively close contact with the family and my prediction about the next area of disharmony, it was not possible to get definite evidence to confirm my postulation nor to suggest an alternative one. There were superficial discontents expressed here and there between the children and their spouses, or between cousins, but there was no definite pattern and these problems seemed to belong more to everyday minor issues than to basic issues in the central family triangle. I even looked for a common pattern that emerged from my multigenerational studies; it had been predicted that conflict between siblings would be perpetuated by the descendents of these siblings far into future generations. It took some time for a definite pattern to emerge in my family. There are several factors which affect the emergence of the pattern, including the basic adaptability of the family (conflict does not occur between people if the adaptability is good), the absence of stress of sufficient degree to cause symptoms to surface, and the number of subtriangles to absorb minor levels of disharmony.

This pattern in my family is identical to many that exist in businesses and staffs of institutions in which the basic problem which exists on the highest administrative level is triangled and retriangled again and again until the conflict surfaces between two employees low in the administrative hierarchy. The three areas in which "undifferentiation" are absorbed in a nuclear family are marital conflict, sickness or dysfunction in a spouse, and projection to one or more children. The total amount of undifferentiation, determined by the basic level of differentiation in the family, is distributed primarily to one area, or any combination of the three areas. In my parental family the level of conflict is very low, the primary mechanism is projection to a child (lower life adjustment of oldest sister), and the other mechanism is physical illness, usually brief medical or surgical illnesses. These areas provide clues about symptoms when family stress mounted.

Aside from the little subsystems of anxiety and concern in each nuclear family, the prevailing stress in my total family was connected with the business. Early in this period, my second brother developed a brief symptom slightly suggestive of a malignancy. Since the "go power" for the family rested with him, anxiety went very high for a week until the possibility of malignancy was ruled out. Thereafter, the stress was related more to health issues in my parents and disposition of the business in case of their deaths. My parents were getting quite old and each serious-appearing illness in either sent out some kind of an alarm, and precipitated some kind of family reaction. The basic reaction in the central family triangle included my father at one corner, my mother, youngest sister, and sister's husband at another, and my second brother and his nuclear family at the other. One of the first changes in the postorganizational period (from my standpoint) was a cool distance between my second brother and me, initiated by him. He and I had always been close and this, I realized in retrospect, continued until the business was reorganized. After that, he was congenial enough in our brief exchanges, but his business and civic activities were demanding. During the period I was working on person-to-person relationships, he was the one important family member with whom it was not possible to develop a relationship. Time planned to see him alone would be converted into a social event. When it became evident that he was avoiding me, I became more persistent in my effort to see him, and he became equally persistent in avoiding me. When I made a summer trip home, he and his wife took a vacation away during the entire period of my visit. Here was a situation where two of the most important figures in the family system could not get together! He was important at home and I was important because of my position as "oldest" and because I had made myself important through my various efforts. As the distance between my second brother and me increased, the stories about him increased. I was hearing all about him and he was probably hearing all about me from the family network, but I could not see him. He rarely wrote letters, so that communication was cut off. One summer I made a concerted effort to meet with my second brother. Expecting that he might again leave during my visit, I waited until the last possible moment, about two days before, to announce my visit. He and his wife left on a trip the following day and returned a few hours before my family was scheduled to leave, just long enough to exchange greetings and superficial comments. The trend of events that are the subject of this presentation began about six weeks later.

An important triangle at work at this time was the one between my mother, my second brother, and me. I had worked very hard on the triangle with my parents and me, assuming that my problem would be solved. Now a new version of the problem had been displaced onto the new triangle. When conflict arose in the business, my mother would communicate by some means, if not directly, that I was on her side, and my brother would react as if this was reality. I began to perceive some of this development on trips. The process would emerge in the form of gossip-type stories which in an emotional system communicate, "We two are together on this issue. We are in agreement about that other third person." One of the better ways to disengage from such a triangling "secret" communication is to go to the third person and report the message in a neutral way. I was out of effective contact with my second brother then and the only move I could make was to tell my mother that I was neutral. She would say that she respected my position and I would assume she was acting neutral about me with others. I would leave town and the family would react as if I was on her side.

Action is required when words fail to detriangle in emotional systems. My mother has always used "secret" communications to facilitate her position in the emotional system. One of my early responses to her communication was to listen, and I thought I could listen without taking sides. In retrospect, this maneuver was one of the key triggers for my early fusions into the emotional system. Listening to such communications without response, pretending that one is not involved, does not fool an emotional system. When I was aware that "no response" was not effective, I began using comments such as, "That's one of the better stories." This method was a little more effective. In retrospect, I undoubtedly was responding while I kidded myself that I was neutral. I had worked much more actively on the triangle with my father, mother, and myself and I had been more effective in detriangling from that. There had been several exchanges about "secrets" that turned the tide in that area. The first one was a letter in which mother communicated some negative story about my father. In the next mail I wrote to my father to say that his wife had just told me this story about him, and I wondered why she told me instead of telling him. He showed the letter to her, and she fussed about not being able to trust me. Several letters such as this, plus similar exchanges when I was with both parents, had been reasonably effective at detriangling me from them. During that period, mother made comments about my reading too much between the lines, and I made comments about her writing too much between the lines.

The triangling pattern in my family of origin, which is the usual one in all emotional systems, was most intense during stress periods. Various family members were grouped on the corners of the primary triangle, except that the grouping would be somewhat different, depending on the emotional issues. The two on the togetherness side of a triangle would talk about the outsider. With various versions of different issues being discussed in four separate households, and with me in reasonably good contact with them all, it was possible to keep a good reading of the family emotional tension. My first brother has hardly been mentioned in this report. His lifelong position in the family has been one of moderate involvement and acting uninvolved, with statements that he would be willing to help anytime if he was needed but that he did not want to "just talk."

The Family Experience

Prologue. The important sequence of events began when my second brother's wife's brother died suddenly of a heart attack. He, like my second brother, was a vigorous business man who was "head of the clan" for his family in another state. His death left my brother's wife as the next most responsible member of her family of origin. The death of such an important family member can "shake" a family system for months. This was the "shock wave" phenomenon I had investigated in some early research, in which a death can be followed by a series of apparently unrelated human problems throughout the family system. This present situation had the characteristics of one in which there could be such a reaction. I reasoned that, sequentially, this death would "shake" my second brother's wife, that my second brother would help her assume responsibility in her family, that he would become involved in her deep anxiety, that my family would react to his anxiety, and the anxiety could amplify minor problems into major ones at vulnerable points in my family. My first thought was to observe carefully and possibly to lend some help if such did occur. About two weeks later there was an indirect report from friends that my older sister was in an anxious, upset state. She is so attuned to emotional forces in the family that a symptom in her is often an early indication of tension in the family system. There were indications that she was probably responding to the pressure in the larger family system rather than to her own nuclear family. The event was noted. About two weeks after that, there was an episode of overt disagreement in the central family triangle of sufficient intensity that it became an "alive" issue for discussion throughout the family. My second brother was pressing my parents for a small block of stock which would give him control of the family business. My father, in the togetherness side of the triangle with my second brother, was agreeable, but my mother was opposed. I had expected the "anxiety wave" issues that autumn to be expressed more as illness, and I was wondering how to deal with that kind of anxiety should the need arise. It is easier to deal with overt conflict than with internalized symptoms, and overt conflict is relatively rare in our family. My thoughts began spinning about ways I could utilize this conflictual episode to interrupt this anxiety wave for the family, and also to utilize it as a way to further my "differentiation of self." In such an anxiety wave period, the person with the most vulnerable heart can have a heart attack, a chronic illness can flare up, a teen-aged child can wreck a car or break a bone, or any of numerous other symptoms could develop in any member of the family. The overt conflict presented new ideas and challenges, but I did not have a clearly defined plan. I was scheduled for a trip home in about two months, so I had time to think the problem through and to devise a working plan. This is the wonderful thing about triangles. One can construct an amazingly accurate hypothesis from which it is possible to plan a predictable result if the differentiating one can contain his own emotional functioning enough to carry through. About three weeks after the conflictual issue, my second brother was immobilized for several weeks with symptoms of a herniated vertebral disc.

The plan. People treat families with great caution, lest the equilibrium be upset. There are situations that automotically disturb families, just as storms disturb a lake, but if one is trying purposely to disturb the surface of a lake, one finds how difficult it is. The carefully worked out specific plans for my visit to the family were some eight weeks in preparation. In my years of family research and therapy, I had diagrammed and successfully blueprinted my way through triangle webs for many other families and I wanted especially to make this effort work for my own family. The over-all goal was to focus on the triangle involving my mother, second brother, and myself, and, preferably, also to include my father. With this configuration there would be the original triangle on which I had done most work, my parents and myself, plus the new triangle in which the conflict developed. My second brother and mother were central figures.

For some years my brother had been avoiding me. The issue of making contact with a family member who retreats and who refuses to relate to issues, had long been a special interest of mine. An immediate goal for this project, then, was to create a situation in which my brother would seek contact with me. It was the development of conflict between my mother and second brother that first motivated this plan; it is far easier to deal with conflict than other mechanisms in such an effort. My aim was to have a conflictual issue around which to work. The recent conflict over the business would still be sufficiently alive during the visit, but to focus on that would make that issue into a *reality* issue rather than a manifestation of an emotional system. In addition, I would be more vulnerable to being triangled with that issue. So, I devised the plan to stir up the family emotional system, using old issues from the past around which to work. Said in another way, the goal was to stir up a "tempest in a teapot" from issues of the past that would highlight the emotional patterns among the principal family members. One other item in the planning was a primary focus. In the past I had done fairly well in detriangling myself from one triangle, only to have the tension slip into another triangle; this pattern had been my undoing. In preparation for all the potential peripheral triangles that could align themselves with issues and prove difficult, I worked out a plan that permitted no "allies" in my effort. In other words, it was an effort to keep the entire family in one big emotional clump, and to detriangle any ally who tried to come over to my side for this project. I had used this rationale before on smaller emotional systems in my practice and I knew the principle was workable. A final part of the plan was to involve my first brother. He is an important part of the family and I wanted to find a way to include him, too. Very early in my planning I called to tell him about the "awful conflict" in the family; that his help was needed; that I was going to be home on a specific date; and I urged that he return home to be part of this family effort. I was sure he would follow his usual pattern of treating the stock transfer as the reality issue, but I was prepared to deal with his introducing the topic of lawyers and determining which side was right.

My greatest effort went into preparing a long letter to my second brother. First I made a list of old emotional issues that focused on my relationship to him and his to me, the family system's relationship to him and to me, and relationships within his nuclear family. It was my purpose to have an issue for all key family members, especially issues that would touch each relationship cleanly. The letter was written and rewritten in order to eliminate hostile or derogatory comments. If the differentiating one becomes hostile or angry he is vulnerable to losing objectivity and either defending or counterattacking when the issues are hurled back at him. I played and replayed these issues so many times that I could be rather objective about each one. The more I did this, the more it was impossible for me to be angry with anyone. In fact, I had only heightened respect for my second brother, who had functioned so well as "head of the clan" at home. I developed a special technique that avoided criticizing him. This technique was to relate "stories" I had heard about him, to tell him that everyone knew these stories but him, state that the family kept warning everyone not to tell him lest he get upset, and to ask why he had not bothered to know what people were saying about him. This sequence is present in every family system—the system talks about the absent one and the system has definite rules about keeping the gossiping "secret." In my letter, my posture to the "stories" was to say they had been going on for years, that some were interesting but most were boring, that the stories seemed to be embellished more during upset periods, that I had long since given up trying to separate fact from fiction in such stories, that I was tired of being admonished about what to tell him and what to avoid telling him, and that this letter represented my right to communicate what I wanted to say directly to him without regard for what the system thought was good for him to hear. This technique, designed to present material in terms of "stories," proved so effective I have since employed it routinely in my practice. One always has an adequate supply of appropriate stories to be used for particular situations.

I started the letter by saying that I had wanted to talk to him for a long time but, since he had been away during my recent trips, I had to resort to putting my ideas onto paper. I mentioned that people were saying things about him in connection with the business. I said I did not understand how this had happened, but there it was. In order to touch on his nuclear family, I said there was a "story" about him and his wife being worried about a problem their son had, and that I had been warned to never say a word about it because he and his wife were so sensitive about it. In one paragraph I emphasized that I had no interest in who controlled the family business but that I recognized his contribution to the business and to the entire family. Then I wrote a full paragraph of "reversals," which is a psychotherapeutic principle I have long used of making a point by saying the opposite. This technique works predictably if the therapist is "outside" the emotional system and can be sufficiently casual and detached. Here was my brother who was working a sixteen hour day for himself, his nuclear family, his parents, the whole extended family system, and all connected with it. He was doing a wonderful job, except that in periods of anxiety he became overly serious and emotionally "uptight." If I were to tell him to slow down and take it easy and not get so overly responsible for everyone, it would merely be what he has been telling himself and trying unsuccessfully to do. Therefore, the "reversals." I wrote him that I was "shifting gears from my previous posture," and would do something I did not ordinarily do—namely, I was going to give him some good sound advice. I implored him to be more responsible. I said that he had the responsibility for his parents and they were not appreciative enough. Maybe he had not worked hard enough to take care of them, or maybe the problem was in not forcing them to appreciate him better. In any case, he should limber up his back and give it the good old college try. I said that he had all the problems to solve in the business, he had to straighten things out with his parents, his wife and children needed more attention, he had additional problems in his wife's family, and there was an immediate problem with his sister's desponden-cy. I ended the letter by saying that I would be home on a specific date, but since I had already said all that was necessary in the letter, it would not be necessary to see him unless he had something to say to me. I signed it, "Your Meddlesome Brother."

By calculation, this letter was mailed exactly two weeks before my trip home. In the same mail I wrote my first brother to tell him the exact date I would be home and I implied that if he cared about his family he would manage to get home on his date to help clear up this terrible situation. In all these letters, I used words such as terrible, awful, pressing, and horrible to describe the family plight. These words were all designed to stir up the "tempest in a teapot" for the purposes of the visit. I also wrote my oldest sister to say I had heard about her distressing upset and I had written her brother to help her out until I got there. I signed that letter, "Your Worried Brother." Then I waited exactly one week to call my parents under the guise of finding out who might meet the plane when I arrived one week later. Actually, I wanted a reading on the results of the letter. My mother said my brother was furious about "that" letter I had written him. I pretended I did not know what letter that could be, saying he had not written me in a long time and that I did not owe him a letter. She said he had several pages I had signed, that he was showing it to people, he was going to have it xeroxed, and that he would take care of me when I arrived. I said I was distressed to hear that something had upset him but I would be glad to see him when I arrived. With this new information, I wrote several other letters within the next hour. One was to my younger sister, who lives near my parents and who functions as the responsible woman in the second generation. I wrote that I had just talked with our mother and had found that my second brother was upset about something I had said in a letter. I said that I found this hard to understand because all I had done was write some of my thoughts on paper and send them to him. I wrote that it was a mystery to me how thoughts that came out of my head could upset him. If he was upset, I said, I was deeply grieved because that could upset the whole family, and as "Big Mother" she had a responsibility to do whatever was necessary to soothe him with whatever Big Mothers do to calm people. I asked her to please treat my letter as confidential because I did not want to upset mother too, and to please advise me immediately what I could do to make amends to Little Brother. I said that if my thoughts were upsetting my second brother, maybe I could think different or "right" thoughts. I signed that letter, "Your Anxious Brother." In the same mail, within the hour, I wrote an exactly opposite message to my mother. I told her that I had known about that letter all the time but I was afraid to let her know because she might tell Little Brother and it would ruin my plan, which was going nicely thus far. I said that since I knew I could trust her (she had pledged me to thousands of secrets in the past), I would let her in on the strategy. I said that my plan was to get Little Brother really angry at me in order to draw the fire off the family situation at home. I told her that I had used a few little personal issues to warm him up, but that I had some big issues to fire him up if he cooled off during the week. I ended the letter by saying that this was all very confidential and that one "leak" would ruin the entire strategy—when one is planning strategy it is not advisable to invite the "enemy" to the briefing sessions. That letter was signed, "Your Strategic Son." Later I heard about my mother's reaction to this letter, which was to say, "I got the craziest letter. I did not know what to do with it, so I burned it." The day before the trip, I received a letter from my younger sister saying that my second brother had spent over two hours with my parents after he received the letter, that they thought it was horrible, and that he had apparently won them over to his side. She said that maybe this was one time Little Brother would not leave town when Big Brother came home—that he was mad enough to stay. She reported that he was really going to have it out with me when I arrived and that my older sister's husband was going to "back me into a corner to prove the lies I had been telling about his wife." Then she added that I had really stirred up the family and she hoped that my strategy worked. She ended up with, "I am back of you if I can be of help. I am really looking forward to your visit this time. It should be very interesting."

I hope the reader is clear about the purpose of these efforts. The conflicting messages were designed to prevent any one segment of the family from getting on my "side." Messages run back and forth in such a family system as if by telepathy. The only letter that was not shown to a circle of others was the "Strategic Son" letter to my mother. My younger sister was the only one reasonably outside the seriousness of the family emotional system, as was conveyed by her comment about looking forward to the "interesting" visit. A red flag had gone up from her comment about "I am back of you," which I handled by telling her that I was going to tell the family she had invited me home to help her with her Big Mother role. She retreated from taking sides with me by acting as if the issues I had raised were all very serious.

My younger sister and her husband and daughter met my wife and me at the airport. The trip was planned so that I would spend two days with my family, then three days at a medical meeting at which my wife's presence was desirable, and then two days back again with my family. My wife had no direct knowledge of what I was doing. From long experience, I have found that a differentiating effort routinely fails if anyone else knows anything about it. To be effective, each action and move must come from within the person who makes the effort. These decisions and actions often have to be made instantaneously and, for better or worse, the *individual* has the responsibility. To discuss the plan with another person *who is part of the system* invites certain failure. The first my wife knew of what was going on was when my younger sister began to discuss bits and pieces of the family events after our arrival at the airport. My wife did not ask a single question nor make positive or negative comments about my family at any time during the trip. This had never happened before. It was Saturday midnight when we arrived at my parents' home. The only comment my mother made about the family occurred Sunday morning when she said she hoped things could work out without hard feelings. I said I was glad she was still a good mother who worried about her children. There was not a word from any segment of the family on Sunday morning. Early Sunday afternoon we were invited to my younger sister's home for an early afternoon meal; included were both of my parents, my wife and myself, and my sister and her husband and daughter. Just as we finished desert and coffee, my second brother telephoned to say he had been checking around town to find me and he would be there in a few minutes. My brother was now seeking me out instead of me chasing him. The inclusion of him and his wife made this into the perfect group for this long-anticipated and rehearsed meeting. Every important triangle in the family system was represented. I had purposely stayed close to my parents all morning, hoping to facilitate a meeting of most of these people, but good fortune was with me when it worked out this way. My immediate goal was to avoid defending anything, or attacking any issues, to be able to avoid getting angry even with provocation, and to have an instant casual response to any comment.

My second brother exchanged pleasantries, but after a minute or two he took out "the letter" and said he was there to discuss the epistle I had written when I was drunk. I said that was an advantage in living where booze was cheap and that if his supply was low, I could get some good prices for him. The meeting went on for two hours and was all personal. The principals in the center were my brother, his wife, and me. My wife and my father were slightly out of the group. My mother moved around just back of the main group. Most of the conversation was between my brother and me and mother, with a few comments from my brother's wife. My brother had reacted most severely to a "story" about him and threatened a libel suit against me. I agreed that it was awful to start such stories and I thought he should find out who started that story and prosecute the person to the full extent of the law. There was more talk about stories, and I expressed surprise he did not know what others said about him. I hoped he would pay more attention to the stories in the future, since he lived there all the time and I only heard them when I visited. His wife had reacted most to the story about their son, to which she said, "I always say nice things about your children." I responded, "I have heard nice stories about all of you, too. There was just not time to remember all of them." Then my brother and his wife began to report negative stories about me, to which I responded with some version of, "That was a fairly amusing one, but there have been some really good ones about me if you had just paid attention and listened better." Mother was pacing back and forth in the back, with comments such as, "I hope I do not die and leave a divided family." At one point toward the end of the meeting, my brother accused me of being in league with mother, and that the whole thing started when she and I took that trip together to see the lands of her ancestors. I said, "You are really intuitive about some things! How did you know about that? You're right. That's when she and I planned the whole thing." Mother responded vigorously with, "That's the biggest lie I ever heard! I will never tell you anything else again." I turned to my brother and said, "Now you see how she tries to wangle out of things when she is caught with the truth." At the end of the meeting, as my brother and his wife were leaving, his wife said, "I never saw such a family in all my life. I think we should do more talking *to* each other and less talking *about* each other."

The end of that Sunday afternoon was one of the most satisfying periods of my entire life. I had actively participated in the most intense family emotion possible and I had stayed completely out of the "ego mass" of my very own family! I had gone through the entire visit without being "triangled" or without being fused into the family emotional system. About two-thirds through the meeting I knew I had been successful for I noted that the family system had lost its emotional punch, and I knew that, if there was not some completely unanticipated event, I would go through the entire meeting without fusing into the system. Even if I had been slightly or moderately triangled, I would have more than achieved my primary mission for the visit, which was to interrupt the anxiety wave in the family. I *knew* that had been accomplished even by the time the family meeting was well under-way. I also *knew* that my postulations about interlocking triangles were accurate by the time the family meeting started. To have completed the meeting without becoming triangled was additional evidence that I had attained the technical excellence to make the theoretical system work. It was the total success of the operation that was surprising, exhilarating, and exhausting. I had spent a dozen years pondering the structure and function of this "undifferentiated family ego mass" and I was so accustomed to each new effort being a partial success that I was hardly prepared for total success. It was equivalent to having finally mastered the secret of the system and having gone all the way to the goal line in one try. Since I believe that one's own life adjustment is dependent on working out a "self" in one's own family of origin, it was equivalent to having reached the summit after a hundred unsuccessful tries. To me the most important long-term accomplishment was the proof that an emotional system has a knowable structure and function, and that one can work out the predictable answers to its problems on a drawing board.

I knew there was follow-up work to be done on Monday, the day after the meeting. To make a differentiating process work, one has to continue in relationship with the family system. Said in another way, it is necessary to keep talking to the system. This is the point where the feeling system dictates withdrawal and comfortable distance, which will result in the system "tightening up" again. On Monday, I knew my brother was still angry and reactive and I would have to seek him out. I didn't want to go see him, but I knew I had to; responsibility overcame the feelings. For the first time in years, I found him alone and willing to talk. There was an exchange of superficial pleasantry and then, after sufficient time to assure myself that he would not mention the family issue about the business, I asked, "Are you still mad at me?" He responded with a detached, "Hell, no!" Then I said that on my way to town I had heard some new stories about him and would he be interested in what others were saying about him? He responded with, "I do not want to hear any more stories." I expressed surprise that a man in his position would not want to know what people said about him, and that to keep him informed I would be willing to write the stories on a piece of paper and send the paper in the mail. He said he would return my mail unopened and unclaimed. I said that I found his attitude hard to understand, but I would respect it, and instead I would tell him a compliment I heard about him as I crossed the street. I had heard someone say that his intentions were good most of the time. He broke into a wide smile, the first of his old "friends-winning" smile I had seen in months. After that I had the first person-to-person talk I had had with him in years. He talked about his effort with the larger family system, his own family, and the business. During this discourse he talked about our oldest sister and how he had been trying to help her, and how she seemed to defeat every effort. At one point he said, "Sometimes I think she is retarded." Immediately after this long talk with him, I drove down to see my older sister, and said ..."Hey, Sis, I have been talking to your brother about your problems and he said you refuse to listen to him. What in the world have you been doing to him to make him talk like that?" In previous years my "detriangling" efforts had been awkward and forced. Now they flowed smoothly and automatically, and I no longer had to discipline myself to do them. I made several more smooth "detriangling" efforts with my parents. That same Monday I wrote a special letter to my first brother, who had not come for the weekend. I chided him about his delinquency and irresponsibility toward the family and reported that I had been home all weekend trying to restore peace and harmony to the family, but that the harder I tried the more I seemed to upset them. I said, "I have been trying to establish free and open communications to calm them down. All I did was tell them some of the stories you have been telling me about them, and this seems to upset them instead of calm them. This weekend has been a complete failure and I do not know where I failed. Since I have failed, it is now up to you to get home immediately to deal with this emergency situation." I later discovered he had been within 65 miles of home that weekend on a business trip, but that the pressure of business had made it impossible for him to get there.

My wife and I were away from home early Tuesday until late Thursday that week. Then we returned home until Saturday noon. For the first time in my life, I had been completely outside the family ego mass all week. There was no major effort on my part those last days, but merely a casual detriangling of each new situation that presented itself. My younger sister and her husband were even more casual and detached than before. They spoke of how "interesting" and "enjoyable" they found the sequence of events. My parents still voiced concern, but they were calmer than they had been in a long time. My brother's wife sought me out, and I had the first serious person-to-person talk with her in many years. Just before my departure, my second brother's younger son came to say goodbye to me, which was unusual for him. He said, "Thank you very much for coming home this week." A week after the trip, my first brother called to talk for an hour. I did much detriangling with him but it was clear that he and his wife were also relatively casual and "outside" the seriousness of the family issues. His wife later wrote me several letters to ask about my "plan and strategy." In the past I had been "undone" by partners and I was not about to get serious with her and risk spoiling my success. I told her I was hurt by her implications of deviousness on my part when I had spent so much time thinking good things about people and doing good things for them. I assured her that my only goal was to restore the basic love and togetherness in the family. Two weeks after the visit I received a long letter from my mother in which she included one concise paragraph about the visit. In it she said, "With all its ups and downs, your last trip home was the greatest ever." Immediately after the visit, I had written to my older sister again, chiding her about my continuing efforts to get various members of her family to "take care of her and her problems." She responded by kidding me for telling everyone else to take care of her while I did nothing to help take care of her. Then she said she was perfectly capable of taking care of herself, that she did not know where she had been for the last forty years, but she had a new outlook and a new lease on life. The issue between my parents and brother about stock and control of the family business completely faded after that "family experience" weekend.

In the almost three-year interim since the family experience, the family has been on the best over-all level of adaptation in many years. There have been anxieties and small crises, but they have been less intense than formerly. I have come to have a new role in the family which I call the role of "the differentiating one." I have had increasing experience with this phenomenon with others and the usual pattern is similar to that in my family. The one who achieves some success at differentiation has a kind of appeal for the entire family. It is as if any member of the family can approach this one and have the advantage of an emotionally detached viewpoint which in turn helps him or her develop a different perspective. It is more a matter of action than words because words often are negative while the action closeness is markedly better. The family sort of comes to expect the differentiating one always to function well in this position. For instance, there have been other periods of mild emotional "uptightness" in the family in which someone would invite me to get involved or return for a visit and would than administer a stern admonition, "But be sure you do not do or say anything to upset the family." This message is a subtle demand for another miracle performance, but differentiation is a self-motivated, self-energized effort and it cannot succeed with outside stimulus.

An interesting event occurred two years after "the experience." In my continuing multigenerational family history effort, I had discovered in a nearby county, a whole segment of my father's family that he had never known about. I arranged two trips to go with him alone to see the land they had owned and the houses where they had lived. Although I thought I had achieved a good person-to-person relationship with him from the former years, the time spent with him on those long drives was so enjoyable there was not time to talk about all the issues that came up automatically. At this time it was possible to talk about the full range of important subjects without avoidance or defensiveness, and we developed a far better relationship than we had ever had. This experience brought a new awareness that I simply did not know what constitutes a really solid person-to-person relationship. The day after those trips, my second brother asked if I had time for a drink before dinner. He and I spent another period going into issues important to both of us. During the talk he thanked me for what I had done for our father, and for all the effort that had gone into finding that segment of Dad's family. He said, "Dad is ten years younger now than he was when you started this effort." My view of the situation was slightly different. I believe that I had done something to change my relationship with my father, which in turn changed his relationship to all he contacted. I do think, however, that the work on his family was the issue around which the relationship changed.

Finally, there is the family perception of a "differentiating step" such as was described here. No two people who were present at that "family experience" or who participated from a distance would have the same view of what happened. A differentiating step has two sides. Only the differentiating one knows the logical, orderly thinking and planning that has to go into such an effort. If anyone else knows about it, then it is doubtful that any differentiation will result from the effort. The other side is the feeling, emotional response, and if this reaction does not occur there is strong doubt that any differentiation will take place. The initial family reaction is negative and takes the form of surprise, anger, and a "you must be crazy" attitude. When one person is doing a differentiating step the others react emotionally, and people do not think while they react. Immediately after the nodal point breakthrough, there will be certain family members who will offer a spontaneous "thank you." If the differentiating one requests or demands an elaboration on the initial expression of appreciation, the response is automatically the opposite of what was expected. At this point there will be comments in the direction of the "togetherness" laws that govern the feeling side of the operation. The comments are likely to consist of devaluing or denying the importance of the event, or may even express a critical opinion if a complaint response is desired. A differentiating effort that is successful has to be for "self" alone. If it is done for self alone and the effort is successful, the system automatically benefits also. If it is done primarily to help others or with the expectation that others will approve and express appreciation, then the effort was for togetherness and not for differentiation; an emotional system does not appreciate such stressful nefarious maneuvers in the service of togetherness.

Post-Conference Clinical Experience

In the years before the breakthroughs with my own family, I had been using the theory, principles, and techniques involved in the differentiation of self in a method I called "family psychotherapy with a single family member." This method involved my "coaching" others as they attempted versions of what I have described with my own family. The results were good, but I still considered formal psychotherapy with husband and wife together to be the most effective of all methods. I urged members of the mental health professions to have formal family psychotherapy themselves as the best possible preparation for the practice of family psychotherapy. A good percentage of my private practice has been devoted to doing family psychotherapy with members of the mental health professions and their spouses; I considered this therapy also as training for the practice of family psychotherapy.

After the breakthrough with my own family of origin, I included my new knowledge about differentiation, illustrated with examples from my own family experience, in formal teaching sessions with psychiatric residents and others in training to learn family psychotherapy. On their own initiative, some of the trainees began to try some of the principles and techniques with their own families of origin. I would first hear about their efforts when they ran into the predictable emotional impasses and then asked for consultation about what had happened and for "coaching" to get themselves free. This coaching was done in the same didactic meetings in which the teaching was done. Over the next months, those who had been most successful with their families developed unusual skill and flexibility as family psychotherapists. They were adept at avoiding intense emotional entanglements with families in their practice, and they could work comfortably with upset and distraught families. They ascribed theis ability as being related to their work with their own families, and a new perspective on what it meant to get "outside the family emotional system." The issue of family psychotherapy for these trainees and their spouses had not been considered. They were doing unusually well in their clinical work, and since my focus was on their efficiency as therapists, I paid little attention to their emotional functioning with their spouses and children. After a year or two I realized that the trainees who had devoted primary attention to their families of origin had automatically made as much, or even more progress, with their spouses and children as similar trainees who had been in formal family psychotherapy with their spouses for the same period of time. The experience with this new method provides strong indications that psychotherapy as we have known it in the past may one day be considered superfluous.

There are some tentative speculations I could make about the efficiency of defining a self in one's parental family. One speculation is that it is easier to make valid observations of emotional forces in the more removed, but equally important, parental family, than in the nuclear family in which one's needs are more intimately imbedded. It is also easier to take an action stand in the parental family than in the nuclear family. From my experience, any progress made with one's parental family is automatically translated into the nuclear family. Another speculation is that the parental family effort requires that the trainee more quickly accept responsibility for his own life, and requires him to accept the notion that he through his own effort can modify his own family system. A trainee is more on his own resources when he deals with the emotional reaction in his own family than when he sees his therapist with his spouse.

This approach to training family therapists is too new for there to be more than early clinical impressions. The method is certainly not for everyone. It requires hard work and dedication. It is not possible for a trainee to make progress until he can contain his own emotional functioning sufficiently to *know* the difference between being inside or outside of an emotional system. Until the trainee is partially outside the system, a differentiating technique is either hollow meaningless words or a hostile assault on the system, and an emotional system knows the difference and reacts accordingly. With trainees partially outside the system, it has been possible to help them avoid time consuming pitfalls, to focus on productive areas, and to achieve a reasonably good beginning process of differentiation in a fraction of the time that my effort required. At the time of my own breakthrough in differentiation, I considered it one of the most significant events in my personal life to that point. It is now proving to be a significant turning point in my professional life.

The presentation to the Family Research Conference included about fifteen minutes of my family history and a few background principles, followed by about fifteen minutes of the clinical experience. For listeners who did not have a reasonably firm grasp of my theoretical system, the brief presentation was mostly an emotional experience. From my standpoint, the goal for me and my family in this presentation was a reasonable success. It was not the success within the "family" of family therapists that the original experience had been with my own family, but the family therapists are not as important to me as my own family, and I was not motivated to work on them in such detail.[1] It is my opinion that most of the participants reacted emotionally to the presentation (it had been planned that way), and that most had no background to regard it as other than a bold, imaginative approach conceived and executed by an intuition that somehow knew what to do at the right time. I hope this presentation has conveyed sufficient additional data for most to know that it was carefully thought through as a conceptual system and that the ability to execute the theoretical assumptions was developed after years of constant practice and modification of techniques to fit the theory. Most of the conference participants reacted as positively to the presentation as my family did. There were those who reacted emotionally to the extent that they considered the presentation to be selfish and hostile and hurtful, but even they were mostly positive in reserving an over-all opinion. Were it not so, then differentiation would not be possible.

Since the 1967 conference there have been concerns from some quarters about my making public this personal report about my family. In the belief that my family is pretty much the same as all families, and that my family is basically grateful for all the dividends that developed from my assumed role as "troublemaker," and in the deep belief that each in his own way, and each with a different reservation, would be basically pleased to have me do a public report about "us all," I had little reservation about this public report. As families move from the compartmentalized, less mature world of secrets and foibles which they assume they are keeping under cover, and into the world of permitting their private lives to be more open and a possible example for others to follow, they grow up a little each day.

Discussion

Note: *Conference participants heard only the final section of this paper, entitled "The Family Experience." The discussion following the original speech has been retained in its original form, even though it refers to a slightly different version of the presentation, inasmuch as the points made and reactions expressed still fit with the revised version. In particular it is hoped that the comments betray the freshness and surprise of the material and its impact on an audience which had been expecting a very different kind of presentation.*

Chairman Watzlawick: I believe I am speaking for everyone present in this room when I say that we are most thankful to Dr. Bowen for a most enlightening and also entertaining lecture—the two adjectives usually don't go together.

Personally, I admire him for his ability to stay out of such emotional systems for twenty-four hours. With me, it is only fifteen minutes. It bears out the old saying that you can't be too careful in the choice of your family. It also reminds me of something that someone said, that if people define a situation as real, then for all intents and purposes it becomes real.

May I now call on the panel to discuss this paper? Dr. Rubinstein, would you care to start off?

Dr. Rubinstein: I would like to start by saying to Dr. Bowen that now I understand why he has delayed writing to me.

I am fascinated because I was triangled throughout your talk, and I found myself writing and writing notes, trying to detriangle myself. I think the concept of the triangle, which has some continuity with what we were talking about yesterday about triads and dyads, is a fascinating one because it brings our clinical experience into the discussion. I have also operated out of the idea that the dyad is an abstract construct and I have wondered many times, in clinical practice, if such a thing as a dyad really exists. For example, in a mother-child schizophrenic relationship, one wonders if there is not always a third party present. It is difficult to conceive that two people can be related so intensely in a symbiotic way without having to differentiate themselves as a unit from a third party. The third party operates as a differentiating factor which solidifies and reassures the existence of the dyad. I agree fully with you, therefore, that probably the building block in human relationship is the triangle, the triad.

In working with couples, I came across some of Norman Paul's ideas about the mourning process, and they influenced my thinking about the techniques we use in clinical practice in marriage therapy. Aside from changing the rules of the game in the relationship between both marital figures, one useful technique has been to open up the emotional system in which each operates in the triangles with their parents, in the presence of the other mate. By opening up these outside emotional systems, some kind of empathic response is created in the other mate. Hopefully, the empathic relationship between both mates is then going to establish a new sort of triangle on a different level. This is why I would like to qualify your term "detriangling." Are we destroying the triangle, are we detriangling, or are we changing the triangles to a different level of functioning?

I wonder to what extent triangling is really necessary to bring empathy into the relationship between both mates. The therapist who becomes part of the triangle has to prepare himself to work through the separation process. How can he get out of the triangle or change his triangular function to a different level? I hope we will have a chance to talk more aobut this.

Chairman Watzlawick: Thank you very much, David. John Weakland is going to be the next discussant.

Mr. Weakland: Dr. Bowen began by saying two true things. He said he was going to depart from his prepared paper and he was going to provide an experience. I think that listening to Dr. Bowen is always an experience, but today was even more so.

I'm going to be very brief, because I don't want to take anything away from the direct impact of the experience which he has provided for us. I think enlightenment in this area comes at the level of experience and not just at the level of ideas, so I will take only one or two minutes, reversing his shift, to return to his prepared paper slightly and to make a couple of general points.

Certainly, the paper he gave me to read, and also the outline which I think was sent around generally, spoke at length about the undifferentiated ego mass and triangles. I must say that I didn't really understand what he was talking about until today—but now I think I do, because he has illustrated it so vividly.

In my opinion, the most important thing he said today, that he did not say in the prepared paper, was to emphasize the importance of getting out of the family ego mass but still keeping one's relationship to it. This sort of going in both directions runs through everything he was telling us today. I think this is very significant, not only for relationships within the families we study but for relationships within our own families. Anybody working in the family field inescapably draws on his own family experience, using this experience in one way or another to inform his work. This is not the kind of work, really, that can ever be put so far away from you that your own life is not involved in it.

So I think that both getting some distance from your own family involvement and yet maintaining some connection is very important to us all. This idea relates to a couple of sentences in his prepared paper that I would like to quote here. He said he believes that, "the laws that govern man's emotional function are as orderly as those that govern other natural systems, and our difficulty in understanding the system is not so much in the complexity of the system as in man's denial of the system." He has a very basic point there. I think such denial often relates to our troubles with our own family involvement. He seems to ask more than we are capable of when he says, "Get with it," and at the same time says, "Get some distance from it." If we do both, we will be better off both in our therapeutic work and, I might say, in our conceptual work. For example, we might be able to look at systems and not dismiss their properties as alien, as we do over and over again with concepts like "mental disorder" or "family disorganization." All our work has been showing more and more that even the most "disorganized" families are highly organized and systematic. If we use such terms and concepts as "disorganization," we don't do anything except obscure the very order that we are looking for.

Chairman Watzlawick: Thank you very much, John. May I now ask Dr. Weiner to comment?

Dr. Oscar R. Weiner: I was really fascinated by Dr. Bowen's talk. I copied down his blueprint and I couldn't help thinking about what this meant to me personally. I found myself kind of wandering a little bit and thinking about going right home and trying it in my own family. Perhaps he has given me something that I might find useful with my own family.

I hope that Dr. Bowen can respond a little later on as to how he really sees himself in this whole family system. The thought that came to my mind, which was kind of verified by what his mother finally told him at the end about what the weekend meant to her, was that perhaps he was being the family healer. I am not quite sure, in terms of the family projection process, what he had seen himself as being before this.

In terms of his discussion of the individual who tries to differentiate himself yet should keep relating to his family, I have found this concept very useful in my own practice. You have spelled out for me what I have already been doing. I have found this procedure very useful in dealing with individual patients who are struggling to differentiate and at the same time continue to show a great deal of resistance to it. I have also begun to send patients back to their families to relate to their families, and I feel that, in a sense, this gets me out of this triangle that exists between the patient, myself, and the patient's family. I arrived at this procedure because I found myself becoming more and more uncomfortable with the burden that I felt patients were placing on me. They were

binding me, resisting growth, development, progress, or whatever you
want to call it, and I have found that sending them back to their own
families somehow placed me in a better position to deal with them. In the
long run it is a much more gratifying experience for the patient because
we both get detriangled and he has a different relationship with his own
family.

Chairman Watzlawick: Dr. Whitaker, would you care to comment?

Dr. Whitaker: Would I care to comment? Boy, what a question! Dr.
Bowen, I wish you were my brother!

Dr. Bowen: Ackerman is.

Dr. Whitaker: When you said you were boring, it was very clear what
you meant. You were boring the hell into me. This is the other end of that
probe we were talking about yesterday, which is the one I would like to
study.

I think one of the other things you said that nobody has had guts
enough to say before is that those people who go into family therapy are
really master manipulators. All this cotton-pickin' talk we give out about,
"We are going to be sincere and we are just playing from ourselves," has
the other side of it, that we are related to the system. It is very intriguing
to me to think about the struggle I have had in terms of trying to
differentiate myself as a "separate," as though I was trying to make
believe that I wasn't relating to this whole. I wonder if there aren't two
groups of us: those who try to separate out from the family or leave home
and never come back, and those who stay home and never go away, and
each of us is trying to solve the impossible problem of this paradoxical
situation in which we go back and forth.

One of the other things that is very inspiring to me is that this thinking
helps explain to me the significance of my functioning with co-therapists.
I don't have to struggle with working with two's, which you do. To me,
working with a co-therapist is a joy. I have the feeling that psychotherapy
ought to be originally taught by working with spouses. It occurred to me
that what happens when I do co-therapy is that I detriangle by a process
of the two of us functioning at one point as a unit and at another point as
two separates. Thus, we are constantly free to detriangulate from
moment to moment.

This business you talk about of getting thrown into a panic at home is
the thing I am more and more sensitive to as a focus for what is going on
in the therapy. I picked up the idea first from the newspaper report of the
American chess master playing with the Russian who won, and he said he
knew that at the moment when he was confused that he had lost. When
this happens to me in the therapeutic situation, I reach over and get hold
of my co-therapist. I have always felt in terms of Lyman Wynne's concept

of the rubber fence, that the process of family therapy consists of standing astraddle this family fence. The problem is, it isn't always rubber. Sometimes the damned thing is of steel and it keeps getting higher and I keep getting worried about what it is going to cut. If I have a co-therapist, I can go in with both feet and hang onto his hand so that I can jump back over and get out; or I can stay out and let him go in and then pull him out when he gets entangled with it.

Chairman Watzlawick: Thank you very much. Dr. Bowen, do you want to respond to any of these comments?

Dr. Bowen: If any of you wonder why I wasn't writing to you, I have just spent a few thousand hours on my own family. I have a folder full of material, the only other copies of those letters about which I spoke. I have spent months on this project and I wanted to utilize this family upset to the full.

I agree with many things all of you say. I don't know about that empathy thing. I don't deal too much in empathy.

Who gets out of a triangle? There is one person who is motivated to do this, if you can find this one. In the average family, if I can get the couple to cooperate, then I do it with them, and if I can't, then I work with the motivated one.

On the question of how do I see myself in my own family, well, it changes from year to year. I used to be myself and go my own way, and I used to sort of stay away and not go back. I think that is one of the biggest delusions that anybody has. I believe it is one of the biggest delusions of psychoanalysis that people have worked things out about their families in their analysis and that they don't have to be involved with them any more.

You talk about resistance to this—it is tremendous. I mean, to force myself to do this was one of the hardest forcing jobs I ever did. It makes you understand a little bit more the resistance of the family member to do it. After I had had this session with my brother, I knew that I had to go back to him the next day. I wished I didn't have to, you know, but I knew I had to go, and that I would go.

Those are all the comment I have at this time. Incidentally, I have had more reports about the way the family situation has settled down. For instance, my oldest sister is on a diet and is losing weight. I have never seen my parents act so alive. They are alive and going like anything. The whole family is.

As for my own emotional part in it, if a person working on a triangle can stay less involved than the others, I think that is to be desired. In other words, I was able pretty much to laugh at my brother while he was shaking his finger at me. But I still get emotional. I get emotional talking about it here. I didn't find a way to get around this last one.

Dr. Whitaker: I hope you won't.

Chairman Watzlawick: Thank you very much, Dr. Bowen. May I invite brief comments from several of the more research- than therapy-minded participants?

Dr. Bell: There was a very interesting book review back in 1916, the heyday of psychoanalysis. Somebody wrote a review that pointed out that no matter what Euclid did, whether he took a square or rectangle, a parallelogram, a circle, the damned thing always came back to triangles. You take two points on a circle and end up with a third point and you have got a triangle. You take a square and you divide that and it comes out a triangle, as was the fashion in the days of the lovely "demonstration" of the universality of the oedipus complex. But two triangles don't make a rectangle, and a circle is something more than a set of triangles.

I guess my question for Dr. Bowen is not really a challenging of the usefulness of conceptualizing these phenomena as triangles, but what strikes me is that there is no triangle that you can triangulate here without taking into account a much broader context. Another possible strategy would be to talk in terms of larger patterns than triangles—a certain cluster analysis or pattern analysis. But these thoughts are from the top of my head. Further down in the more feeling part, I grasp and appreciate this kind of triangular representation, but I always have this problem as a researcher of wanting to organize things a little bit and then try to put them into a classification, preferably into a classification that might allow for some kind of operational statement and testing out.

What came to my mind was the extensive work done by Caplow and others, drawing on the investigations of Georg Simmel on the different processes that occur in sets of relationships. Caplow has done an elegant piece on the theory of coalition in the triad.

The challenge to me here is whether one can identify a number of variables, power, and so on, and show that what is going on here is essentially what has been called the "mores" of triangles. These are not merely personal relationships; they are sets of power relationships that are also affective relationships. Mayber we could sort them out and describe them in a much more orderly way and perhaps even find some way of testing them.

Dr. Minuchin: I am not a researcher but I still want to comment. I also was impressed that, actually, Dr. Bowen was not talking about a triangle, because he was not dealing with geometry. He is so fast on his feet that, simultaneously, at the point at which he was working with one triangle he was using another triangle to superimpose on the first one. So he was working not only with a rectangle that are the seven members of his family, but with fifteen hundred members in the town.

I didn't understand why, in order to give us an image of what he was doing, he used a geometric metaphor. What he was doing, really, was working continuously with all the members of the family, using them, manipulating them actively in the process of helping. He was almost like a sculptor that is working with wax; sometimes the sculptor is caught so that when he is modeling, he is also destroying or creating something anew.

The family that he describes I would call an enmeshed family. He is working with this enmeshed family in the process of separating and detriangulating, but his style is an inclusive style that is the style of the family. In the work that we have been doing, we differentiate two types of family. Evidently all the families of therapists are enmeshed families. This is why we immediately resound to this presentation, but there is also the disengaged family in which the process is not one of detriangulation, of differentiation, of getting out, but a process of reestablishing and creating units.

Dr. Levinger: I will make my comment quickly, and not discuss my delight at hearing the paper. I do want to add that the concept of a triangle can be related very much to the triangular work of a number of prominent social psychologists—for example, Newcomb's ABX, Heider's POX, Osgood's work on understanding communication and attitude change. If A and B are two people and X is a third object—it could be an attitude, object, or any abstraction, or it could be the person of the therapist, or a brother or whoever—this X then is some object to which A and B both relate. And the feelings of A and B toward X, and the balancing of these different feelings, constitute a topic on which there is already a large amount of research.

It seems to me that when Dr. Whitaker talks about "detriangulation," he talks about offering alternative X's to A and B. If A and B get hung up on a particular X where their conflict is maybe at an impasse, then alternatives can be provided. This would be one way one could relate these concepts to existing theory in social psychology. . . .

Chairman Watzlawick: Thank you very much. We will now proceed directly to the next point on our program, a film presentation by Dr. Ackerman.

Dr. Ackerman is going to say a few words. . . .

Dr. Ackerman: I have never seen Dr. Bowen as great as he was this morning. I can't tell you how much I enjoyed that exquisite family tome of his. I am going to talk to him privately about that, especially as he pointed me out as his brother. (Laughter.)

Note

1. I might mention that there was one person present at the conference who sensed that part of the presentation was aimed at the "family" of family therapists. Carl Whitaker, whom I consider one of the most gifted and versatile of all family therapists, made the initial "triangling" move in the meeting with his comment about wishing that he was my brother (the great togetherness), which I dealt with (detriangled) by saying that he could not be my brother since Nathan Ackerman was already my brother. This resulted in some playful byplay on the same subject. My impression is that the emotional impact of the presentation did "one up" the others so well that few but Whitaker would have had a ready response.

Chapter 22

Toward the Differentiation of Self in One's Family of Origin

The one most central theoretical premise of family systems theory concerns the degree to which we all have poorly "differentiated" selfs, or the degree to which we are "undifferentiated," or the degree of our unresolved emotional attachments to families of origin. These are all different descriptive terms to refer to the same phenomenon. The one most important goal of family systems therapy is to help family members toward a better level of "differentiation of self." The theory was developed from family research that focused on the entire nuclear family unit. The theoretical concepts describe the range of ways family members are emotionally "stuck to" each other, and the ways this "stuck-togetherness" continues to operate in the background, no matter how much people deny it or how much they pretend to be separate from the others. The first method of family therapy, developed as part of the research, was directed at the entire family unit. That method was amazingly effective in relieving symptoms but it was not effective as a long-term method for resolving the underlying family "stuck-togetherness." A variety of therapy modifications eventually led to a therapy focus on the two parents and the symptomatic offspring. This was a little more effective at relieving the symptoms, but the young adult son or daughter had little capacity to separate a self from the parents, and neither parent had much ability to separate a self from the other parent. Then came the concept of triangles and the method of family therapy with the triangle consisting of the two spouses and the therapist. This method was so effective that it has been the one most consistent approach to family systems therapy since the early 1960s. There was a sound theoretical basis for saying that "differentiation of self," as described by this theory, takes place only in a triangle, and the most effective method was in the triangle consisting of the two most important family members (the two spouses) and the therapist. When the therapist could remain relatively "differentiated" from the two spouses, they could begin the slow process of each differentiating a self from the other. When the spouses can change in relation to each other, other family members at home automatically change in relation to them. This has all been described in detail in the literature (Bowen 1966, 1971, 1971a). Most of the presentations at this annual Georgetown Family Symposium have been devoted to some facet of the theory about the "differentiation of self" and to variations in this basic method of family systems therapy.

It has long been recognized that the emotional attachment between the spouses is identical to the emotional attachment that each spouse had in his or her family of origin. In any course of therapy it has been routine to encourage each spouse to work systematically toward the differentiation of self in the family of origin. In the average course of therapy there would be times when the primary focus was on the relationship in the marriage, and times when major emphasis would go to differentiation in the extended family. Over-all, the work with the extended family was seen as supplemental to work on the relationship system between the spouses. This paper will report amazing clinical change when the only effort was toward defining self in the family of origin. This was the result of an "accidental" discovery. The first major section of this paper will describe the nodal event that led to a different approach to families; the next section will deal with over-all principles in the defining of a self in one's family of origin, and the last section will deal with the most recent thinking about the success of this approach.

The Nodal Point

The principal message in this paper revolved around one of the most important nodal points in my professional life. It began with a paper at a national conference in March 1967. In it I described my effort toward differentiating myself in my own family of origin. For some twelve years I had been working in a trial and error effort, with knowledge about family emotional process gained from family research. My focus had been on the primary triangle with my parents and myself. Each effort to extricate myself emotionally had always been blocked by the other interlocking triangles in the family of origin. Finally, with knowledge about the functioning of interlocking triangles, I was able to get a surprising breakthrough in the effort with my parents. This was significant. It is not possible to differentiate a self in any single triangle without a method for dealing simultaneously with the interlocking triangles. The knowledge gained from that national meeting was reflected immediately in my own teaching at Georgetown. It became automatic to use the new ideas in teaching psychiatric residents and other members of the mental health professions. There was a different emphasis on the triangle between self and parents, which is the most important primary triangle in life, and the one in which a person develops the triangle relationship patterns that remain relatively fixed in all relationships. There was also a new emphasis in teaching sessions on "person to person" relationships, the ability to see one's own family more as people than as emotionally endowed images, the ability to observe one's self in triangles, and ways to "detriangle" one's self. The new emphasis in teaching was not planned. It occurred automatically after the March 1967 conference.

Within a few weeks the trainees who attended the teaching sessions began to use these concepts in visits to their parental families. This came as a surprise, as it occurred spontaneously, without any suggestion from me. Previous trainees had not done this. After a visit home, they would return to the conference to report the visit, with the successes and the inevitable impasses that occur in such an effort. The visits home were discussed in the conferences, usually attended by fifteen to twenty residents and other trainees, and suggestions were made for the next visit to parental families. This teaching format, started in spring of 1967, has since become a standard format for teaching family concepts to trainees.

Later in 1967 and early 1968 I noticed that this group of residents were doing better clinical work as family therapists than any previous residents. At first I simply considered this an unusually good group of residents. As time passed, I became aware that the difference between these and previous residents was too great for such a simple explanation. The difference appeared related to something I was doing and I began to ask questions. Then it became clear that it was precisely those residents who had done best in the effort with their parental families who were also doing best in their clinical work. The residents provided some clues. Some said that family theory was just another psychiatric theory when they first heard about it. After they could see it work in their own families, it became alive and real. Others said it was the experience with their own families that made it possible to better understand and relate to families in the psychiatric clinic. Still others said it was possible to help families avoid doing things that were nonproductive and hurtful when you had the very same experience with your own family.

None of these residents ever mentioned emotional problems in their own nuclear families. In retrospect this was unusual, since residents are usually quick to seek consultation about their own emotional problems. My mission is to train competent family therapists and this group had been doing unusually well as clinicians. Their superior performance seemed related to the work they were doing with their parental families and there was no reason to ask questions about their emotional adjustment with their spouses and their own children. About a year after this process began, which was late 1968 and early 1969, I did begin to ask questions about their spouses and children. They reported the usual range of problems in their marriages and with their children, but to my amazement, they had made as much progress in dealing with the problems as similar residents whom I had been seeing in once-a-week formal family therapy with their spouses. They had automatically been using things they had learned from their parental families in the relationships with their spouses and their children. This surprise development was a turning point in my professional life.

I had considerable experience in doing formal family therapy with mental health professionals and their spouses. This had started in the early 1960s, when I began suggesting family therapy for residents and their spouses, instead of individual psychotherapy or psychoanalysis, for residents' personal problems. For some eight years a good percentage of my part-time private practice had been devoted to family therapy with mental health professionals and their spouses. There had been extensive experience with those who do well, those who do poorly, and what is average for the group. Through work with this group of highly motivated people who were seriously working in formal family therapy, I had come to know the average amount of time they took for each step in the therapy process. Throughout the years there had been strong emphasis on working out the relationship system in the family of origin, in addition to the primary focus on the relationship in the marriage. In fact, there had been so much emphasis on the extended family that some asked if they could deduct the expense of home trips as a medical expense for tax purposes. Even though I believed this a more legitimate "medical" expense than some that are allowed, I wanted nothing to do with debating this issue with the Internal Revenue Service. In the early 1960s there was one "control" group in which the total focus was on the relationship in the marriage. The hypothesis was that work with the extended family would emerge in the course of therapy. Results with this were disappointing. About 25 percent of these families made some significant change with families of origin, but the average family in that group never made more than a token effort. Most never really got beyond either blaming their parents or benevolently forgiving them. Most tended to become overinvolved in the relationship in the marriage, and the therapy either terminated early or dragged on to an indefinite termination. Except for that one "control" group, there was strong emphasis on teaching about the extended family and on urging spouses to visit their family of origin as frequently as possible. It is difficult for a family to "hear" the idea of the extended family when there are anxiety and symptoms. It is usual for the first part of this kind of therapy to be devoted to the relationship in the marriage and, after anxiety has subsided and there is more objectivity, to devote more and more of the later stages of therapy to the extended family.

The experience with the psychiatric residents in the teaching sessions in the 1967 to 1969 period came as a startling revelation at a time when I was committed to the notion that the fastest and best change in psychotherapy came from working out the relationship between self and the one most important other person in one's life. Here was an experience that contradicted a central theoretical and therapeutic premise. Here was a group, of some fifteen to twenty trainees who met once a week, in which the primary focus was on the primary triangle with the trainee and his parents. None of the trainees or their spouses were in any kind of "therapy." These conferences had no "therapeutic" objective. The amount of time devoted to any one trainee amounted to no more than fifteen to thirty minutes every month or two. There was no more than token "private" time with any resident. This would occur in passing, often in the hospital corridors, when a resident would want a clue about how to respond to a letter or telephone call from the parental family. These residents, and other trainees in the course, were making as much or more progress at change with their spouses and children than similar residents I was seeing weekly in formal family therapy. The observations appeared valid by the most searching criteria I could use at the time. I had many questions, and only a few educated guesses to account for this observation. In the years since 1969, much effort has gone into more careful observation and to devising clinical experiments to clarify some of the variables involved. I have used the teaching approach in a wide variety of teaching sessions with large groups and small groups and in sessions with only one person. Frequency of sessions has been varied from weekly meetings to some that meet three or four times a year. Most of the work has tended to support the validity of the observations made in 1968 and 1969. This work is rapidly changing the course of family "therapy" as practiced at Georgetown. This presentation to the Georgetown Family Symposium was made in October 1971. This paper is being rewritten in October 1974, three years since the original presentation. There is now more solid data to support this approach.

The Differentiation of Self Scale is one of the most important concepts in the total theory. On a simple level it conveys that people are basically different from each other and it is possible to classify them according to these differences. At the bottom of the scale are people with the lowest levels of differentiation, or the highest levels of undifferentiation. The top of the scale is reserved for a theoretical level of complete differentiation. People at each scale level have definably different life styles in terms of the way they deal with the intellect and the emotions. People low on the scale may keep their lives in emotional equilibrium and symptom free, but they are vulnerable to stress, life adjustments are more difficult, and they have a high incidence of human illness and problems. People higher on the scale are more adaptable to stress, have fewer life problems, and deal with problems better. The scale is misleading in that people are not distributed evenly along the scale, and it is not possible to use the scale for making day-to-day estimates of the level of functioning. People are responsive to others in the emotional field and there are frequent shifts in the functional level of differentiation of self, in favorable or unfavorable life situations. It is possible to estimate the basic level of differentiation over long periods of time and this permits the use of the scale for predicting over-all life courses. The concept of triangles is another of the important concepts in the total theory. It has to do with the predictable ways in which people relate to each other in an emotional field. Triangle moves may be so toned down they are barely observable in calm emotional fields. As anxiety and tension increase, the triangle moves increase in frequency and intensity. Less differentiated people are moved about like pawns by emotional tensions. Better differentiated people are less vulnerable to tension.

Dealing with Unresolved Emotional Attachments

There are a variety of ways that people deal with their unresolved emotional attachments to parents. It is necessary to keep in mind that such attachments exist in all degrees of intensity. The degree of unresolved emotional attachment is equivalent to the degree of undifferentiation. The lower the level of differentiation, and the greater the amount of unresolved emotional attachment to parents, the more intense the mechanisms to deal with the undifferentiation. At one extreme are people who use emotional distance from parents by isolating self emotionally while living in physical proximity to the parents. These are psychological mechanisms that operate within the person. When emotional stress is low, such people can relate to each other more spontaneously and freely. When anxiety is higher, they become more reserved and more isolated from each other. These mechanisms are necessary for maintaining the emotional equilibrium of the family unit. To regard such mechanisms as pathological and to attempt to remove the "symptom" without regard for the total family unit can stir anxiety and maladjustment in the family unit. At the other extreme are people so sensitized to the physical presence of the other that some degree of physical distance is necessary for emotional equilibrium. For these people it is "Out of sight, out of mind." Extreme examples of this are people who run away from home and never return, or who return infrequently. There are all gradations of less marked forms of physical distance. Most people use combinations of internal mechanisms and physical distance, with a preference for one type of mechanism. For instance, a person might handle usual levels of anxiety with an internal mechanism such as silence or refusal to speak and only under higher levels of anxiety use physical distance such as walking out of the room. Clinicians are familiar with the hundreds of different combinations of the internal mechanisms and physical distance.

The Emotional Cut-off

We have come to use the term *emotional cut-off* or simply *cut-off* to refer to emotional distancing, whether the cut-off is achieved by internal mechanisms or physical distance. The type of mechanism used to achieve emotional distance is not an indication of the intensity or the degree of unresolved emotional attachment. The person who runs away from home is as emotionally attached as the one who stays at home and uses internal mechanisms to control the attachment. The one who runs away does have a different life course. He needs emotional closeness but is allergic to it. He runs away kidding himself that he is achieving "independence." The more intense the cut-off with his parents the more he is vulnerable to repeating the same pattern in future relationships. He can have an intense relationship in a marriage which he sees as ideal and permanent at the time, but the physical distance pattern is part of him. When tension mounts in the marriage, he will use the same pattern of running away. He may go from one marriage to another, or through multiple living-together arrangements, or his relationships may be even more transient. An intense example of this is the relationship "nomad" who moves from one relationship to another, each time cutting off emotional ties to the past and investing self in the present relationship. The same pattern can apply to work relationships and other areas of his life in which there is an emotional interdependence in relationships. The person who achieves emotional distance with internal mechanisms has a different order of complications. He is able to stay on the scene in periods of emotional tension but is more prone to dysfunctions within himself such as physical illness; emotional dysfunction such as depression; and social dysfunction such as drinking and episodic irresponsibility in relation to others. Depression is one of the better examples. The higher the anxiety in the environment, the more he isolates himself from others emotionally while still appearing to carry on normal relationships in the group. A high percentage of people use various combinations of internal mechanisms and physical distance to deal with the unresolved emotional attachments to their parents.

The principal manifestation of the emotional cut-off is denial of the intensity of the unresolved emotional attachment to parents, acting and pretending to be more independent than one is, and emotional distance achieved either through internal mechanisms or physical distance. One manifestation of the unresolved emotional attachment to parents comes into focus during adolescence. A high percentage of people have a significant amount of unresolved emotional attachment to parents. This is supported by most psychological theories which consider emotional turmoil to be "normal" during adolescence. Family Systems Theory does not support this view. A better differentiated young person who began an orderly process of growing away from his parents in early childhood will continue a smooth and orderly growth process through the adolescent years. The adolescent period becomes a challenge and an opportunity to begin assuming responsibility for self, rather than a fight against the unresolved emotional attachment to the parents. For a high percentage, the adolescent period is one in which there is denial of the attachment to the parents and the assumption of some rather extreme postures in order to pretend to be grown up. The intensity of the denial and the pretending in adolescence is a remarkably accurate index of the degree of unresolved emotional attachment to the parents.

Life Patterns

The degree of unresolved emotional attachment to parents is determined by the degree of unresolved emotional attachment each parent had in their own family of origin, the way their parents handled this in their marriage, the degree of anxiety during critical periods in life, and the way the parents handled this anxiety. The child is "programmed" into the emotional configuration very early in life, following which the amount of unresolved emotional attachment remains relatively fixed except for functional shifts in the parents. Under favorable circumstances and with good fortune in the central family unit, the amount may become less. Under disastrous circumstances, with a high level of parental anxiety, the amount will be greater. There is a variable determined by the ways parents handle anxiety. In broad terms, the amount of anxiety tends to parallel the degree of unresolved emotional attachment in the family. For instance, a family with a higher level of undifferentiation will be a more disorganized family with higher levels of anxiety, and a family with better levels of differentiation will be more orderly with lower levels of anxiety. Families in which the parents handle anxiety well, and in which they are able to stay on a predetermined course in spite of anxiety, will turn out better than the families in which the parents are more reactive and shift life courses in response to anxiety. All things being equal, the life course of people is determined by the amount of unresolved emotional attachment, the amount of anxiety that comes from it, and the way they deal with this anxiety.

One of the most effective automatic mechanisms for reducing the over-all level of anxiety in a family is a relatively "open" relationship system in the extended family. An "open" relationship system, which is the opposite of an emotional cut-off, is one in which family members have a reasonable degree of emotional contact with one another. One has always to be aware that there are wide variations in the frequency and quality of relationships in cut-offs and in openness. Relative openness does not increase the level of differentiation in a family, but it reduces anxiety, and a continued low level of anxiety permits motivated family members to begin slow steps toward better differentiation. The opposite is also true. In an emotional field of sustained high anxiety, the over-all level of differentiation will move slowly toward greater undifferentiation. The following clinical illustrations will help to convey the point about anxiety in a system that is more open. It is fairly common for nuclear families to maintain relative levels of cut-off with families of origin. These are the people who communicate infrequently with parental families and who return home about once a year for brief, superficial "duty" visits. Families in this category have relatively low levels of adaptability to stress, and relatively high levels of anxiety and vulnerability to marital discord, problems with children, and the full range of human problems. Any successful effort that goes toward improving the frequency and quality of emotional contact with the extended family, will predictably improve the family's level of adjustment and reduce symptoms in the nuclear family. This is most striking in the families with more complete cut-offs with their extended families. The level of adaptability to stress is lower, anxiety is higher, and the family is *extremely* vulnerable to all kinds of human problems. To attempt family therapy that focuses directly on problems within the family can be long-term and nonproductive. It might be difficult for such a family to begin more emotional contact with the extended family, but any effort toward reducing the cut-off with the extended family will soften the intensity of the family problem, reduce the symptoms, and make any kind of therapy far more productive. The essential message in this paper is to report on clinical efforts to completely bypass problems in the nuclear family and to focus on working out relationships with the extended family. This is extremely difficult for the therapist and it is impossible for some families to hear this premise or to take action in this direction. In those families in which this has been possible, the results are superior to forms of therapy that focus directly on the problem in the nuclear family.

Family Relationships in Comparison to Social Relationships

People who cut-off with their own parental families are the most vigorous in the effort to create "substitute" families from social relationships. There is a growing trend toward cutting-off from "bad" parental families and finding "good" substitute families. From my theoretical perspective, I believe the trend is a product of the emotional force that moves people toward the emotional cut-off with the past. This is a powerful force in a fair percentage of families and in the total of society. In some twenty years in family research and family therapy, it has been my experience that substitute families are poor substitutes for one's own family, if one's own family still exists. There are exceptions to this in disasters, fragmented families, and a number of other extreme social situations. I speak more about the situations in which an existing family is rejected and a substitute family sought. When people cut-off from their parental families, they tend to seek more congenial relationships among their social relationships. This reduces the immediate anxiety and works well for a time.

If social relationships become significant, the relationships are duplicates of their relationships to their parental families. When they encounter stress, and anxiety increases, they cut-off from the social relationship and seek another, better social relationship. After a few cycles of this, they tend to become more and more isolated. A small percentage of people are able to manage marginally productive lives with numerous superficial relationships, in which no one relationship becomes intense. Over the years I have attempted "family therapy" with people involved in long-term, stable-appearing social relationships. This has induced couples in common-law marriages, single people who have shared apartments for many years, partners in long-term homosexual relationships, people who have been lifelong closest friends, and a wide spectrum of men and women involved in a wide variety of "living together" relationships. I have never had a result that I would be willing to call successful with any of them, not even with common-law marriages in which there have been children. It is as if there is not enough stability in the marriage to sustain change. In these situations, therapy is usually initiated by the partner who is symptomatic. It is common for the other to give lip service to the idea of family therapy, and then find reason to withdraw after a few appointments. The usual "living together" couple either wants to resolve problems so they can proceed to marriage, or they want advice about whether to "split." A small percentage of these go on to marriage after a few appointments. Most continue for a few appointments and separate, following which one is often motivated to go on alone. In summary, the nonfamily relationship may provide a reasonably comfortable existence as long as the relationship is calm, but it has a low tolerance for stress.

Principles and Techniques of Helping People Define a Self in the Extended Family

The terms *defining a self* or *working toward individuation* are essentially synonymous with *differentiation*. The process of differentiating a self has been presented in other papers and is too complex to review in detail here. It requires knowledge of the function of emotional systems in all families and the motivation to do a research study on one's own family. The study requires that the researcher begin to gain control over his emotional reactivity to his family, that he visit his parental family as often as indicated, and that he develop the ability to become a more objective observer in his own family. As the system becomes more "open" and he can begin to see the triangles and the part he plays in the family reaction patterns, he can begin the more complex process toward differentiating himself from the myths, images, distortions, and triangles he had not previously seen. This is a big order and a mission that cannot be accomplished quickly. The effort to help or to supervise someone in this effort has been called "coaching" since it is so similar to the relationship of a coach to an athlete who is working to improve his athletic ability. The initial goal is to get the trainee started. Most of the learning comes as the trainee works toward his goal. The trainee is aware that progress depends on him. This process is quite different from conventional concepts of therapy.

Person to person relationships. Trainees are encouraged to work toward "person to person" relationships in their families. In broad terms, a person to person relationship is one in which two people can relate personally to each other about each other, without talking about others (triangling), and without talking about impersonal "things." Few people can talk personally to anyone for more than a few minutes without increasing anxiety, which results in silences, talking about others, or talking about impersonal things. In its ultimate sense, no one can ever know what a person to person relationship is, since the quality of any relationship can always be improved. On a more practical level, a person to person relationship is between two fairly well differentiated people who can communicate directly, with mature respect for each other, without the complications between people who are less mature. The effort to work toward person to person relationships improves the relationship system in the family and it is a valuable exercise in knowing self.

As a beginning effort, I have suggested to people, "If you can get a person to person relationship with each living person in your extended family, it will help you "grow up" more than anything else you could ever do in life." This admonition is accurate except no one can ever live long enough to complete the task. Success also depends on the response of others. In the process of working toward this, one learns about emotional systems, the way people cling together, the way they drift apart in periods of anxiety, and the power of the emotional process between people who reject and repel each other. A simple admonition is to suggest that people achieve a person to person relationship with each parent. Some people believe they have already developed such relationships with their parents. They mistake the congeniality in calm families in which people relate from the time-honored roles originally assigned them. They are not aware that person to person relationships with their parents will reveal all the emotional problems the parents have had in their relationship, and that they had in their own families of origin.

Many different kinds of problems are encountered in the effort to develop an individual relationship with each parent. This is where it is desirable to have a "coach" who has already had the experience with his own family. Without such help, one unwittingly makes critical decisions based on emotionality and can waste months in fruitless dead-ends. A coach who has had experience can at least guide the trainee away from unprofitable trial and error wandering. It is far better if people go alone to visit their families. A differentiating effort is one that takes place in one self in relation to each other self. It is common for family members to be identified as part of groups and cliques, and for people to relate to the groups rather than to individuals. It is common for parents to write letters signed "Mother and Dad" and for their children to write to "Dear Mother and Dad" or "Dear Family." To take a spouse and children on a trip to visit the parental family results in the parental family relating to the trainee's family as a group, which further impedes the effort toward person to person relationships. Some people mis-hear person to person relationships as "getting to know one's family better." Some have taken spouse and children to visit parental families and have ended up in modified group therapy sessions to talk about "problems." This either can make the emotional climate at home more congenial or can stir up anxiety. In either case it impedes the effort to establish person to person relationships.

Becoming a better observer and controlling one's own emotional reactiveness. These two assignments are so interlinked they are presented together. The effort to become a better observer and to learn more about the family reduces the emotional reactivity, and this in turn helps one become a better observer. This is one of the most profitable efforts one can make. One never becomes completely objective and no one ever gets the process to the point of not reacting emotionally to family situations. A little progress on this helps the trainee to begin to get a little "outside" the family emotional system, and this in turn helps the trainee to a different view of the human phenomenon. It enables the observer to get "beyond blaming" and "beyond anger" to a level of objectivity that is far more than an intellectual exercise. It is fairly easy for most people to intellectually accept the notion that no one is to blame in family situations, but the idea remains intellectual until it is possible to know it emotionally in one's own family. The family gains as one member is able to relate more freely without taking sides and becoming entangled in the family emotional system. It is impossible to tell a family what one is trying to do and still make it work. Telling the others can result in disagreements about the process and build natural resistance into insurmountable hurdles. Telling others also results in group activity which impedes the differentiating result. In the course of such an effort with the family, one comes to have a unique role which is important to everyone, which is highly respected, and which helps to contribute to one's own individuality and responsibility. The person who acquires a little ability at becoming an observer, and at controlling some of his emotional reactiveness acquires an ability that is useful for life in all kinds of emotional snarls. Most of the time he can live his life, reacting with appropriate and natural emotional responses, but with the knowledge that at any time he can back out of the situation, slow down his reactiveness, and make observations that help him control himself and the situation.

Detriangling self from emotional situations. This is an absolute necessity if differentiation of self is the goal. All the work that goes into personal relationships, as well as into learning more about the family through observation and into controlling one's own reactiveness, helps both to create a more "open" relationship system and to reactivate the emotional system as it was before one's cut-off from it. Now it is possible to see the triangles in which one grew up, and to be different in relation to them. The process of detriangling is essentially the same as has been described in doing family therapy with two spouses (Bowen 1971, 1971a). The overall goal is to be constantly in contact with an emotional issue involving two other people and self, without taking sides, without counterattacking or defending self, and to always have a neutral response. To go silent is perceived by the other as an emotional response. There are many details to this process. One part of the process is achieved merely by being in the midst of the family during an emotional issue, and being more objective and less reactive than the others. The family "knows" this when it happens. Differentiation is possible only around an emotional issue about which to relate. Trainees are advised, whenever possible, to be home when there is a natural emotional issue in the family. Trips home when there is a serious illness or a death, or at homecomings or holidays, often provide the levels of family anxiety that are effective for relating to the family. When the family is calm, there not only are no emotional issues about which to relate, but the family system works hard to prevent issues from surfacing. In these situations, it is necessary to introduce small emotional issues from the past, without getting into emotional confrontation. Probably the one biggest error that people make in working with the extended family is emotional confrontation. This may be briefly effective in making the confronter believe he has accomplished something, but the family reacts negatively and it may require months, or even a year or two, to get beyond the family's cut-off with the confronter.

Other issues. There are a number of other important issues in the effort toward differentiation from one's family of origin, but these issues are more in the nature of techniques than over-all principle. In every family, there are times when the trainee is emotionally "locked into" the triangle with his parents. When this occurs, it is counterproductive to keep working against the bloc. Operating latitude is usually possible by focusing on other family members who are emotionally important to the parents. This focus is on a triangle consisting of one parent, the other family member, and self. There are times when the bloc can be productively approached through the trainee's siblings. There are other times when this is not productive and when it can be advantageous to relate to family members in the parents' generation, or to people in the generation before the parents if they are available. Other interesting issues have to do with principles and techniques when one or both parents are dead. Most people have more relatives than they believe they have. It is possible, even when there are only a few living survivors, to use this theoretical system to reconstruct an effective family emotional system for the differentiation of self. The details of this will ultimately appear as a full paper.

Summary. The goal in this section has been to present the over-all principles and techniques that have been found to be most useful in the effort to help people toward the differentiation of a self in their own families of origin. The theoretical issues have been presented in more detail in other papers. Other details of theory and technique are beyond the scope of this brief presentation.

Current Explanations of Results

The surprising observations in the teaching sessions in the 1967 to early 1969 period have been the subject of serious and intensive questioning and clinical experimentation. At the time of the first presentation to the Georgetown Symposium in October 1971, most of the subsequent work tended to support the validity of the original observations. As this paper is being rewritten in October 1974, the further work tends to add even more support to the observations. The teaching method has been used in a variety of teaching situations from small groups of fifteen to twenty people who meet once a week, to much larger meetings of fifty to seventy-five people who meet once a month. The meetings are made up of mental health professionals at the postgraduate level. It is impossible to know the percentage who become interested enough to start serious work on their families of origin, since people have by now heard about this approach and meetings attract people already specifically interested. About fifty percent of those in the small weekly group become sufficiently interested to be regular participants in reporting their efforts to the meeting. None are in any kind of therapy. The results with this group are consistent with the original observations. The large groups meet too infrequently for me to have a clear notion of the total group response. People from the larger groups frequently present results of a major effort after having attended silently for a year or more. I have been surprised at what they could do on their own with no more teaching ideas than could be acquired from sitting in on a dozen sessions of about three hours each. The biggest change has been in my part-time private practice. More and more time has been devoted to coaching individuals about their families of origin. These are people who ask for private practice "coaching." They are members of the mental health professions who have heard about this approach and who want help with their own families. Most are seen for one hour about once a month. Some who live in more distant cities are seen about two hours every two or three months. An increasing number of mental health professionals who ask for formal family therapy are started on this approach. Each spouse is seen separately for work on families of origin. A number of nonprofessional people in my practice have been started on this approach or shifted to it. Given this wide dissemination of practice and teaching, it is hard to know the exact number who have had reasonable exposure to the approach, and who have seriously worked on their own families of origin. In addition, a number of people who have been trained at Georgetown are now practicing their own version of the method. It is my estimate that perhaps five hundred have had reasonable exposure to the ideas in teaching sessions and that about a hundred of these have consistently presented their experience to teaching sessions under my direct supervision. I have exact figures on my practice. The major problem in estimating practice comes from a judgment in separating families in which the focus in the sessions is exclusively on the family of origin from those in which there is a fair degree of focus on the marital relationship. About half of my practice is still with both spouses together, but with an increasing focus on the families of origin of each spouse. When I get to a more careful analysis of the figures, it will be necessary to have several different categories. Over-all, I can say that my practice has shifted heavily toward a focus on the families of origin since the original observation reported here. One need remember that family therapy before that time included considerable focus on the extended families in addition to the primary focus on the interdependence in the marriage. The most accurate count now shows about ninety-five families in my private practice since 1969 who have continued for more than a year and with whom the focus has been almost exclusively on the family of origin with no more than peripheral mention of the relationship in the marriage. The impressions presented here come from both the teaching sessions and the private practice coaching.

In estimating results, note must be taken of those who have had surprising results with relatively little effort and those who have had minimal change after long persistent effort. There are families in which the problem seemed too difficult to expect much change, but in which significant change too place, as well as those that looked relatively easy in which change was slow. In this group I am talking more about averages than extremes. Over-all, the experience since 1969 has closely paralleled the initial observations in the 1967 to 1969 period. The over-all conclusion from that is that *families in which the focus is on the differentiation of self in the families of origin automatically make as much or more progress in working out the relationship system with spouses and children as families seen in formal family therapy in which there is a principal focus on the interdependence in the marriage.* My experience is going in the direction of saying that the most productive route for change, for families who are motivated, is to work at defining self in the family of origin, and to specifically avoid focus on the emotional issues in the nuclear family. I am not yet ready to prescribe this unreservedly, but I do have a group working at this with a more disciplined effort to avoid focus on nuclear family process. If this current impression eventually proves accurate, it has sweeping implications for theory and for the clinical practice of family therapy. This applies to people who live geographically removed from their families of origin. It would not apply to people who live in the parental home, or whose parents live with them, or who are intimately exposed to the parental family in day-to-day living. In the average nuclear family living apart from the parental family, the spouses are intimately involved with each other, and with the children, in the day-to-day emotional and reality issues of living. The spouses are emotionally "fused" with each other and with the children, and it is difficult to get far beyond the fusion or to do more than react and counterreact emotionally. Efforts to gain objectivity and to control emotional reactivity in the nuclear family can remain for long periods on the level of emotional game playing in which the games of each spouse cancel out the potential gains of both.

Certainly there is much to be gained from focusing on the emotional interdependence in the marriage. Twenty years of family therapy experience supports this. Now comes some solid evidence that focus on the family of origin can be even more productive. Why not focus both on the interdependence in the marriage, and on the parental family, and get the potential gain from both approaches? I believe the powerful transgenerational emotional force that goes toward cutting-off from the past may be the most important determining factor in this. There is much clinical experience to support the thesis that people are not motivated to work toward the past when they are involved in a process that offers a solution in the present generation. There are some people who appear to do well with a combination approach, but there are others whose effort with their families of origin are little more than token efforts yielding little or no progress. The latter seem to become so "addicted" to a continuation of their regular family sessions together that urging more work with the extended family results in little more than another token effort. This is in contrast to families whose only effort is made toward the extended family. I still have not had the courage and conviction to focus exclusively on the families of origin, except in the teaching sessions. This has partly to do with my longtime conviction about working out problems in the relationship between the spouses. It has also to do with my search for a way to combine the two approaches more successfully. This is a problem to be solved in the coming years.

When I first began considering this focus on families of origin, it was my belief that only a narrow spectrum of families would be motivated for this approach. I thought it would not make any sense for a family with a major problem in the nuclear family to begin talking about relationships in families of origin. But family resistance has not been as great as I expected. I am reminded of 1954, when I first began thinking about ways to involve the entire family in research, when I believed the only fathers who would be willing to participate would be fathers who were unemployed or retired. I did not believe it would be as easy to involve fathers as it proved to be. At this point I am not sure how widely applicable this family of origin approach will be. Experience thus far indicates it will be easier than I originally thought. It is hard to compare the more conventional family therapy approaches with this family of origin approach. For the family, it is immeasurably easier to do a year or two or three of periodic family therapy visits than it is to undertake the time, expense, and emotional turmoil of visits to parental families. Yet motivated people are willing to really work at this. For the therapist, the extended family approach requires far more skill, more continuing work on himself, and more attention to detail than does more conventional therapy. On the other hand, the extended family approach requires far less direct time with the family. The frequency of appointments with the extended family approach is determined by the amount of work the family member is able to do between appointments. Some can keep the effort alive and productive with appointments as often as once a month.

Some have been seen as infrequently as once or twice a year. The over-all results with the very infrequent appointments have not been rewarding. People tend to let the efforts lapse and to make some kind of visit with their families just before the appointments. Over-all, for a motivated person, half a dozen one-hour appointments a year are more productive than weekly formal family therapy appointments which focus on the relationship between spouses.

This paper has been aimed at presenting an over-all view of a different approach to achieving change in families. The approach is too new for clear answers or for defined procedures in a number of areas. Future reports will be made after more experience.

Summary

This paper reports a striking clinical experience that occurred during a special training course for psychiatric residents and other mental health professionals. Observations suggested that trainees who were not in any type of psychotherapy made as much progress in dealing with emotional issues with their spouses and children as did otherwise comparable residents who participated in formal weekly family therapy with their spouses. This unexpected observation has led to five years of clinical investigation and inquiry for data to support or refute the observation. The evidence supports the validity of the initial observation. This paper is an account of conditions at the time of the observation, a summary of the principles involved in efforts toward differentiating a self in one's family of origin, and current thinking about the accumulated experience of the past five years.

References

Ackerman, N.W. (1956). Interlocking pathology in family relationships. In *Changing Concepts of Psychoanalytic Medicine*, ed. S. Rado and G. Daniels, pp. 135–150. New York:Grune and Stratton.

Ackerman, N.W. (1958). *The Psychodynamics of Family Life*. New York: Basic Books.

Ackerman, N.W., and Behrins, M.L. (1956). A study of family diagnosis. *American Journal of Orthopsychiatry* 26:66-78.

Anonymous (1972). Differentiation of self in one's family. In *Family Interaction*, ed. J. Framo, pp. 111–173. New York:Springer. [chapter 21]

Balint, M. (1957). *The Doctor, his Patient and the Illness*. New York:International Universities Press.

Bateson, G., Jackson, D.D., Haley, J., and Weakland, J. (1956). Toward a theory of schizophrenia. *Behavioral Science, 1:251–164*.

Bayley, N., Bell, R.Q., and Schaefer, E.S. (n.d.). Research study in progress, Child Development Section, National Institute of Mental Health, Bethesda, Md.

Bell, J.E. (1961). *Family Group Therapy*. Public Health Monograph 64. United States Department of Health, Education and Welfare, Washington, D.C.

Benedek, T. (1949). The emotional structure of the family. In *The Family: Its Function and Destiny*, ed. R.N. Anshen, pp. 202–225. New York:Harper.

Benedek, T. (1952). *Studies in Psychosomatic Medicine, Psychosexual Functions in Women*. New York:Ronald.

Birdwhistell, R. (1952). *Introduction to Kinesics.* Louisville: University of Louisville Press.

Birdwhistell, R. (1969). *Kinesics and Context.* Philadelphia: University of Pennsylvania Press.

Boszormenyi-Nagy, I. (1962). The concept of schizophrenia from the perspective of family treatment. *Family Process* 1:103.

Boszormenyi-Nagy, I., and Spark, G. (1973). *Invisible Loyalties.* New York:Harper

Bowen, M. [with the collaboration of Dysinger, R.H., Brodey, W.M., and Basamania, B.] (1957). Study and treatment of five hospitalized families each with a psychotic member. Paper read at annual meeting of The American Orthopsychiatric Association, Chicago, March. [chapter 1.]

Bowen, M. (1957a). Family participation in schizophrenia. Paper read at annual meeting, American Psychiatric Association, Chicago, May.

Bowen, M., [with the collaboration of Dysinger, R.H., and Basamania, B.] (1959). The role of the father in families with a schizophrenic patient. Paper read at the annual meeting of the American Orthopsychiatric Association, San Francisco, May 1958. In: *American Journal of Psychiatry* 115 (11):1017-1020. [chapter 2]

Bowen, M. (1959a). Family relationships in schizophrenia. In *Schizophrenia—An Integrated Approach*, ed. A. Auerback, pp. 147–178. New York:Ronald. [chapter 3]

Bowen, M. (1960). A family concept of schizophrenia. In *The Etiology of Schizophrenia*, ed. D.D. Jackson, pp.346-372. New York:Basic Books. [chapter 4]

Bowen, M. (1961). Family psychotherapy. *American Journal of Orthopsychiatry* 31:40-60. [chapter 5]

Bowen, M. (1965). Family psychotherapy with schizophrenia in the hospital and in private practice. In *Intensive Family Therapy*, ed. I. Boszormenyi-Nagy and J.L. Framo, pp. 213–243. New York:Harper. [chapter 8]

Bowen, M. (1966). The use of family theory in clinical practice. *Comprehensive Psychiatry* 7:345–374. [chapter 9]

Bowen, M. (1971). Family therapy and family group therapy. In *Comprehensive Group Psychotherapy*, ed. H. Kaplan and B. Sadock, pp. 384–421. Baltimore:Williams and Wilkins. [chapter 10]

Bowen, M. (1974) Alcoholism as viewed through family systems theory and family psychotherapy. *Annals of the New York Academy of Sciences* 233:115-122.

Bowen, M. (1974b). Toward the differentiation of self in one's family of origin. In *Georgetown Family Symposium Papers*, I, ed. F. Andres and J. Lorio. Washington, D.C.: Georgetown University Press. [chapter 21]

Bowen, M. (1974a). Societal regression as viewed through family systems theory. Paper presented at the Nathan W. Ackerman Memorial Conference, Venezuela, February. [chapter 13]

Bowen, M. (1975). Family therapy after twenty years. In *American Handbook of Psychiatry*, vol. 5, ed. J. Dyrud and D. Freedman, pp. 367–392. New York:Basic Books. [chapter 14]

Brodey, W.M., and Hayden, M. (1957). Intrateam reactions: their relation to the conflicts of the family in treatment. *American Journal of Orthopsychiatry* 27:349–355.

Caplan, G. (1960). Emotional implications of pregnancy and its influences on family relationships. In *The Healthy Child: His Physical, Physiological, and Social Development*, ed. H. Stuart and D. Prugh, pp. 72–82. Cambridge: Harvard University Press.

Dysinger, R.H. (1957). The action dialogue in an intense relationship: a study of a schizophrenic girl and her mother. Paper presented at annual meeting, American Psychiatric Association, Chicago, May.

Dysinger, R.H. (1959). A family perspective on individual diagnosis. Paper presented at the American Orthopsychiatric Association Meeting, San Francisco, March.

Dysinger, R.H., and Bowen, M. (1959). Problems for medical practice presented by families with a schizophrenic member. *American Journal of Psychiatry* 116(pt. 1):514–517.

Fleck, S., Cornelison, A.R., Norton, N., and Lidz, T. (1957). Interaction between hospital staff and families. *Psychiatry* 20:343–350.

Flugel, J.C. (1921). *The Psycho-Analytic Study of the Family*. 10th impr. London: Hogarth Press, 1960.

Freud, S. (1909). Analysis of a phobia in a five year old boy. *Standard Edition* 10:3–152.

Freud, S. (1914). On narcissism: an introduction. *Standard Edition* 14:69–102.

Group for the Advancement of Psychiatry. (1970). *The Field of Family Therapy, Report Number 78*. New York:Group for the Advancement of Psychiatry.

Hill, L.B. (1955). *Psychotherapeutic Intervention in Schizophrenia*. Chicago:University of Chicago Press.

Jackson, D. (1958). Family interaction, family homeostasis, and some implications for conjoint family psychotherapy. Paper presented at the Academy of Psychoanalysis, San Francisco, May.

Jackson, D. (1966). The marital quid pro quo. In *Family Therapy for Disturbed Families*, ed. G. Zuk and I. Boszormenyi-Nagy. Palo Alto:Science and Behavior Books.

Jackson, D.D., and Bateson, G. (1956). Toward a theory of schizophrenia. *Behavioral Science* 1:251-254

Jackson, D. (1960). *The Etiology of Schizophrenia*. New York: Basic Books.

Jackson, D., and Lederer, W. (1969). *The Mirages of Marriage*. New York:Norton.

Kelly, V., and Hollister, M. (1971). The application of family principles in a community mental health center. In *Systems Therapy*, ed. J. Bradt and C. Moynihan. Washington, D.C.: Bradt and Moynihan.

Kvarnes, M.J. (1959). The patient is the family. *Nursing Outlook* 7:142-144.

Laquer, H.P., LaBurt, H.A., and Morong, E. (1964). Multiple family therapy. In *Current Psychiatric Therapies*, vol. 4, ed. J. Masserman, pp. 150-154. New York: Grune and Stratton

Lidz, R., and Lidz, T. (1949). The family environment of schizophrenic patients. *American Journal of Psychiatry* 106:332-345.

Lidz, R., and Lidz, T. (1952). Therapeutic considerations arising from the intense symbiotic needs of schizophrenic patients. In *Psychotherapy with Schizophrenics*, ed. E.B. Brody and F.C. Redlich, pp. 168-178. New York:International Universities Press.

Lidz, T. (1958). Schizophrenia and the family. *Psychiatry* 21:21-27.

Lidz, T. Cornelison, A., Fleck, S., and Terry, D. (1957). The intrafamilial environment of schizophrenic patients; II. marital schism and marital skew. *American Journal of Psychiatry* 114:241-248

Lidz, T., Cornelison, A., Fleck, S., and Terry, D. (1957). The intrafamilial environment of the schizophrenic patient: the father. *Psychiatry* 20:329-342.

Lidz, T., and Fleck, S. (1960). Schizophrenia, human integration and the role of the family. In *The Etiology of Schizophrenia*, ed. D. Jackson, pp. 323-345. New York:Basic Books.

Lidz, T., Fleck, S., and Cornelison, A.R. (1965). *Schizophrenia and the Family*. New York:International Universities Press.

Limentani, D. (1956). Symbiotic identification in schizophrenia. *Psychiatry* 19:231-236.

Macgregor, R., Richie, A., Serrano, A., and Schuster, F. (1964). *Multiple Impact Therapy with Families*. New York:McGraw-Hill.

Mahler, M. (1952). On child psychosis and schizophrenia. In *Psychoanalytic Study of the Child* 7:286-305.

Mendell, D., and Fisher, S. (1958). A multi-generation approach to treatment of psychopathology. *Journal of Nervous and Mental Diseases* 126:523-529.

Minuchin, S. (1974). *Families and Family Therapy*. Cambridge:Harvard University Press.

Middlefort, C.R. (1957). *The Family in Psychotherapy*. New York:McGraw-Hill.

Mittelman, B. (1948). Concurrent analysis of married couples. *Psychoanalytic Quarterly* 17:182-197.

Mittelman, B. (1956). Reciprocal neurotic patterns in family relationships. In *Neurotic Interaction in Marriage,* ed. V.W. Eisenstein, pp. 81–100.
New York:Basic Books.

Paul, N., and Paul, B. (1975). *A Marital Puzzle.* New York:Norton.

Regensburg, J. (1954). Application of psychoanalytic concepts to
casework treatment of marital problems. *Social Casework* 25:424–432.

Reichard, S., and Tillman, C. (1950). Patterns of parent-child relationships in schizophrenia. *Psychiatry* 13:247–257.

Richardson, H.B. (1948). *Patients Have Families.* New York:Commonwealth
Fund.

Satir, V. (1964). *Conjoint Family Therapy.* Palo Alto:Science and Behavior
Books.

Saxe, J.G. (1949). The blind men and the elephant. In *Home Book of Verse,* ed.
B.E. Stevenson. New York:Holt, Rinehart and Winston.

Scheflen, A (1964). The significance of posture in communication
systems. *Psychiatry* 26:316-331

Scheflen, A. (1968). Human communications: behavioral programs and
their integration in interaction. *Behavioral Science* 13:1

Schilder, P. (1938). *Psychotherapy.* New York:Norton.

Searles, H.F. (1956). The effort to drive the other person crazy. Paper
presented at Chestnut Lodge Symposium, Rockville, Md., October.

Sonne, J., and Speck, R. (1961). Resistances in family therapy of
schizophrenia in the home. Paper presented at conference on
Schizophrenia and the Family, Temple University, Philadelphia,
March.

Speck, R. (1967). Psychotherapy of the social network of a schizophrenic
family. *Family Process* 6:208.

Speck, R., and Attreave, C. (1973). *Family Networks.* New York:Pantheon
Books.

Spiegel, J.P. (1957). The resolution of role conflict within he family.
Psychiatry 20:1-16

Spiegel, J.P. (1960). Resolution of role conflict within the family. In *The
Family,* ed. N.W. Bella nd E.F. Vogel, pp. 361-381. Glencoe: Free Press.

Sterne, Laurence (1762). *The Life and Opinions of Tristram Shandy.* New
York:Modern Library.

Toman, W. (1961). *Family Constellation.* New York:Springer Publishing
Company.

Whitaker, C.A. (1967). The growing edge in techniques of family
therapy. In *Techniques of Family Therapy,* ed. J. Haley and L. Hoffman, pp.
265-260. New York: Basic Books.

Wynne, L., Ryckoff, I., Day, J., and Hirsch, S.H. (1958). Pseudo-mutuality
in schizophrenia. *Psychiatry* 21:205–220.

Index